HISTORY OF AGRICULTURE IN ONTARIO

History of Agriculture in Ontario

1613-1880

ROBERT LESLIE JONES

With a Foreword by
Fred Landon

University of Toronto Press
Toronto and Buffalo

Copyright, Canada, 1946
Published by University of Toronto Press
Toronto and Buffalo

Reprinted 1977
Printed in USA

ISBN 0-8020-2268-5 (cloth)
ISBN 0-8020-6304-7 (paper)
LC 47-27166

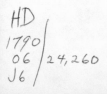

To

MAUDE LACEY JONES

FOREWORD

SCHOLARLY interest in the history of argiculture has greatly increased in the United States in the last quarter century, stimulated by the work of such men as Edwards, Kellar, Gras, Phillips, Moody, Malin and others. It is now twenty-five years since the Agricultural History Society was founded, with the object of promoting study and research in this broad field, and the Society's publication, *Agricultural History*, has in 1946 reached its twentieth volume. The influence which the Society has exerted upon both the teaching and writing of history in the United States has been particularly valuable in broadening the concept of national history in its entirety.

During this period there have appeared a number of extensive studies, examples of which are the *History of Agriculture in the Northern States, 1620-1860*, by Bidwell and Falconer (1925); N.S.B. Gras's *History of Agriculture in Europe and America* (1925); Lewis C. Gray's *History of Agriculture in the Southern United States to 1860* (1933), and in somewhat more restricted fields U. P. Hedrick's *History of Agriculture in the State of New York* (1933) and Ulrich B. Phillips's *Life and Labor in the Old South* (1929). Studies of a more regional or specialized character have been numerous.

This growing interest in agricultural history has shown itself in other ways also. Libraries have set themselves the task of collecting the source materials, both manuscript and printed. Files of the earlier farm journals have been brought together, farm diaries and other records of agricultural activities dug out from attics and old trunks to provide the picture of farm life and farming practices of other days. The library of the Department of Agriculture at Washington is the greatest single depository of this character, but anyone who visits the library of the McCormick Historical Association in Chicago or the libraries of several of the American universities which are active in this field will go away impressed by the volume and variety of material that they have assembled.

In Canada, despite the importance of agriculture in our national economy, we have been tardy in exploring its place in our earlier history and only in the last decade has there been evidence of any general interest in the subject on the part of historians and economists. As Professor Fowke has pointed out,[1] we have as yet no general histories of Canadian agriculture comparable to the works of Bidwell and Falconer, Gras or Gray, mentioned above, nor any work on Canadian agriculture comparable to those of Innis on the cod fisheries and the fur trade or of Lower on the timber trade of Canada.

Furthermore, it is a matter of concern that so little has been done to assemble and conserve the raw materials of the field, so essential to research and writing. There is only one reasonably good collection of early farm journals in the libraries of Canada and even the agricultural college libraries have been so concerned with the problems of the immediate present that they have tended to neglect the building up of collections similar to those in the United States.

All this is preliminary to welcoming a study of the agricultural history of one extensive region of Canada. Professor Jones has for some years past been publishing preliminary studies in this general field and his larger work on the history of agriculture in the Province of Ontario down to 1880 has been awaited with interest. Residence in the United States and acquaintance with the agriculture of states contiguous to Ontario has assisted him to take an objective and discriminating point of view and to provide interesting comparisons and contrasts between Ontario agriculture and that of neighbouring regions of the republic.

In the making of this study Professor Jones has ranged

---

[1] V. C. Fowke, "An Introduction to Canadian Agricultural History" (*Canadian Journal of Economics and Political Science*, VIII, 1942, p. 62).

widely over the available source material. His annotated bibliography, which occupies a large section of the book, should be
welcomed by all students of Canadian history. The list of
newspapers which he consulted is in itself imposing, no less
than thirty-four titles being included, some extending over a
considerable period of years.

Finally, this work is a challenge to further research in
the same and similar fields. The author does not regard his
work as in any way final for the area which he has examined,
and he suggests yet closer investigation of a variety of subjects
related to Ontario agriculture and study also of the history
of particular areas of the province. Some of the topics which
he has mentioned might well be set down for investigation
by graduate students in our universities.

FRED LANDON

University of Western Ontario,
London, Ontario.

PREFACE

Agriculture in its several branches has been, and is now, the foundation on which rests the entire industrial fabric of Ontario. On its prosperity all classes depend— and with a good crop or a bad one, business operations, the abundance of money, and the social comforts of our whole people rise and fall, as do the waters of the sea with the flow and ebb of the tide. CANADA FARMER (Toronto), January 15, 1873, p. 9.

THOUGH agriculture was the dominant industry in Ontario till the end of the nineteenth century, its history has tended to be neglected, except in so far as it is concerned with land settlement and land policy. This volume endeavours to provide a comprehensive description of Ontario agricultural development from the time when Samuel de Champlain set down his observations on the farming practices of the Indians in Huronia to about 1880. The investigations of the Ontario Agricultural Commission in the latter year make it possible to survey the prevailing conditions and tendencies with a fair degree of accuracy. From the economic point of view too, 1880 as a date of termination has much to recommend it. The province had then become adjusted to the effects of termination of reciprocity with the United States, wheat acreage had reached its apogee and the wheat-growing industry was about to decline, and dairying, livestock raising, and fruit-growing had become soundly established. An attempt has been made to deal with all important aspects of agricultural development, among them Indian agriculture, types of settlers, pioneer farming, grain-growing, the grain trade, the live-stock industry, the dairy industry, the fruit industry, farmers' organizations and movements, the relations between the timber trade and farming, and tariff policies and their effects. A work thus concerned with the whole agricultural history of an extensive region over a long period necessarily lacks a clear single theme of the kind expected in the investigation of an institution or a policy, but at least it is hoped that a reasonable synthesis has been achieved.

One of the complicating factors in a history having to do with Ontario is nomenclature. In the French period the land comprised in the province in 1880 was part of New France. From 1763 to 1774 it formed a portion of the unorganized Indian country, except for a narrow strip along the Ottawa River which was included in Quebec. Under the Quebec Act of 1774 it belonged to Quebec. By the Constitutional Act of 1791 it became the separate Province of Upper Canada. By the Act of Union of 1840 it was associated with Lower Canada to form the Province of Canada, but the union was not administratively complete, and the old name of Upper Canada was still commonly used. The official name, Canada West, was much less popular. In 1867, on the formation of the Dominion of Canada, Upper Canada again became a separate province, thereafter known as Ontario.

The research for this volume was conducted in the Main Library of the Department of Agriculture at Ottawa, the Public Archives of Canada, the Library of Parliament at Ottawa, the Ottawa Public Library, the Queen's University Library, the University of Toronto Library, the Victoria College Library, the Ontario Parliamentary Library, the Toronto Public Library, the Harvard University libraries, the Boston Public Library, the New York Public Library, the John Crerar Library at Chicago, the Newberry Library at Chicago, the Cincinnati Public Library, the Detroit Public Library, the University of Michigan Library, and the Marietta College Library. I am deeply grateful to the staffs of these institutions for their helpful co-operation. For copying excerpts, verifying references and quotations, or lending rare periodicals, I am under obligation to most of the libraries just mentioned, as well as to the New York State Library at Albany, the Yale University Library, the Library of Congress, the Library of the United States Department of Agriculture, the Cleveland Public Library, the University of Illinois Library, the Ohio State University Library, and the University of Minnesota Library.

Professor D. G. Creighton of the University of Toronto, Professor Harold A. Innis of the University of Toronto, Professor Frederick Merk of Harvard University, and Professor Gilbert N. Tucker of Yale University, read the manuscript in its initial form of a Harvard University doctoral dissertation. Professor V. C. Fowke of the University of Saskatchewan, Professor Fred Landon of the University of Western Ontario, Dr. O. A. Lemieux of the Dominion Bureau of Statistics, Miss Jean Lunn of McGill University, and Professor James J. Talman of the University of Western Ontario, read it later, in whole or in part. I am indebted to these critics for many valuable suggestions. Professor George W. Brown of the University of Toronto acted as consultant, and my wife, Maude Lacey Jones, served as proof-reader and indexer.

The publication has been supported in part by a grant from the Canadian Social Science Research Council.

ROBERT LESLIE JONES

Marietta, Ohio, May, 1946.

CONTENTS

FOREWORD vii

PREFACE xi

LIST OF ABBREVIATIONS.. xvi

    I. AGRICULTURE BEFORE THE LOYALISTS..................................... 1

    II. AGRICULTURE IN THE LOYALIST ERA, 1784-1812........................ 17

    III. WAR, DEPRESSION AND RECOVERY, 1812-1831............................ 36

    IV. THE AGRICULTURAL POPULATION, 1815-1850.............................. 50

    V. THE BACKWOODSMAN 67

    VI. THE WHEAT FARMER, 1815-1850... 85

    VII. AGRICULTURE IN THE OTTAWA VALLEY TO 1850......................... 109

    VIII. TARIFFS AND PREFERENCES, 1831-1846..................................... 122

    IX. LIVESTOCK AND ITS IMPROVEMENT BEFORE 1850....................... 140

    X. AGRICULTURAL ORGANIZATIONS BEFORE 1850............................ 156

    XI. THE AMERICAN MARKET, 1847-1861.. 175

    XII. FARMING IN THE GRAND TRUNK ERA... 196

    XIII. REPERCUSSIONS OF THE AMERICAN CIVIL WAR.......................... 216

    XIV. THE GRAIN TRADE AND GRAIN GROWING, 1866-1880................. 231

    XV. THE DEVELOPMENT OF THE DAIRY INDUSTRY............................ 250

    XVI. THE LIVESTOCK INDUSTRY, 1866-1880...................................... 266

    XVII. AGRICULTURE ON THE FOREST FRONTIER, 1850-1880................. 289

    XVIII. MISCELLANEOUS ASPECTS OF AGRICULTURE IN THE EIGHTEEN-
          SEVENTIES 304

    XIX. AGRICULTURAL ORGANIZATIONS AFTER 1850............................ 328

    XX. CONCLUSION 353

BIBLIOGRAPHY 361

INDEX 391

LIST OF ABBREVIATIONS

JHC   *Journal of the House of Commons of Canada.*

JLAC   *Journal of the Legislative Assembly of Canada.*

JTBAUC   *Journal and Transactions of the Board of Agriculture of Upper Canada.*

OACR   *Report of the Ontario Agricultural Commission.*

OHSPR   *Ontario Historical Society Papers and Records.*

RAA   *Report on Agriculture and Arts* (i.e., Report of the Commissioner of Agriculture for the Province of Ontario.)

SPC   *Sessional Papers, Canada.*

SPO   *Sessional Papers, Ontario.*

TBA & AAUC *Transactions of the Board of Agriculture and of the Agricultural Association of Upper Canada.*

TBAUC   *Transactions of the Board of Agriculture of Upper Canada.*

CHAPTER I

AGRICULTURE BEFORE THE LOYALISTS[1]

O F the vast territory of Ontario, all that counted from
the agricultural point of view down to 1880 was the
part south of Lake Nipissing, which is now known as Old
Ontario or Southern Ontario. This region, to be sure, is of fair
size. It has an area of about 51,000 square miles (not counting
the surrounding waters), that is, about 4,000 square miles less
than the State of Pennsylvania. It has considerable diversity
of relief, of soil, and of climate. Except for one large segment, all of it is today occupied by farmers who are normally
prosperous.

Four divisions of Old Ontario may be distinguished for
the purpose of studying its agricultural history.[2]

The first division is Eastern Ontario, which includes the
portion of the province between the St. Lawrence and
Ottawa rivers. The western boundary of this region is
marked roughly by the towns of Pembroke, Perth, and
Brockville, or more definitely by the eastern edge of the
spur of the Precambrian Shield which stretches down from
Northern Ontario to cross the St. Lawrence at the Thous-
and Islands. Eastern Ontario is underlaid by nearly
horizontal shales and sandstones, but the soil is mostly
marine till deposited when the Champlain Sea inundated
the St. Lawrence Lowlands. Though the soil is for the
most part fertile enough, agriculture has been handicapped
by a general flatness of terrain, with consequent difficulties
in the way of drainage, and in the case of certain crops,
by a climate which is more rigorous than that of the parts
of the province bordering on the lower Great Lakes. This
division of the province is frequently referred to in the

---

[1]With this chapter in general, cf. Schott, *Landnahme und Kolonisation*, pp. 5-58. For developments during the French régime, with special
reference to the St. Lawrence Valley, see Innis, *Select Documents in
Canadian Economic History.*

[2]Cf. Colby, *Source Book for Economic Geography*, pp. 5 ff., 72-3.
For a good general description of the geography of Old Ontario, see
also Herbertson and Howarth (eds.), *Oxford Survey of the British
Empire*, vol. IV, chap. I.

pages which follow as the Ottawa Valley, according to the local usage, though strictly speaking the Ottawa Valley includes a narrow strip of the Province of Quebec north of the Ottawa. On the other hand, there are a few instances where the term "Ottawa Valley" is used to describe a region larger than Eastern Ontario, that is, to comprise in addition the parts of the Precambrian Shield drained by the tributaries of the Ottawa. These references are almost all in connection with the timber trade, and should cause no confusion.

The second division of Old Ontario may be called the Ottawa-Huron region. It is bordered on the east by Eastern Ontario, and on the south by a line running from Kingston to the southeastern corner of Georgian Bay. It is part of the Laurentian or Precambrian Shield. This means that it is a maze of low hills, sprawling lakes, turbulent rivers, and often of swamps and muskegs. Its surface has been largely denuded of soil by glacial action. Except along some of the streams, such soils as remain are light and infertile. Though the region offers few agricultural possibilities, farming operations have been carried on in certain parts of it for over ninety years. Abandoned or half-cleared farms, tumble-down buildings, and poverty-stricken inhabitants testify to its inability to support a rural population above a subsistence level.

The third and fourth divisions, Central and Western Ontario, together comprise the part of the province south and west of the Ottawa-Huron region. They may be considered as belonging to the St. Lawrence Lowlands, or according to another classification, to the Central Lowlands. They are underlaid, like Eastern Ontario, by sedimentary rocks. Their soil is glacial till of various kinds. East of Toronto there is abundance of lime in at least 80 per cent of the soil, but west of it there is a much higher proportion of acid soil derived from shale. The surface varies. In some places, such as the Essex peninsula, it is decidedly flat; in others it is very rolling; but mostly it is moderately rolling. On the whole, peninsular Ontario is admirably adapted to agriculture. Except in some waste areas, such as the sands of Norfolk, Northumberland, and Prince Edward counties, the marshes at the mouth of the Grand River, and various poorly drained sections, most of the land is at present in use.[3] The most conspicuous physical feature is the Niagara escarpment which, under the name of Hamilton Mountain or Blue Mountains, runs from Queenston Heights northward to Owen Sound and the Bruce peninsula. In Grey County the summit of this escarpment is about 1,000 feet above the level of the adjacent Great Lakes. On the western side of the escarpment a plateau slopes gradually to Lake Huron and Lake Erie. This escarpment is ordinarily considered to mark the dividing line between Central and Western Ontario.

In general the climate of Old Ontario is favourable to agriculture. There is about three weeks' difference in the advent of the growing season between the Essex peninsula and the region south of Lake Nipissing. Ground frosts come late in September in the Ottawa-Huron region and Eastern Ontario, but usually not till October in Central and Western Ontario, for in Central Ontario the climate is moderated by Lake Ontario and Georgian Bay, and in Western Ontario by Lake Huron and Lake Erie. In the Niagara peninsula fruit belt the average length of the growing season is 212 days and the average length of the frost-free period 158 days. Corresponding figures for other parts of Old Ontario are: Essex and Kent counties, 207 and 155; counties along Lake Erie, 203 and 153; shore of Lake Ontario and the Bay of Quinte, 197 and 143-5; shore of Lake Huron and southern part of Georgian Bay, 196 and 148; counties between Ottawa and St. Lawrence rivers, 194 and 131; Renfrew and adjacent counties, 188 and 119; Algonquin Park (the heart of the Ottawa-Huron region), 176 and 93; Muskoka, 182 and 123; region about Lake Simcoe and the Kawartha Lakes, 191 and 130; uplands between Guelph and Owen Sound, 189 and 126; a belt including the second range of counties north of Lake Erie and parts of the first range of counties north of Lake Ontario

---

[3]Chapman, "Adaptation of Crops in Ontario" (*Canadian Geographical Journal*, vol. XXIV, 1942, pp. 253-4); Whitaker, "Agricultural Gradients in Southern Ontario" (*Economic Geography*, vol. XIV, 1938, pp. 112-15). See also Hills, "Pedology, 'The Dirt Science,' and Agricultural Settlement in Ontario" (*Canadian Geographical Journal*, vol. XXIX, 1944, pp. 111-20); and Lee, "Land Utilization in the Middle Grand River Valley" (*Economic Geography*, vol. XX, 1944, pp. 130-51).

(the "South Slopes"), 196 and 135. The average annual precipitation ranges from slightly over 28 inches at Leamington to 38 inches in Muskoka. The only parts of the province where the farmers have much fear of drought are around Leamington and Chatham. The snow which blankets the northern sections of Old Ontario for three or four months, and the southern ones for a shorter time, gave the pioneers an advantage over their contemporaries south of the border in marketing grain, and facilitated the rapid development of the timber trade.[4]

In its primeval state Southern Ontario had three forest belts, which have been classified as the "Carolinian," the "Tolerant Hardwood," and the "Mixed Hardwood and Softwood." The first, which lay along the north shore of Lake Erie, had a number of hardwoods such as the black walnut, the pawpaw, and the tulip-tree, which did not grow elsewhere in Canada. North of it, and including most of the rest of Southern Ontario except the Ottawa-Huron region, was the second belt, with hardwoods such as maple, elm, beech, ash, and oak predominating, but with conifers such as pine, spruce, balsam, and cedar on the sandy or poorly drained soils. The third belt, farther north, was pre-eminently that of the white pine, with red pine occupying a position next in importance.[5] It was the work of three generations of backwoodsmen and farmers to reduce the first two belts to cleared fields, leaving here and there remnants in the shape of woodlots.

Not all Southern Ontario was forest-covered. As in the adjacent parts of the United States there were "oak-plains." These were rather sandy stretches thinly timbered with oaks. Travellers emerging from the woods were astonished when they first glimpsed them. One such traveller, after visiting Long Point in Norfolk County, wrote: "When I first visited this part of the Province, the sudden change which took place in the aspect of nature seemed like magic. The soil became light and sandy, the forests had dwindled away,

---

[4]Chapman, "Adaptation of Crops in Ontario," pp. 248, 250-1; Taylor, "Climate and Crop Isopleths for Southern Ontario" (*Economic Geography*, vol. XIV, 1938, p. 90).

[5]Craig, "Forest Resources of Canada" (*Economic Geography*, vol. II, 1926, pp. 401-3).

and natural groves and copses met the eye in their stead. The fields were beautifully level, and the uncultivated lands had more the appearance of a pleasure-ground than of a wilderness. The trees being small and few in number, and distributed in beautiful clumps, did not at all suggest the idea of a forest, but added charms to the country and variety to the prospect."[6] Oak-plains, in addition to those at Long Point, were found in or near the valley of the Grand River, especially in the townships of Ancaster (Wentworth County), Burford (Brant County), and Dumfries (Waterloo County); in the Niagara peninsula, in the townships of Niagara (Lincoln County) and Stamford (Welland County); in York County along Dundas Street east of the Humber (Scarlett's Plains); and in Northumberland County along the southern shore of Rice Lake. Though oak-plains were easy to clear, they did not become popular with settlers for a long time except as pasture. They were liable to many serious criticisms, as Edward Talbot remarked, "such as the want of timber for building, fencing and fuel." Then he added: "To be obliged to go half a dozen miles for fire-wood, rails, and building materials, would involve an expence, which, in my opinion, no American farmer can at present afford."[7] So great was the prejudice against the oak-plains that it was not till almost 1850 that the Rice Lake Plains, for example, were utilized for the growing of wheat.[8]

Though the Loyalist farmers along the southern fringe of Old Ontario inherited scarcely anything directly from the Indians who preceded them, the agriculture of the aborigines deserves attention. The first European to describe it was Samuel de Champlain. In June, 1613, he and his companions toiled up the Ottawa as far as Allumette Lake. On Allumette Island and in the part of Renfrew County to the south of it they found a tribe of Algonkins. Though these Algonkins depended on hunting and fishing for their subsistence, they practised farming to some extent. Their chief product was Indian corn, but they also had squashes and kidney beans. Two years later, when he

[6]Howison, *Sketches of Upper Canada*, p. 153.
[7]Talbot, *Five Years' Residence*, vol. I, p. 171.
[8]Brown, *Views of Canada and the Colonists* (2nd ed.), pp. 179-80.

again ascended the Ottawa, this time going by way of Lake Nipissing to the Huron country south of Georgian Bay, Champlain found other Indians essentially the same as the Algonkins.   The Nipissings of the vicinity of Lake Nipissing cultivated the land very little, though they dried wild fruits. The Ottawas, whose home was on Manitoulin Island and in the region between Lake Huron and Georgian Bay, were, he wrote, "for the most part great warriors, hunters, and fishermen. . . . In general they plant Indian corn, and other cereals."[9]

When Champlain had coasted along the eastern shore of Georgian Bay to Huronia in modern Simcoe County, he found himself in a new kind of countryside—"the largest part being cleared up," and "thickly settled with a countless number of human beings."   The Hurons, he observed, depended more on agriculture than on the products of the chase.   Their main crop was Indian corn, which they consumed in many forms—as bread, as pudding, as soup, as roasting ears, and in combination with other foods, and which they used in bartering for furs with the Algonkins and Nipissings.   Kidney beans and squashes, as among the Algonkins, were next in importance.   They cultivated sunflowers for the double purpose of making a kind of soup and a hair-oil.   They had dogs, which were "in request at their banquets," and kept bears in captivity, often for several years, to provide another delicacy.[10]

Cultivating maize was a laborious task for the Huron women, for to them it invariably fell.   As it was difficult for them to chop down the trees with their primitive axes, they burned the bases of the trunks to kill them, and cleared the underbrush out of the deadening.   Having done this, they planted the corn in hills about two feet apart, ten kernels to each.   We learn from Gabriel Sagard, who was a missionary among the Hurons less than a decade after Champlain's visit, that the corn was planted in the same hills year after year, without the intervening soil being stirred at all.   According to Champlain, enough seed was

[9]Grant (ed.), *Voyages of Champlain*, pp. 243-4, 249, 279-80, 303.

[10]*Ibid.*, pp. 283-5, 314-17. For the importance of Indian corn in the fur-trading economy of the Hurons, see Innis, *Fur Trade in Canada*, p. 23.

sown each year to provide a supply for three or four years, as the Hurons feared that "a bad year may befall them."[11] Though this remark is a tribute to the sense of providence of the Indians, it may also suggest that maize was not altogether a dependable crop in Huronia.   The Hurons kept their fields in cultivation for a relatively short period, usually not much over five years, though it might be as long as forty, and then abandoned them for new ones.   Sagard ascribed this practice to the increasing difficulty of obtaining fuel in the vicinity of the villages, and to the exhaustion of the soil through lack of manuring.[12]   A more reasonable explanation is that the clearances were overrun with grass, which the Indians could not eradicate with their wooden shovels and pointed stakes.   Under these circumstances they had no choice but to move elsewhere, village and all.[13]

The Hurons and the other Indians supplemented the produce of their fields with nuts, fruits, and berries.   They gathered acorns, chestnuts, and walnuts to eat in their natural state and to grind into flour for use in various dishes.   They picked wild grapes, plums, cherries, cranberries, and crab-apples, and even preserved the last named in maple syrup.   They had strawberries, blackberries, raspberries, gooseberries, and blueberries.[14]   Blueberries seem to have been their favourite small fruit.   Lahontan wrote that "These Berries serve for several uses, after they are dry'd in the Sun, or in an Oven; for then they make Confits of 'em, or put 'em into Pyes, or infuse 'em in Brandy.   The North-Country Savages make a Crop of 'em in the Summer, which affords 'em very seasonable relief, especially when their hunting comes short."[15]

The Hurons, like the other Indians of the Great Lakes region, depended on the maple for their sweetening.   It was stated about 1684 that the "savages of Canada" tapped the maples, and obtained by evaporation about a pound of sugar

---

[11]Grant, *Voyages of Champlain*, p. 327; Hodge, *Handbook of American Indians*, part I, p. 25.

[12]Hodge, *Handbook of American Indians*, part I, p. 586.

[13]Cf. Huntington, *Red Man's Continent*, pp. 155-6.

[14]Grant, *Voyages of Champlain*, pp. 284, 288; Lahontan, *New Voyages*, vol. I, p. 217.

[15]Lahontan, *New Voyages*, vol. I, p. 254.

for every eight pounds of sap. This was evidently a very old procedure. "The savages here," the notice continued, "have practised this art longer than any now living among them can remember."[16]

The other Indian tribes of Southern Ontario in Champlain's time require only brief comment. The Tobacco Nation lived a short distance west of Huronia, and the Neutral Nation had its homeland north of Lake Erie and in northwestern New York. The agriculture of these two tribes differed from that of the Hurons only in the addition of tobacco-growing. Tobacco was cultivated apart from the other crops, and was under the care of the men rather than of the women.[17]

Such then was the agriculture of the aborigines of Old Ontario when the first white men arrived. The members of the Huron-Iroquois family, it is clear, had long before the coming of Champlain made the transition from a nomadic to a "shifting-cultivator" type of culture. The Algonkins, the Nipissings, and the Ottawas were in the midst of the process. Though none of the Indians had quite reached the stage of being sedentary agriculturists, they had done remarkably well considering their lack of draft animals and of implements. One must agree with the authority who, in writing of them and other eastern Indians with the same kind of civilization, has stated that "the more the matter is studied from an unprejudiced point of view the more remarkable appear their achievements in farming."[18]

Almost as soon as the French and Indians came in contact, they borrowed from each other's agriculture. The French were soon making maple sugar, following the Indian technique in every detail till they understood it well enough to improve upon it. They likewise obtained Indian corn

---

[16]Chamberlain, "Maple Sugar and the Indians" (*American Anthropologist*, vol. IV, 1891, p. 382). Among the best descriptions of Indian maple sugar making in the Great Lakes basin is that of Zeisberger, *History of the Northern American Indians*, pp. 48-50.

[17]Grant, *Voyages of Champlain*, pp. 302-4; letter of Father Joseph de la Roche Dallion, July 18, 1627, in Le Clercq, *First Establishment of the Faith*, vol. I, p. 270; Boucher, *True and Genuine Description of New France*, p. 55.

[18]Carrier, *Beginnings of Agriculture in America*, p. 41.

and other products of the soil and the knowledge of their
culture. Shortly after he founded Quebec, Champlain was
growing Indian corn, squashes, and kidney beans in the
manner of the natives.[19] On the other hand the Indians
obtained tools, particularly iron axes, from the whites. Nor
was this all. Even when Champlain first visited the Algonkins of the Ottawa, he observed that they were planting
peas, which they had got from the French.[20] By 1624 the
Recollet missionaries were cultivating the common vegetables of western Europe in their gardens in Huronia,[21] a
demonstration which was not lost on the Indians; and by
1645 the Jesuits were taking young cattle to their missions
among the Hurons.[22]

The small beginnings of the Europeanization of Indian
agriculture were soon reduced to naught by the deadly in-
cursions of the Iroquois. With the westward flight of the
Hurons in 1648-9, and with the subsequent vanquishing of
the Tobacco and Neutral Nations and the other allies of
the Hurons, the Iroquois were unchallenged in Old Ontario.
As they were too much engaged in warfare to colonize their
conquest, they frequented it only for hunting or for gathering wild rice. Terror of the Iroquois kept out other Indians.
Most of the corn fields of the Hurons and their associates
before long were overwhelmed by the forest, like those
abandoned in the ordinary course of cultivation. A few,
for some reason or other, remained as openings, to excite
comment from settlers of a later day and to relieve them
of the necessity of land-clearing.[23] "By this means it comes
to pass," wrote Lahontan of the once populous country of the

---

[19]Saunders, "First Introduction of European Plants and Animals
into Canada" (*Canadian Historical Review*, vol. XVI, 1935, p. 392).

[20]Grant, *Voyages of Champlain*, p. 249. Peas brought from France
did much better in the New World than in the Old. " . . . Peas thrive
very well here, and one never sees any of those worm-eaten peas full
of weevils that one sees in France" (Boucher, *True and Genuine
Description of New France*, p. 47).

[21]Le Clercq, *First Establishment of the Faith*, vol. I, p. 209. They
were also making wine from the wild grapes (*ibid.*, p. 208).

[22]Saunders, "First Introduction of European Plants and Animals
into Canada," p. 399.

[23]Cf. Chapter V, below. For the prevalence and importance of Indian
clearances in eastern North America in general, see Carrier, *Beginnings
of Agriculture in America*, pp. 38-40.

Neutrals, "that the Stags, Roe-Bucks and Turkeys, run in
great Bodies up and down the shoar, all round the Lake
[Erie]."[24] The remnants of the Huron nations lived for a
generation near Michilimackinac, bullied by the Iroquois on
the east and by the Sioux on the west. About 1680 they
descended to the vicinity of Detroit, and became known as
Wyandots. Many of their allies followed, especially after
the founding of Fort Detroit in 1701 gave some assurance of
protection against the Iroquois. The Wyandots came to
have several villages, most of them at the western end of
Lake Erie. One, however, was on the eastern side of the
Detroit River, opposite the fort. In its vicinity was another
village peopled by the Ottawas.

James Smith, a young Pennsylvanian, was among the
Wyandots and their allies as a captive between 1755 and
1759. In his remarks on their diet and their mode of life,
he reveals that they still pursued the agricultural methods
that Champlain had found among their ancestors.[25] Another captive, Charles Stuart, mentions that in 1755 an ex-
pedition of Wyandots (with some other Indians) raided the
English settlements in the modern Fulton County, Pennsylvania, and drove back to their villages near Detroit a
number of horses, cattle, and swine.[26] By 1760, as a
result of this and later depredations against the Pennsylvania, Maryland, and Virginia frontiers, the Wyandots were
"esteemed the richest Indians upon the whole continent,
having not only horses in great abundance, but some black
cattle and swine." Further, corn-growing with them was
on a commercial basis. Major Robert Rogers, who makes
the comment just quoted, adds that "they raise great
quantities of corn, not only for their own use, but [to]
supply several other tribes, who purchase this article from
them."[27]

---

[24]Lahontan, *New Voyages*, vol. I, p. 217.
[25]*Account of the Remarkable Occurrences in the Life and Travels
of Col. James Smith*, pp. 26, 44-6, 50-1.
[26]Bond (ed.), "Captivity of Charles Stuart" (*Mississippi Valley
Historical Review*, vol. XIII, 1926-7, pp. 59-66). James Smith also
mentions horse-stealing by the Wyandots and their associates (*Account
of the Remarkable Occurrences in the Life and Travels of Col. James
Smith*, pp. 32, 36, 81).
[27]Rogers, *Concise Account of North America*, pp. 169-70.

Like their predecessors who had lived in Huronia before the Iroquois conquest, the French missionaries working among the Indians during their western wanderings and afterwards practised agriculture, or rather gardening, on a limited scale.[28]   Then, when the government of New France extended its trading empire into the Great Lakes basin and the Mississippi Valley, and established a chain of military posts to protect it, two of these, Fort Frontenac and Fort Detroit, had some significance in the history of agriculture in Old Ontario. Father Hennepin, who was a missionary at Fort Frontenac between 1676 and 1679, described La Salle's efforts at farming thus :

> The Ground which lies along the Brink of this Lake is very fertile: In the space of two Years and a half that I resided there in discharge of my *Mission*, they cultivated more than a hundred Acres of it. Both the *Indian* and *European* Corn, Pulse, Pot-Herbs, Gourds, and Water-Melons, throve very well. It is true indeed, that at first the Corn was much spoil'd by Grashoppers; but this is a thing that happens in all the Parts of *Canada* at the first cultivating the Ground, by reason of the extream Humidity of all that Country. The first Planters we sent thither, bred up Poultry there, and transported with them Horned Beasts, which multiply'd there extreamly.[29]

It should be added that in another work Hennepin noted that La Salle had only thirty-five head of cattle at Fort Frontenac.[30] This agricultural enterprise ended in a few years, when Denonville abandoned the fort. When it was rebuilt later, there was again some farming. Charlevoix,

---

[28]Its nature is illustrated in an account of an episode which occurred in northeastern Ohio in 1762. At that time Frederick Post, a Moravian missionary, took up his residence there, and set a hired man at cutting down trees, with the intention of growing enough corn for his own use. The Indians made him desist, for they feared that other white settlers would follow him. They told him: "You say, 'that you are come at the instigation of the great spirit, to teach and to preach to us!' so also say the priests at Detroit, whom our Father, the French, has sent among his Indian Children! Well, this being the case, you, as a preacher, want no more land than one of those do, who are content with a garden lot, for to plant vegetables and pretty flowers in, such as the French priests also have, and of which the white people are all fond" (Heckewelder, *Narrative of the Mission of the United Brethren*, p. 63). For a definite contribution made by the French missionaries, see below, p. 73 *n*.

[29]Hennepin, *New Discovery*, pp. 17-18.

[30]Hennepin, *Description of Louisiana*, p. 58.

who visited it in 1721, found that an island opposite the fort was known as Hog Island, because so many pigs were kept there.[31]   But Fort Frontenac remained a military and trading post, and little more.   When Rogers went up the Great Lakes in the autumn of 1760, he noticed that the five hundred acres or so of cleared land around it were overrun with clover and pines.[32]

Agriculture in the vicinity of Fort Detroit had a more substantial development.   The first clearances were made on the western shore, around the fort.   Here there soon appeared the narrow fields and the seigneurial windmills characteristic of the manors along the St. Lawrence.   In 1748 settlers, including some disbanded soldiers, began to occupy the other bank of the river between the sites of Sandwich and Amherstburg.   The new community, called the Petite Côte, had about fifty families in 1760.   James Smith, who was taken by his Indian captors to Detroit in 1757, wrote a description of its appearance.

Opposite to Detroit, and below it, was originally a prairie, and laid off in lots about sixty rods broad, and a great length:[33] each lot is divided into two fields, which they cultivate year about.   The principal grain that the French raised in these fields was spring wheat and peas.

They built all their houses on the front of these lots on the river side; and as the banks of the river are very low, some of the houses are not above three or four feet above the surface of the water; yet they are in no danger of being disturbed by freshes, as the river seldom rises above eighteen inches; because it is the communication, of the river St. Laurence, from one lake to another.

As dwelling-houses, barns, and stables are all built on the front of these lots; at a distance it appears like a continued row of houses in a town, on each side of the river for a long way.   These villages, the town, the river and the plains, being all in view at once, affords a most delightful prospect.[34]

When Henry Hamilton arrived at Detroit in 1776 to assume his duties as lieutenant-governor, the Petite Côte had changed

---

[31]Charlevoix, *Histoire et description générale de la Nouvelle France*, vol. III, p. 195.

[32]Hough (ed.), *Journals of Major Robert Rogers*, p. 179.

[33]For a map illustrating the method of surveying in Sandwich Township, see Schott, *Landnahme und Kolonisation*, p. 57.

[34]*Account of the Remarkable Occurrences in the Life and Travels of Col. James Smith*, pp. 79-80.

little. This was to be attributed to the exclusion of British land-seekers from the western country in accordance with the policy of the Proclamation of October 7, 1763. Hamilton remarked that the settlements on both sides of the river appeared "very smiling," especially on holy days, when the habitants turned out in their finery.[35]

The French Canadians on their holdings along the strait may have been picturesque, but they were slovenly farmers. This was natural enough, for they were usually much more concerned with the fur trade than they were with agriculture. They had no reason to cultivate their land intensively, for it was fertile enough to produce the crops necessary for their sustenance without any great effort on their part, and cheap enough to permit them to leave half of it in fallow every year. Their conservatism and their ignorance of crop rotations did not prevent them from having adequate crops of wheat, barley, oats, peas, buckwheat, Indian corn, and potatoes. Yet, when every allowance is made for their economic situation, it is still true that they were even more backward in their tillage methods than their English contemporaries on the frontier of New York, Pennsylvania, and Virginia. When they had their land cleared, they had only the crudest implements with which to prepare the seed-bed. The most notable was a plough of a kind common in the St. Lawrence Valley and in the Illinois country as well as at Detroit, and which was doubtless the same as the French plough of the seventeenth century. It had a wooden mould-board; short and almost perpendicular handles; no coulter; and an almost straight beam resting on an axle supported by two small wheels.[36] Such a plough was still in use within a few miles of Detroit in 1818. "It was drawn by two yoke of oxen and two horses, and was conducted by three men, who were making as much noise as if they were moving a barn."[37] Incidentally, the French-Canadian *censitaires* of the Petite Côte commonly yoked their oxen by

---

[35]Henry Hamilton to Dartmouth, Aug. 29, 1776, in *Michigan Pioneer Collections*, vol. x, 1886, p. 267.

[36]Hubbard, "Early Colonization of Detroit" (*Michigan Pioneer Collections*, vol. I, pp. 352-3); Reynolds, *Pioneer History of Illinois*, p. 49.

[37]Watson (ed.), *Men and Times of the Revolution*, p. 428.

the horns rather than by the neck, just as did those in the Illinois country, the St. Lawrence Valley, and Old France.[38]

Hamilton reported that the 2,500 settlers on both sides of the river had about 3,000 cattle and about 2,000 sheep. They had had few cattle before 1760, and no sheep at all.[39] Like the habitants of the St. Lawrence Valley, they had a disproportionate number of horses. These they sometimes used for ploughing, but they really kept them for driving to an endless succession of social activities, for almost every family had "a calash for summer and a cariole for winter." They had also swine, which they fattened in the autumn for their next summer's supply of salt pork. In the summer there was plenty of wet prairie, on which the vegetation was abundant, and there was additional grazing on the fallow fields and in the woodlands; but as there were no meadows ("there is no such thing as yet, as a piece of land laid down for Meadow"), the number of livestock was strictly limited. After the snow came, the settlers gave the little wild hay that they had cured to the horses, so that in the mildest winters the cattle almost starved, and in the severe ones, such as that of 1775-6, many of them perished.[40]

The French Canadians of this region did make one distinctive agricultural contribution. This was in fruit-growing. Every farm had an orchard, in which grew peaches, plums, apples, and especially pears. According to tradition pear-seeds, scions, and even trees were brought from Normandy by some of the first missionaries. By the middle of the nineteenth century the "old French pear trees,"

---

[38]Hubbard, "Early Colonization of Detroit," p. 353; Flint, *Letters from America*, p. 238. Yoking oxen by the horns was a practice which gained favour in France in the later Middle Ages, and from it spread to Spain (Clapham and Power (eds.), *Agrarian Life of the Middle Ages*, p. 134).

[39]It was related of these French settlers along the Detroit River that "of the manufacture of wool they were entirely ignorant, using the fleeces to protect their cellar windows from the frost, and like strange appropriations of that valuable article" (Sheldon, *Early History of Michigan*, p. 368).

[40]Hamilton to Dartmouth, Aug. 29, 1776, in *Michigan Pioneer Collections*, vol. X, pp. 266-7. A census of the Detroit settlement in 1782 gave the number of heads of families as 321, and the entire population as 2,291; the number of horses as 1,112; the number of cattle as 1,672; the number of sheep as 447; and the number of swine as 1,370 (*ibid.*, vol. X, p. 613).

which flourished under neglect generation after generation, were as characteristic a feature of the landscape between Amherstburg and Sandwich as the surviving seigneurial windmills.[41]

The few dozen families on the Petite Côte were reduced to a position of comparative insignificance in the agricultural development of Old Ontario by the coming of the United Empire Loyalists. During the American Revolution, transporting foodstuffs from Montreal to posts such as Fort Niagara proved to be both expensive and precarious, but under the conditions of the period there was no alternative, because garrison and fur-trade demand created a shortage in the Detroit settlement.[42]   As a new agricultural community would solve the difficulty, plans were made, beginning about 1780, for the establishment around the posts in the western part of the Old Province of Quebec of refugees from the rebelling colonies. At that time Haldimand announced his intention of assigning lands opposite the fort at Niagara (which was on the eastern side of the river) to Loyalists who had taken refuge with the garrison. They were to pay no rent, were to be furnished ploughs and other farm implements, and were to be bound to sell to the commanding officer any surplus they produced.[43] Five families took up land under this arrangement in 1780. A "Survey of the Settlement at Niagara, 25th August, 1782," shows that there were then 17 families there. They had 236 acres of land under cultivation, owned 49 horses, 61 head of cattle, 30 sheep, and 103 hogs, and in the year 1782 grew 206 bushels of wheat, 926 bushels of Indian corn, 46 bushels of oats, and 630 bushels of potatoes.[44]   These pioneers of Lincoln County were the advance guard of thousands who came to the province on the conclusion of peace in 1783. During that year the government sent out surveyors to divide several districts west of the old French settlements above

---

[41]Hamilton to Dartmouth, Aug. 29, 1776, *ibid.*, vol. x, p. 266; Hubbard, "Early Colonization of Detroit," pp. 355-7; *Michigan Pioneer Collections*, vol. x, p. 70.

[42]Lt.-Col. M. Bolton to Haldimand, March 24, 1779, in *ibid.*, vol. IX, 1886, pp. 428-9.

[43]Haldimand to —, July 7, 1780, *ibid.*, vol. x, 1886, pp. 411-12.
[44]*Canadian Archives Report for 1891*, p. 1.

Montreal into townships wherein the British system of tenure would prevail.[45]   Early in 1784 the Loyalists took up their locations.   This marked the inauguration of a new era in the agriculture of their northern home.

----

[45]For a map of a typical "single-front" township of the survey, see Schott, *Landnahme und Kolonisation*, p. 85.   Maps of later types of surveys are given on succeeding pages.

CHAPTER II

AGRICULTURE IN THE LOYALIST ERA, 1784-1812[1]

T HE Loyalists deserved well of the British government and they were well rewarded. When they came to their locations along the St. Lawrence, the Bay of Quinte, and the Niagara frontier, they obtained not only free grants of land, but a full issue of rations for two years, just as if they were on military service, a stock of the primitive implements of the day, and other articles necessary for making a start in the wilderness. Moreover, during the summer and autumn of 1784 the government sent agents to the Mohawk Valley, the Montreal district, and Vermont to buy seed winter wheat for them. During the same period the Loyalists obtained cattle, which they had either owned previously or now bought, from the Mohawk country. Finally, the government provided grist mills, which operated free of toll till 1791.[2]

However anxious and foresighted the government might be, it could not eliminate all privations, such as those associated with the "hungry year" (1788-9), the worst the Loyalists had to endure. Owing to a crop failure throughout the new settlements in 1788, the people were on the verge of starvation by spring. In 1793 some Quakers on the way to Detroit found that the settlers near Newark in Lincoln County had only too vivid a recollection of their sufferings. According to the narrative :

> They related the dreadful circumstances they were reduced to in this country, by scarcity of bread and provisions of all kinds, in 1789— when they came to an allowance of one spoonful of meal per day, for one person—eat strawberry leaves, beech leaves, flax seed dried, and ground in a coffee mill—catched the blood of a little pig—bled the almost famished cow and oxen—walked twelve miles for one shive

---

[1]With parts of this chapter, cf. Burt, *Old Province of Quebec*, chap. xv, and Shortt, "Economic Effect of the War of 1812" (*Ontario Historical Society Papers and Records*, vol. x, 1913). Hereafter this authority is cited as *OHSPR*.

[2]Cruikshank (ed.), *Settlement of the United Empire Loyalists*, pp. 114, 128, 148, 156, 161, 169; "Petitions for Grants of Land in Upper Canada" (*OHSPR*, vol. xxvi, 1930, p. 122).

[slice] of bread, paid twelve shillings for twelve pounds of meal. One
of the lads who was hired out, carried his little sister two miles on his
back, to let her eat his breakfast, and they gave him none till dinner.
The children leaped for joy at one robin being caught, out of which
a whole pot of broth was made. They eat mustard, potato tops, sassafras
root, and made tea of the tops. The relation was deeply affecting.[3]

If it had not been for assistance from the government, and a
supply of provisions obtained from the Mohawk Valley,
half the Loyalist population, it was said, would have perished.[4]   Even later it was well for them that they were not
altogether dependent on the produce of their fields, but
could obtain on occasion wild meat through hunting or purchase from the Indians, that in the beginning of summer
they could ordinarily kill passenger pigeons in great numbers,
and that the rivers and lakes could provide plenty of bass
and whitefish.[5]   Nevertheless, within ten years the Loyalist
communities were solidly on their feet.   The most flourish-
ing of all was that along the Bay of Quinte, with Kingston
as its commercial centre.   All this region, it was remarked
in 1794, "is settled, and round the whole Bay so thick settled,
that their improvements already meet, and form the appearance of a beautiful old settled country."[6]

On the whole, our judgment must be that the Loyalists
were more fortunate than the generality of pioneers.   As
will be shown later, they had for a dozen years or more an
excellent market for their scant surplus among the newcomers, at the garrisons, and even in the western interior.
When demand slackened along the Great Lakes, they were

---

[3]Lindley, "Account of a Journey to Attend the Indian Treaty"
(*Michigan Pioneer and Historical Collections*, vol. XVII, 1892, p. 579).
For further details of the Hungry Year, see Guillet, *Early Life in Upper
Canada*, pp. 206-14.

[4]John Richardson to John Porteous, Little Falls, May 31, 1789
and June 14, 1789, in Cruikshank (ed.), "John Richardson Letters"
(*OHSPR*, vol. VI, 1905, pp. 23-4).

[5]"Canadian Letters" (*Canadian Antiquarian and Numismatic
Journal*, 3rd series, vol. IX, 1912, pp. 43-4).

[6]Ogden, *Tour through Upper and Lower Canada*, p. 95. It was
reported in 1791 that the Loyalists along the St. Lawrence adjacent to
the French settlements did not "fall much short of having as much
of the land cleared as the French who have been more than a hundred
years in possession" (Campbell, *Travels in the Interior Inhabited Parts
of North America*, p. 123).

able to trade at Montreal throughout the entire open season on the St. Lawrence, not solely when the river was in freshet, as was the case with the Ohio Valley farmers who depended on New Orleans. Again, they had no reason to fear the Indians. From 1783 to 1812 the Upper Canada frontier was one of the quietest of which there is record. Its history is not one of scalping by furtive Indians on the borders of settlement, or of "stations" where men hoed corn under the eyes of a garrison, or of bloody Indian war like that in the Ohio country between 1791 and 1795, but one in which predominantly nomadic Indians, such as the Mississaugas, were little more than hunters for the white population, and "settled" ones, such as the Mohawks and the "Moravian" Delawares, were adjusting themselves to European ways of life.[7]

But their greatest asset was in themselves. They were frontiersmen. Most of them came from New York, with the rest coming from the back country of New Jersey, Pennsylvania, and Vermont. About half had been born in the American colonies, and the other half had at least lived in the backwoods.[8] They had suffered much during the Revolutionary War, and to outward view it might seem that they came to their claims with little except broad shoulders, willing hands, and a determined spirit. Yet they did not fear the wilderness. They knew how to tame the forest, to live in it and in the clearances cut out of it, and to make it profitable. The importance of this knowledge, which we may call their colonial frontier agricultural inheritance, can scarcely be exaggerated. We need only compare the uncertain beginnings of the Pilgrims in Massachusetts in 1620, or the dismal experiences of the misfit group of French émigrés of de Puisaye in York County, with the forthright development of the Loyalist communities to appreciate its significance. A century and a half of frontier expansion had built up a store of information and practices on which the Loyalist backwoodsmen could draw, and which served them as well as it did the pioneers in western New York or in

---

[7]For the Mississaugas, see Weld, *Travels through the States of North America*, vol. II, pp. 85-6; for the others see below, pp. 51-3.

[8]Burt, *Old Province of Quebec*, pp. 360-1.

western Pennsylvania or in the Ohio country. It not only taught them what not to do, but also what to do and how to do it.[9]

The settler had occasion to use the traditional lore of the frontier as soon as he commenced to look for a suitable location. Long observation had convinced the frontiersmen that the native vegetation of a region furnished a reliable indication of its agricultural possibilities. Few pioneers were deceived by land speculators if they were able to tramp over the lots offered for sale. Classifications of soil on the basis of the kinds of trees that grew on them were made everywhere along the frontier, and as a matter of course found their way into the immigration literature. Here is a typical classification :

Land, upon which black and white Walnut, Chestnut, Hiccory, and Basswood, grow, is esteemed the best on the continent. That which is covered with Maple, Beech, and Cherry, is reckoned as second-rate. Those parts which produce Oak, Elm, and Ash, are esteemed excellent wheat-land, but inferior for all other agricultural purposes. Pine, Hemlock, and Cedar land is hardly worth accepting as a present. It is however difficult to select any considerable tract of land, which does not embrace a great variety of wood; but, when a man perceives that Walnut, Chestnut, Hiccory, Basswood, and Maple, are promiscuously scattered over his estate, he need not be at all apprehensive of having to cultivate an unproductive soil.[10]

Once located, the pioneer cleared his land according to the methods he had learnt from his father or his neighbours. He split rails, built worm fences, and erected his log cabin, according to universal patterns. When he began to farm, experience and necessity alike taught him to practise what is called extensive agriculture, that is, a type in which a large production was achieved through applying whatever labour was available to as much land as possible, rather than highly cultivating a limited area. Accordingly, his farming was universally condemned by European observers as wasteful; for they did not realize, for the most part, that cheap land and

---

[9]On the colonial agricultural inheritance, see especially Carrier, *Beginnings of Agriculture in America*. There are some useful remarks on the social adjustment of the Loyalists in Clark, *Social Development of Canada*, pp. 205-7.

[10]Talbot, *Five Years' Residence*, vol. I, p. 159.

high labour costs would have made any other course out of the question. If the pioneer could not look into the future and tell which seed would grow and which would not, he benefited from the succession of colonial experiments in standard and special crops, which had eliminated the most unsuitable, and left him with a few staples, among them Indian corn and most of the cereals of northern Europe. These, he knew, were fairly satisfactory wherever grown, and economical of labour, not like the flax and hemp which well-meaning officials were constantly trying to have produced commercially.[11]

His wife was equally adapted to the frontier. She was acquainted with the technique of various household industries, ranging from spinning and sometimes weaving, to the preservation of fruits by drying, and the making of butter and cheese. Together, they formed a family unit, which became closely integrated with the other similar units on the edge of the wilderness. Thus developed the great varieties of frolics or bees, described in every pioneer history —the logging bees, the barn-raisings, the corn-huskings, the apple-paring bees, the harvesting and threshing bees, and the rest.

These remarks apply not alone to the Loyalists, but to those who came after them in quest of cheap land, the groups of two or three from the back country of New York or Pennsylvania, who would come into Upper Canada, obtain a claim, build a log house apiece, sow a patch of wheat, and depart, to return the next year with their families, poling or rowing their *bateaux* along the shores, or creaking along the bush roads in their covered wagons, with their boxes carefully covered to make them watertight in fording streams.[12] To a considerable extent, they also apply to the British immigrants who came into Upper Canada, such as

---

[11]William H. Brewer, writing of the experiments in special crops during the colonial period, stated: "So extensively did these experiments go on, and so completely had they been tried, that . . . but one species of cultivated plant (sorghum) has been introduced since the Revolutionary War of sufficient importance to be enumerated in the census tables" ("Report on the Cereal Production of the United States," *Tenth Census of the United States*, vol. III, p. 135).

[12]Heriot, *Travels through the Canadas*, p. 152; Ogden, *Tour through Upper and Lower Canada*, p. 103.

the Glengarry Highlanders and the Talbot settlers, who were
shortly absorbed in the colonial population, and acquired its
knowledge.

Armed, then, for the assault on the forest, the Loyalists
quickly passed through the initial stages of pioneering,
following the time-worn procedure to be described in a
subsequent chapter. Soon they had patches of wheat, rye,
oats, buckwheat, and even peas;[13] little fields of the indispensable Indian corn, with squashes, melons, pumpkins,
and gourds, among the rows; and garden plots of flax and
common vegetables. Moreover, as occasion offered, they set
out seedling orchards. As early as 1794, it was remarked
that some of these orchards were already bearing fruit, and
that "Peaches, cherries and currants are plenty among all
the first settlers."[14] Apple trees had not begun to bear at
that time, for the settlement at Niagara was being supplied
with apples from the old French community at Detroit, but
within another decade or so apples were so common throughout all Upper Canada, and peaches in the western part of it,
that they were largely manufactured into cider and peach-
brandy.[15]

When the Loyalists accumulated sufficient capital to acquire some foundation stock, they had oxen, young cattle,
cows, pigs, sheep, and even a few horses, about their clearances. These animals received the minimum of care. Pigs
ran wild in the woods, living off the mast, and were often
hunted down and killed there without any further fattening.
If they were fattened before being slaughtered, it was through
being fed a little Indian corn for a few weeks. Cattle were

---

[13]It is not unlikely that the Loyalists borrowed the cultivation of
peas from the French Canadians. The original Loyalists in the
Niagara peninsula grew none (see above, p. 15), probably because the
pea-bug had rendered the crop uncertain everywhere in the American
colonies except northern New York (Bidwell and Falconer, *History
of Agriculture in the Northern United States*, p. 99). For another
factor in pea cultivation, see below, p. 88. In any case it was not till
1793 that peas were grown in the Bay of Quinte region (La Rochefoucault-Liancourt, *Travels through the United States*, vol. I, p. 499).
[14]Ogden, *Tour through Upper and Lower Canada*, p. 101.
[15]Weld, *Travels through the States of North America*, vol. II, p. 139;
Ogden, *Tour through Upper and Lower Canada*, p. 111; R. Hamilton to
J. Askin, Dec. 16, 1804, in Quaife (ed.), *John Askin Papers*, vol. II,
p. 447; Smith, *Geographical View of Upper Canada*, pp. 9, 21-2, 67.

left to browse in the woods till early in the winter, and then were given little feed except straw and marsh hay, and no shelter except a windbreak. Sheep were said to thrive, but it must be remembered that only enough were kept to provide the family with clothing, on account of the inevitable losses from wolves.[16]

Pioneers on good land anywhere in northern North America ordinarily duplicated this transition from privation to rude abundance, but few, when they had a surplus to dispose of, were so fortunate as the Loyalists. The government had deliberately located them where it did because it hoped that the garrisons at Montreal, Kingston, Niagara, and Detroit, and the developing fur trade of the southwest and northwest, would provide a local market for them. Further to set them on their feet, it followed the policy, beginning in 1786, of paying higher prices for products it purchased from the settlers than it needed to. For example, it paid the garrison contractors, who bought from the farmers, the market price for flour in Lower Canada, plus most of the cost of transporting it above Lachine.[17] No wonder one of the Kingston merchants wrote to his Montreal correspondent that "as long as the British Government shall think proper to hire people to come over to eat our flour, we shall go on very well, and continue to make a figure."[18] Garrison demand likewise stimulated pork-packing along the Bay of Quinte. Here, in the season of 1793-4, the inhabitants cured 480 barrels for the use of the soldiers.[19] The latter, too, were no doubt responsible for the breweries and

---

[16]Ogden, *Tour through Upper and Lower Canada*, p. 98; La Rochefoucault-Liancourt, *Travels through the United States*, vol. I, pp. 462, 502-3. For the sources and characteristics of this livestock, see Chapter IX, below.

[17]John Craigie to Alured Clark, Aug. 2, 1792, in Cruikshank (ed.), *Correspondence of Lieutenant-Governor John Graves Simcoe*, vol. I, pp. 185-6. Hereafter this authority is cited as *Simcoe Papers*.

[18]R. Cartwright to Isaac Todd, Oct. 21, 1792, in Cartwright, *Life and Letters of the Late Honourable Richard Cartwright*, pp. 49-50. Hereafter this authority is cited as *Cartwright*.

[19]R. Cartwright to Major Lothbridge, Oct. 10, 1794, in *Cartwright*, p. 66.

distilleries which soon sprang up, and "consumed no inconsiderable portion of our grain."[20]

For the Loyalists of the Niagara district, as for the old French-Canadian and new British settlers along the Detroit River, the fur trade, especially that of the North West Company, formed an additional market. The western traders seldom cultivated anything larger than a kitchen garden. The inhabitants of such places as Sault Ste. Marie and (after about 1807) Fort William were more or less settled, and had patches of barley, peas, oats, and especially potatoes, but they seldom produced more than enough for their own subsistence.[21] Under these circumstances, most of the supplies of the western fur trade, except pemmican, had to be brought up the lakes. Accordingly, the merchants who furnished them bought provisions at Detroit and Fort Erie, and sent them up the lakes in sailing vessels. In 1793, about 4,000 bushels of Indian corn and about 190,000 pounds of flour were exported from Detroit to "Michilimackinac and the Falls of St. Mary &c. &c."[22] John Askin at Detroit made a contract with the North West Company in 1796 to supply it with 1,200 bushels of hulled corn and 12,000 pounds of flour in each of the three succeeding years.[23] Sometimes the market at Michilimackinac or Sault Ste. Marie was very profitable. This was especially the case when the North West Company and its rivals, such as the X Y Company, were in competition for flour and other provisions.[24] On the other hand, the traders often lost heavily in their speculations. For example, a merchant at Fort Erie, who had suffered from the amalgamation of the X Y Company and the North West Company in 1804, wrote that his disap-

---

[20]R. Cartwright to Davison & Co., London, Nov. 4, 1797, in *Cartwright*, p. 74. Cf. R. Cartwright to Simcoe, Dec. 15, 1794, in *Simcoe Papers*, vol. III, p. 221.

[21]Franchère, *Narrative of a Voyage to the Northwest Coast*, pp. 338, 395. For the difficulties of farming on St. Joseph Island, see the many letters of John Askin, Jr., in Quaife, *John Askin Papers*.

[22]*Simcoe Papers*, vol. II, p. 107.

[23]Quaife, *John Askin Papers*, vol. II, p. 24. He bought some of the corn from the "Moravian" Delawares (Bliss, ed., *Diary of David Zeisberger*, vol. II, pp. 427, 480).

[24]Cf. John Askin to Captain Fearson, March 30, 1800, in Quaife, *John Askin Papers*, vol. II, p. 286.

pointment in the Michilimackinac market was so great that he would not again "be very forward" to try it, "thinking it better to sell at a Saving price at home, than to run great risks for the prospect of an uncertain Advantage."[25] Again, it is clear that by 1807 imports of American agricultural produce at Michilimackinac were of considerable significance.[26] The agricultural export trade up the lakes therefore lost its former attractiveness. Nevertheless, it did retain much of its importance till the War of 1812, even though long before that time it ceased to be the sole dependence, additional to the garrisons, of the western settlers.

The amount of produce which could be absorbed by the garrisons and the fur traders was limited, and even with the most primitive tillage methods, the Loyalists were soon producing a surplus of wheat. The Scottish traveller Campbell in 1791 reported of Kingston that "above 6,000 bolls [one boll equals six imperial bushels] of wheat were bought up and stored here the preceding year, and that at least one fourth more would have been so this one."[27] With the crop of 1792 there was definitely a surplus, which the Kingston merchants began to talk of exporting to Montreal.[28] However, it appears that they did not do so till 1794, when they shipped thither 12,823 bushels of wheat, 896 barrels of flour, and 83 barrels of middlings (biscuit flour), quantities to be compared with the 1,624 bushels of wheat and the 3,596 barrels of flour they furnished to the garrisons at Kingston, York, and Niagara.[29] The wheat and flour trade down the St. Lawrence gained little in volume for the next five years, though the high prices which prevailed in Lower Canada on account of the French Revolutionary War would, in the ordinary course of events, have stimulated further exports. The incipient export trade was checked by the prevalence of the Hessian fly, which, assisted by dry summers, reduced the production of wheat for a number of years, beginning

---

[25]Robert Nichol to John Askin, Aug. 26, 1804, *ibid.*, vol. II, p. 429.

[26]York *Gazette*, Aug. 22, 1807.

[27]Campbell, *Travels in the Interior Inhabited Parts of North America*, p. 140.

[28]R. Cartwright, Jr., to Simcoe, Nov. 12, 1792, in *Simcoe Papers*, vol. I, p. 255.

[29]R. Cartwright to Simcoe, Dec. 15, 1794, *ibid.*, vol. III, p. 223.

with the harvest of 1794,[30] and still more by the sudden development of a market among newcomers on the American side of the St. Lawrence River and the Great Lakes.

The region these new settlers occupied had few permanent residents till after the British evacuation of the western posts in 1796. When more did appear, they were supplied from Upper Canada for several years, as were the American garrisons now occupying the posts at Oswegatchie, Niagara, Presqu'Ile, and Detroit. The demand from the British and American garrisons, and from the American pioneers, caused prices to rule high for several years. Flour, for example, sold in 1797 for $4.00 a hundredweight, and peas for $1.00 a bushel.[31] Some farmers forgot the generosity of the government in the days when there was nothing but the garrison market, and sold to the Americans the supplies which they had contracted to deliver for the use of the British troops.[32] Others simply took high prices for granted, and attempted to profiteer by withholding their supplies from the garrisons in times of scarcity.[33]

If the Upper Canadians for four or five years took advantage of the needs of their neighbours across the border, there was nevertheless a community of interests between them. New Yorkers long had their grain ground at Upper Canadian mills, flour and household articles were freely borrowed, and visits and gossip were exchanged.[34] As time passed, the dimming memories of the Revolutionary War scarcely served to distinguish the Loyalist from the post-Loyalist land-jobber, or either from the northern New York potash burner. The "Yankee pedlar" from Albany paddled

---

[30]*Ibid.*, p. 222; John McGill to Simcoe, May 13, 1796, *ibid.*, vol. IV, p. 263. The cutworm had destroyed the crops in the eastern Loyalist settlements in 1785 (*An Englishman in America, 1785*, ed. by Robertson, p. 58).

[31]R. Cartwright to Davison & Co., Nov. 4, 1797, in *Cartwright*, p. 74.

[32]John McGill to Simcoe, May 30, 1796, in *Simcoe Papers*, vol. IV, p. 284.

[33]John McGill to James Green, June 24, 1798, in Cruikshank and Hunter (eds.), *Correspondence of the Honourable Peter Russell*, vol. II, pp. 191-2.

[34]Hough, *History of Jefferson County*, p. 251; Hough, *History of St. Lawrence and Franklin Counties*, pp. 274, 335-6; Turner, *Pioneer History of the Holland Purchase*, p. 416.

his canoe along the shores of Upper Canada or New York with perfect indifference to the boundary, for, like the Yankee carpenter or mason, he received the same welcome at every clearance.[35]

\ By 1800 the pioneers south of Lake Ontario were not only producing enough for their own needs and that of the adjacent garrisons, but were preparing to send a surplus to Montreal, the only market their transportation facilities permitted them to reach.[36] Accordingly, though advertisements still appeared in Upper Canada newspapers on behalf of the American garrisons,[37] the merchants and millers of the province again turned to Montreal. Even in 1799 the inhabitants of the Loyalist townships along the St. Lawrence were steadily sending their grain there.[38] At this time new settlements as remote as those in Oxford County had wheat to export.[39] By the summer of 1800 flour from mills along Lake Ontario was going down the St. Lawrence in considerable quantities.[40] By midsummer of 1801 the Niagara district exported 5,000 barrels of flour, "which for the first year is really very great."[41] Before the end of 1801, Upper Canada from Kingston westward exported to Montreal 13,963 barrels of fine and superfine flour, 322 barrels of middlings, and 350 bushels of wheat. Of the flour, 2,489 barrels were shipped from the Detroit district.[42] In 1802, a year of exceptionally good demand, Upper Canada exported 11,422 barrels of flour.[43]

From this time on, with few interruptions, there was a

---

[35]Canniff, *History of the Settlement of Upper Canada*, pp. 215-16.

[36]Judge Nathan Ford to Stephen Van Rensselaer, Dec. 30, 1799, in Hough, *History of Jefferson County*, pp. 309-10.

[37]Niagara *Herald*, Jan. 24, Feb. 14, 1801.

[38]Smyth, *A Short Topographical Description of Upper Canada*, p. 8.

[39]Niagara *Canada Constellation*, Sept. 13, 1799.

[40]Elias Smith to Joseph Allen, July 23, 1800, in Elias Smith Papers.

[41]Robert Nichol to John Askin, June 15, 1801, in Quaife, *John Askin Papers*, vol. II, p. 343.

[42]Niagara *Herald*, June 13, 1801; R. Cartwright to General Hunter, Oct. 24, 1801, in *Cartwright*, p. 82. However, as late as 1808 it was said that the cost of transportation ordinarily prohibited the sending of flour from Detroit to Montreal (Charles Askin to John Askin, Feb. 25, 1808, in Quaife, *John Askin Papers*, vol. II, p. 596).

[43]Quebec *Gazette*, April 7, 1803.

strong Lower Canada demand for Upper Canada breadstuffs to export to Great Britain, where a succession of bad crops combined with an occasional shutting off of Baltic wheat supplies to keep the restrictions of the Corn Laws in virtual abeyance.[44] There was also a market in the British West Indies, but American competition kept this from amounting to very much.[45]

The Lower Canada demand made it profitable for Upper Canada capitalists to erect "merchant mills." In 1806 a traveller visited one of these, which was situated in the Niagara peninsula, below St. Johns. He observed that it was four and a half storeys high, that it had two pairs of stones, and that it was equipped with fanning mills, conveyors, and elevators — in other words, with all the inventions then associated with the name of Oliver Evans and the famous mills along the Brandywine. "This mill," continued the visitor, "was built by a young man, who afterwards built mills [below Niagara Falls] for Messrs. Hamilton and Cartwright."[46]

Mills such as these created a local grain market, acreage expanded in consequence, and by 1805 certain parts of Upper Canada, especially the Bay of Quinte region, were beginning to have reputations for good wheat. "The grain," it was claimed, "is heavier and more plump than any that is raised in the territories of the United States, except such as border upon this immense [St. Lawrence] river."[47] It was so superior, indeed, that the small amounts exported without being ground were, like the best spring wheat of Lower Canada, in demand in the west of Scotland for blending with the soft local wheat to produce a satisfactory flour.[48]

---

[44]Ernle, *English Farming Past and Present*, pp. 210-13, 269.

[45]Gray, *Letters from Canada*, pp. 200, 235-7; Bouchette, *Topographical Description of Lower Canada*, pp. 83-4.

[46]Aikins, "Journal of a Journey from Sandwich to York in the Summer of 1806" (*OHSPR*, vol. VI, 1905, p. 18). A description of the inventions of Evans is given in Neftel, "Report on Flour-Milling Processes" (*Tenth Census of the United States*, vol. III, pp. 1 ff.). Descriptions of several grist-mills of the pioneer era are to be found in Guillet, *Early Life in Upper Canada*, pp. 216-31.

[47]Heriot, *Travels through the Canadas*, p. 154. Cf. Boulton, *Sketch of Upper Canada*, p. 38.

[48]Gray, *Letters from Canada*, p. 200.

The most conspicuous figures in the early grain trade of
Upper Canada were the merchants of Kingston and other
villages. For most of them collecting grain, having it
transported, and selling it, were logical additions to their
activities as buyers of peltry, contractors to the garrisons,
importers and forwarders of manufactured goods, and local
bankers. They advanced supplies to the settlers, and received flour or wheat in return.[49] This kind of trade continued year after year. Farmers found that ordinarily
their only outlet for wheat was the merchant to whom they
were indebted, unless they chose to export it to Montreal
themselves. In this period the merchants never paid cash,
at least, not cash in the modern sense. Thus in 1808 a
merchant at York advertised for wheat of good quality,
such as would make superfine flour for export. To those
who were indebted to him for more than one year, he offered
to pay 5s.5d. York currency a bushel; to those indebted
less than one year, 6s.; to those wishing to barter for merchandise, 6s.; and to those wishing to obtain cash, 6s., the
"cash" to take the form of a promissory note payable in eight
months.[50] Another merchant shortly afterwards offered
to pay half in cash, if required, but the balance had to be
taken in merchandise.[51]

When they had bought the wheat, the merchants commonly ground it into flour. This, with the flour they obtained
from the farmers, they had to get to Montreal. The farmers
below Kingston transported much of their grain down the
St. Lawrence on the ice during the winter, but this method
was of little value to those who lived along Lake Ontario.
These turned to rafts of boards or timber for transporting
their flour—not a very satisfactory means, as the flour could
not be kept dry. The merchants, however, were able to
utilize the *bateaux* which brought their imports up the river,
sending them back loaded with flour and other produce. As
soon as the number of *bateaux* was insufficient to carry the
exports, they introduced Durham boats, with a capacity of

---

[49]John McGill to Simcoe, Jan. 8, 1793, in *Simcoe Papers*, vol. I,
pp. 272-3.
[50]York *Gazette*, Feb. 26, 1808.
[51]*Ibid.*, Feb. 3, 1809.

350 barrels of flour. The first of these appears to have left Kingston with a cargo in June or July of 1801.[52]

The merchants consigned their produce to correspondents in Montreal, who sold it on commission. One of these merchants who was in business at Chippawa in 1802 shipped 195 barrels of flour to Montreal, consigned to Auldjo, Maitland & Co. The company paid the freight and the storage and inspection charges, and deducted these expenses from the proceeds, as well as the usual commission of 2½ per cent on the original value of the shipment.[53] The Montreal house then drew at sixty days on the British firm with which it dealt.[54]

Much of the first Upper Canada flour sent to Lower Canada was found to be inferior. To prevent all of it from acquiring a bad reputation, the legislature provided in 1801 for its inspection in the province.[55] That this act was not altogether satisfactory in its operation, we may gather from the fact that after 1806 Upper Canada flour was made subject to re-inspection in Lower Canada.[56]

Though the growing of wheat was rapidly becoming the staple industry of Upper Canada in the years after 1800, other branches of farming had their importance. In the vicinity of such towns as Kingston and York, where civilian and military demand resulted in the establishment of public markets in 1801 and 1804 respectively,[57] farmers were encouraged to produce beef and pork, peas, oats, and potatoes. In inland townships, where transportation was difficult and costly, some began to specialize in dairying, for Michael Smith asserted that Oxford Township, adjacent to the Thames River, was settled by "industrious people, from the states of New

---

[52]Smyth, *Topographical Description of . . . Upper Canada*, pp. 8-9; Robert Nichol to John Askin, June 15, 1801, in Quaife, *John Askin Papers*, vol. II, p. 343; same to same, July 25, 1801, *ibid.*, vol. II, p. 353; R. Cartwright to General Hunter, Oct. 24, 1801, in *Cartwright*, p. 79.

[53]Auldjo, Maitland & Co. to Thomas Cummings, Dec. 31, 1802, in Cruikshank, "Country Merchant in Upper Canada" (*OHSPR*, vol. XXV, 1929, p. 152).

[54]Gray, *Letters from Canada*, p. 200.

[55]41 Geo. III, c. 7 *(Statutes of Upper Canada)*.

[56]*Journal of the Legislative Assembly of Upper Canada, 1821*, p. 473.

[57]Niagara *Herald*, July 18, 1801; Council Minutes, Upper Canada, 1804, Q 298, pp. 51-2.

York and Vermont," who were "famous for making butter and cheese."[58]   Still others, desiring a product which would provide its own transportation, turned to livestock-raising.

Raising livestock on the range had been characteristic of the back country of Virginia and North Carolina in the eighteenth century and of the forest openings and "barrens" (prairies) of the Trans-Appalachian West after the American Revolution.   It was a normal phase of frontier development, therefore, for the inhabitants of the lower Thames Valley to keep their cattle from spring to fall on the wet prairies adjacent to the mouth of the river and Indian-fashion to set fire to the dead vegetation in the autumn to assure fresh pasturage in the spring.[59]   More important in the range-cattle industry than these wet prairies along Lake St. Clair were, however, the oak-plains of the Long Point settlement, where cattle were kept in the open the year around, foraging for themselves, and so being raised very cheaply.   At the age of three or four years, these cattle were driven elsewhere to be fattened.   In 1799 they evidently did not have to be taken beyond the borders of the province to find buyers, but by 1805 so many were being grazed near Long Point that the home market was no longer adequate, and their owners had to drive them as far as Albany, N.Y.[60]   As a matter of fact, it was stated at this time that "the sending of cattle from Upper Canada to the United States for sale, is not confined to any particular district, but is general throughout the Province," because the farmers and drovers considered "the market in the States as superior to that of Canada, both in regard of price and mode of Payment."[61]   From this

[58]Smith, *Geographical View of Upper Canada*, p. 12.

[59]Wallace (ed.), "Captain Miles Macdonell's 'Journal of a Jaunt to Amherstburg' in 1801" (*Canadian Historical Review*, vol. xxv, 1944, p. 171). For the range-cattle industry in eighteenth-century Virginia and North Carolina, see Thompson, *History of Livestock Raising in the United States*, pp. 59-62, 77.

[60]Smyth, *Topographical Description of . . . Upper Canada*, p. 35; Boulton, *Sketch of Upper Canada*, pp. 60-1, 72. Doubtless these exports from the western part of Upper Canada were a consequence of the competition of American cattle at Detroit (John Askin to Isaac Todd, Oct. 17, 1800, in Quaife, *John Askin Papers*, vol. II, p. 318).

[61]General Hunter to Anthony Merry, Nov. 12, 1804, Public Archives of Canada, Letter Book, Military Secretary's Office, C 1212, p. 191.

remark we may deduce that the Upper Canada "growers," whether they were the specialized ones at Long Point or the common settlers with a few surplus steers, were tributary to the cattle fatteners around New York and Philadelphia, just as were the pioneers in the newly opened portions of New York, Pennsylvania, and Ohio. We may assume that cattle-raising with a view to export to the United States continued to be profitable, especially when the animals were kept on the range, for in his description of Upper Canada just before the War of 1812, Michael Smith mentions that the plains of Norfolk County were "thickly settled with rich farmers, who raise great quantities of grain and cattle."[62]

Many farmers found in the by-products of forest-clearing an incidental source of profit. Oak staves, square timber, planks, and boards could be disposed of advantageously at Montreal, at least after about 1800. Potash was more important. As early as 1797 merchants as far west as Queenston were advertising for house and field ashes to be delivered at their potasheries.[63] During the Napoleonic Wars there was a steady overseas demand for potash. Largely in consequence of the United States Embargo Act of 1807-9 and Non-Intercourse Act of 1809-10, prices of potash at Montreal were exceptionally high between 1808 and 1810. At one time they reached $320 a ton. Thousands of barrels of potash were smuggled out of New York State from Oswego eastward in defiance of American customs officers and militia, and on both sides of the frontier much land was cleared simply for the ashes. When Anglo-American commercial relations were resumed after the passage of Macon's Bill Number Two (May, 1810), prices fell from 40 to 60 per cent. This collapse, with a concurrent collapse in the lumber business,

---

[62]Smith, *Geographical View . . . of Upper Canada*, p. 11. This assumption is strengthened by a comment made by a drover encountered by a traveller in the Western Reserve (northeastern Ohio) in 1811, to the effect that "the people along the banks of the lake [Erie] would always have a fine market for their surplus stock to the eastward, and that there would be plenty of people always ready to buy" (Melish, *Travels through the United States of America*, p. 481).

[63]Newark *Upper Canada Gazette or American Oracle*, Feb. 1, Feb. 15, 1797. Provision was made for the official inspection of potash and pearlash in 1801 (41 Geo. III, c. 7).

brought about a depression in parts of Upper Canada which lasted till the outbreak of the War of 1812.[64]

While Upper Canada pioneers were thus making progress in a variety of ways, there arose a problem which was to vex administrators, politicians, and farmers for more than two generations—that of the disposition of waste lands. It is true that the provisions made for granting land to the original Loyalists were wise. Land-jobbing was prevented by a system of drawing lots for parcels of land, and by not permitting the military officers (who were entitled to larger grants in accordance with their rank) to have any advantage in choice. The limited number of the first Loyalists—probably less than 6,000 in all—meant that few were located in 1784 farther back than the third concession.[65] But soon their children either took up unoccupied lots in the vicinity, thus producing a consolidation of settlement in the older townships, or moved north or west to form a second tier of population. "To take advantage of this expansive force and to reward patriotism, the government granted land free to all children of the Loyalists when they came of age." It soon found, to its disappointment, that its policy did not result in a progressive extension of solid settlement. Girls could not clear their grants alone, boys often counted on inheriting their fathers' farms, the allotments were frequently in remote parts of Upper Canada, and ready cash was irresistible. In consequence, "Loyalist rights" became a staple article of commerce. Almost as soon as the rising generation drew them, it sold them to speculators at prices ranging from a gallon of rum for a 200-acre lot to about £6.[66] In this way much of the land all over the province came to be locked up by speculators. A similar condition resulted from the operation of the long-standing practice of the British government of rewarding officers of the army and navy who had served overseas by grants of land ranging up to 5,000 acres, from

---

[64]Shortt, "The Economic Effect of the War of 1812," p. 82; Hough, *History of Jefferson County*, pp. 89, 458-9; York *Gazette*, Aug. 27, 1808; Quebec *Mercury*, March 13, 1809.

[65]Burt, *Old Province of Quebec*, pp. 360-3, 374-5.

[66]Lucas (ed.), *Lord Durham's Report*, vol. II, p. 224; Moodie, *Roughing it in the Bush*, vol. I, p. 196; Croil, *Dundas*, p. 135; Macdonald, *Canada, 1763-1841*, pp. 52-4.

the encouragement given by Simcoe after 1792 to the
"associates" who were supposed to bring in settlers, but who
were actually only land-jobbers, and from the open-handed
generosity of Peter Russell to speculators.[67] The clergy
and crown reserves established in Upper Canada in 1792
were an additional cause of complaint to the pioneer farmers,
for the lots set off in each township according to the checkered
plans, or the reserved blocks, meant that theoretically there
would be parts of almost every township which would remain
in wilderness, possibly for decades, havens for wild animals
and bars to improvements in transportation.[68]

But it is easy to exaggerate the importance of this waste-
land problem. Upper Canada land policy admittedly left
much to be desired, but it was not as bad as Robert Gourlay
represented.   Land speculators were found on every frontier.
It would even seem that the maligned clergy and crown reserves had a definite usefulness, in that they offered a convenient means for a poor man to obtain a piece of land to
rent.   Thus, according to an advertisement of 1803, either
crown or clergy reserves would be rented on a 21-year
lease, at the rate of 10s. provincial currency or three bushels
of wheat per 200 acres, payable annually for seven years,
double these amounts for the next seven years, and treble
them for the third seven.[69] Moreover, there is evidence that
often these small rents went unpaid.[70] As for the land-
jobbers, they had a definite interest in having at least part
of their holdings settled, for otherwise they might have to
wait long for any appreciation in value.   While, therefore,
waste lands held by the crown or by private speculators did
handicap progress, on the whole it appears that there was
so much land readily available—the price of Loyalist rights
shows this—that speculation was but a slight hindrance to
settlement till after the War of 1812.

---

[67]R. Cartwright to Gen. Hunter, Aug. 23, 1799, in *Cartwright*, pp.
94-5; Patterson, *Land Settlement in Upper Canada*, pp. 59, 83.

[68]For a critique of the clergy and crown reserves, see Riddell, "The
Policy of Creating Land Reserves in Canada" (*Essays in Canadian
History Presented to George Wrong*, pp. 296-317).

[69]York *Upper Canada Gazette or American Oracle*, Jan. 1, 1803.

[70]Kingston *Upper Canada Herald*, March 18, 1825.

On the eve of the War of 1812, the Loyalist and other inhabitants of Upper Canada could look back on a quarter-century of notable agricultural advancement. The first of them had occupied a primeval wilderness in what was then the remote interior of North America. They and their successors had now passed from the economy of the back-woodsman to that of the wheat farmer, which they varied by small attempts at diversification. They had an export market overseas, with a backlog in the demand of the garrisons and of the fur traders. In spite of orders-in-council and the recurring threat of Indian troubles in the Old Northwest, they seemed assured of their future.

CHAPTER III

WAR, DEPRESSION AND RECOVERY, 1812-1831

FOR some of the farmers of Upper Canada the War of
1812 was a disaster. They were called to serve in the
militia, and so were unable to get their crops in or to harvest
them; their barns were burnt and their orchards cut down;
and their cattle were driven away by the enemy.[1] But
this was not universally true. Conscientious objectors like
the Mennonites commuted their military service by a tax
and remained on their farms.[2] Military operations centred
on the Niagara frontier, so that the eastern part of the
province saw little except skirmishings. For Upper Canada
as a whole the period was not one of ruin and suffering, but
one of a prosperity which surpassed that prevailing between
1796 and 1800.

The military forces sent to defend the colony created
such a demand for agricultural products that local prices, as
in the early Loyalist era, came to be the Montreal prices with
the cost of transportation up the St. Lawrence added. As
a result everyone thought he was on the high road to wealth,
for he found he could sell anything he owned for double
what it would have brought a few years before. No exports went down the river to Montreal, as the government laid
an embargo on all flour, wheat, and pork in the province as
soon as war was declared.[3] Assured of a market, many of
the farmers sought to profit by the necessities of the military
by withholding supplies to force prices still higher. Accordingly, in 1813-14 martial law was invoked in the Midland,
Johnstown, and Eastern Districts to obtain food for the
garrisons at Kingston and Prescott.[4]

In spite of high prices and the resort to martial law,
the supplies forthcoming in Upper Canada fell far short of

---

[1]Smith, *Geographical View of . . . Upper Canada*, p. 97; Hall,
Travels in Canada, p. 205; Howison, *Sketches of Upper Canada*, p. 79.
[2]Bigsby, *Shoe and Canoe*, vol. I, pp. 293-4.
[3]Smith, *Geographical View of . . . Upper Canada*, p. 97; Kingston
Gazette, May 4, 1814.
[4]Cruikshank, "Study of Disaffection in Upper Canada" (*Transactions of the Royal Society of Canada*, 3rd series, vol. VI, 1912, pp. 40-1).

meeting requirements. The local commanders made up the deficiency by importing flour, pork, and livestock from New York and even from Vermont and New Hampshire. These imports, regulated through trading licences, commenced as soon as sleighing was good in 1812, and continued to the close of the war. By midsummer of 1814, two-thirds of the men under arms in the Canadas were dependent on beef brought in by American contractors.[5] At this time an American general reported that "The road to St. Regis is covered with droves of cattle, and the river with rafts, destined for the enemy. . . . On the eastern side of Lake Champlain the high roads are found insufficient for the supplies of cattle which are pouring into Canada. Like herds of buffaloes they press through the forest, making paths for themselves. . . . Nothing but a cordon of troops from the French Mills to Lake Memphramagog could effectively check the evil."[6]

On the return of peace the disbanded militiamen went back to their farms to add to the population engaged in production, and after an interval a large part of the regular forces departed from the province. Yet for a few years there were comparatively high prices in Upper Canada, so that the province had a semblance of prosperity. These high prices were to be attributed to a number of factors— to a continuance of the war-time policy of easy credit by the Montreal wholesalers to the country store-keepers in Upper Canada, and by the latter to their customers;[7] to the poor harvests of 1815 and especially of 1816 (the "cold summer" in which there was a very severe frost in Western Upper Canada in July), which resulted in such a scarcity that flour sold at York for as much as $16.00 a barrel;[8] and to the demand for livestock to replace that consumed by the troops or driven off by the Americans. Even at the close of 1818 the farmers in the Niagara district had "not got into a

---

[5]Smith, *Geographical View of . . . Upper Canada*, pp. 97-8; Adams, *History of the United States*, vol. VII, p. 146.

[6]Quoted in Adams, *History of the United States*, vol. VIII, p. 93.

[7]Howison, *Sketches of Upper Canada*, p. 80.

[8]O'Reilly, *Sketches of Rochester*, p. 362; "Talbot Settlement and Buffalo" (*Ontario Historical Society Papers and Records*, vol. I, 1899, pp. 139-40). Hereafter this authority is cited as *OHSPR*.

sufficient stock of cattle and hogs since the destruction that
was made during the late war."[9]   The general agricultural
shortage was so great that the inhabitants of New York State
entered the local markets of Upper Canada with their cattle,
their flour, and even their vegetables.[10]

Another factor which helped sustain Upper Canada prices
was the revival of the export trade in wheat and flour.   The
British Isles afforded the most important outlet, as during
the Napoleonic Wars.   Under the new Corn Law of 1815
the colonies in North America enjoyed an advantage over
their foreign competitors, for now the regulations excluded
foreign wheat and flour till the British average price reached
80s. a quarter, while they admitted colonial wheat and flour
at 67s. Under this act, no duties were collected on the
breadstuffs imported from abroad, for the intention was
merely to provide protection for the British farmer.[11]   Deficient crops between 1816 and 1820 on the Continent as well
as in the United Kingdom kept British wheat prices above
67s. Wheat and flour were accordingly shipped down the
St. Lawrence in considerable quantities from 1817 to 1820.
Precarious as the British market was, many Americans obtained farms in the province during these years to take advantage of it.[12]   At this time the fall wheat of Upper
Canada still enjoyed its superior reputation for blending
with the soft wheats of Scotland and the north of England.
On the other hand, exporters found that Upper Canada flour
was declining in British estimation.   It was charged that
it was poorly ground, packed without proper cooling, and
carelessly handled on its way to Montreal, so that on its
arrival at Liverpool it was much inferior to that exported
earlier.   It may be assumed that this development was at-
tributable to a rush of small millers into the trade.   The
deterioration in the quality of the flour soon made little

---

[9]Niagara *Gleaner*, Dec. 31, 1818, quoted in Cruikshank, "News of
Niagara" (*OHSPR.*, vol. XXIII, 1926, p. 56).

[10]Howison, *Sketches of Upper Canada*, p. 80; O'Reilly, *Sketches of
Rochester*, p. 362; Gourlay, *Statistical Account of Upper Canada*, vol.
I, p. 497.

[11]Ernle, *English Farming Past and Present*, p. 446. The background
and the working of this famous Corn Law of 1815 are given exhaustive
consideration in Barnes, *History of the English Corn Laws*, pp. 117-74.

[12]Dalton, *Travels in the United States*, p. 187.

difference, however, for in November, 1820, as a consequence
of an excellent harvest, wheat prices in the British Isles
fell below 67s. a quarter, and Upper Canada wheat and flour
were automatically excluded, or to be more precise, were
forced to remain in bond in British warehouses till such time
as prices would rise again.[13]

Their exclusion accentuated the economic depression from
which Upper Canada had been suffering for over a year,
as an accompaniment of that prevailing in the United States.
It was already the practice in Lower Canada to import
American grain and flour for consumption in the province,
to permit the exportation of the breadstuffs produced locally.
When Upper Canada millers and merchants, with their inferior flour, tried to supplant the Americans in the Montreal
market, they were successful only in bringing about a
glut.[14] Their warehouses filled with flour and grain which
could not be sold, the merchants and speculators ceased to
buy wheat.

Nor was this all. The union of the North West Company
and the Hudson's Bay Company in 1821 made possible the
supplying of all the agricultural requirements of the fur
traders from the Red River settlement instead of from Upper
Canada. Further, the market which had once existed in the
United States for livestock had not revived after the war.
Indeed, New Yorkers and others, even harder hit by the
depression than Upper Canadians, were not only driving
cattle into the province every day, but were coming as far
as 150 miles to sell beef to the newcomers in the back settlements, such as those around Perth and Lanark.[15]

Under these circumstances all prices collapsed. Between
1819 and 1822, the price of wheat dropped from about $1.00
a bushel to 50 cents, livestock values were reduced by half,
and real-estate values by more than half. These changes, it
was declared, represented a decline of from 300 to 400 per

[13]*Journal of the Legislative Assembly of Upper Canada, 1821*, pp.
429-31; Montreal *Gazette*, Feb. 27, 1821.

[14]*Journal of the Legislative Assembly of Upper Canada, 1821*, p.
430; Hodgson, *Letters from North America*, vol. II, pp. 50-1.

[15]Dalton, *Travels in the United States*, p. 187; M'Donald, *Narrative
of a Voyage to Quebec*, p. 29.

cent in the price level since the boom days of the war.[16] When they looked back to that time, with its affluence, many farmers, it was said, "would prefer war, with all its horrors, to the tranquillity which they now enjoy."[17]

Depressions in the United States in the early nineteenth century frequently led farmers to try a new staple, either to replace one which had failed them, or to diversify their production. A similar tendency was manifested in Upper Canada in the early eighteen-twenties in experiments with several crops.

One of these was tobacco. Pickering, writing in 1826, remarked that runaway slaves in western Upper Canada worked at raising tobacco, and ventured a guess that they had introduced its culture into the province. This does not seem probable. Tobacco had been a garden crop for generations among the French Canadians of the St. Lawrence Valley and the Detroit region.[18] In any case, settlers from almost any of the American states had at least a rudimentary knowledge of its cultivation. It was "tried on a small scale near Amherstburgh" before 1819, with the product being "judged equal in manufacture to any obtained from the United States."[19] In the winter of 1822-3, a letter from Amherstburg stated that "there has been some stir this winter in consequence of the Tobacco trade. Next spring I think there will not be less than *one hundred hogsheads* shipped from hence."[20] In 1824 Amherstburg tobacco

---

[16]Cruikshank, "Post War Discontent at Niagara in 1818" (*OHSPR*, vol. XXIX, 1933, p. 46); Talbot, *Five Years' Residence*, vol. II, p. 181.

[17]Bell, *Hints to Emigrants*, p. 152.

[18]Pickering, *Inquiries of an Emigrant*, p. 97. It is most probable that it was derived originally from the Wyandots. According to Parkman, these were chiefly descendants of the old Tobacco Nation (Parkman, *The Jesuits in North America*, p. 426). Cf. Hudgins, "Tobacco Growing in Southwestern Ontario" (*Economic Geography*, vol. XIV, 1938, pp. 229-30).

[19]Stuart, *Emigrant's Guide to Upper Canada*, p. 35.

[20]Quebec *Gazette*, quoted in *American Farmer*, vol. IV, 1822-3, p. 379. Beginning about 1822 there was a similar expansion of tobacco-growing in the hilly country of eastern Ohio. Though it was an outgrowth of conditions similar to those in Upper Canada, it had no discoverable connection with developments in the latter.

seems to have been in demand in towns such as Kingston.[21]
Later, Essex peninsula tobacco was carried down the St.
Lawrence to Montreal or Quebec, where it was manufactured
into cigars. Although the tobacco manufacturers found that
the different varieties grown were coarser and ranker than
tobacco imported from the United States, they apparently
bought the entire crop year after year.[22]

Tobacco culture involved much labour, not heavy according to pioneer standards, but tedious. First the farmer
transplanted the young plants from beds to hills. Then he
hoed them to keep them free of weeds and grass, "budded"
them to prevent the tops from stealing nutriment from the
leaves, and "sprouted" or suckered them three times to remove the side-shoots. He harvested the stalks (with the
leaves still on them) in late August or early September,
suspended them for a few days in the open air, and then
removed them to a shed for curing. During the winter he
stripped the leaves from the stalks, allowed them to sweat
for a few days, and formed them into hands. In the early
spring he packed his crop into hogsheads. As it was considered that one person could not properly manage more than
four acres, or at most five, the shortage of labour characteristic of a new country tended to limit the production of
tobacco. The largest fields mentioned were only of eight
or nine acres. Another limiting factor was that tobacco
prices fluctuated rather widely, sometimes falling to as little
as 5 cents a pound. On the other hand, even at low prices, a
crop yielding 1,500 pounds to the acre, which was said to
be average with tobacco, was not to be despised, for it would
bring the farmer some cash. It was estimated that, at worst,
tobacco would pay for clearing the new land on which it
was almost invariably grown, as well as all the labour costs
involved in its cultivation. Under these circumstances the
first flurry of interest was followed by a very slow expansion
of the industry in Essex and Kent counties. Here, especially
along the Lake Erie shore, hundred-foot tobacco barns dotted
the landscape by 1840. Essex produced 457,111 pounds of

[21]Kingston *Upper Canada Herald*, March 1, 1825.

[22]Murray, *Historical and Descriptive Account*, vol. I, p. 342; *ibid.*,
vol. II, pp. 18-19.

tobacco in 1850 and Kent 313,189. In the other counties of
Upper Canada tobacco-growing failed to become established,
for their combined crop in 1850 was only 6,116 pounds.[23]

Attempts in the early eighteen-twenties to turn colonial
energies to the raising of flax and hemp were ill-starred,
like most similar efforts. As before the War of 1812, almost
all the farmers in Upper Canada grew flax for the purpose
of making grain-bags, towels, household linen, and coarse
clothing, but because they found that there was no established
market for the fibre, they made no response to the reiterated
appeals of officials to extend their acreage. In consequence,
capitalists were reluctant to erect flax mills—a vicious circle.
When a flax mill was opened in Glengarry County in 1818,
it proved so unprofitable that its proprietor was forced to ask
for a government subsidy the next year.[24] In Ohio and
Pennsylvania farmers made money at this time by growing
flax merely for the seed, but those in Upper Canada could
not do this, for there were scarcely any local linseed-oil
mills, and there was no foreign outlet except Ireland. There
was another factor which contributed to the farmers' antipathy to flax as a staple. It was not particularly difficult
to grow flax, but it took much hard work to prepare it for
sale. The flax had to be pulled by hand, and the seed-pods
combed off to provide seed for the next year. When the
stalks were dried, they had to be "retted," that is, spread
out in the weather till the leaves rotted off. Then they went
to the flax-brake, a heavy wooden machine in which they
were so broken up that the woody portions separated from
the fibre. After this followed the operations of swingling
or scutching, which was removing the woody remnants from
the fibre, and of hackling or hatchelling, which was combing
out the tangled fibres (or "tow") and the straight ones (or
flax proper). The oftener the flax was hackled, with combs
of progressive degrees of fineness, the finer the thread (and
so the linen) would be. These factors not only ruined the
prospects of commercial flax culture; they contributed to

---

[23]Pickering, *Inquiries of an Emigrant*, pp. 96-7; Garland (ed.),
"Proudfoot Papers" (*OHSPR*, vol. XXVII, 1931, p. 495); Smith, *Canada,
Past, Present and Future*, vol. I, p. 28; *Census of Canada, 1851-2*,
vol. II, p. 64; Buffalo *Advertiser*, cited in *Cultivator*, April, 1841, p. 61.

[24]*Journal of the Legislative Assembly of Upper Canada, 1819*, p. 146.

the extinction of growing flax even for domestic use. The going out of fashion of the flax patch may be dated from about 1830, when linsey-woolsey clothing began to be replaced by cheap cottons, as it was in the northern United States. By 1850 flax-growing was practically abandoned throughout Upper Canada.[25]

As an answer to the depression of the early eighteen-twenties, hemp proved even more disappointing than flax. There was really nothing new in the attempt to make it a staple. Before the American Revolution it had been the object of frequent experimentation in the seaboard colonies, often with the stimulus of subsidies from the legislatures. During the era of the French Revolution and the Napoleonic Wars the British government had encouraged its production in North America to avert the shortage which would arise from the anticipated loss of Russian supplies. In 1801 the legislature of Upper Canada participated to the extent of voting £250 to buy hemp-seed for free distribution and £500 to provide premiums and bounties. One farmer in Kent County had twelve acres of hemp in 1802. The same year a gold medal was awarded to one at Kingston for growing hemp, and a silver medal to one at York. After 1802, though there are scattered references to hemp culture in the state papers of Upper Canada, the amount of hemp produced was negligible. The little that was marketed was inferior, for according to Charles Askin, the farmers did not know how to cure it, and were unwilling to learn, so that it was usually spoiled. But even if it had been of good quality, it could not have competed in price with Russian hemp in Great Britain, even during the war years. Undeterred by this earlier failure, the provincial legislature in 1822 voted £450 for the purchase and repair of hemp-manufacturing machinery, and then or shortly afterwards offered a premium of £25 to the person growing the most hemp on a plot of land not to exceed five acres. But the machinery never was bought, and the premium never was claimed. The farmers soon found, if they did not already know, that though hemp had a market overseas, they were

[25]Smith, *Canada, Past, Present and Future*, vol. I, p. 249; *Journal and Transactions of the Board of Agriculture of Upper Canada for 1855-6*, pp. 341, 451.

not justified in producing it when their labour would go so much farther in growing grain.[26]   The anxious care of the legislature brought forth little except the *bon mot* of Edward Talbot, that in the matter of hemp, "the two Canadas cannot at present afford a sufficient quantity to hang their own malefactors."[27]

While these special crops were still in the stage of trial or discussion, the farmers of the province passed out of the depression.   Prosperity returned definitely in 1825, and persisted for several years.

One factor which contributed to this rural prosperity was the establishment of a tariff against agricultural imports from the United States.   Previously, in the hope of drawing the commerce of the American West down the St. Lawrence, there had been virtual free trade along the border. The result, as has been mentioned, was that American livestock, meats, and flour came into competition with those of Upper Canada in the markets of Lower Canada, and often in those of Upper Canada as well.   It was with this situation in mind that a Select Committee on Internal Resources of the Upper Canada Assembly in 1821 set forth a proposal which was often to be advanced by Upper Canada farmers in later years.   It suggested that, when the Corn Laws excluded Upper Canadian flour and wheat from the United Kingdom, a protective tariff should be imposed on Lower Canada, to exclude American flour from the only market to which that of Upper Canada could be sent.   This would apply only to what was being imported for consumption in the lower province, not to any merely being exported via the St. Lawrence.[28]

Though it was not passed as a result of this appeal, but as an attempt to systematize the tariffs of the Empire, the imperial Canada Trade Act of 1822 went much farther than the Select Committee had suggested, for it imposed

[26]Quebec *Gazette*, Aug. 27, 1801; *ibid.*, April 7, 1803; Charles Askin to John Askin, Feb. 25, 1808, in Quaife, *John Askin Papers*, vol. II, p. 596; Talbot, *Five Years' Residence*, vol. I, pp. 307-8; Pickering, *Inquiries of an Emigrant*, p. 98; *Canadian Archives Report for 1891*, pp. xlii-iii; *ibid for 1892*, pp. xxiii-iv.

[27]Talbot, *Five Years' Residence*, vol. I, p. 304.

[28]*Journal of the Legislative Assembly of Upper Canada, 1821*, p. 430.

duties on American agricultural products entering both
Canadas—1s. a bushel on wheat, 5s. a barrel on flour, and
corresponding amounts on the whole range of imports.
Three years later, other imperial laws actually prohibited the
importation of salted beef and pork into the Canadas by
land or inland navigation. When it was pointed out that the
fisheries of Lower Canada and Newfoundland, like the
lumber trade, were dependent on the United States for most
of their meat, the new regulations were relaxed in 1826 and
1827 to permit the free importation into the Canadas of
fresh meats from the United States, the importation in bond
of salted meats for re-export to Newfoundland, and the importation in bond of flour for re-export to the British West
Indies and South America.[29]

The duties imposed on American agricultural produce
brought in for consumption by the terms of the Canada
Trade Act and the regulations which followed it were far
from prohibitory. The tariff was no hindrance to the importation of considerable numbers of cattle, pigs, and sheep.
The American timber rafts which came down the St.
Lawrence in the spring frequently had a few yokes of oxen
and two or three hundred pigs aboard.[30] Sometimes Americans drove across the frozen St. Lawrence into eastern
Upper Canada, evading the customs officials, and sold their
beef, pork, flour, and whisky at bargain prices.[31] On the
other hand, there is some evidence that Upper Canadian
farmers packed more pork than they would have done without the slight protection afforded by the tariff.[32] While the
tariff thus seems to have satisfied the farmers fairly well,
it certainly distressed the merchants engaged in the forwarding business.[33] Possibly much of the benefit supposed
to be derived from its operation should actually have been
attributed to the effects of the opening of the Erie Canal

---

[29]Creighton, *Commercial Empire of the St. Lawrence*, pp. 234, 237-9,
247; *Journal of the Legislative Assembly of Lower Canada, 1826*, p. 360.

[30]Hume, *Canada as It Is*, p. 31; Pickering, *Inquiries of an Emigrant*,
p. 141.

[31]Bell, *Hints to Emigrants*, p. 182.

[32]York *Upper Canada Gazette and U. E. Loyalist*, Oct. 27, 1827;
York *Colonial Advocate*, June 2, 1831.

[33]Kingston *Herald*, quoted in Montreal *Gazette*, June 4, 1830.

(1825). With the lowering of freight rates to New York, and a great increase in the consuming population in the western states, the Upper Canada market was not so attractive to Americans as it had been a few years earlier.

Another factor which contributed to the return of prosperity was the development of local outlets for the agricultural surplus. The British immigrants who arrived after 1815 provided an excellent newcomers' market for several years in their respective communities. Ambitious projects, like those of the Canada Company at Guelph and Goderich, created a great demand for provisions. The Pennsylvania Dutch in Waterloo County, for instance, particularly benefited from the foundation of Guelph.[34] Even more important as markets were the construction camps associated with the Welland, Rideau, and Grenville canals.[35] Another local market, one constantly growing in importance with the expansion of the trade in square timber, was especially characteristic of the Ottawa Valley. This was the shanty market, which will be given detailed consideration in Chapter VII.

A final factor in economic recovery was the resumption of the export grain trade. This was made possible in large part by changes in the Corn Laws. By the Corn Law of 1822, the British average price which would exclude colonial wheat was lowered to 59s. Above this point wheat was not admitted free, as in 1815, but was made subject to a duty. This was fixed at 12s. a quarter when the British price was under 67s. (as it proved to be till 1825), 5s. when it was under 71s., and 1s. when it was at or above 71s. In 1825 a temporary regulation permitted Canadian wheat to enter the British Isles at all times, no matter what British prices might be, on the payment of a duty of 5s. a quarter. In 1827 another temporary regulation provided that, while the duty on colonial wheat was to remain at 5s. a quarter when the British home price was below 67s., it was to drop to a nominal 6d. a quarter when the British price exceeded 67s. The same regulation granted colonial flour admission on

---

[34]Fergusson, *Practical Notes made during a Tour*, p. 282.

[35]Report of Duncan McDowell, Sept. 21, 1827, in Picken, *The Canadas*, pp. 130-1; Dunlop, *Statistical Sketches of Upper Canada*, pp. 67-8.

corresponding terms. The Corn Law of 1828 made the regulation of 1827 permanent, and thereby gave Canadian wheat and flour important advantages over those of foreign countries, for the duty on foreign wheat was 1s. a quarter when the price in Great Britain stood at 73s., or above, and increased as the British price fell, till it reached 20s. 8d. when the price dropped to 67s.[36]

Not only did the changes in the Corn Laws assure a market in the British Isles, they incidentally helped to reduce the glut of a few years earlier in Lower Canada. With a duty on American flour, it became easier for Upper Canada flour to supply the deficiency caused by the exportation of wheat from the Richelieu Valley.[37] Again, demand revived in the Maritimes. On the other hand, Canadian flour still had little success in competing in Jamaica and the other islands of the West Indies with American flour, for navigation advantages enabled the shippers of the latter, as in 1830, to reach the Caribbean about three months earlier than their Canadian rivals.[38]

Stimulated by the temporary and permanent modifications in the Corn Laws, by the renewed demand from Lower Canada, and by higher prices in the British Isles on account of bad harvests, the farmers of Upper Canada began to expand their wheat acreage.[39] Their crops varied a good deal in the late eighteen-twenties, with partial failures in 1828 and 1829,[40] but with rising wheat prices, particularly in 1828, they considered themselves prosperous. In 1830 the exports of wheat and flour from the St. Lawrence—principally de-

---

[36]Barnes, *History of the English Corn Laws*, pp. 174, 199, 201; Ernle, *English Farming Past and Present*, pp. 446-7.

[37]Bouchette, *British Dominions in North America*, vol. I, p. 369.

[38]York *Colonial Advocate*, Aug. 11, 1831.

[39]York *Upper Canada Gazette and U. E. Loyalist*, Oct. 27, 1827; York *Colonial Advocate*, June 2, 1831; Tooke, *A History of Prices*, vol. II, pp. 132-6, 194-5, 199. The land under culture in Upper Canada in 1826 was returned to the assessors as 599,744 acres, in 1827 as 645,792 acres, in 1828 as 668,326 acres, in 1829 as 717,553 acres, in 1830 as 773,727 acres, and in 1831 as 818,416 acres. *Census of Canada, 1871*, vol. IV, pp. 92-3, 100-2, 104. There were no separate returns for the land sown to wheat.

[40]York *Colonial Advocate*, Jan. 21, 1830; Pickering, *Inquiries of an Emigrant*, p. 150.

rived of course from Upper Canada—were greater than in any previous year except the abnormal one of 1802.[41] Moreover, the wheat growers heard, as they had in earlier days, "that U C Wheat has brought the highest prices the British markets would afford, and been spoken of by millers as a grain of superior quality."[42]   As at the beginning of the decade, Upper Canada wheat was more in demand in the British Isles than Upper Canada flour.[43]   By 1831 the Upper Canadian farmers could reasonably feel that their economic future was assured.   Even those in the most westerly parts of the province had cause to be satisfied, for the opening of the Welland Canal at the end of the navigation season of 1829 meant the end of the wheat-price differential which transportation difficulties had theretofore imposed.   It was remarked that, in consequence of these favourable developments, the rural inhabitants were making improvements on their farms, and that the value of land was rapidly increasing.[44]

---

[41]The table given below shows the exports of wheat and flour from the St. Lawrence, and therefore roughly illustrates the progress of the grain trade of Upper Canada from the outbreak of the War of 1812 to the year 1830. The return for 1802 is included for reference, though at that time the exports of Upper Canada were still small. The statement gives wheat and flour together in terms of bushels of wheat, one barrel of flour being regarded as equivalent to five bushels of wheat.

1802	1,151,033 bushels	1821	431,658 bushels
....	....	1822	383,520
1812	451,303	1823	535,760
1813	2,585	1824	214,901
1814	6,086	1825	918,031
1815	9,600	1826	396,835
1816	5,675	1827	661,535
1817	335,895	1828	296,314
1818	554,506	1829	99,377
1819	98,325	1830	948,826
1820	535,893		

(Innis and Lower (eds.), Select Documents in Canadian Economic History, pp. 265-6).

[42]Montreal Canadian Courant, March 31, 1830.

[43]York Colonial Advocate, Jan. 21, Sept. 16, 1830.

[44]Colborne to Goderich, Dec. 12, 1831, in Canadian Archives Report for 1899, p. 72.

Before considering the history of the next decade or so, it is advisable to turn to other aspects of the agricultural evolution of Upper Canada. The characteristics of the rural population, the backwoodsman and his life, the wheat farmer and his problems, and the distinctive agriculture of the Ottawa Valley, will therefore be treated in subsequent chapters.

CHAPTER IV

THE AGRICULTURAL POPULATION, 1815-1850

THE agricultural population of Upper Canada after 1815 was of heterogeneous origin. There were French Canadians in the small community in the Essex peninsula, opposite Detroit, which had existed since the heyday of the fur trade. There were Indians and a few Negroes. There were thousands who had once lived in the United States, including the Loyalists and the post-Loyalists. There was a rapidly increasing number of English, Scottish, and especially Irish immigrants. These comprised an essentially new element, for before 1812 few had come from the British Isles. Some of these British people were "assisted" by the home government, for example those in the Military Settlements in eastern Upper Canada and those in the Peterborough Settlement; a few were brought out by private colonizers; but most of them came at their own expense, arriving so quietly and so steadily that scarcely any record of their advent was made.[1] They had a tendency to locate themselves rather clannishly, for the late-comers naturally sought out their relatives and former neighbours, and took up land near them. In consequence, there soon appeared "English settlements," and "Irish sections," and "Scotch lines." The situation in Simcoe County was typical. "In the townships of West Gwillimbury, Tecumseth, Mono, Essa, and Innisfil, the population is principally composed of Protestants from the North of Ireland. The township of Adjala is chiefly inhabited by Roman Catholic Irish, large settlements of whom are also to be found in the townships of Vespra, Flos, and Medonte. Natives of the Island of Islay form the majority in a large part of the township of Oro, in which there is also a large settlement of English. The township of Nottawasaga is almost entirely settled by Highlanders."[2]

---

[1]On the subject of immigration, see the references given in Fowke, "Introduction to Canadian Agricultural History" (*Canadian Journal of Economics and Political Science*, vol. VIII, 1942, pp. 64-6).

[2]*Journal and Transactions of the Board of Agriculture of Upper Canada for 1856-7*, p. 48. Hereafter this authority is cited as *JTBAUC*.

A population so diverse in national and cultural background naturally was not homogeneous in its agriculture. Indeed, there was something about the farming and social customs of each of these groups which was distinctive. Many of these traits were still in evidence at the end of the nineteenth century,[3] and a few of them are to be seen even today.

The French Canadians along the bank of the Detroit River and in the valley of the Thames reproduced in their settlements, with their narrow holdings and their general air of unprogressiveness, the outward appearance of the seigneuries along the St. Lawrence and the Richelieu. Many of them relied on cutting firewood for the Detroit market for their livelihood rather than on agriculture. In any case, as in the eighteenth century, they tilled the soil in a clumsy fashion, with inferior implements and few of them, kept the small livestock characteristic of the valley of the St. Lawrence, and evinced an unaccountable liking for swampy land. If it had not been for their orchards, the casual visitor among them might well have fancied that he was among the parishes of the lower province.[4]

Agriculture among the Indians remained notably backward by European standards. Some Indians, such as the Nipissings and Algonkins of the Oka (Lower Canada) reservation, who hunted in the Ottawa-Huron wilderness, scarcely pretended, when at home, to be farmers at all. Others, such as the numerous bands of Ojibwas (or Chippewas) began to make the transition from their old economy to a settled life in the second quarter of the century, with some guidance

---

[3]"If I could throw upon a screen here before you a picture of a farm settlement on the St. Lawrence below Brockville, another of a group of farms in the German settlement of Waterloo Co., another of a fruit-growing section between Hamilton and Niagara, another of the Paisley Block in Wellington, another of a French settlement in Essex, you would hardly believe that they all represented different sections of the same province, and you would admit that the nationality or origin of the people had much to do with their condition" (James, "Development of Agriculture in Ontario," *Report of the Ontario Bureau of Industries for 1898*, Appendix, p. 25).

[4]Bouchette, *British Dominions in North America*, vol. I, pp. 106-7; Murray, *Historical and Descriptive Account of British America*, vol. I, p. 336; Shirreff, *Tour through North America*, pp. 210-11.

from missionaries.⁵ The "Moravian" Delawares of the
Thames had been more civilized in many respects than their
white neighbours when they came from the Muskingum
Valley in 1792. By 1825, according to Pickering, they were
accustomed to "cultivate as much land and raise as much
stock as the white settlers."⁶ Similarly, the Mohawks of
the Brantford and Bay of Quinte reservations were nominally
farmers. Before 1812, some of the former had grown in
one year as much as 300 bushels of wheat. In 1843, the 500
families on the reserve had waggons, sleighs, ploughs, harrows, 250 horses, 561 oxen, 790 cows, and 83 sheep.⁷ Government agents made similar claims for many of the other
Indians under their charge, listing carefully the number of
acres cleared, the barns, the livestock, and the produce.
Little credence is to be put in their reports. For instance,
Mrs. Jameson tells that in 1837 she "inquired about the
[Ojibwa] Indian settlements at Coldwater and the Narrows;
but the accounts were not encouraging. I had been told, as
a proof of the advancement of the Indians, that they had
here saw-mills and grist-mills. I now learned that they
had a saw-mill and a grist-mill built for them, which they
never used themselves, but *let out* to the white settlers at a
certain rate."⁸ In truth, even among the most advanced

---

⁵For the beginnings of agriculture among them, see *Life and Journals
of Kah-Ke-Wa-Quo-Na-By*, pp. 86-7, 140, 182-3, 190, as well as *Journal of
the Legislative Assembly of Canada, 1844-5*, App. EEE. Hereafter this
authority is cited as *JLAC*.

⁶Pickering, *Inquiries of an Emigrant*, p. 94. Other judgments were
not so favourable. For example, Peter Jones, who was a half-breed
Mississauga, reported in 1828 that "the Moravian Missionaries have
been labouring among this people for a number of years, with very
little success, either in civilizing or christianizing them: they are
much given to intemperance, which is a great barrier to improvement.
I can but admire the patient perseverance of these self-denying men,
who keep up their Missions from one year to another, through dis-
couragements and oppositions of every kind" (*Life and Journals of
Ka-Ke-Wa-Quo-Na-By*, p. 122). For a detailed description of the
agricultural beginnings of these Indians, see Bliss (ed.), *Diary of
David Zeisberger*, vol. II. A good summary, based on Zeisberger and
other sources is Hamil, "Fairfield on the River Thames" (*Ohio State
Archaeological and Historical Quarterly*, vol. XLVIII, 1939).

⁷Smith, *Geographical View of . . . Upper Canada*, p. 40; *JLAC*,
1844-5, App. EEE.

⁸Jameson, *Winter Studies and Summer Rambles*, vol. II, p. 335.
Her account of the limited agricultural progress of Ojibwas such as
these is confirmed in Kane, *Wanderings of an Artist*, pp. 2-10.

Indians, farming was slipshod. Few of them derived their sole support from their fields. They gathered berries, made baskets, worked as raftsmen, or hired with their white neighbours in the harvest season.[9] They had no incentive to compete with the white population in commercial agriculture, and they did not do so.

The Negroes were few in number, and in general, like the Indians, followed somewhat crudely the methods of agriculture which prevailed around them.[10] They made no contributions of their own, unless we accept as fact the discredited guess that they introduced tobacco culture.

At the opposite extreme from the Indians as farmers were the Pennsylvania Dutch, or Germans. Wherever they settled, they were distinguished by their industry and thrift; by their large houses, with harness, ox yokes, and hoes, forks, and other implements hung on pegs under the flaring eaves; by their bank barns (the progenitors of the typical Ontario barn of today) ; and by their carefully cleared fields and their first-rate husbandry. They made Waterloo and Markham townships in particular a delight to British travellers, and parts of the Niagara and Hamilton districts only less so. As in the United States, they shared with the Lowland Scots the reputation of being the best farmers.[11]

More characteristic of Upper Canada as a whole than these small groups were the Americans and "native" Upper Canadians, the latter term being applied indifferently to the descendants of Loyalists and post-Loyalists, as well as to the sons of British immigrants. Collectively, they are best described as "land-butchers." They had no love for well-cleared fields, like the Pennsylvania Dutch, nor for neatly turned furrows, like many of the British immigrants. They

[9]*JLAC 1844-5*, App. EEE; Carruthers, *Retrospect of Thirty-Six Years' Residence*, p. 55.

[10]Landon, "Agriculture among the Negro Refugees in Upper Canada" (*Journal of Negro History*, July, 1936). Descriptions of the farming activities of a considerable number of Negroes are to be found in Drew, *The Refugee.*

[11]Pickering, *Inquiries of an Emigrant*, p. 127; Talbot, *Five Years' Residence*, vol. I, p. 167; "Canadian Settler," *Emigrant's Informant*, pp. 157-8; Gibson, "Conditions in York County a Century Ago" (*Ontario Historical Society Papers and Records*, vol. XXIV, 1927, p. 360). Hereafter this authority is cited as *OHSPR.*

practised, for the most part, the extensive culture characteristic of the frontier. John Lynch of Brampton, in his prize
essay on Bruce County (1855), remarked with truth that
"the native Canadians, especially those who are descended
from the U. E. Loyalists and other Americans, are generally
the most at home in clearing new farms—but as a class,
they are the most miserable farmers in Upper Canada; in
tilling a cleared farm, generally inferior to the most common
laborers from Great Britain and Ireland."[12]

Indeed, many of them should not be considered farmers
at all. Their livelihood came, not from the sale of agricultural produce, but from the increase in the capital value
of their farms in consequence of their being cleared. Such
men may be called professional pioneers. Lynch explained
their activities thus:

It has been remarked of the settlement of Upper Canada, that the
first settlers were not destined to be the permanent occupiers of the land,
and that in the course of a few years, the original settlers are almost
uniformly superseded by an entirely different class of persons.

The task of clearing land—of converting a tract of unbroken forest
into a cultivable farm—is a very different operation from that of tilling
and cultivating the land, after it is brought into that state in which
it may properly be called a farm.

Those different occupations, to a certain extent, require different
tastes and capacities, and have a tendency to require, and to form a
distinct class of persons for each vocation.

Hence it often happens, that when the "original pioneers" as they
are poetically called, have cleared their farms and brought them into
that situation in which the mere *farmer* would consider them just fit
to begin to live on, they become dissatisfied with their lot, they do not
relish the different kind of labour which the altered state of their farms
require, and they long for a new settlement—for the excitement of
chopping, logging and burning brush.

These aspirations are by no means confined to persons who have
always been accustomed to clearing land—it often happens that a
person is forced by circumstances, sorely against his will, to undertake
the life of a "Backwoodsman"—but ten or twelve years' experience in
clearing up his farm gives him a relish for the occupation, which though
rude and rough, is not without its attractions, and he is easily induced
to sell out to some person who wants a *bona fide* farm, and not the materials out of which to manufacture one. An arrangement is then made, sat-

---

[12]*JTBAUC 1855-6*, p. 615.

isfactory to both parties, and the Backwoodsman goes further into the "bush."

. . . I knew a man of this class, of an iron frame, who, during a busy lifetime, cleared up a new farm almost entirely with his own hands, every five or six years, until he came to the ploughing, when he became dissatisfied, and sold out to purchase new land. He declared that he would not live on a farm that required ploughing.[13]

This shifting process has already taken place to a considerable extent, within the County of Bruce, and will probably be continued still further. Many of the earlier settlers in Huron and Kincardine [townships where settlement began in 1849], have within the last three or four years sold out their improvements, and re-purchased in the newer Townships of Elderslie, Bruce, Saugeen and Arran; no other lands in these Townships were brought into the market—and some of these very same persons, as well as others, are now contemplating another move into the new lands of the [Bruce] Peninsula, as soon as they are offered for sale.[14]

Of course, as Lynch mentions, not all those who cleared bush farms did so from love of adventure or other psychological reasons. Sometimes the man who moved into the bush had proved his incapacity as a regular farmer, and so had lost the title to his lot to the holder of the mortgage. Often he was a young man who had served an apprenticeship as a farmer's hired hand,[15] and had thereby earned enough to make a down payment on an uncleared farm. Possibly

---

[13]We are told that another backwoodsman, who lived near Peterborough in the eighteen-twenties, "liked clearing land very much, provided he was the only man in that section who was at it. When he found others flocking in and clearing nearly close to him, or, as he termed it, almost 'under his very nose,' he always sold out and moved away further into the woods. And this moving from clearing 'going on under his nose' always took place as soon as his nearest neighbour was within two or three miles of his farm. Such 'civilization and destruction of timber,' as he termed it, disturbed the game, and this he never could endure" (*Canada Farmer*, Feb. 15, 1872, p. 77).

[14]*JTBAUC 1855-6*, pp. 615-16. Cf. Christie, *Emigrant's Assistant*, pp. 18-20.

[15]The wages of the hired man were not high. In the eighteen-twenties and eighteen-thirties the worker by the day received from 50 cents to $1.00, or $1.25 if he was an expert cradler, in any case plus his board. The permanent worker got from $10.00 to $12.00 a month in summer, $7.00 to $9.00 in winter, or $8.00 to $10.00 the year round, with his board and washing. If he went shantying along the Ottawa, he might earn from $15.00 to $20.00 a month during the winter. As he had few expenses, he was able to save almost everything he earned in the course of the year, and perhaps had something ad-

most commonly of all the backwoodsman was a provident individual with a desire to keep his family more or less together by "setting up" his sons on farms of their own, for the proceeds of the sale of a farm along the "front"[16] would pay for the three or four wild or partly cleared ones in the back settlements. It was the last motive which made possible the report that, in 1854 and 1855, almost all the purchasers of newly opened lands in Huron County were "sons of farmers or farmers themselves, who have sold out farms in older settled parts of Canada."[17]

From one motive or another, in Upper Canada as in the adjacent states, there was an internal emigration always going on from the cleared lands back into the forest. Heriot

ditional from having his wife hire out too. It was generally considered that an ambitious man could save enough in a maximum of four years to be in a position to look around for a farm to rent or even to buy. Lieutenant Coke found one settler near Cornwall who had actually earned enough as a labourer in two years to buy a farm, and who ungraciously attributed his success to the fact that he was not encumbered with a wife ("Canadian Settler," *Emigrant's Informant*, p. 200; Pickering, *Inquiries of an Emigrant*, p. 202; Coke, *Subaltern's Furlough*, pp. 327-8). The wages just mentioned long remained standard in Upper Canada; they were still being paid in the late eighteen-fifties, that is, after the collapse of the inflation of the Grand Trunk era (*New World in 1859*, part III, p. 36; *Transactions of the Board of Agriculture of Upper Canada for 1860-3*, pp. 25, 91).

The hired man had a social status of his own. Whether he was an Irish immigrant or a son of a neighbouring landowner, he was treated by his employer as one of the family. "If a man is good enough to work for me, he is good enough to eat with me," was a common expression. The typical hired man did the hardest chores and was a reservoir of miscellaneous information, and so was always popular with the growing boys. He would sometimes help with the house-work, and could always be depended on to act as a beau for one of the girls. Probably more often than not he married one of them. Certainly he had an excellent opportunity of deciding which one would make the best wife for a farmer. Then, after he had saved enough money to make a down payment on a farm, and to provide himself with some livestock (when the father-in-law did not give the daughter a few head as a dowry), he became an independent farmer, and might keep a hired man of his own.

The above is a summary of a long account of the hired man and his status in New England after the War of 1812; but it applies equally well to Upper Canada (*Ohio Cultivator*, vol. x, 1854, p. 218).

[16]The "front" was a word frequently used in reference to the townships along the St. Lawrence or the Great Lakes. It had no suggestion whatever of "frontier" in the American sense. The Upper Canada equivalent of Turner's "frontier" was "backwoods" or "the bush."

[17]*JTBAUC 1855-6*, p. 529. Cf. *JTBAUC 1856-7*, p. 72.

had noticed it long before the War of 1812, and Howison about 1820 declared that most of the farms in the older parts of the province had lost their original owners.[18] Again, Samuel Strickland, writing in 1852, remarked that "Whitby [township, Ontario County], at the time of which I am speaking [i.e., about 1825], was only partially settled, and chiefly by Americans. . . . At present, the township is well settled, and well-cultivated. Nearly all the old settlers are gone, and their farms have, for the most part, been purchased by old country farmers and gentlemen."[19] The movement to the interior was so steady and so much a matter of course that no one paid any attention to a farmer with his household effects and implements in a covered waggon setting out for the bush.

Not all the "natives" who sought new land found it in Upper Canada. In the days of the impassable Black Swamp in northwestern Ohio, one of the great overland trails from New England and upstate New York to Michigan and beyond lay through western Upper Canada. Emigrants in passage extolled the attractions of the New West. American clock and tin pedlars, American circuit riders, and American teachers, all ubiquitous in the province, added their arguments. Their advocacy, the influence of friends and acquaintances who had crossed the border, dissatisfaction with local conditions, and the lure of cheap land in the western states were responsible for a constant emigration from Upper Canada. Of all these motives, the desire for cheap land was the most important. One of the clock makers tried to convince Mrs. Traill that in Ohio—"rich, highly cultivated, and fruitful"—,"land was much cheaper, both cleared and wild," than in Upper Canada.[20] Indeed,

---

[18]Heriot. *Travels through the Canadas*, p. 152; Howison, *Sketches of Upper Canada*, pp. 170-1.

[19]Strickland, *Twenty-Seven Years in Canada West*, vol. I, p. 17.

[20]Traill, *Backwoods of Canada*, p. 293. The tin pedlars were probably more important than the country store-keepers in the distribution of minor staple articles, especially in the newer settlements. Timothy Dwight wrote in 1797 that "every inhabited part of the United States is visited by these men. I have seen them on the peninsula of Cape Cod, and in the neighbourhood of Lake Erie; distant from each other more than six hundred miles. They make their way to Detroit, four hundred miles farther; to Canada; to Kentucky; and, if I mistake not, to New-Orleans and St. Louis." When his work was published in 1821,

land in the province, as was remarked in 1835, was coming
to be too high in price to attract American immigrants.[21]
It was therefore quite natural that Upper Canada pioneers
should also fall victims to the "Prairie Fever."

While they did remain in the province, they helped, with
the aid of newcomers from the United States, to give it
the distinctively American character so frequently noted by
travellers.   In the Niagara peninsula, for example, Benjamin
Lundy observed that "the appearance of the inhabitants, their
style of building, improving farms and general mode of living
is much like what we meet with in the western parts of
New York."[22]   He might have added that the bee, the
camp meeting, the itinerant preacher, and the temperance
society, were as typical of the backwoods of Upper Canada
as of the American frontier.

It is worth mentioning that the social relationship between Upper Canada and New York continued to be as close
as before 1812.[23]   Political animosities inherited from the
Loyalists, and the new ones created by the War of 1812,
seem to have disappeared very shortly.   It is true that
editors and speech-makers sneered at "Brother Jonathan" at
election time, and that the Upper Canadian farmer liked the
competition of American agricultural produce in his own
markets as little as his descendants did that of New Zealand
butter in recent years, but there is no evidence that the
editorials were taken very seriously, or that the rural population had the slightest antipathy towards individual Americans.   In 1849 it was stated that, in the Brockville region,
the remnants of the Loyalist bitterness had completely dis-

---

an editorial note added that "the business of selling tin ware, has
within a few years undergone a considerable change. Formerly the
pedlar's load was composed exclusively of this manufacture: now he
has an assortment of merchandize to offer to his customers. He carries
pins needles scissars, combs, coat and vest buttons, with many other
trifling articles of hardware; and children's books, and cotton stuffs
made in New-England" (Dwight, *Travels*, vol. II, pp. 54, 55n).

[21]Brantford *Sentinel*, quoted in Montreal *Gazette*, Oct. 13, 1835.

[22]Landon (ed.), "The Diary of Benjamin Lundy" (*OHSPR*, vol.
XIX, 1922, p. 119).

[23]Lucas (ed.), *Lord Durham's Report*, vol. II, pp. 267-8. See also
Garland, "Some Frontier and American Influences in Upper Canada"
(*Transactions of the London and Middlesex Historical Society*, part
XIII, 1929).

appeared; and this was undoubtedly true of the rest of the
province as well. It was surely no accident that Upper
Canadian opinion so strongly favoured the North on the
outbreak of the Civil War, despite British sympathy for the
Confederacy.[24]

A criticism commonly made of the "native" Upper Canadians was that "their manners are somewhat tinctured
with American equality and contempt of distinctions."[25]
Like their American counterparts, they were often ignorant,
vulgar, assertive, and vain. Too many were like some of
the pioneers of the Township of Caledon (Peel County).

It is amusing to see some of these gentry at a tavern, when they
happen to come down to the village to sell their wheat, or transact other
business. Nothing pleases them; nothing is so good as they get in
Caledon! There are no potatoes on the table; they can get potatoes
for supper in Caledon. They do not like *bread;* they get hot cakes for
supper in Caledon. The tea is not as good. Even the salt is not as
salt, the sugar as sweet, nor is the mustard (even when it brings tears
into their eyes) as strong as they get in Caledon! And should any one
at table possessing a little more sense of propriety, attempt good natur-
edly to check their grumbling, they will probably become sulky, and
exclaim loudly that they can talk as much as they like in *Caledon.*
Caledon being in their opinion the *ne plus ultra* of everything that is
desirable or worthy of admiration, and they themselves the "pink of
perfection."[26]

While "native" Upper Canadians, such as these, continued
to move into the bush, or into the American West, their
places were filled, and more than filled, by the great immigration from the British Isles. People fled from the badly
administered laws, the sheer misery, and the potato blight
in Ireland, to escape the effects of the Industrial Revolution
in England and Scotland, and to better their own or at least
their children's economic position in a new world. Each
of the racial groups from the British Isles long continued
to have something distinctive about it from the agricultural
point of view. The Scottish Highlanders were distinguished

[24]Toronto *Globe,* Nov. 20, 1849; *Canadian Agriculturist,* Oct. 1, 1849,
p. 254; Landon, *Western Ontario and the American Frontier, passim.*
[25]Stansbury, *Pedestrian Tour,* p. 151.
[26]Smith, *Canada, Past, Present, and Future,* vol. I, pp. 279-80.
There is a similar description of the pioneers of the Niagara peninsula
in Howison, *Sketches of Upper Canada,* pp. 135-6.

as hard workers, but their living standards remained low.[27] Immigrants from the south of Ireland practised a slovenly agriculture, unless they happened to be located among other British groups. Samuel Strickland, who had excellent chances for observation, declared that "as a general rule, the English, Scotch, and north of Ireland men make much better and more independent colonists than emigrants from the south of Ireland."[28] Lowland Scots, as we mentioned above, had the highest reputation.

Economically nearly all the immigrants, it was remarked, could be divided into three groups. The first consisted of persons without any means at all. If one of these desired to farm, he had to get a start, like the younger sons of many of the native farmers, by working out in the timber trade, as a labourer in a town, as a school-teacher, or as a farmer's hired man. With the little capital thus acquired, he would make a payment on a farm, usually in the backwoods. In the first few years, he cleared his farm between times, and scarcely looked for a crop to sell, relying on making enough to keep his family over the winter on what he could earn on a pilgrimage to the harvest fields along the "front."[29] A man of the second class could buy a farm, if only in the bush, and keep his family for a year or two on what he had left of his savings. He could work all year on his own farm, and would have some grain for sale in the autumn. The third class was composed of those better-off individuals who could buy farms and pay for clearing them, or who could afford cleared farms with their improvements. It included many who aspired to be "gentlemen farmers." It was only the third class that made any modifications in prevailing agricultural methods.[30]

The great majority of the others had been educated to some kind of trade in Great Britain; though this, to be sure,

[27]Jameson, *Winter Studies and Summer Rambles*, vol. II, p. 21; Howison, *Sketches of Upper Canada*, p. 24; Garland (ed.), "Proudfoot Papers" (*OHSPR*, vol. XXVII, 1931, p. 494).

[28]Strickland, *Twenty-Seven Years in Canada West*, vol. I, p. 138.

[29]For examples of the harvesters' movements, see Smith, *Pioneers of Old Ontario*, pp. 178, 185.

[30]*Canadian Agriculturist*, April, 1854, p. 102. Captain Marryatt classified the British immigrants in Upper Canada in the late eighteen-thirties into three similar groups (*A Diary in America*, vol. III, pp. 55-6).

was not considered an impediment to successful farming in
Upper Canada. "It is a common saying in Western Canada,"
remarked an essayist, "that a Spitalfields weaver makes as
good a farmer as any other man."[31]   Nevertheless, farmers
with such a background naturally did merely what was
customary in the neighbourhood. As one authority put it,
"it is truly remarkable, how soon the newly arrived emigrant
from the old country becomes contaminated, and imitates
the bad practices and unprofitable habits and manners of
the old settled Canadian farmers."[32]   The rest of them,
those who had actually farmed in the British Isles, brought
nothing but deep-rooted prejudices with them. As one
British agricultural authority wrote, "having sacrificed themselves at home to their prejudices, they bear them religiously
beyond the Atlantic, and transmit them as heir-looms to
their descendants."[33]   If it was suggested to one of them,
or to the average pioneer farmer for that matter, that his
reduced crops might be increased by adopting a rotation and
raising more livestock, he would scorn the idea as "book
farming" and probably add that he had been farming for
fifteen or thirty years, as the case might be, and he guessed
he knew as much about farming as the next man. He
continued to cherish the belief that peas would not ripen
unless they were planted when the moon was on the wane,
and he sometimes found that he would have to perform
some ceremony over his "elfin-shot" cows to break the spell.[34]

The "improving farmers" were few in number, but they
furnished the agricultural leadership of the province. They
were predominantly Lowland Scotch and English settlers of
the third class mentioned above. While their technique
might be no better than that of the Pennsylvania Dutch,
they made a greater effort to keep abreast of the discoveries
of their time in agricultural science. Often they effected

---

[31]*JTBAUC 1855-6*, p. 326. This remark should not be taken wholly
in a derogatory sense. Cf.: "The great majority of those who now
live by cultivating the soil, were educated to some variety of trade,
but nevertheless many of them manage their farms in a most creditable
manner" (*JTBAUC 1855-6*, p. 218).

[32]Duncumb, *The British Emigrant's Advocate*, p. 179.

[33]Johnston, *Notes on North America*, vol. I, p. 292.

[34]*Canada Farmer*, Aug. 1, 1866, p. 232; *ibid.*, April 15, 1868, p. 121;
Haight, *Country Life in Canada*, p. 99.

improvements which should have been an object lesson to
their whole neighbourhood. It was noted of the Cobourg
region in the eighteen-thirties, that "some Scotch farmers
have settled in the neighbourhood, and, as usual, wherever
they go, you see the signs of their handy work; in fact, they
are excellent landmarks when you want to find out a good
situation."[35] In the early eighteen-fifties, it was said that
most of the Yorkshiremen and the Lowland Scots followed
the practice of renting run-down farms in the older communities, and investing their capital in stock and implements
rather than tying it up in land.[36] Whether they rented land
or bought it, these Britons were foremost in introducing
better crop rotations, pure-bred stock, and labour-saving
machinery. Moreover, they were responsible for some dif-
ferentiation in detail between the agriculture of Upper
Canada and that of the adjacent states—at least, an article in
the Albany *Cultivator* by W. G. Edmundson, former editor of
the *British American Cultivator,* would lead to this conclusion.
Probably he was contrasting in his own mind the country
around Toronto with what he had seen in the Genesee Valley
and in Ohio. He wrote:

> The differences . . . that seem to exist between the western Canadians
> and the American farmers, may be clearly traced to this one fact, that
> the English and Scotch farmers, in establishing their new homes in the
> colony, brought with them their early prejudices and habits, and so
> soon as they became in the ascendancy, all other systems merged into the
> British practice; while on the other hand, the peculiar features of our
> agriculture have been proof against much foreign innovation, and the

[35]William Hutton of Belleville to his brother, June 30, 1834, in
British Farmer's Magazine, April, 1835, p. 105. For the same district
in 1854, cf. *Canadian Agriculturist,* July, 1854, p. 196.

[36]*Canadian Agriculturist,* July, 1854, p. 196; *JTBAUC 1855-6,* pp.
351, 449. As Upper Canada was a land of freeholders, or of persons
who aspired to be freeholders, renting of land was not regarded with
much favour, except in instances such as these, or in connection with
instalment buying. Tenants, it was said, cared nothing for the harm
that might be done through excessive wheat-cropping, while the land-
lords cared little more, because they believed that if they sold the
land, the price would be determined less by its condition than by the
prevailing rate in the neighbourhood. Moreover, if the lease was a
short one (the usual kind), the tenant felt there was no point in
repairing buildings and fences, in planting shade trees, or making
other changes from which his successor would receive most of the
benefit (*JTBAUC 1855-6,* pp. 328, 448).

Europeans of all ranks have readily adopted it, as fast as they have established themselves in their new homes.[37]

There were differences between the agriculture of Upper Canada and that of a state such as Ohio. Upper Canada had little of the corn-and-hog economy of the Miami Valley, and nothing of the cattle-fattening industry of the Scioto Valley. That these differences were to be accounted for solely or mainly by racial inheritance or national origin is, however, doubtful. Climate and markets had much more to do with them.

Gradually, through the early nineteenth century, a "pushing population," as editors liked to call it, cut homes out of the forest and filled in the gaps in the old communities created by the departure of the "first settlers" for the bush. In 1812 a fringe of land along the "front," with a few inland regions such as the vicinity of Yonge Street and part of the Thames Valley, comprised all the inhabited part of the province.[38] By 1851 all of western and central Upper Canada was occupied except for a section in the northwestern corner. East of Lake Simcoe and in the Ottawa Valley more and more land was being taken up along the borders of the Canadian Shield. At this time Upper Canada had 952,004 people; Toronto 30,775; Kingston 11,585; Hamilton 14,112; Bytown 7,760; and London 7,035.[39]

Within the settled area, certain districts became noted for their profitable agriculture. Among these were the Bay of Quinte region, the townships along Yonge Street, those along Dundas Street between Hamilton and Toronto, the vicinity of London, and the Niagara peninsula.[40] "Some of the most beautiful farms I ever saw," reported a visitor from Ohio, "are situated on the Canada side of the river from Buffalo to Niagara."[41]

Even in these old settlements, the remnants of the forest were usually only a few hundred yards from the road. One visitor remarked of Waterloo Township, originally wooded,

[37]*Cultivator*, Dec. 1852, p. 400.
[38]Smith, *Geographical View of . . . Upper Canada*, pp. 48-9.
[39]*Census of Canada, 1851-2*, vol. I, p. 36.
[40]Duncumb, *British Emigrant's Advocate*, pp. 265, 276.
[41]*Western Farmer and Gardener*, vol. III, 1841-2, p. 199.

that "in this township, one can see some distance around, owing to the many clearings and the undulating nature of the ground; whereas, in most of the others, the view is extremely limited."[42]   The only places where the whole country had an open appearance were the oak-plains, which extended from the Grand River to Lake Erie, and the similar Rice Lake Plains north of Cobourg.

It took a long time to clear a whole farm, but this was not the sole cause of the usual limited view.   Everywhere, but especially in the vicinity of the towns, were the lots of wild lands, the holdings of speculators.   In 1838, according to Durham, "a very small proportion (perhaps less than a tenth)" of the land granted to Loyalists, former soldiers, government officials, and mere favourites had been put under cultivation, or even occupied.[43] During the eighteen-forties the government did try to get land into the possession of actual settlers by attaching settlement conditions to the deeds, but the results were disappointing. The men of little capital, who lost no opportunity of attacking large land-jobbers, created a new problem by speculating themselves. The land which they were expected to fence, clear, and live on they left unenclosed, uncleared, and uninhabited.   It was enough for one of them that he could obtain a "right" which had a speculative value by paying down a tenth of the purchase price, and that he could satisfy the settlement conditions by painting his name on a shingle nailed to a tree, cutting down a few saplings, and making an affidavit. If he was fortunate, he could count on an ultimate profit of from £25 to £100 on his small investment, for the government was not likely to dispossess him.[44] Since buying land to hold it for an increase in value was the accepted means of getting wealth, it is not surprising to find that as late as 1854 more than half the land of Simcoe County was still owned by speculators. According to the assessment rolls, there were in the county in that year 324,000 acres of occupied lands and 343,000 acres of unoccupied lands. It was believed, however,

---

[42]Logan, *Notes of a Journey*, pp. 60-1.

[43]Lucas, *Lord Durham's Report*, vol. II, p. 223; cf. Talbot, *Five Years' Residence*, vol. II, pp. 267-8.

[44]*JTBAUC 1855-6*, pp. 631-2, 651.

that the proportion of unoccupied land in this county was higher than in any other county in Upper Canada.[45]

As uncleared lands might be held by their owners till some of the lots in the neighbourhood were in an advanced state of improvement, there were frequently old cleared farms side by side with others in every conceivable state of clearance. James Beaven wrote a description of the appearance of the countryside between Brantford and London in 1845 which would have applied to most of the province.

Here I had an opportunity of witnessing the clearing process in all its stages. In one place might be seen a few trees cut down, and the first rough shanty of boards set up, with which by the bye many of the Irish appear to content themselves altogether for two or three years together. Then about an acre, with the trees felled, and lying irregularly about; about a couple of roods cleared in the centre of it, a small log cottage set up, and the rest planted with potatoes. This would be fenced in perhaps with the boards of the original shanty, nailed to a few stumps and small trees, with their tops cut off and left rooted in the ground, as at first; whilst here and there a stump appears in the midst of the vegetation; and a rough little cow or two might be seen picking about by the road side, or in the still untouched forest. A further step would be, to see some of the tree-trunks laid one on another longitudinally, to form a rude protection to the future field, and the rest cut up in lengths, and drawn together in heaps, and burning with more or less of vigour; whilst interspersed would be the ashes and blackened remains of former heaps, and here and there a curling wreath of smoke, telling of smouldering embers still unquenched. . . .

But we come to another clearing, which is a year further in advance. Here the space for the garden is augumented, and enclosed with a snake-fence; a shed or two is erected, or it may be a little out-house; the whole of the trees are gone from the first clearing, and perhaps from a second, leaving only the stumps; a crop of grain or of Indian corn covers the ground, and the original process is extending itself over a further portion of the forest. Further on the process has advanced another step. The original rough fence of trees no longer appears, but is replaced by the snake fence. What was cropped with grain is laid down to grass; the crops of grain and corn extend on all sides, and the forest recedes into the background: comfortable stables and barns are erected; an addition is perhaps made to the log hut; the chimney, which was of wood, filled in and plastered with clay, is replaced by one of brick or stone, built up from the ground: the waggon or sleigh is lying

---

[45]*JTBAUC 1856-7*, p. 27.

about; a pair of horses may be seen grazing in the pasture, in addition
to the half-dozen of cows and calves; and if the man is an Englishman
or native Canadian [French-Canadian], a few flowers make their appearance in the garden.

As we approach the older settled country, the rough clearings scarcely
appear, such as the first I described: the farm buildings, (all of wood)
become capacious, and are kept in good order. There is a good garden
with upright palings or boards; and a substantial frame-house, painted
white or rough-cast, with its neat verandah, and pretty green French
blinds, shows that the occupier has triumphed over necessity, and possesses both leisure and ability to think of comfort, even perhaps of
elegance.[46]

While we keep in mind this generalized description, let
us consider now the activities of the first group distinguished
by Beaven—the pioneers.

---

[46]Beaven, *Recreations of a Long Vacation*, pp. 58-62. Cf. Brown,
Views of Canada and the Colonists, pp. 65-7.

CHAPTER V

THE BACKWOODSMAN[1]

THE pioneers who chopped clearances out of the forest came into occupation of their holdings in various ways, the precise method ordinarily being determined by the resources they had available. Contrary to an impression rather prevalent among later generations, a considerable amount of money or credit was necessary for getting a start in the backwoods. It was estimated that the man who had £100 currency, in addition to what he paid for his land, had a bare minimum. It would take £20 to buy a pair of oxen, a yoke, a logging-chain, and a harrow, £8 for a cow and a couple of pigs, £22 for a year's provisions, and £50 for erecting buildings and for hiring labour to assist in chopping and logging.[2] Those who lacked money when they arrived in the new settlements had to acquire it by one means or another before they could expect to have a farm of their own.

Some of those who were too impoverished to buy land set themselves down on unlocated or wild lands as squatters. There had been squatters on the crown lands in every surveyed township at least as early as 1794. They continued to be found thereafter everywhere in the new townships. According to the custom of the frontier, the "improvements" they made they could sell to the rightful owner of the property when he came to take possession of it. If they wished to buy the lot on which they were located, they were ordinarily given the first chance when it was offered for sale. Even if they could not sell the improvements nor buy the lot, they could count on not being molested for years.[3]

Squatters were characteristically men who were content to live from hand to mouth. Enterprising pioneers with

---

[1]With parts of this chapter, cf. Guillet, *Early Life in Upper Canada*, and Talman, "Social Life in Upper Canada" (Ph.D. dissertation, University of Toronto, 1931).

[2]*Journal and Transactions of the Board of Agriculture of Upper Canada for 1855-6*, p. 371. Hereafter this authority is cited as *JTBAUC*. See also the estimates in Pickering, *Inquiries of an Emigrant*, pp. 163-5.

[3]MacTaggart, *Three Years in Canada*, vol. I, p. 200; Patterson, *Land Settlement in Upper Canada*, p. 50.

capital insufficient to buy and stock a farm usually managed
to rent one. If a man was willing to go into the real backwoods, he could sometimes make an arrangement with a
speculator, whereby he would clear a specified amount of land,
and in return would be permitted to keep the produce of the
first few years. If he preferred a partly cleared farm, he
could often obtain one on shares.   The landlord found
share-cropping much more advantageous than trying to hire
labourers to work his property.   The usual programme was
that the owner furnished oxen, implements, and seed, and
received in return half the produce of all kinds.[4]   As was
mentioned in an earlier chapter, a poor man could often do
much worse than to rent a clergy reserve lot, for though
the rents were nominally in cash, slowness of collection meant
that in practice he would be renting virtually on a credit
basis.[5]

After the War of 1812, as before, the government of
Upper Canada granted land free to actual settlers and
others. Among those benefiting were the "military settlers"
in the eastern part of the province and Peter Robinson's
Irish immigrants there and in the Peterborough region.
Militiamen, soldiers, and sailors of the late war, like the
children of the Loyalists, continued to be entitled to free
grants, but after 1827 others, even when genuine settlers,
could not obtain them, except in the case of lots along the

---

[4]Grece, *Facts and Observations*, p. 22; Howison, *Sketches of Upper
Canada*, p. 236; Magrath, *Authentic Letters from Upper Canada*, p.
114. By 1860 three other arrangements were the prevailing ones, at
least in Dundas County: (1) the tenant provided his own implements,
stock, and seed, and gave the landlord one-third of the gross produce,
including the hay and straw; (2) the tenant provided his own implements and livestock, and gave the landlord half the produce; (3) the
landlord provided everything and got two-thirds of the gross produce.
The second was the commonest practice (*Transactions of the Board of
Agriculture of Upper Canada for 1860-3*, p. 24).

[5]It was a contention of the Mackenzie faction that the lessees of
clergy reserves were taxed unjustly. "The clergy reserves are . . .
exempt from taxes; but when leased to a poor man, taxes are immediately demanded, and should the lessee, after two or three years
occupation, surrender it up to its clerical owners, it ceases, instanter,
to be liable until re-sold" (M'Leod, *Brief Review of the Settlement of
Upper Canada*, p. 79).

"colonization roads" which began to be opened in 1841, where there were specific settlement requirements.[6]

Ordinary settlers wishing to obtain land of their own therefore had to buy it. Sometimes they bought it directly from the government. Agents of the Department of Crown Lands were located in different parts of the province, but their indifference to their responsibilities, and still more the inefficiency of the placemen in the central office, made getting a deed a tedious process.[7] As most of the readily accessible land had already been alienated by the government anyway, it was on the whole more satisfactory to do business with a land-jobber or with a small speculator of the kind described towards the end of the last chapter. They were ready to take advantage of the inexperienced immigrant, but usually, in consequence of competition among themselves, they sold their lots on favourable terms.[8] The wealthier ones commonly accepted a small down payment, and gave the purchaser five or ten years to pay the balance. The smaller ones, who might have only "rights" to sell, tried to obtain about half the selling price in cash, though they too would give a four- or five-year credit for the remainder.[9] The most conspicuous land speculator of all was the Canada Company, which after 1826 had at its disposal the former crown reserves scattered throughout the province, as well as the Huron Tract. William Lyon Mackenzie and his minions never tired of vilifying the Company. It was, they declared, "an association of European mercantile speculators in those waste lands of the Colony to which the industry of the settled population had given value. . . . We are of opinion, that this monopoly is one of the greatest drawbacks upon the agricultural and commercial prosperity of the Colony—that its formation was an act of injustice and oppression—and that every possible legal effort should be made to root it out of the country."[10]

---

[6]Colborne to Goderich, Feb. 8, 1832, in Q 374, pp. 184 ff. For the colonization roads, see Chapter XVII, below.

[7]Warr, *Canada as It Is*, p. 76.

[8]For an interesting description of the methods of one of them, a country merchant, see Moodie, *Roughing It in the Bush*, vol. I, pp. 181-5.

[9]York *Colonial Advocate*, Aug. 27, 1831; *JTBAUC 1855-6*, pp. 651-2.

[10]*Journal of the Legislative Assembly of Upper Canada, 1835*, App. 11, p. iii. For a Tory defence of the price-raising practice of the Canada Company, see Fidler, *Observations on Professions, Literature, Manners and Emigration*, p. 225-6.

Nevertheless, the Canada Company had a reputation, which it seems to have deserved, of selling land on equitable terms and giving the settlers plenty of encouragement after they took up their locations. Like the small speculators, it leased land to settlers, and allowed them to buy it on the instalment plan.[11]

Having located himself on a lot, the backwoodsman erected a log cabin, and then commenced clearing. If the holding was covered with the common hardwood or mixed forest, he cut out the underbrush and chopped down the trees. Sometimes he felled them into long windrows, which he fired as soon as they were partially dry. This method was dangerous, as the fire could scarcely be controlled. It was therefore considered wiser to cut the trees into logs, which were left to lie where they fell. After he had cut over several acres, the backwoodsman and his neighbours hauled the logs, or the charred remains of trunks ("niggers," they were called), as the case might be, into piles at a logging bee, and set them afire.[12] Samuel Strickland described such a bee in Otonabee Township, Peterborough County, in 1826.

As soon as the ground was cool enough, I made a logging Bee, at which I had five yokes of oxen and twenty men, four men to each team. The teamster selects a good place to commence a heap, generally against some large log which the cattle would be unable to move. They draw all the logs within a reasonable distance in front of the large log. The men with hand-spikes roll them, one upon the top of the other, until the heap is seven or eight feet high, and ten or twelve broad. All the chips, sticks, and rubbish are then picked up and thrown on the top of the heap. A team and four good men should log and pick an acre a day when the burn has been good.

My hive worked well, for we had five acres logged and set fire to the same evening. On a dark night, a hundred or two of these large heaps all on fire at once have a very fine effect, and shed a broad glare of light for a considerable distance. In the month of July in the new settlements, the whole country at night appears lit up by these fires.[13]

---

[11]Warr, *Canada as It Is*, pp. 72, 76. After 1852 it held its lands off the market on account of the rapid appreciation in real-estate values in the province, thus adding to its reputation of being a "monopolist" (*JTBAUC 1856-7*, pp. 173-5).

[12]Christie, *Emigrant's Assistant*, pp. 118-21; Magrath, *Authentic Letters from Upper Canada*, p. 161.

[13]Strickland, *Twenty-Seven Years in Canada West*, vol. I, pp. 96-7.

Not all clearances were made through the agency of the logging bee. Thomas Need, for example, hired a "skilful woodsman" to log, burn, and fence twenty acres of forest for him at £3 7s. 6d. an acre.[14] A few backwoodsmen cleared their land without any outside help, like the violently independent settler Mrs. Jameson met near Chatham. She recounted the following conversation :

"I have a farm hard by—in the bush here."
"How large is it?"
"One hundred and forty acres."
"How much cleared?"
"Five or six acres—thereabout."
"How long have you been on it?"
"Five years."
"And only five acres cleared? That is very little in five years. I have seen people who had cleared twice that quantity of land in half the time."
He replied almost with fierceness, "Then they had money, or friends, or hands to help them; I have neither. I have in this wide world only myself! and set a man with only a pair of hands at one of them big trees there! see what he'll make of it! You may swing the axe here from morning to night for a week before you let the daylight in upon you."[15]

Though the "New England method" of land-clearing just described was the common one throughout Upper Canada, there was another method, the "Southern," which was to be found to some extent everywhere, and was used exclusively on the oak-plains. The trees were simply girdled and left to die. On the oak-plains the few dead trees offered little obstacle to ploughing. In the heavily wooded areas, the method was dangerous, for the decayed limbs were liable to fall on the pioneer or his livestock, and inconvenient, because the trees had to be felled eventually to clear the fields.[16]

From the days of the Loyalists, the most important initial crop for the occupants of the hardwood lands of Upper Canada was often potash. In time almost every farm had

[14]Need, *Six Years in the Bush*, p. 48. The Traills paid $14.00 an acre for the same work (Traill, *Backwoods of Canada*, pp. 131-2).
[15]Jameson, *Winter Studies and Summer Rambles*, vol. II, p. 29.
[16]Campbell, *Travels in the Interior Inhabited Parts of North America*, p. 161; Howison, *Sketches of Upper Canada*, p. 250; Pickering, *Inquiries of an Emigrant*, pp. 64-5.

its potash "factory" with its tubs of leaching ashes and its kettles of boiling lye, and every village had its "pearlash ovens" where potash could be further refined.[17] A few of them even had "saleratus factories" for the manufacture of a crude baking soda from the pearlash. The European demand for potassium salts for use in soaps, fertilizers, and other manufactures sustained the potash market. Most of the potash was obtained as a by-product in land-clearing, but some of it came from the vast accumulation of ashes in the open fireplaces. The potash industry, it should be added, rapidly declined after 1850.[18]

To carry on his clearing and farming, the backwoodsman had a limited stock of tools and implements—axes, spades, shovels, hoes, forks, sickles, scythes, and flails, mostly of American manufacture or made in imitation of American models. His only real labour-saving implement was an A-harrow. This was constructed of heavy timbers framed in a triangle for convenience in passing between stumps. It had nine or more iron teeth, each about an inch and a half in diameter, and tipped with steel.[19]

When he had the trees removed from a few acres, the backwoodsman planted his first crop. With a hoe much resembling a heavy adze, or even with an axe, he cut holes in the turf for his potatoes. Though he did not even hoe them throughout the summer, he was certain of a good return from them in the days before the late blight, and he knew that the ground would be left in good shape for a succeeding crop. Turnips, too, did well on new land, even when it was

[17]The methods of manufacture of potash and pearlash are described in Talbot, *Five Years' Residence*, vol. I, p. 286. It was estimated that good hardwood land would generally yield a barrel of potash an acre.

[18]The prosperity which accompanied the building of railways brought such high prices for all kinds of produce that farmers were glad to give up potash-making, with its unpleasant outdoor work at night. Cooking stoves and box stoves reduced the consumption of wood to a point where the ashes merely sufficed for domestic soap-making. Little hardwood land remained uncleared, and the trees on it were coming to have value as firewood. Finally, the exploitation of the Stassfurt potassium deposits after 1856 ruined the market (Montreal *Witness*, Dec. 27, 1856; *Sessional Papers, Canada, 1861*, no. 23.

[19]*JTBAUC 1855-6*, p. 645. For the superiority of American tools to British, see Montreal *Gazette*, July 20, 1839, and Bird, *The Englishwoman in America*, p. 123.

low and wet. Indian corn, the stand-by of settlers to the south, was not satisfactory in any but the westerly parts of Upper Canada, because it was often destroyed by frost before it could mature; nevertheless, patches of it, with the accompanying squashes and pumpkins between the rows, were characteristic of the backwoods landscape, for they would at least provide roasting ears, as well as green fodder for the livestock. If he came to his lot in the spring, as he usually did, the backwoodsman would have no other crops, for he had to spend too much time in building, fencing, and cutting surface drains through turf and roots to clear any more land. Then, in the autumn, to obtain a little cash for tea and other necessaries, he would sow some wheat broadcast on the unstirred ground among the stumps of his summer logging-fallow, and scratch it in with his harrow. With the wheat, he might sow timothy or red clover seeds, or a mixture of them, but this he did not always do, as a crop of white clover[20] or of red top, a native grass relished by cattle and sheep (though not by horses), would appear spontaneously the next year anyway. The second year, he might sow wheat where the potatoes and Indian corn had been the first. He sometimes sowed wheat after wheat, but this was not considered a good practice, as the crop obtained would be too rank in the straw. Preferably, he chopped and logged enough each year to be able to harrow wheat into four or five acres of new land, and left the older clearings in hay or pasture, or sowed oats or rye or buckwheat in them. Buckwheat was supposed to have the merit of "taming" the soil for a future crop of wheat. In four or five years, weeds and seedlings would overrun the clearance, but by this time the roots of the stumps would have decayed sufficiently to admit of ploughing. The ploughing was of a kind which horrified British travellers, for the backwoodsman merely worked his primitive implement around the stumps, in and out, backwards and forwards, till, somehow or other, he got the soil moved. Then he harrowed it, and sowed wheat. For another four or five years he repeated the procedure, till even the large roots of the stumps were well

[20]It is supposed that French missionaries carried white clover seed through the Great Lakes region and the Ohio Valley (Carrier, *Beginnings of Agriculture in America*, pp. 221, 241).

decayed. Then he hitched his oxen to each stump in turn
and jerked it out. If some of the roots were still sound
he utilized a simple lever or even a screw. As an alternative
he could set fire to the stumps—probably the best method with
pine stumps, which did not decay. Such was the course of
the backwoodsman in the early days of Upper Canada, and
such it continued to be as long as there were wooded areas
being settled.[21]

Not every part of Upper Canada underwent this process.
In many places, but possibly pre-eminently along the Thames
River, there were abandoned Indian clearances, which could
be utilized with little preparation.[22]   Again, on the "natural
plains . . . not entirely clear of timber" in the London district, the pioneer had "but little to do only to fence his land,
and put in the plough, which indeed requires a strong team
at first, but afterwards may be tilled with one horse."[23]

Once his fields were clear of stumps, the backwoodsman
(now no longer entitled to the name) practised tillage methods
identical with those in the older parts of the province, as described in the following chapter.

The settler in the bush kept only enough livestock for
his own needs. If he had a yoke of oxen, two or three cows,
some calves and young cattle, half a dozen sheep, and a litter
of pigs, he was as well off as his fellows. He was not apt
to have any horses till his farm was fairly well cleared, for
they were not so steady and tractable as oxen in working

---

[21]Talbot, *Five Years' Residence*, vol. I, pp. 158, 190, 301; Pickering,
Inquiries of an Emigrant, pp. 158-9; Traill, *Backwoods of Canada*, pp.
194-5; Strickland, *Twenty-Seven Years in Canada West*, vol. I, pp.
32-3, 168-9; Gourlay, *Statistical Account of Upper Canada*, vol. I, pp.
475, 562; *JTBAUC 1855-6*, pp. 340-1, 370-3, 644-5, 648; *Ontario Farmer*,
June, 1869, p. 180.

[22]Heriot, *Travels through the Canadas*, p. 182. Zeisberger, in his
account of the founding of the "Moravian" Delaware settlement at
Fairfield, writes: "The brothers were busy dividing the fields, for
which these great bottoms are needed, but it is such rich land as we
have nowhere had, being like a dung-heap, and very easily cleared. . . .
The brethren were busy clearing land, for which they show real zeal,
the land pleasing them, being the right sort for Indians, such as they
like to have" (Bliss, ed., *Diary of David Zeisberger*, vol. II, pp. 261-2).
The sites of Goderich and Southampton were abandoned Indian clearances (Strickland, *Twenty-Seven Years in Canada West*, vol. I, p. 259;
JTBAUC 1855-6, p. 626).

[23]Smith, *Geographical View of . . . Upper Canada*, p. 5.

among the stumps, and they had to be fed something better than browse, weeds, or beaver hay. On the other hand, he was certain to have hens, ducks, geese, and turkeys.[24]

The backwoodsman found oxen indispensable till his farm was cleared. In fact, oxen remained the common working animals even on old cleared farms till the introduction of machinery such as the reaper. It was not till after 1850 that horses completely supplanted them along the "front." But necessary though oxen and milch cows were to him, the backwoodsman accorded them the worst treatment conceivable. He worked his oxen from early morning to nightfall without food, and then turned them into the woods to browse. He milked his cows at strange hours, and sometimes not at all for days. Fortunately cattle managed to thrive on browse and other coarse feed during the summer. He often provided no shelter for them when winter came, and after the pumpkins were all consumed, gave them nothing to eat but straw. It was estimated that 1,500 cattle perished in London Township, Middlesex County, in 1822 from poor feed and lack of shelter, and corresponding numbers in all the adjacent pioneer townships.[25]

It was natural enough that the pioneer on the fringe of settlement should take little care of his cattle, for he could really afford neither the time nor the labour necessary, but it seems remarkable that even after his farm was mainly cleared he forced them to undergo every privation. He stabled his horses, and his cows when they were milking, but he provided no shelter except open sheds and straw stacks for the grown steers and the young cattle. The advocates of the practice of allowing cattle to shiver around barns and fences said that stabling them would be too expensive and laborious to make it economically profitable.[26] Possibly lack

---

[24]Farmers in the southwestern part of the province often tried to domesticate the wild turkey, taking the young from the nest, or hatching eggs they discovered, but without much success (Smith, *Canada, Past, Present, and Future,* vol. II, p. 405). For a description of Upper Canada livestock, see Chapter IX, below.

[25]Talbot, *Five Years' Residence,* vol. I, p. 178; Strickland, *Twenty-Seven Years in Canada West,* vol. I, pp. 146-7; Traill, *Backwoods of Canada,* pp. 184-5; *JTBAUC 1855-6,* pp. 432, 650.

[26]*Canadian Agriculturist,* Feb. 16, 1860, p. 73; *JTBAUC 1855-6,* p. 327.

of proper feed was even more injurious to the cattle than lack
of shelter. Only a few farmers in the wheat-growing regions fed either hay or turnips. Under these circumstances,
it was, as was remarked of the Niagara peninsula, "a pitiable
sight to go about the country and see the multitudes of poor
cattle, which fill almost every farmer's yards in the spring
of the year."²⁷ The ideal cattle for Upper Canada, thought
the farmers, were those which would "stand starvation best."
When those which did not reach this standard began in the
spring to "lift" (i.e., they were too weak to rise without
assistance), the farmers diagnosed their trouble as "hollow
horn" or "wolf-in-the-tail," and either bored a hole in the horn
and poured in turpentine, pepper, or vinegar, or a mixture
of them, or "killed the wolf" by making an incision near
the end of the tail, putting in pepper and salt, and binding
up the wound. Wolf-in-the-tail was no more than a super-
stition, but hollow horn was really an inflammation of the
sinus brought on by bad care. No matter what the diagnosis
and treatment, the cattle ordinarily recovered if the "cures"
were accompanied by better attention to their general welfare; otherwise the maladies were quite often fatal.²⁸

The backwoodsman did not keep many sheep, in spite of
the remark of the Duke of La Rochefoucault-Liancourt that
sheep were more numerous in the Loyalist community at
Kingston than in any part of the United States he had visited.
Pickering said that the backwoodsman might keep five or
six sheep, or even twenty or thirty, but seldom more—
certainly not large flocks. The champions of sheep-raising
in the new settlements pointed out that sheep need be given
no care in summer and only the barest shelter in winter;
that in an open winter they would live nicely on pea straw

---

²⁷*Canadian Agricultural Reader*, p. 127. See also Chapter IX, below.
It will be understood that the Pennsylvania Dutch were an exception
to this generalization.

²⁸Talbot, *Five Years' Residence*, vol. I, p. 179; Traill, *Backwoods
of Canada*, pp. 185-6; *Farmer's Advocate*, April, 1880, p. 86. The last
authority states that farmers in Western Ontario had then given up
these treatments, and that public opinion would compel the prosecution
of any resorting to them. Nevertheless, my father informs me that
about 1890 they were still being applied in the township of Ross
(Renfrew County). Cf. also, for the same county, an implication in
a letter in the *Farmer's Advocate*, May, 1886, p. 144.

alone; that in Upper Canada they were not affected by ailments such as the foot-rot, so troublesome elsewhere; and that they produced two crops a year, one of wool and one of lambs. Nevertheless, they did require some winter care, at least in the lambing season, and there was much loss from wild animals in the early days of settlement and from dogs later. These factors, combined with a comparative lack of demand for mutton (which was usually unpalatable owing to defective butchering) and low prices for wool, kept the number of sheep in Upper Canada comparatively small till about 1850. That there was little market for wool is demonstrated by the facts that in 1848, at a three-day wool fair at Ingersoll, most of the wool was exchanged for cloth, and that as late as 1853, half the wool grown in the advanced county of Prince Edward was manufactured domestically.[29]

The backwoodsman always had pigs enough to consume the buttermilk, potato skins, and other things which would otherwise go to waste. If he had more than he could thus feed, he let them run in the woods, sometimes till after the first snow fell, precisely as the Loyalists had done. Then, a month or so before he intended to kill them, he shut them up and fattened them on Indian corn, potatoes, or most often, on peas.[30]

Sometimes the pioneer supplemented the meat he obtained from his domestic animals by fishing and hunting. In the spring he could set out in his canoe with a jack light in the bow, and spear the pike or pickerel revealed in the waters. He might join a hunting party of his neighbours, or he might tramp through the woods with only his dog and his gun, but in either case he seldom failed to have two or three fat deer to provide autumn venison. He and his friends slaughtered partridges, wild turkeys, and passenger pigeons in great numbers. He also did a good deal of hunting merely

[29]La Rochefoucault-Liancourt, *Travels*, vol. I, p. 503; Pickering, *Inquiries of an Emigrant*, p. 89; *Agriculturist and Canadian Journal*, June 15, 1848, p. 129; *JTBAUC 1855-6*, pp. 433, 436, 649.

[30]Gibson, "Conditions in York County a Century Ago" (*Ontario Historical Society Papers and Records*, vol. XXIV, 1927, p. 361); *Canadian Agriculturist*, Nov. 1850, p. 249; *JTBAUC 1855-6*, pp. 462, 488, 649. See also below, p. 88.

to rid his clearance of vermin, especially raccoons and squirrels.[31]

Every backwoodsman soon had an orchard of sorts. In eastern Upper Canada he had in it only apples, crab-apples, and plums, but west of Toronto he had in addition peaches, red cherries, and sometimes pears. Though he never drained it, nor cultivated it, nor pruned the trees, nor fenced out the livestock, he had more fruit than he could use. Peaches and apples were so abundant in the Niagara peninsula that passers-by helped themselves as a matter of course, and pigs were turned into the orchards to feed on the windfalls. In this region the pioneer's wife had plenty of dried peaches as well as dried apples for her winter pie-making, and everywhere fresh cider or even cider royal "was brought on the table in jugs-full, as water would be brought in England," as the amazed Isaac Fidler reported.[32] In addition to his orchard fruits, the backwoodsman had various wild ones, such as gooseberries, cranberries, currants, raspberries, and strawberries. None of the backwoodsmen, and few of the old settled farmers, attempted to grow grapes, except as curiosities, as the prevalent impression was that the province was too far north for their successful culture. As late as 1854, fear of severe frosts kept even Niagara peninsula farmers from engaging in viticulture.[33]

The pioneer devoted no more time to his garden than he did to his orchard, and his wife had scarcely more time to attend to it than he. Nevertheless, in spite of its being overgrown with weeds, it produced a quantitatively satisfactory

---

[31]Pickering, *Inquiries of an Emigrant*, pp. 81, 91; Traill, *Backwoods of Canada*, pp. 159-60; Haight, *Country Life in Canada*, pp. 41-2, 74-7. The destruction caused by vermin was thus described by Zeisberger in 1796: "Raccoons, squirrels, bears, wolves, and wild turkeys came in great number, and did great harm to the fields, here indeed not so much, for the Indians scared them away, but among the white people they ruined whole fields. Besides all sorts of vermin [probably mostly squirrels] came from the south, tried to get over the river, and were drowned, whole heaps of which could be seen" (Bliss, *Diary of David Zeisberger*, vol. II, p. 459). For this squirrel invasion of 1796, see also Weld, *Travels through the States*, vol. II, pp. 44-5.

[32]Fidler, *Observations on Professions*, p. 212; Talbot, *Five Years' Residence*, vol. I, pp. 292-4; Pickering, *Inquiries of an Emigrant*, p. 61; Howison, *Sketches of Upper Canada*, pp. 67-8, 200.

[33]*Genesee Farmer*, vol. I, 1831, p. 409; *JTBAUC 1855-6*, p. 452.

supply of various vegetables to add to the melons, squashes, and pumpkins grown in the corn patch. Beets for pickling and greens, radishes, carrots, parsnips, cucumbers, and cabbages were most commonly cultivated. None of these had to contend with insects or other parasites except cabbages, which were much subject to destruction by the cabbage butterfly. Till towards 1850 tomatoes were grown as a garden ornament and not for eating, as there was a prevalent belief that they were poisonous.[34]

The pioneer never thought of buying the sugar needed for sweetening tea, cooking, and making preserves. He had a fairly satisfactory substitute in maple sugar. As soon as the sap began to rise in the spring, he went off to the sugar-bush, tapped the trees with an auger or axe, inserted a chip in the hole, and allowed the wooden troughs he had brought with him to fill with sap. Then he and his boys boiled the sap down in a cauldron suspended over a fire by a thick pole, clarified the syrup by adding the white of an egg or some milk, and boiled the syrup in turn till it granulated. With much industry and some luck he might have as much as 1,000 pounds of sugar as a result, but possibly 500 pounds would ordinarily be all that he could hope for.[35]

The backwoodsman was not altogether dependent on maple sugar for sweetening purposes. Honey-bees were quite common in the new settlements, both in the farmyards and the woods. Those in the woods belonged to swarms which had escaped from their hives, or were descendants of such swarms. If the backwoodsman did not bring bees with him from his old home, he could get all the honey he wanted by searching out "bee-trees." This he usually did by following the common-sense method of melting some wax and honey on a hot stone till a few bees were attracted, marking the direction of their flight when they were gorged, and following it to their hoard. Sometimes he contented himself with smoking the bees out and robbing them of their honey, but at other times he cut down the tree, sectioned out the part of the trunk

---

[34]Talbot, *Five Years' Residence*, vol. I, p. 297; *JTBAUC 1855-6*, p. 330.

[35]Talbot, *Five Years' Residence*, vol. I, pp. 275-6; Bell, *Hints to Emigrants*, pp. 228-30. Maple sugar was possibly the chief salable product of the Indians.

where the bees were, and used it as a hive. It was not necessary for the backwoodsman himself to undertake this work of finding bee-trees, for there were always a few professional "bee-hunters" in the community who would do it for him. In any case, once he had a hive of bees, he was in a position where he could build up a small apiary.[36]

The necessity of providing clothing imposed another set of tasks on the backwoodsman and his family. At odd times throughout the winter, or when he was resting after his dinner in summer, he would dress the flax to make it ready for spinning. Then, usually after the crops were in, he washed his sheep in the nearest creek, permitted them to dry for a few days, and sheared them. The women took the wool, picked it over, and sent it to the carding mill, if there was one at hand. When it came back one of them, or a hired "spinning-girl," would turn it into yarn. After it was spun and dyed, it was handed over to the weaver. When the cloth was in the bolt, it had to be fulled at home if the local carding mill did not do fulling as well as carding. These activities are usually described at considerable length in the pioneer histories, so that no further description of them is needed here.

The pioneer family was of necessity almost self-sufficient. Indeed, long after the farm was cleared, and it was quite possible to purchase manufactured articles, the practice persisted of making at home most of the things needed. A Dundas County writer revealed how the old habit of self-sufficiency still expressed itself as late as 1860.

In summer time, we live upon bacon, beef and pork hams, nicely cured and smoked, and fried with eggs, supplemented with cheese, bread, and butter, all home made, and of the best. In October, we kill a beast. The blacksmith takes a quarter, the shoemaker another, the tailor or the carpenter a third, and ourselves the remaining one. In December, we kill a second, cut it up, freeze it, and pack it away in barrels with straw, where it will keep till the first of April. The hides go to the tanner, who takes one half of each, and gives me the other when tanned; the shoemaker comes to the house once a year and makes out of it

---

[36]Talbot, *Five Years' Residence*, vol. I, pp. 249-52. Talbot describes at length the method used in bee-hunting. Even the "Moravian" Delawares brought in bees from the United States (1793) (Bliss, *Diary of David Zeisberger*, vol. II, p. 316).

boots and shoes for young and old. The tallow is rendered and made into candles, and all the refuse scraps at "killing time" are boiled up with lye, and converted into barrels of soap. And then the women folk spin the wool and weave the stockings, sew the quilts and counterpanes, and make the featherbeds, so that come what may, we are always sure of a living.[37]

The backwoods communities, like the individual settlers, were almost self-sufficient. In general the self-sufficiency was to be accounted for by the lack of markets. Even when settlement had reached the point where there were crossroads communities, each of the blacksmiths, carpenters, weavers, tailors, cobblers, and ministers who lived in them usually kept a cow or two, some pigs, and a yard of poultry, cultivated a small plot of land to feed them, and seldom bought anything except flour. Save when new settlers were coming in, there was no home market in the backwoods. Furthermore, transportation difficulties excluded the pioneers from the towns along the "front." Most of the roads were mere muddy tracks through the forest or along the concession lines. Under these circumstances, even wheat was of little value at the place of production. Thus the pioneers near the southern end of Lake Simcoe were only forty miles from Toronto, but the value of their good crops was halved by the cost of transporting them down Yonge Street.[38]

---

[37]Croil, *Dundas*, p. 199.

[38]*JTBAUC 1856-7*, p. 5. It was doubtless the dependence of the population on agriculture, especially wheat-growing, with the accompanying lack of a large home market, that made central and western Upper Canada appear much less prosperous to the casual traveller than the adjacent parts of the United States. Nevertheless, it should be pointed out that those who belittled Upper Canada were not entirely fair. Usually they saw only a small part of the province. Many of them, who travelled by steamer, saw at close range only the portion between Prescott and the Lower Canada boundary, which, for a variety of reasons, was not impressive agriculturally; and they compared it with the booming country along the Erie Canal, or with a picture in their mind of some western state, as described in an immigration booklet. The region around Cobourg, that around Toronto, and much of western Upper Canada were as prosperous as any of the newer parts of the United States not directly affected by the Erie Canal, and infinitely more prosperous than those parts of New York and New England where the farmers were suffering from the competition of cheap western produce. Moreover, much of the criticism, even that of the authors of *Lord Durham's Report*, was a thoughtless repetition of the ideas of Robert Gourlay, who was obsessed by the wild lands

The life of the backwoodsman was hard and rude.
Writers of local histories have found more romance in it
than did the participants. Canniff Haight tells us that when
his father and mother were married at the beginning of the
century they went to live on a bush farm north of the Bay
of Quinte. Then he adds: "Doubtless there was a good deal
of romance in it. Love in a cot; the smoke gracefully curling;
the wood-pecker tapping, and all that; very pretty. But
alas, in this work-a-day world, particularly the new one upon
which my parents then entered, these silver linings were not
observed. They had too much of the prose of life."[39] There
was certainly little romance in the commonplace episodes
of hunting for "breachy" cattle or fording swollen streams
to reach a grist mill, and not much more in the staple anec-
dotes of the "pioneer history"—tales of settlers lost in the
woods, of perils from wild animals, of semi-starvation in the
"hungry years." Women of refinement, like Mrs. Moodie,
found life in the bush intolerable. On the other hand, it cannot be doubted that to emigrants from the Hebrides or from
the famine areas of Ireland even the remotest backwoods of
Upper Canada must have partaken of the character of an
earthly paradise.

Present-day romanticists, knowing that the first settlers
had plain food and plenty of outdoor exercise, often think that
they escaped sickness. This is a misconception. It was
dietary deficiencies, not red-flannel underwear, that gave the
pioneers the "scratches." Women were old in their thirties,
worn out by child-bearing and exhausting drudgery. Malaria
("agues and intermittent fevers") was nearly universal. The
frontiersmen did not associate it with mosquitoes, but like
Edward Talbot, attributed it to "the effluvia arising from

---

problem. Again, as John Beverley Robinson explained, the critics of
Upper Canada were prone to "think of Buffalo, as if it were a picture
of all America. . . . . They forget the position of Buffalo in the
western world, situated, as it were, between two great inverted funnels,
through the narrow centre of which everything passes from the
expanse of the Atlantic States, to the greater expanse of the far west"
(Pamphlet by J. B. Robinson, quoted in Cobourg *Star*, June 4, 1840).
The Tories of Upper Canada were very sensitive to criticisms of the
economic progress of the province. Cf. Buckingham, *Canada, Nova
Scotia, New Brunswick and the other British Provinces*, pp. 30 ff.

[39]Haight, *Country Life in Canada*, p. 3.

putrid vegetables and from stagnant waters." "In the Summer of 1819," he stated, "agues and fevers prevailed to an alarming extent, in almost every part of the Upper Province, but particularly in the Western Districts."[40] Individuals died of "decline," of "inflammation of the bowels," of diphtheria, and of scarlet fever, and the medical science of the time was helpless. Sometimes an epidemic, like the cholera one of 1832, would strike down a large part of a community.[41]

With their endless round of labour, the pioneer and his family had scant time for recreation. Such recreation as they did have took the form of social mingling. It was for this reason, not merely because the goods were sold on credit, that they attended every auction sale within miles. It was for this reason, too, that the bees—apple-paring, cloth-fulling, logging, barn-raising, and corn-husking—were so characteristic of the backwoods. Unfortunately, like the wakes, they often afforded chiefly an occasion for a carousal. The result was that by the early eighteen-thirties the corn-husking bee was "not now so frequently adopted among the more independent or better class of settlers" as it had formerly been.[42]

It was not till after he was on his clearance for several years that the backwoodsman had many comforts. His open fireplace was inefficient for heating and inconvenient for baking, in spite of its great array of pans and cranes and spits. Tiny windows, uneven floors, crude furniture, and plenty of flies and other insects kept his house from being pleasant, according to the standards in the older settlements. Yet, as Talbot remarked, if he could "keep up his supply of pork and pumpkin-pie, of molasses and sour crout, of tea and Johnny-cake,—which he seldom fails to accomplish,— he feels perfectly indifferent regarding those household conveniences which are not so eminently useful."[43]

---

[40]Talbot, *Five Years' Residence*, vol. I, pp. 360-2.

[41]Landon, *Western Ontario and the American Frontier*, p. 168.

[42]Traill, *Backwoods of Canada*, p. 188. For the cultural deficiencies of the Upper Canada pioneers, see Clark, *Social Development of Canada*, pp. 211-13. See also above, p. 59.

[43]Talbot, *Five Years' Residence*, vol. II, p. 102. For a full consideration of pioneer foods and their preparation, see Guillet, *Early Life in Upper Canada*, pp. 177-207.

In eight or ten years the backwoodsman would progress through the stages outlined by Beaven in the quotation at the end of the last chapter. He would then have a frame house; an assortment of minor buildings, including a granary, a stable, a smoke-house, a milk-house, a pig pen, and possibly an ice-house; and several small barns or one large one, for in Upper Canada it was the practice to put almost all the grain under cover, and as much as possible of the hay, instead of building stacks.[44] Nor was this all. Churches and schools had by this time appeared in his neighbourhood. Trails through the woods were now good roads in winter, and passable in summer. With their improvement, markets were not so inaccessible as formerly. He found that strangers referred to his community as one of "old cleared farms," and realized that he would have to travel twenty or thirty miles to reach the true backwoods.

---

[44]Howison, *Sketches of Upper Canada*, pp. 251-2; Strickland, *Twenty-Seven Years in Canada West*, vol. I, pp. 50-3; Haight, *Country Life in Canada*, p. 112. For descriptions of various kinds of pioneer dwellings, see Guillet, *Early Life in Upper Canada*, pp. 155-76.

CHAPTER VI

THE WHEAT FARMER, 1815-1850

L IKE the adjacent states of the Great Lakes basin, Upper
Canada first established its agricultural reputation as
a producer of wheat. In much of it, therefore, the typical
farmer, as in the Genesee country of New York and the
"backbone counties" of Ohio, came to be the wheat-grower.

The backwoodsman often sowed wheat on land scarcely
reclaimed from the forest, as was mentioned in the preceding chapter. Long after the fields were clear of stumps, he
or his successor relied on wheat as the staple crop. This
was entirely reasonable. Lord Durham wrote (in phrases
borrowed from Canada Company propaganda) that the peninsula between Lake Erie and Lake Huron, "with a smaller
proportion of inferior land than probably any other tract of
similar extent in that part of North America, is generally
considered the best grain country on that continent."[1] The
climate, with its hot summers, was favourable. The grain
was easily transported in bags and its value did not diminish
in storage as long as it was kept dry. In the days before
labour-saving machinery its production necessitated the expenditure of much less capital than other branches of farming. In most of Upper Canada it was far more profitable
than any of the other cereals, some of which, indeed, could
not be sold at all. The Hon. Adam Fergusson, in a speech
delivered at the first provincial exhibition in 1846, thus
summarized the whole question:

In times past, the great and almost sole object of serious interest
to the [Upper] Canadian Farmer, has been to grow wheat as largely,
and to repeat the crop as frequently as any decent return could be
obtained. This system was perfectly natural, if not perfectly wise.
Wheat was found to be always less or more in demand, commanding a
cash payment, while most other articles of farm produce were only
to be disposed of in barter or in trade. Land was cheap and abundant,
and when fields began to exhibit unequivocal symptoms of exhaustion,

---

[1]Lucas, (ed.), *Lord Durham's Report*, vol. II, p. 216.

a new clearing was commenced, and the old pretty much abandoned to nature.[2]

Wheat was by no means the only crop grown by the wheat farmer; it was simply the one which he sold. The census of 1851 shows, especially in its acreage figures, the relative standing of the important grains then produced in Canada West:[3]

	Acres	Bushels
Wheat	798,275	12,682,550
Oats	413,058	11,391,867
Peas	186,643	3,127,681
Indian Corn	72,047	1,688,805
Rye	49,066	318,429
Buckwheat	44,264	579,935
Barley	30,129	625,452

While peas, Indian corn, oats, and barley had a large aggregate production, they were primarily intended to be consumed on the farm, and except in certain areas, did not enter into commerce to any extent. Their bulk and their cheapness made it unprofitable to draw them far to market.

Oats were by far the most important of the coarse grains, mainly because they were considered essential for the keeping of horses, but in the Scottish districts, such as Glengarry, because they formed a staple of human diet. In general their production kept pace with the number of horses. They had the great advantage that they could be grown on nearly every kind of soil; often, it was said, they were simply sown where the soil was too wet or too dirty for any other cereal. As might be expected under these circumstances, the grain was often small and light, "of a miserable description," according to British standards.[4]

---

[2]*Journal and Transactions of the Board of Agriculture of Upper Canada for 1855-6*, p. 36. Hereafter this authority is cited as *JTBAUC*.

[3]*Census of Canada, 1851-2*, vol. II, pp. 61-3. Comparable statistics for 1842 (the first year for which a detailed official agricultural census is available) were: wheat 3,221,989 bushels; oats 4,788,167 bushels; peas 1,191,550 bushels; Indian corn 691,359 bushels; rye 292,969 bushels; buckwheat 352,786 bushels; and barley 1,031,334 bushels (*Census of Canada, 1871*, vol. IV, p. 139).

[4]Murray, *Historical and Descriptive Account*, vol. I, p. 339; Talbot, *Five Years' Residence*, vol. I, pp. 300-1; *Canada Farmer*, March 31, 1873, p. 93.

Indian corn was a much less important crop in Upper Canada than in the northern United States. Only in the southwestern parts of the province could it be counted on to mature. In a few places here—along the alluvial flats of the Thames Valley for example—there were corn fields which rivalled in appearance those on the bottoms along the tributaries of the Ohio and the Mississippi. Elsewhere in the province corn was liable to be destroyed by an early frost. Careful farmers were therefore reluctant to rely on either the blades or the ears for fodder. Many never even attempted to grow corn, and those who did bestowed little attention on it compared with what they gave to wheat. Those who might have been willing to take a chance with the frost objected to the drudgery of hoeing. This seems to have been especially true of British immigrants. It persisted as an important objection till towards 1850, when corn began to be planted in drills rather than in hills, and to be cultivated with a shovel-plough or a corn cultivator.[5] Under these conditions, after about 1825 corn steadily declined in importance relative to wheat. By 1850 its position of comparative insignificance in the province was emphasized by contrast with its position of predominance in even the great wheat-exporting states of the Union. According to the census of 1851, Upper Canada, as already noticed, returned as the crop of 1850, 12,682,550 bushels of wheat and 1,688,805 bushels of corn. The corn figures, incidentally, were probably much too high, owing to the common method of measuring corn in the ear rather than in the kernel. Ohio, according to the census of 1850, returned as the crop of 1849, 14,487,351 bushels of wheat and 59,078,695 bushels of corn.[6] In other words, for every bushel of wheat harvested in Upper Canada there was a little less than a seventh of a bushel of corn, while for every bushel of wheat harvested in Ohio there were slightly over four bushels of corn.

The average Upper Canadian farmer preferred peas to

---

[5]Murray, *Historical and Descriptive Account*, vol. I, p. 340; Talbot, *Five Years' Residence*, vol. I, pp. 155, 299; Stuart, *Emigrant's Guide to Upper Canada*, p. 35; Aylmer (L.C.) *Ottawa Advocate*, quoted in Montreal *Transcript*, Aug. 3, 1844; *JTBAUC 1855-6*, pp. 185, 646-7.

[6]Brewer, "Report on the Cereal Production of the United States," pp. 69, 91.

corn, as they were just as good for fattening hogs, and were a more dependable crop.   Except in the Niagara peninsula, it was not till after 1850 that the pea weevil or "pea-bug," which had practically put an end to pea-growing in the northern United States, began to be troublesome.   On the other hand, peas were not a good initial crop on new land, as it was difficult to cover them with a drag, and the rich soil made the straw too rank; they were therefore not much grown till after the field was ploughed.[7]   A writer mentions "immense pea fields" in western Upper Canada in 1835, into which hogs were simply turned to fatten ("hogging down"); but he adds that peas were often harvested and threshed.[8] As indicated below, they were frequently grown as part of a rotation, to prepare the land for wheat.

Buckwheat was rather generally sown, but mostly as a catch crop, or on shallow or gravelly soil.   Rye was likewise a crop for poor, light land.   It was little used for bread in Upper Canada, except where the population was of German extraction, as even the pioneers soon lost their taste for "rye and Injun."   It was therefore grown mainly to satisfy the demand of the distilleries.   In 1850 about 85 per cent of the rye of the province was produced near the Bay of Quinte, chiefly because there was a large distillery at Kingston.   Rye was commonly sown year after year on the same piece of land; and the same was true of buckwheat.   Barley of the four-rowed kind was grown generally, though not in large amounts, for the breweries, which began to be fairly numerous after about 1825.[9]

Peas and oats likewise had some commercial importance before 1850.   Most of the peas were consumed at home, but many were sold for the lumber camps, and some more were exported to Great Britain, where they had to compete with those produced along the Baltic and the Black seas.[10]   Oats

[7]*JTBAUC 1855-6*, pp. 451, 646.

[8]Duncumb, *The British Emigrant's Advocate*, pp. 187-8. Peas were pulled at harvesting, not cut (Pickering, *Inquiries of an Emigrant*, p. 90).

[9]Murray, *Historical and Descriptive Account*, vol. I, p. 339: *ibid.*, vol. II, p. 29; Talbot, *Five Years' Residence*, vol. I, pp. 300-1: Kingston, *Upper Canada Herald*, March 1, 1825; *Census of Canada, 1851-2*, vol. II, p. 62; *JTBAUC 1855-6*, p. 439.

[10]*Journal d'Agriculture*, fév., 1849, p. 51.

had a limited market in the towns and villages, and in the
Ottawa Valley, as we shall see, they, rather than wheat, formed
the cash crop.

Various special crops were grown in different parts of
Upper Canada, such as tobacco, flax, hops, and fruit. These
are dealt with in other connections. The ordinary Upper
Canadian farmer was not interested in them, except as sidelines. His object was to produce as much wheat as possible.
The statistics from the census of 1851 already given indicate
in a general way how well he succeeded. More specifically,
the census shows that twenty-four of the twenty-six well-
settled counties west of the Bay of Quinte, starting with
Northumberland, had over half of the acreage devoted to
grain sown to wheat. The two exceptions, York and Essex,
had respectively almost 50 per cent and about 45 per cent.
In Grey, Haldimand, Halton, and Lincoln counties, wheat
occupied two-thirds of the cereal area. The predominance
of wheat in counties in the heart of the wheat belt, such as
Peel, may be shown in another way. Wheat each year occupied about one-third of the cleared land, the remainder
being in coarse grains, peas, root crops, naked fallows,
meadows, and pastures.[11] It was with justification that an
investigator (evidently Thomas C. Keefer) remarked, "there
is probably no country where there is so much wheat grown,
in proportion to the population and the area under cultivation,
as in that part of Canada west of Kingston."[12]

The wheat farmers of Upper Canada exhibited a wide
variation in the methods they followed. At one extreme
were those who practised wheat "skinning" or "mining"—a
method of cultivation which had exhausted the soil of certain
parts of Upper Canada as early as 1820.[13] They would sow
wheat year after year till the field returned scarcely half a
crop. Then they would seed it down, allow it to recuperate
for a few seasons, break it up, and again sow wheat. They

[11]*JTBAUC 1855-6*, p. 353.

[12]Andrews, "Report on the Trade and Commerce of the British
North American Colonies" (*House Executive Document*, 32nd Cong., 1st
Sess., 1852-3, No. 136, p. 408).

[13]Howison, *Sketches of Upper Canada*, p. 146; Talbot, *Five Years'
Residence*, vol. I, p. 158.

kept little livestock, and what they did have ran in the woods; but even when they had manure available in the barnyard, and their fields were manifestly becoming worn out, they often neglected it. Visitors who were versed in British agricultural theories and practices were scandalized by the wastage of manure and the slipshod ways of tillage they observed throughout the province. They condemned the agriculture on pioneer clearances and old farms alike. In the latter case there was much to be said for their criticism; but in the former they were prone to overlook the essential point that on newly cleared land better tillage and heavier fertilizing would not have added sufficiently to the product of the soil to justify their use. In other words, when land was cheap and labour dear, "poor" farming was the most profitable kind.

In contrast with the "wheat miners," there were men on many of the old cleared farms in the Niagara peninsula, along the Bay of Quinte, north of Lake Ontario, along Yonge Street, and elsewhere who prided themselves on being efficient farmers. While it was doubtless true that they lacked a regular system of rotation in the English sense,[14] they usually observed a few principles, the most important of which was to avoid two successive crops of any one kind of grain on the same land, and they had a rather common cropping routine. About 1850 in Peel, York, Ontario, Simcoe, and Prince Edward counties specifically it was substantially as follows: in the spring of the first year the meadow or pasture was broken up and a crop of spring grain (usually peas) obtained *or* the field was summer fallowed; the second year a crop of fall wheat (or spring wheat) was obtained; the third year a crop of spring grain (usually oats but sometimes peas or barley) was obtained *or* the field was summer fallowed if the land was very foul; the fourth year, if the crop of the third year was peas, or if the field was summer fallowed, a crop of fall wheat (or spring wheat) was obtained and the field seeded down

---

[14]Thus John Lynch wrote of Simcoe County: "I have not known any farmer to carry out a regular rotation for any considerable length of time, although I have known many who have commenced on various systems, but abandoned them before the cycle was completed, and commenced new rotations which were terminated in a similar manner" (*JTBAUC 1856-7*, p. 34).

otherwise a crop of oats or barley or sometimes even fall or spring wheat was obtained and the field seeded down. The field remained in meadow or pasture for four or five years, after which the process was repeated.[15]

In his prize essay on Peel County, John Lynch described the procedure followed by the farmers of the Toronto region at the point in their rotation where they sowed their fall wheat.

The most general practice among the farmers of this section is, to have rather more than one-third of their cultivated land in wheat—the most of it sown on prepared fallow ground, and the remainder after pease, barley or oats—rather less than one-third being fallow, leaving about one-third for summer grain, vegetables and grass. When land growing spring grain is partially exhausted, or becomes foul with weeds or grass, it is fallowed for the purpose of clearing it, and manured for the purpose of renovating it; but the greater part of the fallow ground will necessarily be that which succeeds fall wheat of the previous year. . . . The operation of fallowing is generally three ploughings with intermediate harrowings to break the clods and level the ground. The manure of the barn-yard (except what may be required for potatos, other root crops and gardens) is spread upon the most needy parts of the fallow, just before the second, or sometimes the third ploughing,—and ploughed under. The last ploughing leaves the land in ridges of from nine to fifteen feet wide, according to the wetness or dryness of the soil, on which the seed is sown and harrowed in; after which the furrows between the ridges are ploughed out, cross-furrows made where they may be necessary, and the junctions of all the furrows and drains carefully cleared out with a shovel, so that no water shall stand in any part of the field.[16]

The naked summer fallow, ploughed lengthwise, then crosswise, and again lengthwise, and harrowed between the ploughings, was an integral part of Upper Canada wheat-farming down to 1850, as it was in the wheat-growing sections of New York and Ohio till about the same date.[17] It had become well established in the province by about 1830,

---

[15]*JTBAUC 1855-6*, pp. 329, 358-60, 430, 437-8; *JTBAUC 1856-7*, p. 50. Even rotations as variable as those outlined were much too elaborate for many farmers, who, according to Lynch, did "regularly pursue that exhausting rotation, fallow and wheat—fallow and wheat" (*JTBAUC 1856-7*, p. 34).

[16]*JTBAUC 1855-6*, pp. 347-8.

[17]Cf. Bidwell and Falconer, *History of Agriculture in the Northern United States*, pp. 263, 325, 328.

possibly owing mainly to the influence of British immigrants, for it was common among those in the Montreal region at the close of the War of 1812.[18] Because the farmer obtained only one crop every two years from the land, the naked summer fallow was often condemned as a waste of a large part of the farm; but it cleared the land of thistles[19] and other weeds, made a better seed-bed, and was often followed by a much better harvest than could be obtained after a smothering crop such as buckwheat, which had no market anyway. No wonder the honest Upper Canadian farmer kept on with it when, as one of them remarked, "he saw that our most successful growers of fall wheat put most dependence on their summer fallows."[20]

On the whole, a rotation emphasizing the naked fallow was approved by observers familiar with the agricultural problems of that day. Lynch for example wrote very sensibly that

This system has certainly succeeded better than any other that has come under my observation; this observation, however, being mostly confined to strong rich lands but lately reclaimed from the forest. On such lands, it is, perhaps, the best plan for the present time, or the plan which will give the greatest and most speedy return. And it is certainly not strange that the farmer should hesitate before giving up a system by which he is rapidly becoming rich, for some other plan which has got to be tried, and of which he is only certain that it will not make him so good a return for his outlay.[21]

But there were many farmers who were convinced that the summer fallow was wasteful, and who eliminated it from their rotations. About 1825 there were a few who ploughed down clover or buckwheat to prepare the land for wheat, and the practice had become not uncommon by 1850. Others, as

---

[18]Grece, *Facts and Observations*, pp. 95, 101, 106; York *Colonial Advocate*, Sept. 26, 1833; Duncumb, *British Emigrant's Advocate*, pp. 194-5; Strickland, *Twenty-Seven Years in Canada West*, vol. I, pp. 32-3. There was very little summer fallowing in the British sense in the continental colonies before the American Revolution (*American Husbandry*, ed. by Carman, pp. 40, 113).

[19]It is said that Canada thistles were introduced into Upper Canada by the men who worked on the *bateaux*. They filled their mattresses with fresh straw at Montreal, and emptied it out, thistles and all, at their destination (Haight, *Country Life in Canada*, p. 244).

[20]*Canadian Agriculturist*, Aug., 1854, p. 226.

[21]*JTBAUC 1855-6*, p. 199.

already shown, used a system in which fall wheat was sown on pea stubble, but this, though it steadily gained in importance, was not till almost 1850 a serious rival of the naked fallow.[22]

In the more progressive wheat-growing districts, the manure available was usually all applied to the summer fallow. Other fertilizers were, on the whole, little used. A few farmers, who could resist the temptation to make potash, sometimes applied unleached ashes to their land.[23] Gypsum, a soil ameliorant rather than a fertilizer, came into use about 1820 in the country adjacent to the Grand River, though not in large amounts at first, as the farmers had to quarry it themselves, and in the absence of mills for grinding it, had to pulverize it with hammers. In the Bay of Quinte region, it was easily obtained from Oswego. Elsewhere in the province, the expense of transportation prohibited its employment. In the two districts named, the better farmers applied it to clover, in preparation for a later wheat crop, especially on sandy soils.[24]

Down to about 1830, the occupant of an old cleared farm had the same limited assortment of implements as the backwoodsman, with the addition of a plough, a waggon, and a grain cradle.[25] After this date, in common with his American contemporaries, he acquired many others. Some of these

[22]Pickering, *Inquiries of an Emigrant*, p. 65; Dunlop, *Statistical Sketches of Upper Canada*, p. 77; *Canadian Agriculturist*, Jan., 1850, p. 31; *JTBAUC 1855-6*, pp. 219, 358-9. Probably because they did not have a rotation involving peas, the wheat farmers of central Ohio seem to have ploughed down clover to a much greater extent than those of Upper Canada (Hildreth, "Ten Days in Ohio," *American Journal of Arts and Sciences*, vol. XXVI, 1834, pp. 232-3).

[23]*Canadian Agriculturist*, Jan., 1850, p. 7; *ibid.*, Dec., 1854, p. 375.

[24]Howison, *Sketches of Upper Canada*, pp. 145-6; Smith, *Canada, Past, Present, and Future*, vol. I, pp. 239-40; *JTBAUC 1855-6*, pp. 430, 448-9; *Report of the Ontario Agricultural Commission*, vol. V, App. N, p. 28.

[25]The grain cradle was a comparatively new implement in North America. While it was used in Elizabethan England for reaping barley, and may have been so used in New England in the Colonial period, it does not appear to have come into general use in the United States till after the American Revolution (Walcott, "Husbandry in Colonial New England," *New England Quarterly*, vol. IX, 1936, p. 235; Gray and Thompson, *History of Agriculture in the Southern United States*, vol. I, p. 170).

were more novel than useful, but gradually reasonably satisfactory models were evolved. The result was that by 1850
the farmer was able to cultivate more land than he had done a
generation earlier, and to do it with less labour on his part.

Among the first implements to be improved was the
plough. Nevertheless, the ploughs in use even in the
eighteen-forties were, by modern standards, most unsatisfactory. Crude home-made ones were not uncommon. These
had a beam made from a crooked oak, a mould-board split
out of a crooked maple, and a straight pole for a handle.
Such an implement, with an L-shaped piece of iron going
through the beam for a coulter, was usually known as a
Loyalist Plough, because it resembled those made in the
earliest days of the province. Others were modifications of
the "bar-share" or "hog-plough" introduced from the United
States about 1808, a kind differing from the Loyalist Plough
only in that it had a bar of iron about two feet long fastened
to the front of the mould-board, with a broad share welded to
it. Still others were copied more or less faithfully from
American cast-iron ploughs, introduced after about 1815.
These had the mould-board and share cast in one piece. A
few were Scotch swing or wheelless ploughs, some of them
being imported, and the rest made in the province. Many
of the latter, as in the country between Kingston and Cobourg,
where they were favourites, were still manufactured with
wooden mould-boards as late as 1849.[26] There was no uni-
formity. The ploughs, it was remarked, embraced "all of
the most improved English and Scottish patterns, with an
almost endless number of mongrels. . . . Almost every county,
and sometimes even township, has a plow in general use, em-
bodying distinct features from those in adjoining counties
and townships."[27] At a ploughing match in connection with
the provincial exhibition at Kingston in 1849, all the ploughs
belonged to three classes. Most of the competitors used a
"Yankee-Canadian" plough, with a cast-iron mould-board and
share, and handles much longer than were customary in the
United States; two or three used Scotch swing ploughs; and

---

[26]*Canadian Agriculturist*, Nov. 1, 1849, p. 286; *ibid.*, Jan., 1850,
p. 9; *JTBAUC 1855-6*, pp. 81, 220; Hind, *et al.*, *Eighty Years' Progress*, p.
40; *Canada Farmer*, Jan. 15, 1874, p. 37.
[27]*Cultivator*, Dec., 1852, p. 400.

one used a Loyalist Plough. This, said the reporter, "did as well as any of the others," for the exhibition of ploughing was "a sorry one," "very crooked and careless."[28]

After ploughing, the farmer prepared the seed-bed with a heavy drag or a harrow. The harrow was greatly improved towards 1850. A Guelph essayist stated in 1852 that "the great clumsy and almost useless things, to which nothing less than a yoke of bulls ought ever to have been hitched, are fast giving place to light, lively working and effective implements."[29] In addition to the harrow, a "cultivator" or "grubber" or "scrabbler" came to be employed in the late eighteen-forties, especially in working fallows. This was essentially a small, heavy harrow with plough handles attached to it. A letter from Waterloo County in 1851 says that the cultivator used there was "the common triangular implement, (with the steel teeth imported from the United States,) and which has been pretty extensively introduced in this section of country, within the last three or four years."[30] The farmer sowed his grain broadcast, as in biblical times, and harrowed it in. The grain-drills introduced before 1850 were a disappointment to those who experimented with them.[31] Wooden rollers were in use in 1851 for smoothing the autumn-sown wheat field in the spring,[32] and probably had been for some time, though certainly not to any extent.

Harvesting the crop was a bugbear to the farmer. The work was arduous, and labourers were much more difficult to obtain than at any other season. Moreover, even the best cradlers seldom exceeded two acres a day, and perhaps an acre and a half would be a good average.[33] An Englishman who visited his brother's farm situated on the road between Dundas and Guelph, thus described a typical harvest scene:

[28]*Canadian Agriculturist*, Oct. 10, 1849, p. 255.

[29]*JTBAUC 1855-6*, p. 220.

[30]*Canadian Agriculturist*, March, 1851, p. 55. For a cut, see Bidwell and Falconer, *History of Agriculture in the Northern United States*, p. 211.

[31]*JTBAUC 1855-6*, p. 228.

[32]*Canadian Agriculturist*, Oct., 1851, p. 232.

[33]Pickering, *Inquiries of an Emigrant*, p. 89; Logan, *Notes of a Journey*, p. 48.

The wheat being ripe, he commenced cutting on the 24th August, when two of his neighbours came with cradles. We all turned out at six o'clock, A.M., there being three cradlers and three binders. My brother and I undertook to put up the corn into stooks. My brother's two bondmen, one of whom was an Englishman, could not keep up with their cradlers, so that he was obliged to assist them in binding; but the other binder, being more active, and having been several years in Canada, kept pace with his cradler. The large thistles, some of them seven feet high, caused us great annoyance. We went home to breakfast at eight, returned in an hour, worked until one, when we had dinner, resumed our labour at two, and continued until six. It is customary to give to every two men a bottle of whisky to mix with the water. . . . The three cradlers cut five acres daily, so that the eighteen acres of wheat were all reaped in less than four days. Much corn is wasted, both because the cradler scatters it about too much, and because the binder is too much hurried to keep up with him. What is left in the field, however, is used for fattening pigs.[34]

It was natural that wheat growers should buy reapers as soon as the high price of wheat and labour made their use economical. In 1833 and 1834 reaping machines were patented in the United States by Obed Hussey and Cyrus McCormick respectively. The first reaper used in Upper Canada was one of the Hussey variety, which was imported into the Cobourg region in 1843. Others were brought into the same district in the two years following. Reapers do not appear to have been used around Toronto till the harvest of 1846. The first McCormick reapers at Cobourg—evidently the first in Upper Canada—were used in 1847.[35]

These early McCormick and Hussey machines were both capable of reaping ten or fifteen acres a day.[36] The Hussey machine left the grain behind it, so that it had to be bound before the reaper went around again. It thus required eleven men to operate it, one driving the horses, one raking off the sheaves from the platform, and nine binding them. The McCormick threw the grain outside the track, so that it was

---

[34]Logan, *Notes of a Journey*, pp. 48-9.

[35]*British American Cultivator*, April, 1847, p. 115; *Canadian Agriculturist*, Aug. 16, 1862, p. 490. For cuts of these early Hussey and McCormick reapers, see Bidwell and Falconer, *History of Agriculture in the Northern United States*, pp. 286, 289.

[36]*British American Cultivator*, Feb., 1874, p. 38.

possible to cut down a whole field without binding a sheaf. On the other hand, the early McCormick was condemned for its flimsiness of construction. As a result, a prominent farmer near Port Hope explained that "within three miles of my residence, three or four of the McCormick machines have been tried for two or three years and abandoned, and the owners are now using the Hussey's machine to their complete satisfaction."[37] The explanation seems to have been that the McCormick reapers imported from the United States were of models already obsolete in that country.[38]

These early reapers were intended to be used for cutting both grain and hay. On the whole, they were negligible factors in harvesting and haying operations down to mid-century. They were, as a matter of fact, of much less significance than the revolving hayrake, which was simply a scantling with teeth on both sides, with handles for the operator and traces or a shaft for a horse. It was introduced from the United States about 1840, and within ten years became very popular.[39]

According to acceptable estimates, the farmer who employed little help outside his family would have, on the average, from 900 to 1,200 bushels of wheat.[40] Threshing the crop was almost as laborious as harvesting it, though there was not the same urgency. Down to 1830, the smaller farmers threshed with the flail. On a cold day, when the work went best, an experienced man could thresh from eight to sixteen bushels, the amount depending on the kind of grain.[41] Among the larger farmers, wheat was often trodden out by horses or oxen, a method which left it so dirty that it was more suitable for the use of the distiller than of

---

[37]*Canadian Agriculturist*, March, 1852, p. 80.

[38]Hutchinson, *Cyrus Hall McCormick*, vol. I, p. 325.

[39]*Canadian Agriculturist*, June 1852, p. 163; *ibid.*, Aug. 16, 1862, p. 490; *JTBAUC 1855-6*, pp. 221, 330, 431. For a cut see Bidwell and Falconer, *History of Agriculture in the Northern United States*, p. 214.

[40]Pickering, *Inquiries of an Emigrant*, p. 113; *Hallowell Free Press*, Sept. 30, 1833. A good average crop would run from twenty-two to twenty-five bushels of fall wheat to the acre (Pickering, p. 114; Talbot, *Five Years' Residence*, vol. I, p. 300).

[41]Cf. Brewer, "Report on the Cereal Production of the United States," p. 140.

the miller.[42]   This means of threshing, as practised by the
farmers of Markham Township, was thus described: "They
thresh with oxen or horses, by laying the barn floor all over
with sheaves, then get the horses or oxen into the barn, shut
the door and make them walk around amongst the untied
sheaves, when it will be to their belly, until the animals are
quite fatigued, then let them stand until they turn it over
and throw it up slack again, and continue to drive them until
it is threshed."[43]

In 1826 Pickering reported that "there are no thrashing
machines in the western part of the province, but I have
heard of a few at the east."[44]   This was doubtless mere
rumour, for as far as can be definitely ascertained, the first
thresher in Upper Canada was one brought from the State
of New York to Northumberland County in 1832.[45]   Another
appeared in Dundas County in 1834.   It was a curiosity in
more respects than one.   "It was one of the American 8 horse
power thrashers, without any separator whatever.   The
whole power was expended in turning the cylinder of 2 feet
diameter at an enormous velocity of 1500 revolutions in a
minute, (the maximum speed of the drum 3 feet in diameter,
of the best British mill is 400).   It literally devoured the
sheaves, required 10 to 12 hands to attend upon it, and left
the barn in a woeful state of confusion.   If kept on full speed
for 10 hours, it would thrash 500 bushels of wheat."[46]   After
about 1840, this kind was completely superseded by the much
smaller Pitt's model and other American threshers made in
imitation of it.   These combined a fanning mill with threshing machinery, and were driven by a "revolving platform"

---

[42]Pickering, *Inquiries of an Emigrant*, p. 80. The Indians had a
peculiar method of threshing wild rice. "They take it to their camps,
and dig a hole in the ground, put a deer-skin into it, then so pour
the rice into it; boys are set to trampling the chaff out with their feet,
after which they fan it, and it is then prepared for use" (*Life and
Journals of Kah-Ke-Wa-Quo-Na-By*, p. 260).

[43]Gibson, "Conditions in York County a Century Ago" (*Ontario
Historical Society Papers and Records*, vol. XXIV, 1927, p. 359).

[44]Pickering, *Inquiries of an Emigrant*, p. 100.

[45]*Canadian Agriculturist*, Aug. 16, 1862, p. 490.

[46]*Ibid.*, Sept. 1, 1860, p. 442.

(or treadmill) horsepower.[47] They proved so popular that it was asserted in 1843 that threshing machines had come into general use throughout the wheat-growing sections of Upper Canada.[48] By 1850 it could be written that "the THRESHING MACHINE, which was looked upon with a good deal of suspicion a few years ago has now become one of the necessaries of the grain grower. The sound of the flail, that simple yet efficient instrument, is now seldom heard in our barns. The hum of the iron spiked cylinder has taken its place. The advantages to the farmer of having his wheat threshed out at once and often immediately after harvest, so that he may sell the moment the price suits him, outweigh every other consideration."[49]

The Upper Canada farmers were as much interested in obtaining new varieties of wheat as they were in new implements.

Fall wheat was the favourite of millers in Canada and Great Britain, as it made a whiter and better flour than spring varieties. As it therefore brought a higher price, few farmers whose land would produce it thought of growing anything else. In the early days of Upper Canada, red wheat (possibly Red Chaff, a smooth red winter wheat) was sown. In the early eighteen-thirties, it was still the favourite along the Bay of Quinte, but farther west the farmers were turning to white wheat, which brought about 6d. a bushel more when exported.[50] Upper Canada white wheat, according to the

[47]*Ibid.*, Sept. 1, 1860, p. 442; *ibid.*, Aug. 16, 1862, p. 490. For a cut see Bidwell and Falconer, *History of Agriculture in the Northern United States*, p. 298.

[48]*British American Cultivator*, April, 1843, p. 53. About the same time clover hullers or "concaves" appeared, particularly in Prince Edward County, which was notable among Upper Canadian counties for its production of clover seed during the eighteen-forties (*JTBAUC 1855-6*, pp. 229, 429, 431). The principle of the concave was that a shaft, covered with tin sheets punched full of holes, was rotated inside a cylinder similarly sheathed with tin. They were dirty to operate, but being driven by horsepower were much faster than threshing with a flail.

[49]*Canadian Agriculturist*, Sept., 1850, p. 199. Still, in 1855 spring grain in Bruce County was "mostly threshed with the flail or with horses" (*JTBAUC 1855-6*, p. 651).

[50]Montreal *Canadian Courant*, March 9, 1833; *Hallowell Free Press*, Oct. 14, 1833. For full descriptions of the various kinds of fall wheats grown in the northern United States (and Upper Canada) in the

grain merchants, was "really a beautiful grain."[51]   Along
the north shore of Lake Ontario about 1830, a favourite kind
was the White Flint.   A little later, the Hutchinson or Kentucky White Bearded enjoyed popularity there.   Soule's
wheat, or Genesee White Flint, was imported into the Peterborough region from Rochester in 1850, though it may well
have been sown elsewhere before this.   Within a dozen years,
it had "become the most valuable variety," and had "almost
driven all others out of cultivation."[52]

There were other factors besides market demand in the
introduction of these new wheats.   For example, the Hessian
fly was still often as destructive as in the time of the Loyalists.[53]   It was checked by better husbandry, and by late
sowing of fall wheat; but in Upper Canada the latter method
was attended by the dangers of winter-killing and of black
stem rust.[54]   Hardy and early maturing varieties of grain,
such as have been mentioned, consequently were introduced
from the United States, one after another, partly on account
of some peculiar excellence each was supposed to have, but
also because poor cleaning and slovenly cultivation resulted
in a constant deterioration of those already grown.

A fundamental disadvantage, which these new fall wheats
could not overcome, was that the only really favourable parts
of the province for fall wheat culture were the Bay of Quinte
region, the western peninsula, and a strip along Lake Ontario
—"a belt of some twelve miles broad, which skirts the lake
from Niagara round as far as the town of Cobourg."[55]   It
was said that, along the Lake Ontario shore east of Cobourg,
and in the country north and west of the town and more than
ten or fifteen miles inland, the fall wheat was winter killed in
three years out of four; it sometimes suffered from black

eighteen-forties and eighteen-fifties, see Klippart, *The Wheat Plant*. For
a briefer description, but one which devotes attention to spring wheats
also, see Emmons, "Agriculture of New York" (*Natural History of
New York*, vol. II, pp. 138-42).

[51]Montreal *Canadian Courant*, Dec. 24, 1833.

[52]*Canadian Agriculturist*, March, 1851, p. 61; *ibid.*, July 16, 1862,
p. 421.

[53]*Canadian Agricultural Reader*, p. 55.

[54]Hind, *Essay on Insects*, pp. 42-3, 60, 70.

[55]Johnston, *Notes on North America*, vol. I, p. 271.

stem rust; and it did not do well on low, wet lands.[56] The
farmers throughout these regions, as well as those in the
townships along the St. Lawrence River, accordingly turned
to spring wheat, just as did their contemporaries in New
York and New England.

Before 1850, the greatest bane of the Upper Canada
farmer, whether he grew fall or spring wheat, was the black
stem rust, which had the effect of shrivelling the grain, and
so reducing the yield.   Rust is still a problem wherever wheat
is sown; but in pioneer Upper Canada, when the weather
was moist and warm, it did untold damage, especially on new
land in low, damp situations.   The rust, with its "unexpected
and universal attacks," was particularly destructive in 1837,
1839, and 1842, more or less so in every other year from
1840 to 1846, and again in 1849 and 1850.[57]

Because the rust attacked the wheat towards the end of
the growing season, the farmers thought that if they could
obtain varieties which would mature a few days earlier than
those they had, their crops would be ripe before the rust
"season" commenced.   Consequently, they introduced one
kind after another, gave them trials, and experimented with
them.   Though their search was based on a scientific fallacy
(for modern rust research has emphasized the development
of rust-resistant varieties rather than that of those which
are merely early maturing), they found a few varieties which
gave promise of being little affected by rust, and one which
was rust-resistant to a remarkable degree.

The first variety of spring wheat to attract much attention
in Upper Canada was the Mediterranean or Italian, which
was brought from the United States about 1830.   Though it
made fairly good flour, it was a grave disappointment in the
backwoods on account of its susceptibility to rust.[58]   It was
replaced by Siberian,[59] which was also imported from the

---

[56]*Canadian Agriculturist*, April, 1854, p. 120; *ibid.*, June, 1854,
p. 166; *ibid.*, Sept., 1856, p. 250.
[57]Hind, *Essay on Insects*, pp. 42-3, 110; Hind, *Eighty Years'
Progress*, p. 57.
[58]*Canadian Agriculturist*, Jan. 16, 1861, p. 55.
[59]"Siberian" wheat was brought from England to New Hampshire
about 1780. Fresh importations were made when the seed showed signs
of degenerating (Patent Office Report, *Senate Executive Document*,
33rd Cong., 1st Sess., 1853-4, No. 27, pp. 128-9).

United States.   In 1839 a Peterborough County farmer sowed
some which he had received as a gift.   John Wade, a seed
merchant of Port Hope, likewise experimented with it about
the same time.   In the beginning Siberian yielded well, and
as it seemed comparatively immune to rust, it gave a great
impetus to the growing of spring wheat north of Lake Ontario
throughout the early eighteen-forties.   Wade was amazed by
its rapidly won popularity.

In two or three years there was quite a rage for it; and although
I had grown it for two years or more,—as fall wheat could be grown
on the front,—I had not noticed its value, and was quite astonished when
I found the demand for it from the back townships, and as a proof of its
value to those townships, I will state that was told me at that time
by a gentleman, one of the most extensive wheat buyers at that time,
in Port Hope, and who for years had bought the crops from the best
farmers in Cavan and Monaghan: that when those farmers depended
only on fall wheat, he might get from 200 to 300 bushels as their yearly
produce; but after this description of spring wheat was introduced,
he got from the same farms from 800 to 1000 bushels annually.[60]

In 1844 Siberian was being sown generally throughout Upper
Canada, but after a few more years, it became subject to
rust, and lost its popularity.[61]

Before the Siberian failed, several other kinds were introduced, including the Bald Club, the Bearded Club, and the
Black Sea, with the Black Sea being the general favourite.
The Black Sea matured early and gave a high yield, but it
was condemned as being vulnerable to both rust and midge.[62]

Of all the varieties of spring wheat introduced into the
province in the nineteenth century, Red Fife was of the
greatest importance.   It has been ascertained that this variety
was identical with "Galician" wheat, which is still grown
about three hundred miles inland from Danzig.[63]   This is
not surprising, for there were many varieties of spring

[60]Canadian Agriculturist, June, 1854, p. 166. Wade credited Siberian
with the same effects in the tract between Port Hope and Grafton
(ibid., Sept., 1856, p. 250).
[61]British American Cultivator, Aug., 1844, p. 113; Canadian Agriculturist, June, 1854, p. 166; ibid., Jan. 16, 1861, p. 55.
[62]British American Cultivator, April, 1843, p. 60; Canadian Agriculturist, July 2, 1849, pp. 171, 174; ibid., Sept., 1852, p. 258; ibid.,
July 16, 1862, p. 422.
[63]Buller, Essays on Wheat, p. 209.

wheats originating in northern Europe grown in Upper Canada in the eighteen-forties. It was remarked in 1843, for example, that a number of farmers near Toronto had for some years been sowing more or less "Dantzic wheat."[64]

So many legends have arisen concerning the origin of the famous Red Fife wheat that it seems worth while to reproduce at length the earliest available printed account of its discovery and development—one which antedates by about twelve years those commonly known.[65] It is a letter from Henry Bawbell of Otonabee (Peterborough County), Secretary of the Otonabee and Asphodel Agricultural Society, to the editor of the *Canadian Agriculturist,* and is dated October 12, 1849.

Eight years ago Mr. David Fife having a friend about to revisit Scotland, requested if an opportunity occurred, that he would forward to this country a small quantity of wheat from some of the northern ports of Europe. On landing at Glasgow he found a vessel discharging a cargo from Dantzic; having procured a portion, he sent it to Mr. Fife, who sowed it the spring following, and it came up various kinds, as might be expected, and the whole was affected by rust, except this variety, of which there was but five ears, and two of them were destroyed by cattle, yet from the remaining three ears he raised the third year half a bushel; from the produce of this he supplied some of his friends with a few bushels, and it began to be noted for not rusting, and one person had twenty-eight bushels from one bushel sown. Next year the Agricultural Society introduced the Club wheat as a change of seed, which being sown along side of the new wheat in many instances, and the former being rusted so as to be worthless, while the latter was not the least injured; so established became its superiority that last spring the Agricultural Society thought it advisable to purchase 260 bushels to distribute amongst its members, rather than it should be taken out of the township, and the principal holder of the wheat refusing to take less than two dollars a bushel for it, that price was given by the Society, and many bushels were sold to the neighbouring townships at the same rate, many people applying for it in vain.

It is rather a late kind of wheat, being 8 or 10 days behind the Club or Siberian, if sown at the same time, and this scorching summer has not suited it so well on dry soils, but on low black ash swales and any

---

[64]*British American Cultivator*, Aug., 1843, p. 117.

[65]For these legends, as well as for more plausible variants of accepted accounts, see Buller, *Essays on Wheat*, pp. 207-15. The well-known narrative of George Esson, which originally appeared in *The Country Gentleman*, April 14, 1859, p. 237, is reproduced in part by Buller, pp. 207-8.

similar place, not too wet for wheat to vegetate, it succeeds well, and its bright yellow appearance confirms the application [appellation] of "*The Golden Grain*" so often applied to wheat, though perhaps some of your readers may think that the price paid for it gives it a better claim to that title.[66]

Till 1848 the new wheat was grown only in Otonabee, but in 1849 its cultivation spread into the adjacent townships, as Bawbell says. So much seed was available at the close of 1849 that some was offered for general sale by the Otonabee and Asphodel Agricultural Society.[67]   Red Fife proved such a complete success in the nearby counties that during the harvest of 1851 the Township of Hamilton Farmers' Club at Cobourg resolved: "That the Township of Hamilton Farmers' Club are unanimous in recommending the 'Fife Spring Wheat' for cultivation, as regards productivness, flouring qualities, perfect freedom from rust, and easy to thrash, it is out of comparison the best ever introduced in this District, for strong clays or low lands."[68]   Under the name of Fife, Scotch, or Glasgow wheat, Red Fife thereafter spread rapidly throughout Upper Canada, so that by 1860 it had almost completely superseded other varieties of spring wheat.[69]   Nor was its popularity long confined to Canada West.   By 1855 it was well enough known in New York to draw a favourable comment from the Albany *Cultivator*; beginning in 1858, it was widely sown in Wisconsin; and by 1861 it won recognition there, and in Minnesota as well, as the best available variety of spring wheat.[70]

Red Fife was the first truly hard spring wheat developed in North America, and ultimately was to lay the foundation of the wheat-growing prosperity of Manitoba and the rest of the northwest.   A Northumberland County contemporary of David Fife declared that "its most marked quality is its

---

[66]*Canadian Agriculturist*, Nov. 1, 1849, pp. 302-3.

[67]*Ibid.*, Nov. 1, 1849, n.p. (advt.)

[68]Cobourg *Star*, Sept. 17, 1851, quoted in *Agricultural Journal and Transactions of the Lower Canada Agricultural Society*, Dec., 1851, p. 372.

[69]*Canadian Agriculturist*, March, 1859, p. 50; *ibid.*, June 1, 1860, p. 245; *Transactions of the Board of Agriculture and of the Agricultural Association of Upper Canada for 1858-9*, p. 113.

[70]*Cultivator*, March, 1855, p. 94; *ibid.*, Dec., 1860, p. 370; *American Agriculturist*, vol. XX, 1861, p. 58; *ibid.*, vol. XXI, 1862, p. 46.

being always free from *rust,* and its bearing to be sown so
late in the season as to escape the *fly* [wheat midge] in great
measure; it is a bald variety, moderately productive, is reckoned rather hard to grind, but makes a good flour."[71] And in
a burst of enthusiasm, John Wade expressed the sentiments
of all his farmer friends when he wrote: "The Fife, the
glorious Fife, I call it, is now as good after being grown 7
years as it was at first, without the least sign or vestige of
failure in any shape except from Weevil [wheat midge]; and
to know that you can be sure of a crop of wheat sown as
late as the 10th of June, and to fill and ripen without a speck
of rust, and yield 20 to 30 bushels an acre, is surely a de-
sideratum. Why sir, ten years ago, it would have been considered incredible."[72]

When the farmer had his crop harvested and threshed,
he could sell it locally or else team it to a distant market.
Almost anywhere in the interior, he could dispose of his wheat
to a miller or a store-keeper. The former paid only in flour,
of course; and in times of depression, or in remote localities,
the latter insisted on paying partly or wholly in trade.[73] In
a few of the larger ports, there were some dealers whose
main business was collecting and shipping grain. On the
return of an export demand for wheat after about 1825,
these dealers did ordinarily pay entirely in cash.[74] Yet on
occasion they too tried to take advantage of the farmer.
Thus, in 1833, a merchant at Hallowell in Prince Edward
County advertised that he would pay cash, and then he tried
to make the sellers take half in merchandise.[75] Again, in the
same year, the wheat buyers at Belleville made an agreement
to keep down prices, and if one of them had not broken the
combine because he was not getting his share of business, the
farmers would have received 6*d.* a bushel less for their wheat
than they eventually did.[76]

---

[71]*Canadian Agriculturist,* July 16, 1862, p. 422.
[72]*Ibid.,* Sept., 1856, p. 250.
[73]Howison, *Sketches of Upper Canada,* p. 113; Talbot, *Five Years'
Residence,* vol. II, pp. 72-3, 181.
[74]Pickering, *Inquiries of an Emigrant,* pp. 113, 150-1; *Hallowell
Free Press,* Jan. 8, Jan. 22, Feb. 5, Nov. 25, 1833.
[75]*Hallowell Free Press,* Nov. 25, 1833.
[76]*Ibid.,* Oct. 14, 1833.

The dealers got the money which they handed over to the farmers from several sources. Sometimes they obtained it as an advance from the commercial houses of Montreal;[77] sometimes they borrowed it at the local bank on their own collateral;[78] sometimes they had it supplied them by merchant millers, such as those at New Edinburgh and Gananoque. A Hallowell buyer for example, "could draw out of the agency of the Midland District Bank in the Village if he chose one thousand pounds per week for the purchase of wheat" for the New Edinburgh mills.[79]

Because these merchants were often engaged in retail activities or in collecting other produce, they were not specialists in wheat-buying. It was important to them not to offend their clients. For these reasons, they made little distinction in price between clean, dry wheat and that which was weedy or smutty. This was a frequent cause of complaint among the careful farmers till the eighteen-fifties.[80]

Though he knew he might be victimized by the dealer in a lakeshore port, the farmer could count on getting a much better price from him than from the crossroads store-keeper. This was mostly owing to the cost of transportation. Wheat was worth 6d. York currency more a bushel at Chatham, for example, than at London, because from the latter point there was a land carriage of twenty-five miles.[81] As a result of this condition it was usual for farmers to draw their loads of forty bushels or so of wheat from Meaford on Georgian

[77]Peter McGill to W. H. Merritt, Aug. 16, 1837, Merritt Papers, vol. IV, quoted in Creighton, "Economic Background of the Rebellions," (*Canadian Journal of Economics and Political Science*, vol. III, 1937, p. 331). The Lower Canada houses were financed in turn by British grain importers. It was remarked in 1831 that several cargoes of wheat from the St. Lawrence had reached Great Britain on a falling market, and that there would be considerable losses in consequence. Then it was added: "Most of the business in the wheat line in this country was, however, done on commission, and the effect will only be felt in cases where houses at home may fail, which we are informed has been the case in some instances" (Neilson's *Quebec Gazette*, quoted in Montreal *Canadian Courant*, Oct. 29, 1831).

[78]York *Colonial Advocate*, July 7, 1831.

[79]*Hallowell Free Press*, Nov. 25, 1833.

[80]William Hutton of Belleville to his brother, June 26, 1834, in *British Farmer's Magazine*, April, 1835, p. 115. Cf. *Canadian Agriculturist*, Dec., 1852, p. 362.

[81]Smith, *Canada, Past, Present, and Future*, vol. II, p. 71.

Bay to Toronto, a distance of well over a hundred miles, and
from the London area through Brantford to Hamilton.[82]
Teaming commenced as soon as part of the harvest was
threshed. In the autumn of 1830, an average of fifty loads
of wheat a day moved over the roads from Brantford to
Hamilton.[83] But the highways of Upper Canada were so
bad at this season that the wiser farmers waited for frost
and snow. Accordingly, at each of the lake ports during the
winter, a daily string of sleighs perhaps a mile long could be
seen waiting to unload.[84]

Though many of them were no more than creek mouths,
with a few flat warehouses beside them, these lake ports were
busy places in the spring. Port Stanley, for example, by
1850 shipped annually about 300,000 bushels of grain.[85]
When the navigation season opened, a gang of men transferred the barrels and bags of grain from the warehouses
to small schooners, which carried them down the lakes to the
mills at Gananoque and elsewhere, or transhipped them at
the foot of Lake Ontario to *bateaux* or Durham boats for
carriage to Lower Canada.[86] However, at least as late as
1826, flour and wheat from the shores of Lake Ontario were
sent to Lower Canada on scows and rafts, which were "towed
by steam boats through the still water and Lakes."[87] The
common method of shipment in bulk, both down the Great

---

[82]Smith, *The Pioneers of Old Ontario*, p. 229; Revelle, *History of
the County of Brant*, vol. I, p. 181.

[83]Hamilton *Gore Balance*, quoted in Montreal *Canadian Courant*,
Oct. 20, 1830.

[84]*British American Cultivator*, May, 1842, p. 65.

[85]Smith, *Canada, Past, Present, and Future*, vol. I, p. 93. Navigable
rivers such as the Thames and the Grand had similar ports.

[86]About 1832 between 300 and 400 Durham boats and between 600
and 750 *bateaux*, mostly laden with wheat and flour, passed the locks in
the St. Lawrence above Montreal, on their way from Kingston or
Prescott to the Lower Canada market (Hind, *Eighty Years' Progress*,
p. 149). The size of the schooners on the lakes may be judged from the
fact that five of them which passed the Burlington Canal early in
1829 had on board a total of 1,900 bushels of wheat and about 550
barrels of flour (*Gore Gazette*, quoted in Montreal *Canadian Courant*,
June 13, 1829).

[87]Lt. Col. By to General Mann, Dec. 6, 1826, in *Canadian Archives
Report for 1890*, p. 78.

Lakes and across the Atlantic, inevitably involved considerable losses from spoilage.[88]

Such then was wheat-farming in Upper Canada between 1815 and 1850, but especially in the period beginning about 1830.   However, the wheat farmer was the typical agriculturist really only in the central and western parts of the province. In the eastern part, that is, the Upper Canada portion of the Ottawa Valley, the timber trade encouraged a different kind of agriculture.   To this we now turn.

---

[88]"The common mode of shipping wheat or other grain in bulk, is the cause of injury. . . . The emptying of loose grain into barges not over dry; spray and moisture on the voyage to the shipping port; exposure to weather while being shipped, damp lining-boards, damp vessels, damp during the voyage; and then again exposed in a lighter and put away in a damp warehouse, or in a low situation on the bank of a river; all tend to the destruction even of the finest parcels of grain" (Brondgeest, "Preservation of Food," *Westminster Review*, vol. L, 1848-9, p. 147). The writer was president of the Montreal Board of Trade, and had been president of the Hamilton Board of Trade.

CHAPTER VII

AGRICULTURE IN THE OTTAWA VALLEY TO 1850[1]

IN the first half of the nineteenth century, lumbering vied with agriculture as the most important industry of the Canadas. Receiving its first impetus during the Napoleonic Wars, it developed rapidly thereafter, primarily because the preferential duties gave colonial timber a decided advantage over the Baltic product in the British market. The export lumber trade soon divided into two distinct branches. In the first, pines were cut, squared, and shipped to the United Kingdom, where they were sawn into boards and finished lumber in the mills of the British importers. In the second, Canadian mills cut saw logs into deals, that is, softwood planks, which were shipped to Great Britain for finishing. The deal trade flourished near the mouths of rivers falling into the St. Lawrence, where local water power was available to operate the mills, and slack-water navigation to carry away the finished material.

Though deals were manufactured at Hawkesbury and elsewhere, it was the square timber trade which became typical of the Ottawa Valley. During the time it flourished, it had striking incidental effects on the economy of this region. As had been true of New France in its relation to the fur trade, the tributary area not concerned directly in the production of the staple was concerned in it indirectly. Lumbering influenced settlement and agriculture so markedly that, as a recent authority declares, "the Ottawa Valley has been a region in itself, with its own character and its own problems."[2]

Along the lower shores of this greatest tributary of the St. Lawrence were immense stands of white pine mixed with

---

[1]Lower, *Settlement and the Forest Frontier*, pp. 43-8. The term "Ottawa Valley" as used in this chapter denotes, in addition to eastern Upper Canada, the adjacent portions of the Ottawa-Huron region, which had an economic affinity with it.

[2]*Ibid.*, p. 10. Writers of the nineteenth century remarked this economic peculiarity, and referred to the Ottawa Valley variously as the Ottawa Country, Central Canada, and even Northern Canada.

hardwood, and above Chats Lake, vast "Norway Plains" of red pine alone. By the close of the War of 1812, lumbermen were sending timber to Quebec from all the lower reaches of the Ottawa and from such easily driven tributaries as the Bonnechere. When they succeeded in fully overcoming the natural obstacles in the main river and its affluents, as they began to do about 1830 through constructing dams and timber slides, they were able to expand their operations widely. They were lumbering near the head of the Deep River, a section of the Ottawa about 150 miles west of Bytown, by 1830; in the vicinity of Lake Temiskaming in 1837 or very shortly afterwards; and near the headwaters of all the tributaries of the Ottawa by 1852.[3] Expensive improvements and remote pineries meant that the small-scale lumbermen, who in the early days spent the winters in taking out rafts for the Quebec market, were nearly all superseded by 1840 by "operators" with extensive limits and hundreds of lumberjacks in their employ. Thus, the firm of the "lumber king" John Egan, the largest on the Ottawa about 1850, had about a hundred shanties and did an annual business of from $800,000 to $1,000,000.[4]

The shanties or camps of such magnates were distant, for the most part, from the settled districts. To them the lumberjacks went in the autumn, some of them long before the first snow. They spent the winter in cutting and squaring timber, and in the spring they went down the river with the drive. The operator had to furnish everything consumed by the men and by the horses and oxen. As early as 1832

---

[3]MacTaggart, *Three Years in Canada*, vol. I, p. 241; Sherriff, "Topographical Notices," (*Transactions of the Literary and Historical Society of Quebec*, vol. II, 1831, pp. 255 ff.) ; *Journal of the Legislative Assembly of Upper Canada, 1839*, Appendix, p. 95; *Journal of the Legislative Assembly of Canada 1847*, App. LL, hereafter cited as *JLAC; Sessional Papers, Canada, 1852-3*, App. MMMM. Hereafter this authority is cited as SPC.

[4]*SPC 1852-3*, App. MMMM. For descriptions of shantying in the period between 1825 and 1850 see MacTaggart, *Three Years in Canada*, vol. I, pp. 240 ff.; Keefer, *Montreal and the Ottawa*, pp. 55 ff.; *JLAC, 1847*, App. LL. For a description of Ottawa Valley shantying in the eighteenseventies, see Grant, *Picturesque Canada*, vol. I, pp. 211-38. For a good modern description of nineteenth-century lumbering, see Guillet, *Early Life in Upper Canada*, pp. 232-51.

it was stated that the lumbermen operating above Chats Lake required at least 2,000 sleigh-loads of supplies. In the six-year period ending in 1850, John Egan & Co. employed annually about 2,000 men and about 1,600 horses and oxen. The men consumed about 6,000 barrels of pork and 10,000 barrels of flour a year, and the horses and oxen about 60,000 bushels of oats and 1,200 tons of hay. In the winter of 1854-5, the same firm employed 3,800 lumberjacks, 200 oxen, and 1,700 horses in its shanties, as well as 400 double-teams of horses in portaging, and the provisions and fodder it had to supply increased in proportion.[5]

The freighting costs on everything going up the Ottawa and its tributaries were so high that every kind of produce raised on the spot bore a price out of all proportion to what could be obtained in the older settlements. It was estimated that the lumbermen paid in transport charges on hay drawn from the agricultural districts an amount equal to two or three times its original cost.[6] No matter what it might cost, they had to have tame hay, for it was exceptional to find a horse that would eat the wild grasses of the beaver meadows. In consequence, their shanties or "establishments" usually

[5]Evidence of T. Davis, in *Journal of the Legislative Assembly of Lower Canada, 1832-3*, App. x; *SPC 1852-3*, App. MMMM. A by-product of the timber trade was the prevalence of lawlessness along the Ottawa, especially between the completion of the Rideau Canal in 1832 and the Rebellion of 1837-8. Many of the Irish labourers laid off by the canal contractors went shantying, and carried on a vendetta with their rivals in the labour market, especially the French Canadians. These "Shiners" were responsible for much violence, including murder, at Bytown. They bullied the farmers of the nearby rural areas, and even maltreated their livestock (as by cropping their ears); and in the country above the mouth of the Madawaska they defied the law with impunity. Early in 1837 Bytown citizens formed a special constabulary to deal with the menace, and later in the year the mobilization of the militia put at government disposal a force which could be turned against the Shiners. Some of the leaders were captured and tried, and by 1841 the reign of terror ended. In the meantime it had done much to hinder the agricultural development of the region west of Bytown (Bytown *Gazette*, March 2, 16, 30, April 6, 20, Oct. 18, 1837; Perth *Bathurst Courier*, Feb. 26, 1841; Toronto *Globe*, Dec. 25, 1856; *ibid.*, Feb. 27, 1857).

[6]Keefer, *Montreal and the Ottawa*, p. 69. In 1847 the freight on a barrel of pork hauled from Bytown to the limits along the Amable du Fond River, a fork of the Mattawan, amounted to from 42s. to 45s., and on a barrel of flour to 30s. (*JLAC, 1847*, App. LL).

included a farm for raising vegetables and hay. Such farms had the additional advantages of making it possible to have produce on hand in the autumn when it was otherwise difficult to obtain it, and of giving employment to the lumbermen's permanent employees during the slack season. As settlement advanced, many of the farms were sold, and in the course of time could not be distinguished from ordinary ones.[7] The farm of John Egan & Co. on the York Branch of the Madawaska near Bancroft was doubtless more systematically managed than most, but it will do as an example. In 1863, after eighteen years of cultivation, there were 310 acres under clearance. The hay, oats, potatoes, and turnips it produced were valued at $2,870. As it cost $1,600 to pay and feed the men and teams employed on the farm, the net profit for the year was $1,270.[8]

As the production of these farms was insignificant in comparison with the quantities required for consumption, the lumbermen came to be encouragers of settlement, even in the most out-of-the-way places. The timber operator preferred to have the good land near his limits settled, because from its occupants he could buy hay, oats, peas, and potatoes cheaper than he could grow them in his establishment or portage them from the "front" up the Ottawa. Moreover, he was assured of a number of experienced men, horses, and oxen always being available for the work of his shanty. The sheltered cash market and the assurance of work made it profitable in turn for the settler to go into the back country. At a time when the prevailing price for hay delivered in the shanties of the upper Ottawa was about £4 per ton (in itself a relatively high figure), farmers in such remote localities as the headwaters of the Madawaska received as much as £10.[9] Thus it happened that after about 1820 squatters began to occupy and clear lands at various places along Chats Lake and above it on the Ottawa, along the Madawaska, Bonnechere, and other rivers, and along the shanty roads leading inland from all of them. By 1838, they had pushed up the

---

[7]Montreal *Gazette*, Feb. 5, 1831; *JLAC 1849*, App. PPPP; SPC *1852-3*, App. MMMM.

[8]*SPC 1864*, No. 5.

[9]*JLAC 1847*, App. LL.

Bonnechere Valley to points well within the "red-pine country."[10]

Unfortunately, settlement such as this had its dark sides. While prosperity in the timber trade brought in its wake a spate of land seekers, a depression was followed by a pause or even a recession in land occupancy. The crisis of 1847, to give one example, caused many of the timber squatters above Chats Lake, who were at the very door of the shanties, to abandon their holdings because their market had temporarily collapsed.[11] Another characteristic trouble was that timber squatters seldom selected their land with an eye to its ultimate agricultural worth, as the careful farmers in the wheat-growing sections tried to do. They preferred a poor and isolated farm near a lumber camp or a shanty road to a better one farther from market. They might indeed get along fairly well at first, because the lumbermen paid them high prices for all they could produce, and besides hired them and their teams in the winter. After a few crops of grain, and perhaps several of hay, the thin vegetable mould of their sandy clearances would be exhausted. About the same time they often found that the shanties were moving away from their vicinity. The stranding which followed settlement of the Norway Plains of the Ottawa-Huron region in the late eighteen-fifties was more widespread than that of the earlier period, but it was not different in character. Occasionally lumbermen would excuse themselves of responsibility for this stranding by charging that it was the policy of the government to lure settlers into the backwoods of the Ottawa Valley by laying out townships at a great distance from the "front." It should therefore be pointed out that before the rich lands of western Upper Canada were disposed of, the government had not the same motives for opening distant townships as in the eighteen-fifties, and that, as a matter of fact, by mid-century, surveys in the Ottawa Valley lagged far behind settlement.[12] A third problem in connection with

---

[10]Sherriff, "Topographical Notices," pp. 250, 252, 260, 265; Montreal *Gazette*, Dec. 27, 1831; Bytown *Gazette*, quoted in Perth *Bathurst Courier*, May 18, 1838.

[11]*SPC 1857*, App. 52.

[12]Evidence of G. Hamilton, W. Hamilton, and A. Russell, *SPC 1854-5*, App. MM.

the settlement which followed lumbering was "timber farming." Beginning in 1826, when Upper Canada land regulations first permitted the sale of lots on credit, unscrupulous
individuals made a down payment to the government on their
grants, stripped them of merchantable timber, and abandoned
them.[13] The interests of such "timber pirates" were an-
tagonistic to those of the lumbermen. An operator might
carefully preserve the best trees in a limit for years, and
then suddenly find that the lots on which they grew had been
opened to location by the Crown Lands Department, usually
at the request of squatters with an eye for a good stand of
pine. Worse, when the lots included slides and other improvements, the new owners were able to charge the lumberman tolls for the use of works he had himself built.[14] Though
the lumbermen were friends of legitimate settlement, they
protested against governmental encouragement of the fraudulent exploitation of their pineries, till finally, in the eighteen-
fifties, the flagrant abuses in the colonization-roads settlement
system brought a partial remedy.

The cash market of the shanties encouraged, while it lasted,
a distinctive type of farming in its vicinity. The best farmers there—those who stayed on their land—naturally concentrated their efforts on growing hay and oats, thinking
themselves additionally fortunate in that these were just the
products most easily grown in the initial years of settlement.
But the kind of farming which resulted was open to criticism.
From a purely agricultural point of view it "meant the clearance off the farm of everything most likely to maintain its
productiveness; of a gradual drain upon and reduction of the
quality of the land, and a most wretchedly parsimonious and
improvident method of keeping stock."[15] However exhausting it was, it was temporarily profitable, and may be justified
wherever it formed a transitional rather than a permanent
phase of farming.

This cannot be said of the practice of those near the shanties known as timber squatters. At best these were neither

---

13Patterson, *Land Settlement in Upper Canada*, pp. 147, 170.

14Evidence of A. Russell, *SPC 1854-5*, App. MM.

15*Report of the Ontario Agricultural Commission*, vol. v, App.
R-1, p. 14.

agriculturists nor lumbermen, but farmers in the summer and shantymen in the winter.[16] At first they combined working throughout the winter for a lumberman very profitably with farming in the summer. Then, as the shanties constantly moved farther away, they were longer in going to work and returning, even if they did not take part in the spring drive. If they engaged in lumbering on their own account, as they were tempted to do, they had no time to devote to their farms. All of them, of course, made very slow progress in their clearing operations in the few months they were not employed in the camps.

The evils of the attempt to combine lumbering and agriculture were found even in the long-settled parts of the Ottawa Valley, though nowhere did they prevail to such an extent as in New Brunswick.[17] Glengarry County apparently suffered more than any other part of eastern Upper Canada from the unsuccessful attempt to unite lumbering on the Ottawa or its tributaries with farming at home. It was once remarked that "if the farmers of the Eastern District [Glengarry, Stormont, and Dundas counties] in general, and more particularly those of Highland Scotch descent, (who perhaps are the most numerous class) would pay but a little more attention to agriculture, and a proportionately less attention to the speculative undertakings of the lumber business, many a good farm would be released from the death grasp of a mortgage."[18] Similar criticisms were made of many of the farmers in Prescott and Russell counties till the eighteen-fifties.[19]

It was possible for the ordinary farmer, especially if he lived in the lower part of the Ottawa Valley, to profit from the timber trade in one of two ways. The first was by working as a teamster in the shanties, or by "portaging"—that is, freighting in supplies—for some operator. If he did either,

[16]Sherriff, "Topographical Notices," p. 250; Montreal *Gazette*, Dec. 27, 1831; Perth *Bathurst Courier*, March 12, 1841; *JLAC 1849*, App. BB.

[17]Cf. Lower, *Settlement and the Forest Frontier*, pp. 31 ff.

[18]Cornwall *Observer*, quoted in Montreal *Transcript*, Sept. 5, 1843. For this condition in the same region at an earlier period see Report on Provincial Progress, Oct. 30, 1830, Q354, p. 304.

[19]Thomas, *History of the Counties of Argenteuil, Quebec, and Prescott, Ontario*, pp. 631, 639, 647.

he made money when there was nothing to do on the farm except the chores; and he got employment for his horses when they would otherwise be idle, and had them in good condition for the spring cultivating besides. Every autumn, therefore, there was an exodus of farmers, hired men, and farmers' sons from the older settlements to portage up the Bonnechere or the Madawaska, or Lower Canada rivers such as the Coulonge, a practice which continued till recent times. The other way of benefiting from the timber trade arose from the circumstance that the farms of the lumbermen and of the settlers adjacent to the shanties could not satisfy the requirements of the lumberjacks and their livestock. Shanty demand was so great that flour, pork, hay, and oats had to be imported. The mess pork which was used came largely from Cincinnati, and the flour from western Upper Canada or lake states such as Ohio. In either case they were imported by way of Montreal or the Rideau Canal. Hay and oats were too bulky to be brought such distances. This factor, added to a geographical one, gave the farmers of the lower Ottawa Valley a virtual monopoly in these two products.

The geographical factor was the lack of means of communication between the shanties in the pineries and the agricultural settlements in central Upper Canada. The Ottawa Valley is hemmed in on its Lower Canada side to almost within sight of Montreal by the Laurentians, and on the west is cut off from Lake Ontario by the rocky country north and west of Kingston. Lumbermen's supplies could be more conveniently obtained at Montreal or Bytown and portaged up the rivers than they could be brought in over hill and dale from Lake Ontario. On account of the existence of the wide unsettled belt north of the Bay of Quinte, it was considered something of a marvel when some lumbermen on the upper Madawaska about 1845 penetrated to the townships in the Peterborough region by means of winter roads which they cut;[20] and as late as 1855 the regular method of supplying the shanties in all the eastern part of the Ottawa-Huron tract was still by way of the Ottawa and its tributaries.[21]

As early as 1830, the demands of the expanding timber

[20]*JLAC 1847*, App. LL.
[21]*SPC 1854-5*, App. MM.

trade of the Ottawa Valley outran the local agricultural production.[22] The result was the development of a considerable internal trade. T. C. Keefer claimed, with some exaggeration, that the import trade of the Ottawa Valley was "greater, for the population, than perhaps any other part of America."[23] "No person who has not witnessed it," he declared in another connection, "can form an idea of the number of teams passing from below to Bytown, and above it, on the Ottawa, in the winter season."[24] "The amount of traffic," wrote another, "would lead one to suppose that he was in the neighborhood of a market town."[25] By the eighteen-fifties it was quite common for twenty sleighs a day to pass given points far up the tributaries of the Ottawa.[26] A concomitant of this import trade was the development of an excellent local market at Bytown. By 1836 it had the reputation of being probably the best in all Upper Canada.[27] When the timber trade was at all prosperous, all kinds of country produce would sell for 10 or 15 per cent more there than they would at any other town in the province, and for cash besides.[28]

The existence of this local market meant that, except in a range or two of townships bordering on the St. Lawrence, eastern Upper Canada did not pretend to raise wheat for export.[29] The merchant flour mills at New Edinburgh and Hawkesbury depended on wheat from the Bay of Quinte and beyond. In nearly all the country above the Rideau Canal, and in Prescott and Russell counties as well, often not enough wheat was grown to satisfy local consumption. Other kinds of farm produce tended to be sold at Bytown or up the Ottawa

---

[22]Sherriff, "Topographical Notices," p. 252. The requirements of the workers on the Rideau Canal were partly responsible for the shortage.

[23]Keefer, *Montreal and the Ottawa*, p. 16. Keefer had been in charge of constructing government "improvements" on the Madawaska and elsewhere in the lumbering country in the mid eighteen-forties.

[24]*JLAC 1847*, App. QQ.

[25]Perth *Bathurst Courier*, Feb. 12, 1841.

[26]*Journal and Transactions of the Board of Agriculture of Upper Canada 1856-7*, p. 170, hereafter cited as *JTBAUC*; *SPC 1859*, App. 17.

[27]Wells, *Canadiana*, p. 25.

[28]*JTBAUC 1855-6*, p. 459.

[29]*British American Cultivator*, April, 1845, p. 102; *Canadian Agriculturist*, Nov., 1854, p. 331.

rather than along the "front" of Glengarry or of Dundas. Even the farmers along the lower reaches of the Ottawa, who had easy and rapid communication with Montreal, did not look to that city for a market. As early as 1832 it was said that no produce of any account arrived in Montreal from the Ottawa Valley;[30] and as late as 1853 there were no agricultural exports for a railway from the country above Bytown.[31] Sometimes even farmers along the banks of the St. Lawrence forsook Montreal, and teamed their surplus far up the Ottawa.[32]

With an outlet at their doors, the more far-sighted farmers in the lower Ottawa Valley resolutely avoided lumbering altogether and sold their produce at high prices to those who did engage in it. Even in the eighteen-twenties farmers of this type near Hawkesbury profited at the expense of the Glengarians cutting pine along the South Nation and Castor rivers.[33] As the area of lumbering operations receded, they followed it by portaging their own produce or that of others up the Ottawa, as has already been mentioned. In the average teaming season of about three months, say from December 15 to March 15, those from the lower Ottawa Valley could make two return trips to Lake Temiskaming, or more to limits which were nearer. Many, however, portaged only to a depot such as Arnprior at the mouth of the Madawaska or Pembroke below the mouth of the Petawawa. Still others took a load of their own oats to a shanty, sold it, worked at skidding timber or local portaging, and did not return home till spring.[34] In any event, all of these men were away from their farms only when their absence was least apt to be harmful.

The shanty market encouraged these farmers of the lower Ottawa Valley to adopt a kind of agriculture much more

---

[30]*Journal of the Legislative Assembly of Lower Canada, 1832-3,* App. T.

[31]*Report . . . of the St. Lawrence and Ottawa Grand Junction Railway Company,* p. 27.

[32]Perth *Bathurst Courier,* March 5, 1841; *JLAC 1847,* App. C, App. LL.

[33]Report of Duncan McDowell, 1827, in Picken, *The Canadas,* pp. 130-1.

[34]Perth *Bathurst Courier,* March 5, April 2, April 9, 1841; *JLAC 1847,* App. C., App. LL.

diversified than that of the wheat-growing sections farther
west. They used methods which met with much disparagement from critics who regarded the wheat-culture technique
of York and Peel counties as an ideal, and they lagged behind
their contemporaries in central and western Upper Canada
in the introduction of improved implements.[35] Even so,
their practices were certainly far in advance of anything
found among the timber squatters or among their own neighbours who tried to combine farming and lumbering. Their
general farming gave them the advantage of not being dependent on a single export crop such as wheat. In the back
townships of the St. Lawrence counties, and in the older parts
of Lanark, Carleton, and Prescott, oats ordinarily formed
the cash crop, but considerable quantities of pork were home-
cured for the shanties, and horses and oxen were raised with
the intention of selling them to the lumbermen.[36]

In the late eighteen-thirties and early eighteen-forties oxen
were generally employed for "straightening out" the "sticks"
in the lumber camps, because most of the horses available
were too light for the purpose. Many of these oxen were
obtained at a cattle fair at Perth. This fair, which was in
existence as early as 1829, was held semi-annually, the fall
one being much the more important. A Methodist circuit-
rider attended it in the autumn of 1839, and reported that
"The Bathurst District annual Fair was held on Tuesday
the 1st instant, when there was a large and excellent collection of horned cattle, and some fine horses. This is the
only annual fair in Upper Canada; it has been held annually
for a number of years in the Bathurst District, after the
custom of the old country. Many oxen are purchased at this
Fair by lumber merchants; and persons attend from sixty
miles distance."[37] The market for surplus oxen thus furnished
by the lumbering industry fluctuated greatly in value, for
when the timber trade was in a state of depression, very few
buyers appeared at the fair.[38]

[35]Perth *Bathurst Courier*, March 9, 1847; *Canadian Agriculturist*,
May, 1854, p. 130.
[36]*JTBAUC 1855-6*, p. 494. Potatoes were also in demand, but the
danger of their freezing prevented their being drawn far.
[37]Toronto *Christian Guardian*, Oct. 30, 1839.
[38]Perth *Bathurst Courier*, Oct. 6, 1837; *ibid.*, Oct. 21, 1841; *ibid.*,
May 10, 1842.

The Trent Valley was the only district in central or western Upper Canada which had a shanty market similar to that
of the Ottawa Valley, and this was an inconsiderable one, for
very little timber was cut there before 1847.[39] Elsewhere
in the province lumbering was carried on mainly by farmers
on their own land, to supply the local sawmills, and as one
phase of their land-clearing operations. Thus, along the
north shore of Lake Erie, where beginning about 1825 there
was an extensive sawn-lumber production for export to Buffalo, Cleveland, and Detroit, the farmers cut sawlogs on their
own holdings as a winter sideline, so that they were able to
grow in the summer most of what they required for winter
consumption, or else to obtain it locally. Even in Norfolk
County, where lumbering was said to engage the farmers
more than agriculture, we find no evidence of extensive importations of pork and flour and fodder such as characterized
the upper Ottawa Valley.[40]

When times were good the rural inhabitants of the Ottawa Valley enjoyed a rude abundance. T. C. Keefer asserted
that "as the lumbering business is conducted on the cash
principle, and wages are highly remunerative, the population
are more able, and do consume more and live better than
any other country population I am acquainted with. . . . I
never saw elsewhere money more plenty, and the means of
comfort more universally diffused than on the upper Ottawa."[41] But it was not always so. Even for the most
successful farmers the dovetailing of agriculture and lumbering had its drawbacks. Prosperity in the timber trade was
reflected in soaring prices for farm produce, but a depression
in the collapse of the shanty market. This was clearly shown
by developments during the decade of the eighteen-forties.
During the early eighteen-forties there was a rapid expansion

---

[39]Poole, *Sketch of . . . Town of Peterborough*, pp. 92-3. Though
square timber making was carried on as far west as Lake Huron by
1850, it was handicapped because the pine in the western part of the
province was often mixed with hardwood, because there were few
streams suitable for floating it to one of the lakes, and because it was
difficult to get it through the open waters of Lake Ontario to reach
the Quebec market.

[40]Smith, *Canada, Past, Present, and Future*, vol. I, p. 118.

[41]Keefer, *Montreal and the Ottawa*, p. 116.

in the timber trade, till exports reached a new height in 1845. Then in 1846, 1847, and 1848 the operators suffered from lower prices and a diminished demand, owing at first to a glut at Quebec, and then to the cessation of the British construction industry following the railway panic of 1847 in the United Kingdom.[42] Consequently, during the two or three years before 1850, many settlers in the remoter parts abandoned their clearances, as has been mentioned, and the rest of the rural population indirectly dependent on the timber trade endured a good deal of distress.

The Ottawa Valley was the only part of Upper Canada with a large consuming population, and therefore it had what was elsewhere completely lacking, a large internal trade. The shanty market encouraged a peculiar type of agriculture near the timber limits, and gave the farmers near the St. Lawrence a domestic outlet to the north as well as an export one at Montreal. This market, with its inherent advantages, could last only as long as the timber trade did not exhaust itself, and, equally important, only as long as poor communications kept prices at the place of consumption far above the levels prevailing along the "front." The changes brought about in the lumbering areas and in the regions adjacent to them by the developments of the late eighteen-fifties in Upper Canada will be described in Chapter XVII.

---

[42]*JLAC 1849*, App. PPPP.

CHAPTER VIII

TARIFFS AND PREFERENCES, 1831 - 1846[1]

A T the end of Chapter III, it was noted that for half a dozen years, beginning about 1825, rural Upper Canada displayed evidences of prosperity. Unfortunately, the decade of the eighteen-thirties, which in consequence opened with fair promise, proved to be one of disappointment. This was to be ascribed to partial crop failures in the province, to a series of abundant British harvests, to a European and North American depression, and most of all, so the farmers thought, to the inequitable operation of the colonial system.

As in the eighteen-twenties, the ordinary market for the surplus wheat and flour of Upper Canada was the United Kingdom. When flour could not be sold profitably in the British Isles, the usual alternatives were the Maritimes and the British West Indies. Neither of these was a satifactory outlet owing to American competition and a rather limited demand. Though the Corn Law of 1828 did give Upper Canada wheat growers an advantage over their foreign competitors in the British market, it offered no assurance of profitable prices. A succession of good British harvests was scarcely less calamitous in Upper Canada than local crop failures. The four years ending in 1835 were, as a series, extraordinary in their production of wheat in Great Britain, with the result that the average annual price between 1832 and 1837 ranged well below 67s. a quarter.[2] In consequence, Upper Canada wheat and flour were only occasionally admitted at the 6d. duty. Sometimes, as in 1834, the sudden increase in duty from 6d. to 5s. had the effect of excluding them from the British market for the time being.[3]

When this happened, Upper Canada grain dealers, warned

---

[1]Part of this chapter is a revision of my article, "Canadian Agricultural Tariff of 1843" (*Canadian Journal of Economics and Political Science*, vol. VII, 1941).

[2]Tooke, *History of Prices*, vol. II, p. 236; Ernle, *English Farming Past and Present*, p. 441.

[3]Cf. Burton, "Wheat in Canadian History" (*Canadian Journal of Economics and Political Science*, vol. III, 1937, p. 214).

by their Montreal correspondents, drastically reduced their quotations on wheat. A Select Committee of the Assembly reported that, in the winter of 1834-5, the prices paid in the Toronto vicinity had fallen to a range of from 32 to 38 cents, and that there was little prospect of improvement. As it was estimated to cost between 40 and 50 cents to produce a bushel of wheat in the country adjacent to Lake Ontario, it was manifest that the wheat growers here, and still more so those in the western parts of the province, were actually operating at a loss.[4] Hard times naturally followed. Even in 1835 it could be remarked that "the inhabitants of Toronto, we believe, never before nor since it was a city, have experienced any thing like the depression in business which this spring has produced."[5]

Wheat was not again exported to the British Isles in any quantity till 1840. The cause lay, not in the low prices overseas, but in other conditions. When Upper Canadian wheat could not be sold at a profit in the United Kingdom, the farmers looked longingly towards the American market, in which, in consequence of the opening of the Erie Canal, increasing industrialization in New England, and crop failures, grain prices in the decade 1830-40 ruled higher than in the British provinces.[6] Usually they could not sell their wheat there, on account of the duty of 25 cents a bushel imposed in 1824. As a matter of fact, only a few hundred dollars' worth of Upper Canada wheat was sold in the United States in any year between 1825 and 1835. But in 1835, 1836, 1837, and 1838 the wheat crop failed in parts of the United States, and wheat was imported from Upper Canada.[7] In all these years, except 1838, the crops were so poor in

---

[4]*Journal of the Legislative Assembly of Upper Canada, 1835*, App. 11, pp. i-ii.

[5]Montreal *Gazette*, May 23, 1835. One result of the depression was a considerable decline in the price of land. In 1839 Buckingham found speculators at Toronto who could get only 2s. 6d. an acre for land they had bought at 10s. fifteen or twenty years before (Buckingham, *Canada, Nova Scotia and New Brunswick*, pp. 49-50).

[6]Cf. Burton, "Wheat in Canadian History," p. 213.

[7]Toronto *Christian Guardian*, Feb. 5, 1840; Report on the Surplus Revenue, Jan. 11, 1837, in Reports of Committees, *House of Representatives*, 24th Cong., 2nd Sess., 1836-7, no. 86, pp. 11-12, 19. The amount of wheat imported from Upper Canada in 1835 was 236,000

Upper Canada that many of the backwoods settlers were on the verge of starvation.[8]   Nevertheless, the deficiency in the United States was so great, and the prices prevailing in consequence so high, that the Upper Canada wheat surplus, such as it was, was shipped to the states of New York, Michigan, and even Illinois.   Little went to Montreal during most of these years, though prices there were high enough to attract wheat from Europe to be milled.[9]

It was only under exceptional circumstances, such as these, that the Upper Canada farmers had access to the United States market.   Ordinarily, indeed, they had to compete with Americans in what they regarded as their own market, that is, Lower Canada.   In the eighteen-twenties, Lower Canada was still exporting wheat of its own growth, but it was able to do so only because it imported other wheat or flour for consumption.   Under the Canada Trade Act of 1822, Upper Canada enjoyed a favoured position in satisfying this demand.   Then, in 1831, in the hope of drawing the grain trade of the western states through the St. Lawrence and otherwise benefiting the commercial community of the Canadas, the Colonial Trade Act[10] was passed by the British parliament.   According to this act, all duties on agricultural produce entering the British North American provinces were repealed.

The Colonial Trade Act made it profitable to import American wheat to grind in the Canadas and ship to Great Britain as Canadian flour; for, in the words of Lord Stanley, the law "made no distinction between flour manufactured from wheat, the produce of the United States, and flour

---

bushels (*ibid.*, p. 19). In 1836 the Rochester millers alone imported 200,000 bushels from Upper Canada (O'Reilly, *Sketches of Rochester*, p. 361).

[8]Traill, *Backwoods of Canada*, (ed. by Caswell), p. 323. Burton says that these failures "played an important part in the fomenting of the rebellion," owing to the high prices of wheat and flour ("Wheat in Canadian History," p. 214).

[9]Jameson, *Winter Studies and Summer Rambles*, vol. I, p. 298; Murray, *Historical and Descriptive Account*, vol. II, pp. 16-17. These exports were accounted for in part by demand in the western states occasioned by abnormal immigration (Quebec *Gazette*, quoted in Montreal *Gazette*, June 11, 1835).

[10]1 William IV, c. 24.

manufactured from wheat the produce of Canada. As long as the flour was manufactured in Canada, it had always been imported into this country as Canadian produce."[11] Ohio and other American flour imported into the Canadas, being at that time already a manufactured product, would have had to pay a special duty on entering the United Kingdom. Therefore, it was either re-exported to the West Indies, or sold in Lower Canada for home consumption.[12] During the eighteen-thirties, the ravages of the midge in the valley of the Richelieu greatly lessened the amount of wheat brought to market in Lower Canada. Indeed, many of the habitants in the old grain-growing parishes no longer had wheat to exchange for the flour they bought for their own use.[13] It seemed unreasonable to the Upper Canada farmers that Americans should have a monopoly of the market south of the border while they were admitted freely by the Colonial Trade Act to that of Lower Canada.'¹

Nor was this the only complaint they had to make. Sometimes, as in 1839, a general crop failure in the upper province resulted in large quantities of American wheat and flour being introduced into that section for home consumption.[14] When this happened, the farming population repeated its demand of the early eighteen-twenties, that if its breadstuffs were to be virtually shut out of the British market by the Corn Laws, and out of the American by the tariff, some legislative action should be taken to assure a profitable outlet in the two Canadian provinces for those who did have grain to sell.

The farmers had other reasons for criticizing the Colonial Trade Act. These help to explain why they persisted in growing wheat in the face of unfavourable legislation and

[11]Speech of March 3, 1843, in *Hansard's Parliamentary Debates*, series 3, vol. LXVII, p. 250. Cf. York *Colonial Advocate*, Aug. 11, 1831.

[12]Rochester, N.Y., *Daily Advertiser*, quoted in York *Colonial Advocate*, Nov. 12, 1831; Montreal *Canadian Courant*, Oct. 27, 1832; *Journal of the Legislative Assembly of Upper Canada, 1835*, App. 11, p. 15.

[13]Cf. Jones, "French-Canadian Agriculture in the St. Lawrence Valley" (*Agricultural History*, vol. XVI, 1942, pp. 141-2).

[14]Toronto *Christian Guardian*, Aug. 28, 1839; *ibid.*, Feb. 5, 1840; *British American Cultivator*, May, 1843, p. 73.

effective competition, instead of turning to dairying or stock-raising. Livestock-raising, except as part of a self-sufficient economy, scarcely existed in Upper Canada in the eighteen-thirties. At first sight, this seems rather strange, as it is now carried on as a major enterprise in much of the province. The lack of commercial stock-raising was attri-buted at the time by some writers to the expense of sheltering and feeding stock during the winter,[15] but it should be re-membered that the average farmer was not convinced of the need of sheltering his animals, and that usually he wintered them on the roughest feeds. The cost of obtaining stock, and the large profits to be made out of the wheat staple in a favourable year on a small investment, were certainly of much greater significance. Moreover, even when the Corn Laws shut their wheat out of the British Isles, farmers were re-luctant to invest anything in stock, as they had no certain home market for meat. Livestock-raising offered few attrac-tions even in the vicinity of urban communities like Toronto, for prices were kept low by competition from the adjacent parts of the United States.

It will be recalled that under the Canada Trade Act of 1822 small duties were imposed on American livestock enter-ing the Canadas. The Colonial Trade Act of 1831, as was previously mentioned, repealed these duties. William Lyon Mackenzie, who had predicted that the act would be disastrous for the yeomen of Upper Canada, pounced on the first evidence he could find of livestock entering the province. "Upper Canada is [now] a very extensive and valuable market for the livestock of the United States. It is almost inconceivable the quantity of fat bullocks, oxen, cows and horses which are brought across duty free from the American frontier."[16] Week after week, especially in the spring, droves of cattle, numbering fifty or sixty head each, continued to be taken over the Niagara at Queenston to be sold to the butchers at Hamilton and Toronto.[17] In western Upper Canada, accord-ing to one traveller, the towns and villages depended on the

---

[15]E.g. Shirreff, *Tour through North America*, p. 369.

[16]York *Colonial Advocate*, Nov. 10, 1831.

[17]*Ibid.*, Nov. 10, 1831; *British American Cultivator*, April, 1843, p. 55; "Ex-Settler," *Canada in the Years 1832, 1833 and 1834*, p. 97.

United States for the sheep and cattle which were slaughtered in them, as did the neighbouring farmers for their working oxen.[18] The market at Montreal, to which the farmers of the eastern part of the province would naturally turn, was supplied to a large extent from Vermont.[19] In most of North America, cattle prices on the edge of settlement were much lower than in regions near the consuming centres, because the animals had to be driven to these centres for sale, but so strong was American competition in Upper Canada that the opposite condition existed in it. Cattle owned in the backwoods were worth too much there to be driven to the "front" for sale, while those raised and fattened in the older townships were cheap.[20]

There can be no doubt that dread of American competition was a strong deterrent to stock-raising. An intelligent immigrant indicated the difficulties he would encounter if he settled somewhere near Lake Erie, and went into the raising of beef and mutton. "My cattle and sheep must be driven a great distance," he wrote, "and this very distance throws me into competition with the Americans from the prairies [of central Ohio, of Indiana, and of Illinois], who are constantly driving bullocks into the market of Toronto, and who could undersell me if I had my farm for nothing, merely because their grazing is unlimited and their pastures finer."[21] The only part of Upper Canada where it cost as little to raise livestock as it did in such regions as the "barrens" of Clark and Madison counties, Ohio, was in the marshes along the southern shore of Lake St. Clair and along the Thames River.

---

[18]Shirreff, *Tour through North America*, p. 369. Notice also: "There has passed up to the Gore District [through Saltfleet Township, Wentworth County] during the last three months of 1842, not less than 4,000 sheep purchased in the United States" (*British American Cultivator*, March, 1843, p. 44).

[19]Fergusson, *Practical Notes Made during a Tour*, p. 62; Montreal *Transcript*, Sept. 28, 1843.

[20]"Ex-Settler," *Canada in the Years 1832, 1833 and 1834*, p. 98; Traill, *Backwoods of Canada*, p. 188.

[21]William Hutton of Belleville to his brother, June 25, 1834, in *British Farmer's Magazine*, April, 1835, p. 109. For further details about the Ohio droving industry, see King, "Coming and Going of Ohio Droving" (*Ohio Archaeological and Historical Publications*, vol. XVII, 1908).

Here droves of semi-feral cattle and especially of semi-feral horses ranged throughout the summer, as cattle were mentioned as doing at the beginning of the century. The owners of the horses branded them in the shoulder before they let them out on the pasture, and caught them with a lasso when they wanted them. They bred the horses for sale, it was stated, but precisely where they disposed of them is not to be ascertained from the evidence at present available.[22]

Cattle formed the most important part of the livestock imported from the United States, with sheep, as our references show, the next in value. In addition to the meat in the form of livestock driven in from the United States, there were large quantities of mess pork imported from Cincinnati. Some of this was used to feed the lumberjacks of the Ottawa Valley, and the rest was re-exported to Newfoundland and the West Indies. In either case it displaced the home-cured product of Upper Canada. In 1833 almost 30,000 barrels of pork from the United States reached Montreal, and not more than 1,800 from Upper Canada.[23] It is only fair to add that there seems to have been little objection offered to the importing of pork, because the Upper Canada farmers in general did not consider swine-raising on a commercial scale profitable. Fresh beef was imported only in negligible quantities, at least till 1843, for when in that year butchers at Hamilton and other centres brought in meat already butchered, it was remarked as a new development.[24]

As a result of this American competition, which was effective even if the drovers diverted at the Niagara frontier only a small proportion of the fat steers they were driving eastward to Albany and New York, the number of local

---

[22]Pickering, *Inquiries of an Emigrant*, p. 134; Bonnycastle, *Canada and the Canadians*, vol. II, pp. 129-30; *Journal and Transactions of the Board of Agriculture of Upper Canada for 1855-6*, p. 520; *ibid.*, for 1856-7, p. 219. Hereafter this authority is cited as *JTBAUC*. It may be conjectured that these horses belonged to the French-Canadian breed, and that their owners were French-Canadians. The French-Canadian settlers around Detroit reared horses in much the same manner as this as late as 1870 (Hubbard, "The Early Colonization of Detroit," p. 354). For the similar raising of horses by the Indians along the Grand River, see below, pp. 143-4.

[23]Montreal *Canadian Courant*, Feb. 5, 1834.

[24]*British American Cultivator*, April, 1843, p. 55.

cattle coming to market in Upper Canada was much smaller than might have been expected from the size of the population. In fact, there were occasions when it was believed that the quantity of cattle kept in the province was actually less than the population required, even for milk. Thus, when in 1838-9 a handful of American drovers appeared in Glengarry, along the Bay of Quinte, and even as far west as Woodstock, and bought some swine and "many hundreds" of cattle, mainly milch cows, the magistrates of the Midland District thought it "highly inexpedient that the country should be further drained of cattle," and tried unsuccessfully to have the provincial administration impose an embargo. The magistrates suggested the embargo largely at the instigation of the butchers of Kingston who contracted to supply meat to the garrison. The butchers contended that the cattle were intended for the "Sympathizers" across the St. Lawrence, though the real basis of their protest was the "unreasonable prices" the Americans paid. When the departure of a few thousand cattle from a region nearly four hundred miles long could cause such concern among responsible officials, and lead them to declare, as they did, that for months veal would be the only meat available in it, it is manifest that Upper Canadian stock-raising was an unimportant industry.[25]

The instance just mentioned was not the only example of Upper Canadian cattle being exported to the United States during the eighteen-thirties. Blois, writing of Detroit in 1838, remarked that "for a few years past, Ohio, Indiana, and Upper Canada have furnished the greater portion of the cattle slaughtered here."[26] The number of cattle from Upper Canada sold there cannot have been large, however. The tariff and the same kind of American competition encountered in Upper Canada made it impossible for the farmers in the western

---

[25]*Journal of the Legislative Assembly of Upper Canada, 1839,* Appendix, pp. 697-700; *Journal of the Legislative Assembly of Canada, 1849,* App. PPP. It was stated that a company of speculators in Utica was responsible for most of the purchases. This is quite likely, as in 1841 some of the milch cows in Herkimer County, N.Y., were described as having been obtained in Upper Canada (*Transactions of the New York State Agricultural Society, 1841,* p. 137).

[26]Blois, *Gazetteer of the State of Michigan,* p. 275.

part of the province to recoup in Michigan what they lost at home.

Owing to the fluctuating character of the grain trade, and to the severe competition of American livestock in the Upper Canadian market, the agricultural interests, as already indicated, strove to have a protective tariff established against American produce. William Lyon Mackenzie attacked the Colonial Trade Act as soon as he was informed of its prospective passage, and commenced a vociferous campaign on behalf of the farmers.[27] Other politicians added to the clamour. At every session of the Upper Canada legislature after 1833, one or another rural representative introduced resolutions in favour of a provincial protective tariff. Some of these passed the Assembly, with the support of both Tories and Reformers, but they were rejected by the Legislative Council, at the instance, it was alleged, of the executive.[28]

This question of a tariff aggravated the cleavage between the agricultural interests of Upper Canada and the commercial interests of Montreal. It has been pointed out by Professor Creighton that this cleavage was one of the fundamental causes of the Rebellion of 1837.[29] The commercial group desired improvements such as the Welland and other canals, and free importation of American agricultural produce, that it might consolidate its position in the grain trade and the rest of the commercial system based on the St.

---

[27]York *Colonial Advocate*, Feb. 17, June 16, July 7, Aug. 25, 1831. The agitation was directed not against the Colonial Trade Act alone, but against the colonial system as a whole. A "general" in the "Patriot Army" wrote: "The laws regulating their trade and commerce, were enacted in the Parliament of the United Kingdom, and continually changed and varied without the Province being consulted, although the value of their labor and property are deeply affected by this ever varying system of legislation. Their trade by sea is carried on exclusively for the advantage of capitalists, residing in England. England claims an exclusive monopoly of the Canadian markets, but allows the Canadians none in hers" (M'Leod, *Brief Review of Settlement*, p. 95). William Lyon Mackenzie had the same idea. "Mr. Poulett Thomson should have remembered that free trade means freedom to all the parties concerned, not to two parties at the expense of a third, who is kept down by one of them" (*Sketches of Canada*, p. 429).

[28]Toronto *Examiner*, July 29, 1840; *ibid.*, Dec. 1, 1841.

[29]Creighton, "Economic Background of the Rebellions" (*Canadian Journal of Economics and Political Science*, vol. III, p. 322).

Lawrence. The timber operators, at this time the largest purchasers of foodstuffs for consumption, desired cheap American pork and flour. On the other hand, the pioneer farmers demanded a revision of the policy which permitted American graziers to compete with them at their very doors; cried down land speculation, especially as expressed in the Canada Company; opposed the squandering of public money on the Welland Canal; and insisted that something should be done for the inland parts of the province.[30] In the Upper Canada Assembly in 1832, W. H. Merritt asserted that the Reformers in their opposition to the Welland Canal were always shouting "monopoly, speculation"; and Peter Perry, one of their leaders, admitted that "we were often told that we were the enemies of public improvements."[31] Rural opposition to the commercial programme was so strong that a recent authority is justified in remarking that "in one sense, the rebellion in Upper Canada was an agrarian revolt."[32]

After the rebellion the agitation for a tariff was renewed when, as has been mentioned, there were in 1840 heavy imports of American wheat and flour. Meetings were held at various places in Upper Canada to petition the government for a duty on all kinds of American agricultural produce, and nearly every rural manifesto of the election of 1841 came out in favour of such protection.[33] In response to this demand, the Upper Canada legislature in 1840 passed an act of the kind requested, but it was disallowed by the Colonial Office. When the agricultural interests then sent a petition to the Queen requesting that the British parliament should pass a measure which would achieve the same purpose, the agents in London of the Quebec and Montreal commercial houses made strong representations against the proposed duty. Partly owing to their activities, and partly to the lobbying of the

---

[30]*Ibid.*, pp. 324-5; *Toronto Christian Guardian*, Feb. 5, 1834.

[31]York *Christian Guardian*, Dec. 12, 1832.

[32]Mackay, "Political Ideas of William Lyon Mackenzie" (*Canadian Journal of Economics and Political Science*, vol. III, p. 18).

[33]Toronto *Examiner*, July 29, 1840, and later numbers. The significant portion of a series of resolutions drawn up by a meeting of farmers at Richmond Hill, December 9, 1840, to demand agricultural protection, is printed in Innis and Lower (eds.), *Select Documents in Canadian Economic History*, pp. 362-3.

other vested groups in the United Kingdom dependent on
the Corn Laws, parliament forced Gladstone to drop his project of thus taxing American produce. As his bill also included
a provision admitting colonial wheat and flour at a nominal
duty, as was done in 1843, the Upper Canadian farmers felt
that the commercial interests had done them a "double injury,"
that is, had helped to exclude their grain from the United
Kingdom by the retention of the 5s. duty, and had permitted
American produce to continue to glut their home market.[34]
It is not surprising, therefore, that Francis Hincks reported:
"We have witnessed with much regret an increasing feeling
of jealousy and distrust between the agriculturists and the
merchants and forwarders. . . . The merchants and forwarders are afraid that a most profitable trade may be taken
out of their hands, while the farmers imagine that the merchants are utterly regardless of *their* interests provided they
can materially advance their own."[35]

In view of this distrust, it was fortunate for provincial
unity that the adoption of a degree of protection was facilitated by a dispatch of March 2, 1842, from the Colonial Secretary to Sir Charles Bagot, which could be interpreted to
mean that, if Canada placed duties on American wheat, the
British parliament would remove or reduce the duties on
Canadian breadstuffs entering the United Kingdom. As a
result, in the autumn of 1842 the Canadian legislature passed
an act (which was proclaimed in effect by the Governor-
General, August 9, 1843) establishing a duty of 3s. sterling
a quarter on American wheat entering Canada. Later, in
November and December of 1843, the legislature imposed
duties on other American agricultural produce, including
livestock, meats, cheese, butter, and coarse grains.[36] In 1846
the duties on wheat imported for consumption, and on livestock, meats, dairy products, and coarse grains were made
permanent.[37]

Did the new duties attain their objective? A distinction
must be drawn between the duty on wheat and those on the

---

[34]Toronto *Examiner*, April 6, 1841.
[35]*Ibid.*, Dec. 1, 1841.
[36]6 Vic., c. 31; 7 Vic., c. 1; 7 Vic., c. 2 (*Statutes of Canada*).
[37]9 Vic., c. 1.

other products. The small duty on wheat did not prevent, nor was it intended to prevent, its importation into Canada on a large scale, with a view to ultimate re-export. The other duties seem to have been more effective, as the following extract suggests: "The loss Canada has sustained in not having one American team pass through Chatham, this year [1844], though 350 passed through the same place in 1843, is not so great as might be supposed. Not one of these teams came to Canada for any other purpose than to advance their own interests, or for their own convenience or pleasure. They most probably came to sell produce in Canada, and take back cash for it, as their tariff is so excessively high that it would not admit of their taking any of our produce or British manufacture [sic], unless they took them as smugglers."[38] The duties of £1 10s. per head on horses, 10s. to £1 on cattle, 5s. on swine, and 2s. on sheep, did succeed in shutting out much livestock, and seem to have made prices rule somewhat higher in western Upper Canada than in adjacent states like Michigan.[39] As a result it was said that "the farmers are devoting much more of their attention to rearing horses, cattle, sheep, and pigs, than was the case ten years ago, when almost all the markets were supplied from the United States."[40] The commercial interests in Montreal felt that they were adversely affected, and sought to have the legislation establishing the tariff repealed.[41]

Nevertheless, it seemed to some observers that the tariff was not bringing about the development of a real livestock or dairying industry. The demand for cheese, for example, was still almost invariably satisfied by imports from New York or Ohio.[42] "Under the operation of this law," it was remarked in 1846, "not one pound weight has been added

---

[38]*Canadian Agricultural Journal*, June 1, 1844, p. 88.

[39]In 1848 half the beef and mutton consumed by the garrison at Amherstburg was imported from Michigan duty free. The local farmers said that they could not afford to raise and feed cattle for what the contractor paid in Michigan (*Agriculturist and Canadian Journal*, May 1, 1848, p. 87).

[40]Bonnycastle, *Canada and the Canadians*, vol. II, p. 211.

[41]*Canadian Agricultural Journal*, March 2, 1846, p. 42.

[42]*Census of Canada, 1851-2*, vol. I, p. XXXVII; *JTBAUC 1855-6*, pp. 56, 263, 453.

to the domestic production [of beef]. The farmer, instead of doubling his industry to fill the vacuum created by the exclusion of American cattle, is absolutely leaving the markets unsupplied."[43] Yet it would appear that dissatisfaction with the tariff was not the reason for the comparative scarcity of cattle at Toronto at this time. The large immigration of the eighteen-forties and the extensive canal-building operations going on in the province together provided a larger, if not sufficiently noticed, outlet than had theretofore existed. More important, the great profits which it seemed possible to make in wheat-growing under the colonial preference of 1843-6 undoubtedly diverted from stock-raising a great many farmers who would otherwise have engaged in it, just as the wheat-growing boom of the Crimean War period did later.

Because historians have directed their attention towards the imperial Canada Corn Act of 1843, they have tended to overlook the significance of the new tariff system as the culmination of the protests of the agricultural population. Nevertheless, it is from this tariff that the beginnings of Canadian protection may be dated. This was recognized by Thomas C. Keefer, when, at the middle of the century, he summarized Canadian tariff policy.[44]

\\During the period in which the Upper Canada farmers were clamouring for an agricultural tariff, they also tried to have the British government bring about modifications in the Corn Law of 1828. At best, they hoped to have their breadstuffs enter the United Kingdom free of duty at all times; at least, they hoped to obtain some reduction in the 5s. maximum duty. Their requests became more urgent when in 1840 it again became possible to export wheat to Great Britain, for in 1840-2 the average British price was under 67s. This meant that only at intervals did Upper Canada wheat enter on the payment of the nominal 6d. duty.[45] Nevertheless, Upper Canada wheat exports expanded rapidly between 1840 and 1843. The increase was to be attributed

[43]Toronto *Examiner*, April 1, 1846.

[44]Keefer, *Canals of Canada*, p. 33. An example of the failure to recognize the importance of this tariff is to be found in Tucker, *Canadian Commercial Revolution*, pp. 103-4.

[45]Creighton, *Commercial Empire of the St. Lawrence*, p. 345; Ernle, *English Farming Past and Present*, p. 441.

to good crops in all these years, especially in 1842, to a marked augmentation in acreage in 1840 and 1842,[46] and to prospective and actual changes in the Corn Laws. [47]

By an act of 1842, the British parliament made it easier for colonial wheat to be sold in the United Kingdom, by establishing 1s. per quarter as the duty whenever the British price was 58s. or more; 2s. when it was 57s.; 3s. when it was 56s.; 4s. when it was 55s., and 5s. whenever it was less than 55s.[47] In 1843, it will be remembered, the legislature of Canada imposed a duty of 3s. sterling a quarter on American wheat and flour imported into the province. This duty was small enough not to interfere seriously with the importation of American breadstuffs, and yet it represented a concession to the local wheat growers. At the same time, partly as an initial step towards free trade, and partly to encourage the milling and forwarding interests of Canada, the famous imperial Canada Corn Act set the nominal duty of 1s. a quarter on all Canadian wheat, and a proportionate amount on wheat flour, imported into the United Kingdom, no matter what the British price might be.[48] Accordingly, after October, 1843, grain from the American West entered Canada in greater quantities than ever before, and was there manufactured into flour, to take advantage of the British custom of permitting flour manufactured in Canada from American wheat to be entered as colonial. As a result, there was a notable expansion in the forwarding and milling industries, with many large mills being erected, especially along the Welland Canal.[49]

---

[46]Toronto *Examiner*, Aug. 5, 1840; *British American Cultivator*, May, 1842, p. 65; *ibid.*, May, 1843, p. 73.

[47]5 and 6 Vic., c. 14 (Ernle, *English Farming Past and Present*, p. 447).

[48]6 and 7 Vic., c. 29 (Ernle, *English Farming Past and Present*, p. 447).

[49]A mill at Gananoque manufactured about 30,000 barrels of flour a year between 1843 and 1846, using both Upper Canadian and American wheat (Smith, *Canada, Past, Present, and Future*, vol. II, p. 297. A minor question concerns the amount of American wheat imported into the Canadas actually reaching England, either in manufactured or unmanufactured form. Dr. Merk thinks that a large part did, basing his opinion on the fact that Canada, according to statistics, had little surplus for export (Merk, "The British Corn Crisis of 1845-6,"

A writer has recently claimed that the benefits received by Upper Canada as a consequence of the Canada Corn Act have been unduly magnified by historians. He points out that though there was an expansion in the amount of wheat produced and exported following the passage of the act, large increases in production and acreage were not new; that the exports of 1841 had been greater than ever before; that prices of wheat were lower in 1843-6 than in 1840-2; that harvest fluctuations in Europe were an important factor; and concludes that at most the preference described above had some "vague influence."[50] This contention does not stand examination. American wheat growers and exporters found that in spite of the provincial duty and in spite of higher freight rates by the St. Lawrence than by New York, it was highly profitable to take advantage of the "Canadian back door."[51] Upper Canada wheat growers had a shorter distance to ship their grain, and no duty to pay on it before it left the province, and so obviously derived more benefit than the Americans. The effects of the preference can be assessed in additional ways. One was in an increase in acreage. The crop of 1843 was excellent, and that of 1844 average, but that of 1845 was not only of high quality, but "twice that of any previous year" in quantity.[52] This would seem to

---

Agricultural History, vol. VIII, 1934, p. 111). The Canadian deficiency was, however, wholly in Lower Canada. As Upper Canada had a large surplus of first-class wheat, it seems probable that it was able to export most of it, either as wheat or flour, and to use flour made from American wheat for its domestic requirements. Cf. MacGibbon, *Canadian Grain Trade,* p. 12.

[50]Burn, "Canada and the Repeal of the Corn Laws" (*Cambridge Historical Journal,* vol. II, 1928, pp. 252, 255-6). The exports of wheat and flour from the St. Lawrence between 1838 and 1849, stated in bushels of wheat (with a barrel of flour considered as the equivalent of five bushels of wheat), were as follows:

1838	296,020 bushels	1844	2,350,018 bushels
1839	249,471	1845	2,507,392
1840	1,739,119	1846	3,312,757
1841	2,313,836	1847	3,883,156
1842	1,678,102	1848	2,248,016
1843	1,193,918	1849	3,645,320

(Hind *et al., Eighty Years' Progress,* p. 291).

[51]Merk, "British Corn Crisis of 1845-6," pp. 110-11.

[52]*British American Cultivator,* Aug., 1843, p. 117; *ibid.,* Sept., 1845, p. 262; *ibid.,* Jan., 1846, p. 3; *ibid.,* Aug., 1847, p. 230; Toronto *Examiner,* Jan. 7, 1846; *ibid.,* Jan. 13, 1847.

indicate a greatly increased acreage, a fairly certain sign of shifting of emphasis to wheat. (According to the editor of the census of 1851-2, the production of wheat in Upper Canada had increased 400 per cent between 1840 and 1850.[53] This expansion was at a much more rapid rate than the expansion of the population, and was made in spite of the comparative failure of the crop in eastern Upper Canada for several years before 1850. Lower prices than in preceding years made little difference, for when he sowed his wheat, the farmer could not tell what the price would be when he had it harvested and threshed; but he did know during these few years what he had never known before—that he had a certain market. It was no accident that the Toronto Board of Trade reported in 1845 that "at no former period in the history of Western Canada has the condition of the agricultural class been so prosperous as at this time."[54] The assured market could, by itself, have brought about a great increase in production. It is true that the failure of the Irish potato crop helped create a demand for colonial wheat in the United Kingdom, but the farmer has always been very much at the mercy of crop conditions in other countries. The contention that the influence of the colonial preference was vague is at variance with a statement made by E. W. Thompson in his presidential address to the Agricultural Association of Upper Canada in 1847. Wheat, he remarked, had "been in brisk demand for the last few years, owing to the failure of the potatoe crop, and the partial failure of the grain crops in Great Britain and Ireland, as well as on the continent of Europe; but especially owing to the preference we enjoyed in the markets of Great Britain."[55] As has already been pointed out, so great was the concentration on wheat during these years that the incipient livestock industry languished.

The wheat-growing prosperity did not benefit every farmer in Upper Canada. This was a consequence of the westward advance of the wheat midge, the advent of which had marked the ruination of wheat-farming in Lower Canada. The midge travelled up the St. Lawrence at an estimated speed

---

[53]*Census of Canada, 1851-2*, vol. I, p. xxxii.
[54]Toronto *Examiner*, Jan. 7, 1846.
[55]*JTBAUC 1855-6*, p. 52.

of ten or twelve miles a year. It had been prevalent around
Montreal shortly before the Rebellion of 1837. It reached
Cornwall probably before 1840, Brockville about 1842, the
Bay of Quinte in 1849. As it spread inland to the outermost
settlements, farmers in one St. Lawrence county after another had to abandon wheat as a staple. The extent of
its depredations may be judged from the fact that about
210,000 bushels of wheat were exported from Brockville in
1843, and not more than 40,000 in 1844. Had it not been
for the expansion in the timber trade farther up the Ottawa
Valley at this time, the farmers in the townships along the
"front of St. Lawrence" would have been in a sad plight.[56]

The pioneer on a new clearance also failed to derive much
profit from the British demand for his wheat, because he
had to consume more of his surplus at home than he expected
to, owing to the failure of his potato crop. The late blight
first appeared in Upper Canada, as throughout North America in general, in 1843. In 1845 it completely ruined the
potatoes in most of the province. It destroyed them again
in 1846, as it was to do for almost every succeeding year till
new and hardier varieties were introduced from the United
States in the eighteen-sixties.[57]

Such then was the situation in Upper Canada in 1846
when the British parliament turned towards free trade by
repealing the Corn Laws. The repeal had immediate reper-
cussions throughout the wheat-growing sections, for the
farmers knew that shortly the prices they received would be
determined directly by those of the world market at Liverpool.
Though it did not hit them as hard as it did the milling and
forwarding interests, which soon found that there was now
little to attract American wheat or flour through the St.

[56]Brockville *Recorder*, quoted in Toronto *Examiner*, Aug. 3, 1842;
Cornwall *Observer*, quoted in Montreal *Transcript*, Sept. 5, 1843;
British American Cultivator, April, 1845, p. 102; *Canadian Agri-
culturist*, July 2, 1849, p. 174; *ibid.*, Nov. 1850, p. 246.

[57]*British American Cultivator*, Sept., 1845, p. 262; *JTBAUC 1855-6*,
pp. 39, 220. The first variety of potato which proved hardy enough
to resist the late blight was the Garnet Chili, which was formally
introduced in the United States in 1857, and which was mentioned as
being grown on a small scale in different parts of Canada West in
1866 (*Transactions of the Board of Agriculture . . . of Upper Canada
for 1864-8*, pp. 503, 517).

Lawrence,[58] it re-emphasized the weakness of their staple-producing colonial economy. Should the farmers keep on with their wheat-growing when there was so little assurance of a market overseas? Could they continue to grow wheat even if they wanted to, with the midge steadily advancing? To what other forms of agriculture could they turn, with their limited domestic market, with world competition in the mother country, and with their virtual exclusion from the United States? What would happen if everyone turned to dairying or to stock-raising? Newspapers and agricultural periodicals argued the issues back and forth, always coming to a single conclusion—that the outlook for the wheat growers of Upper Canada in 1846 was grim. As it happened, new and wholly unforseen developments (described at length in Chapter XI) were shortly to provide a partial solution for the wheat growers' problems.

---

[58]On the effects of the repeal of the Corn Laws on the Upper Canada milling and forwarding interests, see the documents in Innis and Lower, *Select Documents in Canadian Economic History*, pp. 356-8.

CHAPTER IX

LIVESTOCK AND ITS IMPROVEMENT BEFORE 1850

THE "improving farmers" of Upper Canada, like those of the northern United States and of the British Isles, had many interests in the first half of the nineteenth century. These ranged from entomology to Liebig's "mineral theory," but if we judge from the amount of attention it received in the first agricultural periodicals, the most important by far was the improvement of livestock. Scarcely an issue appeared without learned arguments over "breeding in-and-in," or attempts to explain the mysterious phenomena of inheritance (and these without the benefit of Mendel's laws), or accounts of the importation from England of high-priced rams or bulls or boars.

What was the character of the livestock which the advanced farmers thought it wise to improve? The animals commonly found on the farms of Upper Canada were descended chiefly from those which had accompanied the Loyalists and their successors from New York or Pennsylvania, or had been procured by them across the border or in the French-Canadian communities along the St. Lawrence or the Detroit rivers. For years after the first settlement the pioneers of the Niagara peninsula drew heavily upon the supply of both horses and young cattle in the vicinity of the Great Forks of the Genesee River,[1] and those along the Bay of Quinte brought in working oxen from as far away as Connecticut, milch cows mostly from New York but partly from Lower Canada, and horses mainly from Lower Canada. They obtained their sheep from Lower Canada and New York, and their swine presumably from the same sources.[2] As these importations continued year after year, the livestock of Up-

---

[1]Albany, N.Y., *Gazette*, July 15, 1793, quoted in Doty, *History of Livingston County*, p. 251. There was at this time a fairly steady traffic from the Niagara region to Detroit via the Thames Valley, some of it in American cattle (Bliss, ed., *Diary of David Zeisberger*, vol. II, pp. 360, 367, 383, 426, 452).

[2]Canniff, *History of the Settlement of Upper Canada*, p. 221; La Rochefoucault-Liancourt, *Travels through the United States*, vol. I, pp. 502-3.

per Canada, in so far as it did not betray a French-Canadian origin, came to be indistinguishable from that of the adjacent states.

With some exceptions to be mentioned shortly, the farm animals in Upper Canada were poorly bred. Here, as was also the case south of the border, the pigs were most disparaged. They were vicious creatures—the old sows especially being a terror to children—and so wiry that the farmers could scarcely fatten them. They were variously known as "land-pikes" (the commonest name), "razorbacks," "racers," "alligators," "shingle-pigs," and even "cucumber-seeds." "I can compare one of them," wrote a former resident, "to nothing but a small greyhound, with the great head of a rhinoceros, and their ears are like huge plantain leaves."[3] "He has been chiefly notorious in the past," asserted the Ontario Agricultural Commission of 1880, "for somewhat predatory inclinations in which he has been assisted by long limbs, great activity of motion, and a snout that was said to fall short of the truly useful and meritorious if it failed to reach the second row of corn through a snake fence."[4]

The common sheep were described about 1820 as "being rather tall, and frequently horned, with *darkish* legs and faces. A flock will average each about five pounds of wool, of a *fineish* quality."[5] However, the sheep of the French Canadians along the Detroit River were often black, with a little white on their faces, just like those of Lower Canada.[6]

---

[3]"Ex-Settler," *Canada in the Years 1832, 1833, and 1834*, p. 94.

[4]*Report of the Ontario Agricultural Commission*, vol. I, p. 336, hereafter cited as *OACR*. For more information on the perversity of the landpike, see Geikie, *Life in the Woods*, pp. 52-4. For a good cut see *Cultivator*, Jan. 1840, p. 13.

[5]*A Few Plain Directions*, p. 64. Cf. Carman, Heath, and Minto, *Special Report on the Sheep Industry*, p. 344. The five-pound average was doubtless much too high. A more reasonable weight would be two pounds and a half. This was given as an average by Talbot in the early eighteen-twenties, and was also that reported by the census of 1851 (Talbot, *Five Years' Residence*, vol. I, p. 179; *Journal and Transactions of the Board of Agriculture of Upper Canada for 1856-7*, p. 32. Hereafter this authority is cited as *JTBAUC*).

[6]Shirreff, *Tour through North America*, p. 211. The prevalence of black sheep in the flocks of Upper Canada in the eighteen-forties and eighteen-fifties was doubtless to be ascribed to inheritance from these French-Canadian sheep. An Ohio visitor remarked that "a

There were two kinds of common cattle in Upper Canada. The small black or red French-Canadian cattle were found in considerable numbers in eastern Upper Canada,[7] but the predominant cattle in the province as a whole were the so-called "natives." These were, as already indicated, almost identical with the cattle of the northern states, which, by the end of the eighteenth century, were an indistinguishable blend of the various original English, Dutch, Danish, and Swedish breeds.[8] According to the evidence offered by the advertisements for strays in the early newspapers, they were of every conceivable colour—red, brown, yellow, white, black, red and white, black and white, yellow and white, and "yellow-black brindled."[9] Taken one with another, they were poor milkers and producers of tough beef, and seem to have been valued mainly according to their hardiness.

Visitors from the old world sometimes extended their disparagement of Upper Canada livestock to the horses. Nevertheless, the horse of the Upper Canadian farmer was relatively better bred than the rest of his livestock, and much better cared for. This was quite natural, as the backwoodsman did not obtain horses till his farm was fairly well cleared, and he was able to shelter them in some fashion; and there were few farmers who did not take pride in their horses.

There were in early Upper Canada three recognized breeds of horses—the Conestogas (which will be dealt with below), the French Canadians, and the "Indian ponies." The horses

---

noticeable feature in these flocks is the almost universal admixture of black sheep with the white" (*Ohio Farmer*, Nov. 29, 1856, p. 191). An historian stated, with respect to the Upper Canada flocks of the eighteen-forties, that "there were many black sheep among them, and these were prized above others by the farmers' wives, for their wool could be spun into yarn for making the coarse homemade stockings and clothing without the trouble of dyeing" (Carman, Heath, and Minto, *Special Report on the Sheep Industry*, p. 344).

[7]*JTBAUC 1855-6*, p. 462. For a careful description of the pure old French-Canadian cattle, see *Illustrated Journal of Agriculture*, June, 1886, pp. 86-7.

[8]Bidwell and Falconer, *History of Agriculture in the Northern United States*, p. 25.

[9]Advertisements in Newark *Upper Canada Gazette or American Oracle*, 1798; York *Upper Canada Gazette or American Oracle*, 1803-6; *York Gazette*, 1807-9; York *Colonial Advocate*, 1830-1.

called Indian ponies were not, as they ordinarily were south of the border, mustangs obtained through the processes of horse trading from the Indians of the plains west of the Mississippi, but a kind peculiar to Upper Canada and parts of Michigan, Indiana, and Illinois. Henry William Herbert, the leading nineteenth-century authority on North American horses, wrote of them:

On my first visit to Canada, in 1831, I had an opportunity of seeing great herds of these ponies, running nearly wild on the rich meadow lands about the Grand River, belonging to the Mohawk Indians, who had a large reservation on that river, near the village of Brantford. . . .

These little animals, which I do not think any of them exceeded thirteen hands, had all the characteristics of the pure Canadians, and, except in size, were not to be distinguished from them. They had the same bold carriage, open countenance, abundant hair, almost resembling a lion's mane, the same general build, and above all, the same iron feet and legs.

I hired a pair of these, I well remember, both stallions, and they took me in a light wagon, with a heavy driver and a hundred weight, or upwards, of baggage, over execrable roads, sixty miles a day, for ten days in succession, without exhibiting the slightest distress, and at the end of the journey were all ready to set out on the same trip again.

I was new at the time in America, and was much surprised and interested by the performance of this gallant little pair of animals. They were perfectly matched, both in size and color, very dark brown, were twelve hands and a half in height; and where the road was hard and good, could spin along at nearly nine miles in the hour. They were very merry goers.

It was their wonderful sure-footedness, sagacity, and docility, however, which most delighted me. They were driven without blinkers or bearing reins, and where, as was often the case, bridges seemed doubtful, the bottom of miry fords suspicious of quagmires, or the road otherwise dangerous, they would put down their heads to examine, try the difficulty with their feet, and, when satisfied, would get through or over places, which seemed utterly impracticable. . . .

Whence this pony breed of Canadians had arisen, I am unable to say; but I believe it to be almost entirely peculiar to the Indian tribes, whereof I am inclined to think it may have been produced by the dwarfing process, which will arise from hardship and privation endured generation after generation, particularly by the young animals and the mares while heavy in foal.

These animals had, I can say almost positively, no recent cross of the Spanish horse.[10]

The French-Canadian horses were much more numerous than the Indian ponies. They were not confined to the French-Canadian settlements, but were found everywhere in the province. Indeed, as Herbert stated, they might "be regarded as the basis of the general horse" of Upper Canada.[11] These horses in the period before 1850 were indubitably among the best in North America. William Evans, the foremost Lower Canadian agricultural authority of the second quarter of the century, merely expressed prevailing Canadian and American opinion when he wrote: "What is known as the 'Canadian horse' of Lower Canada when of sufficient size, cannot be excelled for agricultural purposes by any horse we have ever seen on this continent. They are strong, active and enduring, and not so liable to diseases as other breeds of horses, indeed they appear to be the breed exactly suited for farmers in Canada, so far as we are capable of judging."[12] Before 1850, however, the original French-Canadian stock was considerably modified, especially in central and western Upper Canada, by crossing with the nondescript horses and mares which were imported in large numbers from the United States. Fortunately the French Canadians were excellent for the purpose of crossing, so that in spite of this mongrelization, there was, at least from the functional point of view, scarcely any deterioration in the colts foaled in Upper Canada.[13]

The common horses of Upper Canada—the French Canadians, the "Americans," and their mixed descendants—were kept both for general farm work and for the road. They satisfied the farmer interested only in drawing his grain to the nearest market town, or his family to church or a political meeting, but they fell short of the standards set up by the

[10]Herbert, *Frank Forester's Horse and Horsemanship*, vol. II, pp. 65-6. Cf. also Beaven, *Recreations of a Long Vacation*, p. 56.

[11]Herbert, *Frank Forester's Horse and Horsemanship*. vol. II, p. 47.

[12]*Agricultural Journal and Transactions of the Lower Canada Agricultural Society*, Oct., 1850, p. 304. Cf. Herbert, *Frank Forester's Horse and Horsemanship*, vol. II, pp. 63-4.

[13]*Ibid.*, p. 64; "Ex-Settler," *Canada in the Years 1832, 1833 and 1834.* p. 101; Gourlay, *Statistical Account of Upper Canada*, vol. I, p. 170; *British American Cultivator*, April, 1843, p. 57.

garrison officers, the lawyers and merchants, and even the country people who liked something more pretentious than a "poor man's horse." The latter groups were certain to have horses that they could boast about as soon as the stumps were cleared out of the trails for even a few miles from the villages. The Military Settlement at Perth was only a little more than a dozen years old when the local editor went to a horse-race in the village. "We were much pleased to notice the wonderful improvement, in the breed of horses, which within these few years has taken place in this settlement," ran his comment. "A few years ago only a solitary horse or so could be found in the township, now the majority of the settlers are supplied with good serviceable horses, and in the town there are some *first rates*."[14]

Light horses with some degree of breeding, or at least of style, were imported from the early years of the colony, first from Lower Canada and the United States, and then from the British Isles. Lower Canada furnished the Canadian Pacer, a saddle horse. This was a cross between the French-Canadian horse and the famous Narragansett Pacer, which was brought into Lower Canada from Rhode Island before the American Revolution and for at least two decades after it. There long remained a demand for these Canadian Pacers on the outskirts of settlement, where the roads were not fit for wheeled vehicles.[15] The United States contributed many horses which passed as Thoroughbreds, but which were really mongrels whose sires had been blooded, more or less. An advertisement of 1805 offering for sale "two young mares and colts by the Horse Morgan Rattler"[16] may indicate that Upper Canada had some stock of the Morgan strain then being developed in Vermont. At a later period horses of considerable

---

[14]Perth *Examiner*, quoted in Montreal *Canadian Courant*, Oct. 17, 1829.

[15]*OACR*, vol. v, App. K, pp. 5, 24; *The Spirit of the Times*, Dec. 12, 1846, p. 499.

[16]York *Upper Canada Gazette or American Oracle*, June 8, 1805. Later—about 1820—one of the sons of the famed Justin Morgan, "the Hawkins Horse," who was foaled in Vermont in 1806 or 1807, was brought to Upper Canada from the Eastern Townships. It is not known where he was kept in Upper Canada, nor what became of him, nor whether he left any descendants in the province. Linsley, *Morgan Horses*, pp. 146-7.

distinction were brought north. "Among the American horses standing in Canada this season," a New York journal of the turf remarked in 1842, "we notice two that are well known in this quarter. We refer to *Manalopan*, a fast two mile horse, and *Stanhope*; the latter stands at $25, the former at $18, and both near the St. Leger Course, Toronto."[17] There were few Thoroughbreds imported from England till after 1815. Richard L. Denison in 1859 did recollect one which had enjoyed a great local reputation around York during his boyhood (he was born in 1814)—"Sultan, a celebrated Arabian Stallion, imported into this country by Col. Smith, about the beginning of this century. Sultan was the progenitor of the best road horses ever owned in this district."[18] Though horse men continually advocated the introduction of such horses on a large scale, their suggestions had little result before about 1830. An illustration of the apathy they encountered was found when in 1828 a bill to appropriate a sum of money to import a good stallion or two from England was defeated in the Assembly·by the vote of the farmer members.[19] Before 1840, however, English blood horses were being regularly imported by private individuals.[20] Owing to the increasing popularity of the roadster after about 1835, there was a tendency among Upper Canadian importers to turn to heavier British horses than the Thoroughbred, that is, to light-draft horses of the Cleveland Bay or the hackney type. In this connection it is significant that there was a good showing of hackneys at the exhibitions in Guelph of the Wellington District Agricultural Society in 1842 and of the Guelph Township Agricultural Society in 1847.[21]

---

[17]*The Spirit of the Times*, April 9, 1842, p. 66.

[18]*Transactions of the Board of Agriculture and of the Agricultural Association of Upper Canada for 1859-60*, p. 50. Hereafter this authority is cited as *TBA&AAUC*.

[19]York *Upper Canada Gazette and U. E. Loyalist*, Feb. 16, 1828. The idea behind this bill was probably derived from Nova Scotia. In 1826 the legislature of that province appropriated £1,000 for the purpose of importing Thoroughbreds from England. Three stallions and two mares were in consequence imported (Haliburton, *An Historical and Statistical Account of Nova-Scotia*, vol. I, pp. 312-13).

[20]Duncumb, *The British Emigrant's Advocate*, p. 81; *British American Cultivator*, April, 1846, p. 114.

[21]*Ibid.*, Jan. 1843, p. 12; *ibid.*, April, 1846, p. 115; *Guelph and Galt Advertiser and Wellington District Advocate*, July 2, 1847. It was stated

If the common horses were not altogether suitable for the saddle or the carriage, they were still less suitable for the heavy work on the farms and in the lumber camps which fell to them as the use of oxen declined. At the beginning of the century there were distinctive heavy-draft horses among the Pennsylvania Dutch farmers north of York and in Waterloo County. These horses belonged to the large, strong Conestoga breed then popular for drawing freighters over the Alleghanies. Unfortunately, these splendid "Pennsylvania horses" were on the way to extinction before 1845. A letter from Eli Irwin of Newmarket in 1846 says: "Not many years since this section of the Home District was noted from one end of Canada to the other for its valuable race of horses; and by the introduction of the small race of English blood-horses from England, to cross upon our large Pennsylvania mares [to produce a farm horse quicker in action than the Conestoga], the whole race is considerably run down and reduced in value."[22] Partly because agricultural leaders frequently advocated the bringing in of British heavy-draft horses, which might give weight and strength to the common horses of the province, the place of the Conestogas began to be filled by the cross-bred progeny of imported Clydesdales and Shires. Importations of British heavy-draft breeding stock began as early as 1836, when a Shire stallion was brought to London and a Clydesdale mare to Pickering (Ontario County).[23] The Shires did not prove altogether satisfactory. In 1854 it was stated that there were in Carleton County "a good many descendants of a large dappled grey English waggon horse, who was imported about fifteen years ago, to

---

of the first showing of hackneys at Guelph that "an experienced horseman would have considered that there was scarcely a thorough good hackney in the lot" (*British American Cultivator*, Jan., 1843, p. 12). Shetland ponies, never much more than a curiosity in Upper Canada, were advertised by an Amherstburg breeder in 1847 (*Ohio Cultivator*, vol. III, 1847, p. 129).

[22]*British American Cultivator*, April, 1846, p. 114. The Conestogas disappeared about the same time in Pennsylvania as in Upper Canada, and for the same reason (John Strohm, "The Conestoga Horse," Report of the Commissioner of Agriculture for 1863, *House Executive Document*, 38th Cong., 1st Sess., 1863-4, No. 91, pp. 179-80).

[23]Plumb. *Types and Breeds of Farm Animals*, p. 130; *Cultivator*, April, 1860, p. 132.

be met with. They are large and strong, but rather too slow for the rapid driving of our winter roads."[24] The Clydesdales, however, met with scant criticism. By the early eighteen-fifties grade Clydesdales were dominant among the heavy drafts of Upper Canada. It was probably this infusion of Clydesdale blood that made it possible for Solon Robinson, the well-known American agricultural editor, who had made tours in practically all the settled areas of the United States, to assert in 1850 that "I can count a greater proportion of good substantial, real serviceable farm horses upon this road [Yonge Street near Toronto] than upon any other that I have ever travelled."[25] The Conestoga inheritance may have been a factor in this region, of course. However, five years later another American agricultural editor, who visited the provincial exhibition at Cobourg, was equally emphatic. Noting that all the heavy-draft horses had more or less Clydesdale blood, he declared that "in farm horses the [Upper] Canadians are altogether ahead of the American farmers."[26]

Improvement of cattle did not begin till after 1825. Even then it encountered obstacles. The settler seldom had the capital needed to buy pure-bred stock. Even if he had the chance to breed from the improved stock of a neighbouring gentleman farmer or of an agricultural society, he preferred to utilize the scrub bull of the man across the road, as it would cost him less; or, if the livestock ran at large, nothing at all. If he did happen to rear an animal better than the average, the butcher or drover was practically certain to obtain it, and the farmer continued to breed from the poorer ones that were left. Even where the farmer had capital and was willing to admit the merits of improved stock, he frequently preferred the natives, on the ground that the purebreds were not suited to Upper Canadian conditions.[27] This point

[24]*JTBAUC 1855-6*, p. 462. This is not surprising, for the Shire at this time was little improved over the old English cart horse (Ernle, *English Farming Past and Present*, p. 355).

[25]Kellar, *Solon Robinson, Pioneer and Agriculturist*, vol. II, p. 406. At Kingston, a few days later, Robinson remarked that "horses are not generally so good as at Toronto, and I fancy that there are few places where they are" (*ibid.*, p. 409).

[26]*Cultivator*, Nov., 1855, p. 353.

[27]*Canadian Agriculturist*, Jan., 1850, p. 8; *ibid.*, Sept., 1860, p. 440; *TBA&AAUC 1859-60*, p. 188.

of view was well expressed by William Hutton, who was far
from being an obscurantist.

It appears to me to be one of the greatest inconsistencies, and
indeed absurdities, with which we farmers can be charged, that we
have individually and collectively, as Societies—taken much pains and
incurred much expense to *improve* our breed of cattle, without making
a simultaneous movement to procure the succulent food, the increased
shelter, the extra supply of clover hay, without which these so called
improved breeds certainly produce no improvement to the farmer.
Without turnips or Mangel Wurtzel, or shelter or hay, our old Canadian
cows are infinitely superior to any of these fancy breeds; they produce
more milk on poor feeding—they stand starvation much longer—they
are better suited to our climate, and are in every way better—unless
we change our system of feeding, and furnish warm and comfortable
housing; if we were to furnish these for our native Canadian cows,
it is doubtful whether they would not in the end pay the farmer better
than either the pure Durhams, Devons, or Herefords.[28]

In spite of the apathy of the ordinary farmers, there was
a considerable introduction of improved cattle before 1850.
The constant exhortations of the agricultural periodicals had
something to do with it. There was the example afforded
by the widely publicized importations of New York, Ohio,
and Kentucky cattlemen. Further, agricultural societies usually made a point of spending part of their funds in obtaining
pure-bred bulls from the British Isles or from some of the
New York or local breeders. Finally, private individuals of
some capital, who had been acquainted with improved breeds
in the Old Country, brought out bulls and cows for themselves,
or as a speculation. Some of these men, such as the Hon.
Adam Fergusson of Waterdown, John Wade of Cobourg,
John Miller of Markham, and F. W. Stone of Guelph, were
stock breeders; others may be classified chiefly as gentlemen farmers. Fergusson, who bred Durhams, sold twenty
bulls by 1853—four to individuals in the United States, six
to agricultural societies in Upper Canada, and ten to gentlemen farmers or enterprising ordinary farmers in Upper Canada.[29] The other breeders doubtless had much the same

---

[28]*JTBAUC 1855-6*, pp. 189-90. Cf. *Canada Farmer*, July 1, 1864,
p. 183.

[29]*Canadian Agriculturist*, March, 1853, pp. 69-70. For the work
of the agricultural societies, see Chapter x.

markets. Primarily as a result of the influence and efforts of these cattlemen, certain districts, of which that around Guelph was by far the most important, came to be distinguished by 1850 for the relative excellence of their cattle.[30]

The first pure-bred cattle in Upper Canada were probably Ayrshires. Even before 1800, Scottish shipmasters usually took a few Ayrshire cows aboard to supply their passengers with milk, and sold them on arrival at Montreal or Quebec.[31] In consequence, there came to be a considerable number of Ayrshires in the Montreal region, with an overflow into eastern Upper Canada. Especially in the latter region, but to some extent farther west, Ayrshires continued to be imported by agricultural societies and private individuals down to 1850.[32]

Except in eastern Upper Canada, the dual-purpose Devons were regarded with more favour than the Ayrshires. The cow was a good milker, while the ox compensated by its comparative sprightliness for its deficiency in size. There were many grade Devons in Upper Canada in the second quarter of the century, and some pure-bred ones, a reflection of their popularity in the United States at this time. By 1850 they were being eclipsed in the estimation of breeders by the Durhams. This is evident from a comparison of the number of entries of the two breeds at the provincial exhibitions. In 1849 there were fifty-four Durhams and ten Devons; in 1850, sixty-five Durhams and eighteen Devons; and in 1851, thirty-seven Durhams and eighteen Devons.[33] After 1850 the Devons began to dwindle in number in Upper Canada, as they did everywhere else in North America except in parts of New England, because they were not looked on as being so good for beef as the Durhams.

By 1850, the improved Durham, or Shorthorn, which was

---

[30]*Ibid.*, Sept. 1, 1849, pp. 226, 237; *JTBAUC 1855-6*, pp. 221-2.

[31]Innis (ed.), *Dairy Industry in Canada*, p. 21.

[32]*Canadian Agriculturist*, May, 1851, p. 104; *ibid.*, Oct., 1863, p. 372; *JTBAUC 1855-6*, p. 429.

[33]*JTBAUC 1855-6*, pp. 116, 146, 206. Some time before 1830, Philemon Wright at Hull, L.C., imported Devons to cross on his natives (Bouchette, *The British Dominions in North America*, vol. II, "Hull"). It is probable that some of their descendants came to be owned in adjacent Carleton County, though there is no direct evidence that this was so.

regarded as an excellent general-purpose breed, was the greatest favourite among stock breeders, especially those in central and western Upper Canada; and this primacy it long retained. Durhams appear to have been first imported from both Great Britain and the United States in 1826, when a cow was brought from New York State to St. Catharines, and a bull and a cow from England to St. Thomas. After this time, there was a steady influx of Durhams, particularly from Great Britain, but also from New York, Pennsylvania, and Ohio.[34] The opinion was sometimes expressed that Durhams were being introduced in preference to other British breeds merely because most of the importers were Yorkshiremen who were acquainted with no other varieties.[35] Actually there was at that time a great craze in the United States for Durhams, and the Upper Canada movement was closely associated with it. The effects of their introduction were manifest in Upper Canada by 1845. "Grade Durhams," it was remarked, "are now very common in every section of the province, but those which may be termed pure or well bred are in the hands of a very few."[36]

There were no other improved breeds of cattle in Upper Canada till after 1850.

Improved pigs were imported from overseas but not in great numbers. They were cheap to buy and transport; the losses in crossing the ocean were small, as they were good sailors; and they matured early and multiplied rapidly. The effects of their introduction in quantity would therefore soon have become apparent. Yet, though there were some of the "English breed" in the Talbot settlement as early as 1823,[37] progress in swine improvement was slow. Few but gentlemen farmers were interested in it. Among these breeders the only pure-bred British pigs to achieve popularity were the Berkshires. The first of these to be imported were, it would appear, a boar and a sow brought from Ireland for a

---

[34]Innis (ed.), *Dairy Industry in Canada*, p. 20; *Canadian Agriculturist*, March, 1863, p. 85; *Canada [Shorthorn] Herd Book*, vol. I, pp. xiii-xiv.

[35]*British American Cultivator*, Feb., 1845, p. 39.

[36]*Ibid.*, Feb., 1845, p. 36. Cf. *Cultivator*, Oct., 1845, p. 311.

[37]Talbot, *Five Years' Residence*, vol. I, p. 180.

settler at Peterborough in 1829.[38] Others from England followed, till in 1845 it was explained that the pigs in Peel County
were "partly Berkshire with a pretty good sprinkling of the
alligator and landpike breeds."[39] A few other breeds were
occasionally mentioned. Thus, in the Guelph region in 1841
there were Hampshires, Shropshires, Montgomeryshires, and
Improved Yorkshires.[40] However, on the whole, the farmers
seem to have been satisfied with their pigs as they were.
Certainly they displayed none of the enthusiasm for developing new varieties so characteristic of the Cincinnati region
at that time. They made their money from grain, and had
little hope of competing effectively in swine-raising with the
nascent corn belt.

Much more was accomplished in sheep-breeding, from
about 1830. Previous to that date, Upper Canadian farmers
had been affected by a backwash of the expansion of Merino-
raising in the eastern states. According to Talbot, Lord
Selkirk introduced the first Spanish Merinos into Upper Canada, presumably at his Baldoon settlement near Lake St. Clair
in 1804.[41] Afterwards, apparently in the late eighteen-thirties as in the United States, there was a noticeable demand
for Saxon as well as Spanish Merinos, with full-bred rams of
either kind bringing from £12 to £15. Those who experimented with them found that their mutton was poor and that their
wool was none too readily salable. There was, too, a general
belief that they were not adapted to the climate.[42] In the meantime, in consequence of depressions in fine-wool growing

---

[38]York *Colonial Advocate*, Feb. 4, 1830.

[39]*Cultivator*, Oct., 1845, p. 311. Cf. *JTBAUC 1855-6*, p. 434.

[40]*Cultivator*, Aug., 1841, p. 133. Thomas Rolph mentioned another—
the Norfolk Thin Rind—in Wentworth County in 1835 (*A Brief Account*, p. 235). This breed resembled the Berkshire rather closely
(*Cultivator*, March, 1841, p. 42).

[41]Talbot, *Five Years' Residence*, vol. I, p. 179. Robert Hamilton
of Queenston, writing to John Askin, Dec. 16, 1804, remarked that
"some hundred more Sheep" belonging to Selkirk were wintering at
Queenston, "on their way upward" (Quaife, *John Askin Papers*, vol. II,
p. 446). A local historian says that these Merinos were brought from
Scotland (*Kentiana: The Story of the Settlement and Development of
the County of Kent*, p. 39).

[42]*British American Cultivator*, Sept., 1842, p. 141; Weld, *Vacation
Tour*, p. 99; *JTBAUC 1855-6*, p. 132.

in the United States, such as that of 1827, thousands of grade Merinos were brought across the border, their owners hoping to make more by disposing of them to the Upper Canada farmers than by slaughtering them for pelts and tallow. The result was that by the early eighteen-forties the common sheep of such regions as Haldimand County had become "a degenerate Merino breed, small in size and of little value for mutton, and the selling price, minus the skin, was often as low as one dollar the carcase."[43]

Fortunately the more progressive farmers did not allow their flocks to deteriorate through the addition of these cast-offs. Many of them had known good sheep on the wolds of Yorkshire or the downs of southern England. They had a liking for mutton, a taste which was then notably absent in the northern United States. They had the example of the British farmers on Montreal Island, some of whom imported Leicesters in 1825, that is, as soon as the embargo on the exportation of sheep from the British Isles was lifted.[44] The first Leicesters introduced into Upper Canada were probably a ram taken to Peterborough County in 1829 and a number of ewes and rams brought out by a gentleman farmer in Durham County about 1831.[45] As early as 1826 Colonel Talbot was considering importing Lincolns, but there seems to be no evidence that he did so. However, there were a few Lincolns in Upper Canada in 1842.[46] Southdowns were imported into Dumfries Township (Waterloo County) and into Prince Edward County in 1833.[47] In succeeding years individuals and agricultural societies obtained many other English sheep. As a consequence, as early as 1837 it could be asserted that "the yearly importation of this kind of stock from England has much improved the flocks of the colony."[48]

---

[43]Clarke, *Sixty Years in Upper Canada*, p. 36. Cf. Fothergill, *York Almanac . . . for the Year 1825*, p. 89.

[44]Montreal *Canadian Courant*, March 16, 1833.

[45]York *Colonial Advocate*, Feb. 4, 1830; *Transactions of the Board of Agriculture of Upper Canada 1860-3*, p. 87.

[46]Pickering, *Inquiries of an Emigrant*, p. 88; *British American Cultivator*, Sept., 1842, p. 141.

[47]Shirreff, *Tour through North America*, pp. 145-6; *JTBAUC 1855-6*, p. 428.

[48]Duncumb, *British Emigrant's Advocate*, p. 83.

By the early eighteen-forties the Leicester, with its heavy carcass and long fleece, which was quite satisfactory for domestic yarn-making, had established itself as the favourite breed among the Upper Canadian farmers who desired something superior to the natives. In 1845 the sheep in Peel— a typical county—were described as "principally of the Leicester breed."[49] Southdowns, though they ranked next in popularity, do not seem to have been so evenly distributed throughout Upper Canada as the Leicesters.[50] Both proved extremely valuable in grading up the existing flocks of native or part Merino blood. One authority asserts that "when the Southdown rams were crossed upon the native or common sheep and the Merino ewes there were great improvements, so great that after a few crosses the flocks became more than doubled in size of carcass and weight of fleece, with a fine wool. . . . So powerfully did the Leicester blood work upon these [natives or grade Merinos] that the sheep of the third cross were nearly equal to the Leicesters as mutton sheep, with the advantage of carrying better fleeces."[51] The only difficulty was that after four or five generations the crosses began to deteriorate or "run out," and pure-bred rams had again to be added to the flock.[52]

One result of the predominance of Leicester and Southdown blood in the flocks of the province was that some of the farmers, notably those along Yonge Street, were able by 1850 to develop a profitable winter sideline, that of stall-feeding sheep for the Toronto market.[53] Another result was that the typical wool of Upper Canada by 1850 was a combing wool, which was shortly to obtain a steady market in the United States, as will be shown in another connection. Little fine wool was produced. The president of the provincial Agricultural Association remarked in 1847 that Upper Canadian manufacturers had to depend on American sources for their fine wool, as they were not able to obtain it locally.[54] While

---

[49]*Cultivator*, Oct., 1845, p. 311.
[50]*British American Cultivator*, Aug., 1842, p. 117; *Canadian Agriculturist*, Oct. 10, 1849, p. 257; *ibid.*, Sept., 1858, p. 198.
[51]Carman, Heath, and Minto, *Special Report on the Sheep Industry*, pp. 344-5.
[52]*JTBAUC 1855-6*, p. 190.
[53]*Ibid.*
[54]*Ibid.*, p. 56.

fairly high prices for fine wool did sometimes encourage the introduction of Merinos, as at Cobourg in 1848,[55] the number of these sheep in Upper Canada, either pure-bred or grade, remained small.

There was scarcely any improvement in poultry before 1850, as there was no market for eggs or fowl except in the towns. It is true that here and there was to be found a gentleman farmer who did make a point of introducing new varieties of poultry; there was, for example, one outside St. Catharines in 1847 who had Chinese, Poland, Bremen, and Irish geese, Muscovy and White Topknot ducks, domesticated wild ducks, pheasants, guinea hens, and even prairie hens from Illinois.[56] However, the "Shanghai mania" or "hen fever" which swept over North America beginning in 1849 did not commence to rage in Upper Canada till 1852. When it did, it brought Shanghai, Royal Shanghai, Buff Cochin China, Black Java, Chittagong or Brahmaputra, Black Spanish or Minorca, Dorking, and Poland or Topnot hens; Bremen and Chinese geese; and Aylesbury, Rouen, Poland, and Muscovy ducks into almost every farmyard.[57]

No aspect of agricultural development attracted more attention before 1850 than the improvement of livestock. So much publicity did it receive that the historian is apt to overlook the fact that the average farmer was still contented with the mediocre natives, and most of the pure-breds obtained abroad were still in the possession of breeders. Upper Canada agriculturalists did not have the inducements to improvement afforded the cattle fatteners of Pennsylvania by the butchers of Philadelphia and New York or the Miami Valley swine raisers by the pork packers of Cincinnati. When we take this fact into consideration, we must in fairness conclude that Upper Canada had made respectable progress in its livestock improvement, quite as much indeed as Ohio or Michigan, the American states with which it might be compared.

---

[55]Cobourg *Star*, quoted in *Agricultural Journal and Transactions of the Lower Canada Agricultural Society*, Nov., 1848, p. 345.

[56]*Cultivator*, Feb., 1848, p. 46.

[57]*JTBAUC 1855-6*, pp. 257, 453, 586; *JTBAUC 1856-7*, pp. 131-2. On the origin and growth of the hen fever in the United States, see Cole, "Agricultural Crazes" (*American Economic Review*, vol. XVI, 1936, pp. 634-7).

CHAPTER X

AGRICULTURAL ORGANIZATIONS BEFORE 1850[1]

T HE agricultural organizations of early Upper Canada were not indigenous, but were imitations of those of Great Britain or of the United States. One of them, the agricultural society, was of recent origin. Another, the market fair, had its roots in the medieval world.

The periodical market fairs, of which Stourbridge fair at Cambridge and St. Bartholomew fair near London were the best English examples, were ancient institutions. Merchants from all over Europe attended such fairs to exchange cloth, iron, tar, salt, and furs for wool or other country produce. Acrobats, jugglers, clowns, and mountebanks resorted to them to amuse (and to rook) the peasants. There were similar fairs, usually on a semi-annual basis, in all the seaboard colonies except Connecticut. They provided an opportunity for farmers to buy or trade livestock, implements, and "domestic manufactures," to engage in horse-racing and to watch the catch-penny antics of the entertainers. These colonial fairs had mostly disappeared before the American Revolution, except seemingly on the borders of settlement, where commercial development was still immature. In England, the fairs by this time had lost most of their economic function and had degenerated into scenes of debauchery and vulgar amusement.[2]

The formation of agricultural societies was a part of the agricultural revolution in eighteenth-century Great Britain. The societies were the creation of gentlemen farmers who found it desirable to meet several times a year to argue technical agricultural questions, such as the best crop rotations, the possibility of the transmutation of wheat into chess, telegony, and outcrossing and inbreeding as methods of livestock improvement. The discussions were frequently opened

---

[1]Cf. Talman, "Agricultural Societies of Upper Canada" (*Ontario Historical Society Papers and Records*, vol. XXVII, 1931).

[2]Neely, *Agricultural Fair*, pp. 7-13, 46; True, "Early Development of Agricultural Societies in the United States" (*American Historical Association Report for 1920*, vol. I, pp. 302-3).

by the reading of a learned paper by one of the members. Occasionally prizes were awarded to members who presented reports on experiments on their own farms. There were similar societies in the United States, beginning in 1785. They were modelled largely on the British societies, but they made even less appeal to the average farmer. Their members were usually merchants, lawyers, physicians, clergymen, and politicians, all with a liking for scientific theory, but with little concern for the economic aspects of agriculture. Their meetings and their published transactions closely resembled those of the philosophical societies.[3]

The first agricultural organization in Upper Canada was akin to these "philosophical" agricultural societies of Great Britain and the United States. In November, 1806, Robert Hamilton, its president, asserted that "the Agricultural Society of Niagara has now subsisted with the utmost harmony for upwards of twenty years—If they have not made a great deal of noise, they flatter themselves that they have done some little good."[4] Hamilton exaggerated the age of the society, for it was not organized till the autumn of 1791.[5] It was to this association, under the name of "The Agricultural Society of Upper Canada," that Lieutenant-Governor John Graves Simcoe promised in 1793 to subscribe ten guineas annually to be spent on a premium for the benefit of agriculture.[6] Practical farming was not a qualification for membership, for many of the members, according to a visitor, were merchants and others not directly engaged in "country business." The group met once a month, dined, and chatted about various aspects of rural affairs—probably the state of the crops, the innovations of Bakewell in breeding, the use of plaster of Paris, the treatment of seed wheat for smut, and the like. The society had a small library on British farm-

[3]Neely, *Agricultural Fair*, pp. 37-8, 43-5; True, "Early Development of Agricultural Societies in the United States," pp. 295-9.

[4]York *Upper Canada Gazette*, Nov. 15, 1806.

[5]Gorham, "Development of Agricultural Administration" (manuscript in the Main Library of the Department of Agriculture, Ottawa), p. 1.

[6]E. B. Littlehales to "Secretary of the Agricultural Society of Upper Canada," April 25, 1793, in Cruikshank (ed.), *Correspondence of Lieutenant-Governor John Graves Simcoe*, vol. I, p. 318. Hereafter this authority is cited as *Simcoe Papers*.

ing, the purchase of which was made possible by the gift received from Simcoe.[7] The only tangible achievement that Hamilton claimed for the society was the introduction, before 1796, of several varieties of fruit into the Niagara peninsula.[8]

The society was already moribund in 1806. Indeed, in 1805 its books had been transferred to the library at Niagara.[9] After 1806 there is no further notice of it. Its disappearance did not indicate a complete absence of interest in agricultural organization in Upper Canada, for there were at least two other "learned" agricultural societies in the province before 1812. One was the Burlington Board of Agriculture, established in Wentworth County in 1806.[10] The other was the Upper Canada Agricultural and Commercial Society, which was organized at York, February 22, 1806, under the leadership of Judge Thorpe. It was intended to be a province-wide association, with local subdivisions, which would keep in touch with the parent society at York, and meet with it in annual conventions at the capital.[11] Thorpe may have borrowed the idea of a provincial society from Simcoe, who had cherished the hope of turning the Niagara society into a province-wide one.[12] On the other hand, Thorpe may have merely thought that such a society would be useful in furthering his political ambitions. The history of Thorpe's organization was brief and unhappy. It held several meetings at York, but the prominent politicians who composed its membership evidently failed to pay their annual fee of $2.00. In September, 1807, it lacked even the money to pay for printing its regulations, and after a final meeting in December "to examine the state of its funds," it disappeared.[13]

---

[7]"Canadian Letters" (*Canadian Antiquarian and Numismatic Journal*, 3rd series, vol. IX, 1912, p. 54).

[8]York *Upper Canada Gazette*, Nov. 15, 1806.

[9]Gorham, "Development of Agricultural Administration," p. 1.

[10]Robertson, "First Agricultural Society in the Limits of Wentworth" (*Journal and Transactions of the Wentworth Historical Society*, vol. IV, 1905, pp. 93-4).

[11]Thorpe to Castlereagh, March 4, 1806, in *Canadian Archives Report for 1892*, pp. 41-3.

[12]Simcoe to Robert Hamilton, Jan. 30, 1796, in *Simcoe Papers*, vol. IV, p. 187.

[13]York *Gazette*, Sept. 26, Dec. 23, 1807.

The market fair appeared in the Niagara peninsula at the end of the eighteenth century, possibly as an extension westward of an institution then of some significance in the Genesee Valley.[14] A Niagara newspaper announced in 1799 that in connection with the "annual fair, as established by proclamation," which was to be held at Queenston the next day, a park was provided for a "show of horses, cattle, sheep, and hogs."[15] As no mention is made of competition or of premiums, it may be assumed that the stock was displayed simply for educational purposes. Presumably most of it belonged to members of the agricultural society at Niagara. A similar provision was made two years later, with the addition of "races and other amusements."[16]

The history of this fair after 1801 is exceedingly obscure. It is possible that it disappeared when regular markets were established, as at York in 1804. There is no mention of it or of any other till the early eighteen-twenties, when Charles Fothergill stated that there were three in Upper Canada. These were being held semi-annually at Port Hope, Cobourg, and York. That at York lasted six days each time, the others four. At the Port Hope fair, which was "well attended and well conducted," the first day was "appropriated to the exhibition of choice stock and the distribution of Premiums;— The *Second* day for the Sale of Horses;—The *Third* for Horned Cattle, Sheep, and Hogs;—and the *Fourth* for articles of Domestic Manufacture."[17] The livestock show of the first day, with its element of competition, reveals that the market fair was acquiring some of the characteristics of the modern agricultural exhibition. However, neither the livestock show nor the fair as a whole was sponsored by an agricultural society. This was also true of the one-day fair at Perth in 1829, which likewise had a cattle show in connection with it. In the late afternoon, when business grew dull, the crowd set off "to the usual race ground," where several

---

[14]There is mention of such an annual fair for selling cattle, horses, and sheep at the Great Forks of the Genesee River (Albany, N. Y., *Gazette*, July 15, 1793, quoted in Doty, *History of Livingston County, New York*, p. 251).

[15]Niagara *Canada Constellation*, Nov. 8, 1799.

[16]Niagara *Herald*, Oct. 17, 1801.

[17]Fothergill, *York Almanac . . . for the Year 1825*, p. 147.

heats were run for "private wagers."[18] Probably the horse-
racing was an outcome of challenges issued and accepted in
the midst of the bargaining over livestock, for the reference
to private wagers would indicate that the fair managers had
not offered any purse.

Other fairs appeared in the eighteen-thirties. The hope
that one at Bytown would provide a cash market for cattle,
grain, and goods of various kinds collapsed when the horse-
race which followed the first (1830) terminated in a riot
with much head-breaking by the lawless Irish lumberjacks
("Shiners"). The authorities then forbade the holding of
any more fairs at Bytown.[19] A quarterly fair was established
at Richmond Hill in 1833 for the purpose of "buying and
selling all kinds of stock, produce and farming utensils, likewise the hiring of labourers."[20] There was a fair, intended
to be annual, in Toronto Township, Peel County, the same
year.[21] In 1836 it was asserted that "that valuable European
custom of holding Fairs semi-annually is fast gaining ground
in this Province," and a recent fair at Napanee was offered
in evidence. At this fair 108 horses, 100 cows, 47 oxen, and
40 young cattle were brought in by farmers for sale, together
with about 1,200 bushels of grain.[22] Other fairs were established in Frontenac County about 1840. These proved a
failure. The farmers, it was charged, did not bring forward
articles to sell.[23] It might better have been said that in
consequence of the American competition described in a previous chapter, the prices offered were no inducement to them
to do so. As a matter of fact, the only Upper Canada fair
which was able to maintain a continuous existence was that
at Perth, which was sustained by the lumbermen's need of
horses and oxen. By 1850, fairs in the province were "so

---

[18]Perth *Examiner*, quoted in Montreal *Canadian Courant*, Oct. 17,
1829.

[19]Montreal *Canadian Courant*, Sept. 8, 1830; *Illustrated Historical
Atlas of the County of Carleton*, p. xi.

[20]York *Colonial Advocate*, Feb. 14, 1833.

[21]*Ibid.*, May 30, 1833.

[22]Kingston *Chronicle*, quoted in Rolph, *Brief Account . . . Made
during a Visit*, pp. 161-2.

[23]*Canadian Agriculturist*, Dec., 1852, p. 363.

few and far between that they are but little known, and less heard of."[24]

Probably most of these fairs came into existence in the fashion of that at Richmond Hill, which was organized at a public meeting held for the purpose. However, some of them were sponsored by agricultural societies in connection with their exhibitions. This was seemingly the case with the Perth fair after the first few years of its existence. The Western District Agricultural Society in 1837 obtained a charter for a semi-annual fair at Sandwich, with the intention of combining the fall one with its exhibition, and the Chinguacousy Township branch of the Home District Agricultural Society about 1845 began to hold a semi-annual "fair and cattle show" at Brampton. At both Sandwich and Brampton premiums were offered for the best cattle, horses, and other livestock, and the animals were then put up for sale, with the owners having the right to bid them in.[25] The Niagara District Agricultural Society likewise had semi-annual fairs and cattle shows in 1847, that in the spring being intended primarily for hiring labourers and exchanging or selling livestock.[26]

The market fairs had some of the characteristics of the agricultural exhibition, but on the whole their contributions to improvement of livestock were only incidental to their commercial function. Their achievements as agents of betterment were therefore trifling in comparison with those of the agricultural societies which appeared soon after Upper Canada recovered from the War of 1812. These new organizations were in general to be classed among the "practical" agricultural societies of the type originated by Elkanah Watson at Pittsfield, Massachusetts. They differed from the learned agricultural societies in that they tried to appeal to men who made their living from farming. Even so, a glance at the lists of their directors shows that it was long before politicians and gentlemen farmers ceased to dominate them.

[24]*Ibid.*, p. 361.

[25]*Address of the Directing President of the Western District Agricultural and Horticultural Society*, p. 11; *Journal and Transactions of the Board of Agriculture of Upper Canada for 1855-6*, p. 351. Hereafter this authority will be cited as *JTBAUC*.

[26]*Cultivator*, Feb., 1848, p. 46.

It is possible that the new associations in Upper Canada were modelled directly on Watson's "Berkshire system," for by 1819 there were many societies in New England based on it, and even a few west of the Alleghanies, but there is no direct evidence to this effect, and it is more likely that they were imitations of the societies established elsewhere in British America (as at Quebec and Montreal in 1817) by settlers from England and Scotland. Certainly the men who brought them into existence were mostly old countrymen. A Scottish visitor to Kingston in 1832 tells that "I rode out . . . to see a ploughing-match, and show of cattle, at the village of Waterloo [now Cataraqui], some miles off; and I could have fancied myself at a similar exhibition at home. The faces round me were almost all Scotch, as was the conversation."[27]

Evidently the first of the new Upper Canada societies was the Upper Canada Agricultural Society at York. Though it resembled the learned agricultural bodies of an earlier day in that it was made up of urban residents rather than of farmers, it differed from them in its activities, for it held a "cattle show" in 1820, at which it awarded prizes to the owners of the three best horses and of the three best bulls.[28] It is impossible to state to what extent this action was an indication of the influence of the Berkshire plan, of which the cattle show, with the offering of prizes, was an integral part. A second society—the Frontenac Agricultural Society—was organized at Waterloo, in July, 1825. Its directors drew up a list of prizes to be offered at an exhibition in October. When the exhibition was held, premiums were accordingly awarded not only for the best livestock, but also for such articles as cheese, flannel, and maple sugar, for the best two acres of wheat, oats, and peas respectively, for the best acre of Indian corn, barley, and potatoes respectively, and for ploughing with horses and oxen respectively.[29] There seems

[27]Alexander, *Transatlantic Sketches*, vol. II, pp. 167-8. On the origin and development of the Berkshire plan, see Neely, *Agricultural Fair*, pp. 50-71.

[28]York *Upper Canada Gazette*, May 18, 1820.

[29]Kingston *Upper Canada Herald*, Aug. 9, Oct. 18, 1825. The prize list is printed in Talman, "Agricultural Societies of Upper Canada," p. 551.

to have been only one other such society in existence before 1830. This was the Northumberland County Agricultural Society established, probably in 1828, at or near Cobourg.[30] These societies had little vitality. That at York had collapsed by 1827, for there was then talk of founding a new one.[31] A similar fate may have overtaken the Frontenac Agricultural Society, for after 1825 there is no mention of it. It is equally likely, however, that it preserved a tenuous existence till about 1830. The fact that its successor, the Midland District Agricultural Society, held its exhibition at Waterloo might argue a continuity of meetings and competitions for prizes there. As for the accomplishments of these societies of the eighteen-twenties, it is enough to notice that their activities were only a vague memory when in 1855 the first historian of agricultural organizations in Upper Canada undertook to investigate them.[32]

Though these societies were failures, the work they attempted seemed potentially useful. Editors and others pointed this out, and campaigned for governmental assistance. Partly influenced by these representations, and partly by the example afforded by recent laws in the neighbouring states, the provincial legislature agreed to subsidize agricultural societies to a limited degree. In March, 1830, it passed a law providing for the payment by the government of £100 to any "district agricultural society" which raised £50 by subscription. (A "district" was a unit of local government which included several counties.) In 1837 a new act—the first had expired after five years—retained the double subsidy principle, but reduced the minimum amount to be subscribed to £25, and fixed the maximum that the government might be called on to pay at £200. A further amendment in 1845 altered the double subsidy to a treble one, with a maximum grant of £250. If, instead of having one society for the whole "district," the constituent counties decided to have separate societies of their own, they could obtain, under all these laws, their proportionate share of the amount otherwise payable

---

[30]Talman, "Agricultural Societies of Upper Canada," p. 551; *Canadian Agriculturist*, Aug. 16, 1862, p. 490.

[31]York *Upper Canada Gazette and U. E. Loyalist*, Oct. 20, 1827.

[32]*JTBAUC 1855-6*, p. 4.

to the district society. In 1851 a final act authorized the formation of county societies (the district as a unit of local administration having disappeared) when fifty persons each subscribed 5s., and promised such societies a maximum subsidy of £250 on the treble basis. These county societies were authorized in turn to support township agricultural societies, provided that the members of a township society raised £17 10s. by subscription.[33]

The law of 1830 stimulated a fresh interest in agricultural societies. A Home District Agricultural Society was formed at York in May, 1830, and four other district societies —the Western, the Johnstown, the Gore, and the Eastern— in time to obtain grants from the provincial treasury in 1831. In addition to these the Durham County Agricultural Society received a grant. On the other hand, the Midland District society, which was organized before November, 1830, did not receive one, presumably because its subscription list was not filled. By the end of 1831 there were societies in the Niagara, the Newcastle, and the Ottawa districts, and in the counties of Kent and Northumberland. The Northumberland County society was a reorganization of the one established in the late eighteen-twenties. The Bathurst District and Leeds County each had a society in 1832, the Prince Edward District one in 1833, and the London District one before 1836. This meant that there was one in every district, at least on paper. In 1841, when two recently created districts, the Brock and the Wellington, had been added to the number, the total government grant to the district societies amounted to £1,607.[34]

---

[33]These acts (11 George IV, c. 10; 7 Will. IV, c. 25; 8 Vic., c. 54; and 14 & 15 Vic., c. 73) are summarized in *JTBAUC 1855-6*, pp. 5-11. Occasionally the societies were subsidized by the municipal governments. The Prescott County society received £88 from the treasury of the Ottawa District in 1844 and again in 1848 (Thomas, *History of the Counties of Argenteuil, Quebec, and Prescott, Ontario*, pp. 475-6). It is also worth mentioning that in 1843 the Canada Company gave the Wellington District Agricultural Society $40.00 to be used for two special prizes for fall wheat at its forthcoming exhibition at Guelph (*British American Cultivator*, Jan., 1843, p. 12).

[34]Gorham, "Development of Agricultural Administration," pp. 5-13; Talman, "Agricultural Societies of Upper Canada," p. 550; *Genesee Farmer*, vol. II, 1832, p. 8; *Hallowell Free Press*, May 28, 1833.

To realize their aim of stimulating agricultural improvement among the practical farmers, the societies of the eighteen-thirties and eighteen-forties sponsored demonstrations of new implements and introduced new or improved seeds. An example of the latter activity was found when the Home District society in 1831 imported seed wheat from England, as well as Dalhousie, Angus, and Potato oats.[35] The Prince Edward District society about 1834 obtained gypsum for its members, and offered premiums to encourage the growing of clover. In 1833 it selected and distributed a number of Leicester and Southdown rams and ewes, the influence of which was noticeable in the flocks of the region twenty years later. At the same time, it purchased two bulls, a small one reserved for the members of the society, and a large one which outsiders might rent.[36] Other societies likewise placed much emphasis on grading up livestock, particularly cattle. The Northumberland County society imported Durhams from New York in 1832. The Home District society sent one of its directors to Canandaigua, N.Y., in 1833, to purchase three or four bulls for an amount not to exceed £100. The "inferior brutes" he obtained were then rented to members of the society. After about 1840, the Bathurst District society at Perth spent much of its funds in introducing improved breeds of sheep, hogs, cattle, and horses.[37] If the state of their funds permitted, the societies held shows or exhibitions at which premiums were given. Though the exhibition of the Home District society seems to have been the only one held in the province in 1830, in 1831 there were at least three in addition to it. These were that of the Gore District society, at Hamilton, that of the Niagara District society, at Clinton, and that of the Kent County society, at Raleigh. There is no reason to doubt that most of the other district and county societies organized under the provisions of the act of 1830 likewise had their exhibitions shortly after their establishment. An obviously incomplete list of

---

[35]York *Colonial Advocate*, Oct. 27, 1831.

[36]*Hallowell Free Press*, May 28, 1833; *JTBAUC 1855-6*, pp. 428-9.

[37]York *Colonial Advocate*, April 18, 1833; Jones, "Diary 1837" (*Willison's Monthly*, July, 1929, p. 15); *Canadian Agriculturist*, May, 1851, p. 106; *ibid.*, July, 1852, p. 207.

1842 announced that the exhibition of the Home District
society would be held at Toronto, that of the Gore District
society at Dundas, that of the Wellington District society at
Guelph, that of the Durham County society at Bowmanville,
and that of the Northumberland County society at Grafton.[38]

The scanty evidence available indicates that the exhibitions of the eighteen-twenties and eighteen-thirties were
imitations of those which their organizers had known elsewhere or had read about. While Upper Canadians probably
based their agricultural societies on old-country models, they
must have been well acquainted with the Berkshire plan of
holding exhibitions, considering the strength of American
cultural influence in the province. Under this plan, the exhibition sometimes opened with a parade from a meeting-place,
such as the town hall or court house, to the town common.
Here the spectators would form a ring, into which the competing animals were led. The judging was sure to be ama-
teurish, with plenty of comments from the by-standers.
After the grain and other articles were judged, there might
be a ploughing match, and during the late afternoon, some
trading or selling of livestock and articles of domestic manufacture. Then the members of the society would go to a tavern
for a banquet, or merely return to the town hall or the court
house for their business meeting. In either case, they listened
to an address on a topic of agricultural interest, delivered by
the president of the society or by some notable outsider. The
speech was ordinarily the last item on the day's programme,
though occasionally "agricultural balls" were held in the
evening. The parade, the ploughing match, the sale, and the
ball were not to be found in every Berkshire exhibition in
the United States, and the parade and the ball do not seem
to have obtained the slightest foothold in Upper Canada; but
both north and south of the border the "show" and the address were regarded as essential. The fact that some features
of the Berkshire plan failed to appear in Upper Canada may
be attributed to the desire of the promoters of the exhibitions

---

[38]York *Colonial Advocate*, Aug. 22, Oct. 27, 1831; *Genesee Farmer*,
vol. II, 1832, p. 8; *Cultivator*, Sept., 1842, p. 141.

to follow English and Scottish prototypes rather than American.[39]

The reports of the societies of the period before 1850 are notably lacking in references to horse-racing in connection with their exhibitions. Horse-racing, it is true, was a popular pastime in Upper Canada, as the references to it earlier in this chapter in connection with the market fairs would indicate. Even so, only one society appears to have attempted to incorporate racing in its programme. This was the Western District Agricultural Society, which in 1837 provided for two races at its fall exhibition, one for trotting horses and the other for saddle horses. Whether these races were held is a matter of doubt, however, for the president of the society admitted that the exhibition of 1837 was a failure, and made no specific mention of any racing.[40] Though the directors of the other agricultural societies knew that horse-racing had the advantage of being certain to draw a crowd, they were aware that it had little other merit. The people attracted by it were not likely to be much interested in agricultural improvement. The race might not end in a riot, as did that at Bytown in 1830, but it was apt to be so disreputable as to discredit the society. So much is clear from the description Edward Talbot wrote of one he attended about 1820.

I once went to a horse-race, that I might witness the speed of their sorry *chevaux*, as they cantered over a quarter of a mile course. Four horses started for a bet of 10,000 *feet of boards*. The riders were clumsy-looking fellows, bootless and coatless. Before they started, every one seemed anxious to bet upon some one or other of the horses. Wagers were offered in every part of the field, and I was soon assailed by a host of fellows, requesting me to take their offers. The first who attracted my notice, said, he would bet me *a barrel of salt pork* that Split-the-wind would win the day. When I refused to accept of this,

---

[39]An adequate description of an Upper Canada exhibition in 1842— that of the Wellington District Agricultural Society at Guelph—will be found in *British American Cultivator*, Jan., 1843, p. 12. For descriptions of American exhibitions held under the Berkshire plan, see Neely, *Agricultural Fair*, p. 64; and Woodward, *Development of Agriculture in New Jersey*, pp. 170-7.

[40]"Report of the Executive Committee of the Western District Agricultural and Horticultural Society" (broadside); *Address of the Directing President of the Western District Agricultural . . . Society*, p. 11.

another offered to bet me 3,000 *cedar shingles* that Washington would distance "every d------d scrape of them." A third person tempted me with a wager of *50 lbs. of pork sausages*, against *a cheese of similar weight*, that Prince Edward would be distanced. A fourth, who appeared to be a shoemaker, offered to stake *a raw ox-hide*, against half its weight in *tanned leather*, that Columbus would be either first or second. Five or six others, who seemed to be partners in *a pair of blacksmith's bellows*, expressed their willingness to wager them against *a barrel of West Indian molasses*, or twenty dollars in cash. In the whole course of my life, I never witnessed so ludicrous a scene.[41]

It was not till about 1865 that "trials of speed" or trotting races became parts of Upper Canada exhibitions, and then the directors admitted them half apologetically, as will be shown in Chapter XIX.

The societies, the activities of which have been described thus far, were all organized on the district or county basis. In addition to them there were scattered and often short-lived societies which drew their support from limited areas. They comprised two distinct types, the "local" or "township" agricultural society, and the "farmers' club."

Possibly the first of the "local" societies to be organized was that of "Colborne and Cobourg," which was in existence before March, 1830. There were several more in the eighteen-thirties, including one for Oro, Orillia, and Thorah townships, Simcoe County, one for Richmond village and its environs, and one for Whitby and Pickering townships, Ontario County.[42] Others appeared in the eighteen-forties, as we know from occasional references to them in the newspapers and agricultural journals. In general, the local societies imitated the activities of the district and county societies, at least to the extent that their resources permitted. The share of the Otonabee and Asphodel society in the distribution of Red Fife wheat was mentioned in Chapter VI. The Kitley Township (Leeds County) society, which in 1849 purchased

---

[41]*Five Years' Residence*, vol. II, pp. 58-9. Organized racing under the auspices of regular turf clubs first became important in Upper Canada about 1840. The best source of information on this subject is *The Spirit of the Times*, which carried accounts of the meets at such places as Toronto, Cobourg, Kingston, Prescott, Cornwall, Caledonia Springs, Niagara, Hamilton, and London.

[42]Talman, "Agricultural Societies of Upper Canada," pp. 546, 550-1.

a bull for the use of its members, was cited as one of several in eastern Upper Canada which had imported livestock.[43] Others gave premiums for root crops in the field. Whenever they could, they held modest exhibitions. In some instances these were scheduled to take place a week or two in advance of the exhibition of the county society. The subscribers of the local society were then encouraged to compete at the county show, one inducement being the waiver of any entry fee.[44]

The "farmers' clubs" were sometimes associated with the local agricultural societies, but usually they were independent of them. They were devoted solely to the discussion of agricultural problems, and so resembled in some respects the earlier learned agricultural societies. Their origins were diverse. Some were modelled on British farmers' clubs, with which many of the better-class immigrants in Canada West had been associated or acquainted. Others were imitations of the farmers' clubs of New York, which received wide publicity in the agricultural press during the middle eighteen-forties. A few, like that at Newmarket, were products of the adult education movement, which in the towns and even small villages took the form of the creation of Mechanics' Institutes, which were combinations of lending libraries and debating societies. One correspondent remarked in 1847 that nearly every township in Upper Canada had a debating society, which argued such subjects as whether the horse or the ox was the more useful.[45] The first farmers' clubs in Upper Canada were organized at Richmond Hill and at Newmarket in 1844, and at Cobourg in 1846. That at Cobourg fell through, was reorganized in 1851, and served as a model for many others. The one at Richmond Hill shortly disappeared. At Newmarket there were several meetings, including one which considered the problem of wheat cultivation. Another club, formed in York Township in 1847, was addressed by several speakers on the system of farm management best adapted

[43]*Canadian Agriculturist*, July 2, 1849, p. 171.

[44]*Ibid.*, Aug. 16, 1862, p. 490; *JTBAUC 1855-6*, pp. 224-5.

[45]*British American Cultivator*, Feb., 1847, p. 44. For an interesting description of these debates, see Haight, *Country Life in Canada*, pp. 20-3.

to the township.[46] Lacking financial resources, such clubs could not attract members by sponsoring competitions. Only a handful of "book-farmers" attended their meetings. The clubs had, therefore, less influence than the township agricultural societies.

The progress of the agricultural societies, whether district, county, or township, was a disappointment to their promoters and friends. Often their lives were brief, on account of lack of interest or of funds. Even when they had a fairly prosperous career, it was sometimes doubtful if they accomplished much, or if what they did accomplish was worth doing. An acidulous critic of the Huron District Agricultural Society (organized in 1842) charged that it had suffered from jealousies and the formation of cliques among its members, from alleged favouritism in the distribution of premiums, from squandering its funds in premiums for articles that had little or nothing to do with agriculture, and from an emphasis on the introduction of improved livestock instead of on the encouragement of neater fields, improved cultivation, and better buildings. "In plain language," his blast concluded, "it might be said that almost the only visible object of the society is, to receive the required amount of subscriptions and the Legislative grant, and to divide the amount 'sum total,' amongst themselves, in the name of premiums for animals that are kept from year to year for the special purpose." These defects in policy were not the monopoly of this society, but were characteristic, so he asserted, of the most of those in the province.[47]

The leaders of agriculture in Upper Canada believed that one cause of the weakness of the societies was merely the absence of common organization, for as yet most of the township societies lacked direct connections with the county societies, while the county and district societies lacked connections with one another. This condition, they thought, could be remedied if there was a provincial society to co-ordinate the activities of the district, county, and township societies, and to bring the inhabitants of Upper Canada and the best

---

[46]*British American Cultivator*, Jan., 1845, p. 2; *ibid.*, Feb., 1845, p. 42; *ibid.*, March, 1845, p. 68; *ibid.*, April, 1846, p. 114; *ibid.*, March, 1847, p. 90; *Canadian Agriculturist*, Aug. 16, 1862, p. 490.
[47]*JTBAUC 1856-7*, pp. 196-7.

of their produce together at an exhibition in one place. They found models in the Highland and Agricultural Society of Scotland, the Royal Agricultural Improvement Society of Ireland, the Royal Agricultural Society of England, and especially in the New York [State] Agricultural Society, which, after nine years of dragging existence, began to flourish in 1841. "Many farmers and others from this Province," we are told, "visited the annual exhibitions of that Society, and became anxious to establish one of the same kind here." W. G. Edmundson, editor of the *British American Cultivator*, was a constant advocate of the creation of such a society. The first step towards setting one up was taken in November, 1843, when a few dozen men, including the officers of some of the district and township societies, gathered at Toronto. They passed resolutions in favour of the establishment of a provincial association, under which the district and county societies should operate. The immediate result of the recommendation was plenty of discussion, but no definite action. In July, 1846, delegates from the county and district societies met at Toronto, on the invitation of the Home District society, and resolved to form an "Agricultural Association of Upper Canada." A second meeting at Hamilton in August adopted a constitution and chose officers. The new society was incorporated the next year. Its board of directors consisted of two delegates from each of the district societies. The delegates were to elect a president, two vice-presidents, and a secretary-treasurer from among themselves.[48]

While the Agricultural Association was still in process of organization in the summer of 1846, its management committee decided to hold a provincial (Upper Canadian) exhibition at Toronto in October, and got out handbills offering premiums in money and books to the amount of about £400. It was a venturesome project, for the Association had no funds at all at the time. However, before and during the exhibition it collected a total of £482—£100 from the Home District Agricultural Society, £97 from seven other agricultural societies, £50 from the Canada Company, about £70 from the sale of admission tickets, and the rest from subscriptions by its members. It had the good fortune, moreover,

---

[48]*JTBAUC 1855-6*, pp. 17-24, 41-2, 45-6. The act of incorporation was 10 and 11 Vic., c. 61.

to find that the steamship and stage lines would carry visitors to the exhibition at half-fare. In view of the infancy of the Association, the exhibition was remarkably successful. About 1,100 items were entered in competition, including livestock, grain, fruit, vegetables, dairy products, and farm implements. The highest premiums were awarded for livestock—£7 10s. for the best bull, £10 for the best stallion, £5 for the best ram, and £5 for the best boar. As no entries were made in certain classes, the premiums paid amounted to only £287. The exhibition was conducted in about the same manner as those of the local societies, though on a more elaborate scale. The exhibits were judged the morning and afternoon of the first day. In the evening a banquet was held, at which addresses were given by the Chief Justice and the Superintendent of Education. During the morning of the second day there was a ploughing match on the outskirts of the city, and in the evening an address by the Hon. Adam Fergusson.[49]

The directors and members of the Association were so well satisfied with this exhibition that they determined to hold one annually thereafter, rotating it among the different districts, according to the plan then and for long afterwards common in the United States. The directors made thorough preparations for the exhibition of 1847, which was to be held at Hamilton. They increased the list of prizes to about £750, including a special prize of £25 offered by the Canada Company for the best twenty-five bushels of fall wheat, the produce of the 1847 crop in Upper Canada. They erected temporary buildings to house manufactures, dairy products, grain, and fruit, and a board fence to confine the livestock and exclude non-paying spectators. Though the number of entries was 1,700, the exhibition was not as great a success as that of 1846, partly because the weather was unfavourable, but mostly because W. G. Edmundson, then treasurer of the Association, departed for the United States before the accounts were settled, taking with him about £289 belonging to it. This left the Association with only £382 in its treasury, an amount which fell £154 short of meeting its liabilities.[50]

---

[49]*JTBAUC 1855-6*, pp. 25-30, 40-4.
[50]*Ibid.*, pp. 42, 47-8, 65-6. An excellent though somewhat facetious description of this exhibition is to be found in *Canada Farmer*, Oct. 9, 1847, pp. 142-3.

Only slightly discouraged by this situation, the Association held its exhibition at Cobourg in 1848. Benefiting from their earlier mistakes, its officers were able to conduct it in a fashion so satisfactory that it served as a model for a decade. They built a high board fence to enclose a circular area of seven or eight acres, a row of pens adjoining the fence for cattle, sheep, and swine, and three sheds near the centre for fine arts, domestic manufactures, flowers, vegetables, and grain. They had the implements set out in a row between the pens and the sheds, and assigned to the horses a place towards the centre of the enclosure. They planned a five-day programme. The first day the exhibits were to be entered and arranged, the second day they were to be judged, and the third and fourth the public was to be admitted to view them. On the afternoon of the fourth day the address was to be given, and in the evening the usual dinner. On the fifth day there was to be a ploughing match. The directors rented the right to locate booths on the grounds, an innovation that showed that grocers and others were counting on a good crowd. Finally, the directors decided to pay all the premiums in money, and when they gave diplomas, to award them to the winners of the highest prize, instead of the lowest, as they had done earlier. The exhibition proved to be so successful that fears that the Association would collapse were ended.[51]

The exhibitions of 1849 at Kingston and of 1850 at Niagara were likewise successful. At the latter, 10,000 tickets for single admissions were sold. This was the first provincial exhibition which was subsidized by the government. The grant was £600.[52]

By the end of 1850, the leaders of the Agricultural Association could feel well satisfied with their accomplishments. They had done something to co-ordinate the activities of the district and county societies. Relying on private financial support, they had provided in the exhibitions an opportunity for the farmers of Upper Canada to become acquainted with better livestock and more modern implements than they could see in their own neighbourhoods. They had succeeded in making the exhibition a social institution, for in 1850 the

---

[51]*JTBAUC 1855-6*, pp. 69-75.

[52]These exhibitions are described in *JTBAUC 1855-6*, pp. 79-82, 112-17, 130-5, 144-8.

steamboats to Niagara were crowded to excess with visitors from every port on Lake Ontario and Lake Erie. As yet they were not vexed with the worries associated with sideshows and horse-racing. They had wrought well, and could look forward with confidence to a future which, as it turned out, was to be one of steady expansion. Their accomplishments in the period after 1850, as well as those of the local societies, will be discussed in a later chapter.

It will be evident from the foregoing account that it is easier to over-estimate the importance of the early agricultural societies than to under-estimate it. Often the interest in agricultural improvement was confined to a handful of public-spirited men in each community. This is sufficiently shown by the limited appeal of the agricultural journals of the eighteen-forties. For those who could benefit from them, these had leading articles on agricultural prospects, discussions of new or approved methods of arable farming, excerpts from other agricultural periodicals, and even whole books serialized, such as a "practical veterinary." Yet in 1841 the *Genesee Farmer* of Rochester, then the only agricultural journal readily available, had a circulation of only 1,500 or so in Upper Canada; and in 1847 the *British American Culti-vator* had only about 6,000 subscribers and the *Canada Farmer* only about 2,000.[53] As there were by 1850 nearly 100,000 occupiers of lots of ten acres or over in Upper Canada, it is surely safe to state that not one farmer in ten ordinarily read an agricultural periodical, except perhaps as it reached him second-hand in the exchange column of his weekly newspaper. The great majority, who had most need of instruction, had an unconquerable aversion to book-farming, unless consulting the almanac for the weather forecasts and the phases of the moon might be dignified by this name. Under these circumstances, it was inevitable that till the Agricultural Association grew in strength, it was a day of small things with the agricultural societies from beginning to end. The most that can be said for them is that their accomplishments were respectable for the time, and worthy of comparison with those of the same era in some of the foremost agricultural regions in the United States.

[53]*British American Cultivator*, Jan., 1842, p. 1; *Agriculturist and Canadian Journal*, Aug. 15, 1848, p. 134; *ibid.*, Dec. 15, 1848, p. 182.

CHAPTER XI

THE AMERICAN MARKET, 1847-1861

I T was pointed out at the end of Chapter VIII that the repeal of the Corn Laws by the British parliament in 1846 caused much disquiet throughout Upper Canada. To what extent were the forebodings of farmers and merchants justified by events?

The milling and forwarding interests in the Province of Canada certainly suffered grave loss. They had heavy stocks of flour on hand when, early in 1847, after a period of speculative activity, British prices suddenly collapsed. They tried desperately to recapture the flour market of the Maritimes, which they had virtually abandoned to the Americans in recent years. They were much encouraged by an arrangement made in 1850 for the free interchange of the natural products of Canada and the provinces of Nova Scotia, New Brunswick, and Prince Edward Island, for this had the effect of eliminating duties on Canadian flour which had ranged from 25 to 75 cents a barrel.[1] Their substantial gains in the Maritimes they nevertheless considered slight compensation for their unfavourable position in the overseas trade. Forwarders, who in the period of the Canada Corn Law

---

[1]Tansill, *Canadian Reciprocity Treaty of 1854*, p. 36; Andrews, "Report on Trade and Commerce" (*House Executive Document*, 32nd Cong., 1st Sess., 1852-3, no. 136, p. 415). Hereafter this authority is cited as Andrews, "Second Report." The measure of the success of the Canada exporters is found in the returns of the imports of the Maritimes from the St. Lawrence Valley and from American ports respectively. Exports of flour from the Province of Canada to the Maritimes by sea are given in the first column; those from the Province of Canada to the Maritimes in bond through the United States in the second; and those from the United States to the Maritimes in the third.

1844 .... 19,530 barrels		
1845 26,694		
1846 35,152		310,091 barrels
1847 66,195		272,299
1848 65,834	7,454 barrels	274,206
1849 79,492	4,311	294,891
1850 140,872	39,723	214,934
1851 154,766	79,806	200,664

(Andrews, "Second Report," pp. 414, 435).

had flourished on the transit grain trade from the American West, found their business at an end. It was to no avail that the Canadian legislature in 1846 repealed the 3s. duty on American wheat, except that imported for consumption.[2] Without the preference it was cheaper to export American oreadstuffs by the Erie Canal than by the St. Lawrence route. Not only did the forwarders lose this profitable trade, but they were threatened with the complete loss of that of Upper Canada as well. A United States Drawback Act of 1846 made it possible to send Canadian products to the seaboard in bond. The first to take advantage of it were a few American speculators who appeared in Upper Canada on the opening of navigation in 1847 to buy wheat for shipment through the Erie Canal.[3] By 1850 more Upper Canadian wheat and flour were being exported in bond through New York than were going down the St. Lawrence.[4]

The farming community in Upper Canada did not suffer from the repeal of the Corn Laws as did the Montreal commercial groups. Till 1849, colonial grain continued to enter Great Britain at 1s. a quarter duty, while foreign grain was still subject to a modified sliding scale.[5] The wheat crops of 1847 and 1848 in central and western Upper Canada were about average, and that of 1849 the greatest which had ever been harvested.[6] Though, as was mentioned in earlier chapters, the agricultural interests dependent on the lumbering industry in the Ottawa Valley were severely affected by

---

2 9 Vic., c. 1 (*Statutes of Canada*).

3Quebec *Mercury*, April 20, 1847, quoted in Burn, "Canada and the Repeal of the Corn Laws" (*Cambridge Historical Journal*, vol. II, 1928, p. 264).

4Exports by the St. Lawrence are given in the first column and those through the United States in the second.

Flour 1850	280,618 barrels	404,103 barrels
Wheat 1850	88,465 bushels	1,353,363 bushels
Flour 1851	371,610 barrels	313,284 barrels
Wheat 1851	161,312 bushels	790,678 bushels

(Andrews, "Second Report," p. 413).

5 9 and 10 Vic., c. 22 (Ernle, *English Farming Past and Present*, p. 447).

6*British American Cultivator*, Aug., 1847, p. 230; *Agriculturist and Canadian Journal*, Aug. 15, 1848, p. 144; Toronto *Examiner*, Sept. 5, 1849.

its collapse in 1847, and the farmers in the St. Lawrence counties were plagued by the wheat midge, those west of the Bay of Quinte had not much to complain about. James Bryce Brown was emphatic on this point. "The farmers of Upper Canada, and towns dependent on them," he wrote in 1851, "have experienced least of the effects [of the repeal of the Corn Laws], and therefore the prosperity of the great western country of Canada goes on very much as usual."[7]

The wheat farmer had, nevertheless, one cause of acute dissatisfaction—the price of wheat during these years was consistently lower than in the United States. The Upper Canada price reflected the decline in British prices from an average of almost 70s. a quarter in 1847 to 38s. 6d. in 1851.[8] That the American price did not fall so fast was due to the cushioning effect of the period of general prosperity which began in 1846-7. This prosperity was stimulated by the discovery of gold in California in 1848, which helped to bring about a rise in commodity prices; by the opening of the British market through the repeal of the Corn Laws in 1846 and the adoption of free trade in 1849; and by the construction of railroads to the Great Lakes and the Mississippi.[9]

As in earlier days, the farmers looked longingly towards the American market, from which they were still excluded by the 25 cents a bushel duty and the usual freight across the lakes of 3 cents a bushel. However, by autumn of 1847, the differential between the export price of wheat in Upper Canada and the Rochester price was more than 28 cents a bushel. Accordingly, at that time some Americans were buying wheat in large quantities at Port Stanley "FOR SHIPMENT TO BUFFALO, *not in bond,* BUT FOR HOME CONSUMPTION!"[10] Early in 1848 others appeared at Toronto and Kingston to purchase grain for the millers of Oswego and Rochester. Before the end of the year, they had

---

[7]Brown, *Views of Canada and the Colonists* (2nd ed.), p. 79.

[8]Ernle, *English Farming Past and Present,* p. 441.

[9]Johnson *et al., History of the Domestic and Foreign Commerce of the United States,* vol. II, pp. 46-8.

[10]London *Western Globe,* quoted in Guelph and Galt *Advertiser and Wellington District Advocate,* Nov. 5, 1847.

bought about 1,400,000 bushels at Toronto.[11] By the autumn of 1849, wheat prices at Toronto and elsewhere north of Lake Ontario were much influenced by the presence or absence of American purchasers.[12] They bought Upper Canada wheat partly to supply the American millers till shipments from the western states could come down the lakes, but mainly to blend with the poor upper-lake wheat to make a good flour.[13] In 1849, of the 623,909 bushels of Upper Canadian wheat imported at Oswego, 243,997 were used by the millers there, and the balance sent to New York in bond.[14]

While Upper Canadian wheat was thus acquiring a merited reputation in the American market, Upper Canadian flour was doing likewise. When it was first sent through to New York in bond, it could not be sold profitably in the United States, on account of the duty which must be paid. However, flour dealers in New York soon found they could get as much for it in the West Indies and the Maritimes as they were getting for American flour. Under these circumstances, by 1850 ordinary Upper Canadian flour rose in price to within 25 cents a barrel of the American variety in New York, and was becoming "an article of large traffic."[15]

Rising prices in the United States soon affected other kinds of Upper Canada agricultural produce. The concentration on wheat for the overseas market had theretofore combined with the American tariff to keep the trade southwards in coarse grains, livestock, and various minor products at a minimum. In 1845, for example, the returns of the American customs officials along the entire frontier of the Province of Canada show exports amounting to only 60,843 pounds of wool, 5,240 dozen eggs, 445 horses (and these almost entirely

[11]*Agriculturist and Canadian Journal*, Feb. 1, 1848, p. 24; "Kingston newspaper," quoted in *Journal d'Agriculture*, juin, 1848, p. 176; Toronto *Examiner*, Sept. 5, 1849. According to the tariff act of July 30, 1848, the duty on wheat and wheat flour imported into the United States was fixed at 20 per cent *ad valorem* (*Reports of Committees, House of Representatives*, 30th Cong., 1st Sess., 1847-8, no. 763, p. 2).

[12]Toronto *Examiner*, Sept. 5, 1849; Montreal *Transcript*, Sept. 8, 1849; *Canadian Agriculturist*, Oct. 10, 1849, p. 282.

[13]*Canadian Agriculturist*, Sept. 1, 1849, p. 252; Montreal *Transcript*, Jan. 5, 1850; Johnston, *Notes on North America*, vol. I, p. 369.

[14]Montreal *Transcript*, Jan. 5, 1850.

[15]Toronto *Globe*, Sept. 7, 1850.

Lower Canada horses), 110 horned cattle, 819 pounds of butter, 4,301 bushels of barley, and a few bushels of other coarse grains.[16]

Though there were always a few American speculators who bought such articles for export to their own country, their activities were scarcely noticed till the early summer of 1849. It was then reported that Americans had been purchasing dairy cows to a great extent in the region north of Brockville. By mid-summer, these drovers were "picking up" cows in various other sections of Upper Canada. In the early autumn they attended the Perth cattle fair, and this time drove off many fat cattle.[17] The trade continued throughout the winter, as the following extract shows:

The purchase of cattle in [Upper] Canada for the American market has been going on during the last few weeks to a considerable extent, and the Kingston *Herald* mentions that 1,000 head have been purchased in that neighborhood alone. We understand that milch cows form a considerable proportion of these purchases, and that the transactions have been to such an extent as seriously to interfere with the increase of our stock next season. . . . It is very evident that our cattle trade with the United States is becoming of very considerable importance, and that there is a likelihood of a rise in the value of the article.[18]

Other dealers, or possibly the same ones, bought many horses in Upper Canada, a large quantity of timber, peas for seed or for manufacturing into "coffee," and a variety of other produce. "During the autumn," the Montreal correspondent of the London *Times* reported, "the exports to the United States have been double what they were before in the

---

[16][Andrews,] "Report of the Secretary of the Treasury . . . [on] . . . the Trade and Commerce of the British Colonies" (*Senate Executive Document*, 31st Cong., 2nd Sess., 1850-1, no. 23, p. 188). Hereafter this authority is cited as Andrews, "First Report." Butter and eggs had been smuggled across the Niagara River to Buffalo for a long time, but it is impossible to estimate the value of this clandestine trade (Martineau, *Retrospect of Western Travel*, vol. I, p. 101).

[17]*Canadian Agriculturist*, July 2, 1849, p. 172; *ibid.*, Aug. 1, 1849, p. 198; Perth *Bathurst Courier*, Oct. 5, 1849. The insignificance of the cattle trade southward before 1849 is emphasized by the fact that in 1847 a Halton County farmer remarked as an unusual development his seeing "a drove of about 200 that were on the way to the lower part of the state of New York" (*Canada Farmer*, Dec. 4, 1847, p. 175).

[18]Toronto *Globe*, March 5, 1850.

most prosperous year during an equal period."[19] According
to the *Globe*, the "demand for farm stock of all descriptions"
throughout the winter of 1849-50 continued to make money
"circulate more freely than common."[20]

Till 1850, it will be noticed, the exports to the United
States were predominantly of timber and cereals or flour,
which could be conveniently shipped by water, and of horses
and cattle, which could be driven. Within the next year or so,
the approach of American railways to the frontier gave an
outlet for all the remaining products. The railroads had not
affected Upper Canada before 1850 for the reason that,
though Buffalo had railway connection with the Hudson River
by seven independent lines as early as 1842, these lines (which
were consolidated into the New York Central by 1850) had
developed little freight traffic because, till the end of 1851,
they had to pay canal tolls as a surcharge on their freight
rates. The first American railway to bulk large in Upper
Canadian agricultural development was therefore the Northern or Ogdensburg Railroad, which was opened in July, 1850,
from Ogdensburg, above the St. Lawrence rapids, to Rouses
Point, where other lines connected it with Boston and New
York. It had been planned and built by Boston capitalists
as part of a plan to divert the trade of the upper lakes from
the Erie Canal and from Montreal. At first the railroad
seemed about to satisfy the hopes of its promoters. Ogdensburg became for a time a prosperous forwarding centre,
supplying much of Upper Canada with merchandise from the
seaboard, and receiving for trans-shipment to New England
produce from Upper Canada and the region of the upper
Great Lakes.[21]

The Ogdensburg Railroad gave the St. Lawrence counties
a new and voracious market. As soon as it was opened, prices
rose rapidly in Prescott, Brockville, and other river towns.
Within a few weeks of its completion the farmers of Leeds
and Grenville were "taking their trips to Boston, by the rail-

---

[19]Quoted in Toronto *Globe*, Feb. 5, 1850.

[20]Toronto *Globe*, March 14, 1850.

[21]Andrews, "Second Report," pp. 66-7, 290, 297-8; *Bytown Packet*,
Aug. 10, 1850.

road from Ogdensburgh, with their produce."[22] In the winter
of 1850-1 the Glengarrians teamed their surplus oats and
peas across to Fort Covington where, in spite of the duty,
better net returns could be obtained than at Montreal. During
and after the summer of 1850, Americans, mostly from
Boston, scoured the country at least as far north as the Rideau
Canal for oats and potatoes and other formerly unexportable
produce.[23] The benefits to that part of Canada West convenient to the railway were thus summarized in 1852: "The
farmers have obtained better prices in New England, than
could be had in Old England or her Provinces. They have
found a ready market for all kinds of coarse grain, cattle,
sheep, beef, mutton, pork, butter, cheese, and even potatoes,
poultry and eggs. Purchasers from the east are continually
in Canada, and the farmers have a market at their own doors.
Every depot on the Ogdensburgh road is a Boston market."[24]
It is not surprising that those interested in the commercial
welfare of Montreal were afraid that the whole trade of the
Ottawa Valley would be diverted to Boston and New York.[25]

Other American railroads soon created a similar demand
along the entire border of Upper Canada. With better transportation facilities and a constantly expanding American
market, Upper Canadian farmers, like those of Lower Canada,
began to look southward rather than overseas. They now
exported barley and rye to satisfy the requirements of some
American brewers and distillers, though not in large
amounts.[26] As for peas, a writer on Oxford County in 1852
remarked that "within the last two years they have commanded a much better price than hitherto, which, in some measure,
is occasioned by the Americans coming over to purchase them
in large quantities."[27] American purchasers sought such farm

[22]Perth *Bathurst Courier*, Nov. 1, 1850.
[23]P. Fleming to C. P. Treadwell, April, 1851, in *Journal of the
Legislative Assembly of Canada, 1851*, App. UU, hereafter cited as
JLAC; Shanly, *Report on . . . Bytown and Prescott Railroad*, pp. 25, 32.
[24]Playfair, *Remarks on Mr. Justice Brown's Report to the Committee
appointed to Promote the St. Lawrence and Lake Huron Railroad*, p. 9.
[25]Keefer, *Montreal and the Ottawa*, pp. 11, 17.
[26]*Journal d'Agriculture*, oct. 1851, p. 309; *ibid.*, janv., 1852, p. 24;
ibid., mars, 1852, p. 91.
[27]Shenston, *Oxford County Gazetteer*, p. 58. Cf. *Journal and Transactions of the Board of Agriculture of Upper Canada for 1855-6*, p. 219.
Hereafter this authority is cited as *JTBAUC*.

products as geese, turkeys, hens, eggs, and butter for the
urban consumers of New York and New England.[28] As, with
the exception of butter, none of these could be sent overseas,
the new outlet was much appreciated. The coarse Leicester
wool of Upper Canada went south in small but increasing
quantity.[29] Hay, which was too cheap and bulky to stand
the expense of transportation for any distance ordinarily,
was actually exported in 1852. When a railroad was built
from Rome, N.Y., to the eastern end of Lake Ontario, a temporary market developed at Kingston. In two weeks, the price of
hay there rose from $5.00 to $10.00 a ton, and "already the
Americans had brought over presses to press it, and were
buying and sending it away [to New York] by the railway."[30]

The export trade in livestock attracted more attention
than that in any other product. The expansion in cattle
exports was typical. After 1849, American drovers swarmed
into the lower Ottawa Valley, the Bay of Quinte region, and
other parts of the province near the border winter and summer. During the winter of 1850-1 they bought so many cattle
in the Perth vicinity that scarcely any were left to be sold at
the spring fair.[31] In Hastings County in 1851, the 348 cattle
shipped to the United States by steamer were but a fraction
of those driven through to cross the St. Lawrence at Kingston
or Gananoque.[32] The cattle trade was most brisk during the
winter and spring of 1851-2, in consequence of a feed shortage (and so of high prices for stock of all kinds) in upstate
New York. It was no longer confined to the easterly parts of
Upper Canada, but flourished in the ranges of townships north
and west of Lake Ontario, and in the Niagara peninsula.
There was scarcely a day throughout the winter that a drove

---

[28]*Journal d'Agriculture*, aôut, 1850, p. 254; *ibid.*, fév., 1851, p. 50;
ibid., juin, 1852, p. 161; *Canadian Agriculturist*, Dec. 1852, p. 363. For
further information on butter exports at this period, see Chapter **XV**,
below.

[29]*JTBAUC 1855-6*, p. 142; *Canadian Agriculturist*, July, 1851, p. 154.

[30]*Canadian Agriculturist*, Dec., 1852, p. 363. There was a prejudice
against Upper Canada hay in the northern states. This was owing
to the presence of the Canada thistle in the hay that was exported
in 1845 to Ohio, where there had been a great drought (Cleveland
Herald, quoted in *Ohio Cultivator*, vol. II, 1846, p. 101).

[31]Perth *Bathurst Courier*, May 2, 1851.

[32]*Canadian Agriculturist*, July, 1852, p. 199.

did not pass along the road from Hamilton to Queenston.[33] In the summer of 1853, it was reported that in spite of the 20 per cent import duty, "immense numbers of sheep and cattle are being driven from all parts of Canada by American drovers to the United States."[34] United States demand meant not only that fat cattle were no longer the drug on the market that they had once been, but that cattle-rustling made its appearance. According to the Guelph *Advertiser*, "the stealing of cattle is becoming of a more common occurrence than formerly, partly caused, perhaps, by the increase of their value, and the additional facilities for their use in the upper country [i.e., towards Owen Sound], where detection is difficult. . . . From the number of cattle missing, it is suggested that there are probably organized bands now cooperating to carry off cattle, having their places of concealment for the day and driving during the night."[35]

Though the trade in horses was numerically much smaller, by 1852 raising horses for sale to American dealers was considered a profitable sideline by many of the farmers in all the Upper Canada counties adjacent to the St. Lawrence or the Great Lakes.[36] At the end of 1851, a Hastings County essayist declared that "the rearing of good horses . . . is at present one of the most profitable of the farmer's pursuits; the prices given for them paying better in proportion than those for any other species of stock."[37] Good farm horses brought from £20 to £25 currency, and roadsters which could trot fast, and so could meet the requirements of the New York or Philadelphia markets, from £30 to £50.[38]

The American railways were especially important in the development of an export trade in Upper Canadian hogs and

---

[33]*Ibid.*, p. 217; *ibid.*, Dec., 1852, p. 362; Guelph *Advertiser*, May 20, 1852; Hamilton *Journal & Express*, quoted in *ibid.*

[34]Brockville *Statesman*, quoted in Montreal *Transcript*, Sept. 5, 1853.

[35]Guelph *Advertiser*, Nov. 11, 1852.

[36]*Canadian Agriculturist*, July, 1852, p. 217; *ibid.*, Oct., 1852, p. 298; *JTBAUC 1855-6*, p. 432. Some horses must have been taken to California by Forty-niners from Upper Canada, just as they were by Forty-niners from Ohio and Michigan, but horses leaving the province as emigrants' effects never attracted any attention.

[37]*JTBAUC 1855-6*, p. 228.

[38]*Canadian Agriculturist*, July, 1852, p. 194; *JTBAUC 1855-6*, p. 432.

sheep, as neither of these could be driven any great distance at a profit. Upper Canadian hogs had to compete in the American market with the domestic corn-fed variety, and this they could do successfully only under extraordinary circumstances, even after the approach of the railroads. One such opportunity resulted from the feed shortage of 1851-2 already mentioned, which had the effect of raising pork prices in the Buffalo region to levels higher than ever before reached. The drovers who bought cattle in Canada West during that winter also took away the few hogs that had not been slaughtered in the fall. When the new hog crop was old enough to travel to the frontier or a steamboat landing, the farmers likewise sold all that they could spare of it to the Americans. A lament came from the township of Cavan (Durham County) that "many, very many, more hogs than ought to have been spared, have been sold in their lean state, taken away from the Province, while many of our own farmers have not so much as one to fatten!"[39] An Oxford County chronicler asserted, with more satisfaction, that "within the last two years the Americans have purchased and drove out of the county a very large number of 'Pigs,' we know of two persons who have purchased upwards of 5,000, at an average price of 15s. each, having purchased at 3 cents per pound 'as they stand.' "[40]

With the advent of the American railways, mutton sheep likewise began to be bought in Upper Canada for eastern American markets. In 1850 fat Leicester wethers were sent from Kingston, and presumably from the rest of the district tributary to the Ogdensburg Railroad, to Boston.[41] By the end of 1851 there was a steady demand for such sheep for shipment to New York or New England all along the border.[42]

---

[39]*Canadian Agriculturist*, Feb., 1853, p. 37.

[40]Shenston, *Oxford County Gazetteer*, p. 63.

[41]*Canadian Agriculturist*, April, 1851, p. 78. The receipts of livestock at the Cambridge Cattle Market in 1849-50 included 1,635 fat sheep and lambs from "Canada" (*New England Farmer*, Nov. 9, 1850, p. 366). It may be presumed that they were mostly, if not altogether, from Upper Canada, as the sheep in Lower Canada were not likely to appeal to mutton lovers.

[42]*Canadian Agriculturist*, July, 1852, p. 217; *ibid.*, Aug., 1852, p. 226; Shenston, *Oxford County Gazetteer*, p. 62.

In 1853 Prince Edward County exported about 10,500 fat and store sheep to the United States.[43]

When the reader turns from this account of the opening of the "New England market" to the statistics of imports of coarse grains, livestock, and miscellaneous products into the United States, he will be surprised to find how small they were, particularly in the case of livestock.[44] In this connection, two things should be noticed. The first is that not much reliance can be placed on the statistics, at least as far as horses and cattle are concerned, for there was notoriously a large illicit trade into the United States in both of them.[45] The other is that the importance of the export trade arose, not out of the actual quantities exported, but out of the fact that the price of the surplus the farmers were able to dispose of outside the province had a remarkable influence on the prices at home. The local prices came to be determined, not by what the butcher or grain dealer or some immigrant chose to pay, but by what an American drover or speculator would give.[46]

---

[43]*JTBAUC 1855-6*, p. 434.

[44]The imports recorded in 1851 will serve as an example. Column I includes "Oswegatchie" (Ogdensburgh) and "Cape Vincent," that is, the region served by the Ogdensburg Railroad; Column II, "Oswego"; Column III, "Niagara" (Lewiston and Niagara Falls) and "Buffalo", which together received the produce of the Niagara peninsula; and Column IV, "Detroit."

	I	II	III	IV
Oats	29,373 bushels	78,771 bushels	4,572 bushels	2,404 bushels
Barley	2,665	23,511	19,682	6,315
Rye	1,781	53,950	87	
Peas	6,494	60,418	1,157	906
Eggs	19,186 dozen	5,050 dozen	4,981 dozen	18,852 dozen
Butter	1,716 cwt.	563 cwt.	203 cwt.	253 cwt.
Wool	70,262 lbs.	82,908 lbs.	211,482 lbs.	20,511 lbs.
Horses	954	101	458	350
Cattle	5,153	35	2,515	347
Sheep	9,301	1,647	1,638	
Swine	1,098		2,771	

(Andrews, "Second Report," pp. 250-3).

[45]Cf. Andrews, "First Report," p. 516. For the smuggling of butter and eggs, see Note 16, above.

[46]Cf.: "From peculiar causes existing in the US a year or two ago, there was a great demand in Canada for provisions to be exported there and . . . the prices rising here suddenly in consequence, immense numbers of cattle were sold for the American market" (Toronto *Globe*, June 2, 1854).

New York, Ohio, Michigan, and Illinois, it might be noticed, were affected in precisely the same way as Upper Canada by the westward extension of the railroads. In other words, between 1849 and 1853 Upper Canada was caught fully in a development characteristic of the whole region tributary to Boston, New York, and Philadelphia.

The opening of the American market was important for several reasons. One was that it made the period one of agricultural prosperity. It is true that wheat crops were abundant in western and most of central Upper Canada in 1850, 1851, and 1852. Nevertheless, the midge, in its advance westward, was at Cobourg in 1853. Moreover, the price of wheat fell steadily till it reached about 3s. (i.e., about 60 cents) a bushel in Toronto in 1851, almost unprecedently low.[47] It was something new for Upper Canada to be prosperous when its staple cereal was so cheap that it could scarcely pay the cost of producing it. Yet it undoubtedly was prosperous. Farmers no longer obtained from their wheat the income they expected, but got it from other articles which formerly had little value. The fact that coarse grains, which had formerly been salable only at distilleries, breweries, livery stables, or lumber camps, as the case might be, could now be exported, was of the utmost importance, especially in the economy of the lower Ottawa Valley and other regions where wheat had failed on account of the attacks of the midge.

The depression in wheat-growing and the growth of trade across the border helped to bring about changes in the basis of agriculture in Upper Canada. A "Report on the State of Agriculture in the County of Prince Edward, 1854," states their origin succinctly: "It was of comparatively little profit to rear fine animals, when there was no demand for beef, mutton, butter, or cheese; consequently the farmer could only depend upon the cereal productions of his land. . . . The increased demand for beef, mutton, wool, butter, and cheese, as also the demand for live stock, to supply the American market, is causing, with good reason, much more attention to be paid to rearing good stock, and to the best and most economical mode of feeding them through the winter." The

---

[47]*Canadian Agriculturist*, Dec., 1851, p. 271; *ibid.*, Jan., 1853, p. 4; *JTBAUC 1855-6*, p. 178.

writer refers also to better farm management in general,
which involved more green crops instead of summer fallow,
more peas for market and as a crop preparatory to wheat,
more roots, and better fertilization from the keeping of more
stock.[48] As will be shown in the next chapter, the trend to
diversification in farming was shortly to be interrupted.

Another result of the opening of the American market
was Upper Canada's first "railway fever"—a sudden interest
in projecting railways leading towards the American border.
This fever raged till the beginning of the Grand Trunk era
in 1853, and there are evidences of it even after that date.
Beginning about 1850, financiers and contractors who had
pushed American railways to the St. Lawrence or the Great
Lakes, like the commercial interests of various cities in the
northern states, prepared to invest in railways in Upper
Canada which would be tributary to their own enterprises.
This is not surprising, as during the late eighteen-forties
and early eighteen-fifties, large amounts of American capital
were invested in other Canadian projects, such as the construction of sawmills. Partly on account of the prospect
of help from American capitalists, partly on account of the
prosperity resulting from the opening of the American market,
partly on account of a well-founded belief that there was no
limit to the amount of produce which might be shipped south
if adequate transportation facilities were provided for its
collection, the communities of Upper Canada developed their
railroad fever. The towns along the St. Lawrence and the
lakes had no intention of contributing towards the building
of a line of railway to parallel the waterway. Their residents
desired, not a "trunk road" to draw their business off to
Montreal, but north and south (or sometimes east and west,
as in the western peninsula) lines to serve as feeders to
American railways. Cornwall, Prescott, Brockville, Kingston,
Belleville, Cobourg, Port Hope, Toronto, Hamilton, Port
Stanley, and the rest could not fail to flourish if they became
the termini of railways stretching inland. The attitude of
the towns in the lower Ottawa Valley was typical. In 1853
Keefer declared that "the sympathy of every river and lake
town is more with their trade across the St. Lawrence to

---

[48]*JTBAUC 1855-6*, pp. 430-1.

the United States, than with that to Montreal."[49] A Perth
editor was even more emphatic when he set forth his opinion
that "so far as the people of this part of the country are concerned, it is not of so much importance to have a railroad
passing through their midst to meet the Trunk Line, as to have
such a road to meet some one of the railroads on the other
side of the St. Lawrence,—the Boston or New York market
being of more importance to us than the Montreal market."[50]

Under these circumstances, it is no surprise to find that
the first railway put under construction in the Ottawa Valley
was the Bytown and Prescott, which was really an extension
of the Ogdensburg Railroad, and as such intended to carry
agricultural produce, as well as sawn lumber from the
Chaudière Falls, to Ogdensburg. The second in eastern
Upper Canada, the Brockville and Ottawa, began to be promoted in 1852 in connection with a line from Watertown to
the St. Lawrence opposite Brockville, a feeder of the New
York Central. Farther west, Kingston business men hoped
that, through a steamer connection, their town would become
the real terminus of the Rome and Cape Vincent Railroad,
at least in summer. Sometimes American interests were much
more important in the organizing of Upper Canada railways
than those of the local communities. In 1852 Oswego forwarders and others were prominent in the formation of a
"Midland Railway" to run from the Bay of Quinte to Georgian
Bay, by way of Belleville and Peterborough. Again, Wads-
worth, Mayor of Buffalo, and his friends, in 1851 planned a
railway which would secure to Buffalo the local trade of the
Grand River Valley. They interested the people of Brantford
in their enterprise, and eventually, though not under the
original management, the Buffalo and Lake Huron Railroad
reached Goderich.[51]

---

[49]Report of . . . the St. Lawrence and Ottawa Grand Junction
Railway Company, p. 34.

[50]Perth Bathurst Courier, Nov. 19, 1852. Cf. ibid., Oct. 10, 1851.

[51]Shanly, Report on the Bytown and Prescott Railroad, pp. 20, 22,
24; JLAC, 1851, App. UU; Perth Bathurst Courier, Nov. 19, 1852;
Report of . . . the St. Lawrence and Ottawa Grand Junction Railway
Company, p. 34; Kingston Daily News, Oct. 8, 1851, and later numbers;
Canadian Merchants' Magazine and Commercial Review, Sept., 1858,
p. 368; Andrews, "Second Report," pp. 90-1, 378; Hind et al., Eighty
Years' Progress, pp. 234-5.

By 1852 a considerable number of railways had been chartered in Upper Canada, designed either as virtual extensions of American lines, or as portage railways to short-circuit the trade of the upper lakes through Upper Canadian ports to the United States. Every one of these lines seemed to threaten disaster to the commercial well-being of Montreal. As a result, though it had long been felt that no railway could compete successfully with such a navigation as that of the St. Lawrence system, the idea of a trunk line developed. The story of the genesis of the Grand Trunk can be read elsewhere. Here it is enough to point out, as has now been done, the relation of the opening of the American market to its beginnings.

A final result of the opening of the American market was an intense interest in the question of reciprocity in natural products with the United States. Reciprocity was advocated in the late eighteen-forties, after the American Drawback Act turned the grain trade of the St. Lawrence system towards the Erie Canal. At this time, it was of course assumed that the only articles which reciprocal trade would benefit greatly were wheat and flour.[52] In 1849 Upper Canada wheat prices were still 25 or 30 cents a bushel lower than those on the other side of the boundary, but during the summer of 1850 United States wheat prices gradually fell till they were more in accord with the Liverpool rates than they had been; by September, the best samples brought 80 cents in Toronto and 84 cents in Oswego.[53] This approximation of price along the border made the Upper Canada farmers feel more and more that they should have some terms arranged for them, whereby their wheat and flour would be admitted to the United States free of duty, especially as they felt that there was a bona fide market for their breadstuffs in the New England states.[54] When the American market expanded to include coarse grains and livestock, the interest of the farmers in reciprocity increased in proportion. "The reciprocity question," declared the Toronto *Examiner*, "has acquired a tenfold importance from

---

[52]Cf. *Agriculturist and Canadian Journal*, Aug. 15, 1848, p. 139.

[53]Toronto *Examiner*, Sept. 5, 1849; Toronto *Globe*, Sept. 7, 1850.

[54]Toronto *Examiner*, quoted in *Bytown Packet*, Nov. 2, 1850; Toronto *Globe*, Feb. 5, 1850.

the facilities which the Ogdensburgh Railroad offers for conveying our produce to the markets of New England."[55]

There are several satisfactory accounts of the tedious
negotiations which preceded the conclusion of the Reciprocity
Treaty.[56] The treaty went into effect in the Province of
Canada in October, 1854, and in the United States on March
16, 1855. Under its terms the products of the forest, the
farm, and the mine were admitted from one country into the
other without the payment of duty.

How did the treaty affect the farming population of Upper
Canada? As the first two years of the period the Reciprocity
Treaty was in force, as well as the last three years, were
characterized by exceptional prosperity in the Province of
Canada, it afterwards became the common thought of Canadians that reciprocity assured prosperity. Actually, the
prosperity of the earlier years was owing mainly to the
boom of the Crimean War and railway-construction era (as
described in the following chapter), while that of the later
years was owing to the abnormal demand for agricultural
produce in the United States during the Civil War. Nevertheless, the Reciprocity Treaty was undoubtedly of great
benefit to Canada.

The trade which developed during the period of its existence was, as has been often remarked, one of convenience. A
disgusted protectionist sneered: "It is true that 'trade' between the two countries has wonderfully increased, but if
Jonathan takes a fancy to John Bull's eggs, and John Bull
is equally fastidious and fancies Jonathan's eggs, we really
do not see what either has gained by the transaction. To our
simple minds the exchange of commodities of this kind, has
been of little benefit to Canada. Toronto has imported from
the United States, what Montreal has exported to the same
country, and had we dealt with one another like Montreal
and Quebec, we would have been equally well supplied, and
our own Railroads, Steamboats, and Canals benefited thereby."[57] Yet the north and south trade in articles which were

---

[55]Toronto *Examiner*, quoted in *Bytown Packet*, Nov. 2, 1850. Cf.
Journal d'Agriculture, fév., 1851, p. 50.

[56]The best recent study is Masters, *Reciprocity Treaty of 1854*.

[57]*Canadian Merchants' Magazine*, March, 1858, p. 524.

statistically the same when entered at a customs port was often based on differences in quality, on times of harvesting, or on local market demands. Thus, as we shall see, Canadian barley was found to be the best that American brewers could obtain; heavy mutton sheep like the Leicesters were not much raised in the United States, nor fine-wool breeds in Canada; Toronto fall wheat was required by American millers for blending with the softer grain of the upper-lake region; peas could not be matured for seed in most of the United States, nor Indian corn in most of Canada; and if the heavy immigration of 1855-7 into the western states made it profitable to ship coarse grains from Toronto to Chicago, the crop failures of 1857 and 1858 made it necessary to import similar supplies from Chicago for consumption in Toronto and other Upper Canadian towns.[58] As has been indicated, all these articles had been exported to the United States before 1855, and they were to continue to be exported thither after the abrogation of the treaty. All that the Reciprocity Treaty did was to establish the trade in agricultural produce between Canada and the United States on a much firmer basis than might otherwise have been possible.

The Reciprocity Treaty contributed to the further shifting of the Upper Canada grain trade from the St. Lawrence route to the Erie Canal, though it must be remembered that much of the "Canadian" grain, especially the Indian corn and the wheat, was first imported from the United States and then re-exported. Moreover, the treaty was responsible for a great increase in the consumption of Upper Canadian wheat and flour in the United States. The millers in Oswego and Rochester often found it more convenient to purchase small lots of 4,000 or 6,000 bushels at Toronto, and obtain them in a week, than to have to purchase 10,000 or 12,000 bushels at some of the upper-lake ports, as they had to do to make certain of low freight charges; this demand, it seems, was especially strong in the spring, before the upper lakes were fully open to navigation.[59] A great deal of the Toronto wheat

---

[58]*Ibid.*, Aug. 1857, p. 559; Masters, *Reciprocity Treaty of 1854*, pp. 191-2.

[59]*Canadian Merchants' Magazine*, April, 1857, p. 54; *ibid.*, June, 1857, p. 284.

found its way much farther than Oswego or Rochester, as we are informed that "purchases continue to be made on orders from millers in the New England States, whom we now look upon as regular and good customers for all the grain shipped from this point."[60] It was largely used for blending with wheat from the western states, "in order to produce flour which passes inspection as 'extra Genesee'."[61]

To fill the deficiency created by these exports, much American flour was imported for consumption. At the same time, the free entry of American wheat encouraged the expansion of the milling industry. Millers imported spring wheat from the American northwest, and made a cheap flour from it for consumption in Lower Canada, as they did from Upper Canada spring wheat. Till 1858, moreover, they were able to mill American wheat and export the flour to the United States. Many of the cheaper grades of this flour were re-exported from the United States to the Maritimes and elsewhere. On the other hand, "Canadian Extra" flour was said to be gradually replacing the famous Genesee Valley flour in New York, and was sent direct from Upper Canada to regular customers there, in Boston, and in the other manufacturing towns of New England.[62]

On the eve of the American Civil War, the American dealers disappeared from the Toronto market. New England millers had been able to store great quantities of grain from the western states, and speculators could not obtain money from their accustomed sources on account of the financial stringency.[63] The grain trade, it was obvious, was in an uncertain position. None could tell what effect the approaching conflict would have on the demand for flour, wheat, and coarse grains in the United States, nor on exporting through the Erie Canal.

The Reciprocity Treaty accelerated the trade in cattle which had already developed. Around Perth and in its hinterland in both 1855 and 1856 American drovers collected about

---

[60]*Ibid.*, July, 1857, p. 373. Cf. Toronto *Globe*, Sept. 18, 1857.
[61]*Canadian Merchants' Magazine*, April, 1857, p. 54.
[62]*Ibid.*, p. 55; Masters, *Reciprocity Treaty of 1854*, pp. 193-5.
[63]*Annual Report of the Toronto Board of Trade for 1860*, p. 7.

6,000 head to fatten.[64] North of Lake Ontario, few cattle had been raised for export before the treaty came into effect, but many were in the years after 1855. In 1859 several hundred were driven away to the United States from Durham County, and about five hundred from the one township of Otonabee in Peterborough County.[65] Farther west, cattle were being bought for export at this time seemingly on an even larger scale, especially in counties such as Waterloo and Wellington.[66] Most of the Upper Canada cattle exported during this period found their way to the Buffalo and Albany markets, or through Montreal to the Boston market. Though many were fat cattle, the most of them were of the feeder type. A few were intended to build up or replenish the herds of American dairymen.[67] The only hiatus in the cattle trade seems to have been in 1858, when the depression in the United States and Canada put an end temporarily to the visits of the cattle drovers. The result was that large numbers of cattle were turned over to the village store-keepers in payment of accounts. The merchants were unable to fatten them conveniently, and so had no alternative to sending them to the already glutted Montreal market.[68]

There was likewise a steady demand for horses throughout Upper Canada during these years. Some of those bought by the American dealers were roadsters. Addington and Prince Edward counties were for a while claimed by local patriots to stand supreme in this kind of horse, but by the early eighteen-sixties eastern Upper Canada in general was

[64]Prescott *Telegraph*, quoted in Montreal *Witness*, Dec. 19, 1855; Perth *Bathurst Courier*, Sept. 19, 1856; Kingston *Chronicle and News*, Oct. 10, 1856; Brockville *Recorder*, quoted in Montreal *Witness*, Oct. 10, 1857.

[65]*Canadian Agriculturist*, Jan. 16, 1861, p. 58; *ibid.*, May 16, 1861, p. 315. It was remarked of the Toronto region in 1857 that "of late years, the Americans have been the chief purchasers of our surplus . . . cattle" (Toronto *Globe*, Sept. 11, 1857).

[66]Guelph *Advertiser*, quoted in *Canadian Agriculturist*, Nov., 1859, p. 259; *Canadian Agriculturist*, Feb. 16, 1861, pp. 122, 126; *ibid.*, June 1, 1861, p. 347; *ibid.*, July 1, 1861, p. 408.

[67]*Canadian Merchants' Magazine*, June, 1858, p. 204; Guelph *Advertiser*, quoted in *Canadian Agriculturist*, Nov., 1859, p. 259; *Canadian Agriculturist*, June 1, 1861, p. 347; *ibid.*, July 1, 1861, p. 408.

[68]Montreal *Witness*, Nov. 6, 1858.

noted for the excellence of its roadsters.[69] The rest of those exported were intended for farm service. For several years before 1859 American speculators were accustomed to buy such horses in the Niagara peninsula and to sell them in the southern states.[70] This represented an extension into Upper Canada of the horse-buying area tributary to Cincinnati, then the most important horse market in the United States.[71]

The Reciprocity Treaty stimulated the export trade in wool from Upper Canada to the United States. Before 1855, the quantity exported from the Province of Canada seldom exceeded $100,000 in value. Beginning in 1855, it ranged between about $300,000 and $400,000.[72] The increased demand for Leicester wool was paralleled by one for Leicester mutton. "We need not be afraid of raising too many sheep," declared a farmer at Cobourg, "for our neighbors on the other side of the Lake are prepared to buy all we have to spare, since

---

[69]*JTBAUC 1855-6*, p. 432; *JTBAUC 1856-7*, p. 154; *Genesee Farmer*, Oct. 1863, p. 321.

[70]*Canadian Agriculturist*, July 1, 1861, p. 406. It is probable that such horses were reared as a sideline to wheat-growing, as they were in western New York and eastern Ohio about this time (Bidwell and Falconer, *History of Agriculture in the Northern United States*, p. 446). The report of the Haldimand County Agricultural Society for 1859 states: "For a man with one hundred and fifty or two hundred acres of cleared land, two brood mares are the most profitable stock he can have. Raise foals every second year; by so doing you get showier and better foals; sell them at two years old for $60, this will afford a good profit" (*Transactions of the Board of Agriculture of Upper Canada for 1860-3*, p. 105). Hereafter cited as *TBAUC*.

[71]Horses were at this time being brought to Cincinnati from Indiana, Illinois, Michigan, Wisconsin, and Iowa, and were being exported thence not only to Georgia, Alabama, and Louisiana, but even to Mexico (*Ohio Cultivator*, vol. x, 1854, pp. 148-9).

[72]Harvey, *Reciprocity Treaty*, p. 21. One factor in the exporting of wool to the United States was that standards there were much less rigorous than in the British market. Little wool, it was said, went to England from Durham County in 1859. "It is generally bought for the American market. The buyers from that market put a regular price upon Canadian wool, not according to quality, but all at one price, the only distinction being washed and unwashed. The agents employed get a certain percentage per pound, therefore in purchasing they make no distinction in quality; the per centage to them on a pound of dirt is equal to a pound of wool, there is, therefore, a premium held out for bringing it in without bestowing the least care upon it, but all this tends to depreciate the sample" (*TBAUC, 1860-3*, p. 92).

brother Jonathan has become so fond of English mutton."[73]
In the summer of 1859, the farmers of Otonabee Township
sold about five hundred sheep to American jobbers, and other
parts of Upper Canada reported similar exports.[74]

After 1855 Upper Canada hogs were exported to the
United States for a special reason. When the Reciprocity
Treaty went into force, and the plentiful supply of cheap
hogs in the United States made the fat mess pork cheap in
Upper Canada in turn, there came to be a surplus of hogs in
Upper Canada, especially of the lighter kind, which became
available for export. As a result, in certain districts great
numbers of scrub pigs came to be raised to be sold on foot
to American drovers at about 4½ cents a pound. The farmers
considered that it was much more profitable to sell them thus
than to fatten them. The trade was said to be particularly
important in Simcoe County. Otonabee Township, however,
exported about 1,000 of these store pigs in 1859.[75]

Other kinds of farm produce, such as timothy seed,[76]
oats, barley, peas, butter, eggs, and poultry were always in
demand south of the border. As there was nothing new or
distinctive about the trade in them during the first part of
the reciprocity period, it does not seem necessary to do more
than mention it.

Though on the whole Upper Canada's American agricultural market during the first six years of the reciprocity
period was little different from that of the preceding period,
its development was somewhat masked by economic complica-
tions arising within the province during what may be called
the Grand Trunk era. These will now be given consideration.

---

[73]*Canadian Agriculturist*, Aug., 1859, p. 186.

[74]*Ibid.*, Jan. 16, 1861, pp. 62-3; *ibid.*, Feb. 16, 1861, p. 126; *ibid.*,
May 16, 1861, p. 315; *ibid.*, June 1, 1861, p. 347.

[75]*Ibid.*, May 16, 1861, p. 315; *ibid.*, June 1, 1861, p. 342; *ibid.*, July
15, 1861, p. 432. For developments in the Upper Canadian pork-packing
industry at this time, see Chapter XIII.

[76]Timothy seed from Glengarry had a limited but assured market
because it was grown on new land, and so was large and heavy in
character; and it enjoyed in the United States the general reputation
for superiority common to northern seed (Montreal *Witness*, April
1, 1857).

CHAPTER XII

FARMING IN THE GRAND TRUNK ERA

THE early eighteen-fifties were not prosperous years for the farmers of central and western Upper Canada who placed their reliance entirely on wheat. Many whose fields brought forth abundantly were discouraged by the low prices prevailing in the three or four years before 1853. Others found that the attacks of the midge left them with only half a harvest. Still others, who were as yet unaffected by the midge knew only too well that their land was becoming so hard and weedy that it would scarcely produce ten bushels to the acre. Though he was exaggerating for effect, E. W. Thompson, president of the Agricultural Association of Upper Canada, made an illuminating remark in his annual address at the provincial exhibition in 1847. He said:

It is mortifying to hear remarked by those lately arrived from Great Britain, where the land is cultivated in a very superior manner, that some parts of Canada look as if the people had farmed themselves out. Yet mortifying as it is, these are the remarks we are compelled to listen to, and cannot contradict. Facts are stubborn things; for in many parts of Canada such an exhausting course of culture has been pursued, without adding what was necessary to sustain the productive powers of the soil, that it has become so reduced, and the yield consequently so small, as to scarcely adequately remunerate the cultivator for the expense of harvesting, leaving him minus all the other expenses, as well as interest of his capital.[1]

Three years later his successor, J. B. Marks, added a postcript—"the farms on the whole line in the old settled Townships from Montreal to Hamilton, and round the banks of the lakes, rivers, and bays, for a space of eight or nine hundred miles, with few exceptions, are what is in Canada termed, worn out."[2]

If such farms were cultivated in better, that is, more intensive fashion, the cost of producing wheat was so high that the owners could not compete in ordinary times with

---

[1]*Journal and Transactions of the Board of Agriculture of Upper Canada for 1855-6*, p. 54. Hereafter this authority is cited as *JTBAUC*.

[2]*JTBAUC 1855-6*, pp. 138-9.

pioneers on the virgin soil of the frontier. As a consequence, they naturally turned to stock-raising, dairying, or mixed farming, or at least they did if they had a market for their products. It will be remembered that one of the important effects of the opening of the American market was to encourage farmers to rely less on wheat, and to produce coarse grains and livestock for export.

Nevertheless, in spite of this incentive to diversification, and in spite of every hindrance, wheat continued to be regarded as the staple of central and western Upper Canada during the eighteen-fifties. It was idle to expect farmers like those of Chinguacousy Township, Peel County, who had "annually in the ground about one hundred acres of wheat, which produces from three to four thousand bushels,"[3] to give up their wheat-growing. Such men had always depended on wheat, and were reluctant to abandon it; they had an idea, as was said, "that nothing they can raise will bring cash except wheat."[4]   Moreover, even if they desired to do so, few had the capital necessary to go into stock-raising or dairying on a scale which would return them the same income as did their wheat. Furthermore, if they had a crop failure one year, their natural tendency was not to gamble with something else the next, but to put a wider acreage than before under wheat, in the hope that their total production would bring them a profit, no matter how low the price of wheat might be. Many, too, would not admit that they had exhausted their farms. The climate had changed, they said, or was changing. When several near crop failures had the effect of "resting" the soil, and they once again obtained an abundant harvest, or when the vagaries of nature filled a field where theoretically there should have been nothing but thistles, they assumed that the climate was once more normal. But the greatest factor in the continuance of wheat-growing was the high prices which prevailed in the middle eighteen-fifties.

These high prices were wholly owing to conditions in Europe. In 1853 the wheat crop failed over nearly all Europe, and especially in the Danube basin, with the result that the

---

[3] *JTBAUC 1855-6*, p. 350.
[4] Smith, *Canada, Past, Present, and Future*, vol. II, p. 525.

price of wheat in Liverpool jumped from 38s. to 68s. a quarter. In 1854, 1855, and 1856 the Crimean War shut out Russian wheat from the British Isles. The result was that wheat, which had sold for about 60 cents a bushel in the Toronto market in 1851, brought $1.40 to $1.60 in 1854, and about $2.40 in 1856.[5] In consequence of these high prices, there was a large increase in the acreage sown to wheat, with a turning away on the part of many from the diversified agriculture they had tentatively begun to develop before 1853.[6] Wheat crops in 1853, 1854, and 1855 were about average or a little better, except where the midge prevailed.[7] Under these circumstances, high prosperity was reported from almost every part of the wheat-growing region.

The prosperity was accentuated by other factors. The most obvious of these was railway construction. The Grand Trunk and many of the other railways chartered earlier began in 1853 to pour immense sums of money into the province, buying land for rights of way, hiring teams and labourers and so raising wages, and providing through the growth of a consuming population local outlets for all kinds of farm produce.[8] Another factor was the expansion in the lumber trade. A third was that increasing local demand for meat in the western states on account of the inrush of immigrants meant that relatively less livestock came east, so that a vacuum was created in the eastern states which the Upper Canadian farmer, as was mentioned in the preceding chapter, was partly able to fill with his livestock.

Never had the farmers of Upper Canada believed them-selves to be so prosperous as during the years from 1853 to 1857. "In Canada," declared the *Globe* at the beginning of the boom, "we have passed through a year of commercial

---

[5]Montreal *Transcript*, Oct. 12, 1853; *Canadian Agriculturist*, Sept., 1854, p. 285; *Canadian Merchants' Magazine*, March, 1859, p. 167.

[6]Toronto *Globe*, Sept. 7, 1855; *Transactions of the Board of Agriculture and of the Agricultural Association of Upper Canada for 1859-60*, p. 92. Hereafter this authority is cited as *TBA&AAUC*.

[7]Toronto *Globe*, Jan. 6, 1854; *Canadian Agriculturist*, Aug. 1855, p. 253; *JTBAUC 1855-6*, p. 301.

[8]For the effects of railway construction, cf. Shortt, "Railroad Construction and National Prosperity" (*Transactions of the Royal Society of Canada*, 3rd series, vol. VIII, 1915, pp. 300 ff.).

prosperity unexampled in the history of the province."[9] Beginning in 1854, the prices of rural real estate climbed, even in remote localities. "Improved farms have advanced within the last year, from 25 to 50 per cent,"[10] it was stated of Hastings County early in 1855, and a few months later it was reported of the relatively new settlements along Lake Huron that "land (partly cleared farms) in the immediate neighbourhood of Goderich, has increased in value during the last year immensely."[11] Some farmers were wise enough to profit from the inflation. Most of them seem to have done so by erecting better houses and barns, for the agricultural press was filled with references to extensive building in different parts of the province. A typical notice came from Huron County in 1855. Here, it was said, "nearly every lot presents its frame barn or improved mansion, many of them just in course of erection."[12] Others were able to buy livestock, to introduce better methods of cultivation, and to obtain improved implements.

The introduction of the major labour-saving devices, especially reapers, was hastened by a shortage of farm labourers. In the winter of 1852 an essayist from Wellington County declared that "labour is very scarce and dear. Good servants are scarce, and bad ones seldom stay long in one place."[13] The California gold rush increased employment in the lumber camps, and high wages on the construction gangs of American railroads served to draw off not only the immigrants from whose ranks casual labourers on the farms had been largely recruited, but even the sons of the farmers. By 1853 Upper Canada was embarked on its own railroad programme, and the shortage of hired help became acute, especially in the vicinity of Toronto. In 1854 farmers in counties such as Simcoe were beginning to buy reapers on account of the high wages demanded by the harvesters, and in 1855 a large proportion of the crop not only in such old counties as Ontario and Norfolk but even in new ones such as Huron was cut by

---

[9]Toronto *Globe*, Jan. 6, 1854.
[10]*JTBAUC 1855-6*, p. 528.
[11]*JTBAUC 1855-6*, p. 530.
[12]*JTBAUC 1856-7*, p. 180.
[13]*JTBAUC 1855-6*, p. 223.

the reaper.[14] "The demand for improved implements in this vicinity," asserted a Toronto editor, "and, so far as we can learn, throughout Upper Canada, has more than doubled within the last year."[15] By the end of 1857 reapers and mowers were used on nearly every farm of any extent in Durham County,[16] and an agricultural editor justly remarked: "Notwithstanding defects of construction, badness of material, ignorance of workmen, and the difficulties of stumps, stones and water-furrows, the REAPER and the MOWER have established themselves as permanent 'institutions.' No farmer who cultivates over 75 acres, and whose fields present a suitable surface, can afford to be without one of these machines at the present price of labor."[17] Of course the depression of 1857 and the failure of the harvests of 1857 and 1858 checked the introduction of machinery for a number of years.

During this period the Hussey and McCormick reapers of earlier years were displaced by others. The Hussey machine was quite outmoded by 1857.[18] McCormicks, which came to dominate the field in the United States, soon lost their early leadership in Upper Canada. The sales of McCormicks, even of the improved kind, dwindled steadily, till only three were sold in Canada West in 1857. The explanation was that the machines, after the $15.00 duty was paid, could not compete with those manufactured in the province.[19] As a result of the disappearance of the Hussey and McCormick reapers, reapers manufactured under licence from Burral, Manny, and other American patentees, or made more or less in imitation of those so manufactured, were all that the farmer had to choose from. By 1860 some of these machines had evolved into self-rakers, that is, reapers equipped with revolving rakes which swept the grain from the front of the platform off to the ground behind.[20]

14*JTBAUC 1856-7*, pp. 32, 84, 198, 258.
15*Canadian Agriculturist*, June, 1855, p. 181.
16*TBA&AAUC 1858-9*, p. 100.
17*Canadian Agriculturist*, June, 1857, p. 156.
18*Ibid.*, Oct., 1857, p. 260.
19Hutchinson, *Cyrus Hall McCormick*, vol. II, pp. 646-8.
20*Canadian Agriculturist*, July, 1854, p. 223; *ibid.*, Oct., 1857, p. 260; *ibid.*, Aug. 16, 1862, p. 490. There are good cuts of one manufactured at Port Hope in *L'Agriculteur*, nov., 1859, pp. 35-6.

Mowers and reapers were at first usually combined in the one implement, the reaper being made into a mower by removing the platform, lowering the cutting bar, and (sometimes) increasing the speed of the knives.[21] Such a combined reaping-and-mowing machine would, it was said, cut more hay in a day than thirty or forty men with scythes.[22] When, after about 1852 or 1853, simple mowers came into use, most of the Upper Canadian manufacturers followed one general model—that of a Buffalo manufacturer called Ketchum. This was doubtless because Ketchum's was the first mower to meet with widespread approval on its introduction into the province.[23]

Other kinds of labour-saving machinery likewise came to be more extensively employed in the eighteen-fifties than earlier. By 1855 heavy cultivators, mounted on wheels, and drawn by two horses, had become fairly common.[24] Seed-drills, by this time much resembling modern seeders, were no longer rarities.[25] A few farmers were importing gang ploughs from New York by 1854 or 1855, in some cases to take the place of the cultivator, and in others simply to cover seed. They had four small ploughs fastened to an adjustable beam which in turn was mounted between two wheels.[26] A new type of hayrake (named for its American patentee, Delano) was introduced into Carleton County about 1853 and into other parts of the province shortly thereafter. It had twenty-four ash teeth independently attached to an axle mounted on wheels. The driver stood on a platform and lifted the teeth with either a lever or a treadle to drop the hay in the windrow.

---

[21]*L'Agriculteur*, nov., 1859, p. 33.

[22]Perth *Bathurst Courier*, July 18, 1856.

[23]*Canadian Agriculturist*, Aug., 1852, p. 240; *ibid.*, July, 1854, p. 223; *ibid.*, Aug. 16, 1862, p. 490. For a cut see Bidwell and Falconer, *History of Agriculture in the Northern United States*, p. 294.

[24]*JTBAUC 1856-7*, p. 89; *Ohio Cultivator*, vol. XIV, 1858, p. 325. These had been manufactured in New York State since 1846 (*ibid.*, vol. II, 1846, p. 172). For a cut see Bidwell and Falconer, *History of Agriculture in the Northern United States*, p. 303.

[25]*JTBAUC 1855-6*, pp. 348, 431, 496; *JTBAUC 1856-7*, p. 32. For a cut of a drill of the eighteen-fifties, see Bidwell and Falconer, *History of Agriculture in the Northern United States*, p. 299.

[26]*JTBAUC 1855-6*, pp. 496, 577.

This machine, it was stated, could rake about sixteen acres a day.[27]

This improved machinery was at first obtained in the United States, usually at Rochester. However, as soon as a real demand arose in Upper Canada, local workmen, as already suggested, began to construct reapers and other machines on the American models. This they could readily do, as the United States manufacturers did not always patent their implements in Canada. In 1860 it was said that "so great has the supply become from our home manufacturers that an American-made machine is now as great a rarity as a Canadian one was a few years ago"; and at the provincial exhibition at Hamilton in that year there was not a single implement shown by an American manufacturer.[28] The local importance of the agricultural implement factories was great. The largest and most important of these plants, that of Joseph Hall at Oshawa, a branch of a factory first established at Rochester, may be taken as typical. In 1864 it was to turn out 700 mowers, as well as a number of reapers, horsepowers, threshing machines, and ploughs. It used wrought iron from Glasgow, cast iron (for wheels) from a foundry at Three Rivers, Sheffield steel for mould-boards, cutter bars, etc., and Kent County white ash for the wooden parts.[29] When it is considered that every town and important village had one or more small factories of this kind, the importance of the industry in the creation of a home market for agricultural produce may be realized.

The period of prosperity was characterized by a mania for real-estate speculation, especially along the new railways. It was stated in 1855 that, at the stations along the Northern Railway, "land formerly worth no more than £1 per acre, has been sold in quarter acre lots as high as £400 per acre, and from that to £50 and £100 per acre."[30] So great was the interest in town sites that in Huron County, according to its

[27]*Canadian Agriculturist*, Sept. 1, 1860, p. 442; *JTBAUC 1855-6*, p. 496; Copleston, *Canada*, pp. 116-17.   For a cut see Bidwell and Falconer, *History of Agriculture in the Northern United States*, p. 297.

[28]*Transactions of the Board of Agriculture of Upper Canada for 1860-3*, p. 50. Hereafter this authority is cited as *TBAUC*.

[29]*Canada Farmer*, July 1, 1864, p. 180.

[30]*JTBAUC 1856-7*, p. 53.

essayist, "surveying and map-making, and handbill-printing, and auctioneering, became profitable occupations, and the multitude of paper towns and villages exhibited on the walls of every country bar-room suggests the idea of a gallery of amateur landscape painters, or the more alarming idea that Canada is just about to resolve herself into one enormous city!"[31] Farmers, even those remote from the railroad lines, did not escape the mania. The effect of prosperity on many, especially in the country west of Toronto, is only too truly pictured in the following paragraph:

Elated by the amount of money coming into their hands during the Crimean war and the railway inflation, a large number lost control of themselves and acted foolishly. Extravagance was the order of the day. They built houses and bought farms, and speculated on village lots to a lavish extent. Many who had been thought sober, sedate people, took the land fever very badly, with fatal results. Instead of improving the property they already had, erecting convenient farm buildings, and introducing new and more efficient methods of husbandry, they thought of nothing but additional land, and with reckless eagerness bought often without even taking the trouble of looking at their purchase. Reckoning on the war lasting for a generation, they spent all their ready cash in making the first payment on these new purchases; nay, even mortgaged the homestead for this purpose, fully assured that they would meet all the instalments as they came due with perfect ease.[32]

Yet in the midst of the boom, the farmers north of the Great Lakes were being scourged by the attacks of the wheat midge. As those who studied the habits of the insect were convinced that it travelled westward at the rate of ten or twelve miles a year, and as it was prevalent no farther west than Cobourg in 1853, they announced that it would be a considerable time before western Upper Canada was affected. But they were mistaken. In 1856 the midge crossed from the United States along both the Niagara and the Detroit rivers, and caused such havoc in the counties from Toronto to the Detroit River that the estimated loss to the farmers was $2,500,000, even though in desperation they turned to every expedient they had heard of or could invent to check its progress—smoking the flies when they were depositing their

---

[31]*JTBAUC 1856-7*, p. 188.

[32]*Canada Farmer*, Oct. 16, 1871, p. 381. Cf. *TBA&AAUC 1859-60*, p. 220, and *TBAUC 1860-3*, pp. 172-3.

eggs, fumigating with sulphur, early sowing and late sowing, and the introduction of new "fly-proof" varieties of wheat.[33]

By the spring of 1857, there were signs that the great boom was coming to an end. Railway construction was virtually at a standstill, with a consequent reduction in expenditure. Owing to the Crimean War's termination in the spring of 1856, the price of wheat in the Upper Canada markets dropped a third by early 1857.[34] The wheat crop was poor in 1857 from the Bay of Quinte to Lake Huron, being estimated at about 30 per cent below average, and again the midge was chiefly responsible.[35] Worse, before the crop could be sold, the boom gave way to the deep commercial depression which followed the crisis precipitated by a run on American banks in the late summer. Between June and October, the price of wheat at Toronto fell from $1.80 a bushel to about 92 cents;[36] and the *Globe* inquired: "Is there one large buyer of wheat, or oats, or corn, or barley or timber now in the market from one end of the Province to the other? Not one, that we hear of."[37]

In the spring of 1858, a competent observer wrote that "from all parts of Canada, we hear nothing but the same unvaried story of hard times, dull trade and scarcity of money."[38] When the crop of 1858 in central and western Upper Canada turned out to be a severe failure from the ravages of rust and midge,[39] and could be sold only at low prices, the wheat growers were discouraged. Many had already been forced to abandon wheat as unprofitable, so that it could be remarked with truth that, on account of the midge, Canada West was "in a fair way to go out of wheat growing."[40] Others, while they gave up fall wheat, did not adopt other kinds of farming, but merely cultivated spring varieties.

---

[33]Hind, *Essay on Insects*, pp. 80-2, 84-5, 95-101.

[34]Montreal *Witness*, March 21, April 4, 1857.

[35]*Canadian Agriculturist*, Aug., 1857, p. 199; *ibid.*, Feb., 1859, p. 25.

[36]*Canadian Merchants' Magazine*, Oct., 1857, p. 93; *ibid.*, March, 1859, p. 167.

[37]Toronto *Globe*, Oct. 9, 1857.

[38]Montreal *Witness*, May 8, 1858.

[39]*Canadian Agriculturist*, Aug., 1858, pp. 175-6; *Canadian Merchants' Magazine*, March, 1859, p. 167.

[40]*Canadian Agriculturist*, Feb., 1859, p. 25.

The result was that, by 1861, the Upper Canada acreage devoted to spring wheat was more than twice that sown to fall wheat (951,637 acres to 434,729 acres).[41]

The effects of the depression and the bad crop were especially disastrous in the country north and west of Lake Ontario. The report of the West York Agricultural Society for 1858 stated:

> The hired laborer who was tempted to sink his little accumulations in the renting of a farm, and buying stock upon credit at extravagant prices,—the tenant farmer who was tempted to convert his lease into a freehold and burden himself with heavy payments for a series of years,—the proprietor who was tempted to add by purchase to the acres he already possessed, and mortgage his homestead in security, have each in many instances been obliged to fall back from the position they had been too ready to assume, happy if they could escape from their involvements without a serious diminution of their original means, while the seller of land has been equally embarrassed by being disappointed in the receipts of his instalments.

> We do not mean to imply that such a position of affairs is universal, but merely that it is common.[42]

By the end of 1859 the worst of the depression was over. During the summer of that year the imminence of war in Italy between Napoleon III and Austria enhanced the price of breadstuffs.[43] Again, in both 1859 and 1860 the midge was not nearly so destructive as it had threatened to be, with the result that the 1859 wheat harvest was good, and the 1860 one excellent.[44] In fact, by 1860 the depression was at an end in central and western Upper Canada, as the comment of a Haldimand County farmer indicates: "This Spring there is more abundance, less poverty, all over, than there has been for many years. . . . There is now a healthier and more uniform state of things all over the country, than I ever knew."[45]

---

[41]*Census of Canada, 1861*, vol. II, p. 91.

[42]*TBA&AAUC 1859-60*, pp. 220-1.

[43]*Farmers' Journal and Transactions of the Lower Canada Board of Agriculture*, June, 1859, p. 217.

[44]*Canadian Agriculturist*, Aug. 1, 1860, p. 353; Montreal *Witness*, Dec. 31, 1859; *ibid.*, Jan. 5, 1861.

[45]*Canadian Agriculturist*, Aug. 16, 1860, p. 398.

A few of the wheat-growers of central and western Upper Canada profited by their hard experience, and began to turn to other crops or to mixed farming. However, as the prices of other farm products fell during the depression, by far the largest number saw no reason to turn from their "everlasting wheating." As a result, by 1861 or 1862, portions of the Thames Valley had become a "striking example" of a once fertile region that had been almost ruined,[46] but there were many others. Though it had to compete more and more with other forms of agriculture, and had difficulties of its own, wheat-growing was still in 1860 the characteristic type of farming north of the Great Lakes.

Eastern Upper Canada did not follow the same course of development during the eighteen-fifties as central and western Upper Canada. It had no feverish prosperity during the Crimean War, and it did not suffer so severely from the depression of 1857-60. As neither of its two north and south railways reached farther than sixty miles or so from the St. Lawrence till after 1860, the shanty market, with its advantages and defects, continued to be characteristic of the whole upper part of the region. Though there were, as always, considerable fluctuations in the lumber trade, on the whole it steadily expanded, mainly because the prosperity which prevailed in the northern states during the settlement boom of the eighteen-fifties created a great demand for sawn lumber from the Ottawa Valley. On the other hand, the timber trade overseas declined considerably during the Crimean War period.[47]

Though in the lower Ottawa Valley the farmers shared, as earlier, in the vicissitudes of the lumber industry, they became more independent of the lumbermen than they had been, and placed their reliance on the export trade across the St. Lawrence. Indeed, in this part of the province, the export market for livestock, coarse grains, and dairy produce was responsible for the extension of mixed farming. This type of agriculture was well established by 1859, as an extract from the report of the North Lanark Agricultural Society reveals: "The mixed system of agriculture practised by the

[46]Hind et al., Eighty Years' Progress, p. 54.
[47]Harvey, Reciprocity Treaty, p. 24.

farmers in the County of Lanark, where a fair proportion
of the various grain and root crops are cultivated, and animals
of different kinds kept for their products is, we conceive,
much superior to that in the western section of the Province,
where many farms are devoted almost exclusively to the
production of wheat, by which the soil must very soon be
exhausted, and where a failure of that particular crop is
attended with the most disastrous consequences."[48] About the
middle of the decade, it again became possible to grow wheat
in the lower Ottawa Valley. The midge, it was generally
believed, remained only from five to seven years in one locality.
It did in fact pass from the lower Ottawa Valley by 1858, and
had not been troublesome in some places for several years
before this.[49] Even so, most of the farmers along the "front"
of the St. Lawrence counties found it to their advantage not
to concentrate on wheat-growing as they had done in earlier
years, but to keep on with their mixed farming and to sell
their coarse grains to the lumbermen or the exporters.[50]

Not having a wheat surplus, and not having railroad-
building on as large a scale as farther west, the Ottawa
Valley was much less affected by the speculation of the Grand
Trunk era than central and western Upper Canada. The
commission merchant who edited the Montreal *Witness* remarked before the crash of 1857 that "in all Canada that lies
east of Kingston, or perhaps we might say Belleville, there
has been no extraordinary speculation or high scale of expenditure to cause a revulsion. Indeed, we look upon the
business of Canada East and the eastern part of Canada
West as more sound and prosperous than for several years."[51]
When the depression came, the coarse grains on which eastern Upper Canada depended did not fall in price as did wheat.
Further, though the lumber trade was hurt for a time by a
falling off in British demand, rising prices overseas early
in 1859 caused much activity to prevail in the shanties of the
Ottawa, greatly to the advantage of the rural population

---

[48]*TBAUC 1860-3*, p. 120.
[49]Hind, *Essay on Insects*, p. 80; *JTBAUC 1856-7*, p. 249; *Canadian Agriculturist*, Oct., 1858, p. 230.
[50]*TBAUC 1864-8*, p. 338.
[51]Montreal *Witness*, April 4, 1857.

dependent on them.[52] The commercial observer just quoted was therefore substantially correct when he stated that "Lower Canada and the Ottawa country are, however, not nearly so much depressed as the western [part of the] province."[53]

Though Upper Canada agriculture during the eighteen-fifties was still dominated by wheat-growing, dairying and livestock-raising developed an importance undreamed of in the period before the agricultural tariff of 1843, and fruit-growing gave promise of a significant future. A discussion of the progress of dairying at this time will be found in Chapter xv. The other two branches of agriculture mentioned will be given some attention here.

The first great impetus to the development of a livestock industry came with the opening of the American market, as was pointed out in the preceding chapter. After 1853, not only did the export market become more important, especially after the Reciprocity Treaty went into force, but the local demand for meat in Upper Canada vastly increased, owing to the requirements of the railway labourers and of the incoming settlers. During the railway-construction and wheat-growing boom, the call for meat at such places as Toronto sometimes outran the supply. By 1855 the average price of pork had doubled, while cows which earlier would have brought only £4 sold for £9 or £10. In addition, even the completion of the railways, which destroyed the stage and teaming businesses in many parts of Upper Canada, did not diminish the demand for horses. By 1859, that is, in the middle of the depression, horses which would in 1854 have brought about £20 sold at Toronto for £50.[54]

Owing to the demand at home and across the border, the quantity of livestock in Upper Canada increased rapidly during the eighteen-fifties. We find reports from different sections commenting on the great growth in the number of cattle.[55] Sheep became so profitable that more were raised

[52]Ibid., May 12, 1858; ibid., Jan. 29, May 4, 1859; ibid., Jan. 5, 1861.
[53]Ibid., April 2, 1859.
[54]Toronto Globe, Jan. 2, 1854; TBA&AAUC 1859-60, p. 51; Widder, Information for Intending Emigrants, p. 14.
[55]Cf. JTBAUC 1855-6, pp. 451, 453, 520; JTBAUC 1856-7, p. 83; TBA&AAUC 1859-60, p. 216.

than ever before; so large was the increase in Elgin County, for example, that the wool clip of 1859 was double that of any previous year.[56]

Hog-raising did not, however, keep pace with the other branches of the livestock industry. Several reasons may be given. Till about the time of the Reciprocity Treaty, pork was produced in considerable quantities wherever there was a satisfactory demand. Such a region was Lanark County, where the requirements of the lumbermen made the pork of pigs fattened on peas, oats, and barley a staple product.[57] After about 1855, not only was there competition from American pork, but the pea crops frequently failed on account of the attacks of the pea-bug. Without a supply of peas, the Upper Canada farmer fattened few hogs, for the use of corn for this purpose was characteristic only of Essex and Kent counties. Moreover, when he had peas, he now usually found that they would bring more if sold to a merchant than if marketed in the form of pork. In general, it was a settled conviction that it was unprofitable to keep more pigs than were sufficient to eat up the scraps.[58] Thus, except when railway-building or the rapid growth of communities led to an increased local demand, or the exceptional prosperity of the lumber trade did the same, pork was not one of the major items sold from an Upper Canadian homestead. The farmers were in consequence only too well satisfied when, as was shown in Chapter XI, they had an opportunity of selling their swine as store pigs to American drovers.

Though the livestock industry made respectable progress, it nowhere in Upper Canada became the typical form of agriculture during the eighteen-fifties. Only in counties such as Waterloo and Wellington did it give evidence of triumphing over wheat-growing. Indeed, it would be fair enough to state that while the increase in the number of livestock was great throughout Upper Canada, it did not keep pace with the expansion of the population or the demands of the export

---

[56]*Canadian Agriculturist*, Jan. 16, 1861, pp. 62-3.

[57]*JTBAUC 1856-7*, pp. 77, 246.

[58]*JTBAUC 1855-6*, p. 451; *JTBAUC 1856-7*, p. 246; *Canadian Agriculturist*, June 1, 1860, p. 246; *Canada Farmer*, Aug. 1, 1864, p. 214.

market or even the demands of the home market,[59] except in those districts where wheat-farming could no longer be carried on successfully.

The trade in cattle, particularly that southward, led to an extension of the institution of cattle fairs. This development was not peculiar to Upper Canada, for it was found in the Kentucky Bluegrass and in the grazing regions of Ohio at the same time. In 1849 the only fair in Upper Canada of any significance was that at Perth. To this were gradually added various others in the lower Ottawa Valley, for the convenience of the American drovers who were constantly seeking out cattle.[60] However, the cattle fair which came to be recognized as the most important in Upper Canada was that at Guelph. It was established some time before 1852, but it did not really flourish till towards 1860. It was held monthly, with the largest amount of business being done in May and October. At the fair of October, 1859, there were 1,500 head of cattle on the ground. The buyers here during the late eighteen-fifties were dealers from Toronto, Montreal, Albany, New York, and Boston.[61] The success of the Guelph fair led to the holding of fairs in neighbouring communities, Elora beginning in 1852, and Mount Forest in 1859.[62] The importance of these fairs at this time and afterwards will be discussed in Chapter XVI.

In pioneer Upper Canada little attention had been given to fruit-growing except for mere home consumption, though farmers in the Niagara peninsula shipped peaches, apples, and sometimes other fruit to York, Kingston, and even Lower Canada from shortly after the War of 1812.[63] About 1840

---

[59]Cf.: "There are many persons here present [at Newmarket] who saw the Toronto Christmas market. Was it a show of Canadian beef? . . . We import our beef. Soon we may have to import our wheat" (*TBA&AAUC 1859-60*, p. 47).

[60]Two of these fairs were held at Portland and Kitley respectively (Brockville *Recorder*, quoted in Montreal *Witness*, Oct. 10, 1857).

[61]*Canadian Agriculturist*, Nov., 1852, p. 340; *Wellington Mercury*, May 4, 1859, quoted in *ibid.*, May, 1859, p. 103; Guelph *Advertiser*, Oct. 6, 1859, quoted in *ibid.*, Nov., 1859, p. 259; *TBAUC 1860-3*, pp. 160, 164.

[62]Connon, *Early History of Elora*, p. 132; *TBAUC 1860-3*, p. 102.

[63]*A Few Plain Directions*, p. 90; "Canadian Settler," *Emigrant's Informant*, p. 79; Jameson, *Winter Studies and Summer Rambles*, vol. I, p. 271; Preston, *Three Years' Residence*, vol. II, p. 3.

a few of the advanced farmers had such varieties of apples
as the Fameuse (or Snow), the Pomme Grise, the Bourassa,
the Baldwin, the Rhode Island Greening, and the Early
Harvest. The cultivated cherries they had were all of the
sour kind, the commonest being the Kentish. Most of them
had plums, some wild, some tame, some blue and some yellow,
but none of an improved variety. Pears were not grown,
except along the Detroit River, and grapes only in hot-
houses.[64] During the late eighteen-forties farmers began to
improve their orchards. Many new varieties of fruit were
introduced from both England and the United States; nurseries were set out, at first in connection with American ones,
but soon independently; and American tree-peddlers and
fruit-grafters with scions travelled through Upper Canada
every spring, often imposing on the farmers, but more often
giving them good value.[65] As a result, by 1855 a nurseryman
was able to list such varieties of apples as the Fall Pippin, the
Esopus, the Spitzenberg, the Yellow Bellflower, the Baldwin,
the Roxbury Russet, the St. Lawrence, and the Ribston Pippin
as being offered for sale on the Toronto market.[66]

During the eighteen-fifties fruit-growing came to be an
important sideline on many farms from the Bay of Quinte
to the Essex peninsula. This was owing partly to the fact that
the railroads brought urban markets within range, partly
to the devastation caused by the midge on the wheat farms,
and partly to a realization that regions such as the Niagara
peninsula had climatic advantages. By 1859 the fruit crop of
the Niagara Electoral Division (part of Lincoln County) was
estimated at 30,000 barrels, and peaches, plums, grapes, pears,
and apples were being exported to Toronto, Buffalo, Montreal,
New Brunswick, and even to Great Britain.[67] The chief
hindrances to the development of the industry were competition from American fruit in Upper Canada markets, and a
feeling of uncertainty about the climate and about pests of

---

[64]*TBA&AAUC 1859-60*, p. 31.

[65]Strickland, *Twenty-Seven Years in Canada West*, vol. II, pp. 152-3;
Smith, *Canada, Past, Present and Future*, vol. II, pp. 205, 418-19;
Ohio Cultivator, vol. XIV, 1858, p. 325.

[66]*TBA&AAUC 1859-60*, p. 31.

[67]*TBAUC 1860-3*, p. 123.

various kinds. Black knot and curculio destroyed the plums, sometimes to the extent of 90 per cent of the crop; fire blight caused much damage to the pears; and the codling moth, the apple-tree borer, and especially the bark louse sometimes reduced the profits of the apple orchard to next to nothing.[68] Under these circumstances, no person in Upper Canada went into fruit culture before 1860 as his sole business.[69] Nevertheless, it did offer such promise in the Niagara peninsula at least that a Fruit Growers' Association was organized there in 1859.[70]

When Upper Canada's first important period of railway construction came to an end with the depression of 1857-60, it left more than memories of a boom and of a financial crisis. Almost every part of Canada West was now within reasonable distance of a railway. Districts which had once been considered out of the way, merely because they were thirty or forty miles from navigable water, found their isolation at an end. Inland villages now got their merchandise from Montreal or Toronto in a few days, instead of having to wait weeks or even months for it. Merchants established new stores near the stations, and greater competition brought lower prices for the manufactured goods the farmer had to buy, and higher prices for the agricultural produce he offered in trade.[71] The railroads contributed to the expansion of the livestock industry by providing improved facilities for shipping, and brought about significant changes in the grain trade, which will be discussed in Chapter XIV.

What precisely were the effects of the decade of the eighteen-fifties on the individual farmer? In other words, how did his agriculture in 1860 differ from that which he had practised in 1850? Fortunately there is available a careful description of a Dundas County farm in 1859, which shows with accuracy the prevailing idea of what a practical agriculturalist should be. It may well be compared with the description of the activities of the wheat farmer as given in Chapter VI.

---

[68]*TBA&AAUC 1859-60*, pp. 38-40, 154.

[69]*Ibid.*, p. 32.

[70]*Report of the Ontario Agricultural Commission*, vol. I, p. 16.

[71]*JTBAUC 1856-7*, p. 5; Perth *Courier*, Oct. 14, 1859; Croil, *Dundas*, p. 302.

The following system is pursued by one of our best and most successful farmers, evidently the right man in the right place, the President
of our Agricultural Society. His farm embraces 500 acres, whereof
300 are cleared. His whole farm is enclosed with cedar fences, proof
against all intruders, by which means his cattle have the exclusive and
unrestricted privilege of roaming through the woods, with all the
benefits thereto appertaining.

Of his cleared farm 120 acres are devoted to pasture, 100 acres
to meadow, and 80 to tillage. His stock consists of 20 milch cows, 6
working horses and two brood mares, with 60 sheep. He makes from
10 to 20 acres of summer fallow every year, to which he applies all
the manure made upon the farm, and as much more as he can procure
from the neighbouring village of Morrisburgh. The proportion of
different grains is regulated entirely by the adaptation of the different
fields entering into his rotation. He sows each year a certain portion
of fall wheat and rye, and carefully avoids running into extremes. He
ascribes his success mainly to the diversity of his productions. He
employs cheap labor, say three at $8 per month for the year round,
and keeps a sharp look out upon them; he generally has an apprentice
or two, who work gratuitously, and are paid off with $100 or so when
they come of age. In hay and harvest time he employs 6 of the best
men that can be had, at from 75c. to $1 per day. At these times he can
conceive it to be important to be strong-handed, and always takes time
by the forelock. He begins to cut his clover hay in the end of June;
and by the time the timothy is ripe, he cuts it down in the morning,
spreads it out immediately, and puts it in the barn before night. He
uses a horse-rake, but no reaper, and the greater portion of his grain
he thrashes with the flail, just as it is required for his cattle. He
raises 8 calves, and sells as many head of cattle at 3 or 4 years old;
two colts at 4 years old yield him yearly $100 each. He has his own
wool made into cloth for his own wear, eats his own mutton, and has
always some to sell. He has neither Ayrshire cows nor Clydesdale
horses, but has great faith in both, and will take the first opportunity
to get into these breeds.

He wages a war of extermination against wild mustard, thistles,
and quack, and very rarely do his crops disappoint his expectation. He
has 8 wells with chain pumps, and keeps his cattle trough always full
of water, and supplies them with abundance of salt in summer. All
his grain is freely salted as it is stowed away in the barn, and the
straw is highly relished by his cattle in winter. His brood mares run
on the straw yard, and suckle their colts all winter till the 1st of April,
when the colt is weaned and cared for. His cattle are fed in winter
on straw, with a very little hay, and neither root nor grain, and in
spring never need to be *tailed*. He carefully removes all surface water,

but does not underdrain his land. Every thing is profitable, but hay excels them all. His average return of hay is 1¼ tons per acre, his maximum 2¾, and his minimum ½ ton. He sells largely every year of hay at an average price of $10 per 2000 lbs. He states the average yield of hay for 1859 from the whole County to be not exceeding ½ ton per acre. He considers roots too expensive, and his principle is to keep no more stock than he has abundance of food for. . . .

It is a mystery to him to hear intelligent and industrious men speak of farming as unprofitable, and the summing up of his evidence leaves no doubt in our minds that his system PAYS! which he corroborates by the following figures:——In 1832, he went on to a farm of 250 acres, with 2 horses and 2 cows, and $400 of debt. In 1840 he purchased 250 acres adjoining, for which he paid in cash down $4000. Up to 1860 he has spent at least $4000 cash in buildings and fences, besides other large improvements. He has cleared for the last 20 years more than $600 per annum, and has now $10,000 at interest at 10 per cent. He values his farm at $14,000, and is quite satisfied that it yields him not less than 10 per cent. per annum clear of all expenses.[72]

Possibly the changing conditions of rural life were nowhere more clearly manifested than in the farmer's home. Even before 1850 the system of self-sufficiency had been breaking down on the old cleared farms along the "front." Sheriff Ruttan of Cobourg, one of the old school, in a speech at the provincial exhibition at Kingston in 1849, found much to deplore in the increasing comfort of the farmers north of Lake Ontario. "The old-fashioned home-made cloth has given way to the fine broadcloth coat; the linsey woolsey dresses of females have disappeared, and English and French silks [been] substituted; the nice clean-scoured floors of the farmers' houses have been covered by Brussels carpets; the spinning wheel and loom have been superseded by the piano; and, in short, a complete revolution in all our domestic habits and manners has taken place." Ruttan went on to decry such innovations, on account of the debt he claimed they had

---

[72]*TBAUC 1860-3*, pp. 21-2. Among the expenses were taxes. As everywhere in Upper Canada, these were surprisingly low. "The Municipal assessed taxes come to 2c in the $4; additional school tax, 1½c. in $4; voluntary religious tax, 1½c. in $4; total tax for School, Church, and State, 5c. in $4; or at the rate of 1¼ per cent. on the value of property. *E.g.*—A farmer who owns 100 acres of land, which with his personal property is valued at $2,000, would pay municipal taxes, $10; school tax, $7.50; for religion (if he paid his share) $7.50; in all $25 per annum" (*TBAUC 1860-3*, p. 29).

produced.[73] He was exaggerating, of course, but the tendency
was unmistakable. In most of Upper Canada cooking and
box stoves, especially the former, were common by 1856, and
the open fireplace was disappearing.[74] The stoves were usually bought from peddlers, who gave almost unlimited credit
so long as the purchaser had title to his land. "Parties bought
stoves that had not a herring to cook on them, and others
got them who did not know which part of them to put the fire
in a year before, and if they were not getting them on the
credit system they would not have one in the course of their
lives." So wrote a Bruce County critic of the extravagance
of the middle eighteen-fifties.[75] At the provincial exhibition
of 1858, coal-oil lamps made in Upper Canada were displayed,
as well as a "family sewing-machine,"[76] and soon the agents
got both of them into farm-houses. All in all, rural standards
of living were steadily rising.

The decade of the eighteen-fifties was indeed a revolutionary one in Upper Canada rural life. Farmers turned from
the overseas market to that of New York and New England.
They began to shift, gropingly enough, from their "everlasting
wheating" to other branches of agriculture. They acquired
new kinds of implements. They built better houses and larger
barns, and abandoned the candle and the fireplace. So extensive were the changes that, in dealing with this era, the
present-day student feels that he is concerned, for the first
time in Upper Canadian history, with an agricultural economy
essentially modern in its characteristics.

---

[73]*JTBAUC 1855-6*, p. 97. Ruttan attributed the popularity of these
"luxuries" to the bad example set by wealthy immigrants. Similar
objections to the passing of the self-sufficient economy were made in the
United States (Bidwell and Falconer, *History of Agriculture in the
Northern United States*, pp. 255-6).

[74]Montreal *Witness*, Dec. 27, 1856.

[75]*TBAUC 1860-3*, p. 172.

[76]*TBA&AAUC 1858-9*, p. 171.

CHAPTER XIII

REPERCUSSIONS OF THE AMERICAN CIVIL WAR[1]

T HE Civil War which broke out in the United States in April, 1861, had profound and lasting effects on the agriculture of the northern states. Upper Canada had developed such an intimate economic relationship with the United States in the preceding decade that of necessity many phases of American war-time evolution had their counterparts in the province. Farmers experimented with tobacco, flax, and other special crops, expanded their barley-growing, and devoted more attention to livestock-raising and to dairying.

The wheat-growers of Upper Canada, remembering the soaring prices of the Crimean War period, expected that the war in the United States would create a demand for their wheat greater than had theretofore existed. In this they were disappointed. It was during these years that the agricultural production of the western states increased phenomenally, owing to the heavy immigration to the prairies, the introduction of labour-saving machinery, and the demands of the British market following the European crop failures of 1860, 1861, and 1862. So great was American wheat production that it not only took care of domestic needs fully but made possible a jump in exports to higher levels than ever before. There were 4,155,000 bushels of wheat and 2,612,000 barrels of flour exported in 1860 from the United States, and in 1862, 37,290,000 bushels of wheat and 4,882,000 barrels of flour.[2]

As soon as the war broke out, American orders for wheat grown in Upper Canada began to fall off. Nevertheless, much of this wheat continued to find a market in New York or New England. Millers at Toronto and other centres imported wheat from the western states to grind into flour for use in Lower Canada, the Maritimes, or Great Britain, thus enabling dealers to dispose of their better varieties of fall wheat in the United States for blending purposes, as they had done for

---

[1]Cf. Landon, "Some Effects of the American Civil War on Canadian Agriculture" (*Agricultural History*, vol. VII, 1933).

[2]Johnson *et al.*, *History of the Domestic and Foreign Commerce of the United States*, vol. II, p. 56.

more than a decade. Moreover, Upper Canada spring-wheat flour began to find a satisfactory outlet south of the border. However, except in 1865, when the United States absorbed all the best Upper Canadian wheat and flour, war-time demand for breadstuffs did not, on the whole, come up to expectations.[3]

With other cereals it was different. The amounts of oats and barley exported to the United States during the Civil War in several years exceeded in value the exports of wheat. In the fiscal year 1862-3, 2,563,325 bushels of oats were exported by inland carriage to the United States from the Province of Canada, in 1863-4, 9,549,994 bushels, and in 1864-5, 4,207,211 bushels. Only a minor fraction was American grain re-exported. Thus, according to Canadian statistics, the value of Canadian oats sent to the United States in 1863 was $2,097,688, while that of American oats imported was only $17,637.[4] Almost all the Canadian oats exported were grown in Lower Canada or eastern Upper Canada, as we can deduce from the American returns just referred to, for 97 per cent of the oats shipped across the border in 1862-3, 90 per cent of those in 1863-4, and 96 per cent of those in 1864-5, entered at Whitehall, Burlington, and other ports south of Montreal. The farmers in the regions mentioned relied more and more on oats as a cash crop. Before the end of the war, it could be remarked that "oats and barley are the chief staples of a large portion of Upper Canada [oats chiefly in eastern Upper Canada], and we may say of all Lower Canada."[5]

The export trade in barley soon attracted more attention than that in any other grain. Barley had been grown exten-

---

[3]Toronto *Globe*, Jan. 30, 1862; *Canada Farmer*, Feb. 1, 1866, p. 41; Montreal *Witness*, Jan. 17, 1866; Patterson, *Report on the Trade and Commerce of Montreal for 1864*, p. 37; Report of J. Potter, United States Consul-General at Montreal, Nov. 2, 1865 (*House Executive Document*, 39th Cong., 1st Sess., 1865-6, no. 56, p. 29). For further information about the grain trade in general during this period, see Chapter XIV, below.

[4]Harvey, *Reciprocity Treaty*, p. 20; *House Executive Documents*, 38th Cong., 1st Sess., 1863-4, vol. XVII, p. 235; *ibid.*, 38th Cong., 2nd Sess., 1864-5, vol. XV, p. 275; *ibid.*, 39th Cong., 1st Sess., 1865-6, vol. XVII, p. 543.

[5]Montreal *Witness*, Jan. 21, 1865.

sively in Lower Canada after the failure of the wheat crop, though it was not till after the opening of the American market that there was a satisfactory outlet for it. During the eighteen-fifties American demand became so insistent that in the autumn of 1859 about 600,000 bushels were exported from Lower Canada to Albany.[6] In spite of this, the ordinary Upper Canada farmer was not much interested in barley as a cash crop, unless he was near a brewery. It was said in 1860 that before 1858 the annual marketable surplus of barley in Upper Canada had not amounted to more than 50,000 or 60,000 bushels. High prices for barley in 1858, with the continued uncertainty of the wheat crop, resulted in a much larger acreage in 1859 than was usual. Nevertheless, where wheat could be grown it was preferred, for barley sold in the Toronto market in 1859 for only 60 to 65 cents, whereas fall wheat brought from $1.18 to $1.25. As late as 1862 a farmer in the vicinity of Cobourg, where barley within a very few years became a staple, could remark that it was not extensively grown.[7]

The fact that the trade in barley developed so rapidly during the Civil War period is to be explained by conditions in the United States. The influx of Germans and other Europeans had by 1860 produced a great demand for beer, which was intensified by the internal revenue tax placed on whiskey during the war. It was estimated that the consumption of beer in the United States increased about sixteen-fold between 1860 and 1865.[8] The chief barley-growing region in the United States during the preceding generation had been upstate New York, especially the Mohawk Valley, the Finger Lake section, and the country adjacent to Lake Ontario. Here the conditions of soil and climate were admirably adapted to the cultivation of a high-quality grain.[9] This region

---

[6]*Canadian Agriculturist*, June 1, 1860, p. 246.

[7]*Ibid.*, Jan. 2, 1860, market report; *ibid.*, July 16, 1862, p. 423; *Annual Report of the Toronto Board of Trade for 1860*, p. 9; *Transactions of the Board of Agriculture of Upper Canada for 1860-3*, p. 90. Hereafter this authority is cited as *TBAUC*.

[8]Fite, *Social and Industrial Conditions in the North*, pp. 81-2. The tax on whiskey was raised from 25 cents a gallon to $2.00.

[9]Weaver, "Barley in the United States" (*Geographical Review*, vol. XXXIII, 1943, pp. 59, 65).

was said to be "barley-sick" by 1865. At any rate, New York State barley was losing its favour with the brewers, who believed that Canadian barley made better beer, and therefore, at least in Philadelphia, sometimes paid as much as 20 or 30 cents more a bushel for it. It appears that the brewers preferred a four-rowed barley, such as was usually grown in Upper Canada, while the New York farmers were turning to a two-rowed variety.[10]

With the help of free entry to the United States under the Reciprocity Treaty, the barley trade consolidated itself during the Civil War. The exports to the United States from the single port of Toronto will illustrate its expansion:[11]

	Bushels	Value
1858	720	$444
1859	54,532	38,583
1860	246,106	165,065
1861	251,167	127,255
1862	226,033	176,875
1863	376,761	329,055
1864	435,944	370,921
1865	1,197,207	938,706
1866	1,212,432	716,506
1867	955,095	738,357

As early as 1863 New York farmers were losing control of their own market for barley. Thus in 1862, out of the 2,814,700 bushels received at Albany (where almost all the Canadian barley went), only about 500,000 had been produced by New York farmers, and it was asked, "Why should they abandon its culture thus largely to the Canadians?"[12]

The Civil War was responsible for considerable attention being devoted to special crops in Upper Canada. These were sorghum, hops, tobacco, and flax.

Of these, sorghum (or "Chinese Sugar-cane") was least important. It had been introduced into the Peterborough region in 1857, shortly after its appearance in the United States. South of the border there was much experimentation with it during the war, in the hope that sugar could be

---

[10]Canada Farmer, April 2, 1866, p. 106; ibid., April 16, 1866, p. 112.
[11]Ibid., Feb. 15, 1868, p. 60.
[12]Country Gentleman, quoted in Genesee Farmer, May, 1863, p. 150.

manufactured from it to replace the Louisiana sugar which was no longer available. Upper Canada was only mildly affected by the movement, presumably because plenty of sugar was available from the West Indies, as well as from the sugar-maples. A small proportion of the sorghum actually grown was used in the manufacture of an unpalatable molasses, and the rest as cattle feed. The limited quantity of molasses made was due in part to the lack of proper machinery for pressing and boiling. In Essex County the experiments with the crop were considered to have been so far successful that at the conclusion of the war plans were being made for the expansion of the acreage devoted to it.[13]

During the war there was a great craze for hop-growing in certain parts of the United States, Wisconsin for example, and this American tendency was reflected in an increased production of hops in Upper Canada for export. Hops had been grown since the eighteen-twenties, but always on a small scale, for there was no market except the local breweries. None of the few commercial hop-yards exceeded seven or eight acres. The total production of hops in Upper Canada in 1850 was only 113,527 pounds, with Middlesex County contributing 20,968; Brant 18,942; Prince Edward 13,224; and Peel 11,346. Hops throughout were a gambler's crop, for prices ranged from 12 to 50 cents, and yields fluctuated widely.[14] During the Civil War the old yards, especially those along the Bay of Quinte, were extended in area, and new ones appeared as far west as Essex County. It was estimated that the expense of growing an acre of hops would average $70.00 or $80.00, but even so, if an acre bore 1,200 pounds, as it might do, which could be sold at 15 cents a pound, there would be a profit of about $100 an acre; and during the last year of the war, Upper Canadian hops brought from 30 to 40 cents a pound. But such yields were not to be depended on,

---

[13]Clark's Sorgo Journal, vol. I, 1863, p. 104; Transactions of the Board of Agriculture and of the Agricultural Association of Upper Canada for 1858-9, p. 126, (hereafter this authority is cited as TBA&AAUC); TBAUC 1864-8, pp. 341, 494-5.

[14]Pickering, Inquiries of an Emigrant, p. 96; Census of Canada, 1851-2, vol. II, p. 64; Canadian Agriculturist, July 2, 1849, p. 171; TBA&AAUC 1858-9, p. 213. The last authority includes a careful description of the methods of culture employed in a hop-yard at Oshawa.

for beginning about 1865, the crops in Prince Edward County were severely blighted. At best the industry was highly speculative, and it was well that the scarcity of cheap labour kept farmers in general from engaging in it.[15]

Tobacco had long been grown on a small-scale commercial basis in Essex and Kent counties, as was pointed out in Chapter III. After 1854, when tobacco entered Canada free of duty, Montreal cigar manufacturers had obtained their requirements from the United States, and its cultivation in western Upper Canada had been partially abandoned. During the Civil War, tobacco again became a fairly profitable crop, bringing from 5 to 7 cents a pound for manufacture at Toronto or Montreal. But even in the Essex peninsula, no one at this time went exclusively into the growing of tobacco.[16]

Flax had almost gone out of cultivation in Upper Canada by 1850, on account of the cheapness of cotton. The few patches still found were for the production of linseed. This condition was much regretted by many leaders of agricultural thought, who believed that flax would make an ideal staple. This was true in many ways, and it was certainly desirable to diversify the farm production of Upper Canada. But there were two great objections to flax. It was a crop which required a considerable amount of labour, mostly unpleasant, and the average farmer preferred the low costs of extensive farming to the high ones of intensive; and there was no satisfactory market for flax in Canada. To assist in establishing what it regarded as a desirable branch of agriculture, the Canada Company gave prizes at the provincial exhibitions for the best samples of flax and hemp, beginning in 1852, and in 1853 it presented to the Board of Agriculture of Upper Canada a flax-scutching machine it had specially imported from England. The same year the provincial government sent a deputation to England and Ireland to obtain the most reliable information on the subject of flax culture. In

---

[15]*Canadian Agriculturist*, Sept., 1863, p. 331; *Canada Farmer,* May 1, 1866, p. 136; *ibid.*, Sept. 15, 1866, p. 283; *Ontario Farmer*, June, 1869, p. 163; *ibid.*, Aug., 1869, p. 236. The blight had not appeared in Upper Canada as late as 1858 (*TBA&AAUC 1858-9*, p. 213).

[16]*Canadian Merchants' Magazine*, June, 1857, p. 218; *Report of the Ontario Agricultural Commission*, vol. I, p. 523; *ibid.*, vol. V, App. O, pp. 3-4. Hereafter this authority is cited as *OACR*.

1859 the Board of Agriculture distributed a quantity of flax-seed among the farmers. None of these attempts at promotion was successful. The only private commercial venture in flax production during the eighteen-fifties of any significance was that of W. D. Perine, who about 1855 erected a scutching mill at Doon in Waterloo County, a favourable location owing to the presence of a population of German extraction. He offered the farmers seed on credit, with information on the proper methods of culture, and then purchased the seed and fibre they produced. At first the farmers were much prejudiced against cultivating flax for him, and indeed, till 1861 his prospects of success were none too bright, for there was still no market for fibre anywhere in Upper Canada. As late as 1859 his mill exported only 60 tons of flax and tow, apparently its whole manufacture. All went to the United States.[17] With the outbreak of the Civil War, and the shutting off of Southern cotton, an excellent future for linens and flax seemed assured. The Canadian government again authorized an agent to collect the latest information on flax culture in Ireland, and imported a number of "Rowan's new patent flax-scutching machines" which it set up at several places in Upper Canada. When farmers could estimate that they netted $20.00 to $25.00 an acre in the land under flax, as they did in Hastings County in 1864, it is not surprising that many of them went into the industry extensively, though not exclusively. Fifteen or twenty acres would be the ordinary maximum on account of the difficulty of obtaining labour. However, in 1863 a Colonel Mitchell in Halton County and Perine in Waterloo County had together more than 3,000 acres. The number of acres sown to flax in Upper Canada in 1864 was estimated at about 10,000. By 1866 there were three linen factories in Canada West, which manufactured cordage and grain bags, each employing about two hundred hands the year round; there were three linseed-oil mills, which took such seed as was not needed for sowing; and there were about a hundred scutching mills. In spite of the existence of the

---

[17]*Journal and Transactions of the Board of Agriculture of Upper Canada for 1855-6*, pp. 282-3, 311; *TBA&AAUC 1858-9*, pp. 213; *ibid.* 1859-60, p. 348; *TBAUC 1860-3*, p. 150; *Canadian Agriculturist*, March 1, 1860, p. 107; *Canada Farmer*, Jan. 1, 1864, p. 1; *ibid.*, Dec. 1, 1864, p. 362.

linen factories, most of the fibre grown during this period
went to the United States.[18]

Of more permanent importance than the special crops
furor was the impetus given to the Upper Canada livestock
industry and export trade. The heavy requirements of the
Northern army and civilian population greatly increased the
demand for Upper Canadian horses, sheep, and cattle from
the outset of the war. The agricultural journals and the
newspapers bore constant witness to the importance of the
trade. A resident of Haldimand County afterwards described
it thus: "The country was full of American buyers. I have
seen these men bring over two or three shot bags filled with
coin. In going back the bags were empty, but in exchange
there were from fifty to four hundred sheep in a drove.
Twenty dollar American gold pieces were common, and cows
that had been selling around eighteen dollars jumped to forty
dollars, a big price for that time."[19]

The swine-raising and pork-packing industries were at
first affected by the Civil War in different ways from the trade
in horses, sheep, or cattle. After the Reciprocity Treaty came
into force, packing houses had been established, at Toronto
about 1855, and a little later at Hamilton, as well as at
Montreal. Most of these packed both the fat mess pork and

[18]*TBAUC 1860-3*, p. 345; *Canadian Agriculturist*, June 16, 1862,
p. 357; *Canada Farmer*. Jan. 1, 1864, pp. 1-2; *ibid.*, Feb. 1, 1865, p.
35; *ibid.*, Oct. 15, 1866, p. 313; *Revue agricole*, juillet, 1864, p. 290.

[19]Smith, *Pioneers of Old Ontario*, pp. 283-4. Unfortunately, it
is impossible to give precise statistics for this trade, as the horses,
cattle, sheep, and swine imported into the United States under the
provisions of the Reciprocity Treaty were lumped together as "animals
of all kinds" and merely assigned a rough monetary valuation. In the
returns for the ports of entry from the Oswegatchie [Ogdensburg]
collection district on the east to the Milwaukee one on the west it may
be assumed, however, that (except at Buffalo and Detroit) practically
all the animals were of Upper Canada origin. In the fiscal year 1861-2
the "live animals" imported into the United States between Ogdensburg
and Milwaukee were valued at $870,226; in 1862-3 at $671,043; in 1863-4
at $2,151,681; in 1864-5 at $4,320,347; and in 1865-6 (8½ months) at
$5,897,272. In these statistics suitable allowance must be made for the
greenback inflation in the United States (*House Executive Documents*,
37th Cong., 3rd Sess., 1862-3, vol. XIII, p. 234; *ibid.*, 38th Cong., 1st Sess.,
1863-4, vol. XVII, p. 230; *ibid.*, 38th Cong., 2nd Sess., 1864-5, vol. XV,
p. 270; *ibid.*, 39th Cong., 1st Sess., 1865-6, vol. XVII, p. 538; *ibid.*, 39th
Cong., 2nd Sess., 1866-7, vol. XVII, p. 382).

lean pork. The mess pork was liked in the British North
American provinces, especially among the lumbermen, but
the British consumer insisted upon a much leaner pork, which
was produced from comparatively small hogs, that is, those
weighing about 220 pounds. Upper Canada pea-fed pork
was more popular in Great Britain than American corn-fed
pork, but while the Reciprocity Treaty remained in effect,
the packers at Toronto and Hamilton obtained most of their
hogs from Chicago, as there were not enough available locally
of the kinds they needed at the prices they were willing to
pay.[20]

During the Civil War, American pork-packing expanded
phenomenally, because it was more profitable to feed grain
to hogs and then send the pork east than to pay the high
grain rates which resulted from the congestion on northern
railroads after the closing of the Mississippi.[21] At times,
in consequence, Chicago mess pork had a virtual monopoly
of even the Toronto market.[22] Upper Canadian packers,
therefore, concentrated their efforts on the packing of bacon
and hams for the United Kingdom. By 1865 several of the
packers were using about 50,000 hogs apiece each year. Operating on this comparatively large scale, they were able to
introduce some system into the business. To make sure that
they got no frozen or half-bad meat, they tried to induce the
Upper Canadian farmers to sell their hogs alive, by offering
higher prices for them on the hoof. They also endeavoured
to have them raise hogs of the bacon type, though without
very much success.[23] During the summer of 1864, about half
the hogs bought by Hamilton packers were Upper Canadian,
nine-tenths of these coming from Oxford County, where they
were probably raised as by-products of the dairy industry.[24]

Canadian pork was able to enter the British market profitably only during part of the year, that is, after the stock of

---

[20]Montreal *Witness*, Jan. 23, 1861; *Canada Farmer*, July 15, 1864,
p. 199; *OACR*, vol. IV, App. H, p. 83.

[21]Fite, *Social and Industrial Conditions*, p. 17.

[22]Toronto *Globe*, Jan. 30, 1862; *Canada Farmer*, Feb. 1, 1865, p. 41.

[23]*Canada Farmer*, July 15, 1864, p. 199; *ibid.*, Aug. 1, 1864, p. 214,
ibid., Aug. 1, 1865, p. 232.

[24]*Ibid.*, Nov. 1, 1864, p. 309.

bacon cured by English and Irish packers had become exhausted, and before the appearance of the new cure in November. To take advantage of this short season, one firm at Hamilton in 1863 cured and packed pork during the summer, by using the refrigerating principle in its cooling-houses. By shipping its pork by the cool St. Lawrence route, it had it reach the British market as a cure at once mild and new.[25]

By 1864, the price of pork in the United States was so high that many Upper Canadian farmers were tempted to raise hogs for export; and indeed, the next year, after the war had come to an end, great numbers were reported to be "on the tramp" towards the railway stations, for shipment to the United States. In the first few months of 1866, that is, till the Reciprocity Treaty expired, immense droves were taken to the United States, some by way of Montreal to Boston, and others, especially from the country along the line of the Buffalo and Lake Huron Railway, to Buffalo. In fact, it was stated that at this time more Upper Canadian hogs were being packed in Buffalo than in Toronto. After this, the 20 per cent American duty effectually shut out Upper Canadian hogs.[26]

Owing to the increased demand for wool to supply the Federal army with clothing, and to take the place of the cotton no longer obtainable from the south, the northern states witnessed a great expansion in the sheep-raising industry from 1861 to 1865. All the northern states were affected more or less. In some parts of northern New England, the number of sheep doubled, and in Wisconsin it is said that it quadrupled during the war.[27]

The Upper Canadian farmers benefited scarcely less from the demand for wool than did those south of the border. At the beginning of the war, wool in Toronto brought on the average from 20 to 25 cents a pound; by 1863, it was bringing

---

[25]*Ibid.*, March 1, 1864, p. 57; *ibid.*, March 15, 1864, p. 72; *ibid.*, Sept. 15, 1865, p. 280.

[26]*Ibid.*, March 1, 1864, p. 57; *ibid.*, Aug. 15, 1865, p. 256; *ibid.*, Oct. 16, 1865, p. 320; *ibid.*, Feb. 15, 1867, p. 59.

[27]Fite, *Social and Industrial Conditions*, p. 3; Wilson, "Rise and Decline of the Sheep Industry" (*Agricultural History*, vol. IX, 1935, pp. 22-3); Hibbard, *History of Agriculture in Dane County, Wisconsin*, p. 147.

40 cents and even 50 cents, prices comparable to the dollar a pound in greenbacks which prevailed in the northern states. As a result, the amount exported increased from year to year. In 1860 the exports of wool from Toronto, then as later a less important city than Hamilton in the wool trade, were no more than 32,500 pounds, worth $8,800; by 1865 they climbed to an estimated 300,000 pounds, worth $138,000. American demand continued through 1865 to the termination of the Reciprocity Treaty. This was contrary to expectations, as it was the general opinion that it would cease abruptly at the end of the war. That it did not do so was attributed to the fact that the worsted mills going into operation in the eastern states required combing wool, of which there was little in the United States, but an abundance in Upper Canada.[28]

There was an equally lively demand for mutton in the United States during the war. As a result, the trade in live sheep which had developed before 1861 continued unabated. Most American buyers preferred large sheep, like the grade Leicesters and Cotswolds, because they gave more mutton than the smaller breeds, and Upper Canadian farmers had long raised these kinds. In 1863 it was said that most of the fat-sheep surplus of Upper Canada was disposed of in New York State.[29]

The natural effect of the sustained demand in the United States for wool and mutton was a great increase in the number of sheep in Upper Canada. Many farmers turned to sheep-raising, just as they did after 1864 to dairying, to

---

[28]*Canada Farmer*, May 15, 1865, p. 149; *ibid.*, Feb. 1, 1866, pp. 40-2, The wool imported into the American collection districts between Ogdensburg and Milwaukee (including some shipped through Upper Canada from the western states) amounted in the fiscal year 1861-2 to 1,338,895 pounds; in 1862-3 to 1,151,363 pounds; in 1863-4 to 2,482,344 pounds; in 1864-5 to 2,378,727 pounds; and in 1865-6 (8½ months) to an unstated amount valued at $700,047 (*House Executive Documents*, 37th Cong., 3rd Sess., 1862-3, vol. XIII, p. 244; *ibid.*, 38th Cong., 1st Sess., 1863-4, vol. XVII, p. 241; *ibid.*, 38th Cong., 2nd Sess., 1864-5, vol. XV, p. 280; *ibid.*, 39th Cong., 1st Sess., vol. XVII, p. 549; *ibid.*, 39th Cong., 2nd Sess., 1866-7, vol. XVII, p. 389).

[29]*Genesee Farmer*, Oct., 1863, p. 321. One farmer in Albany County, N.Y., purchased 453 head of Leicesters and Leicester crosses in Upper Canada in the autumn of 1862, and sold them the following spring as fat sheep (*ibid.*, May, 1863, p. 150).

find an advantageous means of escape from the ills their excessive wheat-cropping had brought. In 1865 the sheep industry had become important enough in the peninsula of Upper Canada to warrant the formation of a Wool Growers' Association, which was designed to foster sheep-farming in general, but especially in fine wool.[30] A year earlier, an agricultural editor could observe with truth that "the two most inviting channels for agricultural enterprise, are cheese-making and sheep-rearing."[31]

On account of the brisk market for wool, many farmers were tempted to invest in fine-woolled sheep. French and Spanish Merinos were obtained from some of the best flocks of central New York in 1862 and later, and at the provincial exhibition of 1864 there were seventy-four Spanish Merinos and sixty-seven French Merinos entered.[32] But though the Merinos were profitable till the war ended, they were not highly regarded by the average farmer; and when the price of wool fell after the war, the flocks diminished so rapidly that in 1880 there were scarcely any in Ontario.[33]

Another development of the Civil War period was the introduction of the factory manufacture of cheese. It will be dealt with in Chapter xv.

It should not be thought that the period of the war was one of unqualified prosperity in Upper Canada. In spite of the American demand for livestock, coarse grains, and lumber, there was a considerable depression by the winter of 1864-5. There had been partial failures of the wheat crop for several years in the western and central parts.[34] Moreover, during 1864 the depreciation of the United States currency had an adverse effect on the trade across the border. Thus, we are told of the Brockville region in 1864 that "this section of the country has for the last ten years depended very much

---

[30]*Canada Farmer*, Aug. 1, 1864, p. 211; *ibid.*, March 1, 1865, p. 75; *ibid.*, May 15, 1865, p. 149; *ibid.*, Feb. 1, 1866, p. 42.

[31]*Ibid.*, March 1, 1864, p. 53.

[32]*Canadian Agriculturist*, June 16, 1862, p. 367; *Canada Farmer*, April 15, 1864, p. 103; *ibid.*, Nov. 1, 1864, p. 328.

[33]*OACR*, vol. I, p. 321. The long-woolled sheep bore heavier fleeces, and there was little difference in the prices obtainable for the two kinds of wool (*Canada Farmer*, Aug. 1, 1865, p. 229).

[34]*Canada Farmer*, May 15, 1865, p. 149.

upon the United States for a market for their products. During the past season, the Americans, owing to the great depreciation of their currency, have purchased but little from us."[35]

It should be noticed that the Ottawa Valley, as during the depression of 1857, had much less cause for complaint than the more westerly parts of Upper Canada. Though the crops here were only fair during these years, the coarse grains which its farmers grew brought comparatively good prices in the United States. The lumber trade southwards was severely demoralized from the outbreak of the war till late in 1862, but by the middle of 1863, high prices in the United States made it more satisfactory than it had been since 1857. Even when this temporary weakness of the industry on which so many of them depended directly or indirectly was taken into consideration, it was true that most of the farmers in this section of Canada West experienced a real prosperity during the whole Civil War period.[36]

A return current of prosperity set in throughout the rest of Upper Canada on the opening of navigation in 1865, when the Army of Northern Virginia was on the road to Appomattox. Partly owing to an abundant harvest, Upper Canada exported more wheat, flour, and coarse grains "than in any like period for many previous years."[37] Another product equally in demand at this time was butter. American speculators penetrated into the most remote settlements, and paid good prices for the worst grease. Moreover, much wool and many hogs, as has been mentioned, were shipped across the border. The trade in live sheep was brisker than ever before. American dealers scoured all Upper Canada for horses, seeking out those still in the possession of farmers, and offering up to $800 a pair for them. American cattle drovers swarmed through the countryside, forcing local buyers practically out of business, and brought immense herds to the

---

[35]*TBAUC 1864-8*, p. 193.

[36]Montreal *Witness*, April 12, 1863; Toronto *Globe*, May 31, 1865.

[37]Report of D. Thorton, United States Consul at Toronto, Feb. 7, 1866 (*House Executive Documents*, 39th Cong., 1st Sess., 1865-6, no. 56, p. 31).

depots.[38] So many of the cattle bought were milch cows, which were in great demand in New York, that fears were expressed that the dairy interest would suffer as a result;[39] but probably the greatest number, as usual, was made up of feeders. "Butchers and speculators," it was stated, "are stocking the mountain pastures of New Hampshire extensively with Canadian cattle."[40] Apparently the export trade in livestock attained these large proportions because the opening of the southern market was tending to drain the north of its cattle and other animals. The fact that the trade in all these articles was so great, though the American currency was still much depreciated with reference to the Canadian, was probably owing to the circumstance that there were "high prices in the United States due to paper money inflation, while yet there was gold in the country for export."[41]

At the end of 1865, the Upper Canadian agricultural community could look back on a season of exceptional prosperity. American dealers had swept the country clean of livestock, butter, wheat, flour, and coarse grains. The result was that Upper Canadians assumed an attitude of indifference to the approaching termination of the Reciprocity Treaty. "The high prices the Americans have been paying lead to the opinion that no serious effects of the abrogation of the Reciprocity Treaty will be felt for years at least," remarked one authority.[42] As the chief agricultural journal of Upper Canada put it: "There has been no time since the treaty was negotiated when our country has been so well prepared for the effects of its abrogation."[43] The American consul at Toronto noted that "the failure of the negotiation for the renewal of the reciprocity treaty has caused no apparent curtailment of preparations for the next year's business. . . . There are many parties who talk of the increase of trade

[38]*TBAUC 1864-8*, pp. 337, 353, 355, 363; Montreal *Witness*, Sept. 20, 1865; *Perth Courier*, Sept. 22, Oct. 6, 1865; *Canada Farmer*, April 15, 1865-April 2, 1866, *passim*.

[39]*Canada Farmer*, Nov. 1, 1865, p. 331; *ibid.*, April 2, 1866, pp. 105, 107; *ibid.*, May 1, 1866, p. 144.

[40]*Ibid.*, July 15, 1865, p. 213.

[41]Haynes, *Reciprocity Treaty*, p. 34 *n.*

[42]Montreal *Witness*, Jan. 17, 1866.

[43]*Canada Farmer*, April 2, 1866, p. 105.

between Canada and England as likely to yield the same if not larger returns than have been realized by the exportation of the same articles to the United States. But the difference between expectation and facts is shown by the results from shipments of grain, flour, and other products to England during the past twenty years."[44]

The Reciprocity Treaty thus ended on a wave of speculative optimism which, as the last sentence suggests, had slight justification in past experience. Actually, the termination of the treaty had little effect on the export to the United States of horses and lumber and barley, but in other respects, as we shall see, it gave rise to new agricultural problems.

---

[44]Report of D. Thorton, Feb. 7, 1866, p. 32.

CHAPTER XIV

THE GRAIN TRADE AND GRAIN-GROWING, 1866-1880

SEVERAL of the changes in the grain trade of Upper Canada between the repeal of the Corn Laws and the termination of the Reciprocity Treaty have already been discussed—the transference of the exports of the western states, and even of those of Upper Canada, to the Erie Canal; the growth in the volume of Upper Canada wheat and flour entering the United States for domestic consumption; and the development of an American market for peas and coarse grains. There were other significant changes during these years in the grain trade, both transit and domestic, which should be dealt with before we turn to developments in grain-growing and the grain trade after 1866.

During the eighteen-fifties Montreal and the St. Lawrence system steadily lost ground to the Erie Canal and New York in the competition for the grain of the Great Lakes region. The decline was, of course, relative. Montreal did have a large absolute increase in her grain trade after the completion of the canals. In 1846, there were exported from the St. Lawrence 3,312,757 bushels of wheat, including flour estimated as wheat at the ratio of a barrel of flour to five bushels of wheat; in 1853, 6,597,193 bushels; in 1856, 9,391,531 bushels; and in 1860, 8,431,253 bushels.[1] The promoters of the Grand Trunk had been certain that it would draw through Montreal the grain trade which had been lost to the Erie Canal. It is true that its construction did, in a measure, counterbalance the advantages possessed by New York in the Erie Canal and the New York Central Railroad. With the completion of the Grand Trunk, and the establishment of a regular line of steamers between Quebec and Liverpool, there was almost at once a great falling off in the receipts of flour and grain at Oswego and other American lake ports and an increase at Quebec and Montreal, and American flour from as far west as Iowa began to pass over the railway to Portland in the

---

[1]Hind, *Eighty Years' Progress*, p. 291.

winter.[2] Nevertheless, the New York route was still favoured over the Montreal one, even by the Upper Canada shippers of grain for export. Thus, in the five years from 1855 to 1859, the shipments of grain and flour by way of Buffalo and Oswego were about twenty times those by way of Montreal.[3]

The outbreak of the American Civil War gave a decided impetus to the transit grain trade. The receipts of American wheat and Indian corn at Kingston for transfer to vessels bound for Oswego or Montreal will serve as an illustration. In 1860, they amounted to approximately 1,184,000 bushels of wheat and 219,000 bushels of Indian corn; in 1861 to 2,851,000 bushels and 1,013,000 bushels respectively; in 1862 to 5,079,000 bushels and 1,913,000 bushels; in 1863 to 3,135,000 bushels and 654,000 bushels; in 1864 to 1,813,000 bushels and 122,000 bushels; and in 1865 to 1,687,000 bushels and 640,000 bushels.[4] Before 1861 Montreal had exported on the average about 500,000 bushels of wheat (not including flour) a year. In 1861 it sent overseas approximately 5,585,000 bushels, in 1862, 6,501,000; in 1863, 3,741,000, and in 1864, 2,407,000.[5] More grain, it was reported, "reached Montreal in 1861 and 1862, than in all the previous years since the opening of the canals."[6] The sudden increase in 1861 was partly owing to the closing of the Mississippi, which had the effect of blocking southern outlets for western grain, and partly owing to the circumstance that dealers in the American Northwest, who now turned perforce to the European market, considered the northern route by Montreal and the Gulf of St. Lawrence less endangered by Confederate commerce raiders than that by New York.[7] At the end of the Civil War,

---

[2]Detroit *Free Press*, quoted in *Canadian Merchants' Magazine*, April, 1858, p. 53; Portland *State of Maine*, quoted in *ibid.*, Feb., 1858, p. 449.

[3]*Sessional Papers, Canada*, 1860, no. 11 (hereafter cited as *SPC*). On the factors affecting the competition between the St. Lawrence Waterway and the Erie Canal in the transit grain trade at this time and later, see Innis and Lower (eds.), *Select Documents in Canadian Economic History*, pp. 471-86.

[4]Patterson, *Statements relating to the Home and Foreign Trade . . . for 1877*, p. 37.

[5]*Ibid.*, p. 95.

[6]Hind, *Eighty Years' Progress*, p. 183.

[7]Masters, *Reciprocity Treaty of 1854*, p. 185.

there was a sudden drop in the exports of flour and wheat from Montreal. The reason for this was that in 1865 the United States absorbed all the best Upper Canadian wheat and flour, as well as most of its own domestic crop.[8] Then the exports via the St. Lawrence revived, and continued to grow steadily, mainly in consequence of the supplies received from the American West. In 1875, when the receipts of wheat alone at Montreal were nearly 8,000,000 bushels, it was said that this did "represent an immense trade, but a large part of it is merely the handling of wheat bought in the Western States for through shipment."[9] In spite of the considerable absolute increase in its grain trade, Montreal failed to match the development of its old rival, New York. However, about 1875 or 1876, it did surpass Oswego in the amount of grain handled.[10]

The expansion of the trade through the St. Lawrence was facilitated by improvements in the methods of handling grain. So far-reaching were they that by 1863 the tonnage of flour going down the river was only a third that of wheat, whereas ten years earlier it had been three times as great.[11] By the early eighteen-sixties steamers were plying between Lake Michigan ports and Sarnia or Collingwood, and transferring their cargoes at these points to the railroads, which transported them to Lake Ontario ports, where they were loaded into steamers or sailing vessels. The aeration of the grain at the time of transfer was claimed to be an incidental advantage of the trans-shipping.[12] In the meantime, many of the ships engaged in the grain trade on the Great Lakes— particularly the broad and long sailing vessels—had been built too large to pass through the Canadian canals. Accordingly, to provide an auxiliary to the Welland Canal, the Hon. W. H. Merritt fostered a company which constructed a portage railway across the Niagara peninsula, to carry grain from vessels on Lake Erie and discharge it into others on Lake Ontario.[13] In the middle eighteen-seventies schooners from

8*Canada Farmer*, Feb. 1, 1866, p. 41; Montreal *Witness*, Jan. 17, 1866.
9Montreal *Witness*, quoted in *Farmer's Advocate*, Dec., 1875, p. 223.
10*Farmer's Advocate*, June, 1877, p. 129.
11Hind, *Eighty Years' Progress*, p. 183.
12*Agriculture of the United States in 1860*, p. cliii.
13Hind, *Eighty Years' Progress*, pp. 236-7.

Chicago or Milwaukee brought their cargoes of 18,000 or 20,000 bushels of wheat or Indian corn to Kingston, where they were trans-shipped to barges which were towed to Montreal. Larger upper-lake boats, usually steamers, carrying 30,000 or 35,000 bushels, could not pass through the Welland Canal, so their cargoes were unloaded at Port Colborne, taken by rail across the Niagara peninsula, transshipped at Port Dalhousie for Kingston, and again at Kingston for Montreal. Occasionally the Chicago boats ran only to Collingwood, and the grain was sent from there by rail to Toronto, and trans-shipped at the latter place for Kingston. Sometimes shipments were made direct from Chicago to Montreal in schooners or small steamers, but these unloaded about a third of their cargoes at Kingston before proceeding to Montreal.[14]

The fact that the average through-rate from Chicago to Montreal in 1877 was only 10 or 11 cents a bushel is to be accounted for by the development of bulk handling facilities. At Kingston, as early as 1856, there was at least one floating elevator, capable of unloading 3,000 bushels an hour from the lake boats into St. Lawrence or Oswego Canal barges.[15] In the late eighteen-seventies, Kingston had five floating elevators, together capable of transferring 250,000 bushels in twelve hours; and Montreal had seven elevators for transferring grain from the Kingston barges, four for emptying railway cars, and twelve floating ones in the harbour.[16] By 1866, elevators were being built at such points as Collingwood, where grain was received from the upper-lake boats.[17]

The grain trade within Upper Canada was profoundly affected by the advent of the railways. The markets at such places as Goderich and Kincardine began to decline in importance, as the grain they formerly would have received

---

[14]Patterson, *Statements relating to the Home and Foreign Trade . . . for 1877*, p. 22.

[15]*Canadian Merchants' Magazine*, April, 1857, p. 28.

[16]Patterson, *Statements relating to the Home and Foreign Trade . . . for 1877*, pp. 23-4.

[17]*Canadian Handbook and Tourists' Guide*, p. 140. For a description of an elevator built at Toronto in 1863, see *Canadian Agriculturist*, May, 1863, p. 198.

was carried off by the railways to Toronto and elsewhere.[18] The creek-mouth shipping ports soon disappeared. Yet, at ports such as Whitby, with its excellent harbour and its railway into the back country, the old state of affairs continued. At Whitby, too, farmers still teamed their grain in to the dealers from considerable distances.[19] At the close of the American Civil War, most of the towns and villages along the shore of Lake Ontario were becoming noted as barley ports. They maintained their reputation till the barley trade across the lake was crippled by the McKinley Tariff. Now nothing remains of them but a few rotting wharves.[20]

One of the striking results of railway construction was the rise of Toronto as a primary grain market, that is, a place for the large-scale collection of grain and flour for shipment to domestic markets for home consumption, or to the seaboard for export. The rapid growth of the Toronto grain trade was thus described in 1856:

> Toronto is becoming a very important wheat market. Enjoying an excellent geographical position, within a few hours' sail of the south shore of the lake, where there are numerous mills and a good market, as at Rochester, Wilson, Oswego, Ogdensburg, &c., in the midst of a most fertile country, into which now radiate railways, East, West, North and Northwest, with abundant facilities for purchase, storage, and shipment; and possessing men of business, energy and tact, we believe that Toronto is speedily becoming the leading market in the Provinces. The receipts of wheat for the past two months, are 275,000 bushels per week; of this about 35,000 bushels in each week have been purchased on the market, while a great deal of it has been sold by country dealers to our wholesale buyers, in lots of 1,000 bushels and upwards, being what is termed, "shipping parcels."[21]

By 1865 the pre-eminence of Toronto as the leading grain market of Canada West admitted of no doubt, for the prices there tended to determine those in the lesser ports.[22]

The rise of the city as a grain market resulted in the

---

[18]*SPC 1870*, no. 49.

[19]Smith, *Pioneers of Old Ontario*, p. 164.

[20]There is a slight amount of information about these barley ports, particularly Bowmanville, in Martyn, "Loitering along Lake Ontario" (*Canadian Geographical Journal*, vol. XIII, 1936).

[21]*Canadian Agriculturist*, Oct., 1856, p. 288.

[22]*Canada Farmer*, May 15, 1865, p. 149.

formation of the Toronto Exchange in 1855. Similar exchanges had already appeared in the United States and at Montreal, owing to the need of a specialized commercial organization where buyers and sellers or their agents could come together conveniently. The Toronto Exchange was organized by the merchants, millers, and brokers of the city and the surrounding country, partly as a stock exchange but mainly as an exchange for dealing in wheat and flour and other products of the soil.[23]

To facilitate dealings such as those on this exchange, as well as to overcome the difficulty of keeping grain shipments of different qualities and of different owners distinct when they were handled by elevators, the provincial legislature passed a grain-grading act in 1863. Flour, it will be remembered, had been inspected since the first shipments down the St. Lawrence in the days of the Loyalists. That this was done in perfunctory fashion we may deduce from the fact that in the eighteen-thirties the British buyers thought so little of the inspectors' brand that they always bought according to their own judgment.[24] By the eighteen-fifties it had become the custom of the millers to stamp a barrel of flour they would like to have considered very superior as Extra Superfine, one of second quality as Fancy Superfine, one of third quality as Superfine, one of fourth quality as Superfine No. 2, and one of fifth quality as Fine. The inspectors at places like Toronto had authority under the law to alter these designations, and did so daily.[25] Though merchants and grain dealers were thus conversant with the idea of inspection and grading, wheat was not officially graded in Upper Canada till five years after a grain-grading system had been established at Chicago. The Grain Inspection Act of 1863[26] provided that there should be inspectors at Quebec, Montreal, Kingston, Toronto, Hamilton, London, and any other cities which might have a Board of Trade; that there should be three grades for winter wheat—No. 1 and No. 2 White and

---

[23]*Canadian Agriculturist*, March, 1857, p. 73; *Annual Report of the Toronto Board of Trade for 1855*, p. 10.

[24]York *Christian Guardian*, Dec. 26, 1832.

[25]*Canadian Merchants' Magazine*, Nov., 1857, pp. 357-8.

[26]26 Vic., c. 3.

No. 1 Red—, and three for spring wheat—Extra, No. 1, and No. 2; that all unsound, very dirty, or damp wheat should be classed as Rejected; that peas, barley, rye, and oats might also be graded; that certificates of inspection should be issued; and that inspection was not to be compulsory. The act was evidently intended to apply mainly to shippers. To what extent was it effective? At Montreal in 1864 one-twelfth of the receipts of wheat was inspected, and one-seventh of the exports. Peas, barley, corn, oats, and rye were seldom graded. In 1870 grain dealers, even at Toronto, manifested little disposition to purchase from the farmers on the basis of inspection, though they sometimes did so. There is some evidence that grading was of more importance by 1880, especially in Waterloo, Wellington, Bruce, and Grey counties.[27]

Another revelation of maturity in the grain trade was to be found in its methods of financing. In an earlier chapter it was pointed out that in the eighteen-thirties banks, millers, and Montreal forwarders were accustomed to advance money to dealers for the purchase of wheat. By 1860 bank financing was so important that farmers threshed as soon as possible and brought their crops at once to market. "They *must* send them forward; they cannot keep them [for speculation]; banks wont loan money to them to hold on to their crops, but will loan plenty to dealers to pay for produce."[28] The failure of the Commercial Bank, which was followed by a run on other banks, completely paralysed the Ontario grain trade for about a month in the autumn of 1867.[29] Another method of financing became important about 1860, when arrangements were made whereby advances could be obtained by dealers on warehouse receipts and bills of lading.[30] Even earlier,

---

[27]Patterson, *Report on the Trade and Commerce of Montreal for 1864*, pp. 56, 62-3, 66, 69; *Canada Farmer*, May 15, 1871, p. 181; Toronto *Globe*, Jan. 14, 1870; Toronto *Weekly Globe*, Sept. 5, 1879.

[28]*Canadian Agriculturist*, Nov. 1, 1860, p. 556. Cf.: "The banks . . . continue to supply the necessary funds for the removal of the immense product at the usual rate of seven per cent" (Hamilton *Times*, quoted in *Canada Farmer*, Oct. 15, 1866, p. 315).

[29]Report of D. Thurston, United States Consul at Toronto, Jan. 1, 1868 (*House Executive Document*, 40th Cong., 2nd Sess. 1867-8, no. 160, pp. 135-6).

[30]Innis and Lower (eds.), *Select Documents in Canadian Economic History*, p. 491.

on the opening of the "New England market," there was another factor of much significance in the financing of the grain trade in Upper Canada. It was remarked in 1860 of Toronto that "ever since, and, indeed, before the ratification of the Reciprocity Treaty, we have always had throughout the winter, a small army of Americans, who were either speculators or representatives of important milling interests in the Eastern States. To these men our smaller dealers disposed of round lots of from five to ten thousand bushels as fast as they could be got together. . . . Our dealers made fair profits without losing heavily by a decline; and farmers realized the highest prices on the continent." These Americans paid the Upper Canadian dealers from whom they purchased with drafts on New York banks. The dealers cashed them and paid the farmers in Canadian currency. Accordingly, the grain trade of Toronto was largely financed during these years by American funds.[31]

Though the dealers now invariably paid them in cash, the farmers were just as critical of them as ever. The following passage shows that they had a real grievance in the treatment they received from the commission merchants at the shipping ports and the railway stations.

The present plan by which farmers have to sell their grain is most unfair. The buyer has all the advantage and the seller none. The farmer drives eight, or perhaps ten miles into market; when there, he must either sell his grain at the price ruling that day, or drive back his load; the latter he will not do for the sake of a few cents per bushel, and consequently he sells his grain at a sacrifice.

Again, there comes on a heavy rain. The buyers say among themselves: "two or three cents per bushel less for this rain;" the farmers will sooner sell even at a reduced figure than get drenched to the skin.

In the barley season, such matters as these particularly affect the daily variation of prices. It is a notorious fact, that when there are only a few teams on the market, a larger price is offered to draw the

[31]*Annual Report of the Toronto Board of Trade for 1860*, p. 7. The rest of the financing process in the late eighteen-fifties was this: "In the usual course of trade, exporters send breadstuffs, cotton, etc., abroad, and draw 60 day drafts upon the proceeds. These proceeds, constituting foreign exchange, are sold to importers of foreign goods, and the proceeds used in paying for the crops brought from the interior" (*American Agriculturist*, vol. xx, 1861, p. 28).

farmers, and that when on the succeeding days the latter put in a strong attendance, the inevitable fall in price takes place.[32]

There is no doubt that the bait was effective, for the Upper Canada grain market had long been notoriously sensitive to price changes. As early as 1852 a Wellington County essayist could write that "an advance of a penny per bushel in the price of grain at Guelph, is known in every part of the County within twenty-four hours of such advance taking place."[33]

After Confederation barley encroached more and more on wheat as the most important cereal of Ontario growth entering into the grain trade. The steady gain in the production of barley at the expense of other grains as well as of wheat in the period between 1860 and 1880 will be clear from the returns of the census.[34]

| | 1860 | | 1870 | | 1880 | |
	Acres	Bushels	Acres	Bushels	Acres	Bushels
Spring wheat	951,637	17,082,774		7,891,989		7,213,024
			1,365,905		1,949,135	
Fall wheat	434,729	7,537,651		6,341,400		20,193,067
Oats	678,337	21,220,874		22,138,958		40,209,929
Peas	460,595	9,601,396		7,653,545		
						9,434,872
Beans				107,925		
Indian corn	79,918	2,256,290		3,148,467		8,096,782
Rye	70,376	973,181		547,609		1,598,871
Buckwheat	74,565	1,248,637		585,158		841,649
Barley	118,940	2,821,962		9,461,233		14,279,841

The prime reason for the expansion of the barley industry was that the abrogation of the Reciprocity Treaty brought no check in the exporting of the grain to the United States. An association of American brewers presented a memorial to Congress in 1866, in which it was stated "that if the barley now grown in Canada was reduced one-half, it would cripple

---

[32]*Canada Farmer*, May 15, 1871, p. 181. Cf. *ibid.*, March 15, 1866, p. 88.

[33]*Journal and Transactions of the Board of Agriculture of Upper Canada for 1855-6*, p. 219.

[34]*Census of Canada, 1861*, vol. II, pp. 91-2; *Census of Canada, 1871*, vol. III, pp. 150-1; *Census of Canada, 1881*, vol. III, pp. 226-7.

the manufacture of malt liquors to such an extent as to involve a loss to the United States treasury, annually, of about $2,000,000."[35] American brewers then and for some time thereafter were able to satisfy only a third of their barley requirements from the domestic crop, but this was not the only reason for their dependence on Ontario. The barley they obtained from north of the border was superior to that of the western states, as was shown in quotations prior to the end of reciprocity. Early in 1866 western barley was quoted in Chicago at from 30 to 60 cents for common to good grades, while "choice grades of Canada" brought from $1.20 to $1.30.[36] Ontario barley came, indeed, to have the reputation of being the finest grown in North America. An American investigator explained why this was so:

Barley, as well as being one of the staple articles of export [from London], is also one of the most important, on account of the position Canadian barley has taken among the brewers and maltsters of the United States; in fact, it has become virtually a necessity in the manufacture of ale and beer on account of its peculiar properties, which are in all probability climatic and due in a measure to the soil. At any rate it produces a better color and more extract than the barley raised in the United States, as well as makes a beer with a delicate flavor, which will keep better in hot climates and stand export without deterioration. In nearly all first-class breweries in the United States, I understand, a proportion of it, from 25 to 75 per cent., is mixed with native barley, in order to attain the results mentioned above.[37]

This admitted superiority virtually nullified the United States duty of 15 cents a bushel, for in spite of increasing American competition, Ontario barley still sold in the eighteen-eighties for about 10 cents a bushel more than that from the western states.[38] Under these circumstances the trade increased from

---

[35]*House Executive Document*, 39th Cong., 1st Sess., 1865-6, no. 128, p. 113.

[36]*American Agriculturist*, vol. xxv, 1866, p. 89.

[37]"Report of Commercial Agent Washington on the Exports from London, Canada, to the United States" (*House Executive Document*, 49th Cong., 1st Sess., 1885-6, no. 253, p. 609). The best Ontario barley was grown along the Bay of Quinte (*Canada. Farmer*, Dec. 30, 1873, p. 453).

[38]Report of United States Consul at Hamilton, 1886 (*House Executive Document*, 49th Cong., 2nd Sess., 1886-7, no. 171, p. 804).

year to year. According to American statistics, there were exported direct from Ontario to the United States approximately 3,612,000 bushels of barley in 1868; 5,114,000 in 1869; 5,169,000 in 1870; 3,587,000 in 1873; 4,997,000 in 1874; 8,236,000 in 1875; 7,521,000 in 1876; and 6,701,000 in 1877.[39] It might be added that by 1890 the Dominion of Canada was exporting almost 10,000,000 bushels of barley a year to the United States, almost entirely from Ontario and Quebec. The imposition of a duty of 30 cents a bushel by the McKinley Tariff of October, 1890, reduced the trade to small proportions, and at the same time ruined the malting industry in upstate New York which had been largely dependent on it.[40]

There were other outlets for Ontario barley, but these were much less important than the American. Breweries catering to an extensive trade were in operation about 1867 at Prescott, Kingston, Toronto, Hamilton, and London, and these provided a local market.[41] There was an unreliable demand in the United Kingdom. Some brewers there liked the Canadian four-rowed barley because they could make from it a light beer (which was in demand among the upper classes as a stomachic), whereas from their home-grown two-rowed barley they could make only strong ales and porters. In any case, most of the barley shipped overseas was the growth of Quebec rather than of Ontario. Whatever its origin, Canadian barley failed to gain any real footing in the British Isles before 1880. The exports overseas from Montreal reached 901,000 bushels in 1867; 451,000 in 1868; 251,000 in 1870; and 1,091,000 in 1877; but in no other year from 1867 to 1877 did they exceed 250,000 bushels.[42]

---

[39]Patterson, *Report on the Trade and Commerce of Montreal for 1870*, p. 21; Patterson, *Statements Relating to the Home and Foreign Trade . . . for 1877*, p. 79.

[40]MacGibbon, *Canadian Grain Trade*, p. 21; Weaver, "Barley in the United States" (*Geographical Review*, vol. XXXIII, 1943, p. 69).

[41]Small, *Products and Manufactures of the New Dominion*, pp. 137-8.

[42]Toronto *Weekly Globe*, Jan. 4, 1878; MacGibbon, *Canadian Grain Trade*, p. 22; Patterson, *Statements relating to the Home and Foreign Trade . . . for 1877*, p. 95.

The lack of a strong British demand for barley made little difference in Ontario so long as the American one was sustained. Barley became the staple crop of the country from Kingston west to the head of Lake Ontario. The crop of 1880, as already noticed, was 14,279,841 bushels. The electoral ridings of Lennox and Addington produced 997,714 bushels; Prince Edward 876,432; Hastings East, Hastings West, and Hastings North 886,619; Northumberland East and Northumberland West 811,606; Durham East and Durham West 783,948; Victoria South and Victoria North 556,942; Ontario South and Ontario North 797,332; York East, York West, and York North 1,002,399; and Peel and Cardwell 596,277. Only two western Ontario counties had a production in excess of 500,000 bushels. The ridings of Wellington South, Wellington Centre, and Wellington North had 671,170, and those of Middlesex East, Middlesex West, and Middlesex North 565,239. In this part of the province barley did not compete successfully with fall wheat.[43]

The growing of barley on the extensive scale indicated inevitably involved a tendency towards soil exhaustion through excessive cropping. A Northumberland County farmer was emphatic on this point. "All of us can remember how some years ago, what with dry weather, and the midge, it was hardly possible to grow a crop of wheat worth harvesting; [sic] Then we took to raising barley as a substitute; and now, as a natural result, in many of our fields we can hardly tell which is master, barley, thistles, or charlak."[44] Aside from soil exhaustion, the chief disadvantage of the industry was the great fluctuation in price to which the grain was subject. It was said that the reason for the capricious prices was that the market was controlled by a few men—presumably either the American brewers or else the grain-pit operators. Barley growing was in consequence always more or less speculative in character.[45]

None of the other coarse grains was of much importance

---

[43]*Census of Canada, 1881*, vol. III, pp. 192-226.

[44]*Canada Farmer*, Feb. 15, 1873, p. 44.

[45]*Ibid.*, Dec. 30, 1873, p. 453; *Report of the Ontario Agricultural Commission*, vol. I, p. 369. Hereafter this authority is cited as *OACR*.

as an article of trade. The exporting of oats to the United States was crippled by the termination of the Reciprocity Treaty, though there was occasionally some traffic across the border. Thus, about 1870 two townships in Glengarry County shipped approximately 200,000 bushels to New England. Moreover, especially after 1870, a good deal of Ontario oats was manufactured into oatmeal, some of which was sold in the United States. On the whole, it seems that most of the Ontario oats surplus went to England, either as grain or oatmeal, but the quantity thus disposed of was seldom large.[46] Rye was negligible as an export crop. Farmers felt that it was a reflection on them or their farms if they cultivated it. One witness before the Ontario Agricultural Commission expressed the prevailing prejudice—"he had no land poor enough for rye." Some grain dealers at Perth shipped rye to Belgium and Germany in the few years preceding 1880, and for some time after 1880, but the market was not satisfactory owing to American competition. They bought the grain from the farmers on the sandy soils of western Lanark County and western Renfrew County.[47] Indian corn entered into the grain trade to some extent, but only on a provincial basis. It was a valuable crop in Essex, Kent, Norfolk, and Elgin counties. Of the 8,096,782 bushels returned as the Ontario crop of 1880, Essex riding produced 1,103,179; Kent 801,227; Bothwell 469,790; Elgin East 466,581; and Norfolk South and Norfolk North together 681,057. In this region it was fed as grain to hogs and cattle. Most of the surplus of Essex County, amounting to about 100,000 bushels a year, went to a local distillery, while that of Kent County went eastward to livestock feeders. Outside the counties mentioned corn was extensively cultivated as a

---

[46]Montreal *Witness*, March 8, 1871; Toronto *Globe*, Jan. 4, 1870; Toronto *Weekly Globe*, Jan. 31, 1879; Patterson, *Statements relating to the Home and Foreign Trade . . . for 1877*, p. 95; *Journal of the House of Commons, Canada, 1876*, App. 7, p. 4.

[47]*OACR*, vol. I, pp. 378-9. The limited export market for rye was crippled in the middle eighteen-eighties by the raising of the German tariff (Report of Albert Roberts, United States Consul at Hamilton, Nov. 16, 1887, *House Executive Document*, 50th Cong., 1st Sess., 1887-8, no. 402, p. 516).

green fodder, especially for dairy cattle, without any attempt being made to save the ears.[48]

During the eighteen-seventies the surplus of peas could usually be disposed of either in Great Britain or the United States. The amount of peas shipped to these two countries fluctuated. The steadiest demand in the United States came (as in the eighteen-sixties) from the sheep feeders, and this varied in accordance with the price. The quantity exported overseas was ordinarily determined by the availability there of supplies from the Baltic and Black seas, together with the price of Indian corn in Europe. After 1870 a large proportion of the peas exported to Great Britain was intended to be used as seed rather than as fodder. This had long been true to a considerable extent of those exported to the United States; indeed, it was asserted that, without Ontario seed-peas, there would have been scarcely any pea culture in North America. Yet even this profitable trade in seed-peas was threatened. The pea-weevil which, it will be remembered, had been troublesome during the eighteen-fifties, spread so rapidly during the eighteen-sixties and eighteen-seventies that it was only in Eastern Ontario and in the country north and west of Toronto that it was not forcing farmers out of the crop.[49]

To fill the deficiency created by the exports of peas and barley, Ontario (like Quebec) drew on the western states. Lumbermen sometimes imported oats, not so much on the ground of cheapness, as on that of the American crop being earlier. Farmers in grazing regions found that American Indian corn was much the cheapest grain they could buy for finishing their livestock. Others, who made a practice of

---

[48]*OACR*, vol. I, pp. 374-8; *Census of Canada, 1881*, vol. III, pp. 213, 217, 223, 225, 227. Silos had not as yet appeared in Ontario.

[49]*Country Gentleman*, quoted in Ohio State Board of Agriculture, *Annual Report for the Year 1863*, p. xxix; Toronto *Globe*, Jan. 14, 1870; *Canada Farmer*, June 15, 1875, p. 118; *OACR*, vol. I, pp. 170-3, 373-4. The leading pea-growing regions in Ontario in 1880 were the ridings of Wellington South, Wellington Centre, and Wellington North with 787,649 bushels; Grey South, Grey East, and Grey North with 760,346 bushels; Bruce South and Bruce North with 619,856 bushels; and Simcoe South and Simcoe North with 549,388 bushels (*Census of Canada, 1881*, vol. III, pp. 192-226). These statistics include a small quantity of beans.

selling their barley and oats, likewise bought Indian corn to replace them.[50]

While Ontario barley was acquiring a reputation for itself in the American market, Ontario wheat was steadily losing the one it had long held. After 1866 exports of it to the United States steadily declined, though it is true that on some exceptional occasions, such as in 1866 itself, crop failures south of the border created a considerable demand.[51] The white wheat of the province was coming into disfavour in the New York market by 1868, mainly because it was so heavily impregnated with smut; indeed, it was selling for less than sound spring wheat.[52] Under these circumstances, the tariff effectively kept it out of the United States. The story was the same with flour. The demand in the United States held up well in 1866 and 1867. Then it shrank rapidly, though at least one Ontario miller about 1876 continued to sell his 10,000 to 20,000 barrels of flour there, a quota he had maintained since before 1866. With the new "patent process" of grinding flour, introduced at Minneapolis about 1870, the American millers were able to manufacture such a high-class spring-wheat flour that Canadians could not compete with them at New York. Moreover, though the leading Ontario millers did adopt the patent process by 1874, they suffered greatly from the dumping of lower-grade American flours in the Maritimes, at that time their best market.[53]

The loss of the share of the American flour and wheat market which had been profitable for twenty years or so was merely one aspect of the decline of the Ontario wheat industry. It has been shown previously that, during the eighteen-fifties, there were many indications that wheat was failing as a staple in central and western Upper Canada. The

[50]Toronto *Weekly Globe*, May 12, 1876; *ibid.*, Jan. 31, 1879; *JHC 1876*, App. 7, p. 4.

[51]*Canada Farmer*, Feb. 15, 1867, p. 58. For the chief developments in the wheat-growing industry in the United States between 1867 and 1882, see Veblen, "The Price of Wheat since 1867" (*Journal of Political Economy*, vol. I, 1892-3, pp. 68-94).

[52]*Canada Farmer*, Jan. 15, 1869, p. 28; *ibid.*, Feb. 15, 1870, p. 74.

[53]*Ibid.*, Feb. 15, 1867, p. 58; *ibid.*, Feb. 15, 1868, p. 60; *JHC 1876*, App. 3, pp. 69, 75, 78.

wheat midge combined with soil exhaustion to make the crop unprofitable in most of the older settlements. However, after 1860 the midge gradually came to occupy a less prominent place in Upper Canada agriculture. While certain sections sometimes suffered grievously from its ravages, as did York and Peel counties in 1864, the insect was not as troublesome as it had been earlier. After 1869 it ceased to do any appreciable mischief, and by 1872 it had virtually disappeared. While it is probable that the vanishing of the midge was to be attributed mostly to its being attacked by parasites, as the entomologists insisted (though without any proof), the farmers certainly helped by turning to other crops, by following the advice of the agricultural journals to sow spring wheat instead of fall and to sow it either too early or too late to be affected by the midge, and by developing "midge-proof" varieties of wheat. These owed their immunity to the fact that they grew quickly and matured early, or else matured late.[54]

In spite of the discovery of midge-proof wheat, of the passing of the midge, and of occasional high prices, farmers in the older parts of central and western Upper Canada placed less and less reliance on wheat as their main crop. The midge-proof wheat was soft, and so inferior for milling.[55] The old fall wheat, as has been mentioned, was affected by smut. The yield per acre declined steadily on the average long-cultivated farm. Complaints of soil exhaustion became more common than ever before, though farmers were not disposed to attribute the condition to their own wasteful agricultural methods. "In various parts of this province," declared one editor, "the complaint is made that it no longer pays to grow wheat, and many regard the land as poverty-stricken from some occult cause only to be sought in the realms of meteorology and climatology."[56] Many farmers found more profit in other branches of agriculture than in

---

[54]*Canada Farmer*, Aug. 1, 1864, p. 211; *ibid.*, July 15, 1865, p. 217; *ibid.*, March 31, 1873, p. 97; *OACR*, vol. I, p. 160; *ibid.*, vol. III, App. E, p. 24.

[55]*Canada Farmer*, Nov. 1, 1866, p. 328.

[56]*Ibid.*, Jan. 15, 1864, p. 4.

growing wheat—in dairying, in wool-growing, in livestock husbandry, in other grains. Early in the eighteen-sixties fall wheat was abandoned in most of the country between the Bay of Quinte and Toronto, and by the end of 1866 barley had largely replaced fall wheat in the other older settled districts of central Upper Canada. Fall wheat was then disappearing so fast from the vicinity of Toronto that little was being teamed into the city.[57] Even spring wheat, which had been fairly successful when the fall wheat was worst affected by the midge, was becoming a complete failure in many places by the eighteen-seventies. The Red Fife, the best kind of all, had sadly deteriorated. It was so nearly worn out by 1877 that a large importation of it was made from Manitoba for seed.[58]

There were factors which helped to delay the westward passage of the wheat industry, even in the older settlements. One was the evident disappearance of the midge. Another was comparatively high prices for wheat. Thus, the fall-wheat crop of 1871 was one of the largest ever produced in Ontario, and as it had been little harmed by the midge, the quality was high. When it sold for $1.35 a bushel in Toronto —largely owing to the Franco-Prussion War—one editor, who ten years earlier would have been delighted with the crop and the price, half deplored both, fearing that the Ontario farmers who were just emerging from the old thriftless plan of cultivating wheat almost exclusively might, unthinking, make it once more their chief dependence.[59] Again, wheat continued to be grown as successfully in the new townships as formerly it had been in the older. For example, in the late eighteen-sixties Bruce County exported on the average 300,000 to 400,000 bushels of wheat a year, and in 1880 the reclaimed lands of the Essex peninsula were bringing forth abundant crops.[60] Finally, fall wheat was still profitable throughout

---

[57]*Canadian Agriculturist*, July 16, 1862, p. 421; *Canada Farmer*, Aug. 15, 1864, p. 239; *ibid.*, Feb. 15, 1867, p. 58; *ibid.*, Feb. 15, 1868, p. 60.

[58]*Canada Farmer*, Jan. 15, 1875, p. 18; Toronto *Weekly Globe*, Jan. 25, March 29, 1878; *OACR*, vol. I, pp. 343-4, 362-5.

[59]*Canada Farmer*, Oct. 16, 1871, p. 381.

[60]*Ibid.*, Oct. 1, 1867, p. 296; *OACR*, vol. IV, App. G, pp. 57-9, 75.

Western Ontario when grown as part of a scheme of mixed farming, and the same was true to a lesser degree of spring wheat. As a consequence of these factors, the wheat acreage of Ontario continued to increase till 1880. At that time Middlesex and Huron counties were the leading producers of fall wheat. The three ridings of Middlesex accounted for 2,080,881 bushels and the three ridings of Huron for 2,080,357 bushels. Their chief competitors were the ridings of Elgin East and Elgin West with a combined total of 948,693 bushels, Oxford South and Oxford North with 837,785 bushels, Perth South and Perth North with 1,083,063 bushels, Bruce South and Bruce North with 1,360,747 bushels, and Kent with 950,167 bushels. The largest producers of spring wheat were the ridings of Grey South, Grey East, and Grey North, with a combined total of 855,489 bushels, Ontario South and Ontario North with 647,430 bushels, Durham East and Durham West with 558,859 bushels, Victoria South and Victoria North with 556,955 bushels, Wellington South, Wellington Centre, and Wellington North with 543,190 bushels, and Simcoe South and Simcoe North with 530,086 bushels.[61]

After 1880 the acreage devoted to wheat in Ontario steadily declined. It was already evident at that date that the industry was being pushed more and more into the new settlements, and that it had ceased to be the main dependence of the Ontario farmer. "As far as Ontario is concerned," it was asserted, "the end of exporting wheat is not far off. . . . We have sold wheat till in an average year we lose money by every bushel sold."[62] Fundamentally, the decline and passing of wheat as a staple in Ontario was made inevitable by the expansion of the railways which opened the prairies of the American West and later of the Canadian Northwest. These distant regions now had the cheap lands and the agricultural machinery requisite for successful extensive farming. The agriculturists of Ontario kept abreast of developments in farm machinery,[63] but their land was too valuable for con-

---

[61]*Census of Canada, 1881*, vol. III, pp. 192-226.
[62]Toronto *Weekly Globe*, July 12, 1878. Cf. *OACR*, vol. I, p. 361.
[63]For the new farm machinery, see pp. 309-13, below.

centration on wheat. The result was that when the high-quality grain of the West poured into the European market, the Ontario farmers turned to more profitable branches of agriculture than wheat-growing—to barley-growing, stock-rearing, dairying, or mixed farming.

Though the wheat-growing industry was declining in relative importance, it had long since left its imprint on the economic structure of the province. Its needs had contributed to canal and railway building. Those engaged in it had operated schooners and steamboats, warehouses and elevators. Others, like the bankers and retail merchants, in fact whole communities, had been scarcely less dependent on it for a livelihood than had the farmers. It had provided an export staple which enabled the province to obtain a return flow of merchandise and capital. Finally, it had called into existence a type of economic organization which could be extended, and indeed already was being extended, to meet the requirements of the wheat-growers of western Canada.[64]

[64]Cf. Innis and Lower (eds.), *Select Documents in Canadian Economic History*, p. 730.

CHAPTER XV

THE DEVELOPMENT OF THE DAIRY INDUSTRY[1]

THE manufacture of cheese and butter, especially the latter, was carried on in Upper Canada as a household industry from the earliest settlement. If the farmer had a surplus of either, he sold it to the store-keeper who disposed of it to his other customers, or exported it to Montreal. Both butter and cheese were being sent down the St. Lawrence as early as 1801.[2] Though Michael Smith mentioned dairy farmers in Oxford Township before the War of 1812, as was indicated in Chapter II, dairying on a commercial basis was found on very few farms till after 1850. Actually, a dairy farm in certain parts of the province was so rare as to be a curiosity.[3]

There were many hindrances to the expansion of commercial dairying. In the case of butter, there was little local demand, because even the village householders kept cows and made their own, and the universally inferior quality of that exported through Montreal to the West Indies or the Maritimes or (after 1843) to the British Isles, kept prices low.[4] In the case of cheese, the local demand in Upper Canada was considerably in excess of the production, but it was almost invariably satisfied by imports from the United States.[5] Several reasons may be suggested. Cheese made in small quantities was inconstant in quality, and therefore could not command as high a price as the product of the Mohawk Valley or of the Western Reserve. Again, in domestic cheesemaking, especially in Upper Canada, the entire labour had

---

[1]Cf. Innis (ed.), *Dairy Industry in Canada*.

[2]R. Cartwright to General Hunter, Oct. 24, 1801, in Cartwright, *Life and Letters of the Late Honourable Richard Cartwright*, p. 82.

[3]Jameson, *Winter Studies and Summer Rambles*, vol. II, p. 19.

[4]Montreal *Canadian Courant*, Oct. 27, 1832; *Journal d'Agriculture*, juin, 1849, p. 179.

[5]*Journal and Transactions of the Board of Agriculture of Upper Canada for 1855-6*, pp. 56, 262, 453. Hereafter this authority is cited as *JTBAUC*. It was only partially true, however, that "the demand for American Cheese in Canada causes its production in such large quantities in Ohio" (*Census of Canada, 1851-2*, vol. I, p. xxxvii).

to be performed by the women of the family; hence it was said, when a considerable dairy industry had actually been established, "that the old method of cheese-making has done more to injure the health of women in cheese-dairying districts than any other cause."[6] But probably the greatest hindrance to the expansion of cheese-making was the larger profit to be made in wheat on a comparatively small capital investment and with much less labour than dairying would entail. It was not till after the midge and soil exhaustion rendered the Upper Canada wheat crop precarious that many farmers thought seriously of embarking on specialized dairying, and even then cheese-making developed slowly till manufacturing in factories was inaugurated in 1864.

However, by 1850 certain parts of Upper Canada—Oxford County, the region along the Bay of Quinte, and the St. Lawrence counties—produced cheese in fairly large quantities. In the lower Ottawa Valley and along the Bay of Quinte cheese-making was carried on at this time partly on account of the failure of the wheat crop and probably partly on account of the infiltration of Americans who were acquainted with the processes, as the New York cheese industry was then well established in Jefferson and St. Lawrence counties, just across the St. Lawrence River.[7] In Oxford County the influence of such farmers as Hiram Ranney and James Harris was important. The production of cheese in these districts increased rather slowly during the eighteen-fifties. Thus, in 1850, Upper Canada manufactured 2,292,600 pounds, with Oxford County contributing 315,650, Leeds 120,720, Hastings 102,825, and Glengarry 97,586; ten years later, Upper Canada had 2,687,172, Oxford County 457,348, York 218,465, Glengarry 122,627, Ontario 110,853, and Northumberland 108,273.[8] The slow expansion of production was in part owing to effective competition, for large quantities of cheese continued to be imported from the United States,[9] and in part owing to the fact that the high wheat prices of the middle eighteen-fifties

---

[6]*Canada Farmer*, April 15, 1864, p. 102.

[7]Bidwell and Falconer, *History of Agriculture in the Northern United States*, p. 422.

[8]*Census of Canada, 1851-2*, vol. II, p. 65; *ibid., 1861*, vol. II, p. 95.

[9]*Canadian Merchants' Magazine*, June, 1857, p. 196; *Canadian Agriculturist*, Aug. 1, 1860, p. 377.

discouraged cheese dairying. Moreover, a factor in farm economy tended to restrict cheese production, even as a sideline. There was little difference in the prices of butter and cheese during the eighteen-fifties, and little more labour was required in the manufacturing of cheese, but the raising of pigs created a demand for buttermilk rather than whey, and so farmers ordinarily favoured butter-making rather than cheese-making.[10]

A few of the early commercial cheese-makers deserve mention. Bradish Billings of Bytown as early as 1841 sold 2,000 pounds of cheese a year; at the end of a decade, he was manufacturing annually 15,000 pounds from the milk of fifty-six cows.[11] Before 1850 there were a few dairymen in Glengarry operating on much the same scale.[12] However, the largest producer in Upper Canada before 1850, and the best known, was Hiram Ranney. He left Vermont for the Eastern Townships in 1831, spent four years there, and then established himself on a farm a few miles from Ingersoll. Here he began in 1841 to make cheese from the milk of five cows, and peddled his product in Ingersoll, Brantford, London, and Hamilton. Sometimes he was nearly a week in disposing of his load, a fact which explains the reluctance of most of his neighbours to enter the business. In 1853 and later years his average production was from 15 to 18 tons from the milk of a hundred cows. Some of it was Stilton cheese, and some Pineapple cheese, but the most was "common," that is, of the Cheddar type. By 1863 he was able to sell all that he made to the store-keepers of Guelph—evidence that a home market was developing. When he died, honoured as "the dairy patriarch of South Oxford," Ranney left an estate valued at $70,000, and he had started with almost nothing.[13]

According to the census of 1851, there was little regional specialization in butter-making in Upper Canada, though per

---

[10]*JTBAUC 1855-6*, p. 491.

[11]Bytown *Gazette*, Nov. 25, 1841; *JTBAUC 1855-6*, p. 461.

[12]Innis, *Dairy Industry in Canada*, p. 44.

[13]*Canadian Agriculturist*, Sept., 1854, p. 284; *Canada Farmer*, Feb. 1, 1864, pp. 22-3; *Farmer's Advocate*, Jan., 1874, p. 8. Ranney gave a description in detail of his methods in *Transactions of the Board of Agriculture and of the Agricultural Association of Upper Canada for 1858-9*, pp. 214-15.

capita production was heaviest around Toronto, in the St.
Lawrence counties, and along the Bay of Quinte. Of the
16,064,532 pounds reported for 1850, York County had
812,477, Leeds 758,606, Lanark 674,927, Northumberland
626,689, Hastings 588,500, Middlesex 557,970, Prince Edward
556,010, Stormont 534,305, and Grenville 518,624.[14] At this
time butter-making was increasing in importance rapidly,
owing primarily to the opening of the American market. It
was estimated that in the three years from 1849 to 1851 butter
production increased 372 per cent.[15] Early in 1853 a Peel
County correspondent declared that "at the profits of the past
year, this has been one of the most profitable branches of
farming."[16] Within a few years most of the butter of the
Brockville district was finding its way to New England, the
farmers selling it at their own doors for cash.[17] Moreover,
the prosperity of the railway boom era in Canada West made
butter a lucrative article to produce for local consumption.[18]
Butter-making did not become a distinct industry, however, as
it was still carried on either as a sideline to wheat-growing
or as part of a scheme of mixed farming.

The high prices for cheese which prevailed during the
American Civil War tempted many farmers in Upper Canada
into dairying. The province was a well-watered region, with
plenty of rich grass. There was a large domestic market
already in existence, as was shown by the importations of Ohio
and New York cheese, and a potential one in the British Isles
which American cheese men were already entering. There
was need of finding a substitute for wheat, which of late years
had been an uncertain crop in central and western Upper
Canada, and often poor in yield. All that was necessary for
the development of cheese-making on a large scale was the
introduction of the factory system.[19]

The manufacturing of cheese in factories was begun in

---

[14]*Census of Canada, 1851-2*, vol. II, p. 65.

[15]*Ibid.*, vol. I, p. XXXIV.

[16]*JTBAUC 1855-6*, p. 361.

[17]*Canadian Agriculturist*, Dec., 1852, p. 363; *ibid.*, Feb. 1, 1861,
p. 89. For the activities of an American butter speculator at Cobourg
in 1854, see Weld, *Vacation Tour*, pp. 93 ff.

[18]*JTBAUC 1855-6*, p. 361; *JTBAUC 1856-7*, p. 77.

[19]*Canada Farmer*, March 1, 1864, p. 53.

1851 in Herkimer County, N.Y. During the early eighteen-sixties it was frequently suggested that the system should be adopted in Upper Canada, just as it was suggested that it should be in states such as Ohio and Wisconsin. The first Upper Canadian dairyman to look into the possibilities of the proposal was Hiram Ranney, who about 1862 or 1863 visited some of the factories in Herkimer County. He came away convinced that his own dairy methods were just as efficient. Some of his fellow farmers in Oxford County were soon satisfied that the American system really was a superior one.[20] Early in 1864 one of them, Andes Smith of Norwich, who had a hundred milking cows of his own, put into operation the first cheese factory in British North America, with an American from Herkimer County in charge. A few miles away Harvey Farrington, a cheese maker from Herkimer County, shortly afterwards began production.[21] The following year there were four factories in operation in Oxford County (which enthusiastic editors labelled "the Herkimer of Canada") and another at Athens, a few miles from Brockville.[22] In 1866, when the ending of the Reciprocity Treaty cut off the American supply of cheese entering Canada by restoring the old Canadian tariff, the high prices paid for cheese (about 12½ cents) created a veritable mania for factory cheese-making. From Oxford County came the report: "To use a recent coinage, farmers have 'cheese-on-the-brain,' which is fast approaching a mania equal [to] that produced

---

[20]Ibid., Feb. 1, 1864, p. 23.

[21]Ibid., Nov. 1, 1864, p. 310; ibid., Aug. 1, 1865, pp. 230-1. Though the Canada Farmer is quite definite in its references to the Smith factory as being the pioneer one, John A. Ruddick claims that the Farrington factory was first, principally on the ground that Farrington began to erect a building for it in the autumn of 1863 (Innis, Dairy Industry in Canada, p. 47). Smith used a building theretofore devoted to dairy-cheese making. But the point is academic. Little else is heard of Smith, while Farrington became the recognized leader of the cheese-factory movement. "Mr. Ferrington [sic], we believe, gave Canadians more information about manufacturing cheese on the factory system than any other individual in Canada. . . . All western [Ontario] dairymen who have attended the conventions have known the great benefits derived from his information. . . . He never allowed nationality, party, sect, greed and gain to influence him" (Farmer's Advocate, April, 1883, p. 102).

[22]Canada Farmer, Aug. 1, 1865, pp. 230-1; Montreal Witness, July 29, 1865.

in other localities by 'oil-on-the-brain.' It is extending so rapidly into every township, that there is scarcely a concession where preparations are not being made for cheese making."[23] A correspondent of a western Upper Canada newspaper told how this mania developed in Lobo Township, outside London:

Last spring our enterprizing citizen, J. W. Scott, proposed to start a cheese factory, and in order to bring the matter before the people and ascertain what amount of support he could get, he put up notices and called a meeting in his school-house, which a few of his neighbors attended, more from curiosity than from anything else. After Mr. Scott had presented the matter to this meeting in its most favorable aspect, he went round to see what support he could get, and nineteen gallons of milk per day was all he could get promised him, which would be the amount obtained from about six cows. However, to his praise be it spoken, nothing daunted, Mr. Scott concluded to go on with his factory at least for one year, by way of experiment, and, when he started his factory on the first of May last, it was with the milk of thirty cows, principally his own. The cheese factory business with us at that time was so little understood that Mr. Scott became the butt of ridicule for engaging in such an enterprise. The boys gave him the nickname of Cheese Factory: and some of his neighbors declared that rather than give their milk to Scott to make money out of them, they would feed it to their hogs. But the scheme worked well, and before two months had passed, those very individuals who ridiculed the enterprise at its outset, went off and purchased more cows, and were found among Mr. Scott's best supporters; so that in a short time he had the milk of one hundred cows to manufacture from. This was not the only way in which the change of opinion showed itself. The report spread like wildfire, "Scott and those fellows who are furnishing milk for his factory are making money hand over fist," and in less than two months, Tom, Dick and Harry, all over the township, were talking about starting cheese factories.[24]

The writer adds that this one township as a result would have five factories in operation in 1867. Early in 1867 it was remarked that "cheese factories are now springing up in nearly every section of the country so rapidly that it is difficult to keep track of all the new institutions."[25] In East Zorra Township, adjacent to Woodstock, there were in 1867 "ten or

---

[23]*Transactions of the Board of Agriculture of Upper Canada for 1864-8*, p. 511. Hereafter this authority is cited as *TBAUC*.

[24]London *Advertiser*, quoted in *Canada Farmer*, Jan. 15, 1867, p. 29.

[25]*Canada Farmer*, May 15, 1867, p. 150.

twelve factories almost in sight of each other and preparations for further extension next season."[26]   By midsummer of the same year, it was estimated that there were about 235 in Ontario.[27]   This estimate is rather misleading, for many of the new "factories" were, for several years, really only enlargements of the old dairies.   However, many of them, including Ranney's, operated on the factory principle, more or less.[28] Thus, the author of the account of the movement in East Zorra goes on to say: "I said factories, but I should explain that some only make up the milk of their own dairies, others take milk from their near neighbours, and others gather from a long distance."[29]

Contrary to expectations, prices of cheese were not high in 1867; much of the product was poor; factories were too close together, and thus too small for profitable work; and, as was therefore inevitable, some of the new factories lost so much that they were unable to operate in 1868.[30]   Nevertheless, though many factories failed from mismanagement or over-competition, the number rapidly increased.   According to the census of 1870-1, there were 323 cheese factories in Ontario, 150 of which were in the three counties of Middlesex, Elgin, and Oxford, with a large proportion of the rest being concentrated in the Belleville and Brockville districts.   In 1880, there were 550 factories in the province.[31]   By this time many of the smaller factories were being absorbed in large combinations under one manager.   Outstanding among these combinations was the "Allengrove" association of D. M. McPherson of Lancaster, which was formed in 1871.   In 1879 it was operating thirteen factories in Glengarry County and in Huntingdon County (Quebec), and later it had a much greater number under its control in the same region.[32]

[26]*Ibid.*, Sept. 2, 1867, p. 266.

[27]*Ibid.*, Aug. 15, 1867, p. 246.

[28]*Ibid.*, Sept. 16, 1866, p. 275; *ibid.*, Sept. 16, 1867, p. 277; *TBAUC 1864-8*, p. 511.

[29]*Canada Farmer*, Sept. 2, 1867, p. 266.

[30]*Ibid.*, Feb. 15, 1869, pp. 57, 61.

[31]*Census of Canada, 1871*, vol. III, pp. 368-70; *ibid.*, *1881*, vol. III, pp. 404-6.

[32]*Report of the Ontario Agricultural Commission*, vol. I, p. 405. Hereafter this authority is cited as *OACR*.

In the first factories, two methods of organization were followed. In one, the proprietary, the owner of the factory bought the milk from the farmers, sending his own waggons around the countryside to collect it. Many patrons preferred this arrangement, as all the risks of making and marketing the cheese fell on the owner. In the other system, which was called the "American," a number of farmers united in a syndicate, chose a board of directors, and appointed one of their number to act as manager. The manager provided a building and the necessary equipment, hired a competent cheese-maker, and received usually 2 cents a pound on all the cheese produced. The rest of the proceeds from the sale of the cheese was then divided among the patrons in proportion to the quantities of milk they supplied. In this system the farmers ordinarily delivered their own milk. One such factory, the "Front of Sydney," the first in the Belleville district, during its first season (1866) of 165 days received 581,371 pounds of milk from 220 cows. The expense of drawing the milk, manufacturing the cheese, providing boxes, and paying freight was $1,555. As the amount of cheese sold was 59,498 pounds, worth $7,706, the net proceeds of the nineteen share-holders was $6,151. This meant that each cow netted an average of $28.00.[33]

The overseas cheese export trade depended on the making of a better product through the extension of the factory system, and on adaptation to the demands of the British market. Even during the days when cheese was made in the dairy, small amounts had been exported to Great Britain.[34] When the factory system began to spread, it was therefore thought that Upper Canadian cheese would capture a large share of the British market, for the kind made was an imitation of Cheddar, an English variety in popular demand. This it failed to do at first. One reason lay in the inferiority of the cheese to its American competitor. Many people rushed into the new industry at the urging of farmers who thought that the more competition there was, the higher the prices of milk would be. Most of them had not the least idea of

---

[33]*Canada Farmer*, July 15, 1865, p. 213; *ibid.*, Feb. 15, 1867, p. 54. Smith's was proprietary, Farrington's "American."

[34]*Canadian Agriculturist*, July, 1852, p. 217.

proper sanitary methods. They kept pigs in a sty beside
their factory to feed on the whey, with the result that the
neighbourhood was pervaded by a sickening stench; they
made no effort to keep flies away from the curd; and they
did not bother to scour their vats and other equipment. The
consequence was that when the president of the American
Dairymen's Association visited some of the Ontario factories in
1867, he had to report, "I tried many cheeses in various factories, and found many of good quality; candor compels me to
add that I also found many that were execrable."[35]

Faced by the possible loss of their scarcely gained export
market, the cheese-makers of Ontario tried to improve the
quality of their product. They were soon able to do so, partly
on account of the adoption of various improved devices being
manufactured in the United States, but mainly on account of
the educational work carried on by their own voluntary
organizations. In the summer of 1867, about two hundred
dairymen met at Ingersoll and formed a Canadian Dairymen's
Association, for the double purpose of making it possible to
benefit from one anothers' practical experience through
annual discussions, and to develop a profitable method of
marketing their cheese in the United Kingdom. In 1872 a
new organization appeared in the Belleville district, called
the Ontario Dairymen's Association. The two societies were
united between 1873 and 1877 under the name of the Dairymen's Association of Ontario. In 1877, on the termination
of the amalgamation, there appeared the Dairymen's Association of Western Ontario and the Dairymen's Association of
Eastern Ontario. The annual meetings of all these organizations were largely devoted to addresses by visiting dairymen
from the United States, or to discussions among the members
about improvements in factory methods.[36]

Their influence was shown in a steady raising of standards
for Ontario cheese. Not every cheese-maker could keep
abreast of the improvements, so the poorer ones were forced
out of business, and this too contributed to a higher average
quality in the product. By 1880 so many changes had been

---

[35]*Canada Farmer*, Jan. 1, 1868, p. 6.

[36]*Ibid.*, Aug. 15, 1867, pp. 246, 249; Innis, *Dairy Industry in Canada*,
pp. 78-80; *Report on Agriculture and Arts for 1872*, p. xiv.

introduced that it could be asserted with truth that "the dairying system has . . . attained a high degree of excellence of late years. The cheese made at our factory in 1866, and which then commanded the highest price, would now be regarded as a fifth or sixth rate article, if saleable at all."[37]

A second early difficulty in the shipment of factory cheese overseas was marketing. In the beginning, the cheese was bought by a country merchant or small cheese dealer, who sold it to a commission dealer in Montreal, who had it shipped to Great Britain, and buyer, commission dealer, and shipper had to have their profits. In England the cheese passed through the hands of an importer, of a broker who acted as intermediary between the importer and the middleman, of a middleman or wholesaler, and of a retail grocer. This British system was so well integrated that the Ontario producers found that the appointing of an agent of their own to dispose of their cheese would fail to avail them anything, and would certainly antagonize these vested interests.[38] On the other hand, the expansion of production made it profitable for Ontario speculators to make a profession of buying cheese from the makers and shipping it direct to the United Kingdom. They shortly replaced the small-scale cheese buyers of 1864 and 1865. One of them, Edwin Caswell of Ingersoll, bought practically the whole output of Oxford County in 1866. Three years later, he and another dealer paid out $319,000 for cheese for export.[39] The cheese boards established at Ingersoll, Stratford, and Belleville in 1873 further facilitated orderly marketing on the part of the producers.[40] The putting into operation of a weekly refrigerated cheese-and-butter train between Stratford and the Montreal docks, beginning in 1877, gave assurance that the cheese would reach Liverpool in good condition.[41]

With the improvement in the quality of Ontario cheese through the elimination of the less efficient producers and the

---

[37]Evidence of K. Graham, Belleville, in *OACR*, vol. IV, App. G, p. 127.
[38]*Canada Farmer*, March 15, 1866, p. 86; *ibid.*, Sept. 2, 1867, p. 263.
[39]*Ibid.*, Sept. 15, 1866, p. 275; *Ontario Farmer*, Feb., 1870, p. 36.
[40]Toronto *Globe*, Feb. 8, 1873.
[41]Patterson, *Statements relating to Home and Foreign Trade . . . for 1877*, p. 120.

gaining in experience of the rest, the export trade expanded. By 1870 Ontario cheese was coming into favour in the British Isles. In 1869, 2,594,544 pounds, worth $350,000, were shipped overseas from Woodstock and Ingersoll; in 1873, 3,935,111 pounds, worth $442,760, from Belleville, an amount estimated at only one-fifth of the provincial output; and in 1879-80 (fiscal year), something less than 40,368,678 pounds from Ontario.[42] Of course the export trade does not tell the whole story, for with the improvement in quality, the domestic consumption of factory cheese greatly increased.

During the years that factory cheese-making was expanding, important changes took place in the butter trade and in butter-making. During the late eighteen-forties and the eighteen-fifties, the overseas trade from the Province of Canada had steadily increased. The establishment of a Canadian steamship line to Great Britain in 1858 was an important factor in this development. In 1863-6 the butter sent to Great Britain was valued at about $2,918,000, or approximately two and a half times the value of that sent to the United States.[43] There were large shipments later. Thus, a single retail firm at Perth in 1871 gathered 2,800 boxes, worth $50,000, for export, and two firms at Renfrew in 1880 shipped twenty carloads direct to Liverpool.[44] Nevertheless, ordinary Ontario butter continued to be so inferior in quality that each year dealers found it less able to compete with European or even American butter. During the late eighteen-seventies, when common Ontario and Quebec butter sold in England at an average price of 7d. a pound, American butter brought an average of 12d., French butter an average of 14½d., and Irish butter an average of 15d. The competition of these butters, and of those of Denmark, Holland, and Sweden, was not, however, the only deterrent to the overseas trade. By 1880 Australian butter, shipped in hermetically sealed cans, and Dutch oleomargarine (which was only half as expensive as butter, and was preferred by

---

[42]*Ontario Farmer*, Feb., 1870, p. 36; *Canada Farmer*, Feb. 16, 1874, p. 74; *OACR*, vol. I, p. 404. The last figure includes a small amount from the Quebec factories.

[43]*Canada Farmer*, June 15, 1867, p. 182.

[44]Small, *Resources of the Ottawa District*, p. 34; Smallfield, *Lands and Resources of Renfrew County*, p. 11.

many British consumers) were likewise threatening. The result was that the value of butter exported from Ontario to Great Britain, which had exceeded that of cheese till 1873, declined rapidly thereafter. The quantity of butter exported from Canada—meaning mostly Ontario—was 897,000 pounds less in 1879 than it had been in 1871. This retrogression continued after 1880.[45]

One reason for the low price overseas of Ontario butter was its slovenly method of manufacture. The farmers in the western part of the province became so engrossed in wheat-growing, and later in stock-raising and cheese-making, that they did not bother to make it properly.[46] However, much

---

[45]*Canada Farmer*, Feb. 16, 1868, p. 61; *Farmer's Advocate*, April, 1881, p. 100; Ruddick, *Historical and Descriptive Account of the Dairying Industry*, p. 44; Montreal *Star*, quoted in *Illustrated Journal of Agriculture*, Dec., 1880, p. 125; *ibid.*, March, 1884, p. 36.

[46]The following description (seemingly original) of a Wardsville humourist is essentially accurate: "I wad jist gie u a bit inklin o tha way tha mak buter in our parts, an then you can gess abot the greese. In the fust place, tha don't stabel their kows, but feed em all winter on straw, an u ma expekt in the spring like this, tha com out sae pur, that unless the sun is sinin vera brite, it will tak too of em to cast a shadoo. Tha are also covered with so long an shaggy hares, that when u are mylkin the pale is half full of hares. Aftr mylkin a boy an a dorg is sent wi em to the sumrfoler to pastr till evnin when the boy and the dorg is cent aftr em agin, an u ma xpekt tha com hom kanterin. Tha ar nou so restles tha will not stand to be mylkd, for which tha git a gude hamrin. Tha are now klosd in the yard till mornin. Mean whyle, the mylk is removed to the darey, where it is filtrd thro a kalndr straanr, to tak out som of the hares. The dary is sometims a gude one, but in ten kases out of one it is a pur konstructd bildin, with shelf abov shelf, an plenty of holes for vntlaton—the upr story bein genraly ocypd by the poltry. Imeditly B. hind is the syne stye, in ordr to be konvenent for the sour milk; or it may be a log bildin, chinkd an plastrd, with a hole 5 feet deep inside. On the groun floor, the mylk dishes is plasd: as there is no vntilaton here, the mylk molds B-4 it sours. After remainin in this state a konsidrabel tim, the kream is skimd in-2 a pork barrl, or othr vesel big enuf to hold it till a rany dae coms, when all the men is in. This tim havin arivd, the kream is put in-2 a churn, an workd for abot an our, withot synes of buter. Hot water is now added in konsidrabel quantityes, when the buter is on hand rite awa. It is now removd in-2 a tub or other vesel for the purpos, in ordr to get some of the butermylk out, after which it is saltd an mad in-2 roles for markt. A boy is now cent aftr the old mare, to tak it 2 the store, and bein redy 1 or 2 rols is put in eithr end of a grain bag, an put on the hoss, an the boy dispatchd with the instruktions to get hiest markt price, as it is new" (*Canada Farmer*, May 15, 1868, p. 150. Cf. *OACR*, vol. I, p. 417).

of its bad reputation resulted from the way it was handled. The store-keepers paid the same price regardless of quality, and sold it without grading, for the buyers were more concerned about a low price than about palatability. The merchants packed it just as they received it, in layers of every degree of freshness and of colour, and in rough kegs or dirty crocks. No wonder, then, that in the British market it was quoted among the lowest grades; and that it was said that half of it was too bad even for cooking, and was therefore sold only for axle grease or for smearing sheep.[47]

Though Ontario butter in general had a poor reputation, Eastern Ontario butter had a deservedly high one. This made it possible to sell it in New York when ordinary Ontario butter was excluded by the 4 cents a pound duty. At the end of the American Civil War, butter from Dundas County brought 50 cents a pound in Boston and New York under the labels of "Orange County [N.Y.]" or "Vermont" butter.[48] A few years later it was remarked that "it is well known to the trade that in the Eastern Townships, bordering on the State of Vermont, and in the vicinity of Brockville, there is produced rich, sweet, marketable butter—butter that is very seldom handled by Canadian buyers at all—that made in the Eastern Townships being generally contracted for by Americans before a pound of it is gathered, shipped to Boston, rebranded and sold for the highest price under the name of 'Vermont Dairy,' while that from Brockville is also taken by Americans and finds its way to market to be sold as St. Lawrence County [N.Y.] butter at an excellent per centage of profit."[49] Too, by 1865 the butter of this "Brockville district," which included the country as far north as Smiths Falls and Perth, was favourably known in the United Kingdom, as it continued to be till after 1880. During the eighteen-seventies that of the "Morrisburg district," which included territory as far north as Winchester, became equally famous. This butter was so

---

[47]*Canada Farmer*, June 1, 1867, p. 167; *ibid.*, Feb. 15, 1868, p. 61; *OACR*, vol. I, p. 416.

[48]*TBAUC 1864-8*, p. 489.

[49]*Canada Farmer*, July 15, 1872, p. 260.

uniformly graded that it could be sold by cable at any time in the British Isles.[50]

Little butter was made in factories in Ontario before 1880. In the autumn of 1867 a factory was built near Port Hope for the purpose of manufacturing butter as well as cheese, that is, butter from the cream and cheese from the skim milk, as was a fairly common practice in the adjacent states. Two years later another, erected in Port Hope, was said to be doing a good business.[51] After this, nothing is to be learned of them, probably because they were in practice simply cheese factories. The first successful creamery in the modern sense was opened in 1876 by two enterprising store-keepers at Teeswater, who had read about butter factories in the United States, had gone to see how they were operated, and then had hired a man who had worked in one to open a factory for them in their village. In 1876 they churned the cream of 120 cows, in 1879 of 700. They sold their butter in Glasgow for about 50 per cent more than the prevailing price for Ontario dairy butter. In 1876 and 1877 they made only butter, but in 1878 they also manufactured skim cheese.[52] Their success led to the establishment of four other factories within a radius of twenty miles, and others elsewhere, so that there were twenty-three in Ontario in 1881.[53] Compared with the rate of expansion of factory cheese-making in the middle eighteen-sixties, this was a slow development. Why was there so much difference? For one thing, these first butter factories followed a plan of obtaining cream which was extremely costly, that is, they gathered the milk from the farmers, thus hauling six times as much liquid over the country roads as they would have done if the cream had been skimmed. Then they had only primitive methods of recovering the butter fat, for there were no cream separators in Ontario

[50]*Ibid.*, Feb. 1, 1866, p. 41; *ibid.*, June 1, 1867, p. 168; *OACR*, vol. I, p. 417; *ibid.*, vol. IV, App. J, p. 24; *Illustrated Journal of Agriculture*, Feb., 1880, p. 147.

[51]*Ontario Farmer*, July, 1870, p. 210.

[52]*Farmer's Advocate*, April, 1879, p. 81; *OACR*, vol. I, p. 422. One of these men, Moses Moyer, within a few years came to hold much the same position in the Ontario creamery industry as Farrington had held in the cheese-factory industry (*Farmer's Advocate*, Oct., 1885, p. 297).

[53]*Census of Canada, 1881*, vol. III, p. 483; *OACR*, vol. I, p. 422.

till 1884, when one of the De Laval factory variety was installed in a creamery in Ameliasburgh Township (Prince Edward County). Finally, they were handicapped through the fact that the best dairy districts had already turned to the manufacturing of cheese.[54]

Raw-milk dairying in the vicinity of urban centres was an industry which was just beginning to be important in 1880. It was still on a small-scale, unorganized basis, and was characterized by complete disregard for the most elementary sanitary principles.[55]

The growth of the dairy industry after the introduction of the factory manufacture of cheese had some disadvantages. Dairying required a good deal more labour throughout the year than did the seasonal business of wheat-growing. It was criticized for its tendency to retard the introduction of pure-bred cattle in the districts where it prevailed. Of course, this was a natural result of the farmers' interest in the milking rather than the beef-producing qualities of their stock. Again the pursuit of dairying was incompatible with the extensive raising of cattle for beef. It was said of Oxford County in 1869 that "calves with a lean and hungry look, called in this section of the country 'factory calves,' may be the result of 'cheesing' them out of their milk."[56] Moreover, the farmers raised few of their calves. Some, in accordance with a custom which had prevailed in the cheese-dairying regions of North America for generations, "deaconed" or killed them when they were a few days old.[57] Others, such as those in Oxford County, which was near the chief livestock region in Ontario, sold their calves to drovers who auctioned them off among the cattlemen.[58]

---

[54]Innis, *Dairy Industry in Canada*, p. 37; *OACR*, vol. I, p. 422-3; *Farmer's Advocate*, July, 1884, p. 195.

[55]Innis and Lower (eds.), *Select Documents in Canadian Economic History*, pp. 562-3; Innis, *Dairy Industry in Canada*, pp. 69-70.

[56]*Ontario Farmer*, Aug., 1870, p. 247.

[57]Evidence of G. Matheson, Perth, in *OACR*, vol. IV, App. G, p. 52. Cf. also: "It has become quite a common practice among dairymen to purchase their cows in spring, and sell them off in the fall, under the impression that the saving in the expense of keeping them over winter is thereby a great gain. . . . The calves that come in spring are, to save the trouble of raising, sold cheap to the butcher when three or four weeks old" (*Canada Farmer*, May 16, 1870, p. 184).

[58]Information furnished by Professor Harold A. Innis.

Whatever disadvantages the growth of the factory-cheese industry had, they were more than counterbalanced by its advantages. The farm work associated with milk production was continuous, but not unduly hard, and it could be carried on as a family enterprise, with no dependence on hired workers. The returns did not fluctuate so much as they did in other branches of farming, especially wheat-growing. The British market and the growing domestic market ordinarily absorbed all the cheese that could be produced, usually at fair prices. The shift from wheat-growing to dairying, or to mixed farming involving dairying, contributed to the improvement of agricultural practices. Farmers began to better their herds, not so much through the introduction of purebreds, as through the acquisition of individual grade cattle that had shown themselves to be good milkers. They cared for their cattle better. They kept more of them,[59] with the result that the land received more manure, and they laid down a greater acreage in pasture.[60] In general, as a Lanark County farmer who had been driven out of wheat-growing into dairying explained to the Ontario Agricultural Commission: "Dairying is more profitable than grain growing. The farm has improved under this system. We could hardly live on the farm previously."[61]

---

[59]For the increase in the number of milch cows from 1851 to 1881, see below, p. 287 n.

[60]Cf. *Ontario Farmer*, Feb., 1871, p. 59.

[61]Evidence of P. Clark, Smith's Falls, in *OACR*, vol. IV, App. G, p. 109.

CHAPTER XVI

THE LIVESTOCK INDUSTRY, 1866-1880

THE history of the livestock industry in Ontario before
Confederation has been treated in several preceding
chapters—the day of small things and little hope in Chapter
VIII, the beginnings of the improvement of breeds in Chapter
IX, the expansion of the eighteen-fifties in Chapters XI and
XII, and the effects of the American Civil War in Chapter
XIII. The present chapter will show that, after the termination
of the Reciprocity Treaty, the industry became solidly estab-
lished in Ontario, and this in spite of a world-wide depres-
sion and a partial loss of markets.

Before describing the economic aspects of post-Confedera-
tion stock-raising, we shall find it advisable to continue the
account of the introduction of improved breeds from the date
at which the treatment in Chapter IX ended, that is, from
about 1850.

There was a sharp difference in motivation between the
early period and the later one. Before 1850 gentlemen farmers
of a scientific or patriotic turn of mind were the prominent
importers. After 1850, though such men still had their importance, breeders who made their living from selling
improved stock tended to displace them. This was because
the expansion of domestic and foreign markets encouraged
a much more extensive introduction of improved breeds
among ordinary farmers. As the Ontario Agricultural Commission of 1880 explained, "if a Canadian farmer were raising
cattle for his own market alone, it would be only commonly
prudent to keep none but improved stock . . . but if he looks,
as he must look, to the British market as his standard, he is,
with common cattle, hopelessly behind, and while his wiser
neighbours will be getting their $75 to $80, or even $100 for
a good grade beast, he will be left to go a-begging to the
local butcher to relieve him of his rubbish at the latter's own
terms."[1] The observation applied to other kinds of livestock,

---

[1]*Report of the Ontario Agricultural Commission*, vol. I, p. 241.
Hereafter this authority is cited as *OACR*.

and was as true of the eighteen-fifties as of the eighteen-
seventies. Thus, when Upper Canada sheep began to enter
the American market about 1850, whole flocks in Prince
Edward County were sold, so that their owners could get
better breeds.[2] So too, the increase in local consumption
and the expansion of the export trade during the boom of
the eighteen-fifties encouraged farmers everywhere to improve
their horses, cattle, and sheep.[3] The demand in the United
States during the Civil War had a similar effect, as was shown
in Chapter XIII in connection with wool-growing.

Before 1850 Upper Canada farmers had taken much more
interest in improving their horses than their other livestock,
and the same was true after 1850. Horsemen continued to
bring Thoroughbreds into the province from Kentucky and
Virginia, as well as from England, but they made little effort
to perpetuate the breed in its purity. There was so little
demand for race-horses in Ontario by 1880, in consequence
of the demoralization of the turf, that the leading breeder of
them was then selling almost all his young stock in the United
States.[4] As far as the ordinary farmer was concerned,
Thoroughbreds really derived their importance between 1850
and 1880 from the fact that they were crossed with common
horses to produce roadsters. The preference for roadsters
became even more pronounced than it had been earlier, for by
the eighteen-fifties there were plank or gravel roads,
and the coming, actual or prospective, of the railway

---

[2]*Journal and Transactions of the Board of Agriculture of Upper
Canada for 1855-6*, p. 434. Hereafter this authority is cited as *JTBAUC*.

[3]*Transactions of the Board of Agriculture and of the Agricultural
Association of Upper Canada for 1858-9*, p. 129; *ibid., for 1859-60*, p.
188. Hereafter this authority is cited as *TBA&AAUC*. A resident of
the Township of Hamilton, Northumberland County, was able in 1862
to name eight farmers in the township who had made importations of
sheep from the United Kingdom and to add that "many others of our
farmers have either imported or procured from imported stocks." He
also remarked that sheep had been improved more than any other
kind of livestock, and that "it has become very uncommon to see any
of the old common breeds, even among those sheep that are still turned
out to pasture on the roadsides and woods during summer" (*Canadian
Agriculturist*, July 1, 1862, p. 395).

[4]*JTBAUC 1855-6*, p. 519; *TBA&AAUC 1859-60*, p. 245; *OACR*, vol.
I, p. 439; *The Spirit of the Times*, Jan. 12, 1856, p. 571.

gave even farmers a taste for speed. Nothing delighted them more than a "2.40" roadster attached to a light buggy. Richard Denison, who had a farm on the outskirts of Toronto, in 1859 asserted that "trotting is practised by most of us, and slow indeed is the man who never becomes excited enough to try his horse or team against some fellow traveller, and I do believe that a day never passes without a trot or more across the front of my farm, it being the first clear place on the road after turning out of the city throng."[5] Several families of trotting horses came to be well represented in Upper Canada. During the eighteen-fifties and eighteen-sixties there were many Morgans and Black Hawks, but these, though well liked, failed to gain in Upper Canada the overwhelming popularity that they then enjoyed in the United States. This was unquestionably because Upper Canadian horsemen were convinced that the Morgans and Black Hawks were in no whit superior to some families developed within the province in the same way as these two strains were developed in Vermont, that is, by crossing Thoroughbreds or half bloods with the common horses. The two leading indigenous Standardbred families, especially after about 1865, were the Clear Grits and the Royal Georges. The Royal Georges, which took their name from a horse foaled at Toronto in 1844, had not only some Messenger blood, but also a good deal of French-Canadian.[6] After 1850 the French-Canadian horses in Upper Canada more and more lost their separate identity, and were absorbed in the trotting stock or the general farm stock, for the deterioration of the parent race in Lower Canada made it

---

[5]*TBA&AAUC 1859-60*, p. 54. The phrase "2.40 horse" is not to be taken too literally. In the United States and Canada, it was noted, "those who can trot 1 mile in 2 minutes and 40 seconds are considered up to the mark as 'fast' horses. From this has arisen the common remark of '2.40,' when applied to anything which is done fast. Thus they have 2.40 men, 2.40 women, 2.40 steamboats, 2.40 workmen, same as there are 2.40 horses and if we can believe one common idea in England, it is that all America, everything in it, and which is done in it, is 2.40" (*The New World in 1859*, part IV, pp. 59, 61).

[6]*TBA&AAUC 1858-9*, p. 107; *TBA&AAUC 1859-60*, p. 338; *OACR*, vol. I, pp. 444-54; *Transactions of the Board of Agriculture of Upper Canada for 1860-3*, p. 105 (hereafter cited as *TBAUC*); Busbey, *Trotting and Pacing Horse in America*, pp. 226-7; Wallace, *Wallace's American Trotting Register*, p. 49.

increasingly difficult to obtain satisfactory sires there.[7] By 1880 these once-famous horses were but seldom mentioned. The draft horses of Upper Canada tended after mid-century to be both heavier and better-actioned than comparable horses in the eastern United States. Most of them were grade Clydesdales, for the heavy-draft horses imported from the British Isles continued to be predominantly of this breed. During the eighteen-fifties there were also brought from overseas a few Yorkshires and a few Cumberlands—both of which "breeds" were evidently themselves crosses between the Clydesdale and the Shire—and then and later a few Shires. The only other heavy-draft breed of any significance in Upper Canada before 1880 was the Suffolk Punch, the first of which arrived in Oxford County in 1854. As the Suffolk Punch had cleaner legs and sounder feet than the Clydesdale, it was gradually gaining on it in favour by 1880.[8] There were some Percherons in Ontario before 1880, but most of these were inferior specimens, and so they enjoyed none of the popularity that Percherons then had in Illinois and Iowa and were subsequently to win in Ontario.[9]

After 1850 the Durhams retained their primacy as the most popular breed of improved cattle, except in the dairying regions, where the Ayrshires were the favourites.[10] As a

---

[7]Jones, "The Agricultural Development of Lower Canada" (*Agricultural History*, vol. XIX, 1945, p. 220).

[8]*JTBAUC 1855-6*, p. 541; *TBAUC 1860-3*, p. 46; *Farmer's Advocate*, March, 1881, p. 50; *OACR*, vol. I, pp. 457-8. It was stated in 1883 that "Suffolk Punches are in great favor in various parts of Canada. . . . They are bred and raised to a considerable extent in the counties of Wellington, Waterloo, [and] Oxford, and some are found in Brant and South Ontario" (*Farmer's Advocate*, July, 1883, p. 203).

[9]*OACR*, vol. I, pp. 460-3; *Report on Agriculture and Arts for 1879*, p. 71 (hereafter cited as *RAA*); *Illustrated Journal of Agriculture*, Dec., 1879, p. 117; *ibid.*, May, 1882, p. 11. The Percherons were much more popular in Quebec than in Ontario. They were brought in beginning in 1866, for the purpose of building up the race of French-Canadian horses (*Revue agricole*, janv., 1867, p. 99; *ibid.*, fév., 1867, p. 134; *ibid.*, avril, 1868, p. 209).

[10]An idea of the relative importance of the various improved breeds of cattle in Upper Canada at different dates after 1850 may be obtained from the entries at the seven provincial exhibitions held at Toronto between 1850 and 1880. It must be remembered that these statistics are rather misleading in the case of the minor breeds, because often

result, down to 1880 the typical cattle of the province were Durham grades. Devons, which, till about 1865, breeders showed at the provincial exhibitions in numbers about as great as those of the Durhams, appear to have made much less appeal to the average farmer, especially as his need of oxen diminished. Witnesses who appeared before the Ontario Agricultural Commission agreed that they were deficient in the quantity of milk they gave, in propensity to fatten rapidly, and in size.[11] Other breeds, such as the Galloways, introduced in 1853 and valued for their size and hardiness, the Herefords, of which there were a very few as early as 1852, and the Polled Angus, introduced in 1861, were still limited to a few breeders' herds in 1880.[12] The first Jerseys appeared in Ontario in 1877, though there had been a few around Montreal for about ten years before this. However, when the Ontario Agricultural Commission made a careful examination of the merits and shortcomings of the various breeds, it concluded that the Jersey was suitable only for private family use or for butter-dairying.[13] The Commission went on to state that of the other breeds mentioned, it was manifest that the Durham and the Hereford were best adapted for up-

---

every animal in the province belonging to them was entered in competition by the professional breeders for advertising purposes. This remark does not apply to the Durhams, Devons, or Ayrshires.

	1852	1858	1862	1866	1870	1874	1878
Devons	30	102	110	106	71	44	45
Durhams	81	135	142	92	188	258	283
Ayrshires	21	47	100	91	127	151	129
Herefords	5	8	32	32	27	44	27
Galloways		45	79	59	52	39	47
Polled Anguses				12			
Jerseys or Alderneys							27

(*JTBAUC 1855-6*, p. 271; *TBA&AAUC 1858-9*, p. 216; *TBAUC 1860-3*, p. 324; *TBAUC 1864-8*, p. 326; *RAA 1872*, p. 211; *RAA 1875*, p. 193; *RAA 1879*, p. 209).

[11]*OACR*, vol. I, pp. 252-4. The Devons had disappeared by about 1900 (Bailey, ed., *Cyclopedia of American Agriculture*, vol. I, p. 17).

[12]*JTBAUC 1855-6*, pp. 271, 301; *TBAUC 1860-3*, pp. 47-8, 227-8; *Farmer's Advocate*, Oct., 1881, p. 234. A few West Highland cattle imported from the Isle of Skye by an Upper Canada breeder were shown at the provincial exhibition at Toronto in 1852 *(Agricultural Journal and Transactions of the Lower Canada Agricultural Society*, Oct., 1852, p. 304).

[13]*RAA 1879*, p. 209; *OACR*, vol. I, pp. 269-70.

grading Ontario herds; and that of the two, the Durham would prove the more satisfactory for breeding as far as the ordinary farmer was concerned, owing to the great number already in the province.[14]

The question arises as to how great the improvement in cattle actually was. Possibly it was less than in the State of New York, for an Upper Canada delegate to the state fair at Albany in 1859 remarked the superiority of the Durhams and Devons there to those exhibited in Upper Canada.[15] Again, the Ontario Agricultural Commission received returns from 409 townships. Of these, 53 reported no improved stock (by "stock" was here meant cattle) at all; 113 a small quantity; 126 considerable improvement; and 117 general improvement.[16] However, though the quantity of improved stock seems small at first thought, it must be remembered that the gains made through up-grading had been the achievement of virtually a single generation of farmers.

After 1850 the improving sheep raisers of Upper Canada no longer depended solely on the Leicesters and Southdowns. A few of them imported Spanish and Saxon Merinos during the eighteen-fifties, but these failed to gain any foothold before 1860.[17] A reporter at the provincial exhibition of 1860 admitted that he was not competent to assess the merits of the fifty or so Merinos he saw there. "All animals of these two breeds [Spanish and Saxon] are so decidedly foreign in their appearance, and differ so essentially from what we are generally accustomed to regard as useful and valuable sheep, that we look upon them rather as curiosities than anything else."[18] The popularity they enjoyed during the years of the American Civil War they lost abruptly as soon as the conflict was over. Sheep which produced a long comb-

[14]*OACR*, vol. I, pp. 274-6. The Ontario Agricultural Commission also recommended the introduction of the Holstein. The first of this breed were brought into Ontario in 1882-3 (Ruddick, *Historical and Descriptive Account of the Dairying Industry*, pp. 14-15).

[15]*TBA&AAUC 1859-60*, p. 338.

[16]*OACR*, vol. I, p. 231.

[17]*JTBAUC 1855-6*, p. 453; *TBA&AAUC 1859-60*, p. 339; *Canadian Agriculturist*, March 16, 1861, p. 186; *ibid.*, May 1, 1861, p. 281.

[18]*TBAUC 1860-3*, p. 49.

ing or "lustre" wool were the Upper Canada ideal. The
Leicester did this, and so it continued to be the most numerous
breed throughout Canada West. Much resembling it, though
larger and coarser, was the Lincoln, so it also had its adherents
after 1850. However, the chief long-wool rival of the Leicester
was the Cotswold, the first of which was brought to Northumberland County in 1854. There was a good deal of crossing
of the Cotswold on the existing Leicester flocks, usually,
according to the sheep men, to their detriment. A few Romney
Marsh (or Kent) sheep were kept in Welland County in 1854,
and between 1854 and 1865 several breeders tried to stimulate
interest in the Cheviot, but neither of these long-wools met
with much approval.[19] In the middle eighteen-seventies, owing
to a development in the woollen industry which will be explained later in this chapter, and to the increasing importance
of the lamb trade, which put a premium on lambs with a
tendency to mature early, the long-wools met with severe
competition from the middle-wool or Down sheep. Of the
middle-wools, the Southdown remained after 1850 the most
important. The Hampshire Down (introduced into Upper
Canada in 1860), the Shropshire Down (introduced in 1861),
and the Oxford Down (introduced by 1868) were still being
promoted none too successfully by breeders till after 1870.
Then the Shropshire and the Oxford, though they did not as
yet threaten to overtake the Southdown, began to rise in

---

[19]*JTBAUC 1855-6*, pp. 406, 453; *TBAUC 1860-3*, pp. 48, 229; Carman,
Heath, and Minto, *Special Report on the . . . Sheep Industry*, p. 345.
As in the case of cattle, an idea of the relative popularity of the
various improved breeds of sheep, especially among importers and
breeders, may be obtained from the entries at the provincial exhibitions
at Toronto:

	1852	1858	1862	1866	1870	1874	1878
Lincolns				}	167	148	184
Leicesters	79	188	227	363 }		45	85
Cheviots		15	19				
Cotswolds		39	62	142	155	185	244
Southdowns	39	49	99	103	61	104	107
Shropshires }				36	16	26	15
Hampshires }							
Merinos	33	29	51	91	61	38	

(*Authorities*: same as in Note 10).

favour among the farmers, as they continued to do after 1880.[20]

The comparative unimportance of the Upper Canada swine industry was reflected in the relative slowness of improvement in the stock the farmers kept, one in striking contrast to developments in the American corn belt during these years. The only improved hogs that had attained much popularity in Upper Canada before 1850 were the large Berkshires. After 1850 these lost their pre-eminence to other breeds. Among the heavy competitors of the Berkshires, those weighing about 600 pounds, the most important was the Yorkshire. The Cumberland Improved, which seems to have closely resembled the Yorkshire, also had its champions.[21] In the late eighteen-fifties these oversize hogs began to be replaced by smaller and finer breeds, which when dressed would weigh 300 pounds or less. The Suffolks and the Improved Berkshires ranked about equal in popularity among these, with the Essex having some adherents in the eighteen-sixties and eighteen-seventies.[22] The lard-type Poland Chinas, brought in from the Miami Valley, were finding favour in the Essex peninsula in the late eighteen-seventies, though elsewhere in Ontario they were still a curiosity.[23] Though by 1860 there was considerable improvement in the hogs of the better farming regions, such as that

---

[20]*TBAUC 1860-3*, pp. 48, 229; *OACR*, vol. I, pp. 313, 318; Carman, Heath, and Minto, *Special Report on the . . . Sheep Industry*, p. 347; *American Agriculturist*, vol. XXVII, 1868, p. 403. During the eighteen-nineties the Shropshires outdistanced all others in popularity (Bailey, *Cyclopedia of American Agriculture*, vol. I, p. 17).

[21]*TBAUC 1860-3*, p. 230; *Canadian Agriculturist*, May 16, 1861, p. 315

[22]*Canadian Agriculturist*, Sept., 1858, p. 198; *TBA&AAUC 1859-60*, p. 247; *TBAUC 1860-3*, pp. 23, 49, 230. The following table gives the entries of improved hogs at the provincial exhibitions at Toronto, 1862-78.

	1862	1866	1870	1874	1878
Yorkshires	45	30	33	35	68
Large Berkshires	18	6			
Improved Berkshires	55	56	74	78	214
Suffolks	39	40	50	51	147
Essexes			26	34	42

(*TBAUC 1860-3*, p. 324; *TBAUC 1864-8*, p. 326; *RAA 1872*, p. 211; *RAA 1875*, p. 193; *RAA 1879*, p. 209).

[23]*OACR*, vol. I, p. 334; *Farmer's Advocate*, Nov., 1881, p. 268.

around Cobourg ("It is seldom that we now see those specimens of the *genus sus* known by the names of *Landpikes* or
razorbacks, which used to be common"),[24] long afterwards
the less progressive farmers still thought near-relatives of
the landpikes good enough to turn table-scraps and swill into
fat pork.   In 1880 it was really only in Essex and Kent
counties that the grading up of hogs was making much gain.[25]

The improvement of poultry requires only a brief notice.
The "hen fever," which, as was mentioned in Chapter IX, was
much in evidence in the early eighteen-fifties, had run its
course by 1859.   Of the fowls then introduced, the Dorkings
and Brahmas gave most satisfaction in the following generation, and the Cochins least.   Some new breeds were brought
into the province after the passing of the hen fever, including
the Plymouth Rock in the eighteen-sixties and the White
Leghorn before 1880.[26]

Though the subject of livestock improvement occupied
much space in the agricultural press after Confederation, it
was much less significant than the adjustments being made by
Ontario farmers in response to extending or changing markets.

The abrogation of the Reciprocity Treaty had little effect
on the trade with the United States in horses.   The rapidly
expanding iron and steel industry in Pennsylvania, the
brewers, and the draymen required thousands of heavy-draft
horses. Street cars utilized roadsters or general-purpose ones.
Ontario horses, whether heavy draft or light draft, were
regarded as so superior to those of the midwestern states
(owing to a belief that their being fed on oats made them
stronger boned than any fed on corn) that they brought from
$25.00 to $50.00 a head more than their rivals.   In consequence it was declared in 1880 that the brewery horses—which
were often kept for their advertising value as much as for
hauling—throughout the northern United States were nearly
all of Canadian (mostly Ontario) origin.   Horses were reared
all over Ontario for the American market, but the best evidently came from Perth County and its neighbours, from the

---

[24]*Canadian Agriculturist*, July 1, 1862, p. 395.

[25]*OACR*, vol. II, p. 74.

[26]*TBA&AAUC 1859-60*, p. 247; *OACR*, vol. I, pp. 477-83; *Farmer's
Advocate*, March, 1881, p. 57.

country about Toronto, and from Carleton County and its vicinity. In the last region, the lumber industry had long encouraged the breeding of heavy drafts. Horses with some evidence of Clydesdale blood were most sought after. Boston provided the most profitable outlet. The horses in demand there and throughout southern New England were large and showy coach and carriage horses of a kind procurable nowhere except in Canada—that is, in Ontario and southwestern Quebec—and in Kentucky. Philadelphia and New York were, however, very important markets. Ontario horses which went to New York or Philadelphia were sold to American dealers, who boarded them out among Pennsylvania farmers to condition them, and then disposed of them to draymen or brewers or mining companies. The extent of the trade can be judged from the fact that a single dealer at Seaforth handled an average of two hundred horses a year between 1860 and 1880, purchasing them all within a radius of twenty-five miles.[27] About 1880 Manitoba-bound Ontario farmers took a considerable number of horses with them, and some of these were sold along the way in Iowa and Minnesota. Western Ontario dealers likewise shipped horses to these two states, as well as to the farming regions of the Dakota and Montana Territories and the lumbering areas of Michigan. It was asserted in 1885 that a third of the horses then being exported from the vicinity of London went to these western states and territories.[28]

The end of the American Civil War did not interrupt the expansion of Upper Canada sheep-raising. Nevertheless, the industry was not as profitable as it had been. With the crop of 1866 there came a collapse in wool prices. It is true that the wool factors were misled by orders from manufacturers into thinking that the demand was as great as ever, and continued to pay from 35 to 37 cents a pound, but all of them lost

---

[27]OACR, vol. I, pp. 432, 435-7; OACR, vol. II, p. 37; OACR, vol. v, App. K, pp. 42, 64-5; Illustrated Historical Atlas of the County of Carleton, p. XI; National Live Stock Journal, vol. IX, 1878, p. 9.

[28]OACR, vol. II, p. 91; Johnston, History of the County of Perth, pp. 162-3; Innis and Lower (eds.), Select Documents in Canadian Economic History, pp. 552, 753-4; "Report of Commercial Agent Washington on the Exports from London, Canada, to the United States" (House Executive Document, 49th Cong., 1st Sess., 1885-6, no. 253, pp. 608-9).

heavily, and by the next year the price had dropped to about 25 cents. Then the Ontario wool producer felt fully the effects of the fall in the price of cotton, which diminished the need for wool in the province as well as in the United States. In addition, there was the handicap of the American tariff, the lack of an adequate British market, and the dead weight of the surplus in the hands of the dealers, which was made worse by the very large clip of 1867.[29] The lowered price made sheep-raising less attractive than before, but there were two other factors contributing to its decline. One was losses from the dogs kept by villagers and other farmers—for no farmer would ever admit that *his* dog was a sheep killer. An act passed by the Canadian legislature in 1863 to prevent dogs running at large[30] was only a futile gesture so far as ending the dog menace was concerned. The other factor was the extension of dairying. It was said of the North Riding of Oxford, for instance, that the development of the factory system of cheese-making brought about a "depreciation in sheep and a premium on cows."[31]

This does not mean that sheep-raising went the way of the other furors of the American Civil War period. The combing wool of Ontario remained a specialty, with a ready market for a number of years in the United States. Its production centred at Hamilton. The United States consul there, who appears to have been something of an authority on the wool trade, thus reported in 1870:

> The class of wool grown in this section of the country is composed of Leicester, Cotswold, Lincoln, Southdown, and Merino, pure-bred and crossed; this also applies to many other sections of Canada, the first three being what is called combing-wool, the Leicester and Lincoln being the most desirable, having less noils than the Cotswold, and principally purchased for American manufacturers.

---

[29]*Canada Farmer*, Feb. 15, 1867, p. 59; *ibid.*, June 15, 1867, p. 185; *ibid.*, July 1, 1867, p. 201.

[30]*TBAUC 1864-8*, p. 74; *OACR*, vol. v, App. R-2, p. 15.

[31]*TBAUC 1864-8*, p. 511. Cf.: "There are no farms in Ontario devoted exclusively to sheep-raising. The clip comes from the small farmers in all parts of the province, and as soon as a cheese factory is started in their vicinity they drop sheep-raising and turn their attention to the production of milk for the creameries and cheese factories" (Report of Albert Roberts, United States Consul at Hamilton, Nov. 16, 1887, *House Executive Document*, 50th Cong., 1st Sess., 1887-8, no. 402, p. 520).

These varieties are also crossed with the Southdown, producing a shorter wool than the pure-bred, but a wool much sought after by American buyers for the past two years. This retains the luster and is found suitable for fine worsted goods.

About one-third of the wool raised in this district is what is termed clothing-wool, grown on the Southdown and Merino sheep, pure and crossed [i.e., the common sheep], and on another class called the old [French-] Canadian sheep. . . . . The wool grown on these sheep is very fine and short. The other two-thirds of the wool grown is long-combing and very desirable stock, from its fine silky appearance and luster, such as is required by the manufacturers of the best braids, alpacas, and other worsted goods.

These combing-wools are grown for a short distance east of this city and for some distance west, Hamilton being the most important point for wool in Canada, and where the largest wool business is done. South of this, along the shores of Lake Erie, the wool is principally finer; and north of this, as well as east, it is principally long, but of a coarser staple than that grown in this section, and not suitable for making the same kind of goods as wool produced in this neighborhood.[32]

In the late eighteen-seventies the manufacturers of New England and the Philadelphia region ceased to buy this combing wool. Fashions had changed, and worsted goods like the alpacas were now unsalable. Combing wool was equally a drug on the market in Ontario. The demand was now for a medium wool, which could be used in the manufacture of tweeds, serges, and underclothing. The small woollen mills which were beginning operations throughout the province provided the most important outlet for it.[33]

While the American demand for combing wool continued, many Ontario sheep raisers benefited in another way. The United States tariff of 1867, combined with the requirements of the manufacturers, kept prices of such wool high. The result was that sheep men as far distant as Maine, Oregon, and California obtained pure-bred Cotswolds and Leicesters, especially the former, from breeders in Ontario. This trade was

---

[32]Report of F. R. Blake, Dec. 31, 1870 (*House Executive Document*, 42nd Cong., 2nd Sess., 1871-2, no. 22, pp. 540-1. Cf. *OACR*, vol. IV, App. H. pp. 85-6).

[33]*Monetary and Commercial Times*, quoted in *Ontario Farmer*, July, 1870, p. 202; *Monetary and Commercial Times*, quoted in *Farmer's Advocate*, Sept. 1881, p. 215; *OACR*, vol. I, pp. 313, 319, 323-4.

not entirely new. In 1859 F. W. Stone of Guelph shipped to San Francisco a Leicester ram, five Southdown rams and three Southdown ewes, and ten Cotswold rams and six Cotswold ewes. Toward 1880 the Americans bought mostly Southdowns, Shropshires, and Oxfords. By 1880 some Ontario breeders were selling all they could raise of these breeds to Americans.[34]

After 1866 the ordinary farmer was able to benefit from his sheep being largely of the mutton type. There was a constantly expanding market for mutton in the United States, which American sheep raisers were wholly unable to fill. Thus, though the exporting of sheep to the United States appears to have declined somewhat after 1866 owing to the 20 per cent duty, for several years before 1876 about 500,000 lambs were sent across the border annually, as well as a number of fat wethers. By 1880 one of the dealers, who operated in Lanark, Carleton, and Renfrew Counties, was accustomed to buy 9,000 or 10,000 lambs every year at from $3.00 to $7.00 apiece, and to send them to Boston or New York. The lamb trade was seasonal. The eastern cities obtained their lambs from Chicago from January to April, from the middle states from May to August, and from Ontario, Quebec, and the northern states from then till Christmas.[35] It might be added that the lamb trade was one branch of Ontario agriculture not affected by the McKinley Tariff. In the eighteen-seventies lamb-raising for the American market was not confined to any particular part of Ontario, nor was it the dominant type of agriculture anywhere, unless possibly on the edge of settlement in Lanark and Renfrew counties.[36]

The termination of the Reciprocity Treaty and conditions in succeeding years affected the export trade in cattle ad-

[34]*Cultivator*, Sept., 1859, p. 291; *OACR*, vol. I, pp. 300-1; Carman, Heath and Minto, *Special Report*, pp. 345-6; *Farmer's Advocate*, Jan., 1881, p. 22.

[35]*Canada, Farmer*, June 15, 1872, p. 193; *ibid.*, Nov. 15, 1876, p. 219; *OACR*, vol. I, p. 302; *ibid.*, vol. IV, App. 1, p. 59. There was also a considerable local demand for lambs during the summer, before the export season opened. This was of fairly long standing. Cf. Copleston, *Canada*, pp. 112-13.

[36]Kirkwood and Murphy, *Undeveloped Lands in Northern and Western Ontario*, p. 145; *Journal of the House of Commons, Canada, 1877*, App. 6, p. 227; *ibid., 1884*, App. 1, p. 115. Hereafter this authority is cited as *JHC*.

versely. By 1867 American demand had resolved itself into a search for milch cows, mainly for the dairies of New York State, where Upper Canadian cows were highly esteemed.[37] After this date the expansion of the Ontario dairy industry resulted in a rapid decline in the number of cows sent to the United States, though some fat cattle and many more feeders —about 5,000 in all annually—did continue to find their way to New York, Boston, Philadelphia, and Pittsburgh. On the whole, however, the export trade grew progressively less attractive. The 20 per cent duty was a considerable obstacle, but more important was the competition of the American Northwest and Southwest, which drove prices in New York, Chicago, and Boston even lower than they were in Ontario.[38] By 1876 good beef was being sold off the experimental farm of the Ontario Agricultural College for as little as 4½ cents, and it was said that "the shippers consider it an established fact that the trade of Canada with the United States is now at an end."[39]

The trade did not come entirely to an end. A good many Durhams and Herefords for breeding purposes were still exported.[40] Calves, especially in the neighbourhoods of Detroit and Buffalo, were bought up by American hucksters, their selling price being reckoned at $1.00 for each week of their existence.[41] Occasionally feeders were exported, as the following extract shows: "This spring [1880] some 5,000 or 6,000 of cattle were taken from the west of the province to the Buffalo market. As a rule they come mostly from the northern part of the country, and are a very inferior class of cattle,

[37]*Canada Farmer*, May 15, 1867, p. 155; *ibid.*, June 1, 1868, p. 171; *ibid.*, May 15, 1869, p. 198; *ibid.*, May 16, 1870, p. 184.

[38]*Ibid.*, June 15, 1870, p. 224; *ibid.*, Aug. 15, 1870, p. 303; *ibid.*, Sept. 15, 1871, p. 331; *ibid.*, April 15, 1874, p. 152; Toronto *Weekly Globe*, Sept. 1, 1876.

[39]*Farmer's Advocate*, Sept., 1876, p. 168.

[40]*Ibid.*, Feb., 1880, p. 27; *OACR*, vol. I, p. 249. This trade was one which lent itself to fraudulent practices. According to a law which went into effect January 1, 1871, all animals of a superior description, and adapted for breeding purposes, were admitted into the United States free of duty. Till 1886 "hordes of scrubs" were exported to the United States thus on the plea that they were to be used for breeding (*House Executive Document*, 49th Cong., 2nd Sess., 1886-7, no. 171, p. 855).

[41]*OACR*, vol. I, p. 291; *OACR*, vol. IV, App. G, p. 72.

but they are taken down to the Genesee Flats, and after remaining there for a time, they are turned out good cattle. Higher prices are paid for them than for Michigan and Indiana cattle, as it is said that they grow better. In that instance Canada is acting as a cattle-raising country for an adjoining cattle-feeding country."[42]

Faced with the total loss of their American market, Ontario dealers, like those of Quebec, began to consider sending their surplus livestock overseas. The first shipment of livestock from the St. Lawrence basin, twenty-five head of fat cattle, arrived at Liverpool June 3, 1875; it was sent by a Montreal man, purely as a speculation. In 1876 Ontario shippers entered the business, sending overseas sheep and horses as well as cattle.[43] Little came of the trade in horses. The British demand was for light and active horses for use as drivers or for drawing street-cars. Few such horses were available in Ontario or in the United States at the prices the dealers were able to pay ($120 being the maximum). At the end of 1880 there was only one firm in all North America engaged in exporting horses to Great Britain, Hendrie & Douglas of Toronto.[44] In contrast, the trade in mutton sheep expanded rapidly, as is shown by the statistics of exports from the Dominion: 1875-6 (fiscal year), none; 1876-7, 3,170; 1877-8, 11,985; 1878-9, 54,721; 1879-80, 109,506. Virtually all these sheep came from Ontario. Qualitatively they left much to be desired, owing to the practice of exporting the best lambs to the United States.[45] The exports of cattle made similar progress, for Ontario shippers had some advantages over their American competitors. Ocean rates from Montreal as well as from New York had been driven down by the depression of 1873; and the Grand Trunk cut its rates as much as did the American railways. In 1876 the freight from Montreal to Liverpool was actually less than the duty collectable under the United States tariff. Moreover, beginning

[42]*OACR*, vol. IV, App. I, p. 13.

[43]Montreal *Witness*, July 8, 1875; Toronto *Weekly Globe*, July 7, Nov. 3, 1876; Trafford, *Horses of the British Empire*, vol. II, p. 244.

[44]Toronto *Weekly Globe*, July 21, 1876; *Farmer's Advocate*, Jan., 1881, p. 2.

[45]*OACR*, vol. I, p. 303. Lambs were little exported, as they did not stand the voyage well.

in 1879 American cattle were subjected to a so-called embargo, established by a British order-in-council. This provided that cattle from the United States should be slaughtered within ten days of their arrival at a British port, to prevent their infecting the local animals with pleuro-pneumonia. Canadian cattle were not similarly "scheduled" till 1892, when the trade overseas had become fairly well consolidated. Because they did not have to be slaughtered on arrival, but instead could be sold to the cattle fatteners of Scotland and Ireland for further conditioning, they brought about $20.00 a head more at Liverpool and Glasgow than the American cattle.[46]

The growth of the export market in horses, cattle, and sheep was accompanied by an expansion of the domestic market as the result of industrialization. Sometimes outlets were found in unexpected places. The driving of cattle north or west to the shanties of the Ottawa Valley is an example. This trade, though not large, was an interesting by-product of the American Civil War. The high price of American pork during those years caused the lumbermen of the Ottawa to try the experiment of using fresh beef instead of salt pork in their establishments. It was so successful that for many years small droves of cattle, often laden with bags of oats, salt, or beans, passed through the towns along the Ottawa River, bound for the shanties farther west and north.[47]

On account of the demand for feeder cattle during the American Civil War, several new monthly fairs were established in the region north and west of Guelph—one at Goderich in 1864, others at Fergus, Harriston, and Georgetown in 1865, and one at Waterloo early in 1866.[48] In addition, fairs were held sporadically at places such as Brantford and Chatsworth, usually in connection with the exhibitions of the agricultural

---

[46]Toronto *Weekly Globe*, Nov. 3, 1876; *Farmer's Advocate*, Jan., 1881, pp. 2, 6; Drummond, "Marketing of Canadian Live Stock" (Mss. Thesis, 1930, in Main Library of the Department of Agriculture, Ottawa), pp. 12-13, 16. On the technical problems involved in the livestock trade to the British Isles, see Innis and Lower, *Select Documents in Canadian Economic History*, pp. 554-6.

[47]*Sessional Papers, Ontario, 1868-9*, no. 7, pp. 48-9; Kingston *Daily News*, Jan. 11, 1871; Grant, *Picturesque Canada*, vol. I, p. 224.

[48]*Canada Farmer*, Dec. 1, 1864, p. 362; *ibid.*, June 1, 1865, p. 171; *ibid.*, June 15, 1865, p. 186; *ibid.*, Nov. 1, 1865, p. 331; *ibid.*, Feb. 1, 1866, p. 43.

societies.[49] Eastern Upper Canada also had its fairs. In the
upper Ottawa Valley in September, 1865, there were three
fairs held at Eganville, Douglas, and Renfrew, respectively,
for the special purpose of collecting cattle for export to the
United States.[50] After the termination of the Reciprocity
Treaty, fairs continued to develop. There were few north of
Lake Ontario, probably owing to the ease with which livestock
could be sent off by the Grand Trunk. There were still some
in the lower Ottawa Valley, though they received little notice
in the local newspapers or in the agricultural periodicals published at Toronto or London.[51] The most conspicuous and
important fairs came to be concentrated in the stretch of
country bounded by the towns of Brantford, Woodstock, Stratford, Listowel, Walkerton, Durham, Orangeville, and
Brampton, which is about a hundred miles long and fifty miles
wide. "In one particular section of this Province," it was
asserted in 1872, "the Fair has become deeply rooted, and
will in all probability continue to increase with each succeeding year. We allude to that section in which are situated
Guelph, Galt, Mount Forest, Durham, &c., &c."[52] In this
region there were by 1875 ordinarily at least twenty-five
monthly cattle fairs, as well as a number of quarterly ones.[53]
Many of them were integrated with and tributary to that at
Guelph, that is, they were held a few days in advance of the
latter, so that the cattle sold at them could be driven to Guelph

---

[49]*Ibid.*, April 1, 1864, p. 90; *ibid.*, March 15, 1865, p. 96.

[50]Ottawa *Citizen*, quoted in Montreal *Witness*, Sept. 20, 1865.

[51]*Canada Farmer*, Oct. 15, 1866, p. 318; Ottawa *Citizen*, Sept.
19, 1936.

[52]*Canada Farmer*, April 15, 1872, p. 141.

[53]It may be assumed that the most successful cattle fairs in central
and western Ontario were those which managed to maintain the
steadiest existence. Cattle fairs were mentioned as having been held, or
as about to be held, in 1869, 1871, 1874, 1877, and 1882 at Elora, Fergus,
Guelph, Harriston, and Orangeville; in 1869, 1871, 1874, and 1877 at
Bosworth, Clifford, Drayton, Elmira, Mount Forest, and Teviotdale;
in 1871, 1874, 1877, and 1882 at Brampton, Erin, and Mono Mills; in
1871, 1874, and 1877 at Durham, Listowel, Masonville, New Hamburgh,
and Waterloo; and in 1874, 1877, and 1882 at Hillsburgh (*ibid.*, Feb. 15,
1869, p. 74; *ibid.*, April 15, 1869, p. 156; *ibid.*, Dec. 15, 1869, p. 473;
ibid., Jan. 16, 1871, p. 35; *Ontario Farmer*, Feb., 1869, p. 44; *Farmer's
Advocate*, July, 1874, p. 99; *ibid.*, July, 1877, p. 152; *ibid.*, Oct., 1882,
p. 281).

for shipment. On the average about three hundred cattle would be brought for sale at each of these fairs. Horses were occasionally offered, but only in small numbers, and more often a flock or two of sheep,[54] but usually the trade was in cattle only. These fairs flourished till the eighteen-eighties, when the arrival of railways nearly everywhere in the settled parts of Old Ontario robbed them of their former importance.[55]

When the cattle fair became well established in any locality, it benefited the farmers and those dependent on the agricultural community. The farmer no longer had to rely on the local butcher or on itinerant drovers for a market. He could sell small lots of cattle as advantageously as large droves. He could not be victimized through his ignorance of prices, for competition assured that he would get nearly what his stock was worth. He was paid in cash. And, a matter of much significance, he learned that the better the stock, the higher the price. As a result of all these advantages in the marketing of his stock, the farmer raised more animals, and his farm profited. The cash in the hands of the farmers gave the local merchants an exceptional opportunity to dispose of the goods on their shelves. On the other hand, pedlars, medicine vendors, and lightning-rod agents often fleeced innocent individuals from the back concessions. The activities of these persons, and the drunkenness and fighting which customarily prevailed, were the greatest drawbacks of the fairs.[56]

The drovers appreciated the fairs possibly even more than the farmers. In the parts of the province where there were no fairs, the drover had to scour the countryside in his buggy, "picking up" a steer here and three or four somewhere else. Then he had to collect his purchases, and hire labourers or boys to help drive them to a railroad station or urban market. Where the cattle fairs were established, he could associate with other drovers, and they could drive and pasture their

---

[54]There were occasionally separate sheep fairs, as at Galt in 1870 (*Ontario Farmer*, Nov., 1870, p. 335).

[55]For the decline of the fair at Durham, cf. Marsh, *History of the County of Grey*, pp. 293-5. The Durham fair turned into a horse fair.

[56]*Canada Farmer*, June 1, 1868, p. 169; *ibid.*, March 15, 1872, p. 116; *ibid.*, April 15, 1872, p. 141; *ibid.*, May 15, 1872, p. 170; *Ontario Farmer*, Aug., 1870, p. 249.

herds together, having first branded them for purposes of identification. Thus all concerned cut their overhead expenses considerably.[57] These advantages were especially apparent in the Guelph vicinity.

It is not the monthly fairs held in Guelph alone, that draw such large numbers of buyers from a distance to that locality, but the series of fairs held upon consecutive days in the villages around Guelph. For instance a buyer demanding a large number of stock for shipments, stays at Mount Forest, and for several consecutive days can work down through Mount Forest, Durham, Fergus, Elora, &c. to Guelph, collecting as he goes a large herd for shipment upon the railways.

There are hundreds of farmers who cannot spare time, nor the expense, of driving their two or three beeves perhaps 30 or 40 miles to the large city, but who can drive them to the villages in their own locality, and it is comparatively inexpensive for the buyer to drive his herd, increasing as it goes alone [along] at each fair held upon his route to the point of embarkation.[58]

During the eighteen-seventies the chief cattle-raising region in Ontario came to be that in which the fairs mentioned flourished, that is to say, Wellington and Waterloo counties, with contiguous portions of Peel, Halton, Wentworth, Brant, Oxford, Perth, and Dufferin counties. Wellington County was notable as the centre of the fattening industry. In 1869 it was reported that "there is hardly a farmer in the county of Wellington who does not now fatten from four to ten head of oxen, hence the continually increasing amount of fat cattle pouring in from that quarter."[59] In 1880 enthusiasts asserted of the same county that "more turnips are raised and more beef sold in Wellington than in any other county in Ontario," and that "Wellington possesses better herds and more good stock than any [other] county in the Dominion. Durham blood is largely diffused and a poor beast is becoming a rarity."[60]

The neighbourhood of London and St. Thomas was another good region. By 1880 a considerable grazing industry had developed in Middlesex County. The graziers here raised only a few calves each year, and obtained their feeders at three or four years of age in Huron, Lambton, Elgin, and Kent

[57]Ottawa *Citizen*, Sept. 19, 1936.
[58]*Canada Farmer*, May 15, 1872, p. 170.
[59]*Ibid.*, Jan. 15, 1869, p. 4. Cf. *Ontario Farmer*, Jan., 1870, p. 1.
[60]*OACR*, vol. II, pp. 615-16.

counties. They kept them over the winter, then grazed them till the middle of the next summer. Some of the farmers were accustomed to have from 200 to 250 steers on grass.[61] In Huron, Bruce, and Grey counties, cattle-raising was an important branch of farming, though the animals there had the reputation of being much inferior to those around Guelph or London.[62] Drovers obtained many good steers in the counties between Belleville and Toronto, but very few along the Bay of Quinte or farther east, where dairying had become dominant; in fact, so unsuitable for beef were most of the cattle east of Kingston that in 1880 one fattener at Cardinal obtained all his feeders from the shores of Lake Huron.[63]

It was only under exceptional circumstances that the Ontario farmer made raising cattle for market his sole occupation. Ordinarily he kept them for the general purposes of the farm. A Northumberland County resident noted that

Some keep cattle strictly for breeding purposes, raising stock to sell for breeders. In that case they must keep a breed that is in demand—for which they can find a ready market. Others, again, keep cattle chiefly for giving milk, either for selling new or else for making into butter and cheese. . . . The number of cheese factories that have grown up amongst us of late years has caused some of our farmers to turn their attention chiefly to keeping cows to supply these factories with milk. Others, again, depend chiefly on feeding, turning their cattle into beef. Most of us, however, use them for all these purposes, breeding from them what stock we want, milking them, and, when no longer profitable for these purposes, we turn them into beef.[64]

After Confederation, as earlier, hog-raising on a commercial basis amounted to little, taking Ontario as a whole. Parts of the province, such as the Ottawa Valley, did not even raise enough pork for their own consumption. In 1880 commercial hog-raising was still confined to corn-growing Essex and Kent counties, and to the dairying districts where there was an abundance of whey or buttermilk; elsewhere the farmers could not compete with the corn-fed hogs of the United States. In Essex County farmers on hundred-acre lots

---

[61]*OACR*, vol. II, pp. 251, 340; *OACR*, vol. IV, App. G, p. 65; *OACR*, vol. IV, App. I, pp. 20-1.

[62]*OACR*, vol. IV, App. I, pp. 10, 13. See above, pp. 279-80.

[63]*OACR*, vol. IV, App. G, p. 43; *OACR*, vol. IV, App. I, p. 4.

[64]*Canada Farmer*, Jan. 15, 1872, p. 31.

were accustomed to fatten twenty hogs a year, all of which
went to the packers at London, Hamilton, Toronto, or
Montreal. In 1880 the pork crop of Essex County was estimated to be worth about $400,000 a year.[65]

The Essex peninsula hogs provided the packers with pork
suitable for the lumbermen. It was not adapted to the
demands of the British market, where what was required
was a lean pork. Packers engaged in this overseas trade,
the most important of whom was William Davies of Toronto,
found it difficult to get swine in Ontario of the proper and
uniform quality. Davies could get less than three thousand
a year in the province, even counting those he bought in Essex
and Kent counties. He actually preferred a lean (not thin)
hog fattened on peas or barley, because his business was curing
bacon and hams, but the local farmers failed to provide it.
They did not feed their swine carefully throughout their
careers, but turned them out along the roadside or into bare
pastures, threw them the garbage, and in the autumn shut
them up for a few weeks, hoping that by stuffing them they
could fatten them adequately. The result was that Ontario
packers relied on Chicago hogs.[66]

Poultry and eggs remained minor products of most Ontario
farms, often indeed only pin-money ones for the farmers'
wives, but the trade in them was of considerable importance
in the aggregate. This was especially true of eggs, particularly after they began to be admitted free of duty to the
United States in 1871. However, even in 1867 a dealer at St.
Marys found it profitable to construct cold-storage warehouses for the eggs he exported across the border. In
September, 1878, the merchants of Guelph shipped $13,000
worth to the United States. About 1880 the "egg king of
Canada" at Seaforth employed eight or ten teams in collecting
eggs from country store-keepers, and shipped about 75,000,000
eggs a year to New York. The trade was seasonal, beginning
in March, when supplies from the South began to fall off,
reaching a peak in June, when Canadian eggs virtually

---

[65]*JHC, 1876*, App. 7, p. 28; *OACR*, vol. I, pp. 332-5; *OACR*, vol. IV,
App. G, p. 87.

[66]*OACR*, vol. I, pp. 335-8. The packing methods employed by Davies
are described in Timperlake, *Illustrated Toronto*, pp. 284-6.

monopolized the market, and coming to an end in November with the reappearance of southern eggs. Not many eggs were shipped to Great Britain before the season of 1880-1 (when large quantities were), primarily because French competition was too strong.[67] Poultry exports were on a much smaller scale than those of eggs. Nevertheless, it was stated of Essex County in 1880 that "in our part of the country we can always get a high price for spring chickens in the Detroit market."[68] Too, during the eighteen-seventies dealers all over Ontario shipped a good deal of poultry every year to Boston or New York. At the end of the decade the development of refrigerated steamships made it profitable for them to send geese, turkeys, and chickens to the British Isles for the Christmas trade. They frequently obtained the poultry for both the American and the overseas markets at special poultry fairs. The most important of these was the Turkey Fair at Smiths Falls, which was stated in 1883 to have been in existence for twenty-seven years, and which was patronized by farmers within a radius of from thirty to forty miles.[69]

The growth of the American market, of the domestic market, and after 1875, of the British market, for livestock, and the development of the dairy industry, were responsible for a large increase in the number of livestock kept,[70] and for

[67]*RAA 1879*, p. 192; *OACR*, vol. I, pp. 478, 483-4; Johnston, *History of the County of Perth*, p. 165; *Farmer's Advocate*, Jan., 1881, p. 11.

[68]*OACR*, vol. I, p. 184.

[69]*RAA 1879*, p. 192; *Farmer's Advocate*, Jan., 1877, p. 5; *ibid.*, Feb., 1881, p. 26; *ibid.*, Jan., 1884, pp. 11-12.

[70]Livestock in the province, 1851, 1861, 1871, and 1881:

	1851	1861	1871	1881
Horses				
Horses over 3 years....		277,258	368,585	473,906
Colts and fillies..........		100,423	120,416	116,392
Total	201,670	377,681	489,001	590,298
Cattle				
Milch cows..................	297,070	451,640	638,759	782,243
Bulls, oxen, or steers	192,140	99,605		
Calves or heifers........	255,249	464,083		
Other horned cattle....			716,474	896,661
Total	744,459	1,015,328	1,355,233	1,678,904
Sheep	1,050,168	1,170,225	1,514,914	1,359,178
Swine	571,496	776,001	874,664	700,922

Census of Canada, 1851-2, vol. II, p. 65; *ibid., 1861*, vol. II, p. 94; *ibid., 1871*, vol. III, pp. 110-1; *ibid., 1881*, vol. III, pp. 130-1.

a bettering of their quality. What was the importance in
Ontario agriculture of this consolidation of the livestock
industry? No matter what the purpose for which they were
raised, the cattle, sheep, and horses greatly benefited the
worn-out wheat farms. Even when reared only as part of a
diversified economy, without expectation of much profit from
them, they protected the farmer against the evil of single-crop
price fluctuations. By feeding his coarse grains to his animals,
he obtained, in a sense, a better price for the produce of his
fields than he could get from an elevator operator. He kept
his land more in pasture and less in cereals. He built better
stables and barns. As the Ontario Agricultural Commission
said, "the farmer begins to grow roots and coarse grains
and feed his stuff to his own cattle when he raises his cattle
with an object, and has stock worth caring for. Good feeding
is the first necessity of good stock, and good stock means
above everything good farming with all that the phrase
implies."[71]

[71]*OACR*, vol. I, p. 242.

CHAPTER XVII

AGRICULTURE ON THE FOREST FRONTIER, 1850-1880[1]

IN an earlier chapter, the agriculture of the Ottawa Valley was described, with particular emphasis being laid on the importance of the shanty market. During the late eighteen-fifties and early eighteen-sixties, the government of the Province of Canada attempted to utilize the shanty market in promoting the settlement of the area between the Ottawa River and Georgian Bay. Now known to have been a tragic mistake, its scheme at the time seemed well thought out, and promised to solve at least two current difficulties of the administration—the demand of the lumbermen for better communications, and the clamour of potential settlers for cheap land.

During the eighteen-forties there had been a great increase in Upper Canadian immigration. The consequence was that, by the middle eighteen-fifties, the supply of crown lands in the fertile peninsula of Upper Canada was exhausted. This occasioned much disquiet, for a steady influx of pioneers was considered an essential of colonial prosperity. Moreover, owing to the boom of the time, real estate in the older settlements had advanced so much in price that it was beyond the reach of the ordinary immigrant or native. It was unthinkable that no provision should be made for them, even though the only crown land available in Upper Canada was north of Lake Huron, or in the country between the Ottawa River and Georgian Bay—the Ottawa-Huron region.[2]

A select committee on the management of the public lands heard opinions in 1855 on the subject of opening to settlement the last area, nearly all of which was within the Canadian Shield, and much of which was already notorious as "red-pine country." One witness, A. J. Russell, the Crown Timber Agent at Bytown, advocated the limitation of settlement there to tracts of good land sufficiently extensive to support a popu-

---

[1]Cf. Lower, "Assault on the Laurentian Barrier" (*Canadian Historical Review*, vol. x, 1929), and Lower, *Settlement and the Forest Frontier*.

[2]*Sessional Papers, Canada, 1857*, App. 25. Hereafter this authority is cited as *SPC*.

lation large enough to keep up roads and schools. Other
witnesses, among them T. C. Keefer, who as early as 1846
had advocated colonizing the region,[3] evidently exercised more
influence on the committee, though it failed to make any
definite recommendations.[4] It was therefore without the
approval of the Select Committee, indeed, wholly on his own
responsibility, that later in the year the Hon. P. Vankoughnet,
Commissioner of Crown Lands, committed the administration
to a policy of settlement in the Ottawa-Huron region by means
of "free grants" along "colonization roads." In doing so, he
declared that the ready market for settlers' produce in the
lumber camps made it the most advantageous district for
colonization that the government had at its disposal.[5]

The only new thing in this policy was the application of
the principle of free grants along colonization roads to the
lumbering areas. Free grants along leading roads had been
known in Upper Canada since Simcoe opened Yonge Street
northwards from York, but they had first become important
through the Land Act of 1841, which provided that free allotments of not more than fifty acres could be made along roads
in any new settlement.[6] The first of these roads had been
opened in the preceding year. This was the "Garafraxa" or
Owen Sound Road, which ran from Fergus to Owen Sound.
The free grants, which carried with them the right to purchase the 150 acres adjacent to them, were so popular that
the road was soon settled throughout its entire length, and
the government was encouraged to open others on the same
terms. One of these, the "Toronto and Sydenham" (usually
known as the "Toronto Line"), was opened in 1849 from
Chatsworth to Shelburne. Another, the Durham Road, was
cut out some time before 1853 between Lake Huron at Kincardine and the Garafraxa Road. A third, the Elora and
Saugeen Road, which was practically completed in 1855, ran
northwest and then north from Elora to Southampton. All

---

[3]*Journal of the Legislative Assembly of Canada, 1847*, App. LL.
Hereafter this authority is cited as *JLAC*.

[4]*SPC 1854-5*, App. MM.

[5]*SPC 1857*, App. 25; *Thompson's Mirror of Parliament*, nos. 7 & 8,
pp. 5-6.

[6]Morrison, "Principle of Free Grants in the Land Act of 1841"
(*Canadian Historical Review*, vol. XIV, 1933, pp. 392-3, 404).

these roads gave connection with older ones leading to Toronto or Hamilton; all were opened on the free-grant principle; and all were exceedingly popular with the poorer settlers.[7]

In the meantime, to aid the lumbermen, the government opened several important roads, some leading west from the Ottawa River, and others north from Lake Ontario. In 1852 it completed one (ever since known as the Government Road) from Arnprior to Pembroke, to enable the lumbermen to get their anchors, axes, and foodstuffs past the rapids in the summer, and to make them independent of the weak river ice in autumn and spring. In 1854 it completed another, the "Ottawa and Opeongo," westward from the mouth of the Bonnechere River to the Great Opeongo Lake, roughly along the backbone between the Bonnechere and Madawaska rivers. Both roads, it was hoped, would ultimately terminate on Georgian Bay. The lumbermen with limits in the remote interior might then be able to get their supplies cheaper from the West than they could over the portage roads from the lower Ottawa. Eventually there were five main roads in the Ottawa-Huron region running north and south—the Hastings, the Addington, the Frontenac, the Bobcaygeon, and the Muskoka—and four which ran from east to west—the Mississippi, the Peterson, the Opeongo, and the "Pembroke and Mattawan." These roads were systematically located over a wide area. From the point of view of the lumbermen, who needed only good winter roads, they were an immediate success. They made it possible to bring larger quantities of supplies into the shanties, and at a much lower cost per ton than formerly.[8]

It was pointed out in Chapter VII that the lumbermen in the Ottawa Valley in the eighteen-thirties and eighteen-forties were interested in having the good lands near their limits settled. It is therefore not surprising that when the Crown Lands Department came to lay out the Opeongo Road the lumberman John Egan and some of his associates prevailed on it to open the eastern border of the Ottawa-Huron region

[7]*Journal and Transactions of the Board of Agriculture of Upper Canada for 1855-6*, pp. 367, 369, 641-2. Hereafter this authority is cited as *JTBAUC*.

[8]Perth *Bathurst Courier*, Oct. 22, 1852; *SPC 1854-5*, App. MM.; *SPC 1858*, App. 45; *SPC 1861*, no. 23. For their location, see the map in Schott, *Landnahme und Kolonisation*, p. 257.

to settlement, by setting off a tier of fifty-acre lots on each side of the road to be granted to actual settlers on the same terms as on the colonization roads in the Upper Canada peninsula. The rapid swarming of squatters in the early eighteen-fifties into the area through which the Opeongo Road ran, just west of the old settlements in the Bonnechere Valley, augured well for a scheme of directed colonization. It was therefore with the support of a certain class of lumbermen as well as that of influential politicians like the Hon. Malcolm Cameron (who had been advocating a free-grant road on the Owen Sound principle between the Bonnechere and Mada-waska rivers since 1841), that Vankoughnet made his decision. As a result of it, the quondam bush trails became colonization roads, in order that the plan tentatively applied to the lower Opeongo Road might be extended throughout much of the Ottawa-Huron country.[9]

Free grants were shortly made available along three roads —the rest of the Opeongo Road in 1855, and the Addington and Hastings roads in 1856. The free-grant system was later extended to some of the lots along the Bobcaygeon, Muskoka, Mississippi, and Frontenac roads.[10] However, the bulk of the land in the vicinity of all the roads was intended to be sold. To do otherwise would be to belittle them, and, in any case, as Vankoughnet explained, "he was not prepared to throw open the country to any host of marauders that might come here."[11] To enable immigrants to make their way through the extensive broken country separating their holdings from the older settlements to the south and east, the government improved the roads sufficiently to permit of waggon traffic; but all this meant in practice was that the work gangs moved the bigger stones and the fallen trees out of the way, and laid corduroy causeways through the swamps. Worse, till the autumn of 1862, the contractors from the front townships, with the men they hired there, considered their job finished when they had chopped the road out, and left it to grow up in underbrush forthwith. After 1862 the settlers did the

---

[9]*Bytown Packet*, Aug. 17, 1850; Perth *Bathurst Courier*, April 23, Oct. 22, 1852; evidence of A. J. Russell, in *SPC 1854-5*, App. MM; *SPC 1861*, no. 15.
[10]*SPC 1858*, App. 45; *SPC 1862*, no. 11.
[11]*Thompson's Mirror of Parliament*, nos. 7 & 8, p. 7.

work on a day-labour basis, but they were too few to accomplish even as much as the contractors, and invariably they looked on their pay as a subvention. The lumbermen cared little whether the roads were passable in summer or not; and the government was far away and had other uses for its funds. Under these circumstances, no permanent improvement was effected in any of the colonization roads.[12]

This fact did not hinder the government from anxiously fostering settlement along the roads. It gave lots of a hundred acres on easy conditions—cultivation of twelve acres within four years, construction of a cabin, and continued residence.[13] It established an agency at Ottawa in 1857 to look after immigrants, and distributed in Europe pamphlets in English, German, French, and Norwegian.[14] These particularly emphasized the insatiable produce market created by the lumbermen—"the vast amount of lumbering all along the Madawaska and its tributaries will require more than the Settlement can yield for years."[15] Politicians and railroad promoters held out the hope that when the Quebec and Lake Huron Railway went up the valley of the Madawaska or of the Bonnechere to Georgian Bay it would bring a rush of immigrants and a rise in land values as had the Illinois Central, the land-grant railway on which it was modelled. The colonization roads would assure access to the older communities in the meantime.[16]

Contrary to expectations, the settlers who came to take up lands along the colonization roads or in their vicinity were numbered not in thousands but only in dozens. The overwhelming majority of such as did come was composed of farmers who had been brought up in Upper Canada, or who had lived some years in it. Many had owned small farms in

[12]*SPC 1857*, App. 54; *SPC 1867-8*, no. 6, pp. 1ff.; Toronto *Globe*, May 9, 1865.

[13]*SPC 1857*, App. 54.

[14]*SPC 1858*. App. 41; *SPC 1859*, no. 19. On the immigration campaign, see Gates, "Official Encouragement to Immigration" (*Canadian Historical Review*, vol. xv, 1934).

[15]*JTBAUC 1856-7*, p. 170.

[16]Speech of John A. Macdonald, June 17, 1856, in Debates of the Parliament of Canada, 1856 (scrapbook of newspaper clippings in Library of Parliament, Ottawa).

the near-by settlements, and had sold them to purchase larger ones for themselves and their sons.[17] Many others went primarily to work in the shanties, and many more, especially after 1860, to engage in lumbering on their own account by taking the pine off their grants.[18]

The colonization roads had really been opened to attract European immigrants. This they failed to do. The extensive governmental advertising brought only a few poverty-stricken Poles and Germans into the Ottawa-Huron region. It is easy to explain the failure. The American states with which the Province of Canada came into competition for settlers were all assisted in their propaganda by land, railway, and shipping companies, which sent their agents to the agricultural exhibitions and other rural gatherings.[19] More important was the attraction of the prairies, now that railroads touched the Mississippi, steel ploughs that would scour were available, and low costs made it possible to grow wheat at a profit in Iowa and Minnesota. Farmers, farmers' sons, country storekeepers, day labourers, and lawyers from one end of Canada West to the other sold their properties for what they would bring, and joined the European immigrants making their way

---

[17]*SPC 1858*, App. 45; *Bytown Gazette,* quoted in Montreal *Witness,* Jan. 7, 1860; *Canada, 1862,* p. 18.

[18]Langton, "On the Age of Timber Trees" (*Transactions of the Literary and Historical Society of Quebec,* vol. v, 1862, p. 75); evidence of Ezra Stephens, *JLAC 1863* (1st Sess.), App. 8.

[19]"The agents of the Illinois Central are flooding the Province Show at Kingston with their books and pamphlets" (*Lower Canada Agriculturist,* Dec., 1862, p. 125). Cf. also: "In all the public places throughout our country . . . , in railway stations and out houses—in the saloons of steamboats and the public rooms of hotels—on the doors of our school-houses and at the cross roads of townships—on the frontier and far back in the interior of our new settlements—everywhere, in fact, where readers can be found, the placards of an unscrupulous class of American land speculators are to be seen. It is impossible to take a drive into the back townships, a quiet sail down the river, or a dusty jolt by the railway, without meeting, at every turn and stepping place, flaming posters, offering for sale western lands, which if we are to believe their words, are 'unequalled in richness, cheap in price, and easy of access to market.' These Yankee lands are not 'rude forests' of beech and maple, elm and basswood, but 'beautiful prairies that require no clearing.' All that is necessary for the farmer to do, is to turn over the sod, harrow in the seed, and then prepare to reap the harvest" (Ottawa [Valley] correspondent of the *Bytown Gazette,* quoted in *Canadian Merchants' Magazine,* Aug., 1857, p. 406).

up the St. Lawrence and the Great Lakes to the American
West. The exodus from Upper Canada, like that from New
York, was compared despairingly to that from Western
Europe in the days of Peter the Hermit. By the late eighteen-
fifties the practical question was no longer that of promoting
immigration into Upper Canada, but of preventing emigration
from it. There seemed to be no prospect of accomplishing
this aim as long as there was no industrialization. So it
happened that, before 1860, the frontier of Upper Canada
moved into the United States.[20]

Under these circumstances the failure of the wooded free
grants to appeal to any but a few impecunious natives in the
regions adjacent to them was quite what should have been
expected. By the end of 1860 the free grants had lost even
this limited popularity. New settlers no longer appeared to
take up grants; older ones abandoned their clearances; and
in certain localities it was only a question of time till not a
person would be left.[21] The situation was aggravated by
abuses in connection with the grants. The poor Polish immigrants did intend, it is true, to hew homes for themselves
out of the wilderness, as their ancestors had done in the
Posen section of Prussia, but they found it difficult to clear
their pine land and unprofitable to cultivate it. On the other
hand, the current opinion was that if a native of Upper
Canada or an immigrant of several years' experience acquired
a lot in the pineries, either by free grant or purchase, it was
almost invariably merely to cut the timber.[22] Early in 1859
the Department of Crown Lands therefore felt forced to take
action against fraud on the part of settlers. This was in a
timid regulation which provided that "squatter's rights" would
no longer be recognized as giving any equity in the land.[23]

Stories began to reach the older parts of Upper Canada of
distress approaching starvation among the colonization-roads
settlers, especially the Poles and Germans. The lumbermen
who had been the friends of genuine settlement began to com-

---

[20]*Canadian Merchants' Magazine*, June, 1857, pp. 269-70; *Canadian
Agriculturist*, April, 1861, p. 253.

[21]*SPC 1860*, no. 12; *SPC 1861*, no. 23; *SPC 1863*, no. 5.

[22]Perry, *Staple Trade of Canada*, pp. 40, 42.

[23]*SPC 1859*, App. 17.

plain, with reason, that irresponsible persons were stealing
their timber under the guise of land-clearing, and destroying
the woods as a result of uncontrolled fires in their slashings.[24]
The Toronto *Globe,* impressed by the agitation in the United
States which culminated in the Homestead Act of 1862, kept
on insisting that the system of free grants should be extended,
so that the whole public domain, including the wilderness
north of Lake Huron and Sault Ste. Marie, would be free to
location.   Crown land, it declared, should not be held for
speculative purposes, but should be "regarded as a foundation
of the prosperity which a pushing and increasing population
alone can render available."[25]   The government, kept in
ignorance of the true state of affairs by the optimistic reports
of its land agents and surveyors, remained smugly confident
of the ultimate success of its policy, but those who were really
acquainted with the progress of the settlement were convinced
that the Ottawa-Huron region would prove utterly worthless
as the site of an agricultural population.

Why had the scheme failed? Two reasons were fundamental—the character of the land and the weakness of the
shanty market.

Before the government's colonization policy was inaugurated, lumbermen such as the Hamiltons and Gilmours, and
other well-informed individuals such as A. J. Russell, pointed
out the natural obstacles in the way of its achievement. In
general the roads ran along the ridges, whereas the best land
was found in the valleys. But even on the bottoms there was
little first-class land. Walter Shanly, who made an exploratory
survey of the country north of the line of the Opeongo Road
for the proposed Quebec and Lake Huron Railroad, found that
there was scarcely any in the part of the Ottawa-Huron area
he traversed, with the exception of a few spots such as the
vicinity of the headwaters of the York River. Some of the
government surveyors in the colonization-roads settlements
shortly reported that in a few townships there was not enough
soil to hold their stakes, and that in others there was nothing

---

[24]Cf. A. Gilmour to W. McDougall, Feb. 9, 1863, in *JLAC 1863*
(1st Sess.), App. 8, and the speech of the Hon. James Skead in Debates
of the Parliament of Canada, 1863, 2nd Sess., p. 29.

[25]Toronto *Globe,* Dec. 31, 1859; cf. *ibid.,* Feb. 5, 1863.

but sand. These statements were scarcely an exaggeration, as can be attested by modern summer campers in northern Hastings County.[26]

It is obvious that people on land such as that of the Ottawa-Huron region could not hope to compete with those on the prairies in the markets of Europe. Yet, poor as the land was, lumber squatters in the preceding quarter century had made a good living in many parts of the Ottawa Valley no better adapted to agriculture. New conditions, however, contributed to the immediate failure of the shanty market, on which so much reliance had been placed by the pamphleteers. Prices had earlier been high for the produce of the isolated clearings in the region officially opened by the colonization roads, owing to the difficulty and cost of communication with Bytown and the lower Ottawa Valley; but the cutting-out of the colonization roads, even only as lumbermen's winter trails, made it possible to team in foodstuffs at comparatively low rates. In 1858 one lumbering firm on the upper Madawaska River, which had never had flour delivered at its shanties for less than $7.00 a barrel, nor oats for less than 50 cents a bushel, obtained them for $5.25 and 35 cents, respectively. In the winter of 1859-60 the Gilmours and other firms with limits in the country behind Perth brought in hay and oats from Lower Canada, and even after paying the freight on the Grand Trunk, saved money, and at the same time reduced local prices. In the same winter the lumbermen along the Hastings Road got most of their supplies from Madoc and Belleville, rather than from the pioneers in their own neighbourhood.[27] This competition was before long so serious for the settlers far up the Opeongo Road that many of them were forced to sell their produce at the country stores in the older communities near the Ottawa River, a proceeding which neither they nor the government had contemplated when they took up their land.[28] Outside competition in their own market, impassable roads to the outer world, scanty surpluses or even none, and the

[26]*SPC 1857*, App. 5; speech of the Hon. W. McDougall, Aug. 21, 1863, in Debates of the Parliament of Canada, 1863, 2nd Sess., pp. 23-4.

[27]*SPC 1858*, App. 45; *SPC 1860*, no. 12; *Perth Courier*, Dec. 30, 1859; *ibid.*, Jan. 13, 1860.

[28]*SPC 1867-8*, no. 6, pp. 57-8.

rapid recession of the lumbering industry together meant that the thinly rooted colonization-roads settlements could not prosper.

Fortunately, the Hon. William McDougall, Commissioner of Crown Lands in the administration of John Sandfield Macdonald (1862-4), was less of a doctrinaire than his predecessors. Admitting in his first report that most of the Ottawa-Huron region was not suitable for colonization, he began to ascertain what areas should be closed to settlement because they were purely pine lands, and decided to make no further surveys till the number of settlers or prospective settlers showed that there was clearly an urgent necessity.[29] In a speech in the Assembly he amplified his policy. There was no point, he asserted, in bringing in paupers at government expense, and watching over them and even feeding them afterwards. The best way to encourage immigration was to provide good government, to reduce taxes, and to encourage business, so that there would be plenty of work at fair wages. Then the satisfied settlers would prove to be better immigration agents than any that could be hired.[30] His commonsense attitude was fully approved in 1863 by a select committee of the Legislative Assembly, established to consider "the lumber trade of Canada in relation to the settlement of the country." This committee found from the evidence of a number of qualified witnesses that the criticisms being made of the colonization-roads system in the Ottawa-Huron region were fully justified.[31] The next year a select committee on the Ottawa and Georgian Bay territory, impressed by the weight of similiar opinions, recommended that any new colonization roads should be confined to areas found fit for settlement.[32] In 1865 the declining interest of the politicians in the colonization roads was well shown by the report of another select committee, this time on emigration and colonization, for "in view of the general expectation that a very large area of fertile land . . . is shortly to be placed under the control

---

[29]*SPC 1863*, no. 5.

[30]Speech of Aug. 21, 1863, in Debates of the Parliament of Canada, 1863, 2nd Sess., p. 24.

[31]*JLAC 1863* (1st Sess.), App. 8.

[32]*JLAC 1864*, App. 8.

and supervision of the Canadian legislature," it was wholly devoted to the territories of the Hudson's Bay Company in the Northwest.[33]

However, the lumbermen did not allow the government to forget the evils of fraudulent occupation and of an increasing fire-hazard in their timber limits, and pressed for such action on the part of the Department of Crown Lands as would exclude settlement from the country between the Ottawa River and Georgian Bay.[34] It was unfortunate for Upper Canada that, on account of the preparations for Confederation, the government had no time to put in force an effective policy discriminating between agricultural and non-agricultural land.

After Confederation the Dominion and provincial governments decided on a joint immigration policy, whereby the Dominion government was to maintain emigration offices in the United Kingdom and on the continent of Europe and to defray the costs of quarantine, and the provincial governments were to put into effect a liberal scheme of settlement. Ontario's chief contribution, the Free Grants and Homestead Act of 1868, took the form of an expansion of the earlier colonization-roads enterprise.[35] As the act reserved to the crown the pine on the lots granted, the *Globe* assailed it as "paltry" and "stingy" in comparison with the homestead laws of the United States, but admitted that it was a "long step in the right direction."[36] In 1868-9 the Ontario government opened forty townships in the Ottawa-Huron country as free grants. Free lots might be taken up anywhere in the townships, not solely along colonization roads. Then, to make the free grants more attractive, it gradually extended its colonization-roads system. It maintained the leading roads it had previously opened — the Opeongo, the Frontenac, the Muskoka, and the rest — and in addition made grants for the construction of short branch roads which would afford access to the communities

---

[33]*JLAC 1865*, App. 6, p. 37.
[34]Toronto *Globe*, Feb. 26, 1867.
[35]*SPC 1869*, no. 76, p. 6.
[36]Toronto *Globe*, Jan. 28, Feb. 6, 1868.

being formed in the forty townships.[37]   Even so, it first directed seekers of free land to the Muskoka and Parry Sound districts, mainly because they were easily reached by water. The statistics of location show that these areas received more than half of the free-grant settlers after 1870. The rest took up lots in the region to the south and east which had nominally been settled earlier. The free-grant policy was no more successful after Confederation than it had been before. The settlers were poor and often shiftless as well. Every year grants were cancelled on account of the non-fulfilment of settlement duties.[38] Further, the shanty market once more proved unreliable. For a number of years the Muskoka pioneers did obtain 50 cents a bushel for oats and $9.00 a ton for hay, with the freight added, but by 1880 the lumbermen were bringing in oats so cheaply by way of Collingwood that it was evident that the shanty market was doomed.[39] In that year only a belt of townships across the northern part of Frontenac, Addington, Hastings, Peterborough, Victoria, and Simcoe counties, together with all of Haliburton County, still could depend on the lumbermen.[40] The rest of the free-grant area was in reach of railways. When the shanty market collapsed, the settlers in the Ottawa-Huron region wore out their light soil in a few years and became wholly dependent on employment in the lumber camps for a livelihood. When the good timber was cut down, or destroyed by fires, and the lumbermen moved away, the pioneers were stranded. At that time one well acquainted with the Ottawa-Huron area pronounced a judgment with which nobody would disagree today: "No greater mistake was ever made in political economy than the attempt to open up and colonize this country with the view of developing its agricultural resources."[41]

---

[37]Kirkwood and Murphy, *Undeveloped Lands*, pp. 46-7; *Sessional Papers, Ontario, 1871*, no. 7, pp. 17-19; *ibid., 1884*, no. 34, pp. 70-9. Hereafter this authority is cited as *SPO*.

[38]*SPO 1871*, no. 30, p. 2; *SPO 1877*, no. 1, pp. 52-3; *SPO 1882-3*, no. 4, pp. 17-18.

[39]*Report of the Ontario Agricultural Commission*, vol. v, App. R-1, p. 14; *ibid.*, vol. v, App. R-2, p. 27. Hereafter this authority is cited as *OACR*.

[40]*OACR*, vol. II, pp. 126, 176, 206, 286, 324, 460, 518-19, 543.

[41]Fraser, *Shanty, Forest and River Life*, p. 107. The most disastrous failure in the Ottawa-Huron region was not in the free grants, however,

It is easy to criticize the government of Ontario for the free-grants fiasco, with its legacy of a scattered and poverty-stricken population. However, during the same generation, other settlers, who owed nothing to governmental encouragement, were passing through the same unfortunate cycle. They had followed the lumbermen up the Ottawa Valley till by 1875 there was not a spot of arable land left unoccupied in the whole distance from Allumette Lake to the mouth of the Mattawan River.[42] These people were much affected by the depression in the lumber industry which followed the collapse of the construction trades in the United States in 1873, and which was augmented by a new American tariff which made it difficult for Ontario lumber to compete with that of Michigan. Hard times, then as earlier, resulted in considerable emigration.[43] In spite of this, new settlements of the peculiar kind associated with the lumber industry continued to be made long after 1880, not only in the Nipissing District, but in the country to the north of it which soon came to be called New Ontario.

Farmers in the upper part of the Ottawa Valley, but on the fairly good land near the Ottawa River, especially those in Renfrew County, profited by their position between the shanties and the railroads farther south as late as 1880.[44] In the eighteen-seventies farmers in Lanark and Carleton counties still portaged their hay, oats, and pork up the Ottawa

---

but in Haliburton County. Here the Canadian Land and Emigration Company, an association of English investors, had purchased ten townships from the Department of Crown Lands in 1862. The directors of the Company were so inexperienced that they were fleeced out of their valuable timber by the Ottawa Valley lumbermen, and the settlers they sent out from England were soon left in a hopeless situation (*SPC 1862*, no. 11; Thompson, *Up to Date*, pp. 43-4, 65-6).

[42]Kirkwood and Murphy, *Undeveloped Lands*, pp. 162-6.

[43]*SPO 1874*, no. 26, p. vii; *SPO 1877*, no. 11, p. vii; *SPO 1880*, no. 4, p. ix; *Journal of the House of Commons, Canada, 1876*, App. 3, p. iii. Hereafter this authority is cited as *JHC*.

[44]*OACR*, vol. II, pp. 518-19. An example of shanty market encouragement: "Western grumblers about the high price of hay, may find consolation in the statement of the Arnprior *Times* that on the Upper Ottawa hay has reached a fabulous price: even in Pembroke it readily brings $40 a ton. We learn that one gentleman in the village of Cobden has been offered $100 a ton delivered at the Mattawan, about 100 miles above Pembroke. Hay recently brought $35 a ton in Ottawa" (*Canada Farmer*, May 15, 1869, p. 197).

in seasons of prosperity, sometimes to the remote limits
above Lake Temiskaming and along the Kippawa River. A
witness from Carleton County told a Select Committee of the
House of Commons in 1876 that "the farmer here has a home
market where he can dispose of his coarse grain to a better
advantage than to use it for fattening cattle, on account of
the large lumbering interest carried on here, except barley,
for which they find a better market in the United States
than at home."[45] But in Lanark and Carleton counties, and
to some extent in Renfrew County, it was found advisable to
turn to articles which might be exported, including butter
and livestock as well as barley.[46] It was recognized that it
would not be long till the shanty market would disappear in
these counties, as it had already virtually done in Prescott
and Russell counties. Here, as early as 1870, it had been reduced to supplying part of the requirements of the lumbermen operating up the Gatineau Valley and in other fairly
accessible sections along the north shore of the Ottawa
River.[47]

Few of the squatters near the pineries had much hope of
finding salvation in diversified agriculture. Their soil was
so poor that only the Poles and Germans seemed to be able
to make a living from it, and they only by the utmost
industry and frugality.[48] It was not only that lumbering
receded; the advent of the railways (especially the Canada
Central) destroyed the sheltered position which the squatters had previously enjoyed. Many in the poorer and remoter
localities were literally starved out; by 1880 the backwoods
part of the Ottawa Valley was remarkable for the vast
number of its abandoned clearances and buildings.[49]

------

[45]*JHC 1876*, App. 7, p. 26.

[46]*JHC 1884*, App. 1, pp. 115-20; Kirkwood and Murphy, *Undeveloped
Lands*, p. 145; Smallfield, *Lands and Resources of Renfrew County*, p. 5.

[47]"The surplus coarse grains, grown on the south side, together
with pork, butter, hay, &c., now actually find their principal market
on the north shore, to supply the lumbering establishments" (Legge
and Macdonald, *Report on Explorations of Routes North and South Sides
of Ottawa River*, p. 3).

[48]*JHC 1884*, App. 1, p. 112.

[49]Fraser, *Shanty, Forest and River Life*, p. 102.

By 1880 the pressure on the provincial government to expand the free-grant system had already diminished. This was not because Ontario farmers did not want land, but because they preferred a farm on the prairies to one on the Canadian Shield. With the opening of Manitoba, people lost interest in the Ottawa-Huron region. Not till long after 1880 did the province make any serious effort to turn the territory into a forest reserve.[50] Till the tourist industry began to contribute to its rehabilitation through bringing a new local summer market, the area remained one of low living standards and marginal agriculture.[51]

---

[50]Algonquin Park was established in 1893.

[51]For brief descriptions of modern conditions in part of this region, see Kirkconnell, *Victoria County Centennial History*, pp. 87-8, and Lower, *Settlement and the Forest Frontier*, pp. 71-2.

CHAPTER XVIII

MISCELLANEOUS ASPECTS OF AGRICULTURE IN THE EIGHTEEN-SEVENTIES

I N the four preceding chapters emphasis has been laid in turn on different phases of Ontario agriculture in the period before 1880. This chapter completes the picture of farming in the eighteen-seventies. What was the character of the rural population? What was the appearance of the countryside? What general economic factors modified agriculture? What implements were in use? What improvements were being made in fencing and in drainage? What happened to the special crops of the era of the American Civil War? What new ones attracted attention? What progress was evident in fruit-growing? What changes were there in farm practices? These questions and others will be answered.

Fundamentally the agricultural population of Ontario in the eighteen-seventies was what it had been for over a generation. The chief modification was the presence of a smaller proportion of immigrants, for the typical farmer was a native son. The people still had their eyes set on new land in the enticing West, so that there was a constant shifting in farm ownership. Reasons for the continued migration were the same as in the eighteen-fifties. Some farmers lost their homesteads because their inefficient methods brought on a mortgage foreclosure. Well-to-do ones left because they thought it wise to sell their high-priced land and invest the proceeds in cheap farms in the West for their sons, or because they succumbed to restlessness or to the advertisements of railroads and prairie land companies. Many of them went to Manitoba after the collapse of the Red River Insurrection of 1870-1. Then, as one observer put it, "there has been a Western States fever, and Australian, Californian, and South American fever; and now we have an attack of Red River on the brain."[1] The movement to Manitoba grew from year to year, as did that to the states and territories of the Upper Mississippi Valley. In 1880 the Grand Trunk agent at

---

[1]*Canada Farmer*, July 15, 1871, p. 262.

Ottawa sold 886 adult through-tickets to Manitoba (with which rail communication had been opened via Chicago in 1879), 616 to Minnesota, 358 to the Dakota Territory, and 331 to Illinois. Emigrants usually went in special trains, in family or community groups, and took with them farm implements and stock of every description.[2]

Sometimes the emigrants sold their farms to old neighbours, and sometimes to newcomers from the Old Country. In the easternmost counties, especially Prescott, Russell, and Glengarry, the purchaser was often a French Canadian, usually from the triangle of Quebec west of the Ottawa River. French Canadians had begun to occupy the low-lying parts of Prescott and Russell during the eighteen-fifties, and then went on to buy the farms of emigrating English-speaking settlers. When the French Canadians came to be a majority, or approached being one, there were clashes between them and the older inhabitants over the control of the township councils and the hiring of school-teachers. These disputes accelerated the rate of departure of the English-speaking group, whether Presbyterian or Irish Catholic, and the community became dominantly French Canadian much earlier than would otherwise have been possible. The incoming French Canadians introduced nothing new into the agriculture of eastern Ontario. At worst they clung to the traditional practices of the St. Lawrence Valley, and at best they imitated as well as they could what they saw of the farming of the remaining English-speaking inhabitants.[3]

In appearance the Ontario of 1870-80 was vastly changed from the Upper Canada of the eighteen-thirties and even of the eighteen-forties. Then the typical landscape in all but the longest-settled regions was one wherein the primeval forest was only a few hundred yards from the trail along the concession line, smoke rose from the logging-fallows, and occasional cabins denoted the homes of pioneers. By 1870 there was so little good land left to be cleared that the country had

---

[2]*Manitoba Liberal*, cited in *Canada Farmer*, July 15, 1872, p. 242; *Sessional Papers, Canada, 1879*, no. 9, App. 20; *Journal of House of Commons, Canada, 1880-1*, App. 1, pp. 16-20.

[3]Barbezieux, *Histoire de la province ecclésiastique d'Ottawa*, vol. I, pp. 187, 236, 339, 346.

a naked look. The farmers hated trees so much that many of them now lacked even a woodlot, and were buying cordwood for their own use. Creeks ·which once had turned water-wheels were now dry throughout most of the year, and fall wheat and clover were being winter-killed through the absence of a windbreak. Foresighted individuals pointed out the dangers inherent in the destruction of the remnants of the forest, but the farmers were generally indifferent. They went on selling their remaining wood in the nearest towns or to the railways and steamboats, and rejected all suggestions that they should relieve the bleakness of their farmyards by planting a few shade trees.[4]

The farmers might care nothing for trees, but they did have standards of beauty. They liked to see the line of forest receding, fields being cleared of stumps, and new buildings going up. They would slave for years gathering foundation stones, cutting sawlogs for timbers and siding, and hauling home planks and boards and bricks. So well did they succeed in their building programme that by 1880 about 45 per cent of them had farm-houses of brick, stone, or first-class frame construction, and about 54 per cent had first-class barns, stables, and sheds.[5] However much of the rawness of an earlier day might remain, it was manifest that they had ended the struggles incidental to the opening of a new country. No wonder, then, that when the *Canada Farmer* compared the Upper Canada of the early eighteen-forties with the Ontario of 1873 it burst into a paean. "Privation has given place to comfort and abundance. The Canadian farmer wheels it to market and church in a modern and handsome vehicle drawn by a fine team of horses, instead of jumbling slowly along in an ox-cart. The mower and reaper do the work of the back-breaking scythe and cradle. Sewing-machines and pianos have crept into the

---

[4]*Canada Farmer*, Nov. 29, 1873, p. 424; *Report on Agriculture and Arts for 1872*, p. 63. Hereafter this authority is cited as *RAA; Report of the Ontario Agricultural Commission*, vol. I, pp. 123-4. Hereafter this authority is cited as *OACR*.

[5]*OACR*, vol. I, pp. 560-1. The increased value of the buildings involved an additional expense for the farmers. By 1880 most of them were carrying fire insurance (*Farmer's Advocate*, March, 1881, p. 68).

house, and girls disport themselves in the latest fashions. The railroad whistle, whose shrill sound means near markets, can be heard in almost every rural homestead."[6]

One factor of great significance in the development of Ontario agriculture after Confederation was the growth of a home market. It was associated with the extension of old industries and the beginning of new ones. Lumbering, for example, had spread throughout all the accessible parts of Ontario by 1880. By this time all the lower limits in the Ottawa Valley had been so thoroughly denuded that the timber supplies had largely to be drawn from the Province of Quebec, that is, from the remote forests at the headwaters of the Kippawa, and sawmills could be found the whole way along the shore of Georgian Bay and Lake Huron as far as Sault Ste. Marie. At the same time the expansion of railways made possible the erection in the forests of efficient little mills which operated the year round and formed the nuclei of industrial villages, often, unfortunately, ephemeral in character. Mining was of comparatively little importance as late as 1880. However, there was copper-mining north of Lake Superior beginning in 1845, gold-mining in Hastings County for a few years after 1866, iron-mining along the Rideau Canal after 1855, phosphate-mining in the same region after 1863, petroleum-mining near Petrolia beginning in 1859, and salt-mining near Goderich beginning in 1866. These activities did bring about the formation of distinctive mining communities, especially in the granite wilderness north of Lake Superior. The miners here had to import nearly everything they consumed, either from the United States or from the Owen Sound region, as they could easily do by water. In the older agricultural communities, mining was usually a part-time activity for the farmers of the neighbourhood, just as shantying or pilotage might be. However small the pay-roll of the individual mine or quarry might be, the miners did create a local market for considerable quantities of agricultural produce. The farmers, moreover, profited by the demand for timber for derricks and shafts. Before the advent of railways, the greatest expense

---

[6]*Canada Farmer*, Aug. 15, 1873, p. 283.

in mining was that of transporting the ores to a waterway;
but this was really a signal advantage to many persons in
the vicinity of the mines, who would, without the employment
thus afforded, have been dependent on the meagre output
of their farms for a livelihood. Manufacturing was negligible
as an industry before 1850. Labour costs were high and
capital scarce. Upper Canada was in a "colonial" relation to
both New England and the United Kingdom with respect to
manufactures, and what markets existed were supplied with
the hardware and textiles produced by cheaper labour and
capital. During the eighteen-fifties, the articles made in the
crossroads villages by coopers and blacksmiths and weavers
began to be replaced by factory products, partly on account
of the cheapening of transportation through the construction
of railways, partly on account of an increased demand from
a larger population, partly on account of the inflow of
American capital in several important branches of manufacture. Some villages had large sawmills, others woollen
mills, and still others, as has been mentioned in another
connection, small agricultural implement works. During the
American Civil War, manufacturing made significant progress. By 1870, factories for the manufacture of woollens and
cottons, boots and shoes, furniture, stoves, doors and sashes,
agricultural implements, and a host of other products were
multiplying throughout Ontario, though none of them was
very large. Municipalities, moreover, were beginning to compete with one another for new industries by offering concessions. Most of these industries were dependent mainly on local
raw materials, such as grain, animal produce, and lumber in
its various forms. The growth of urban communities
more or less dependent on the factories involved an expansion
of the home market for all kinds of agricultural products.[7]

Another economic development of direct interest to the
farming population was a revival of railway construction.
The financial failure of the Grand Trunk and of many of the
lesser lines built at the same time had prejudiced the public
against railways, but by 1867 the prosperity which

---

[7]Cf. the appropriate sections of Innis and Lower (eds.), *Select
Documents in Canadian Economic History.*

accompanied the closing year of the Reciprocity Treaty, and the natural influence exercised by the great railway-building boom in the United States which followed the termination of the Civil War, prepared the way for a second railway-building era in Ontario. The first proposals were for light narrow-gauge railways, for the purpose of carrying cord-wood to places like Toronto. Within a few years, promoters turned their attention to railways of the kind already in existence, and less was heard about the cheap transportation of cordwood. Some of them hoped to develop an extensive traffic in sawn lumber or in ores. Others intended to tap the grain trade of the American West by constructing lines from ports on Lake Ontario to Georgian Bay, or more ambitiously, from Montreal to Sault Ste. Marie. Business interests in every important town sponsored lines to draw the trade of the interior from other centres to their own, or to retain what they were threatened with losing. An answering speculative interest in railways on the part of the public led to the chartering of a great many in Ontario, and even to the complete or partial construction of some of them before the crisis of 1873. As Ontario emerged from the depression, the construction of railways was resumed. Before 1880 new lines were built in various parts of western Ontario, from Lake Ontario ports northward to tap the lumbering or mining regions, and from Montreal up the Ottawa Valley almost to Lake Nipissing. At the same time many of the older ones, such as the Northern and the Great Western, were extended. As a result, very few of the agricultural areas in the older parts of Ontario were left without railway accommodation.[8]

The history of the introduction of farm machinery into Upper Canada to the end of the eighteen-fifties was traced in Chapter XII. During and after the period of the American Civil War, more farmers than ever before availed themselves of labour-saving devices. In 1866 it was remarked that the demand was so strong that the manufacturers had difficulty in satisfying it. In 1868 so great was the scarcity of labour

---

[8]For the details of their extension, see Bladen, "Construction of Railways in Canada" (*Contributions to Canadian Economics*, vol. v). See also Trout and Trout, *Railways of Canada for 1870-1*, pp. 37, 150, 154, 251.

that mowers, reapers, and other implements were being bought by even the farmers of the newer settlements. By 1870 there were 36,874 reapers and mowers in use in Ontario. By 1880 labour-saving machinery was almost universally used, the only exception being in the remoter regions where the land still had too many stumps. At this time farmers were so thoroughly convinced of the need of implements that the Ontario Agricultural Commission warned them against buying novelties which had nothing to recommend them except the glib tongue of an agent.[9]

What implements did the ordinary Ontario farmer of the eighteen-seventies have? In 1873 the *Canada Farmer* had a series of articles describing the machinery in use on most of the farms. From the descriptions and illustrations given there, and from other scattered items of a similar kind, the following summary is made.[10]

To turn over the sod, the farmer had a choice of a variety of ploughs. He might own a double-furrow sulky plough, but he relied on the "common plough," that is, a walking plough with a replaceable point and a standing coulter. Sometimes this plough had a small wheel to regulate the depth of the furrow, and less often, a rolling or disk coulter. American observers noticed that the Ontario plough had much longer handles than theirs, a longer point with a narrower wing, and a mould-board that turned a narrower furrow.[11] To break up the soil, the farmer had a wheel-cultivator with long, shovel-shaped teeth. It differed from the modern cultivator chiefly in that the teeth were seemingly of cast

[9]*Canada Farmer*, Jan. 1, 1867, p. 8; *Ontario Farmer*, March, 1869, p. 66; *Census of Canada, 1871*, vol. III, p. 110; *OACR*, vol. I, p. 561.

[10]An advertisement for an auction sale on a 107-acre farm adjacent to Newcastle village mentions some equipment not described below, but equally typical. "There will be sold on the premises . . . a Wood's patent reaping machine, a Buckeye mower, a sulky rake, chop mill, straw cutter, 6 ploughs, 3 pairs harrows, 1 roller, 2 waggons, a pair of trucks, a top buggy, an open buggy, a democrat waggon, a covered cutter, a pair of bob sleighs, a pleasure sleigh, a long sleigh, &c., &c., &c." (Toronto *Weekly Globe*, April 4, 1879).

[11]*Canada Farmer*, May 2, 1864, p. 113; *ibid.*, Jan. 30, 1873, p. 32; *American Agriculturist*, vol. XXVII, 1868, p. 402. In spite of the missionary work of the agricultural journals, few farmers used subsoil ploughs, and then with little satisfaction (*OACR*, vol. I, pp. 401-3).

iron rather than steel, and so were rigid, and in that they lacked replaceable plates.[12] As disks had not come into use, he levelled and pulverized the seed-bed with a set of harrows of the "40-tooth diamond Scotch" model which as early as 1860 was said to be superseding all others.[13]

For seeding, the farmer might use a hand-seeder or a horse-drawn one. Some of the latter kind scattered the grain broadcast, but the best of them had rubber tubes with steel points to conduct the grain from the box into the earth.[14] His roller, if he had one, was usually the "pioneer roller," that is, a-large log with bolts driven into either end to serve as an axle to carry the frame, though a few iron ones were in use.[15]

The farmer cut his hay with a mower of a standardized type—the "Buckeye model"—much like a modern one in essentials. It had two fairly small driving wheels, an arrangement which had proved more satisfactory than the single driving wheel (like a binder's) which was still found on a few of the cheaper makes.[16] His tedder, if he was able to afford one, was not unlike those of today. His hayrake had independently suspended spring-teeth, with a gearing operated by a treadle for lifting them to empty the hay.[17] If he had a hay-loader, it was certain to attract neighbourhood attention, such a rarity would it be.[18] Unless he had a large barn, in which the hay would have to be pitched several times to get it to the back of the mow, he was likely to know hayforks, cars, and tracks only through report, as they were still uncommon in Ontario.[19]

---

[12]*Canada Farmer*, April 30, 1873, p. 135.
[13]*Canadian Agriculturist*, Sept. 1, 1860, p. 443.
[14]*Canada Farmer*, May 15, 1873, pp. 154-5.
[15]*Ibid.*, March 15, 1873, p. 78.
[16]*Ibid.*, June 30, 1873, p. 215. Buckeye mowers (patented in the United States in 1856) were being manufactured at Smiths Falls in 1859 (*Canadian Agriculturist*, Sept. 1, 1861, p. 517). The attachment for harvesting peas did not come into use till about 1890.
[17]*Canada Farmer*, July 15, 1873, p. 235; *Illustrated Journal of Agriculture*, May, 1880, pp. 30-1.
[18]Cf. *Farmer's Advocate*, Sept., 1876, p. 172.
[19]*Canada Farmer*, Aug. 15, 1873, p. 274; *ibid.*, Sept. 15, 1873, p. 315. The modern type of hay fork was being advertised at the end of the period (*Farmer's Advocate*, Feb., 1881, p. 48).

The reaper that he used in his grain harvesting might be one of several kinds then on the market. After Confederation the self-raker was standard equipment on reapers manufactured in the province. In 1866 the "Marsh Harvester" was manufactured and sold in Ontario. It had already been experimented with for two or three years in the United States. It was the first to use elevating canvases on the principle still employed. These did not bring the grain to a mechanical binder, but to a man who stood on a platform at the side of the machine. After it had been tried for seven years in Ontario, the *Canada Farmer* regretfully stated that the Marsh Harvester, like the other machines then available for binding grain, did not "appear to be adapted to general use."[20] Wire-binders proved unsatisfactory, as in the United States, when they were introduced in the middle eighteen-seventies. It was a great advance in Ontario agriculture when the binder of the type known to the present generation, utilizing twine to tie the sheaves, came into use in 1880.[21]

The farmer relied on a hired thresher instead of owning one, because the machines had become large and expensive. The common type was an improved form of the old Pitt model, though a more satisfactory kind working on a different principle was on the market. The ordinary thresher had a capacity of from 300 to 500 bushels of wheat in a short winter day. It was usually driven by an old-fashioned horsepower, either of the sweep or treadmill ("railroad") type, with the person who "travelled" the outfit furnishing two teams out of the four teams of horses required.[22] It was seldom that a steam engine was used as

---

[20]*Canada Farmer*, Aug. 1, 1867, p. 227; *ibid.*, April 15, 1869, pp. 122-3; *ibid.*, July 30, 1873, p. 255. Self-rakers manufactured at Brockville and Smiths Falls are pictured in *Illustrated Journal of Agriculture*, July, 1880, pp. 46-7.

[21]*Farmer's Advocate*, Sept., 1880, p. 201. For an analysis of the significance of the evolution of reaping machinery in the eighteen-seventies, see Veblen, "The Price of Wheat since 1867" (*Journal of Political Economy*, vol. I, 1892-3, pp. 83-6).

[22]*Canada Farmer*, April 15, 1864, p. 105; *ibid.*, Sept. 15, 1873, p. 315; *ibid.*, Oct. 15, 1873, p. 356.
Custom threshing was responsible for a social phenomenon, which appeared about 1850 and has not yet quite disappeared—"the threshing."

a source of power in the early eighteen-seventies. A portable engine, the first in Upper Canada, was in operation in the vicinity of Cobourg in 1861, but it was not popular with the farmers, on account of the trouble of drawing water for it.[23] Though this prejudice was prevalent for a long time, ultimately the efficiency of the steam engine came to be recognized. By 1878 it was said that "threshing by steam is coming into general use," and that the fire-insurance companies were complaining of the hazards the engines created around the barns.[24]

In the eighteen-seventies the farmer might have some of his hay pressed, though in 1874 it was observed that hay-pressing was still comparatively new in most of the province. Much of the hay actually pressed was not baled on the farm, but at the railroad station, where a dealer would set up a machine.[25] One variety of baler compressed the hay with a screw into cylindrical bundles; the other kind, which was

---

Isabella Bird wrote: "When a person wishes to thrash his corn, he gives notice to eight or ten of his neighbours, and a day is appointed on which they are to meet at his house. For two or three days before, grand culinary preparations are made by the hostess, and on the preceding evening a table is loaded with provisions. The morning comes, and eight or ten stalwart Saxons make their appearance, and work hard till noon, while the lady of the house is engaged in hotter work before the fire, in the preparation of hot meat, puddings, and pies; for well she knows that the good humour of her guests depends on the quantity and quality of her viands. They come in to dinner, black (from the dust of a peculiar Canadian weed [i.e. from smut]), hot, tired, hungry, and thirsty. They eat as no other people eat, and set all our notions of the separability of different viands at defiance. At the end of the day they have a very substantial supper, with plenty of whisky, and, if everything has been satisfactory, the convivial proceedings are prolonged till past midnight" (*The Englishwoman in America*, pp. 205-6).

[23]*Canadian Agriculturist*, Aug. 16, 1862, p. 490; *Canada Farmer*, June 1, 1864, p. 159.

[24]Toronto *Weekly Globe*, March 7, 1879. Cf. also *Farmer's Advocate*, Aug., 1876, p. 152. The traction engine came into use in the early eighteen-eighties (*ibid.*, May, 1883, p. 163).

[25]*Canada Farmer*, Nov. 16, 1874, p. 424; *Farmer's Advocate*, Jan., 1881, p. 22. Till 1875 most of the hay reaching markets like Toronto was in the loose form, though baled hay was being sold at Toronto in 1860 (*Canadian Agriculturist*, March 16, 1860, p. 134. Cf. also above, p. 182).

more popular, had gearing and a plunger much like the modern presses.[26]

No problem had caused the Upper Canada farmer so much thought and labour as his fencing. On the advice of agricultural journals he tried many kinds of hedges—thorn, willow, cedar, and osage orange. Some of these winter-killed, and none of the others proved to be of any use. The result was that, where stones were scarce, the fences continued to be generally of the old snake or worm type, though along the fronts of the farms they were often of boards or pickets. Constant repairing of the wooden fences, with the materials becoming ever scarcer, plagued the farmers till almost 1880, when barbed wire began to be strung in the more prosperous sections.[27]

Much of the land in Ontario was so flat as to require thorough underdraining, but ordinary farmers made less progress in this till 1880 than in other aspects of agriculture, partly because they did not understand its necessity, partly because they considered the capital expenditures involved beyond their means. Most of them contented themselves with running "clearing-up furrows" between the lands for surface drainage. Till about 1860 the few who did underdrain on a small scale used hemlock scoops, pine or cedar rails, or stones. After 1860 they could obtain tile, and those who could afford it utilized it. To help others to do so, the Ontario Tile Drainage Act of 1878 (41 Vic., c. 9) authorized a farmer, under certain conditions, to borrow up to $1,000 from his municipality for the purpose of tile-draining, and to repay the loan over a period of twenty years. The local council in turn borrowed the money from the province.[28]

Many parts of Ontario required arterial drainage to make the rich soil worth anything. In the Essex peninsula and in the flat lands of Prescott, Russell, Glengarry, and other

[26]*Farmer's Advocate*, Sept., 1876, p. 173; *ibid.*, Sept. 1877, p. 201.

[27]*Journal and Transactions of the Board of Agriculture of Upper Canada for 1855-6*, pp. 221, 357; *ibid.*, *for 1856-7*, pp. 221, 223; *Canadian Agriculturist*, Aug. 16, 1862, p. 489; *OACR*, vol. II, *passim*.

[28]*Canadian Agriculturist*, Dec., 1854, p. 375; *ibid.*, Oct. 16, 1861, p. 637; *ibid.*, Aug. 16, 1862, p. 489; *Canada Farmer*, June 15, 1867, p. 187; *OACR*, vol. I, pp. 392, 401.

counties of Eastern Ontario much of the country was still in bush and swamp till the eighteen-sixties, with farming operations being confined to the higher places. About the time of Confederation, arterial drainage began to be carried out, especially in Western Ontario, to relieve large areas of stagnant water in the spring and autumn. The movement was facilitated by an amendment to the Municipal Act in 1866. This measure, amplified as the Provincial Drainage Act of 1872, gave the municipal councils the right, when a majority of the resident owners petitioned for the deepening of a stream or for the draining of a property, to borrow money for carrying out the project, and for levying rates for its payment.[29] By 1880 great changes had been wrought in parts of Russell County in Eastern Ontario and in Middlesex, Lambton, and other counties in Western Ontario.[30] Perhaps the effects were most evident in Essex County. "The Ontario Drainage Act for the reclamation of wet lands," it was stated, "has done wonders for Essex. Under this act thousands of acres have been brought into cultivation, and are today yielding a profitable return from land that was, till recently, all but worthless."[31]

Four special crops, it will be remembered, attracted experimenting farmers during the American Civil War — sorghum, hops, tobacco, and flax. None of these proved able to withstand the new conditions created by the termination of the war. Sorghum continued to be grown in Essex County, but only on a small-scale domestic basis. The farmers' wives used the syrup in making apple butter, but there was no market for it, as it was inferior to corn syrup.[32] Hop growing likewise retrograded. Prices held up well for two years, but the bottom fell out of the United States market in 1868, and commercial production began to decline in Ontario. There were 1,188,940 pounds gathered in the province in

---

[29]*Transactions of the Board of Agriculture of Upper Canada for 1864-8*, p. 499. Hereafter this authority is cited as *TBAUC;* 39 Vic., c. 26 (*Statutes of Ontario*).

[30]*Farmer's Advocate*, March, 1877, pp. 51-2; *OACR*, vol. IV, App. G, pp. 59, 81, 84.

[31]*OACR*, vol. II, p. 90.

[32]*OACR*, vol. I, pp. 525-6.

1870, the chief contributing counties being Middlesex with 174,529, Northumberland with 171,514, Prince Edward with 148,997, and Halton with 117,071. After 1870 such farmers as did persist in the enterprise were at the mercy of sudden and violent price fluctuations. By 1880 hop production had fallen to 615,967 pounds, with only three electoral ridings having over 50,000 pounds. These were Prince Edward, which had 136,266; Grenville South, which had 117,628; and Northumberland East, which had 64,494.[33] Tobacco-growing went the same way. The Ontario crop of 1870 was 399,870 pounds, of which 353,844 pounds were grown in the ridings of Essex, Kent, and Bothwell, that is, in Essex and Kent counties. Tobacco continued to be steadily abandoned throughout the following decade. The crop of 1880 was a mere 160,251 pounds. The ridings of Essex, Kent, and Bothwell were responsible for 33,625 pounds, 9,813 pounds, and 12,901 pounds respectively, amounts which may be compared with the 24,484 pounds of Prescott and the 24,656 pounds of Russell, electoral divisions in which tobacco was grown as a crop for home consumption by French Canadians. Tobacco requires very rich soil and considerable labour. That grown in Essex and Kent counties was at best only second or third grade, and so was unable to compete at Montreal with Southern varieties. Under these circumstances, tobacco growing in the Old Belt remained dormant till after 1880.[34] The flax industry too languished. With an abundant supply of cotton available to textile factories, the prices in the United States fell steadily. Soon after the close of the Civil War not more than $12.00 or $14.00 a ton could be obtained in Canada West — not enough to cover the costs of production. The Ontario linen mills failed and closed by 1868, and most of the scutching mills with them. Yet flax-growing did not dwindle as did hop-growing and tobacco-growing. The Ontario production in 1870 was 1,165,117 pounds, with Perth County contributing 410,495 pounds, Wellington 222,348, Elgin 118,991, and

---

[33]*Ontario Farmer*, June, 1869, p. 163; *ibid.*, Aug., 1869, p. 236; *Census of Canada, 1871*, vol. III, pp. 207, 209, 211, 213; *Census of Canada, 1881*, vol. III, pp. 240-7; Toronto *Weekly Globe*, March 14, 1879.

[34]*Census of Canada, 1871*, vol. III, pp. 207, 213; *Census of Canada, 1881*, vol. III, pp. 240-7; *OACR*, vol. I, pp. 523-4.

Oxford 107,851. In 1880 the crop of flax (with an insignificant amount of hemp) still amounted to 1,073,197 pounds. The electoral ridings of Perth North, Oxford North, Wellington Centre and Wellington North together, and Huron South and Huron Centre together, accounted respectively for 331,636, 125,565, 198,453, and 137,286 pounds. There was a tendency for flax-growing to be confined to the part of the population which was of German extraction, for this held its labour cheap. The fibre was mostly sold in the United States, and the seed (for which there was a fairly good demand, though production was small) to mills at Toronto and Baden.[35]

In the eighteen-seventies there were two minor special crops in Western Ontario. White beans were grown in parts of Kent County in the early part of the decade, and in parts of Essex County as well before the end of it. The crop of 1870 was 107,925 bushels. That of 1880 was not listed separately in the census, but presumably it was much larger. Farmers with the proper soil considered white beans profitable, as they were readily salable in the United States, especially among the lumbermen of Michigan.[36] Men on high, dry, and light soils sometimes raised potatoes as a special crop, though Ontario potatoes were much inferior to those of the Maritime Provinces. Even low-lying Kent County exported a good many in 1880, partly to the United States and partly to the Ontario urban centres to the eastward.[37]

[35]*Canada Farmer*, March 1, 1867, p. 74; *ibid.*, July 1, 1868, p. 195; St. Thomas *Journal*, quoted in *ibid.*, Aug. 15, 1868, p. 253; *Census of Canada, 1871*, vol. III, pp. 206, 208, 212; *ibid., 1881*, vol. III, pp. 240-7; *OACR*, vol. I, pp. 521-3.

[36]*RAA 1875*, p. 60; *Census of Canada, 1871*, vol. III, pp. 150-1; *OACR*, vol. I, pp. 524-5.

[37]*OACR*, vol. IV, App. G, p. 63. The Colorado potato beetle first appeared in Ontario in 1872, having crossed the St. Clair River. "We supposed that it would have gradually come eastward, but to our surprise, it took advantage of the railways and canals, and spread itself with great rapidity, even to the remoter parts of the Province." However, it did not do as much damage as might have been expected, because the farmers had been acquainted through their farm journals and newspapers with the use of Paris green as an insecticide (*OACR*, vol. I, pp. 167-8).

Two special branches of agriculture — bee-farming and market-gardening — require only brief mention. Bee-farming in the province was a little-noticed activity till almost 1880, though a few persons had been engaged in it for many years on a small scale. One of them in a single year had a yield of 75,000 pounds of honey. In 1880 he was importing Cyprian and Holy Land queens and breeding them on two isolated islands between Parry Sound and Collingwood to discover if they were superior to Italian queens. The domestic demand was sufficient to absorb practically the whole supply of Ontario honey, less than 8,000 pounds being exported in 1880.[38] Market-gardening had developed in the eighteen-fifties on the outskirts of urban communities. One market gardener in Halton County had sales of $1,200 in 1859, an amount said to be considerably below those of the preceding few years. About 1865 a steamer was operated on the lower Ottawa solely for the purpose of supplying Montreal with vegetables and other produce. About the same time there was a good deal of market-gardening for Detroit, especially on the part of the French Canadians near Windsor. The industry expanded considerably during the eighteen-seventies, especially between Hamilton and Toronto, where many of those engaged in it came to emphasize the growing of small fruits as well as vegetables.[39]

A third special branch of agriculture in the eighteen-seventies deserves a lengthier description. This is fruit-growing, the beginnings of which were outlined in Chapter XII. During the eighteen-sixties it steadily increased in im-

---

[38]*OACR*, vol. I, pp. 220, 222, 228-9. Within a few years, however, according to a statement of Professor Daniel Wilson in 1884, the exports of honey from Ontario amounted to 1,200,000 pounds annually ("Ontario," *Encyclopaedia Britannica*, 9th ed., vol. XVII, p. 775).

[39]*TBAUC 1860-3*, p. 108; Thomas, *History of the Counties of Argenteuil, Quebec, and Prescott, Ontario*, p. 31; *Canada Farmer*, May 1, 1866, p. 136. Market gardening for Detroit seems to have fallen on evil days by 1880, on account of American competition. "The glory of the ancient market-days has departed. The black-eyed, olive-skinned maidens, in short petticoats, from the Canada shore, no longer bring 'garden-sauce and greens,' the French ponies amble not over our paved streets, and little brown-bodied carts no longer throng the market-place" (Farmer, *The History of Detroit and Michigan*, vol. I, p. 793).

portance, owing to the failure of the wheat crop, the expansion of urban centres, the construction of railroads, and the general rise in living standards. Unfortunately, it is impossible to describe its development quantitatively, for the government made no effort to collect statistics concerning it. This fact must be kept in mind in connection with the references to local production and shipments found below.

Apples were the most important Ontario fruit of the eighteen-seventies. They were grown everywhere in the province, though not very successfully in the eastern part on account of the climate. Elsewhere the only handicap was the codling moth. The local consumption was great, but still there was a surplus for export, particularly in Prince Edward County and its western neighbours and in the Niagara peninsula. The shippers sent some of the surplus to New York, but they tended to concentrate on the British market. Their first shipments thither were decidedly speculative, and sometimes, as in 1871, resulted in serious losses. By 1874 Ontario apples were, however, selling in London and Glasgow for as much as, or even more than, those of the Genesee Valley. Ontario-grown apples had an advantage over American-grown apples of the same varieties in that though they were smaller, they were hardier, and therefore had a reputation as better keepers. By 1880 they and their American competitors had displaced both local and continental apples in most of the cities of the United Kingdom. The quantity exported overseas in 1879-80 was about twelve times as great as in 1868-9, being worth about $300,000. Those exported to the United States in the same fiscal year were valued at about $50,000. The apple most in demand for export was the Baldwin. In 1880, 4,250 barrels out of 4,500 in a shipment to Glasgow, and 3,974 out of 4,259 in one to London, were Baldwins. So well was the trade established by 1880 that British buyers were appearing in Toronto and Montreal to purchase apples for shipment.[40]

Peaches ranked next in importance to apples among Ontario fruits. The main peach area was the "Grimsby

---

[40]*RAA 1872*, pp. 142, 255; *RAA 1875*, pp. 299, 301; *OACR*, vol. I, pp. 43, 53-4.

country," the narrow belt between the Niagara Escarpment
and Lake Ontario, and stretching from Hamilton to the
Niagara River. A minor area extended along the shore of
Lake Erie in Elgin and Norfolk counties. Yellows provided
the only threat to the industry. About 1875 this disease,
which had recently destroyed many of the peach orchards of
western New York, got a strong foothold in the vicinity of
Niagara Falls, and thereafter created much panic among the
peach growers. The market for peaches was mostly in the
towns of Ontario, though in 1880 some were shipped by the
Intercolonial as far as Halifax, and others, after the season
had passed for New Jersey, Delaware, and New York
peaches, to the near-by cities of the United States.[41] No
better description of the industry about 1880 can be found
than that in *Picturesque Canada.*

It has been roughly calculated that one thousand five hundred acres
are under cultivation as peach-orchards in the Niagara district, the
number of trees being three hundred and seventy-five thousand, and
their produce a million baskets of fruit annually. Niagara, Stamford
and Grimsby are the chief peach-growing townships. Every farm has
a peach-orchard; orchards of two thousand trees are common, and
every year new orchards are planted and the yield increases. In
Stamford there is a peach-orchard of eleven thousand trees, and three
years after being transplanted they bore twenty thousand baskets of
peaches. The Crawford peaches grow here to an enormous size, measuring from nine to nearly twelve inches in circumference; they have an
exquisite flavour and fragrance, at once sweet, piquant, and aromatic,
with a rich mellow pulp, overflowing with juice; and the trees bear so
abundantly that, with every precaution, the branches often break
down under their heavy load of fruit. Peach-trees generally grow
about fifteen feet high in the orchards, and are planted in rows eighteen
feet apart. . . . The peach harvest begins towards the end of July
and continues to the middle of October. Men and women gather the
ripe fruit into baskets carried on the arm; children are not employed,
as the peaches require careful handling. The baskets, when filled, are
taken to sheds prepared for the purpose, where women pick out all

---

[41]*RAA 1879*, pp. 273, 292; *OACR*, vol. I, pp. 72-3, 76-8. It is probable
that the peach growers of the Niagara peninsula owed much (especially
in the introduction of new varieties of the fruit) to their American
neighbours, for the chief peach-growing region of New York between
1840 and 1860 was on Grand Island in the Niagara River (Hedrick, *A
History of Agriculture in the State of New York*, p. 383).

damaged fruit and cover the baskets with coarse pink gauze. They are then sent in wagons to the nearest railway station, where a "peach car" is always provided, in which they are despatched to their destination. Every day the platforms at the stations are crowded with piles of pink-covered peach baskets, in waiting for the trains which are to carry them to all the large towns in the Dominion—Halifax and St. John's included. The demand for this delicious fruit far exceeds the supply, and early in the season baskets of twelve quarts bring two dollars each, the price gradually falling to seventy-five, or even sixty cents a basket, till later in the season, when peaches begin to get scarce, and the price rises again. The baskets in which they are packed furnish a special industry, and the factories for making them are kept busy all the year round. They are supplied to the peach growers at the rate of three-and-a-half cents each, and are always thrown in with the peaches. Great quantities of this favourite fruit are preserved by canning, and canning factories have been established in the district and at Toronto, which are doing a considerable trade, domestic and foreign.[42]

Grapes ranked third in importance among Ontario fruits in the eighteen-sixties and eighteen-seventies. The development of the industry owed much to the Vine Growers' Association, chartered in 1866, which carried on an educational programme, and had a share in the marketing. The only obstacle encountered was the grape rot, and this did not cause trouble till 1878. Most of the grapes were grown in that part of the Niagara peninsula below the Escarpment. There was a minor centre on Pelee Island, an outgrowth of the industry on the adjacent islands belonging to Ottawa County, Ohio. The most popular grape for market was the Concord. Other leading varieties were the Isabella (which ripened so late that it monopolized the end-of-the-season trade), the Clinton (a wine grape), the Delaware (a table and wine grape), and the Catawba (a wine grape which was virtually confined to Pelee Island). By 1880 the viticulturists of the Niagara district were shipping thousands of baskets annually to Toronto and smaller towns. They used the rest of their grapes for the manufacture of wine. The growers on Pelee Island sold all their grapes for wine-making. One winery at St. Catharines had a fifty-acre vine-

---

[42]Grant, *Picturesque Canada*, vol. I, pp. 391-3, 395.

yard of its own, and a firm near Niagara was said to manu-facture from 600 to 800 gallons of wine every year.[43]

Plums were grown on a fairly large scale in the Owen Sound region, some of the orchards having thousands of trees. Black knot was a problem here, but the curculio (which was responsible for the ending of plum-growing else-where in Ontario) had not yet appeared. One firm shipped 2,273 bushels in 1880. The usual markets were Toronto, Buf-falo, Detroit, Port Huron, and Sault Ste. Marie.[44] A few pears, mostly Bartletts, were grown in the Niagara penin-sula and along the shore of Lake Erie, and marketed wholly in the province or at Montreal. The business was made pre-carious by the fire blight. Remarkably enough, this disease did not harm the old French pear trees along the Detroit River.[45] Cherries in the Niagara peninsula suffered so much from black knot, curculio, and birds that the fruit growers disputed among themselves as to whether it was worth while to attempt to grow them or not.[46]

Strawberries were the most generally cultivated small fruit. They had a market in the towns and villages, though in the smaller communities the wild berries were effective competi-tors. One strawberry grower near Goderich had eight acres of plants in 1878, from which he obtained 800 bushels of berries. The chief strawberry region, however, was the southern part of Halton County, especially around Oakville. About 1880, 126,000 quart baskets were shipped from the Oakville station annually.[47] Raspberries were still to be had in such abundance in the woods and pastures that few tried to cultivate them. Blackberries were grown to a limited extent but they were not profitable, partly because the wild thimble-berries were still plentiful, partly because they ripened at the

---

[43]*TBAUC 1864-8*, pp. 75, 510; *RAA 1875*, p. 246; *RAA 1879*, p. 275; *OACR*, vol. I, pp. 113-16, 121; Grant, *Picturesque Canada*, vol. I, p. 395. The wine-making processes employed in the Niagara peninsula are described in *OACR*, vol. I, pp. 116-18.

[44]*RAA 1875*, p. 300; *Farmer's Advocate*, Dec., 1881, p. 306; *OACR*, vol. I, pp. 80, 82.

[45]*OACR*, vol. I, pp. 60-5, 71.

[46]*RAA 1875*, pp. 295, 298; *OACR*, vol. I, p. 85.

[47]*RAA 1879*, p. 65; *OACR*, vol. I, pp. 96, 102.

same time as peaches. Black currants had a small but fairly certain market among confectioners.[48]

It is well to remember that, in spite of the tendency towards specialization shown in different parts of the province, the average farmer was not a specialist. When he could no longer depend on wheat or the shanty market, he ordinarily turned to mixed farming, though he might have specialties as important sidelines. He grew coarse grains to feed his stock, or for sale if prices were favourable, fattened a few cattle for market, sold a dozen lambs or a horse now and then, and sent his milk to a cheese factory or creamery, or manufactured it into butter at home. Though varying greatly from district to district and from farm to farm in the extent of its adoption, this mixed farming was by 1880 the typical form of agriculture in Ontario.[49]

While critics approved this diversification of interests, they were far from satisfied with what they saw in the line of crop rotations. This was especially true of those who looked to the highly developed systems of the British Isles as standards.[50] Nevertheless, it was probably true in 1880 "that a very considerable proportion of the farmers of Ontario do endeavour, as far as they can, to carry out something like a systematic rotation of crops, while others are, perhaps, almost unconsciously, falling into a similar plan or practice."[51] Progressive farmers used fairly lengthy rotations, lasting seven or eight years, providing they did not break them off in the middle. The chief differences between their rotations and those mentioned in Chapter VI as being characteristic of the better farmers of the late eighteen-forties and early eighteen-fifties were a more pronounced tendency to grow peas as a crop preparatory to fall wheat; the introduction of a root or other hoed crop into the rotation, also before fall wheat; and a diminished dependence on the summer fallow.[52] Most

---

[48]*RAA 1875*, p. 298; *OACR*, vol. I, pp. 90-1, 102-3.
[49]Cf. *OACR*, vol. I, p. 231.
[50]Cf. evidence of George Buckland (*OACR*, vol. IV, App. G, p. 156).
[51]*OACR*, vol. I, p. 360.
[52]*OACR*, vol. I, pp. 155, 359; *OACR*, vol. IV, App. G, p. 135; *OACR*, vol. V, App. K, p. 97. The use of roots in the rotation was by no means general. "In a number of townships the area devoted to root cultivation is small, and in too many utterly insignificant" (*OACR*, vol. I, p. 379).

farmers, however, simply kept cropping away, planting their fields with whatever they thought would yield and sell best, and sowing peas or clover when the land got dirty. As a result, many of those in Kent and Essex counties overcropped with wheat,[53] just as those along the Bay of Quinte and north of Lake Ontario did with barley.[54]

A tendency to abandon the summer fallow became manifest in the eighteen-fifties, as was pointed out in Chapter XI, when the opening of the American market enabled the Upper Canada farmer to diversify his production. The decline in its importance was pronounced by the early eighteen-seventies. It was stated in 1875 that "among the many changes and improvements in agriculture, even within the memory of many of our readers, not the least is in bare fallows."[55] Its partial disappearance came about as a consequence of the passing of wheat as the provincial staple, the rise in the value of land, the introduction of better implements, and the realization that by having clover or buckwheat or roots in a rotation it would be possible to smother or eradicate the weeds and have a crop besides. Farmers, too, found that they could gain some of the advantages of the regular summer fallow through the "pin-fallow" or "half-fallow," and still not lose a crop.[56] However, in spite of this tendency, the summer fallow had wholly disappeared by 1880 only in the older regions where the farmers had turned to spring wheat or to barley. Where they still could grow fall wheat profitably, as in the newer parts of Bruce, Grey, and Simcoe counties, they still placed reliance on the naked fallow.[57]

It was in consequence of the unsystematic cropping re-

---

[53]*OACR*, vol. I, pp. 353-5.

[54]Cf. above, p. 242.

[55]*Farmer's Advocate*, Oct., 1875, p. 183.

[56]The meaning of half-fallow and pin-fallow is probably explained in the following sentence: "Sometimes land is *rag* or *bastard* fallowed—that is, the land is ploughed and harrowed immediately after the hay crop is taken off, and then allowed to lie till after harvest, when it is cross ploughed and harrowed" (*Canadian Agriculturist*, July 16, 1862, p. 421).

[57]In Simcoe County in 1880, one-third of the fall wheat was sown on pea stubble, and two-thirds on naked fallow after an oat crop (*OACR*, vol. I, p. 351).

ferred to in the last paragraph but one, that the criticism was often made, as by the provincial Commissioner of Agriculture in 1880, that "to a large extent, land in Ontario is being indifferently farmed and even gradually exhausted, [and] that the aids of science for its recuperation are sparingly invited."[58] Certainly very few farmers chose to invest anything in expensive commercial fertilizers, such as the bone or mineral superphosphates then on the market, or even in gypsum. In 1880 the Ontario Agricultural Commission had to report that the practice of applying plaster to clover and roots was confined to the more enterprising farmers; and it was estimated that no more than 8,000 tons of it were sold in Ontario in 1879.[59] On the other hand, a considerable number of farmers did plough under the second crop of red clover as a green manure, and others ploughed under buckwheat.[60] The overwhelming majority, however, was content with utilizing the barnyard manure. It was therefore fortunate that the increased attention paid to dairying and livestock-rearing meant that more of it was available.

The Ontario of 1880 was from an agricultural point of view a far different place from what it had been even twenty years before. People felt that they were living in a much altered world, as is evidenced by the popularity at that time of subscription pioneer histories. The first hard struggles incident to a new country were long since over, but the recent phases of transition had not been easy ones. There were poor crops in most of the province in 1870, 1872, 1874, 1875, and 1876, the last being one of the most disastrous on record.[61] As was pointed out in Chapter XVI, livestock prices had fallen drastically for a time, owing to western American competition and the depression of 1873. However, the eighteen-

[58]*RAA 1879*, p. viii.

[59]*OACR*, vol. I, p. 561; *OACR*, vol. V, App. N, p. 29.

[60]*OACR*, vol. I, p. 355; *JHC, 1884*, App. 1, p. 115. Red clover was still the only kind sown in Ontario. A few experimenters had tried alsike in the eighteen-fifties, but they did not like it. In 1880 its use was restricted to bee-keepers (*Transactions of the Board of Agriculture and of the Agricultural Association of Upper Canada 1859-60*, p. 186; *Farmer's Advocate*, March, 1881, p. 65).

[61]*RAA 1872*, p. 508; *RAA 1875*, p. 394; Toronto *Weekly Globe*, Feb. 7, 1879.

seventies closed in a spirit of optimism, which was largely owing to the beginning of the exportation of cattle and sheep to the British Isles. Farmers once again were certain that they were making money, and were showing it by constructing new barns and otherwise improving their properties.[62]

In January, 1880, the Commissioner of Agriculture for Ontario, the Hon. Samuel C. Wood, proposed that an investigation should be made of agriculture in Ontario, partly to assemble information about prevailing practices, partly to make it possible to chart a course for the future. He pointed out that his suggestion was not new, for two committees of the legislature of the Province of Canada had been appointed in 1864, one to consider measures for the advancement of agriculture in general, the other for the promotion of viticulture. Neither had accomplished anything. Wood had two objections to having a committee of the Ontario legislature undertake an agricultural investigation — the session was too short, and there would be danger of partisan politics. A royal commission on the British model would do the work more efficiently and with less criticism.[63] As a result of his recommendation, the government shortly afterwards appointed a number of men who had long been leaders of agriculture to serve as the Ontario Agricultural Commission. They made a careful examination of many witnesses on most subjects of agricultural interest, and incorporated this evidence in a five-volume report. Its investigation convinced the Commission that the advances of Ontario farmers in recent years gave a sound basis for continued expansion. "While there is a very large amount of very defective farming among them," it reported, "it cannot be questioned that, by no portion of the industrial population has greater progress in the last quarter of a century been made."[64]

The Commission was right, of course. The technical improvements in farming described in this chapter and preceding

---

[62]Toronto *Weekly Globe*, June 2, 1877; *ibid.*, April 12, 1878; *Farmer's Advocate*, Dec., 1877, p. 273.

[63]*RAA 1879*, pp. x-xii.

[64]*OACR*, vol. I, p. 230.

ones were indications that Ontario was keeping fully abreast of American agricultural development. The rural population could look backward with no little pride in its accomplishments, and forward with reasonable hope of advancement. It was clear that the province would thereafter develop agriculturally along lines already well established.

CHAPTER XIX

AGRICULTURAL ORGANIZATIONS AFTER 1850

THE organizations concerned with the promotion of agriculture in Upper Canada after 1850 were mostly continuations or modifications of those developed earlier. Similarly, most of their activities were either elaborations of those of the earlier associations or outgrowths of them. However, there also appeared the small beginnings of governmental encouragement and supervision, the first provision for formal education in agriculture, and for an interval, a widespread association primarily interested in co-operative purchasing.

It will be recalled that in 1846 an Agricultural Association of Upper Canada came into existence to co-ordinate the efforts of local societies engaged in agricultural improvement, and to have charge of a provincial (Upper Canada) exhibition. After a few years its members were convinced that a more elaborate and powerful organization was needed for the task. In April, 1850, the Association submitted a memorial to the legislature, which on August 10 passed an act (13 and 14 Vic., c. 73) incorporating the recommendations. The act, which went into operation in 1851, provided for a semi-official Board of Agriculture of Upper Canada composed of ten members—the Inspector-General (finance minister) of the Province of Canada, the Professor of Agriculture at the University of Toronto (of whom more hereafter), and eight men elected by the members of the Agricultural Association. The Board elected its own chairman. The Board had fairly extensive powers, including the right to collect statistics; to operate experimental or model farms; to introduce new or improved plants or animals; to publish its own transactions and, if it chose, an agricultural journal; to supervise and co-ordinate the work of the county and township agricultural societies; and to supervise the Agricultural Association. Under this arrangement, the essential function of the Agricultural Association was to manage the provincial exhibitions. As its directorate was now to be composed of the members of the Board of Agriculture, plus the presidents of the county societies, the

Association was in effect conducted as part of the Board of Agriculture.[1]

From 1851 to about 1865 the Board of Agriculture exercised a vital influence on agricultural organization in Canada West. Some of the functions assigned to it by the act of 1850 and confirmed by the Agricultural Statute of 1857 (20 Vic., c. 32) were routine ones. Thus, it collected and published the proceedings and financial reports of the county agricultural societies, in which were incorporated the returns of the township societies as well. Then, on the basis of these returns, it assigned to the county societies their own and the township societies' shares of the government grants. The only other direction the Board gave the societies was to send Professor Buckland of the University of Toronto around the province for a few months in the summer to visit them and give lectures. The only outright exercise the Board made of its power to introduce new or improved plants or animals was to distribute $2,000 worth of flaxseed to farmers in 1859, as was mentioned in Chapter XIII, but indirectly, through the Agricultural Association, it did a great deal by offering attractive premiums at the provincial exhibitions, especially on newly imported livestock. Other parts of the programme of the Board were, in one way or another, educational. These included the publication of its own transactions and other agricultural information, the establishment of an experimental farm and the opening of a veterinary college. Each of these deserves special description.

By the act of 1850 the Board of Agriculture had the right, as already noted, to publish its own transactions, and if it thought it desirable, to publish an agricultural journal as well. For the first few years it communicated its proceedings and the agricultural information it collected, including its prize essays, to the *Canadian Agriculturist* of Toronto. In 1858 it acquired the copyright of this journal, which it published till the end of 1863, with the busy Professor Buckland and the secretary of the Board doing the editorial work. At intervals

---

[1]*Journal and Transactions of the Board of Agriculture of Upper Canada for 1855-6*, pp. 121-2, 128, 158-60. Hereafter this authority is cited as *JTBAUC*.

the Board republished its own proceedings and other agricultural material which it considered to have permanent value. Ultimately there were six volumes, the first two being entitled *Journal and Transactions of the Board of Agriculture of Upper Canada,* the third and fourth *Transactions of the Board of Agriculture and of the Agricultural Association of Upper Canada,* and the last two *Transactions of the Board of Agriculture of Upper Canada.*[2] Another action of the Board deserves the special gratitude of the economic historian. On its own responsibility it offered, as one of its first acts in 1851, prizes for reports on the agriculture of certain counties. In the next five years it awarded prizes for fifteen such reports. In 1860 it revived the offer in a somewhat different form, by confining it to the annual reports of township and county agricultural societies. These essays it published first in the *Canadian Agriculturist,* and later in its own *Journal and Transactions* or *Transactions.*[3]

When the Agricultural Association petitioned the legislature in 1850 to amend the existing agricultural societies bill, it suggested that the new Board of Agriculture should establish an experimental farm. The Senate of the University of Toronto agreed that such a farm might be made from part of the lands belonging to the University, because thus it would have the advantage of supervision by the Professor of Agriculture. The newly organized Board visited the grounds of the University in July, 1851, and picked a suitable fifty-acre plot. The first work was done on it in 1852. The Board did not intend that the farm should be ambitious (and costly), but it did expect that the professor could use it to give practical illustration to his lectures, to test imported seeds and plants, and to try out new implements. It was even possible that the

---

[2]Landon, "Agricultural Journals of Upper Canada" (*Agricultural History,* vol. IX, 1935, p. 173); *Transactions of the Board of Agriculture and of the Agricultural Association of Upper Canada 1858-9,* p. 20; *ibid. for 1859-60,* p. 348. Hereafter this authority is cited as *TBA&AAUC.*

[3]*JTBAUC 1855-6,* pp. 166, 240; *Transactions of the Board of Agriculture of Upper Canada 1860-3,* p. 206. Hereafter this authority is cited as *TBAUC.* For further information about these prize essays, see below, pp. 386-7.

farm would pay its own way. This it failed to do. In the fiscal year 1856-7 the expenses of seeds, labour, and building materials came to £347, and the produce brought only £200; in 1858 expenses were £72 and income £10. It was an educational as well as a financial failure, evidently because the professor was so overburdened by his other functions that he had little time to supervise it. In 1860 the Board in disgust sold the spring crops in the field, the straw in the barn, the grain in the granary, and the tools and implements, and rented the fifty acres to a practical farmer. This renting arrangement continued till 1871, when the Council of the Agricultural and Arts Association sold the experimental farm premises back to the University of Toronto for $2,000.[4]

Mention has been made several times of the Professor of Agriculture at the University of Toronto. Though he was not in this capacity an employee of the Board of Agriculture, his associations with it were so close that it is well to consider his functions here. In its memorial of April, 1850, the Agricultural Association stressed the importance of establishing a chair of agriculture at the University of Toronto. The Senate of the University approved the recommendation the following January. A year later the provincial government appointed George Buckland, then secretary of the Board of Agriculture, to fill the position. Buckland gave his first course of lectures in the winter of 1852-3. Then and in succeeding years he taught the history, science, and practice of agriculture, while other members of the faculty contributed lectures in chemistry, botany, entomology, geology, and mineralogy. Though the University provided five scholarships worth £30 a year each, very few students attended. It was stated in 1855 that the classrooms were "almost tenantless." After limping along dismally for a few years longer, the experiment collapsed, though the chair of agriculture remained in nominal existence.[5]

---

[4]*JTBAUC 1855-6*, pp. 122, 128, 162, 165-6, 246-7; *JTBAUC 1856-7*, p. 349; *TBA&AAUC 1858-9*, p. 227; *TBAUC 1860-3*, pp. 1-2; *Report on Agriculture and Arts for 1872*, p. 197. Hereafter this authority is cited as *RAA*.

[5]*JTBAUC 1855-6*, pp. 128, 162, 212, 275, 573. It appears that in 1859-60 Assumption College at Sandwich was proposing to establish

The teaching of agriculture at the University of Toronto really failed because farmers considered it too theoretical for their sons. This criticism could not be made of the veterinary college which to some extent took its place. In 1861 the Hon. Adam Fergusson persuaded a Scottish veterinarian to come to Upper Canada, and induced the Board of Agriculture to appoint him as its veterinary surgeon. He gave a few lectures at Toronto in 1861-2, and inaugurated a regular course of them in 1862. These dealt with the physiology of animals, their diseases, their history, breeding, and management, and other appropriate subjects. Students attended two sessions and were required to serve an apprenticeship under a qualified veterinarian for two summers. By the end of 1867 fifteen students graduated from this one-professor Ontario Veterinary College. At this time, in addition to the regular course, a six-weeks' one was provided during the winter in association with University College. This was free of cost to *bona fide* young farmers. It dealt with the anatomy and diseases of farm stock, and evidently with little else. During the eighteen-seventies the Ontario Veterinary College (now under the auspices of the Agricultural and Arts Association) began to flourish. In 1879 it had eight professors and assistants, and graduated thirty-two students.[6]

Another agency which should have had much to do with agriculture before Confederation, but which actually had very little, was a department of the government called the Bureau of Agriculture. This department was established in November, 1852 (16 Vic., c. 11). Its head was called the Minister of Agriculture. Theoretically the purpose of the Bureau (Department after 1862) was to centralize the organization of the agricultural societies by bringing the Board of Agriculture and the Agricultural Association of Upper Canada, as well as the corresponding Board and Association in Lower Canada, under a member of the Executive Council. Actually it was concerned

---

a farm school, more or less in imitation of that already in operation at Ste. Anne, Kamouraska County, Lower Canada (*L'Agriculteur*, janvier, 1860, p. 101). President V. J. Guinan of the College informs me that nothing came of the suggestion.

[6]*TBAUC 1864-8*, pp. 92, 439, 623-4; *RAA 1879*, pp. 217-18.

almost entirely with immigration, colonization roads, the collection of statistics, and the registration of patents and copyrights. The ministers were changed every time there was a realignment in the government. There were ten of them between 1852 and 1867, with four occupying the office in 1858.[7] Till Confederation, according to the *Canada Farmer*, "the Agricultural Bureau was of but small practical value, having very little actual connection and sympathy with farming as a business and a national interest. This was, doubtless, partly owing to the fact that our Ministers of Agriculture knew nothing of farming except in theory, and, perhaps, were not well up even in that."[8]

After Confederation the name of the Board of Agriculture was changed to "Council of the Agricultural and Arts Association," and that of the Agricultural Association to "Agricultural and Arts Association." As the president of the Council acted as president of the Association, and as the activities of the Council tended to be more and more restricted to the management of the provincial exhibition, the Association lost its former importance. The only new activities the Council undertook were the issuing of the *Canada [Shorthorn] Herd Book* (which was severely condemned for its deficiencies by the cattle breeders) and the sponsoring of four annual sectional ploughing matches between 1873 and 1878. Both Council and Association had clearly outlived their usefulness before 1880. They were under continual attack in the agricultural press and in the provincial parliament. Nevertheless, they existed till Janary 1, 1896, when they were dissolved by act of the legislature.[9]

After Confederation the Bureau of Agriculture and Arts in the Ontario government succeeded the Department of Agriculture of the Province of Canada, the office being under the

[7]*JTBAUC 1855-6*, pp. 271-2; Gorham, "Development of Agricultural Administration in Upper Canada during the Period before Confederation" (Mss. in Main Library, Department of Agriculture, Ottawa), pp. 29-33, 40, 47-51.

[8]*Canada Farmer*, Jan. 15, 1868, p. 24.

[9]*RAA 1875*, p. 18; *RAA 1879*, p. 212; Hopkins, *Historical Sketch of the Ontario Department of Agriculture*, pp. 3-5; *Farmer's Advocate*, April, 1881, pp. 81, 94.

supervision of a Commissioner of Agriculture. This official at different times had charge also of immigration, public works, and the Mechanics' Institutes. The Bureau had a much larger jurisdiction than its predecessor, especially in practice. It took over administration of the grants to the local agricultural societies. It made grants, under legislative authority, to the Agricultural and Arts Association, and to private organizations such as the Fruit Growers' Association of Ontario, the Entomological Society of Ontario, the Ontario Poultry Society, and the dairymen's associations.[10] Yet, in the final analysis, the functions of Commissioner and Bureau were merely administrative. They had little share in shaping governmental policy towards agriculture, if indeed the government could be said to have such a policy. When, therefore, the Commissioner of Agriculture and Arts in 1880 suggested the appointment of the Ontario Agricultural Commission, it was partly with the hope that one result of the investigation it would undertake would be to extend the authority of Commissioner and Bureau.[11]

The first Commissioner of Agriculture, the Hon. John Carling, was an exception to the generalization about the lack of policy-making, for he was responsible for the initial official steps which led to the establishment of the Ontario Agricultural College. Of course, the idea of opening a school of agriculture in the province was not original with him. As early as 1857 one of the delegates to the meeting of the Agricultural Association at Brantford advocated one in Upper Canada, pointing out that Great Britain had set an example.[12] From this time on there was a sporadic agitation among editors and politicians, who deplored the failure of the professorship of agriculture at the University of Toronto, declared truly enough that the Veterinary College was a specialized institution, and warned that the United States, with its Morrill Act

---

[10]In 1879 the grants to the electoral division societies (for themselves and the township societies) amounted to $59,168, and those to the Agricultural and Arts Association, the Poultry Society, the dairymen's associations, the Fruit Growers' Association, and the Entomological Society respectively to $10,000, $700, $3,000, $1,300, and $750 (*RAA 1879*, p. 424).

[11]*RAA 1879*, pp. viii-ix.

[12]*JTBAUC 1856-7*, p. 298.

of 1862 providing for land grant colleges to "teach such branches of learning as are related to agriculture and the mechanic arts" would before long far outstrip Ontario in farming progress. In 1869 Carling had the Rev. W. F. Clarke (then editor of the *Ontario Farmer* and previously of the *Canada Farmer*) visit the more important agricultural colleges of the United States, with the purpose of submitting a plan for the development of one in Ontario. As a result of the report Clarke submitted the next year, the provincial government went ahead with plans for a college with an experimental farm in connection with it. The government first purchased land at Mimico, but as the site had some objectionable features, the new administration decided to locate the college at Guelph. Here the Ontario Agricultural College opened in 1874 with thirty-one students. By 1880 it had 162. It was still, however, far from attaining the place of prominence in the agricultural life of the province that it achieved in succeeding years. Good Conservatives condemned it as a political job, in consequence of the changing of the site, and loyal Liberals failed to see what practical benefit it could confer on the average farmer.[13]

The local agricultural societies increased slowly in number after 1850. In 1857 there were 42 county societies (one for every county) and 182 township societies. Under the provisions of the Agricultural Statute of 1857 the electoral division replaced the county as the administrative area for the large societies, and horticultural societies were given the same status as the township societies. This arrangement added only a few to the number of the smaller societies, but almost doubled that of the larger ones. In later years there was little change in the number of electoral division societies, but there were more township ones, occasioned from the formation of units in the newly settled regions, the establishing of horticultural societies, and the reorganization of dormant societies. In 1878 there were 88 electoral division societies and 286 township and horticultural ones.[14]

---

[13]*RAA 1872*, pp. 14-15; *RAA 1875*, pp. xiii-xv; *Report of the Ontario Agricultural Commission*, vol. v, App., P, pp. 57-9.

[14]*TBA&AAUC 1858-9*, pp. iii, 10, 12; *RAA 1879*, pp. 422-3, and *passim*.

The agricultural societies engaged in a variety of activities after 1850. The Tilbury East Township society (Kent County) owned two threshing machines in 1856, one bought in 1848 and the other in 1855.[15] The Prince Edward County society purchased an agricultural library in 1852 for the use of its members.[16] A few societies held spring exhibitions, usually restricted to stallions. This was really a method of subsidizing the importation of improved animals. In 1878 eleven electoral division societies were still holding their "spring shows." They were much criticized on the ground that the usual result was to award premiums year after year to the same inferior horses.[17] The West Middlesex society held an annual farmers' picnic at Port Stanley, beginning in 1866, and the Hullett Township society (Huron County) had an annual farmers' dinner, beginning in 1863.[18] However, the activities thus far enumerated are not to be considered altogether typical. Those that were are listed in the subjacent table.[19] A glance at it shows that, while the societies of the

[15]*JTBAUC 1856-7*, p. 75; *TBAUC 1860-3*, p. 115.
[16]*JTBAUC 1855-6*, p. 437.
[17]*JTBAUC 1856-7*, pp. 97-261; *RAA 1879*, p. 83, and *passim*. In the early eighteen-fifties a few societies tried subsidizing private individuals who brought improved bulls and stallions into their localities, but the plan proved less satisfactory than the purchasing of stock by the societies for the joint use of their members (*JTBAUC 1855-6*, pp. 228, 532; *JTBAUC 1856-7*, p. 80).
[18]*TBAUC 1864-8*, p. 504; *Farmer's Advocate*, July, 1881, p. 153; *ibid.*, May 1883, p. 134.
[19]The first two columns indicate the activities of the societies in 1854 and 1855, the last two those of 1878. In computing the figures in the first two columns it was assumed that if an activity was mentioned in 1854 it applied also to 1855, and *vice versa*.

	County societies 1854 and 1855	Township societies 1854 and 1855	Electoral division societies 1878	Township societies 1878
Number	41	about 175	88	286
Kept livestock for use of members	11	42	1	12
Imported livestock for sale to members	4	5	3	6
Imported seed grain, plaster, roots, &c., for sale to members	12	18	2	11
Imported implements for sale to members	2	4	1	0
Offered premiums for standing crops	4	7	0	5
Furnished agricultural periodicals to members	14	41	4	15
Held ploughing matches	5	26	16	22
Held exhibitions	41	152	84	253

eighteen-seventies preserved many of the features which characterized them in the eighteen-fifties, they had a tendency to emphasize the exhibition at the expense of everything else. In 1880 the Commissioner of Agriculture noted with regret that "comparatively few of the Ontario Agricultural Societies do more than hold an annual exhibition."[20]

Till after 1870 the provincial exhibition held under the auspices of the Agricultural Association was the most important one in Ontario. Even in the early eighteen-fifties it was drawing crowds of 30,000. During the eighteen-seventies it began to lose its pre-eminent position. One reason was that it began as a migratory exhibition, and such it continued to be. It was held at Brockville, 1851; Toronto, 1852; Hamilton, 1853; London, 1854; Cobourg, 1855; Kingston, 1856; and Brantford, 1857. From 1858 to 1874 it had a four-year cycle— Toronto, Kingston, Hamilton, and London. Then it was held at Ottawa, 1875; Hamilton, 1876; London, 1877; Toronto (the last time), 1878; Ottawa, 1879; and Hamilton (the last time), 1880. The peripatetic plan was kept in Ontario long after it was given up by most of the state fairs south of the border. Critics had pointed out that it involved sheer waste in erecting temporary buildings and much difficulty in obtaining accommodation for visitors. Nevertheless, it had met with approval because it allowed each section of the province to benefit from seeing improved livestock and implements, and by enlisting local support it helped to cut down expenses.[21] Whatever were the merits of the procedure in the eighteen-fifties and early eighteen-sixties, they had disappeared by 1870. Strong local agricultural societies began to encroach

---

(*JTBAUC 1855-6*, pp. 509-61; *JTBAUC 1856-7*, pp. 62-107; *RAA 1879*, pp. 2-205). The ploughing matches at the provincial exhibitions were discontinued, beginning in 1852, partly because the ground was usually too dry for a satisfactory contest, but mostly because only a few contestants appeared, and these from the immediate locality (*JTBAUC 1855-6*, pp. 144, 213).

[20]*RAA 1879*, p. ix. In spite of their deficiencies, the Upper Canada agricultural societies were much in advance of those in Lower Canada. For the latter, see Jones, "The Agricultural Development of Lower Canada" (*Agricultural History*, vol. XIX, 1945. pp. 222-3), as well as *Illustrated Journal of Agriculture*, Aug., 1879, pp. 49-51.

[21]*JTBAUC 1856-7*, pp. 298-9; *RAA 1875*, p. 190; Hopkins, *Historical Sketch of the Ontario Department of Agriculture*, p. 4.

on the field of the provincial exhibition. At first the two
most important were the Western Fair at London and the
Central Fair at Hamilton. As early as 1871 there were 6,130
entries at the Western Fair, with premiums amounting to
$5,445, while the premiums at the Central Fair came to $4,125.
The same year the provincial exhibition at Kingston, though
subsidized by the government of Ontario through a grant
made to the Agricultural and Arts Association, had only 6,682
entries and $12,951 in prizes.[22] In 1879, after considerable
agitation, an "Industrial Exhibition" was established at
Toronto under an incorporated Exhibition Association. This
really meant the beginning of the end of the provincial
exhibition. The president of the Council of the Agricultural
and Arts Association recognized as much, for in his annual
address in 1879 he went so far as to suggest that legislative
action should be resorted to "by which judicious arrangements should be made for the proper control of these rival
shows, so as not to impair the great usefulness and provincial
celebrity of this association."[23] Yet there was more involved
than upstart rivalry. The provincial exhibition suffered from
bad management. It was asserted that it was controlled by a
small ring of breeders in their own interests,[24] and that many
of the judges employed were mere favourites of the directors
and were completely unqualified for their responsibilities.[25]

[22]*RAA 1872*, pp. 58, 89, 209.

[23]*RAA 1879*, p. 212.

[24]Early in 1881 a member of the provincial legislature, in seeking
to have the annual grant to the Agricultural and Arts Association
terminated, stated that "he thought there was too much of a ring
influence in the conduct of the Provincial exhibition, [one which] if not
as large, [was] at least as corrupt, as the Tammany ring. One very
significant fact was that the small breeders did not come to exhibit
at the Provincial fairs, and this was because they had come to learn
that they had to be within a charmed circle if they desired to obtain a
prize on thoroughbred stock. Very frequently the mere names of ex-
hibitors was deemed sufficient to carry away prizes" (*Farmer's Advocate*, March, 1881, p. 55).

[25]"At the last Provincial Show held in London [1877] a laughable
circumstance took place. . . . A breeder of Southdown sheep from near
Toronto was there with some pens of sheep. The morning upon which
the judges were to make their awards the owner was seen among his
sheep getting them in order to appear neat and trim before the judges.
While thus engaged an elderly gentleman with a judge's badge pinned
to his coat collar came that way, and looking on, addressing the

The provincial exhibition dragged on during the eighteen-eighties, being held twice at Kingston, thrice at London, twice at Ottawa, and twice at Guelph. Kingston and Ottawa had been notoriously poor centres for the exhibition theretofore, Guelph was a small town, and London had its own Western Fair. The Industrial Exhibition at Toronto offered most of the advantages of a permanent provincial exhibition. The last provincial exhibition was held in 1889. The Ontario government refused to provide a grant for any more of them.[26]

If a local agricultural society of the period after 1850 was able to raise any funds at all, it was almost certain to hold an exhibition. By the early eighteen-seventies it was commonly felt by the public that, while there could not be too many agricultural societies, there could be, indeed already were, too many exhibitions, which awarded prizes for inferior animals, field products, and implements. A tendency was therefore manifest to combine those of several townships, or those of several townships and the electoral district, into a "union show" or "central fair." One such combination was the Central Fair at Cobourg, established in 1875, for the electoral divisions of East Durham, West Durham, West Northumberland, East Peterborough, West Peterborough, and Victoria.[27]

The exhibitions of the larger societies in any case expanded at the expense of those of the smaller ones. As their attendance grew, their directors began to exact an admission fee. As early as 1855 four societies charged admission, the Halton, Oxford, and Waterloo County societies, and the Pickering Township (Ontario County) society. They did so from motives not altogether mercenary. At the Halton County exhibition at Milton the directors, "in order to avoid and prevent the

---

breeder, said, 'what do you ca' thae black-faced beasties?' The proprietor replied that they were Southdown sheep. The judge (save the mark!) remarked. 'Soothdoons, are they? I believe I am a jedge o' thae things the day.' " The writer also asserts that equal incompetence was displayed by the judges at the provincial exhibition at Hamilton in 1880 (*Farmer's Advocate*, April, 1881, p. 94).

[26]Hopkins, *Historical Sketch of the Ontario Department of Agriculture*, p. 4.

[27]*RAA 1872*, pp. ix, 14, 120-1; *RAA 1879*, p. 21.

indiscriminate rush of spectators into the grain, &c., Hall, adopted the system of charging all persons not members of the Society, the small sum of one York shilling each, and by this means the sum of twelve pounds five shillings was realized, and disorderly persons excluded from the hall."[28] By 1870 the larger societies generally charged admission (usually 10 cents) and many of the smaller ones were beginning to imitate them.[29]

When the exhibitions became securely established, their directors found it desirable to obtain grounds of their own and to erect permanent buildings on them. In 1855 only four county societies — Kent, Middlesex, Simcoe, and Oxford — had permanent buildings or even grounds, but the next year the opinion was expressed that soon all societies would have to provide them.[30] Many did so, as is evidenced by the reports of the societies during the late eighteen-fifties and the eighteen-sixties. The property of the South Wellington Agricultural Society at Guelph in 1871 was typical of the best class. It consisted of thirty-three acres of land surrounded by a board fence eight feet high. In the enclosure were four buildings — a main hall for "ladies' work," dairy products, fruits, flowers, etc., and three small ones, one for the display of implements, one for grain and roots, and one for poultry. There was a row of horse stalls 600 feet long, a row of cattle pens 900 feet long, and a row of sheep and pig pens 500 feet long. In front of the horse stalls was a fenced ring (*not* a race track) about 400 feet in diameter for the exhibition of heavy-draft, general-purpose, and carriage horses, with a judges' stand in the centre. There were several smaller rings for showing cattle.[31]

Why was it that crowds of from 3,000 to 5,000 people were in attendance at some of the larger electoral district exhibitions in the eighteen-seventies? One explanation, embodied in the report of the East Lambton society for 1878, fails to

---

[28]*JTBAUC 1856-7*, p. 71.
[29]*RAA 1872*, p. viii.
[30]*JTBAUC 1856-7*, pp. 80, 97, 227.
[31]*RAA 1872*, p. 179. The similar but less pretentious buildings of the South Renfrew Agricultural Society at Renfrew, newly built in 1874, cost $4,500 (*RAA 1875*, pp. 130-1).

satisfy — "it is a fact beyond contradiction that the majority of those paying for entrance tickets, go expressly to see the Ladies' handiwork."[32] Neither did the farmers and their families attend because they were obsessed by a desire to see better livestock than their own, nor, as was asserted often enough, merely because they hoped to obtain a premium. Essentially the reason was that the exhibition provided a form of communal recreation.

In pioneer days communal recreation had found expression in bees in which neighbours participated actively. The exhibition furnished a type of recreation in which the people were entertained. At the larger exhibitions, outsiders, who had no connection with agriculture at all, provided the entertainment. When the exhibitions began to attract crowds, their directors were able to rent concessions for booths for the sale of groceries and other commodities. From this they found it but a step to admit pedlars, quack doctors, and sideshows, the last ranging from shooting-galleries and two-headed calves to alleged embalmed mermaids. They justified their policy by insisting, as was true, that if the sideshows were kept out, they would merely set up outside the grounds, where the directors would have no control over them. By letting them in, the society made a little money.[33] As the exhibitions throughout the province were held during September and early October, there was considerable clashing in dates. The result was that the smaller ones were often neglected by all but the most down-at-heel medicine vendors and lightning-rod agents. It was therefore mostly among the township exhibitions and the smaller district ones that alternatives to the sideshows were found. At the Russell County exhibition in 1866 two young women read essays on "the requirements of a good farmer's wife."[34] Two societies in Ontario County in 1871 had turnip-hoeing matches, one with sixty competitors.[35]

---

[32]*RAA 1879*, p. 83.

[33]*Farmer's Advocate*, Nov., 1881, pp. 265, 279. On the problem of the midway at the exhibitions of the period in the United States, see Neely, *Agricultural Fair*, pp. 201-9.

[34]*Cultivator and Country Gentleman*, Dec. 6, 1866, p. 365.

[35]*RAA 1872*, p. 114.

Others later had baby contests.[36] A few in the early eighteen-seventies had brass bands on the grounds, either hired or as competitors for prizes; in 1878 at least twenty-eight electoral division societies and at least twenty-three township societies had them.[37] One local society in Wentworth County in 1879 gave prizes for a competition which it called "Ladies Horse Riding." This attraction had appeared in central Ohio in 1851, and, under the pretentious title of "female equestrianism," had spread rapidly thereafter throughout the northern United States.[38]

Horse-racing (trotting) was an integral part of most of the American state and local exhibitions beginning in the eighteen-fifties. It was therefore natural that it should obtain a foothold, though a much smaller one than in the United States, in those of Upper Canada. It was a gradual process. The delegates from the Agricultural Association who attended the exhibition of the United States Agricultural Society at Boston in 1855, the New York State Fair at Watertown in 1856, and the New York State Fair at Albany in 1859 came back each time disgusted with the over-emphasis on trotting horses. They pointed out that the useful features of the exhibitions failed to attract the public, while there were evils, especially gambling, inseparable from the presence of the jockeys.[39] However, before long the directors of the Agricultural Association relaxed their attitude slightly, for in 1863 the trotting horses entered at the provincial exhibition at Kingston appeared in sulkies, giving the ground something of the appearance of a race-course. Even so, there was no racing, at least on the exhibition grounds.

---

[36]*Farmer's Advocate*, Nov., 1881, p. 265.

[37]*RAA 1872*, pp. 44, 132, 157, 191, 194; *RAA 1879, passim.*

[38]*RAA 1879*, p. 197; Jones, "A History of Local Agricultural Societies in Ohio to 1865" (*Ohio State Archaeological and Historical Society Quarterly*, vol. LII, 1943, pp. 133-4); Neely, *Agricultural Fair*, pp. 193-4. A good idea of the appearance of a township exhibition in the eighteen-eighties may be obtained from a drawing of that held in Delaware Township (Middlesex County) in 1885 (*Farmer's Advocate*, Dec., 1885, p. 356).

[39]*JTBAUC 1855-6*, p. 661; *JTBAUC 1856-7*, p. 208; *TBA&AAUC, 1859-60*, p. 338. On racing at exhibitions in the United States at this time, see Neely, *Agricultural Fair*, pp. 93-4, 191-6, and Demaree, *The American Agricultural Press, 1819-1860*, pp. 216-22.

Doubtless there was some on the streets of the city on a private basis.[40] Three years later the Welland electoral division society, being in a part of Upper Canada where American influence was exceedingly strong, evidently did permit trotting races.[41] After this many of the exhibitions had trials of speed, but how many it is impossible to state. Ignorance on this point arises from the fact that in their reports the societies scarcely ever mention racing, probably because the purses were raised independently among the lovers of horseflesh, and so did not enter into the book-keeping of the societies. There are, however, many references scattered through the reports to "special prizes" and "donations." It is reasonable to assume that these were frequently given to encourage trotting. Sometimes the trotting race was an impromptu like that in Louth Township (Lincoln County) in 1871.

The Directors gave a special prize for style and speed, which was the means of creating amusement for the crowd and elicited a spirited competition among those who entered for it. We were pained to see so many accidents happen while competing for the prize, and would recommend that, on future exhibitions, if we cannot procure a suitable place for showing, the prize be discontinued, as life and property are endangered by speeding horses on a narrow street, and we had a striking instance of the truth of it at our last fair. We also think that horse trots are quite foreign to the object for which such an association as ours was organized.[42]

Directors of a conservative cast of mind agreed with the concluding observation, but others insisted that offering prizes for trials of speed was a reasonable use of the funds of an agricultural society, because the ability to trot fast was a

---

[40]*TBAUC 1860-3*, p. 343.

[41]"Your Committee being generously offered the sum of 100 [*sic*] by the people of Welland towards enlarging the grounds of the society and that the track for exhibition purposes might be extended, it was thought advisable for the interests of this society to accede to this offer, and on this condition—that the donors might have the use of [the] track when not required by the society" (*TBAUC 1864-8*, p. 520). The same influence was manifest in Middlesex County. "We know that some Londoners have for the past 18 years striven to make these races a grand part of the attraction, but as yet they have not entirely eclipsed the agricultural departments" (*Farmer's Advocate*, June, 1883, p. 166).

[42]*RAA 1872*, p. 87.

desirable quality in a horse, and giving him a chance to compete against others was an effective method of bringing it to public notice, and so of enhancing his value. Even the provincial exhibition succumbed, for in 1881 it was mentioned in passing that, in preparation for the one to be held at London, "a good track for horses is being made."[43]

As was shown in Chapter X, there were a few farmers' clubs in Upper Canada before 1850. Others were organized sporadically thereafter. The *Canadian Agriculturist* and the *Canada Farmer* record the proceedings of about thirty between 1852 and 1870. Nearly all of them were in the older settled regions north of Lake Ontario and Lake Erie. Some of them, and these the least successful, met for informal conversations on agriculture, that is, to drink whiskey and squabble over politics; but usually the subject was prearranged, some person was made responsible for opening it, either by a paper or an extemporaneous address, and then a discussion followed. The information in the paper was usually drawn from agricultural text-books or the files of farm journals, but the discussions which followed were based on the practical experience of the members. As a consequence the reports of these meetings printed in the *Canadian Agriculturist* and the *Canada Farmer* are first-rate sources for the student of the agricultural history of Upper Canada. The activities of the Brighton and Cramahe Farmers' Club (Northumberland County) in 1865-6 will serve as an illustration of what the clubs tried to do, though this club was much more enterprising than most. It had ten meetings at which lectures were given, and two which passed wholly in discussion. The subjects of the lectures (some of which lasted over two sessions) were: preparing the soil for spring crops, bee-keeping, pigs and their management, "the farmer's spare hours and how to use them," the dairy and its management, sheep and their management, and the improvement of Upper Canada agriculture. The last was an address by Professor Buckland. The wives of the members attended two meetings. The club also held an annual picnic.[44] Few of the clubs had an extended

---

[43]*Farmer's Advocate*, Sept., 1881, p. 201.
[44]*Canada Farmer*, Nov. 1, 1866, p. 330; *ibid.*, Feb. 15, 1867, p. 62.

life. After attending one or two meetings of the local club, the average farmer paid no attention to its activities. He could not be disabused of the idea that, theoretically or practically, there was really little, if anything, new to be learned about farming. As the clubs did not appeal to the cupidity of prospective adherents as did the later Grange movement, their membership was invariably small. They had almost entirely disappeared by 1880. Yet their history should not be considered altogether one of failure. To some extent they anticipated the better features of the programme of the Grange, and they were the ancestors of the Farmers' Institutes which appeared in 1885.

The Grange (or "Patrons of Husbandry") was an organization which entered Ontario from the United States. Founded in 1867 by a government clerk in Washington who envisaged a secret society which would relieve the drabness of rural life, it had grown rapidly after 1870 in the states of the upper Mississippi Valley, where farmers ascribed their desperate economic situation to bad treatment by the railways, and used the organization as a political instrument in their fight against them. In Ontario the people were not so dependent on the railways, for they had nearly everywhere easy access to navigable water, the competition between waterways and railways kept freight rates relatively low, and neither the Montreal nor the eastern American market was distant. Nevertheless, Grangerism did for a time have a mushroom growth in Ontario. An organizer from Vermont, who had set up the first Canadian grange in the Eastern Townships in August, 1872, established the first in Ontario at L'Orignal (Prescott County) early in 1874, another near Winchester (Dundas County) shortly afterwards, and several others in the western part of the province before spring. There were 75 local granges in Ontario and Quebec by January 1, 1875, and 711 in the Dominion by January 1, 1879. Though a few of these were in Quebec, the Maritimes, and Manitoba, the great majority was in Ontario, especially in the part of the province west of Kingston. These local granges, like their counterparts in the United States, were united through district granges and a Dominion Grange, the last holding annual conventions, beginning in September, 1874.[45]

In Ontario the purpose of the Grange was not to procure legislation regulating the railways, but to eliminate the middleman as far as possible. The farmers had much reason to complain of the treatment they received from grain dealers, store-keepers, tree-pedlars, and implement agents. It seemed to them that co-operation offered a means of preventing further exploitation. Accordingly the members of the granges gave their orders for implements, apple trees, tea, and groceries to the local secretary, who transmitted them through the division grange to the manufacturers, nurserymen, and wholesalers. Manufacturers and dealers, hard hit by the prevailing depression, often made liberal offers to the granges. By purchasing in bulk and by paying cash the farmer was supposed to save the profits of three or four middlemen as well as the amount the local merchant usually charged to cover credit risks. However, it seems that poor goods were fobbed off on the farmers at the bargain prices, and even when the grangers obtained genuine discounts on standard goods, they found that there were inevitable losses when the barrels of sugar or chests of tea were parcelled out in their lodge rooms or in adjacent barns.[46] For a time the Grange engaged in the wholesaling of implements and other articles on its own account, but without any success. The implements the Grange supplied were cheaper than those of the agents, but the Grange did not service them afterwards.[47] Other co-operative enterprises were even more unfortunate. For example, the grangers at Napanee, then a great barley port, built an elevator of stone with a capacity of 100,000 bushels, only to have it collapse as soon as it was filled with barley.[48]

---

[45]Wood, *A History of Farmers' Movements in Canada*, pp. 33-5, 52, 60. For the locations of these units, see *Canada Farmer*, 1874-6, *passim*. and *Farmer's Advocate*, 1874 ff., *passim*.

[46]*Canada Farmer*, Nov. 15, 1875, p. 213; *Farmer's Advocate*, Aug., 1874, p. 117; *ibid.*, Jan., 1880, p. 7; *ibid.*, March, 1880, p. 62.

[47]Wood, *History of Farmers' Movements*, pp. 73-4. This wholesaling, like the other activities of the Grange, was an imitation of the practices of the parent organization in the United States.

[48]*Farmer's Advocate*, March, 1880, pp. 62-3.

The Grange had a social aspect, which usually took the form of annual June picnics under the auspices of the division granges. Those at Port Hope and Port Stanley in particular were attended by thousands of excursionists from a wide area.[49] Nominally, too, the grangers were supposed to discuss the principles and improvement of agriculture, but most of them entered the organization to save a few dollars on some purchase, and were little interested in anything else. A North Bruce farmer explained that one reason he refused to join was that "two-thirds of the members calculated to get rich out of the proceeds of the Grange, the social or moral aspect being no advantage to them, which, I think, should be the greater part."[50]

By 1880 the Grange was collapsing in Ontario. At the end of 1879 the fifteen local granges in the London Division had dwindled to three, and these feeble ones; and the same condition prevailed in most of the other counties in western Ontario, where the movement had had its greatest strength. Even the annual report of the Grange acknowledged signs of decay in parts of the heritage. It is said that by 1884 there were only 12,500 members of the organization left in the Dominion.[51] On the whole, the Grange in Ontario fell far short of the importance it attained in the western states. There was really no great agricultural discontent, in spite of the depression of 1873, and the least successful farmers were migrating to the American West or to Manitoba. No enduring association could be built on the mercenary motives which brought many farmers into membership. The chief importance of the Grange was not in its temporary activities, but in its being a parent or forerunner of other farmers' organizations.

The Grange in Ontario never had any political significance, though the way in which politicians contended for invitations to speak at the annual picnics indicated that they were fearful (or hopeful) that it might have. There was, on the other

---

[49]Toronto *Weekly Globe*, June 9, 1876; *ibid.*, June 8, 1877; *Farmer's Advocate*, July, 1878, p. 167.

[50]*Farmer's Advocate*, March, 1876, p. 58. Cf. *ibid.*, Oct., 1879, p. 230, and *ibid.*, Jan., 1880, p. 7.

[51]*Ibid.*, pp. 7, 15; Wood, *History of Farmers' Movements*, p. 68.

hand, a political party in Upper Canada in the eighteen-fifties and early eighteen-sixties which was tinged with agrarianism. This was the Clear Grit party. Agrarian movements have appeared in different parts of the world whenever the rural population has felt itself menaced by urban interests — in the engrossing of land by speculators, in an unequal incidence of taxation on urban and rural property, in excessive interest charges on mortgages, in mortgage foreclosures, in discriminating freight rates, in unfair tariffs. Bitterly resenting any of these abuses, or combinations of them, farmers have joined in attempts to remedy them, often giving a moral flavour to their protests. Such in general has been the background of the agrarian movements which have existed in the United States, Ireland, Western and Central Europe, and elsewhere, in modern times.[52] Agrarianism was not new in Upper Canada, for the branch of the Reform party led by William Lyon Mackenzie in the eighteen-thirties had been in many respects an agrarian one. It was in this sense, rather than in the borrowing of American political ideas, that it was a counterpart of Jacksonian Democracy in the United States.[53] It has been pointed out in Chapter VIII that Mackenzie and his followers had real grievances in the land policy of the government and in the inequitable operation of the Colonial Trade Act. Yet, even so, their movement was at least as much political as it was economic. It struggled against an entrenched oligarchy, an unreasonably favoured church, and the Orangemen whose violence assured the success of the administration at elections.[54] Further, it was sectional in its appeal, for Mackenzie had no following in the eastern parts of Upper Canada. This lack of influence was probably owing in varying degree to the proximity of eastern Upper Canada to Montreal and an overseas market, to the existence of the

---

[52]Cf. Johnson, "Agrarian Movements" (*Encyclopedia of the Social Sciences*, vol. I, pp. 490-2).

[53]For various suggestions about American political influences, pro and con, cf. Landon, *Western Ontario and the American Frontier*, pp. 152-4, and New, "Rebellion of 1837 in its Larger Setting" (*Canadian Historical Association Report for 1937*, pp. 15-16).

[54]Landon, *Western Ontario and the American Frontier*, pp. 151 ff.; Lucas (ed.), *Lord Durham's Report*, vol. II, pp. 161 ff.

local shanty market, to the predominantly British character of the inhabitants of the Military Settlements, and to the efficiency and popularity of the Tory political machine, especially the Orange lodges. Whatever the reason, the result was that, as the *Bytown Gazette* declared afterwards, "when Mackenzie was in all his glory of radicalism, he only prowled about the outskirts, but never ventured among our loyal men of Bathurst."[55] After the rebellion, 824 persons were arrested in the province on the charge of treason, but only eight of these came from east of Belleville, and against none of them was there sufficient evidence to proceed to trial.[56]

After the suppression of the rebellion, agrarianism again revealed itself in the demand for an agricultural tariff. However, after the adoption of the provincial tariff in 1843 (see Chapter VIII), the farmers were less vociferous than before. The prosperity of the wheat-growers during the period of the Canada Corn Law, and then the operations of the American drawback laws, which permitted the grain and flour of western and central Upper Canada to be exported via the Erie Canal, eliminated some of the discontent. Then, in 1849, the radical or Clear Grit Upper Canada wing of the disintegrating Reform party was organized. Its leaders, it has been asserted, "preached the gospel of a triumphant democracy. They derived their political opinions to a large extent from the doctrines and experience of the neighbouring American states."[57] It seems that they might equally well have derived them from the British Chartists.[58] Nevertheless, the reforms

---

[55]*Bytown Gazette*, n.d., quoted in Hill, "Bytown Gazette" (*Ontario Historical Society Papers and Records*, vol. XXVII, 1931, p. 409).

[56]Lindsey, *Life and Times of William Lyon Mackenzie*, vol. II, pp. 373, 400.

[57]Allin and Jones, *Annexation, Preferential Trade and Reciprocity*, p. 51.

[58]The programme, as outlined in the Toronto *North American* in 1850, advocated the establishment of an elective legislative council; widening of the franchise; vote by ballot; biennial parliaments; representation by population; secularization of the clergy reserves; termination of the special privileges theretofore accorded the Anglican Church; making legal proceedings simpler, and so less expensive; and throwing open the St. Lawrence to American shipping, so that the Upper Canada farmer might have the lowest possible freight rates (Dent, *Canadian Portrait Gallery*, vol. IV, pp. 148-9).

they demanded were clearly such as would appeal to the rural districts. The party had in general, therefore, the same point of view as the followers of Mackenzie. It was antipathetic to middlemen and money-lenders, to land speculators, to forwarding interests, to special privileges in church or state, and to promoters of canals or railways, like the Grand Trunk, who dipped into the public treasury. The *Globe*, its organ after 1854, proclaimed itself to be the spokesman of "the intelligent yeomanry of Upper Canada."[59]

Though the Clear Grit party had its agrarian aspects, we should err if we considered that it was dominated by them. Like the Mackenzie faction, it was sectional in its appeal. Its strength lay in wheat-growing central and western Upper Canada. At the great Reform Convention of 1859 only eighteen of the 570 delegates came from east of Kingston.[60] The Ottawa Valley, indeed, was the political stronghold of John A. Macdonald, a fact which requires explanation, for parts of it were newer and rawer than western Upper Canada, and the Reform party in it had received great accessions after 1840 in immigrants from the United Kingdom.[61] An economic reason was the timber industry, with its semi-feudal relations between lumber kings and those dependent on the shanty market. A political reason was that the region was opposed to George Brown's panacea of Representation by Population because it was not increasing in population as fast as western Upper Canada, and therefore stood to be injured rather than benefited by making electoral districts equal in population.[62] But undoubtedly the greatest reason was "practical politics." From the union of Upper Canada and Lower Canada in 1841 to Confederation, the practical politicians of the Ottawa Valley always desired three things: the improvement of the Ottawa River for the passage of timber; the establishment of Bytown

---

[59]Underhill, "Some Aspects of Upper Canadian Radical Opinion" (*Canadian Historical Association Report for 1927*, p. 47). Cf. Morrison, "Background of the Free Land Homestead Act of 1872" (*Canadian Historical Association Report for 1935*, p. 63).

[60]Toronto *Globe*, Nov. 10, 1859.

[61]*Bytown Packet*, Dec. 8, 1849.

[62]Ottawa *Citizen*, June 7, 1856, quoted in Montreal *Witness*, June 25, 1856; Montreal *Witness*, July 11, 1866; Toronto *Globe*, June 2, 1872.

(Ottawa) as the capital of the united province; and the canalization of the Ottawa River to Lake Huron. To realize any or all of these desires, the members of the Legislative Assembly representing the ten or so eastern Upper Canada constituencies and the two or three Lower Canada ones north of the Ottawa River were willing to be bribed to support the administration. In the days of governmental majorities of two or three or half a dozen, the Ottawa Valley members succeeded in making themselves an effective pressure group.[63] The *Globe* was nearly justified when it inquired how long the people of the Ottawa Valley would "still countenance their members in being the hewers of wood and the drawers of water for the government, despised and ridiculed by the people of all other sections."[64]

Though an element of agrarianism certainly existed in the Clear Grit party, it is exceedingly easy to over-emphasize its importance. The Clear Grits were strong in the rural sections of western Upper Canada not so much because they appealed to the economic aspirations of the farmers as because they offered a political instrument for throwing the "corruptionists" out of office. Party spirit ran high, and there were few farmers who would allow their economic interests to prevail over their loyalty to their political machine. Indeed there were few who could resist the temptation to turn their agricultural organization into vehicles for the promotion of the

---

[63]A few examples of their success: (1) About 1853 the government of the day obtained their support for the Grand Trunk by undertaking a useless canal between Lake Deschenes and Chats Lake, two expansions of the Ottawa (Hind *et al., Eighty Years' Progress*, p. 158). (2) In a speech in the Assembly in 1856 the Hon. A. T. Galt referred to the fact that at a public meeting a number of the supporters of the Cartier-Macdonald government "had pointed to some sort of engagement to make their political support contingent on the government taking up certain improvements" (Debates of the Parliament of Canada, Scrapbooks of newspaper clippings in Library of Parliament, Ottawa, Feb. 20, 1856). (3) In 1864 the Hon. L. H. Holton, Minister of Finance in the Dorion - J. S. Macdonald government, told a delegation from Ottawa that if the government was defeated the resulting confusion would make it impossible to move the provincial administration to Ottawa that year, and therefore he hoped it would not be beaten by the votes of the Ottawa Valley members, an involuntary tribute to their power (Toronto *Globe*, Feb. 5, 1864).

[64]Toronto *Globe*, Nov. 26, 1859.

welfare of their party. By the early eighteen-eighties the Dairymen's Association of Western Ontario was so riddled with politics that it was no longer of any practical value in the promotion of dairying.[65] There is no doubt that a common cause of the failure of township agricultural societies was electing officers, appointing judges, and even awarding prizes, on a party basis.[66] One township society—that of Ameliasburgh in Prince Edward County — had a sensible solution for the problem. "A great secret of the success of this Society," we are told, "consists in a by-law passed by the Society many years ago for the simultaneous election of a Reformer and Conservative as President and Vice-President. Thus, a Conservative President, who acts but one year, is succeeded the next year by the Vice-President, who is a Reformer. The successful working of this plan sets aside all theory averse to it."[67]

To complete the description of agricultural organizations in Ontario before 1880, it is only necessary to point out that in addition to the agricultural societies, the farmers' clubs, and the Grange, there were several associations, the activities of which did much for the promotion of agriculture, either directly or indirectly. Of these, the Fruit Growers' Association, the dairymen's associations, and the Entomological Society of Ontario (founded in 1868) have been mentioned in other connections. There was a Poultry Association of Ontario in existence in 1868, which held shows and meetings. It seems to have become moribund by 1874, for a new Ontario Poultry Society was then established at Guelph.[68] Another organization, this one concerned primarily with marketing problems, was the Association of the Live Stock Dealers of Western Ontario, founded at Stratford in 1876.[69]

---

[65]*Farmer's Advocate*, March, 1882, p. 67.
[66]*Ibid.*, Jan., 1881, pp. 1, 3.
[67]*Ibid.*, July, 1884, p. 195.
[68]*TBAUC 1864-8*, p. 569; *RAA 1875*, p. 165.
[69]Toronto *Weekly Globe*, June 23, 1876.

CHAPTER XX

CONCLUSION

THE history of agriculture in Ontario before 1880 is but a segment of the history of agriculture in the upper St. Lawrence Valley and the basin of the Great Lakes. Nevertheless, Ontario agriculture always differed considerably in detail from that of the adjacent states, as it did (except in a few places) from that of Quebec.

Climate was one of the factors responsible. In all but the southwestern portion of the province it discouraged the large-scale production of Indian corn, and so made impossible the corn-and-hog economy of the bottom lands of the Ohio Valley. It restricted the area in which fall wheat could be grown, and so forced many farmers to rely on spring wheat. At the same time, it encouraged the cool-weather crop of peas, and so contributed to the popularization of a wheat-growing rotation involving a legume rather than a hoed crop. The usually adequate snowfall protected meadows and fall-sown wheat from winter-killing, facilitated the marketing of farm produce, and promoted the expansion of the timber trade, on which the prosperity of eastern Upper Canada depended. Cold winters which necessitated good stabling and plentiful supplies of forage were, however, a deterrent to the expansion of the livestock industry, though by no means the only one.

Geography was no less important. The agricultural portion of the province throughout our period was confined to the country north of the St. Lawrence, Lake Ontario, and Lake Erie, and south and east of the Precambrian Shield. This meant, on the one hand, that there were few settlers outside the shantying regions who were not within reach of a grain-shipping port, and, on the other hand, that the northward expansion of population was drastically limited. When, during the eighteen-fifties, the advancing fringe of settlement reached the rocks, sand, and muskeg of the Ottawa-Huron area, it paused, and native sons and immigrants turned to the prairie lands of the upper Mississippi Valley. Then and in succeeding decades, as one authority has put it, "all the vitality which a moving frontier absorbs from a people, and gives back again, was lost to the communities of Canada. The export of men was draining the very life blood of Ontario rural settlements."[1]

The markets that were available did much to shape the development of Ontario agriculture in ways at variance with those of the northern United States. The outstanding feature in the history of farming south of the border in the early nineteenth century was the expansion of the consuming population within the national limits, whether in the mill towns of New England or in the cotton fields of the South. This meant that, during the second quarter of the century, the farmer in central Ohio, for example, was able to fatten his cattle for the butchers of Baltimore, Philadelphia, New York, or Boston, to fatten hogs for the packers of Cincinnati, to raise horses and mules for the southern plantations, to shear Merinos for the woollen mills of New England, and to grow wheat for export through New Orleans, New York, or Montreal. His Upper Canada counterpart had no such variety of outlets. His home market was, indeed, a paltry one till after 1850, save in so far as the lumbermen along the Ottawa created a demand. He depended, therefore, on exporting his produce. His chief outlet was in Great Britain and the Maritime Provinces, for, after the days of the Loyalists, he was ordinarily excluded from the United States. As flour and wheat were the staples of the Maritimes and overseas trade, the Upper Canada farmer at that time naturally concentrated on wheat-growing at the expense of other branches of agriculture. It was not till after 1850, when the American railroads opened the "New England market" and the Reciprocity Treaty increased its profitability, that rural Upper Canada had an incentive to diversification of farming. After the abrogation of the Reciprocity Treaty, the overseas market once more became a dominant influence in agriculture, encouraging as it did the extension of dairying and stock-raising.

Another factor helped to differentiate the agriculture of

[1]Mackintosh, "Economic Factors in Canadian History" (*Canadian Historical Review*, vol. IV, 1923, p. 24).

Upper Canada from that of the northern United States, but it was so intangible that it is difficult to assess its true significance. This was the influence of the settlers in the province, especially the "improving farmers" from the British Isles. Such men introduced improved livestock, experimented with seed grains, and fostered agricultural organization. Yet it is doubtful if the province would have been much different agriculturally if there had been no British immigration, that is, if it had been settled entirely by an overflow from New England or upstate New York or Ohio. Its general techniques of farming were always those common in the New World, and the European immigrant adjusted himself to them. Economic forces were more powerful than transplanted predilections, and Upper Canada reacted to them in the same manner as the neighbouring states.

In surveying the development of agriculture in Ontario, we find it advantageous to divide it into several periods, though, as might be expected, students are in disagreement as to the number of them and to the dates to be assigned to them. Professor Landon suggests, for example, that there were three periods — the pioneer one, from the advent of the Loyalists to the Rebellion of 1837; that of improvement in livestock, of the zenith and decline of wheat-growing, of the introduction of farm machinery, from the rebellion to Confederation; and that after Confederation.[2] William Johnson, ex-president of the Ontario Agricultural College, proposed what would seem to be a better division in his testimony before the Ontario Agricultural Commission in 1880. His first period was that of frontier forest clearings, which terminated, he considered, about 1826, that is, when the Welland and Rideau Canals were in course of construction, and the Canada Company began to colonize the Huron Tract. His second period lasted from 1826 to about 1854, and so comprised the era of the construction of canals, plank and gravel roads, and the first railways, of the expansion of settlement to the outermost limits of good land, and of the growth of the wheat and timber staples.

---

[2]Landon, "The 1860's a Period of Transition in Upper Canada Agriculture" (*Ontario Agricultural College Review*, April-May, 1937, p. 4).

His third period was that of the Reciprocity Treaty, one of
rapid and often unhealthy expansion. His final period, 1866-80,
was characterized by the expansion of such branches of agriculture as cheese-dairying, by soil depletion, and by world-wide
competition in farm produce.[3] It will be noticed that neither
Landon nor Johnson mentions the pre-Loyalist period, a day of
small things, but one with an interest of its own. The present
volume assumes a division into five periods, the first being the
pre-Loyalist one of Indian agriculture in Huronia and of
French-Canadian agriculture along the Petite Côte, and the
other four being as outlined in the paragraphs following.

The "pioneer period" inaugurated by the Loyalists had the
features characteristic of wooded-region frontier economy in
the temperate zone of North America. Isolated clearances, log
cabins, self-sufficing families, co-operative activities, an
absence of churches, schools, and roads, land speculation,
barter economy owing to lack of money, and shifting from the
local market provided by newcomers and garrisons to an overseas one, emphasizing wheat, were all typical. Then gradually,
as settlers with capital bought out the backwoodsmen, as
crossroads villages and shipping ports sprang up, and as the
blacksmith, the minister, the tavern, and the general store
appeared, Upper Canada lost its pioneer rawness. The passing
of the distinctive life of the backwoods occurred at different
times. By the outbreak of the War of 1812, the Niagara peninsula, the townships along the St. Lawrence, the Bay of
Quinte, and Lake Ontario, and to a considerable extent the
townships bordering Lake Erie, constituted an old settled
country. While much of the cultivable land of Upper Canada,
particularly in the Ottawa Valley and in the region adjacent
to and inland from Lake Huron, was still in process of occupation by 1850, pioneer conditions as the North American understood them were not characteristic of the province as a whole
after about 1830.[4] This is the date, incidentally, which has

---

[3]*Report of the Ontario Agricultural Commission*, vol. v, App. P,
p. 49.

[4]Many Ontarioans have gained their most lasting impressions of
rural life in early Upper Canada from a selection in one of the public
school readers entitled "Country Life in Canada in the Thirties," an
adaptation from Canniff Haight's *Country Life in Canada Fifty Years*

been given for the passing of frontier life from Ohio[5]—a matter of some significance, considering that the early development of Ohio in many respects paralleled that of Upper Canada.

The period which followed, or rather overlapped, that of the pioneers may be described as that of the wheat farmer. It began in the older settlements in the early eighteen-hundreds, and was most characteristic of the province as a whole in the eighteen-thirties and early eighteen-forties. It was a time when the typical farmer had a fairly well-cleared holding, had a frame house and a large frame barn, kept horses as well as oxen, ordinarily pursued an exhausting scheme of cultivation, and sold so much wheat every year that he had money to buy good farms for his sons. Though he was still self-sufficing in many things, he was within easy reach of grist mills, sawmills, and grain dealers. His chief handicap lay in his dependence on wheat, the ultimate market of which was beyond the limits of the province. He found other kinds of farm produce unprofitable, especially between the passage of the imperial Colonial Trade Act of 1831 and the adoption of the provincial agricultural tariff of 1843. During this interval American farmers with lower costs of production could use Upper Canada as a dumping ground for their cattle, sheep, and cheese, while the United States tariff prevented the Upper Canadians from taking advantage of the demand in the urban communities of New England, New York, and Pennsylvania. The period as a whole was therefore not only one of dependence on wheat, but of a persistent campaign to obtain modifications in the Corn Laws, and of a rural agitation against the British colonial policy which permitted the easy entrance of competing American produce into Upper Canada. In the Ottawa Valley, where wheat was not of much importance, the

---

Ago. It should be pointed out that this book, vivid and accurate as it is, does not describe pioneer life at all, strictly speaking, but rather life in a community of old cleared farms along the Bay of Quinte. It is this fact which gives the work its unique value. At the time of which Haight wrote, some of the land around the Bay of Quinte had been under cultivation for almost half a century.

[5]Bidwell and Falconer, *History of Agriculture in the Northern United States,* p. 166.

prosperity of the farmers was tied to the advances and reces-
sions in the square-timber trade with the British Isles. The
economy of the province throughout revealed the weaknesses
of a staple-producing area in a colonial relationship to the
overseas market.

The period *par excellence* of the wheat farmer terminated
in the late eighteen-forties, when the British parliament
adopted the policy which culminated in the repeal of the Corn
Laws. In the period which followed, the dominant theme was
the influence of the American market. In the five or six years
before 1854 high prices in the United States — a consequence
of the discovery of gold in California and of the railroad-
construction boom — nullified the protective features of the
American tariff as far as Upper Canada was concerned. In
the dozen years the Reciprocity Treaty was in force, there
was no artificial barrier in the way of agricultural commerce
between the northern states and Upper Canada. With an
outlet next door for his livestock, wool, butter, and coarse
grains, as well as for his wheat, the quondam wheat farmer
responded by diversifying his production. While the Crimean
War encouraged a continued reliance on wheat, factors such as
the ravages of the midge and the depression of 1857 had a
counteracting effect. The period was notable for other developments — the speculative frenzy of the Grand Trunk era, the
first large-scale introduction of labour-saving machinery
(especially the reaper and the mower), many importations of
improved livestock, the inauguration of factory cheese-making,
the expansion and consolidation of agricultural organizations,
and an attempt to use the shanty market as the basis for
agricultural settlement of the Ottawa-Huron country. The
period ended amid the exceptional prosperity of 1865-6, for
which the demands of a United States repairing the devastation of the Civil War were responsible.

The period between 1866 and 1880 was one of adjustment
to the changes resulting from the abrogation of the Reciprocity Treaty and to world-wide competition in the European
market. Specific developments of note were the collapse of
special crops like flax, hops, and tobacco, which had been
profitable during the American Civil War; the expansion of the

trade with the United States in lambs and horses, and a gradual loss of that in cattle; the establishment of barley-exporting to the United States, and the decline and virtual termination of wheat- and flour-exporting thither; the recognition that wheat-growing on the old scale had passed westward from the province; the expansion of factory cheese-making, with its dependence on the British market, and the beginning of creamery butter-making; the opening of an export trade to the British Isles in cattle and sheep; a brief attempt at farmers' co-operation in the Grange movement; and the distinction achieved by certain districts in special branches of agriculture, such as fruit-growing (the Niagara peninsula), cattle-rearing (the Guelph and London regions), and dairying (Oxford and Hastings counties). By 1880 Old Ontario was a region wherein there was slight possibility of placing new areas under cultivation, one whence there was a steady migration to the newly opened prairies of Manitoba and the upper Mississippi Valley. It was one, too, wherein general farming with tendencies to specialization had replaced the once-common reliance on wheat alone. The raw and economically weak province of the eighteen-thirties and eighteen-forties had grown into the mature and strong one of the days of the National Policy.

To bring this volume to a close, it seems worth while to mention those aspects of the agricultural history of Ontario before 1880 which deserve further research.[6] There is a place for histories of the branches of agriculture, such as grain-growing, fruit-growing, livestock husbandry, and dairying, as well as of the development of financial and transportation facilities associated with them. There should be a study of German (Pennsylvania Dutch) influences, and possibly of those of other distinctive groups. There is an acute need of reliable statistical data, as it is most unsatisfactory to the

---

[6]For suggestions for research in agricultural history, made with particular reference to the United States, but applicable in almost every detail to Ontario, see the extracts from Schmidt, "Topical Studies and References in the Economic History of American Agriculture," reprinted in Schmidt and Ross, *Readings in the Economic History of American Agriculture*, pp. 17ff., as well as Edwards, "Objectives for the Agricultural History Society" (*Agricultural History*, vol. XVIII, pp. 187 ff.)

agricultural historian to have to rely on trade and navigation returns and the decennial censuses.[7] Perhaps the most fruitful field for investigation is to be found in the agricultural development of special sections in the post-pioneer era, say the Essex peninsula, the Niagara peninsula, the Guelph region, the Toronto region (York, Ontario, Peel, and Simcoe counties), the Cobourg-Peterborough region, the Bay of Quinte region, the Rideau Canal region, and the Glengarry region. The completion of projects such as these is a prerequisite to the production of a definitive history of agriculture in Ontario.

---

[7]Some statistics relating to Upper Canada prices are included in *Statistical Contributions to Canadian Economic History.* Otherwise the materials necessary for statistical analysis are sadly lacking. The Commissioner of Agriculture for Ontario admitted in 1880 that "no machinery is provided, as in Great Britain or the United States, for the collection by the Bureau [of Agriculture and Arts] of general or statistical information relating to agriculture" (*Report on Agriculture and Arts for 1879*, p. viii).

BIBLIOGRAPHY

SECONDARY MATERIALS

The student who undertakes research in the agricultural history of Ontario must carry on his work with little help from previous historians. That he must do so is to be attributed to the fact that the field has attracted little attention. Of course many of the authors of standard histories do have chapters which purport to outline agricultural development, but for the most part they never get much beyond the hominy-block and the "romance" of pioneer life. When they do, they ordinarily content themselves with generalizations based on census data or on earlier writers like themselves. Of slightly more value are several brief surveys dealing specifically with the history of agriculture. C. C. James (Deputy Minister of Agriculture for Ontario, 1892-1912) wrote three short descriptions of the progress of Ontario farming, which may be found in the Appendix to the *Report of the Ontario Bureau of Industries* (Toronto, 1898), in *Canada and its Provinces* (edited by A. Shortt and A. G. Doughty, 23 vols. Toronto, 1915), vol. XVIII, and in the *Cyclopedia of American Agriculture* (edited by L. H. Bailey, 4 vols., New York, 1907-9), respectively. The documents in *Select Documents in Canadian Economic History, 1783-1885* (edited by H. A. Innis and A. R. M. Lower, Toronto, 1933), and the notes on them, together comprise a history of Canadian agriculture—mainly that of Ontario—during the period covered. Unfortunately this volume is of very slight value for the years after 1845, owing to a complete absence of references to the agricultural periodicals.

Though the present volume is the first that attempts to deal with the agricultural history of Ontario on an extended scale, there have been some studies of single aspects of it, especially land settlement and its related problems, as well as monographs and articles on subjects with a tangential relationship to it. For a further discussion of this rather fragmentary secondary material, the reader is referred to V. C. Fowke, "An Introduction to Canadian Agricultural History" (*Canadian Journal of Economics and Political Science*, Toronto, vol. VIII, 1942). This article was reprinted in *Agricultural History* (Washington), vol. XVI, 1942.

While the present book is based mainly on primary materials, many secondary works have been consulted in its preparation. The titles included below really fall into several groups: (1) books, mono-

graphs, or articles on the history of the economic development of
Ontario actually cited, quoted or referred to in this volume; (2) books
or articles on the history of the economic development of regions outside Ontario either cited or quoted; (3) a few political or general
histories either cited or quoted; (4) a number of books, monographs,
or articles, neither cited nor quoted, but consulted in the preparation
of the work, and recommended to the attention of future students in the
field; these are distinguished by an asterisk; (5) a small number of
Ontario local histories either cited or quoted. Here it may be stated flatly
that such local histories are, as a class, almost valueless for the
study of agricultural history, as they never get much beyond the
period of the pioneers. Their descriptions of pioneer life are accurate
enough in general, though mainly based on reminiscences, but the
student will prefer contemporary accounts, which are equally available.

ADAMS, HENRY. *History of the United States of America* [1801-17]
(9 vols., New York and London, 1891).

ALLIN, C. D., and JONES, G. M. *Annexation, Preferential Trade and
Reciprocity. An Outline of the Canadian Annexation Movement of
1849-50 with Special Reference to the Question of Preferential Trade
and Reciprocity* (Toronto and London, 1911).

BAILEY, L. H. (ed.). *Cyclopedia of American Agriculture* (4 vols., New
York, 1907-9).

*BALL, C. R. "The History of American Wheat Improvement" (*Agricultural History*, Washington, vol. IV, 1930).

BARBEZIEUX, ALEXIS DE. *Histoire de la province ecclésiastique d'Ottawa
et de la colonisation dans la vallée de l'Ottawa* (2 vols., Ottawa, 1897).

BARNES, D. G. *A History of the English Corn Laws from 1660 to
1846* (London, 1930).

BIDWELL, P. W., and FALCONER, J. I. *History of Agriculture in the
Northern United States, 1620-1860* (Washington, 1925).

BLADEN, M. L. "Construction of Railways in Canada to 1885" (*Contributions to Canadian Economics*, Toronto, vol. V, 1932).

*BUCK, SOLON. *The Granger Movement: a Study of Agricultural
Organization and Its Political, Economic and Social Manifestations,
1870-80* (Cambridge, 1913).

BULLER, A. H. R. *Essays on Wheat, Including the Discovery and
Introduction of Marquis Wheat, the Early History of Wheat Growing
in Manitoba, Wheat in Western Canada, the Origin of Red Bobs and
Kitchener, and the Wild Wheat of Palestine* (New York, 1919).

BURN, D. L. "Canada and the Repeal of the Corn Laws" (*Cambridge Historical Journal*, Cambridge, vol. II, 1928).

BURT, A. L. *The Old Province of Quebec* (Minneapolis and Toronto,

BURTON, F. W. "Grain Trade" (*The Encyclopedia of Canada*, edited by W. S. Wallace, 6 vols., Toronto, 1935-7, vol. III).
"Wheat in Canadian History" (*Canadian Journal of Economics and Political Science*, Toronto, vol. III, 1937).

BUSBEY, HAMILTON. *The Trotting and the Pacing Horse in America* (New York, 1904).

CANNIFF, WILLIAM. *History of the Settlement of Upper Canada with Special Reference to the Bay Quinte* (Toronto, 1869).

CARMAN, EZRA, HEATH, H. A., and MINTO, JOHN. *Special Report on the History and Present Condition of the Sheep Industry in the United States* (Washington, 1892).

CARRIER, LYMAN. *The Beginnings of Agriculture in America* (New York, 1933).

CHAMBERLAIN, A. F. "Maple Sugar and the Indians" (*American Anthropologist*, Washington, vol. IV, 1891).

CHAPMAN, L. J. "Adaptation of Crops in Ontario" (*Canadian Geographical Journal*, Montreal, vol. XXIV, 1942).

CLAPHAM, J. H., and POWER, EILEEN (eds.). *The Agrarian Life of the Middle Ages* (*Cambridge Economic History of Europe from the Decline of the Roman Empire*, Cambridge, vol. I, 1942).

CLARK, S. D. *The Social Development of Canada: An Introductory Study with Select Documents* (Toronto, 1942).

COLBY, C. C. *Source Book for the Economic Geography of North America* (Chicago, 1921).

COLE, A. H. "Agricultural Crazes: a Neglected Chapter in American Economic History" (*American Economic Review*, Evanston, vol. XVI, 1926).

CONNON, J. R. *Early History of Elora, Ontario, and Vicinity* (Elora, 1930).

CRAIG, R. D. "The Forest Resources of Canada" (*Economic Geography*, Worcester, Mass., vol. II, 1926).

CREIGHTON, D. G. *The Commercial Empire of the St. Lawrence, 1760-1850* (Toronto, New Haven, London, 1937).
"The Economic Background of the Rebellions of Eighteen Thirty-Seven" (*Canadian Journal of Economics and Political Science*, vol. III, 1937).

CRUIKSHANK, E. A. "The News of Niagara a Century Ago" (*Ontario Historical Society Papers and Records,* Toronto, vol. XXIII, 1926). "Post War Discontent at Niagara in 1818" (*Ontario Historical Society Papers and Records,* vol. XXIX, 1933). "A Study of Disaffection in Upper Canada in 1812-15" (*Transactions of the Royal Society of Canada,* Ottawa, 3rd series, vol. VI, 1912).

DEMAREE, A. L. *The American Agricultural Press, 1819-1860* (New York, 1941).

DENT, J. C. *The Canadian Portrait Gallery* (4 vols., Toronto, 1880-1).

DOTY, LOCKWOOD. *History of Livingston County, New York: From its Earliest Traditions to its Part in the War for Our Union* (Geneseo, 1876).

DRUMMOND, N. A. "Marketing of Canadian Live Stock" (Ms. thesis, 1930, in Main Library of the Department of Agriculture, Ottawa).

EDWARDS, E. E. "Objectives for the Agricultural History Society during its Second Twenty-Five Years" (*Agricultural History,* vol. XVIII, 1944).

ERNLE, LORD. *English Farming Past and Present* (3rd ed., London, 1922).

FARMER, SILAS. *The History of Detroit and Michigan* (2 vols., Detroit, 1884).

FITE, E. D. *Social and Industrial Conditions in the North during the Civil War* (New York, 1930).

FOWKE, V. C. "An Introduction to Canadian Agricultural History" (*Canadian Journal of Economics and Political Science,* vol. VIII, 1942).

GARLAND, M. A. "Some Frontier and American Influences in Upper Canada prior to 1837" (*Transactions of the London and Middlesex Historical Society,* London, vol. XIII, 1929).

GATES, P. W. "Official Encouragement to Immigration by the Province of Canada" (*Canadian Historical Review,* Toronto, vol. XV, 1934).

GORHAM, R. P. "The Development of Agricultural Administration in Upper Canada during the Period before Confederation" (Ms. in the Main Library of the Department of Agriculture, Ottawa).

GRAY, L. C., and THOMPSON, E. K. *History of Agriculture in the Southern United States to 1860* (2 vols., Washington, 1933).

GUILLET, E. C. *Early Life in Upper Canada* (Toronto, 1933).

HAMIL, F. C. "Fairfield on the River Thames" (*Ohio State Archaeological and Historical Quarterly,* Columbus, vol. XLVIII, 1939).

HAYNES, F. E. *The Reciprocity Treaty with Canada of 1854-66* (Baltimore, 1892).

HEDRICK, U. P. *A History of Agriculture in the State of New York* (Geneva [?], N.Y., 1933).

HERBERTSON, A. J., and HOWARTH, O. J. R. (eds.). *The Oxford Survey of the British Empire* (6 vols., Oxford, 1914).

HIBBARD, B. H. *History of Agriculture in Dane County, Wisconsin* (Madison, 1904).

HILL, H. P. "The Bytown Gazette" (*Ontario Historical Society Papers and Records*, vol. XXVII, 1931).

HILLS, G. A. "Pedology, 'The Dirt Science,' and Agricultural Settlement in Ontario" (*Canadian Geographical Journal*, vol. XXIX, 1944).

HODGE, F. W. *Handbook of American Indians North of Mexico* (*House Document*, 59th Cong., 1st Sess., no. 926, Washington, 1907).

HOPKINS, J. C. *Historical Sketch of the Ontario Department of Agriculture* (n.p., 1912).

HOUGH, F. B. *History of Jefferson County in the State of New York, from the Earliest Period to the Present Time* (Albany and Watertown, 1854).
History of St. Lawrence and Franklin Counties, New York, from the Earliest Period to the Present Time (Albany, 1853).

HUBBARD, BELA. "The Early Colonization of Detroit" (*Michigan Pioneer Collections*, Lansing, vol. I, 1877).

HUDGINS, BERT. "Tobacco Growing in Southwestern Ontario" (*Economic Geography*, vol. XIV, 1938).

HUNTINGTON, ELLSWORTH. *The Red Man's Continent: a Chronicle of Aboriginal America* (New Haven, Toronto, London, 1919).

HUTCHINSON, W. T. *Cyrus Hall McCormick* (2 vols., New York and London, 1930, 1935).

INNIS, H. A. (ed.). *The Dairy Industry in Canada* (Toronto, New Haven, London, 1937).
The Fur Trade in Canada: an Introduction to Canadian Economic History (New Haven, 1930).
(ed.). *Select Documents in Canadian Economic History, 1497-1783* (Toronto, 1929).
and LOWER, A. R. M. (eds.). *Select Documents in Canadian Economic History, 1783-1885* (Toronto, 1933).

JAMES, C. C. "Agriculture in Canada" (*Cyclopedia of American Agriculture*, edited by L. H. Bailey, vol. I).

"The Development of Agriculture in Ontario" (*Report of the Ontario Bureau of Industries for 1898*, Toronto).

"History of Farming [in Ontario]" (*Canada and Its Provinces*, edited by A. Shortt and A. G. Doughty, 23 vols., Toronto, 1915, vol. XVIII).

JOHNSON, ALVIN. "Agrarian Movements" (*Encyclopedia of the Social Sciences*, edited by E. R. A. Seligman and Alvin Johnson, 15 vols., New York, 1930-5, vol. I).

JOHNSON, E. R. *et al. History of the Domestic and Foreign Commerce of the United States* (2 vols., Washington, 1915).

JOHNSTON, W. *History of the County of Perth from 1825 to 1902* (Stratford, 1903).

JONES, R. L. "The Agricultural Development of Lower Canada, 1850-1867" (*Agricultural History*, vol. XIX, 1945).

"The Canadian Agricultural Tariff of 1843" (*Canadian Journal of Economics and Political Science*, vol. VII, 1941). See note 1, Chapter VIII.

"French-Canadian Agriculture in the St. Lawrence Valley, 1815-1850" (*Agricultural History*, vol. XVI, 1942).

"A History of Local Agricultural Societies in Ohio to 1865" (*Ohio State Archaeological and Historical Society Quarterly*, vol. LII, 1943).

KELLAR, H. A. *Solon Robinson, Pioneer and Agriculturist* (2 vols., Indianapolis, 1936).

Kentiana: The Story of the Settlement and Development of the County of Kent (Chatham [?], 1939).

KING, I. F. "The Coming and Going of Ohio Droving" (*Ohio Archaeological and Historical Quarterly*, vol. XVII, 1908).

KIRKCONNELL, WATSON. *Victoria County Centennial History* (Lindsay, 1921).

LANDON, FRED. "The Agricultural Journals of Upper Canada (Ontario)" (*Agricultural History*, vol. IX, 1935).

"Agriculture among the Negro Refugees in Upper Canada" (*Journal of Negro History*, Washington, July, 1936).

"The 1860's a Period of Transition in Upper Canada Agriculture" (*Ontario Agricultural College Review*, Guelph, April-May, 1937).

"Some Effects of the American Civil War on Canadian Agriculture" (*Agricultural History*, vol. VII, 1933).

Western Ontario and the American Frontier (Toronto, New Haven, London, 1941).

*LEAVITT, C. T. "Attempts to Improve Cattle Breeds in the United States, 1790-1860" (*Agricultural History*, vol. VII, 1933).

LEE, CHU-FEN. "Land Utilization in the Middle Grand River Valley of Western Ontario" (*Economic Geography*, vol. XX, 1944).

LINDSEY, CHARLES. *Life and Times of William Lyon Mackenzie: With an Account of the Canadian Rebellion of 1837, and the Subsequent Frontier Disturbances* (2 vols., Toronto, 1862).

*LOEHR, R. C. "Influence of English Agriculture on American Agriculture, 1775-1825" (*Agricultural History*, vol. XI, 1937).

LOWER, A. R. M. "The Assault on the Laurentian Barrier, 1850-1870" (*Canadian Historical Review*, vol. X, 1929).
Settlement and the Forest Frontier in Eastern Canada (Toronto, 1936).

LUCAS, SIR C. P. (ed.). *Lord Durham's Report on the Affairs of British North America* (3 vols., Oxford, 1912).

MACDONALD, NORMAN. *Canada, 1763-1841: Immigration and Settlement. The Administration of Imperial Land Regulations* (London, New York, Toronto, 1939).

MACGIBBON, D. A. *The Canadian Grain Trade* (Toronto, 1932).

MACKAY, R. A. "The Political Ideas of William Lyon Mackenzie" (*Canadian Journal of Economics and Political Science*, vol. III, 1937).

MACKINTOSH, W. A. "Economic Factors in Canadian History" (*Canadian Historical Review*, vol. IV, 1923).

MARSH, E. L. *A History of the County of Grey* (Owen Sound, 1932).

MARTYN, HOWE. "Loitering along Lake Ontario" (*Canadian Geographical Journal*, vol. XIII, 1936).

MASTERS, D. C. *The Reciprocity Treaty of 1854: Its History, Its Relations to British Colonial and Foreign Policy and to the Development of Canadian Fiscal Autonomy* (Toronto, 1937).

MERK, FREDERICK. "The British Corn Crisis of 1845-6 and the Oregon Treaty" (*Agricultural History*, vol. VIII, 1934).

MORRISON, H. M. "The Background of the Free Land Homestead Act of 1872" (*Canadian Historical Association Report for 1935*, Toronto).
"The Principle of Free Grants in the Land Act of 1841" (*Canadian Historical Review*, vol. XIV, 1933).

NEELY, W. C. *The Agricultural Fair* (New York, 1935).

NEW, C. W. "The Rebellion of 1837 in Its Larger Setting" (*Canadian Historical Association Report for 1937*).

PARKMAN, FRANCIS. *The Jesuits in North America in the Seventeenth Century* (Boston, 1894).

PATTERSON, G. C. *Land Settlement in Upper Canada, 1783-1840*, in *Report of the Ontario Department of Archives for 1920* (Toronto, 1921).

PLUMB, C. S. *Types and Breeds of Farm Animals* (Boston, 1906).

POOLE, T. W. *A Sketch of the Early Settlement and Subsequent Progress of the Town of Peterborough and of each Township in the County of Peterborough* (Peterborough, 1867).

REVELLE, F. D. *History of the County of Brant* (2 vols., Brantford, 1920).

REYNOLDS, JOHN. *The Pioneer History of Illinois, containing the Discovery, in 1673, and the History of the Country to the Year Eighteen Hundred and Eighteen* (Belleville, Ill., 1852).

RIDDELL, R. G. "The Policy of Creating Land Reserves in Canada" (R. Flenley, ed., *Essays in Canadian History Presented to George Mackinnon Wrong for his Eightieth Birthday*, Toronto, 1939).

*RIDDELL, WALTER. "Farming in Northumberland County, 1833 to 1895" (W. R. Riddell, ed., *Ontario Historical Society Papers and Records*, vol. XXX, 1934). See below, p. 387.

ROBERTSON, H. H. "The First Agricultural Society in the Limits of Wentworth—1806" (*Journal and Transactions of the Wentworth Historical Society*, Hamilton, vol. IV, 1905).

*ROBINSON, F. V. "Survey of Agriculture in Upper Canada, 1830-50" (M. A. Thesis, University of Western Ontario, 1938).

RUDDICK, J. A. *An Historical and Descriptive Account of the Dairying Industry of Canada* (Ottawa, 1911).

SAUNDERS, R. M. "The First Introduction of European Plants and Animals into Canada" (*Canadian Historical Review*, vol. XVI, 1935).

SCHMIDT, L. B., and ROSS, E. D. (eds.). *Readings in the Economic History of American Agriculture* (New York, 1925).

SCHOTT, CARL. *Landnahme und Kolonisation in Canada am Beispiel Südontarios* (Kiel, 1936).

SHELDON, E. M. *The Early History of Michigan, from the First Settlement to 1815* (New York, 1856).

SHORTT, ADAM. "The Economic Effect of the War of 1812 on Upper Canada" (*Ontario Historical Society Papers and Records*, vol. X, 1913).

"Railroad Construction and National Prosperity; an Historic Parallel" (*Transactions of the Royal Society of Canada*, 3rd series, vol. VIII, 1915).

SMITH, W. L. *Pioneers of Old Ontario* (Toronto, 1923).

Statistical Contributions to Canadian Economic History (2 vols., Toronto, 1931).

TALMAN, J. J. "Agricultural Societies of Upper Canada" (*Ontario Historical Society Papers and Records*, vol. XXVII, 1931).
"Social Life in Upper Canada, 1815-1840 (Ms, Ph.D. Dissertation, University of Toronto, 1931).

TANSILL, C. C. *The Canadian Reciprocity Treaty of 1854* (Baltimore, 1922).

TAYLOR, GRIFFITH. "Climate and Crop Isopleths for Southern Ontario" (*Economic Geography*, vol. XIV, 1938).

THOMAS, C. *History of the Counties of Argenteuil, Quebec, and Prescott, Ontario, from the Earliest Settlement to the Present* (Montreal, 1896).

THOMPSON, J. W. *A History of Livestock Raising in the United States, 1607-1860* (Washington, 1942).

*TOON, C. C. "Some Aspects of Agricultural Development in Canada West between 1850 and 1870" (Ms, M. A. Thesis, University of Western Ontario, 1938).

TRAFFORD, SIR HUMPHREY DE. *The Horses of the British Empire* (2 vols., London, 1907).

TRUE, RODNEY. "The Early Development of Agricultural Societies in the United States" (*American Historical Association Report for 1920*, Washington, 1925).

TUCKER, G. N. *The Canadian Commercial Revolution, 1845-51* (New Haven, 1936).

TURNER, O. *Pioneer History of the Holland Purchase of Western New York* (Buffalo, 1849).

UNDERHILL, F. H. "Some Aspects of Upper Canadian Radical Opinion in the Decade before Confederation" (*Canadian Historical Association Report for 1927*).

VEBLEN, T. B. "The Price of Wheat since 1867" (*Journal of Political Economy*, Chicago, vol. I, 1892-3).

WALCOTT, R. R. "Husbandry in Colonial New England" (*New England Quarterly*, Boston, vol. IX, 1936).

WEAVER, J. C. "Barley in the United States: a Historical Sketch" (*Geographical Review*, New York, vol. XXXIII, 1943).

WHITAKER, J. H. "Agricultural Gradients in Southern Ontario" (*Economic Geography*, vol. XIV, 1938).

WILSON, H. F. "The Rise and Decline of the Sheep Industry in Northern New England" (*Agricultural History*, vol. IX, 1935).

WOOD, L. A. *A History of Farmers' Movements in Canada* (Toronto, 1924).

WOODWARD, C. R. *The Development of Agriculture in New Jersey, 1640-1880: A Monographic Study in Agricultural History* (New Brunswick, N.J., 1927).

OFFICIAL RECORDS

Government records of one kind and another constitute in the aggregate sources of great value for the study of agricultural history. Those used in the preparation of this study fall into several classes:

(1) MANUSCRIPT OFFICIAL RECORDS OF THE PROVINCE OF UPPER CANADA. As there was nothing secret or mysterious about agriculture, the manuscript official records are much less useful in tracing its development than they are in investigations of other fields of history. Nevertheless, there is much information scattered through the correspondence of the lieutenant-governors with the governors at Quebec and with the Colonial Office, most of it concerned with the details of early settlement. Fortunately, several collections of documents leave the student little to search for in the original. Among these are H. A. Innis and A. R. M. Lower (eds.), *Select Documents in Canadian Economic History, 1783-1885* (Toronto, 1933); E. A. Cruikshank (ed.), "Petitions for Grants of Land in Upper Canada, 1796-99" (*Ontario Historical Society Papers and Records*, vol. XXVI, 1930); E. A. Cruikshank (ed.), *Correspondence of Lieutenant-Governor John Graves Simcoe* (5 vols., Toronto, 1923 ff.); E. A. Cruikshank and A. F. Hunter (eds.), *Correspondence of the Honourable Peter Russell* (3 vols., Toronto, 1932 ff.); and the *Reports* of the Public Archives of Canada (Ottawa). After the War of 1812 the manuscript official correspondence, except on such matters as land policy, contains little of value from the agricultural point of view, and that little is easily found elsewhere.

(2) MANUSCRIPT OFFICIAL RECORDS OF THE OLD PROVINCE OF QUEBEC AND OF THE PROVINCE OF LOWER CANADA. After 1792 there is little found in the Lower Canada correspondence that is not also in the Upper Canada. However, in the period before Upper Canada was set off from the lower province, there is a considerable amount of information. A fair selection from it will be found in the *Michigan Pioneer Collections* (Lansing), and in E. A. Cruikshank (ed.), *Settlement of the United Empire Loyalists on the Upper St. Lawrence and Bay of Quinte in 1784 : a Documentary Record* (Toronto, 1934).

(3) PRINTED OFFICIAL RECORDS OF UPPER CANADA. These records include a wide variety of material, ranging from the volumes of *Statutes* through the journals of the legislature to miscellaneous parliamentary papers. The last were published from 1825 to 1840 under the title of "Appendixes to the Journal of the Legislative Assembly of Upper Canada," and may be conveniently consulted through the *General Index to the Journals of the Legislative Assembly of Upper Canada, 1825-40.* They are of much value for the study of certain aspects of agriculture. Some of them are routine reports of the various departments of the government; others are made up of tabled correspondence between provincial officials and the Colonial Office; and many of them present the reports of special or standing committees on certain subjects, and the evidence taken before them. Often the titles of the documents furnish scarcely any clue to their content. Thus, in the recurring reports on the canals, there is much information respecting the grain trade.

(4) PRINTED OFFICIAL RECORDS OF LOWER CANADA. These correspond to the official records of Upper Canada, and have considerable value for the study of Lower Canada agriculture. As they were concerned, however, almost exclusively with the problems of *habitant* farming, they throw little light on developments in Upper Canada, even in the parts adjacent to Lower Canada, except in connection with the timber trade of the Ottawa Valley.

(5) PRINTED OFFICIAL RECORDS OF THE PROVINCE OF CANADA. These continued in ever-expanding form the parliamentary papers of Upper Canada and Lower Canada. They may be consulted through the *General Index to the Journals of the Legislative Assembly of Canada, 1841-51,* and the *General Index to the Journals of the Legislative Assembly of Canada, 1852-66.* Possibly they are most useful for the relations between agriculture and land settlement, and between agriculture and lumbering. In some of the reports of the Board of Works or of the Commissioner of Public Works the relation between agriculture and lumbering in the Ottawa Valley is discussed at considerable length (especially in the *Journal of the Legislative Assembly of Canada, 1847,* App. LL, and in the *Journal of the Legislative Assembly of Canada, 1849,* App. BB). On the settlement of the Ottawa-Huron region and on the clash between the lumberman and the farmer which resulted, the reports of two committees are of outstanding significance —the "Report of the Select Committee on the Management of the Public Lands" (*Sessional Papers, Canada, 1854-5,* App. MM), and the "Report of the Select Committee on the State of the Lumber Trade of Canada in Relation to the Settlement of the Country" (*Journal of the Legislative Assembly of Canada, 1863,* first session, App. no. 8). On the details of settlement in the lumbering areas after 1855 there is a welter of material in the Reports of the Commissioners of Crown

Lands (commencing with *Sessional Papers, Canada, 1857*, no. 25) and in the Reports of the Ministers of Agriculture (commencing with *Sessional Papers, Canada, 1857*, no. 54).

(6) PRINTED OFFICIAL RECORDS OF THE DOMINION OF CANADA. Aside from the censuses of 1870-1 and 1880-1, and the trade statistics, there is not much of value in these records, with the exception of the "Report of the Select Committee on the Agricultural Interests of the Dominion" (*Journal of the House of Commons, Canada, 1876*, App. no. 7).

(7) PRINTED OFFICIAL RECORDS OF THE PROVINCE OF ONTARIO. The important sources found among these records are the *Statutes* of Ontario; the annual reports of the Commissioner of Crown Lands (printed in the *Sessional Papers*), which have much scattered information on agriculture in the Ottawa-Huron region; the annual reports of the Commissioner of Agriculture; and the *Report* of the Ontario Agricultural Commission. The last two deserve special consideration.

The annual report of the Commissioner of Agriculture, or to give it its full title, the *Annual Report of the Commissioner of Agriculture and Public Works* (or *Arts*) *for the Province of Ontario*, was really a continuation of the semi-official publication called the *Transactions of the Board of Agriculture of Upper Canada*, which is described farther on in this bibliography. During the eighteen-seventies it ordinarily contained an analysis of the reports of the agricultural and horticultural societies; the report of the Council of the Agricultural and Arts Association, including a description of the provincial exhibition; the report of the Ontario Veterinary College; the report (sometimes) of the Ontario Agricultural College; the report of the Fruit Growers' Association; the report of the Entomological Association; and an introduction by the Commissioner intended to bind these diverse elements together.

The *Report of the Ontario Agricultural Commission* (5 vols., Toronto, 1881) is of exceptional value, as the members of the body collected evidence on agriculture from a large number of competent witnesses. The *Report* has, however, two defects. One is that most of the witnesses relied on their memories, so that their description of events or conditions of even a decade earlier do not always agree with the evidence of the farm journals of the eighteen-sixties and early eighteen-seventies. A striking example is the completely inaccurate account of the wheat midge's activities. Except on certain subjects, such as horse-breeding, the *Report* is therefore reliable only for its description of nearly contemporary conditions. The other defect is a complete absence of investigation into the agricultural societies and their operations. It is true that the members of the Commission were authorized to look into the organization and functioning of these societies, but they decided that the work could be performed better by the Executive Council of the province, which would in any event have to accept responsibility for any changes that might be necessary.

(8) PRINTED OFFICIAL RECORDS OF THE UNITED KINGDOM. Comparatively little use has been made of these records, because most of the information they contain is readily accessible elsewhere. Some of them are nevertheless indispensable. Among these are the *Report from the Select Committee on Emigration from the United Kingdom* (London, 1826) and *Lord Durham's Report on the Affairs of British North America* (edited by Sir C. P. Lucas, 3 vols., Oxford, 1912).

(9) PRINTED OFFICIAL RECORDS OF THE UNITED STATES. These are valuable for the trade in agricultural products between Upper Canada and the United States. The most important is the report of I. D. Andrews entitled "On the Trade and Commerce of the British North American Colonies and upon the Trade of the Great Lakes and Rivers" (*House Executive Document*, 32nd Cong., 1st Sess., 1852-3, no. 136). Evidently the parts of this report dealing with Upper Canada were written by T. C. Keefer, an excellent authority. Only less important are the annual reports of the American consular officials at Toronto, Hamilton, and other centres, which began towards the end of the American Civil War, and continued past the time covered in this volume. Their value lies in the fact that they make it possible to trace changes in agriculture, particularly in its commercial aspects, from year to year in the same localities.

PRIVATE RECORDS

Some use has been made of these. The most significant are those left by some of the early merchants who were engaged in the fur, provision, or grain trades. The journals and letters of a Port Hope merchant (Elias Smith Papers, 1799-1800) are deposited in the Baker Library of Harvard University. The correspondence of others has been published, notably that of John Askin of Detroit and Sandwich, as the *John Askin Papers* (edited by M. M. Quaife, 2 vols., Detroit, 1928-31); that of John Richardson as "The John Richardson Letters" (ed. by E. A. Cruikshank, *Ontario Historical Society Papers and Records*, vol. VI, 1905); that of Robert Nichol of Fort Erie as "A Country Merchant in Upper Canada, 1800-1812" (ed. by E. A. Cruikshank, *Ontario Historical Society Papers and Records*, vol. XXV, 1929), and as "Additional Correspondence of Robert Nichol" (ed. by E. A. Cruikshank, *Ontario Historical Society Papers and Records*, vol. XXVI, 1930); and that of Richard Cartwright of Kingston as *Life and Letters of the Late Honourable Richard Cartwright*, (ed. by C. E. Cartwright, Toronto, 1876).

A collection of papers in the Ontario Archives (Manuscripts of Papers on Agricultural Subjects, 1853-1893, by Walter Riddell) consists of the manuscripts of articles and miscellaneous comments submitted to various agricultural publications. It contains little that the student will fail to find in the *Canadian Agriculturist* or the *Canada Farmer*.

CONTEMPORARY WORKS OF TRAVEL, DESCRIPTION, ETC.

The titles included below may be classified into several divisions, sometimes more or less overlapping: (1) works of travel or description, including gazetteers and immigration pamphlets; these are evaluated in the following paragraph; (2) diaries; (3) works of reminiscence, which are usually of little importance; (4) a few histories which are chiefly valuable for their accounts of events or conditions of their own day; (5) promotional publications of the early railways, which are useful for the economic aspects of agriculture; (6) works on such rather technical phases of agriculture as horse breeding; (7) miscellaneous reports, articles, and books with some bearing on agriculture.

Travel books, immigration pamphlets, gazetteers, and topographical descriptions constitute probably the best source material for studying the agriculture of the province before 1840; after this date, they decline steadily in importance. No part of North America was more fully described by travellers than Upper Canada. As might be expected, their accounts vary greatly in value. The best are the narratives of men who resided in the province for some time, like Talbot, Pickering, Howison, and Strickland. Two of these, Howison and Talbot, have been condemned for their aristocratic prejudices, but these do not destroy their usefulness as agricultural observers. Also of much value, though for a different reason, are books and pamphlets by certain travellers (beginning with Champlain) who simply passed through the province, or else resided in it for only a short time. Though they often made superficial and erroneous judgments, these writers must not be neglected, because, as visitors, they often remarked things to which the natives were so much accustomed that they did not think it worth while to include them in their statistical accounts or narratives of pioneer life. The ordinary casual traveller, however, contributed little to our store of information about agriculture; not one in a dozen of the "summer visits" or "agricultural rambles" or "subaltern's furloughs" deserves more than a brief glance. Travel books, taken as a whole, emphasize pioneer life and agriculture. For this reason, those who rely on them to the exclusion of other sources may obtain a distorted view of early farming. They may, indeed, fail to recognize the existence of the cleared farm stage entirely. Immigration pamphlets tend to gloss over pioneer difficulties, and sometimes to glorify the work of the Canada Company.

The list following is restricted to the titles which are actually cited or quoted in this volume.

An Account of the Remarkable Occurrences in the Life and Travels of Col. James Smith, during his Captivity with the Indians in the Years 1755, '56, '57, '58, & '59 (edited by William Darlington, Cincinnati, 1870).

Address of the Directing President of the Western District Agricultural and Horticultural Society (Sandwich, 1838).

Agriculture of the United States in 1860: Compiled from the Original Returns of the Eighth Census (Washington, 1864).

AIKINS, CHARLES. "Journal of a Journey from Sandwich to York in the Summer of 1806" (*Ontario Historical Society Papers and Records*, Toronto, vol. VI, 1905).

ALEXANDER, J. E. *Transatlantic Sketches, comprising Visits to the Most Interesting Scenes in North and South America, and the West Indies. With Notes on Negro Slavery and Canadian Emigration* (2 vols., London, 1833).

American Husbandry (edited by H. J. Carman, New York, 1939).

ANDREWS, I. D. "Report on the Trade and Commerce of the British North American Colonies and upon the Trade of the Great Lakes and Rivers" (*House Executive Document*, 32nd Cong., 1st Sess., 1852-3, No. 136).

BEAVEN, JAMES. *Recreations of a Long Vacation; or a Visit to Indian Missions in Upper Canada* (London and Toronto, 1846).

BELL, WILLIAM. *Hints to Emigrants in a Series of Letters from Upper Canada* (Edinburgh, 1824).

BIGSBY, J. J. *The Shoe and Canoe or Pictures of Travel in the Canadas* (2 vols., London, 1850).

[BIRD, ISABELLA.] *The Englishwoman in America* (2nd ed., London, 1856).

BLISS, E. F. (ed.). *Diary of David Zeisberger, a Moravian Missionary among the Indians of Ohio* (2 vols., Cincinnati, 1885).

BLOIS, J. T. *Gazetteer of the State of Michigan* (Detroit and New York, 1838).

BOND, B. W., JR. (ed.). "The Captivity of Charles Stuart, 1755-57" (*Mississippi Valley Historical Review*, Cedar Rapids, vol. XIII, 1926-7).

BONNYCASTLE, SIR R. H. *Canada and the Canadians in 1846* (2 vols., London, 1846).

BOUCHER, PIERRE. *True and Genuine Description of New France, commonly called Canada, and of the Manners and Customs and Productions of that Country* (ed. by E. L. Montizambert, Montreal, 1883).

BOUCHETTE, JOSEPH. *The British Dominions in North America or a Topographical and Statistical Description of the Provinces of Lower and Upper Canada, New Brunswick, Nova Scotia, the Islands of Newfoundland, Prince Edward, and Cape Breton* (2 vols., London, 1831).
A Topographical Description of the Province of Lower Canada, with Remarks on Upper Canada (London, 1815).

BOULTON, D'ARCY. *Sketch of his Majesty's Province of Upper Canada* (London, 1805).

BREWER, W. H. "Report on the Cereal Production of the United States" (*Tenth Census of the United States*, Washington, 1883, vol. III).

BRONDGEEST, J. T. "Preservation of Food" (*The Westminster Review*, American edition, New York, vol. L, 1848-9).

BROWN, J. B. *Views of Canada and the Colonists* (Edinburgh, 1844; 2nd ed., rev., Edinburgh, 1851).

BUCKINGHAM, J. S. *Canada, Nova Scotia, New Brunswick, and the Other British Provinces in North America, with a Plan of National Colonization* (London, 1843).

CAMPBELL, PATRICK. *Travels in the Interior Inhabited Parts of North America in the Years 1791 and 1792* (ed. by H. H. Langton, Toronto, 1937).

Canada, 1862: For the Information of Emigrants (Quebec, 1862).

Canada [Shorthorn] Herd Book (Toronto, 1867).

Canadian Agricultural Reader, Designed Principally for the Use of Schools (Niagara, 1845).

Canadian Handbook and Tourist's Guide; Giving a Description of Canadian Lake and River Scenery and Places of Historical Interest with the Best Spots for Fishing and Shooting (Montreal, 1867).

"Canadian Letters: Descriptive of a Tour thro' the Provinces of Lower and Upper Canada, in the Course of the Years 1792 and '93" (*Canadian Antiquarian and Numismatic Journal*, Montreal, 3rd series, vol. IX, 1912).

"CANADIAN SETTLER." *The Emigrant's Informant or a Guide to Upper Canada* (London, 1834).

CARRUTHERS, J. *Retrospect of Thirty-Six Years' Residence in Canada West: Being a Christian Journal and Narrative* (Hamilton, 1861).

CHARLEVOIX, P. F. X. DE. *Histoire et description générale de la Nouvelle France, avec le journal historique d'un voyage fait par ordre du roi dans l'Amérique septentrionnale* (3 vols., Paris, 1744).

CHRISTIE, A. J. *The Emigrant's Assistant: or Remarks on the Agricultural Interest of the Canadas* (Montreal, 1821).

CLARKE, CHARLES. *Sixty Years in Upper Canada* (Toronto, 1908).

COKE, E. T. *A Subaltern's Furlough: Descriptive of Scenes in Various Parts of the United States, Upper and Lower Canada, New Brunswick, and Nova Scotia, during the Summer and Autumn of 1832* (London, 1833).

COPLESTON, MRS. EDWARD. *Canada: Why We Live in It and Why We Like It* (London, 1861).

CROIL, JAMES. *Dundas, or a Sketch of Canadian History* (Montreal, 1861).

DALTON, WILLIAM. *Travels in the United States of America and Part of Upper Canada* (Appleby, 1821).

Debates of the Parliament of Canada, 1854-63 (Scrapbooks of newspaper clippings in the Library of Parliament, Ottawa; mainly from the Toronto *Globe*, the Toronto *Leader*, and the Quebec *Morning Chronicle and Mercury*).

DREW, BENJAMIN. *The Refugee: or the Narrative of Fugitive Slaves in Canada* (Boston, 1856).

DUNCUMB, THOMAS. *The British Emigrant's Advocate: Being a Manual for the Use of Emigrants and Travellers in British America and the United States* (London, 1837).

DUNLOP, WILLIAM. *Statistical Sketches of Upper Canada for the Use of Emigrants, by a Backwoodsman* (London, 1832).

DWIGHT, TIMOTHY. *Travels; in New-England and New-York* (4 vols., New Haven, 1821).

EMMONS, EBENEZER. "Agriculture of New York" (*Natural History of New York*, 5 vols., New York, Boston, and Albany, 1842 ff., vol. II).

An Englishman in America 1785: Being the Diary of Joseph Hadfield (ed. by Douglas S. Robertson, Toronto, 1933).

"EX-SETTLER." *Canada in the Years 1832, 1833, and 1834* (Dublin, 1835).

FERGUSSON, ADAM. *Practical Notes Made during a Tour in Canada and a Portion of the United States in MDCCCXXXI* (2nd ed., Edinburgh and London, 1834).

A Few Plain Directions for Persons Intending to Proceed as Settlers to his Majesty's Province of Upper Canada (London, 1820).

FIDLER, ISAAC. *Observations on Professions, Literature, Manners, and Emigration in the United States and Canada, Made during a Residence There in 1832* (New York, 1833).

FLINT, JAMES. *Letters from America: Containing Observations on the Climate of the Western States, the Manners of the People, the Prospects of Emigrants, etc., etc.* (ed. by R. G. Thwaites, *Early Western Travels*, vol. IX, Cleveland, 1904).

FOTHERGILL, CHARLES. *The York Almanac and Royal Calendar of Upper Canada for the Year 1825* (York, 1825).

FRANCHERE, GABRIEL. *Narrative of a Voyage to the Northwest Coast of America in the Years 1811, 1812, 1813, and 1814; or the First American Settlement on the Pacific* (ed. by R. G. Thwaites, *Early Western Travels*, vol. VI, Cleveland, 1904).

FRASER, JOSHUA. *Shanty, Forest and River Life in the Backwoods of Canada* (Montreal, 1883).

GARLAND, W. F. (ed.). "The Proudfoot Papers" (*Ontario Historical Society Papers and Records*, vols. XXVII, XXVIII, 1930, 1931).

GEIKIE, J. C. *Life in the Woods; A Boy's Narrative of the Adventures of a Settler's Family in Canada* (Boston and New York, 1865).

GIBSON, DAVID. "Conditions in York County a Century Ago" (*Ontario Historical Society Papers and Records*, vol. XXIV, 1927).

GOURLAY, ROBERT. *Statistical Account of Upper Canada* (2 vols., London, 1882).

GRANT, G. M. *Picturesque Canada: the Country as It Was and Is* (2 vols., Toronto, 1882).

GRANT, W. L. (ed.). *Voyages of Samuel de Champlain, 1604-1618* (New York, 1907).

GRAY, HUGH. *Letters from Canada Written during a Residence There in the Years 1806, 1807 and 1808; Shewing the Present State of Canada, its Productions — Trade — Commercial Importance and Political Relations* (London, 1809).

GRECE, C. F. *Facts and Observations respecting Canada and the United States of America Affording a Comparative View of the Inducements to Emigration Presented in Those Countries* (London, 1819).

HAIGHT, CANNIFF. *Country Life in Canada Fifty Years Ago: Personal Recollections and Reminiscences of a Sexagenarian* (Toronto, 1885). See above p. 356n.

HALIBURTON, T. C. *An Historical and Statistical Account of Nova-Scotia* (2 vols., Halifax, 1829).

HALL, FRANCIS. *Travels in Canada and the United States in 1816 and 1817* (London, 1818).

HARVEY, ARTHUR. *The Reciprocity Treaty: Its Advantages to the United States and to Canada* (Quebec, 1865).

HECKEWELDER, JOHN. *A Narrative of the Mission of the United Brethren among the Delaware and Mohegan Indians, from its Commencement, in the Year 1740, to the Close of the Year 1808* (Philadelphia, 1820).

HENNEPIN, LOUIS. *A Description of Louisiana* (ed. by J. G. Shea, New York, 1880).
A New Discovery of a Vast Country in America, extending above Four Thousand Miles, between New France and New Mexico (London, 1699).

HERBERT, H. W. *Frank Forester's Horse and Horsemanship of the United States and British Provinces of North America* (2 vols., New York, 1857).

HERIOT, GEORGE. *Travels through the Canadas: Containing a Description of the Picturesque Scenery on Some of the Rivers and Lakes; with an Account of the Productions, Commerce, and Inhabitants of those Provinces* (London, 1807).

[HILDRETH, S. P.] "Ten Days in Ohio; from the Diary of a Naturalist" (*American Journal of Arts and Sciences*, New Haven, vol. XXV, 1834).

HIND, H. Y. *Essay on the Insects and Diseases Injurious to the Wheat Crops* (Toronto, 1857).
et al. *Eighty Years' Progress of British North America Showing the Wonderful Development of its Natural Resources, by the Unbounded Energy and Enterprise of its Inhabitants* (Toronto, 1863).

HODGSON, ADAM. *Letters from North America Written during a Tour in the United States and Canada* (2 vols., Edinburgh and London, 1824).

HOUGH, F. B. (ed). *The Journals of Major Robert Rogers: Containing an Account of the Several Excursions He Made Under the Generals Who Commanded upon the Continent of North America During the Late War* (Albany, 1883).

HOWISON, JOHN. *Sketches of Upper Canada, Domestic, Local and Characteristic: To Which are Added Practical Details for the Information of Emigrants of Every Class* (Edinburgh and London, 1821).

HUME, G. H. *Canada as It Is* (New York, 1832).

Illustrated Historical Atlas of the County of Carleton, Ontario (Toronto, 1879).

JAMESON, ANNA. *Winter Studies and Summer Rambles in Canada* (2 vols., New York, 1839).

JOHNSTON, J. F. W. *Notes on North America: Agricultural, Economical and Social* (2 vols., Edinburgh and London, 1851).

JONES, H. J. "Diary 1837" (*Willison's Monthly*, Toronto, July, 1929).

KANE, PAUL. *Wanderings of an Artist among the Indians of North America from Canada to Vancouver's Island and Oregon through the Hudson's Bay Company's Territory and Back Again* (London, 1859).

KEEFER, T. C. *The Canals of Canada* (Toronto, 1850).
Montreal, [and] the Ottawa (Montreal, 1854).

KIRKWOOD, A., and MURPHY, J. J. *The Undeveloped Lands in Northern and Western Ontario* (Toronto, 1878).

KLIPPART, J. H. *The Wheat Plant: Its Origin, Culture, Growth, Development, Composition, Varieties, Diseases, etc. etc.* (Cincinnati, 1859).

LAHONTAN, BARON. *New Voyages to North America. Containing an Account of the Several Nations of that Vast Continent* (2 vols., London, 1703).

LANDON, FRED. (ed.). "The Diary of Benjamin Lundy Written during his Journey through Upper Canada, January, 1832" (*Ontario Historical Society Papers and Records*, vol. XIX, 1922).

LANGTON, JOHN. "On the Age of Timber Trees, and the Prospects of a Continuous Supply of Timber in Canada" (*Transactions of the Literary and Historical Society of Quebec*, Quebec, vol. V, 1862).

LA ROCHEFOUCAULT-LIANCOURT, DUC DE. *Travels through the United States of North America, the Country of the Iroquois, and Upper Canada in the Years 1795, 1796 and 1797* (2 vols., 2nd ed., London, 1800.)

LECLERCQ, CHRISTIAN. *The First Establishment of the Faith in New France* (ed. by John G. Shea, 2 vols., New York, 1881).

LEGGE, CHARLES, and MACDONALD, DUNCAN. *Report on Explorations North and South Sides of Ottawa River, for the Montreal Northern Colonization Railway from Grenville to Ottawa City* (Montreal, 1871).

Life and Journals of Kah-Ke-Wa-Quo-Na-By: (Rev. Peter Jones,) Wesleyan Missionary (Toronto, 1860).

LINDLEY, JACOB. "Account of a Journey to Attend the Indian Treaty, proposed to be held at Sandusky, in the Year 1793" (*Michigan Pioneer and Historical Collections*, Lansing, vol. XVII, 1892).

LINSLEY, D. C. *Morgan Horses: A Premium Essay on the Origin, History, and Characteristics of This Remarkable American Breed of Horses* (New York, 1857).

LOGAN, JAMES. *Notes of a Journey through Canada, the United States of America, and the West Indies* (Edinburgh, 1838).

M'DONALD, JOHN. *Narrative of a Voyage to Quebec, and Journey from Thence to New Lanark in Upper Canada* (2nd ed., Glasgow, 1822).

MACKENZIE, W. L. *Sketches of Canada and the United States* (London, 1833).

M'LEOD, D. *A Brief Review of the Settlement of Upper Canada by the U. E. Loyalists and Scotch Highlanders, in 1783: and of the Grievances which compelled the Canadas to have Recourse to Arms in Defence of their Rights and Liberties, in the Years 1837 and 1838* (Cleveland, 1841).

MACTAGGART, JOHN. *Three Years in Canada: an Account of the Actual State of the Country in 1826-8. Comprehending its Resources, Productions, Improvements, and Capabilities; and Including Sketches of the State of Society, Advice to Emigrants, &c.* (2 vols., London, 1829).

MAGRATH, T. W. *Authentic Letters from Upper Canada; with an Account of Canadian Field Sports* (Dublin, 1833).

MARRYATT, CAPTAIN. *A Diary in America, with Remarks on its Institutions* (Part Second, 3 vols., London, 1839).

MARTINEAU, HARRIET. *Retrospect of Western Travel* (2 vols., Cincinnati, 1838).

MELISH, JOHN. *Travels through the United States of America in the Years 1806 & 1807, and 1809, 1810 & 1811; Including an Account of Passages betwixt America & Britain, and Travels Through Various Parts of Britain, Ireland, and Canada* (Philadelphia, 1818).

MOODIE, SUSANNAH. *Roughing it in the Bush: or, Life in Canada* (2 vols., New York, 1852).

MURRAY, HUGH. *Historical and Descriptive Account of British America; Comprehending Canada Upper and Lower, Nova Scotia, New Brunswick, Newfoundland, Prince Edward Island, the Bermudas, and the Fur Countries* (3 vols., 2nd ed., Edinburgh, 1839).

NEED, THOMAS. *Six Years in the Bush: or Extracts from the Journal of a Settler in Upper Canada, 1832-38* (London, 1838).

The New World in 1859 being the United States and Canada, Illustrated and Described (New York and London, 1859).

NEFTEL, KNIGHT. "Report on Flour-Milling Processes" (*Tenth Census of the United States*, vol. III).

OGDEN, J. C. *A Tour through Upper and Lower Canada* (2nd ed., Wilmington, 1800).

O'REILLY, HENRY. *Sketches of Rochester; with Incidental Notices of Western New York* (Rochester, 1838).

PATTERSON, W. J. *Report on the Trade and Commerce of Montreal for 1864* (Montreal, 1865).
Statements relating to the Home and Foreign Trade of the Dominion of Canada, also Annual Report of the Commerce of Montreal for 1877 (Montreal, 1878).

PERRY, G. H. *The Staple Trade of Canada* (Ottawa, 1862).

PICKEN, ANDREW. *The Canadas as they at Present Commend Themselves to the Enterprize of Emigrants, Colonists, and Capitalists, Comprehending a Variety of Topographical Reports Concerning the Quality of the Land, etc., in Different Districts, and the Fullest General Information* (2nd ed., London, 1836).

PICKERING, JOSEPH. *Inquiries of an Emigrant: Being the Narrative of an English Farmer from the Year 1824 to 1830* (3rd ed., London, 1832).

PLAYFAIR, A. W. *Remarks on Mr. Justice Brown's Report to the Committee Appointed to Promote the St. Lawrence and Lake Huron Railroad, via Peterborough, Contrasted with a More Inland Route, via Smith's Falls, Perth, etc.* (Perth, 1852).

PRESTON, T. R. *Three Years' Residence in Canada, From 1837 to 1839, with Notes of a Winter Voyage to New York, and Journey thence to the British Possessions* (London, 1840).

Report of the Directors and Chief Engineer of the St. Lawrence and Ottawa Grand Junction Railway Company (Montreal, 1853).

"Report of the Executive Committee of the Western District Agricultural and Horticultural Society" (broadside, Sandwich [?], 1837).

ROGERS, MAJOR ROBERT. *A Concise Account of North America: Containing a Description of the Several British Colonies on that Continent including the Islands of Newfoundland, Cape Breton, &c.* (London, 1765).

ROLPH, THOMAS. *A Brief Account, together with Observations, Made during a Visit in the West Indies, and a Tour through the United States of America, in Parts of the Years 1832-3, together with a Statistical Account of Upper Canada* (Dundas, 1836).

SHANLY, WALTER. *Report on the Location, Surveys and Estimates of the Bytown and Prescott Railroad* (Bytown, 1851).

SHENSTON, T. S. *The Oxford County Gazetteer: Containing a Complete History of the County of Oxford* (Hamilton, 1852).

SHERRIFF, ALEXANDER. "Topographical Notices of the Country Lying between the Mouth of the Rideau and Penetanguishine, on Lake Huron" (*Transactions of the Literary and Historical Society of Quebec*, vol. II, 1831).

SHIRREFF, PATRICK. *Tour through North America, together with a Comprehensive View of the Canadas and the United States. As adapted for Agricultural Emigration* (Edinburgh, 1835).

SMALL, H. B. *The Products and Manufactures of the New Dominion* (Ottawa, 1872).
The Resources of the Ottawa District (Ottawa, 1872).

SMALLFIELD, ALBERT. *Lands and Resources of Renfrew County, Province of Ontario: a Handbook* (Renfrew, 1881).

SMITH, MICHAEL. *A Geographical View of the Province of Upper Canada; and Promiscuous Remarks on the Government* (3rd ed., Philadelphia, 1813).

SMITH, W. H. *Canada, Past, Present and Future: Being a Historical, Geographical, Geological and Statistical Account of Canada West* (2 vols., Toronto, 1852).

SMYTH, W. D. *A Short Topographical Description of His Majesty's Province of Upper Canada in North America* (London, 1799).

STANSBURY, P. *A Pedestrian Tour of Two Thousand Three Hundred Miles in North America* (New York, 1822).

STRICKLAND, SAMUEL. *Twenty-Seven Years in Canada West: or the Experience of an Early Settler* (2 vols., London, 1853).

STROHM, JOHN. "The Conestoga Horse" (Department of Agriculture Report for 1863, *House Executive Document*, 38th Cong., 1st Sess., 1863-4, No. 91).

STUART, CHARLES. *The Emigrant's Guide to Upper Canada: or Sketches of the Present State of that Province, collected from a Residence there during the Years 1817, 1818 and 1819* (London, 1820).

TALBOT, E. A. *Five Years' Residence in the Canadas: Including a Tour Through Part of the United States of America in the Year 1823* (2 vols., London, 1824).

"The Talbot Settlement and Buffalo in 1816" (*Ontario Historical Society Papers and Records*, vol. I, 1899).

THOMPSON, G. S. *Up to Date or the Life of a Lumberman* (Peterborough, 1895).

THOMPSON, SAMUEL. *Thompson's Mirror of Parliament* (Quebec, 1860).

TIMPERLAKE, J. *Illustrated Toronto Past and Present* (Toronto, 1877).

TOOKE, THOMAS. *A History of Prices, and of the State of the Circulation, from 1793 to 1837; Preceded by a Brief Sketch of the State of the Corn Trade in the Last Two Centuries* (2 vols., London, 1838).

TORONTO BOARD OF TRADE. *Annual Reports*, 1855, 1860.

TRAILL, MRS. C. P. *The Backwoods of Canada: Being Letters from the Wife of an Emigrant Officer Illustrative of the Domestic Economy of British America* (London, 1836). New edition (ed. by E. Caswell, Toronto, 1929).

TROUT, J. M., and TROUT, EDWARD. *The Railways of Canada for 1870-1, Shewing the Progress, Mileage, Cost of Construction, etc.* (Toronto, 1871).

WALLACE, J. H. *Wallace's American Trotting Register, Containing All That is Known of the Pedigrees of Trotting Horses, Their Ancestors and Descendants* (New York, 1871).

WALLACE, W. S. (ed.). "Captain Miles Macdonell's 'Journal of a Jaunt to Amherstburg' in 1801" (*Canadian Historical Review*, Toronto, vol. XXV, 1944).

WARR, G. W. *Canada as It Is: or the Emigrant's Friend and Guide to Upper Canada Being a Sketch of the Country* (London, 1847).

WATSON, W. C. (ed.). *Men and Times of the Revolution: or Memoirs of Elkanah Watson, including Journals of Travels in Europe and America, from 1777 to 1842* (New York, 1856).

WELD, C. R. *A Vacation Tour in the United States and Canada* (London, 1855).

WELD, ISAAC. *Travels through the States of North America and the Provinces of Upper and Lower Canada, during the Years 1795, 1796 and 1797* (4th ed., 2 vols., London, 1807).

WELLS, W. B. *Canadiana: Containing Sketches of Upper Canada and the Crisis in its Political Affairs* (London, 1837).

WIDDER, F. *Information for Intending Emigrants of All Classes to Upper Canada* (Toronto, 1855).

WILSON, DANIEL. "Ontario" (*Encyclopædia Britannica*, 9th ed., New York, vol. XVII, 1884).

ZEISBERGER, DAVID. *History of the Northern American Indians* (edited by A. B. Hulbert and W. N. Schwarze, Columbus, 1910).

NEWSPAPERS

In the preparation of this volume a considerable number of newspapers was consulted. Except for a few stray items, and some advertisements, newspapers are rather disappointing as a source of information till about 1825. Before that date, events as well as conditions of agricultural significance went unnoticed, doubtless because the population of the community was so small that everything of local interest was known without publication. After 1825 the newspapers steadily gain in value. In general, the information they contain is concerned with the commercial aspects of agriculture—crops, marketing problems, land policy, tariff policy, and the like. After about 1860 there is little of agricultural interest in the newspapers, except for the surveys of the commercial operations of the preceding year, which they usually printed some time in January. On the whole, the most important newspapers were those published at Toronto (earlier York). Of these, the *Colonial Advocate*, the *Examiner*, and the *Globe* supply the most material. The newspapers of Montreal derive their value from the fact that that city was the commercial capital of the St. Lawrence Valley. The *Witness* was unique in that, being edited by a produce dealer, it appealed less to urban business men than to a rural constituency, much of which was in Upper Canada. Of the village or town weeklies consulted, the most useful was the Perth *Bathurst Courier*. The files of newspapers actually searched, with their dates, follow. Some of them were of such little worth that no mention is made of them in the references in this volume.

Bytown Gazette and Ottawa and Rideau Advertiser, 1836-45
Bytown Packet, 1849-51
Cobourg Star, 1837-41
Guelph Advertiser, 1849-53
Guelph and Galt Advertiser and Wellington District Advocate, 1847-9
Hallowell Free Press, 1832-3
Kingston Chronicle and News, 1854-8
Kingston *Daily News*, 1851, 1871
Kingston Gazette, 1812-15
Kingston Gazette and Religious Advocate, 1829-30
Kingston *Upper Canada Herald*, 1825
Montreal *Canadian Courant*, 1829-34
Montreal *Gazette*, 1827-40
Montreal *Transcript*, 1841-54
Montreal *Witness*, 1852-6 (weekly); 1857-71 (biweekly); 1872-6 (triweekly); 1877-8 (weekly)
Newark ("West Niagara") *Upper Canada Gazette or American Oracle*, 1793, 1796-8

Niagara *Canada Constellation,* 1799-1800
Niagara Herald, 1801-2
Ottawa *Citizen,* 1859-60, 1866-9, Sept. 19, 1936
Perth *Bathurst Courier,* 1835-57
Perth Courier, 1857-66
Quebec Gazette, 1800-3
Quebec Mercury, 1808-11
Toronto *Christian Guardian,* 1834-41
Toronto *Examiner,* 1840-9
Toronto *Globe,* 1849-53 (triweekly); 1854-7 (weekly); 1859-72 (daily);
   1876-9 (weekly)
York *Christian Guardian,* 1832-3
York *Colonial Advocate,* 1830-3
York *Courier of Upper Canada,* 1832
York Gazette, 1807-9
York *Loyalist,* 1828
York *Upper Canada Gazette,* 1820
York *Upper Canada Gazette and U. E. Loyalist,* 1826-8
York *Upper Canada Gazette or American Oracle,* 1798-1807

AGRICULTURAL PERIODICALS AND RELATED PUBLICATIONS

Beginning in 1842, with the advent of the *British American Culti-vator,* farm journals and related publications provide the best source material for the agricultural history of Upper Canada.

There were before this date and afterwards a few farm journals in Upper Canada which either never got beyond the prospectus stage, or else were published only a few months, or else were thought so little worthy of preservation that no copies are now known to be in existence. Among these were the *Upper Canada Farmer,* announced as about to be published at Cobourg in 1837; the *Canadian Cultivator and Farmer's Magazine of Useful Knowledge,* which evidently had a short career at St. Catharines in 1839; and the *Canadische Bauernfreund,* mentioned in 1851 as being published at Preston. Other journals are represented in libraries by scattered issues. Among these are the *Farmer and Mechanic* of Toronto, which appeared in 1848, and the *Newcastle Farmer,* which was published at Cobourg between 1846 and 1848. All of these journals are, however, interesting merely as curiosities. The important farm journals of Upper Canada and Ontario were these: the *British American Cultivator* (1842-7), the first *Canada Farmer* (1847), the *Agriculturist and Canadian Journal* (1848), the *Canadian Agriculturist* (1849-63), the second *Canada Farmer* (1864-76), the *Farmer's Advocate* (1866 ff.), the *Ontario Farmer* (1869-71), and the *Weekly Globe* (1877 ff.). Together they provide a continuous history, month by month, of agricultural development in the province. The reader who is interested in them will find further information in Fred Landon, "The Agricultural Journals of Upper Canada (Ontario)" (*Agricultural History*, Washington, vol. IX, 1935).

For the historian, the most valuable portions of these farm journals are the editorial comments, the market reports, the excerpts from local newspapers, the reports of the proceedings of farmers' clubs, the descriptions of the exhibitions, and the letters from correspondents. One journal, the *Canadian Agriculturist*, had also a number of prize essays. As these appeared subsequently in the *Journal and Transactions* (or the *Transactions*) of the Board of Agriculture of Upper Canada, discussion of them is postponed for the time being. However, in 1862 the *Canadian Agriculturist* published an essay by Walter Riddell which was not written for a prize and which was therefore not included in the publications of the Board of Agriculture. The essay—"Hints for an Agricultural Report of the Township of Hamilton"—is a detailed account of the progress of farming in the vicinity of Cobourg from about 1830 to 1862. A paraphrase of it, with some unreliable additions, may be found as "Farming in Northumberland County: 1833 to 1895" (ed. by W. R. Riddell), in *Ontario Historical Society Papers and Records*, vol. XXX, 1934. It must be remembered that in even the best of the farm journals, such as the second *Canada Farmer*, the material of interest to the historian is incidental to the great mass of practical advice offered to the subscribers. As the indexes are invariably poor, the volumes have to be read carefully, page by page.

The agricultural journals of Lower Canada and Quebec have been used to supplement the material found in those of Upper Canada and Ontario. In general, the farm periodicals published at Montreal during the period covered by this volume are distinctly inferior to those published at Toronto, Hamilton, or London. They tend to be highly theoretical in their approach to agricultural problems and practices; they incorporate few newspaper clippings; and they have almost no rural correspondence.

A good deal of information has been derived from American farm journals, especially from those which circulated north of the border. They have frequent items on agriculture in Upper Canada, some of which are not to be found in the journals published in the province. The only one of these American farm journals really indispensable for the study of Upper Canadian farming is, however, the Albany *Cultivator*.

Closely allied with the farm journals in subject matter was the publication known first as the *Journal and Transactions of the Board of Agriculture of Upper Canada*, then as the *Transactions of the Board of Agriculture and of the Agricultural Association of Upper Canada*, and finally as the *Transactions of the Board of Agriculture of Upper Canada*. It had an emphasis different from that of the ordinary farm journals, though in its early years much of its material also appeared in the *Canadian Agriculturist*. It contained reports from the county and township agricultural societies, speeches delivered at the provincial exhibitions, and prize essays. There is much useful if fragmentary information in the agricultural society reports, there are often acute generalizations in the speeches of the presidents of the Agricultural Association, but it is from the prize essays that the *Journal and Transactions* derives its unique value. In 1851 the Board of Agriculture decided to offer prizes for the four best reports submitted by county agricultural societies, and in 1852 it threw the prizes open to general competition. Between 1852 and 1856 it awarded prizes to the authors of fifteen county essays, and published the essays in the *Journal and Transactions*, and as has been previously mentioned, in the *Canadian Agriculturist*. These essays were on the following counties, the dates being those in which they were entered in competition: Hastings, 1852; Wellington, 1852; Grey, 1853; Peel (two essays), 1853; York, Ontario, and Peel together, 1853; Carleton (two essays), 1854; Prince Edward, 1854; Welland, 1854; Bruce, 1855; Simcoe (two essays), 1855; Addington, 1856; Huron, 1856. In 1857 the Board published in its *Transactions*, and then separately, an essay on economic entomology, for which the Bureau of Agriculture had awarded a prize of £40. This was Professor H. Y. Hind's *Essay on the Insects and Diseases Injurious to the Wheat Crops* (Toronto, 1857), a valuable history of wheat pests, especially the midge. Then, after a lapse of a few years, the Board of Agriculture again offered prizes for the best county and township agricultural society reports. The best, that on Dundas County, shortly after its publication in the *Transactions* appeared in a somewhat modified form as James Croil's *Dundas, or a Sketch of Canadian History* (Montreal, 1861). The great value of the county prize essays arises from the fact that their authors, who were instructed to describe the farming methods actually prevailing in their localities, did so conscientiously. Some of them produced works of exceptional clarity and insight, especially John Lynch of Brampton, who wrote four of the essays, one on each of Peel, Simcoe, Grey, and Bruce counties. None of the adjacent states had descriptions of its agriculture in the eighteen-fifties so complete and penetrating as those found in these prize essays. They are therefore indispensable to the historian of agriculture (and only slightly less valuable to the student of general economic development) in Upper Canada between 1845 and 1855. In spite of this, the present volume is the only one ever published which makes any use of their wealth of material.

The *Canadian Merchants' Magazine*, published at Toronto during the late eighteen-fifties, though intended, as its title suggests, primarily for the business community, devoted sufficient attention to agriculture, particularly in its trade aspects, to justify its inclusion in the list below.

A list of the farm journals and related publications actually consulted in the preparation of this study follows:

L'Agriculteur (Montreal), 1858-62

Agricultural Journal and Transactions of the Lower Canada Agricultural Society (Montreal), 1848-52

Agriculturist and Canadian Journal (Toronto), 1848

American Agriculturist (New York), 1859-68, 1876

American Farmer (Baltimore), 1819-28

British American Cultivator (Toronto), 1842-7

British Farmer's Magazine (London, Eng.), 1835

Canada Farmer (Eastwood, publ., Toronto), 1847

Canada Farmer (Brown, publ., Toronto), 1864-76

Canada Agricultural Journal (Montreal), 1844-6

Canadian Agriculturist (Toronto), 1849-58

Canadian Agriculturist and Journal of the Board of Agriculture of Upper Canada (Toronto), 1858-9

Canadian Agriculturist and Journal and Transactions of the Board of Agriculture of Upper Canada (Toronto), 1860-3

Canadian Merchants' Magazine and Commercial Review (Toronto), 1857-9

Canadian Quarterly Agricultural and Industrial Magazine (Montreal), 1838

Clark's Sorgo Journal (Cincinnati), 1863

Country Gentleman (Albany), 1853-9

Cultivator (Albany), 1838-60

Cultivator and Country Gentleman (Albany), 1866

Farmer's Advocate (London), 1874-86

Farmer's Journal and Transactions of the Lower Canada Board of Agriculture (Montreal), 1859-60

Genesee Farmer (Rochester), 1831-4, 1847-8, 1863

Illustrated Journal of Agriculture (Montreal), 1879-86

Journal and Transactions of the Board of Agriculture of Upper Canada (2 vols., Toronto), 1855-6, 1856-7

Journal d'Agriculture (Montreal), 1848-52

Lower Canada Agriculturist (Montreal), 1862-3

Michigan Farmer (Jackson, Detroit), 1845-9

National Live Stock Journal (Chicago), 1876-81

New England Farmer (Boston), 1822-4, 1829-31, 1849-50, 1859-60

New York State Agricultural Society *Transactions* (Albany), 1841-60

Ohio Cultivator (Columbus), 1845-60

Ohio Farmer (Cleveland), 1852-8

Ohio State Board of Agriculture *Reports* (Columbus), 1846-65

Ontario Farmer (Toronto, Hamilton), 1869-71

Prairie Farmer (Chicago), 1849-52, 1862-3

Revue agricole, manufacturière, commerciale et de colonisation (Montreal), 1861-8

Spirit of the Times (New York), 1840-57

Transactions of the Board of Agriculture and of the Agricultural Association of Upper Canada (2 vols., Toronto), 1858-9, 1859-60

Transactions of the Board of Agriculture of Upper Canada (2 vols., Toronto), 1860-3, 1864-8

Weekly Globe (Toronto), 1877-9 (also listed among newspapers)

Western Agriculturist (Columbus), 1851

Western Farmer (Cincinnati), 1839-40

Western Farmer (Detroit), 1841

Western Farmer and Gardener (Cincinnati), 1840-6

INDEX

Abandoned farms, 2, 113, 302

Addington County: essay, 388; grain-growing, 242; livestock industry, 193-4; shanty market, 300; *see also* Addington Road, Bay of Quinte, Midland District

Addington Road, 291, 292

Adjala Township: settlement, 50

Agrarianism, 130-2, 347-52

Agricultural advantages of the Loyalists, 19

Agricultural and Arts Association (of Ontario), 332, 333, 334, 334n

Agricultural Association of Upper Canada, 137, 170-1, 196, 328-9, 333, 342

Agricultural background of the Rebellion of 1837, 124n

Agricultural conventions, *1843*, *1846*, 171

Agricultural history of Ontario, periods in, 355-9

Agricultural journals, 140, 174, 386-9

Agricultural societies: development, 156-8, 162-4, 164n, 168-9, 335-7; functions and achievements, 103-4, 149, 150, 153, 159-61, 165-8, 168-9, 170, 173-4, 281-2, 336-7, 340, 352; *see also* Agricultural Association of Upper Canada, Exhibitions, Farmers' clubs

Agricultural Society of Upper Canada, 157-8, 158, 159

Agricultural statutes: *1850*, 328; *1857*, 329, 335

Agriculture (for Ontario), Commissioner of, 333-4

Agriculture of (the Province of) Canada, Bureau of. *See* Bureau of Agriculture of (the Province of) Canada

Agriculture of (the Province of) Canada, Department of. *See* Department of Agriculture of (the Province of) Canada

Agriculture of Ontario and the northern United States compared: British influences, 62-3, 354-5; cattle fairs, 210; comparative prosperity, 81n; exhibitions, 166-7, 342; grain-growing, 87, 93n, 101, 194n, 353; Granger movement, 345-7; implements, 310; livestock industry, 127, 147n, 148, 150, 151, 152, 155, 194n, 268, 269, 271, 354; pioneering, 18-9, 215n; railway-construction effects, 186

Albany, N.Y.: grain market, 218, 219; livestock market, 31, 193, 210; New York State Fair at, 342

Albany County, N.Y.: livestock industry, 226n

Algonquin Park, 303n

"Allengrove" cheese-factory combine, 256

Allumette Island (P.Q.): Indian agriculture, 5

Alsike, 325n

Ameliasburgh Township: agricultural society, 352; dairying, 263-4; politics, 352

American Civil War: effects on American agriculture, 216, 218, 219-20, 220, 224, 225; effects on Upper Canadian agriculture, 192, 216-30, 232-3, 253, 281, 309

American influences on Ontario
agriculture: agricultural organizations, 161-2, 169, 171, 345-7;
dairy industry, 30-1, 251, 254,
258; exhibitions, 166-7; fruit-
growing, 320n, 321; grain trade,
238; Granger movement, 345-6;
horse-racing, 342-3; livestock
industry, 31, 149; pioneering,
19-20; wool-growing, 194n, 226
Amherstburg region: fruit-growing, 14-5; livestock industry,
133n, 147n; settlement, 12-3;
tobacco-growing, 40-1; see also
Essex County
Ancaster Township: oak-plains, 5
Apples, 7, 14, 22, 78, 212, 319;
domestic markets for, 210, 211;
exported to British Isles, 211,
319; exported to the United
States, 319; pests affecting, 212;
varieties of, 210-1, 319
Arnprior: shanty depot, 118
Arran Township: settlement, 55
Ashes as a fertilizer, 93
Askin, John, merchant, 24
Asphodel Township: agricultural
society, 103
Association of the Live Stock
Dealers of Western Ontario, 352
Assumption College: proposed
farm school, 331n
Athens: cheese factory, 254
Aylesbury ducks, 155
Ayrshire cattle, 150, 270n

Baden: linseed-oil mill, 317
Baldoon: sheep-raising, 152
Barley, 13, 86, 86n, 88, 217-9, 238-9,
239-42, 302; domestic market for,
241; exported to British Isles,
241; exported to the United
States, 178-9, 181, 218-9, 240-1;
production statistics, 86, 86n,

239, 242; shift from wheat to,
218, 242, 247; superiority of
Ontario, 219, 240
Barley ports, 236, 346
Barns, 53, 84, 199, 203, 306, 326
Bateaux in grain trade, 29-30, 107,
107n
Bathurst District: agricultural
society, 164, 165; cattle fair, 119;
livestock industry, 165
Bay of Quinte: climate, 3; dairy
industry, 251, 252-3; grain-
growing, 22n, 28, 88, 90, 99, 117,
138, 240n, 324; gypsum, 93; hop-
growing, 220; Indian agriculture,
52; livestock industry, 129, 140,
182, 285; pioneering, 82; pork-
packing, 23; settlement, 17, 18,
63, 356, 357n; soil exhaustion,
324; superior farming, 63; trade
with the United States, 129, 182;
see also Addington County,
Frontenac County, Hastings
County, Lennox County, Prince
Edward County
Beans, 7, 317; exported to the
United States, 317
Bears, 6, 78n
Bee hunters, 79-80
Beef imported from the United
States, 39, 45, 128, 210n
Bees (honey), 79-80, 80n, 318, 325n
Bees (husking, etc.), 21, 83, 312n
Belgium: grain market, 243
Belleville: cheese board, 259; dairy
market, 259, 260; railroads, 187,
188; shanty market, 297
Belleville region: dairy industry,
256, 258; see also Hastings
County
Berkshire swine, 151-2, 273, 273n
Berries, 7, 78, 322-3
Billings, Bradish, dairyman, 252
Binders, 312

Black Hawk horses, 268

Black Java hens, 155

Black Sea wheat, 102

Black stem rust of wheat, 101, 204

Board of Agriculture of Upper Canada, 221-2, 328, 329, 329-30, 330-1, 332, 333; proceedings and transactions, 329-30, 387-8

Bobcaygeon Road, 291, 292

Bonnechere Valley: lumbering, 110; portaging, 116; settlement, 112-3, 292

Boston, Mass.: dairy market, 262; egg and poultry market, 287; exhibition at, 342; flour market, 192; livestock market, 184, 193, 210, 225, 275, 278, 279; Ogdensburg Railroad and, 180; speculators from in Upper Canada, 181

Bosworth: cattle fair, 282n

Bothwell (electoral district): grain-growing, 243; tobacco-growing, 316

Bounties for hemp, 43

Bowmanville: exhibition, 165-6; grain market, 235n

Brahmahputra hens, 155, 274

Brampton: cattle fairs, 161, 282n

Brant County: hop-growing, 220; livestock industry, 269n, 284; oak-plains, 5; see also Brantford region, Gore District, Grand River Valley

Brantford: Agricultural Association meeting at, 334; cattle fair, 281-2; dairy market, 252; provincial exhibition at, 337; railroad interests, 188

Brantford region: grain-growing, 52; Indian agriculture, 52; livestock industry, 52; see also Brant County

Bremen geese, 155

Breweries, 23-4, 88, 241

Brighton and Cramahe Farmers' Club, 344

British American Cultivator, 174

British influences on Ontario agriculture: agricultural organizations, 162, 171; compared with American influences, 21-2, 53, 61, 354-5; farming improvements in general, 61-3, 354-5; grain-growing, 86, 87; livestock industry, 149, 151, 153; settlement, 50

British Isles: agricultural market in general, 354; dairy market, 250, 257, 259-60, 262-3, 263, 358-9; egg and poultry market, 287; flour and grain market, 25-6, 27-8, 28, 38-9, 46-7, 47-8, 88, 122, 124-5, 134-5, 136n, 204, 216, 232-3, 241, 243, 244; fruit market, 211, 319; immigration from, 50, 59-60; livestock market, 280-1, 359; pork market, 224, 224-5, 286; source of livestock, 146, 147-8, 151, 151-2, 152n, 153, 267, 267n, 269, 270, 272, 273; wool market, 226n

British West Indies: dairy market, 250; flour market, 28, 47, 122, 125

Brock District: agricultural society, 164

Brockville: implement factory, 312n; provincial exhibition, 337; railroad interests, 180, 187

Brockville and Ottawa Railway, 188

Brockville region: dairy industry, 253, 256, 262; grain-growing, 138; livestock industry, 179; politics, 58-9; trade with the United States, 179, 227-8; see also Leeds County

Bruce County: essay, 388; grain-growing, 99n, 237, 244n, 247, 248, 324; Granger movement, 347; land speculation, 215; livestock industry, 285; settlement, 55

Bruce Township: settlement, 55

Buckland, Professor George, 329, 331, 344

Buckwheat, 13, 22, 73, 86, 88, 92, 239, 324; production statistics, 86, 86n, 239

Buff Cochin China hens, 155, 274

Buffalo, N.Y.: dairy market, 179n; egg market, 179n; fruit market, 211, 322; grain market, 177; livestock market, 184, 193, 225, 279; packing industry, 225; railroad interests, 188; Robinson, John B., on, 82n; smuggling at, 179n

Buffalo and Lake Huron Railroad, 188, 225

Bureau of Agriculture and Arts (Ontario), 333-4

Bureau of Agriculture of (the Province of) Canada, 332-3

Burford Township: oak-plains, 5

Burlington Board of Agriculture, 158

Butter, 252, 253, 261-2, 302; exported to British Isles, 250, 260, 263; exported to British West Indies, 250; exported to Maritime Provinces, 250; exported to the United States, 178-9, 179n, 181-2, 228, 253, 253n, 262; manufacturing methods, 261-2; production statistics, 253; speculators, 253n, 262

Bytown. See Ottawa

Bytown and Prescott Railway, 188

Caledon Township: pioneers, 59

Caledonia Springs: horse-racing, 168n

California: emigration to, 183n, 199; livestock market, 183n, 278

Calves, 264, 264n; exported to the United States, 279

Cambridge, Mass.: cattle market, 184n

Cameron, Hon. Malcolm, and colonization roads, 292

Canada Central Railway, 302

Canada Company: exhibition grants, 164n, 171, 172; flax-growing encouragement, 221; hemp-growing encouragement, 221; land speculation, 69-70, 70n, 131

Canada Corn Act (imperial), 1843, effects of, 135-7

Canada Farmer, 174

Canada Herd Book, 333

Canada Trade Act (imperial), 1822, 44-5, 124

Canada West. See Ontario

Canadian Agriculturist, 329, 330

Canadian Dairymen's Association, 258

Canadian Land and Emigration Company, 301n

Canadian Pacers, 145

Canneries, 321

Capital required by pioneer, 67

Cardinal: cattle-fattening, 285

Cardwell (electoral division): grain-growing, 242

Carleton County: dairy industry, 302; essays, 388; grain-growing, 119, 302; implements, 201; livestock industry, 119, 147-8, 150n, 274-5, 278; pork-packing, 119; shanty market, 119, 301-2; see also Military Settlements, Rideau Canal region

Carling, Hon. John: Commissioner of Agriculture for Ontario, 334; establishment of Ontario Agricultural College, 335

Caswell, Edwin, cheese dealer, 259

Cataraqui (formerly Waterloo): exhibitions, 162, 163

Cattle (beef): development of industry *before 1812*, 10, 11, 14, 14n, 15, 31-2, *1812-1850*, 126-30, 133-4, *1850-1867*, 179, 182-3, 192-3, 228-9, *1867-1880*, 264, 278-81, 281-5, 359; exported to British Isles, 280, 280-1; exported to the United States, 31-2, 129, 129n, 149, 178-9, 179, 179n, 182-3, 185n, 192-3, 193n, 210, 223, 228-9, 278-80; imported from British Isles, 151, 270; imported from Quebec, 9, 11, 140, 150; imported from the United States, 10, 17, 37, 38, 39, 45, 126-7, 127-8, 133n, 140, 140n, 151, 165; improvement, 148-51, 165, 265, 269-71, 284; kinds or breeds of *(see also* Ayrshire cattle, etc.), 142, 150-1, 269-71; methods of raising, 14, 22-3, 31-2, 75-6, 128, 149, 213, 243-4, 244, 284-5; production statistics, 287n; rustling, 183; shanty market for, 119, 281

Cattle fairs: *before 1812*, 156, 159; *1812-1850*, 119, 159-61, 161, 179; *1850-1880*, 210, 210n, 281-4

"Cattle shows" at cattle fairs, 159, 161

Cavan Township: grain-growing, 102; livestock industry, 184; trade with the United States, 184

Central Fair: at Cobourg, 339; at Hamilton, 337-8

Champlain, Samuel de, on Indian agriculture, 5-8, 9

Chatsworth: cattle fair, 281

Cheese: boards, 259; dealers, 259; development of dairy manufacturing of, 30-1, 250-2, 253; development of factory manufacturing of, 254-9; exported to British Isles, 257, 259-60; exported to the United States, 181; imported from the United States, 133, 250; marketing difficulties, 259; production statistics, 251, 260; *see also* Dairy industry

Cheese-and-butter factories, 263

Cheese-and-butter train, 259

Cherries, 7, 22, 78, 211, 322

Cheviot sheep, 272, 272n

Chicago, Ill.: grain trade, 191, 233-4, 234, 236; source of pork, 224; source of swine, 224, 286

Chinese geese, 155

Chinguacousy Township: agricultural society, 161; cattle fair, 161; grain-growing, 197

Chippewa: grain trade, 30

Cincinnati, Ohio: livestock market, 194, 194n; source of pork, 116, 128

Civil War, effects of American. *See* American Civil War

Clark County, Ohio: livestock industry, 127

Clarke, W. F., and Ontario Agricultural College, 335

Clear Grit horses, 268

Clear Grit party, 347-8, 349-51

Clergy reserves, 34, 68, 68n

Cleveland Bay horses, 146

Clifford: cattle fair, 282n

Climate of Southern Ontario, 3-4, 353

Clinton (Lincoln Co.): exhibition, 165

Clover: red, 73, 92, 99n, 325, 325n; white, 12, 73, 73n

Clover hullers ("concaves"), 99n
Club wheat, 102
Clydesdale horses, 147-8, 269, 275
Cobden: shanty market, 301n
Cobourg: agricultural society, 168;
    cattle fair, 159; dairy market,
    253n; exhibitions, local, 339,
    provincial, 1 4 8, 1 7 3, 3 3 7;
    farmers' club, 104, 169; horse-
    racing, 168n; railroad interest,
    187
Cobourg region: essay, 387; grain-
    growing, 100-1, 186, 203, 218;
    implements and machinery, 96,
    313; livestock industry, 154-5,
    194-5, 273-4; superior farming,
    81n; tenant farming, 62; trade
    with the United States, 194-5;
    see also Northumberland County
Codling moth, 212, 319
Colborne and Cobourg Agricultural
    Society, 168
"Cold summer" (1816), 37
Coldwater, Indian agriculture near,
    52
Collingwood: elevators, 234; grain
    trade, 233, 234; shanty market,
    300
Colonial Trade Act (imperial),
    1831, 124-5, 126, 130, 130n, 357
Colonization roads, 290-3, 297-8,
    299-300
Colorado potato beetle, 317n
Commercial Bank, effects of fail-
    ure, 1867, 237
Commissioner of Agriculture (for
    Ontario), 333-4
Committees of the Canadian legis-
    lature on: immigration and col-
    onization, 1865, 298-9; lumber
    trade and settlement, 1863, 298;
    management of the public lands,
    1855, 289-90; Ottawa-Huron
    region, 1864, 298

Concaves (clover hullers), 99n
Conestoga horses, 147, 147n
Connecticut: source of livestock,
    140
Conventions, agricultural, 1843,
    1846, 171
Corn: 6-7, 8-9, 10, 15, 22, 24, 73,
    86, 86n, 87, 239, 243-4; domestic
    markets for, 243; imported from
    the United States, 244-5; pro-
    duction statistics, 86, 86n, 239,
    243
Corn Laws, 27-8, 38-9, 46-7, 122,
    135; effects of repeal, 138-9, 175
Cornwall: horse-racing, 168n; rail-
    way interest, 187
Cornwall region: grain-growing,
    138; see also Stormont County
Cotswold sheep, 272, 272n, 276,
    277-8
Coulonge River (P.Q.), portaging
    up, 116
Council of the Agricultural and
    Arts Association, 333
Cradle scythe, 93, 93n
Cream separators, 263-4
Creameries, 263-4
Crimean War, agricultural effects
    of, 198, 204, 206, 358
Crop rotations, 12, 90-3, 186-7,
    206-7, 323-4, 324n
Crops: 1788, 17; 1794, 25-6; 1815,
    37; 1816, 37; 1828, 47; 1829, 47;
    1835, 123-4; 1836, 123-4; 1837,
    101, 123-4; 1838, 123-4; 1839,
    101, 125; 1840, 101; 1841, 101;
    1842, 86n, 101; 1843, 101, 136;
    1844, 101, 136, 138; 1845, 101,
    136; 1846, 101; 1847, 176; 1848,
    176; 1849, 101, 176; 1850, 86,
    101, 186; 1851, 186; 1852, 186;
    1853, 198; 1854, 198; 1855, 198;
    1856, 203; 1857, 200, 204; 1858,
    200, 204; 1859, 205; 1860, 205,

239; *1870*, 239, 325; *1871*, 247;
1872, 325; *1874*, 325; *1875*, 325;
1876, 325; *1880*, 239, 242, 248
Crown Lands Department criticized, 69
Crown reserves, 34, 69
Cultivators: corn, 87; field, 95, 201, 310-1
Cumberland horses, 269
Cumberland Improved swine, 273
Currants, 22, 323
Cutworm, 26n

Dairy industry: advantages and disadvantages, 250-1, 264, 265; American influences, 30-1, 251, 254, 258; development, 30-1, 229, 243-4, 250-65, 287n, 359; effects on beef-cattle industry, 279, 285; effects on swine raising, 224, 285; effects on wool-growing, 276, 276n; organizations, 258, 334, 334n, 352; refrigerated train, 259; shift from wheat to, 227, 251, 253; see also Butter, Cheese, Milk
Dairymen's Association of Eastern Ontario, 258, 334n
Dairymen's Association of Ontario, 258
Dairymen's Association of Western Ontario, 258, 334n, 352
Dakota Territory: emigration to, 304-5; livestock market, 275
Davies, William, packer, 286
Debating societies, 169
Delaware Township: exhibition, 342n
Department of Agriculture of (the Province of) Canada, 332-3
Depressions: *1810-2*, 32-3; *1819-25*, 39-40; *1834-8*, 123, 123n; *1846-9*, 121; *1857-60*, 193, 204-5, 207-8; *1864-5*, 227-8; *1873-8*, 325

Detroit, Mich.: firewood market, 51; fruit market, 322; garrison market, 15, 23, 26; livestock market, 31n, 129-30, 140n, 279; poultry market, 287; vegetable market, 318, 318n
Detroit settlement: agriculture in early, 12-5, 51; fruit-growing, 14-5, 22, 211; fur-trade supply source, 15, 24; grain-growing, 10, 12, 13; grain trade, 27, 27n; Indian agriculture, 10; livestock industry, 10, 14, 14n, 128n, 141; tobacco-growing, 40; see also Essex County
Devon cattle, 150, 150n, 270, 270n
Diseases of pioneers, 82-3
Distilleries, 23-4, 88, 243
Dogs, 6; as sheep menace, 77, 276
Doon: flax-mill, 222
Dorking hens, 274
Douglas: cattle fair, 282
Drainage Act, *1872*, 315
Draining, 91, 213-4, 314-5
Drawback Act of 1846, effects of American, 176
Drayton: cattle fair, 282n
Drovers, 264, 278, 283-4; from the United States, 129, 179, 183, 184, 185, 192-3, 194, 195, 210, 228-9, 279; organization of, 352
Ducks, 155
Dufferin County: livestock industry, 284
Dumfries Township: livestock industry, 153; oak-plains, 5
Dundas: exhibition, 165-6
Dundas County: draining, 213-4; essay, 388; farm described, 213-4; grain-growing, 213; Granger movement, 345; hay-growing, 214; implements, 98, 213; labour, 213; livestock industry, 213; lumbering, 115; self-sufficiency

in, 80-1; tenant farming, 68n; see also Eastern District, Morrisburg region, St. Lawrence River counties

Dundas Street, good farms along, 63

Durham boats in grain trade, 29-30, 107, 107n

Durham cattle, 150-1, 269-70, 270-1, 279, 284

Durham County: agricultural society, 164, 165-6; exhibition, 165-6; grain-growing, 242; implements, 200; livestock industry, 153, 184, 193; trade with the United States, 193, 194n; wool-growing, 194n; see also Cavan Township, Lake Ontario counties, Monaghan Township, Newcastle District, Port Hope region

Durham Road, 290

East Zorra Township: dairy industry, 255-6, 256

Eastern District: agricultural society, 164; lumbering, 115; War of 1812, 36

Eastern Townships (P.Q.): dairy industry, 262

Edmundson, W. G.: and Agricultural Association of Upper Canada, 171; and provincial exhibition, 172; on influence of British settlers, 62-3

Egan, John, lumberman, 110, 111, 112, 291-2

Eganville: cattle fair, 282

Eggs: exported to British Isles, 287; exported to the United States, 178-9, 179n, 181, 181-2, 286-7

Elderslie Township: settlement, 55

Election of 1841, tariff issue in, 131

Elevators, 234, 346

Elgin County: dairy industry, 256; flax-growing, 316-7; fruit-growing, 320; grain-growing, 243, 248; livestock industry, 284-5; wool-growing, 208-9; see also Lake Erie counties, London District, St. Thomas region, Talbot settlement, Thames Valley

Elmira: cattle fair, 282n

Elora: cattle fair, 210, 282n, 284

Elora and Saugeen Road, 290

Embargo Act of 1810 (American), 32

Embargo on agricultural exports, 1812, 36

Emigration from Ontario, 57-8, 294-5, 301, 302, 304, 305, 353-4, 359

England. See British Isles

Entomological Society of Ontario, 334, 334n, 352

Erie Canal, 45-6, 231

Erie, Lake, counties. See Lake Erie counties

Erin: cattle fair, 282n

Essa Township: settlement, 50

Essays, prize, 330, 341, 387-8

Essex County: climate, 3; distillery, 243; draining, 314-5, 315; grain-growing, 89, 243, 247, 324; hop-growing, 220; livestock industry, 209, 273, 274, 285-6, 286; poultry industry, 287; settlement, 51n; soil exhaustion, 324; sorghum-growing, 220, 315; tobacco-growing, 41-2, 221, 316; see also Amherstburg region, Detroit settlement, Pelee Island, Thames Valley, Western District, Windsor region

Essex swine, 273, 273n

Exhibitions (local): *before 1850*, 162, 166-8, 169; *1850-1880*, 336-7, 339, 341-4; admissions, 339-40; baby shows, 342; banquets, 166; brass bands, 342; contests, 341-2; "female equestrianism," 342; horse-racing, 167-8, 343-4; livestock shows, 162; ploughing matches, 162, 166, 337n; sideshows, 174, 341; speeches, 166; "spring shows," 161, 336

Exhibitions (provincial): *1846*, 85-6, 171-2; *1847*, 172, 172n; *1848*, 173; *1849*, 94-5, 173, 214-5; *1850*, 173-4; *1851-1881*, 202, 215, 221, 227, 271, 328, 329, 333, 337-9, 342-3, 344; admissions, 171, 173; banquets, 172, 173; horse-racing, 344; livestock shows, 150, 172, 173, 270n, 272n, 273n; ploughing matches, 172, 337n; speeches, 172, 173

Experimental farms, 330-1, 335

Extensive agriculture, 13, 20-1, 53-4, 89-90

Fairfield: Indian agriculture, 74n

Fairs (exhibitions). *See* Exhibitions (local), Exhibitions (provincial)

Fairs (markets). *See* Cattle fairs

Fallowing, 91-3, 186-7, 213, 323, 324, 324n

Farm school (proposed) at Assumption College, 331n

Farmers: classes, 60; origin, 55-6

Farmers' clubs, 169-70, 344-5

Farmers' Institutes, 345

Farms, lumbermen's, 111-2

Farrington, Harvey, dairyman, 254, 254n, 257n

Fences, 20, 213, 314

Fergus: cattle fair, 281, 282n, 284

Fergusson, Hon. Adam: livestock breeder, 149; on wheat-growing, 85-6, 172; sponsor of veterinarian, 332

Fertilizers, commercial, 93, 324-5

Fife, David, discoverer of Red Fife wheat, 103-4

Finger Lake region, N.Y.: grain-growing, 218

Firewood, 51, 306, 309

Fishing, 18, 77

Flax, 22, 42, 42-3, 221, 221-3, 316-7, 329, 358-9; exported to the United States, 222-3, 317

Flos Township: settlement, 50

Flour: exported to British Isles, 25-6, 27-8, 38-9, 46-7, 122, 124-5, 136n, 216; exported to British West Indies, 28, 47, 122, 125; exported to Maritime Provinces, 47, 122, 175, 175n, 216, 245; exported to the United States, 26, 176, 178, 192, 217, 228, 233, 245; exported to upper Great Lakes region, 24; imported from the United States, 37, 39, 45, 116, 125, 131; inspection, 30, 236; milling (*see* Milling industry)

Forest regions of Southern Ontario, 4

Fort Erie: source of supplies for upper Great Lakes region, 24-5

Fort Frontenac, agriculture at, 11

Fort Niagara, N.Y.: garrison market, 23, 25, 26

Fort William, agriculture at, 24

Franco-Prussian War, agricultural effects of, 247

Free grants, 68-9, 290, 293, 299-300

Free Grants and Homestead Act, *1868*, 299

French influence on Indian agriculture, 9

French Revolutionary War, agricultural effects of, 25, 43
French-Canadian agriculture, 11-5, 22n, 40, 51, 66, 128n, 141, 142, 305, 318, 318n
French-Canadian cattle, 142
French-Canadian horses, 14, 128n, 144, 268-9
French-Canadian sheep, 141n, 277
"Front," meaning of, 56n
Frontenac County: agricultural society, 163; cattle fairs, 160; shanty market, 300; see also Bay of Quinte, Frontenac Road, Kingston region, Midland District
Frontenac Road, 291, 292, 299-300
Fruit, 6, 7, 14-5, 78, 158, 210-2, 318-23, 359; exported to British Isles, 211, 319; exported to Maritime Provinces, 211, 320, 321; exported to Quebec, 210, 211, 322; exported to the United States, 211, 319, 320, 322; imported from the United States, 211; shift from wheat-growing to, 318-9
Fruit Growers' Association, 212, 334, 334n
Fulton County, Pa.: source of livestock, 10
Fur trade, agricultural market provided by, 24-5, 39

Galloway cattle, 270, 270n
Galt: sheep fair, 283n
Gananoque: milling industry, 106, 107, 135n
Garafraxa Road, 290
Gardening, market, 318, 318n
Gardens, 78-9
Garrison market, 15, 23-4, 25-6
Gatineau Valley (P.Q.): shanty market, 302

Geese: exported to the United States, 181-2; improved breeds, 155
Genesee Farmer, 174
Genesee Flats, N.Y.: livestock industry, 279-80
Genesee Valley, N.Y.: cattle fairs, 159; fruit-growing, 319; grain-growing, 85, 192; source of livestock, 140; see also Genesee Flats
Geography of Ontario, agricultural effects of, 353-4
Georgetown: cattle fair, 281
Germany: grain market, 243, 243n
Glengarry County: dairy industry, 251, 252, 256; draining, 314-5; flax-mill, 42; grain-growing, 86, 181, 243; livestock industry, 129; lumbering, 115; settlement, 21-2, 305; timothy-seed growing, 195n; trade with the United States, 129, 181, 243; see also Eastern District, St. Lawrence River counties
Goderich: cattle fair, 281; grain market, 234-5; Indian clearance, 74n; railway interest, 188
Goderich region: fruit-growing, 322; land speculation, 199; salt-mining, 307; see also Huron County
Gore District: agricultural society, 164, 165, 165-6; exhibition, 165, 165-6; livestock industry, 127n
Gourds, 22
Government Road (Renfrew County), 291
Grafting of fruit-trees, 211
Grafton: exhibition, 165-6
Grafton region: grain-growing, 102n; see also Northumberland County
Grain Inspection Act, *1863*, 236-7

Grain trade: *before 1812*, 25-6, 27-8, 29-30; *1812-1850*, 38-9, 48*n*, 105-8, 122-5, 131-2, 134-8, 175-8; *1850-1867*, 175*n*, 176*n*, 189-90, 191-2, 216-9, 231-3, 235-6; *1867-1880*, 234-5, 239-45; dealers in, 29-30, 102, 105, 106, 177-8, 236, 238, 238-9; financing of, 30, 106, 106*n*, 237-8, 238*n;* inspection, 30, 236-7; primary markets in, 106-7, 234-6; transportation in, 29-30, 106-7, 107-8, 108*n*, 233-4; *see also* Barley, etc., Flour, Milling industry
Grand Island, N.Y.: fruit-growing, 320*n*
Grand River Valley: grain markets, 107*n;* gypsum-mining, 93; livestock i n d u s t r y, 143-4; marshes, 2-3; oak-plains, 5; railroad interest, 188
Grand Trunk Railway, 189, 198, 231-2, 308-9
Grange. *See* Patrons of Husbandry
Grape rot, 321
Grapes, 7, 78, 211, 321-2; markets for, 211, 321-2; varieties of, 321
Grasshoppers, 11
Great Britain. *See* British Isles
Great Western Railway, 309
Grenville C a n a l : construction market, 46
Grenville County: dairy industry, 253; hop-growing, 316; trade with the United States, 180-1; *see also* Johnstown District, Rideau Canal region, St. Lawrence River counties
Grey County: essay, 388; grain-growing, 89, 237, 244*n*, 248, 324; livestock industry, 285; *see also* Owen Sound region
"Grimsby country": fruit-growing, 319-20

Grimsby Township: fruit-growing, 320
Grist mills, 17, 28
Guelph: agricultural society, 340; cattle fair, 210, 282-3, 284; dairy market, 252; exhibitions, local, 146, 146*n*, 164*n*, 165-6, 167*n*, provincial, 339; grain market, 239; Ontario Agricultural College, 335; Ontario Poultry Society, 352
Guelph region: implements, 95; livestock industry, 150, 152, 183, 278, 359; trade with the United States, 278; *see also* Wellington County
Guelph Township: agricultural society, 146; exhibition, 146
Guinea hens, 155
Gypsum, 93, 165, 325

Hackney horses, 146, 146*n*
Haldimand County: depression of 1857-60, 205; grain-growing, 89; livestock industry, 153, 194*n*, 223; trade with the United States, 223; *see also* Lake Erie counties, N i a g a r a District, Niagara peninsula
Haliburton C o u n t y: lumbering, 300*n;* settlement, 300*n;* shanty market, 300
Halifax, N.S.: fruit market, 320, 321
Hallowell: grain market, 105, 106
Halton C o u n t y : agricultural society, 339; exhibition, 339-40; flax-growing, 222; fruit-growing, 322; grain-growing, 89; hop-growing, 315-6; livestock industry, 179*n;* market gardening, 318; trade with the United States, 179*n; see also* Dundas

Street, Gore District, Lake Ontario counties

Hamilton: agricultural convention, *1846*, 171; brewery, 241; dairy market, 252; exhibitions, local, 165, 337-8, provincial, 172, 202, 337, 339*n;* grain market, 106-7, 236-7; horse-racing, 168*n;* livestock and meat market, 126, 128; packing industry, 223-4, 225, 286; population, *1850*, 63; railway interest, 187; wool market, 226, 276

Hamilton region: wool-growing, 276-7; *see also* Wentworth County

Hamilton Township: essay, 387; farmers' club, 104; livestock industry, 267*n*

Hampshire Down sheep, 272, 272*n*

Hampshire swine, 152

Harris, James, dairyman, 251

Harriston: cattle fair, 281, 282*n*

Harrows, 72, 95, 311

Harvesting, 95-6; machinery (*see* Binders, Reapers)

Hastings County: dairy industry, 251, 253, 359; essay, 388; flax-growing, 222; grain-growing, 242; land speculation, 199; livestock industry, 182, 183; mining, 307; shanty market, 300; trade with the United States, 182; *see also* Bay of Quinte, Belleville region, Hastings Road, Lake Ontario counties

Hastings Road, 291, 292, 297

Hawkesbury: milling industry, 117; shanty market, 118

Hay, 14, 111, 112, 114, 214; exported to the United States, 182, 182*n;* imported from Quebec, 297; pressing of, 182, 313-4; shanty market for, 111, 112, 300,

301*n*, 302*n; see also* Clover, Timothy, Red Top

Haying machinery: balers, 313-4; forks, 311, 311*n;* loaders, 311; mowers, 200, 201, 310, 311, 311*n;* rakes, 97, 201-2, 311; tedders, 311

Hedges, 314

Hemp, 43-4, 221

"Hen fever," 155, 274

Hens: exported to British Isles, 287; exported to the United States, 181-2, 287; improved breeds, 155, 274

Hereford cattle, 270-1, 279

Herkimer County, N.Y.: dairy industry, 129*n*, 253-4

Hessian fly, 25-6, 100

Hillsburgh: cattle fair, 282*n*

Hired man, 53, 55, 55*n; see also* Labour, agricultural

Hollow horn, 76, 76*n*

Holstein cattle, 271*n*

Home District: agricultural society, 161, 164, 165, 165-6, 171; exhibition, 165, 165-6; livestock industry, 147, 165

Home market, 81, 81*n*, 307-8

Honey, 79, 318, 318*n;* exported, 318, 318*n*

Hop blight, 221*n*

Hops, 220-1, 315-6, 358-9

Horse fairs, 119, 283, 283*n*

Horse-powers, 98-9, 312

Horse-racing, 159, 159-60, 167-8, 342-4

Horses: *before 1812*, 10, 14, 14*n*, 15, 22, 140, 145, 147; *1812-1850*, 74-5, 75, 128, 142-8, 179; *1850-1867*, 147-8, 183, 208, 267-9, 274-5, 287*n; 1867-1880*, 267-9, 274-5, 287*n;* dealers in, 275, 280; exported to British Isles, 280; exported to Manitoba, 275; exported to the United States, 178-9, 179, 183, 183n, 193-4, 228, 267, 274-5; imported from British Isles, 146, 147-8, 267, 269; imported from Quebec, 140, 145, 145n; imported from the United States, 10, 126, 140, 144, 145-6, 267; improvement of, 145-8, 267-9, 336; kinds or breeds of (see also Black Hawk horses, etc.), 142-8, 267-9; methods of raising, 14, 128, 143, 194n, 213; shanty market for, 119; superiority of Ontario, 148, 148n, 274

Horticultural societies, 335

Houses, 65-6, 199, 203, 306

Hull, P.Q.: livestock industry, 150n

Hullett Township: agricultural society, 336

"Hungry year" (1788-9), 17-8

Hunting, 77-8

Huntingdon County, P.Q.: cheese factories, 256

Huron County: agricultural society, 336; barns, 199; essay, 388; flax-growing, 317; grain-growing, 248; implements, 199-200; land speculation, 202-3; livestock industry, 284-5; settlement, 56; see also Goderich region, Huron District, Seaforth region

Huron District: agricultural society, 170

Huron Township: settlement, 55

Huron Tract, 69, 355

"Huronia," 6-8, 9

Hutchinson wheat, 100

Illinois: emigration to, 304-5; grain market, 124; implements in, 13-4; livestock industry, 142-3, 194n, 269; railway influences, 186; source of livestock, 127

Illinois Central Railroad and emigration, 294n

Immigration: methods, 21; policy, 68-9, 293, 294-5, 298-9

Implements: introduction, 72, 199-202, 213, 309-14; manufacturing of, 202; see also Cultivators, etc.

Indian agriculture, 5-10, 19, 51-3; abandoned clearances, 7, 9, 74; bee-keeping, 80n; fruit-growing, 7; grain-growing, 5-6, 6, 9, 52; influences on French agriculture, 8-9; livestock-raising, 6, 10, 10n, 52, 143-4; land-clearing, 6-7, 74n; maple sugar, 7-8, 79n; tillage methods, 6-7; tobacco-growing, 8, 40n; vegetable-growing, 5, 6

Indian corn. See Corn

Indian menace, absence of, 19

"Indian ponies," 142-4

Indiana: livestock industry, 129, 142-3, 194n, 280; source of livestock, 127

Industrial Exhibition (Toronto), 338, 339

Ingersoll: cheese board, 259; dairy convention, 258; dairy market, 252, 260; wool fair, 77

Innisfil Township: settlement, 50

Insurance, fire, 306n, 313

Iowa: flour trade, 231-2; horse market, 275; livestock industry, 194n, 269

Ireland. See British Isles

Irish geese, 155

Italian War of 1859, effects of, 205

Jefferson County, N.Y.: dairy industry, 251

Jersey cattle, 270, 270n

Johnstown District: agricultural society, 164; War of 1812, 36

Journal and Transactions of the Board of Agriculture of Upper Canada, 329-30, 387-8

Keefer, T.C., 117n, 373; on colonization policy, 290; on Ottawa Valley, 117, 120; on tariff of 1843, 134; on wheat-growing, 89
Kent County: agricultural societies, 164, 165, 336, 340; bean-growing, 317; climate, 3; exhibition, 165; grain-growing, 243, 248, 324; hemp-growing, 43; livestock industry, 209, 274, 284-5, 285-6, 286; potato-growing, 317; soil exhaustion, 324; tobacco-growing, 41-2, 221, 316; *see also* Lake Erie counties, Thames Valley, Western District
Kentucky: cattle fairs, 210; competitor in horses with Ontario, 275; source of horses, 267
Kincardine: grain market, 234-5
Kincardine Township: settlement, 55
Kingston: breweries and distilleries, 88, 241; elevators, 234; exhibitions, provincial, 173, 214-5, 337, 339, 342-3; fruit market, 210; garrison market, 23, 25, 36, 129; grain trade, 25, 29-30, 177, 232, 233-4, 234, 236-7; horse-racing, 168n, 342-3; population, *1850*, 63; railway interest, 187, 188; trading centre, 18, 30
Kingston region: hemp-growing, 43; livestock industry, 76, 148n, 179, 184; trade with the United States, 179, 182, 184; *see also* Frontenac County
Kippawa River (P.Q.), lumbering along, 301-2
Kitley Township: agricultural society, 168-9; cattle fair, 210n

Labour, agricultural, 55n, 60, 161, 199, 199-200, 213, 309-10
Lake Erie counties: Carolinian forest belt, 4; climate, 3-4; lumbering, 120; settlement, 356; wool-growing, 277; *see also* Elgin County, Haldimand County, Kent County, Norfolk County
Lake Ontario counties: climate, 3-4; grain-growing, 89, 90, 100, 100-1, 102, 107, 123, 242, 247, 324; livestock industry, 182, 285; settlement, 356; soil exhaustion, 196, 324; trade with the United States, 182; *see also* Durham County, Halton County, Hastings County, Northumberland County, Ontario County, Peel County, York County
Lake Temiskaming region: lumbering, 110, 301-2; portaging to, 118
Lambs, 272, 278n; exported to British Isles, 280n; exported to the United States, 278; *see also* Sheep
Lambton County: agricultural society, 340-1; draining, 315; exhibition, 340-1; livestock industry, 284-5; *see also* Western District
Lamps, kerosene, introduction of, 215
Lanark: trade with the United States, 39
Lanark County: agricultural society, 206-7; dairy industry, 253, 265, 302; grain-growing, 119, 243, 302; livestock industry, 119, 209, 278; mixed farming, 206-7; pork-packing, 119; shanty market, 119, 209, 301-2; *see also* Bathurst District, Military

Settlements, Perth region, Rideau Canal region
Land Act of 1841, 290
Land regulations, 33, 64, 114, 290-2, 295, 299-300
Land speculation, 33-4, 64-5, 68, 69-70, 70n, 199, 202-3, 205
Land-clearing, 6, 54-5, 65-6, 68, 70-1
"Landpike" (common) swine, 141, 152, 273-4
Lectures sponsored by Board of Agriculture of Upper Canada, 329, 344
Leeds County: agricultural societies, 164, 168-9; dairy industry, 251, 253; livestock industry, 168-9; trade with the United States, 180-1; see also Brockville region, Johnstown District, Rideau Canal region, St. Lawrence River counties
Leicester sheep, 153-4, 165, 271-2, 272n, 276, 277-8
Lennox County: grain-growing, 242; see also Bay of Quinte, Midland District
Libraries, agricultural, 157-8, 336
Lincoln County: exhibition, 343; fruit-growing, 211; grain-growing, 15, 89; livestock industry, 15; oak-plains, 5; pioneer difficulties, 17-8; settlement, 15; vegetable-growing, 15; see also "Grimsby country," Grimsby Township, Niagara District, Niagara peninsula, Niagara Township, St. Catharines region
Lincoln sheep, 153, 272, 272n, 276
Linen factories, 222, 316
Linseed-oil mills, 42, 222, 317
Listowel: cattle fair, 282n
Live Stock Dealers of Western Ontario, Association of the, 352

Livestock industry: before 1812, 10, 11-2, 14, 22-3, 31-2, 140-1; 1812-1850, 37, 37-8, 74-7, 119, 125-6, 133-4, 140-55; 1850-1867, 179-80, 182-5, 186-7, 193-5, 208-10, 223-7, 228-9, 266-74, 287n; 1867-1880, 264, 266-88, 302, 358-9; improvement of breeds in (see also Cattle, etc.), 155, 266-7, 329, 336n
Lobo Township: cheese factory, 255
London: brewery, 241; dairy market, 252; exhibitions, local, 338, provincial, 337, 337-8, 338n, 339, 344; grain market, 236-7, 240; horse-racing, 168n, 343; population, 1850, 63; pork-packing, 285-6
London District: agricultural society, 164
London region: grain trade, 106-7; land-clearing, 74; livestock industry, 147, 275, 284, 359; superior farming, 63; trade with the United States, 275; see also Middlesex County
London Township: livestock industry, 75
Long Point: livestock industry, 31, 31-2; oak-plains, 4-5; trade with the United States, 31
L'Orignal: Granger movement, 345
Louth Township: exhibition, 343
Lower Canada. See Quebec
"Loyalist rights," 33, 68-9
Loyalist settlement, 14-6, 17
Lumbering, 32-3, 109-10, 120, 120n, 187, 206, 207-8, 301, 307; effects on agriculture, 111-2, 113-5, 120-1, 307; encouragement to settlement, 112-5, 291-2, 301

Lumbermen, antagonism between farmers and, 114, 295-6, 299

Lynch, John, essayist, 388; on crop rotations, 90n, 91n; on grain-growing, 91, 92; on native-born farmers, 54; on professional pioneers, 54-5

McDougall, Hon. William, colonization policy of, 298

Mackenzie, William Lyon: *Bytown Gazette* on, 349; hostility to Canada Company, 69; on American livestock competition, 126; opposition to colonial system, 130, 130n; political weakness in Ottawa Valley, 348-9

McKinley Tariff, *1890*: effects on barley industry, 236, 241; effects on livestock industry, 278

Macon's Bill Number Two (United States), *1810*, 32

McPherson, D. M., dairyman, 256

Madawaska Valley: lumberman's farm, 112; portaging, 116; settlement, 112; shanty market, 112, 116, 293, 297

Madison County, Ohio: livestock industry, 127

Madoc: shanty market, 297

Manitoba: emigration to, 303, 304, 359; horse market, 275; source of wheat, 247

Manitoulin Island: Indian agriculture, 6

Manufacturing, growth of, 202, 308

Manure, 91, 325

Maple sugar, 7-8, 8n, 79, 79n

Maritime Provinces: agricultural market, 354; dairy market, 250; flour market, 47, 122, 175, 175n, 216, 216-7, 245; fruit market, 211, 320, 321; *see also* New Brunswick, Nova Scotia, Prince Edward Island

Markham Township: Pennsylvania Dutch influence, 53; threshing with horses, 98

Market, "newcomers," 46

Markets, influence of on agricultural development: *before 1812*, 23-33; *1812-1850*, 38-40, 46-8, 81n, 117-8, 122-4, 125-30, 175-80, 354; *1850-1867*, 179-86, 190-5, 197-9, 206-10, 216-9, 223-30, 266-7, 354; *1867-1880*, 257-63, 274-81, 354

Markets (town) established, 30

Marks, J. B.: on soil exhaustion, 196; president of the Agricultural Association of Upper Canada, 196

"Marsh harvesters," 312

Masonville: cattle fair, 282n

Mattawan Valley: shanty market, 111n

Meaford, wheat-teaming from, 106-7

Meat imported from the United States, 37, 39, 45, 116, 128, 133n, 210n, 224

Mechanics' Institutes, 169

Mediterranean (Italian) wheat, 101

Medonte Township: settlement, 50

Melons, 11, 22

Mennonites and War of 1812, 36

Merino sheep, 152-3, 154-5, 227, 271, 272n, 276-7

Merritt, Hon. W. H.: on opponents of Welland Canal, 131; railway promoter, 233

Miami Valley, Ohio: livestock industry, 155; source of swine, 273

Michigan: bean market, 317; grain market, 124; livestock industry, 133, 142-3, 194n, 280; livestock market, 275; railroad effects, 186; source of livestock, 133n; *see also* Detroit settlement

Michilimackinac, Mich.: agricultural market, 24-5

Middlesex County: agricultural societies, 336, 340, 343n; dairy industry, 253, 256; draining, 315; exhibition, local, 342n, 343n; grain-growing, 242, 248; hop-growing, 220, 315-6; horse-racing, 343n; livestock industry, 75; *see also* Lobo Township, London District, London region, Thames Valley

Midland District: agricultural society, 163, 164; exhibitions, 163; livestock industry, 129; trade with the United States, 129; War of 1812, 36

Midland Railway (proposed), 188

Military Settlements: livestock industry, 145; settlement, 50, 68

Milk, raw, 264

Miller, John, livestock breeder, 149

Milling industry, 28, 39, 106, 117, 125, 135, 192, 216-7, 245

Milton: exhibition, 339-40

Milwaukee, Wis.: grain trade, 233-4

Mimico: proposed site of Ontario Agricultural College, 335

Mining, 307-8

Minnesota: emigration to, 304-5; grain-growing, 104; horse market, 275

Minorca hens, 155

Missions, agriculture at, 9, 11, 11n

Mississippi Road, 291, 292

Mitchell, Colonel, flax grower, 222

Mixed farming, 118-9, 206-7, 323

Mohawk Valley, N.Y.: grain-growing, 218; source of supplies, 17, 18

Monaghan Township: grain-growing, 102

Mono Mills: cattle fair, 282n

Mono Township: settlement, 50

Montana Territory: horse market, 275

Montgomeryshire swine, 152

Montreal, P.Q.: agricultural society, 162; elevators, 234; fruit market, 211, 319, 322; garrison market, 23; grain trade, 25-6, 27-8, 29-30, 231-2, 233, 236-7, 237, 241; livestock market, 127, 193, 210; packing industry, 223, 285-6; potash market, 32; tobacco market, 40-1, 221; trading centre, 18-9; vegetable market, 318

Montreal region (P.Q.): grain-growing, 91-2, 138; livestock industry, 153, 270; source of supplies, 17

Morgan horses, 145, 145n, 268

Morrisburg region: dairy industry, 262-3

Mount Forest: cattle fair, 210, 282n, 284

Mowers, 200, 201, 310, 311, 311n

Moyer, Moses, dairyman, 263n

Municipalities: and agricultural societies, 164n; and draining, 314, 315

Muscovy ducks, 155

Muskoka District: climate, 3, 4; settlement, 300; shanty market, 300

Muskoka Road, 291, 292, 299-300

Mutton imported from the United States, 133n

Napanee: cattle fair, 160; grain market, 346

Napoleonic Wars, effects of, 27-8

Narragansett Pacers, 145

"Native" livestock: cattle, 142, 148-9; sheep, 141, 141n; swine (see Landpike swine)

Negro agriculture, 40, 53, 53n

New Brunswick: effects of lumbering on agriculture, 115; fruit market, 211; reciprocity with, 175; see also Maritime Provinces

New Edinburgh: milling industry, 106, 117

New England: agricultural societies, 161-2; dairy market, 181-2, 253; egg and poultry market, 181-2; flour and grain market, 181, 189, 191-2, 216; hired man in, 55n; livestock industry, 150, 225; livestock market, 184, 275; milling industry, 191-2, 192; tin pedlars of, 57n; see also Boston

"New England market," 177-85, 354, 358

New Hamburgh: cattle fair, 282n

New Hampshire: livestock market, 229; source of supplies, 37

New Jersey, immigration from, 19

New York, N.Y.: dairy market, 181-2, 262; egg and poultry market, 181-2, 286-7; flour and grain market, 178, 192, 231-2, 245; fruit market, 319; hay market, 182; livestock market, 183, 184, 210, 275, 278, 279

New York (State): dairy industry, 133, 251, 279; farmers' clubs, 169; fruit-growing, 320; grain-growing, 22n, 85, 218-9, 219; grain market, 124; immigration from, 19, 21, 30-1; livestock in-dustry, 31-2, 194n; livestock market, 179n, 226; malting industry, 241; potash industry, 32; railroad influences, 186; settlement, 26-7; smuggling, 32; source of livestock, 37, 38, 39, 140, 146, 151, 165, 227; source of other supplies, 37, 38, 133; see also Genesee Valley, Herkimer County, Mohawk Valley

New York Central Railroad, 180, 188, 231

New York State Agricultural Society, 171

New York State Fairs, 171, 342

Newark. See Niagara

Newcastle: farm inventory, 310n

Newcastle District: agricultural society, 164

Newmarket: farmers' club, 169

Niagara (Newark): agricultural society, 157-8; exhibitions, provincial, 173-4; horse - racing, 168n; pioneer difficulties near, 17-8; winery, 321-2

Niagara District: agricultural society, 161, 164, 165; exhibition, 165

Niagara Escarpment, 3

Niagara peninsula: American character, 58; cattle fairs, 159; climate, 3; fruit-growing, 22, 78, 158, 210, 211, 212, 319, 319-20, 320n, 321, 322, 359; grain-growing, 22n, 27, 88, 90; livestock industry, 37-8, 76, 140, 182-3, 194; milling industry, 28; oak-plains, 5; portage railway, 233; settlement, 17, 51n, 59n, 356; source of fur-trade supplies, 24; superior farming, 63; trade with the United States, 182-3, 194; War of 1812, 37-8; see also

Haldimand County, L i n c o l n County, Welland Canal, Welland County, Wentworth County

Niagara Township: fruit-growing, 320; oak-plains, 5

Nipissing District: Indian agriculture, 5-6; settlement, 301; *see also* Mattawan Valley

Non-Intercourse A c t (United States), *1809*, 32

Norfolk County: fruit-growing, 320; grain-growing, 243; implements, 199-200; livestock industry, 32; lumbering, 120; oak-plains, 4-5; *see also* Lake Erie counties, Long Point

Norfolk Thin Rind swine, 152*n*

North Carolina: livestock industry, 31

North West Company, 24, 24-5, 39

Northern Railway, 202, 309

Northumberland County: agricultural societies, 162-3, 164, 165, 165-6; dairy industry, 251, 253; exhibition, 165-6; farmers' clubs, 344; grain-growing, 5, 89, 104-5, 242; hop-growing, 315-6; implements, 98; livestock industry, 165, 267*n*, 272, 285; oak-plains, 5; soil exhaustion, 242; *see also* Cobourg region, Grafton region, Lake Ontario counties, Newcastle District, Trent Valley

"Norway plains," 109-10, 113

Norwich: cheese factory, 254

Nottawasaga Township: settlement, 50

Nova Scotia: influence on horse improvement, 146*n*; reciprocity with, 175; *see also* Maritime Provinces

Nurseries, 211

Oak-plains, 4-5, 31, 64, 71, 74

Oakville: strawberry-growing, 322

Oats: 13, 15, 22, 86, 86*n*, 89, 114, 165, 217, 239; domestic markets, 89, 119; exported to British Isles, 243; exported to the United States, 181, 217, 243; imported from Quebec, 297; imported from the United States, 244; production statistics of, 86, 86*n*, 239

Ogdensburg, N.Y.: forwarding centre, 180; interest in railways, 188

Ogdensburg Railroad, 180, 180-1, 184, 188, 189-90

Ohio: cattle fairs, 210; "female equestrianism," 342; flax-growing, 42; grain-growing, 85, 87, 93*n;* hay market, 182*n;* livestock industry, 31-2, 32*n*, 63, 127, 129, 155, 194*n*, 354; pioneer era, 356-7; railway effects, 186; source of cheese, 133; source of flour, 116; source of livestock, 127; tobacco-growing, 40*n*

Ontario (Upper Canada, Canada West): description, 1-5; Central, 2-3; Eastern, 1-2; Southern, 1-5; Western, 2-3

Ontario, Lake, counties. *See* Lake Ontario counties

Ontario Agricultural College, 279, 334-5, 335

Ontario Agricultural Commission: appointment, 326, 334; on implements, 310; on livestock, 141, 266, 270-1, 288; on progress of Ontario, 326; report, 372-3

Ontario C o u n t y : agricultural societies, 168, 339; dairy industry, 251; essay, 388; exhibitions, 341; grain-growing, 90-1, 242, 248; implements, 199-200;

livestock industry, 147, 269n; settlement, 57; see also Home District, Lake Ontario counties

Ontario Dairymen's Association, 258

Ontario Poultry Society, 334, 334n, 352

Ontario Veterinary College, 332

Opeongo Road, 291, 291-2, 297, 299-300

"Orange County (N.Y.) butter," 262

Orangeville: cattle fair, 282n

Orchards, 22, 36, 51, 78

Orillia Township: agricultural society, 168

Oro Township: agricultural society, 168; settlement, 50

Osage-orange hedges, 314

Oshawa: hop-growing, 220n; implement factory, 202

Oswegatchie, N.Y.: garrison market, 26

Oswego, N.Y.: grain trade, 177, 189, 191, 231, 233; interest in Upper Canada railways, 188; milling industry, 177-8, 191

Otonabee Township: agricultural society, 103; grain-growing, 103-4; land-clearing, 70; livestock industry, 193, 195; trade with the United States, 193, 195

Ottawa (formerly Bytown): cattle fair, 160, 167; dairy industry near, 252; exhibitions, provincial, 337, 339; politics, 350-1, 351n; population, 1850, 63; railway terminus, 188; shanty market, 117, 117-8, 301n; Shiners at, 111n

Ottawa County, Ohio: fruit-growing, 321

Ottawa District: agricultural societies, 164, 164n

Ottawa Valley: agriculture in general, 109-21, 206-8; area, etc., 1-2; cattle fairs, 210, 282; dairy industry, 251; economic peculiarity, 109, 116; grain-growing, 117, 186, 207; hay-growing, 111, 112; land speculation, 207; livestock industry, 119, 182, 210, 281, 285; lumbering, 109-11, 206, 207-8, 228, 357-8; mixed farming, 118-9, 206-7; politics, 348-9, 350-1, 351n; railways, 187-8, 309; settlement, 112-4, 301, 356; shanty market, 116, 116-7, 117-8, 281, 301-2; Shiners, 111n; trade with the United States, 182, 206, 228, 302; see also Carleton County, Dundas County, Glengarry County, Grenville County, Lanark County, Leeds County, Prescott County, Renfrew County, Russell County, Stormont County

Ottawa-Huron region: climate, 3; description, 2, 3, 296-7; emigration from, 302; settlement, 113, 289-90, 291-6, 298-9, 299-302; shanty market, 116, 297-8, 300; stranding of settlers, 300

Owen Sound region: fruit-growing, 322; livestock industry, 183; mining market, 307; see also Grey County

Owen Sound Road, 290

Oxen, 13-4, 75

Oxford County: agricultural society, 339, 340; cheese dealers, 259; dairy industry, 251, 254-5, 256, 264, 276, 359; flax-growing, 316-7; grain-growing, 27, 181, 248; livestock industry, 184, 224, 264, 269, 269n, 284; trade with the United States, 181, 184; wool-growing, 276; see also

Brock District, East Zorra Township, Oxford Township, Thames Valley

Oxford Down sheep, 272-3

Oxford Township: dairy industry, 30-1

Parry Sound District: shanty market, 300

Passenger pigeons, 18

"Patent process" in flour manufacturing, 245

Patrons of Husbandry, 345-8

Pea weevil, 9n, 22n, 88, 209, 244

"Peach cars," 321

Peaches, 14, 22, 78, 319-21; domestic markets, 210-1, 320; exported to British Isles, 211; exported to Maritime Provinces, 211, 320, 321; exported to Quebec, 210, 211; exported to the United States, 211, 320; yellows in, 320

Pearlash, 71-2

Pears, 14-5, 78, 211, 322; domestic markets, 211, 322; exported to British Isles, 211; exported to Maritime Provinces, 211; exported to Quebec, 211, 322; exported to the United States, 211; fire blight in, 212, 322

Peas, 9, 9n, 11, 12, 13, 22, 22n, 86, 86n, 87-8, 88-9, 209, 239, 353; crop rotations involving, 90-1, 92-3, 323-4; domestic markets, 88; exported to British Isles, 88, 244; exported to the United States, 179, 181, 244; method of harvesting, 88n, 311n; pioneer crop, 88; production statistics, 86, 86n, 239, 244n; see also Pea weevil

Pedlars, 26-7, 57, 57n, 211, 215, 310, 341, 346

Peel County: cattle fair, 160; dairy industry, 253; essays, 388; grain-growing, 89, 90-1, 91, 197, 242, 246; hop-growing, 220; livestock industry, 152, 154, 284; see also Chinguacousy Township, Dundas Street, Home District, Lake Ontario counties

Pelee Island: grape-growing, 321

Pembroke: shanty depot, 118, 301n

Pembroke and Mattawan Road, 291

Pennsylvania: flax-growing, 42; immigration from, 19, 21; livestock industry, 147n, 155, 275; source of livestock, 10, 140

Pennsylvania Dutch, 46, 53, 61, 76n, 147, 222, 317; see also Mennonites

Percheron horses, 269, 269n

Perine, W. D., flax-grower, 222

Perth: agricultural society, 165; cattle fair, 119, 159-60, 160, 179, 182, 210; dairy market, 260; grain market, 243; horse-racing, 145

Perth County: flax-growing, 316-7; grain-growing, 248; livestock industry, 274-5, 284; see also Huron District

Perth region: dairy industry, 262; livestock industry, 145, 182, 192-3; railroad interest, 188; shanty market, 297; trade with the United States, 39, 192-3; see also Lanark County

Peterborough: railroad interest, 188

Peterborough County: grain-growing, 100, 102, 103-4; land-clearing, 70; livestock industry, 151-2, 153, 193; pioneering, 55n; settlement, 50, 68; shanty market, 116, 300; sorghum-growing, 219; trade with the United States,

193; *see also* Otonabee Township, Trent Valley

Peterson Road, 291

Petite Côte. *See* Detroit settlement

Petrolia: petroleum industry, 307

Philadelphia, Pa.: grain market, 219; livestock market, 183, 275, 279

Pickering Township: agricultural societies, 168, 339; exhibition, 339; livestock industry, 147

Picnics, farmers', 336, 344, 347

Pigs. *See* Swine

Pioneer era: cropping methods, 72-4; domestic activities, 80, 80-1; passing of, 214-5, 356-7; self-sufficiency, 80-1

Pioneers: characteristics of, 58-9; professional, 54-5, 55n

Pittsburgh, Pa.: cattle market, 279

Ploughing, 13-4, 73, 91

Ploughing matches, 94, 162, 172, 333, 336n

Ploughs: common, 13, 15, 94-5, 310; gang, 201; subsoil, 310n; sulky, 310

Plums, 7, 14, 78, 211, 212, 322; black knot in, 212, 322; curculio in, 212, 322; domestic markets, 211, 322; exported to British Isles, 211; exported to Maritime Provinces, 211; exported to Quebec, 211; exported to the United States, 211, 322

Plymouth Rock hens, 274

Poland China swine, 273

Poland ducks, 155

Poland geese, 155

Poles in Ottawa-Huron region, 294, 295, 302

Polled Angus cattle, 270, 270n

Population of Upper Canada, *1850*, 63

Pork: exported to British Isles, 224, 224-5, 286; imported from the United States, 37, 45, 116, 128, 224; shanty market for, 116, 119

Pork-packing industry, 23, 45, 119, 223-5, 285-6, 286n

Port Colborne: grain trade, 234

Port Dalhousie: grain trade, 234

Port Hope: cattle fair, 159; cheese-and-butter factories, 263; farmers' picnics, 347; railway interest, 187

Port Hope region: grain-growing, 102n; implements, 97; *see also* Durham County

Port Huron, Mich.: fruit market, 322

Port Stanley: farmers' picnics, 336, 347; grain market, 107, 177; railway interest, 187

"Portaging" to shanties, 115-6, 118, 301-2

Portland: cattle fair, 210n

Portland, Me: grain trade, 231-2

Potash, 32-3, 71-2, 72n; inspection act, *1801*, 32n

Potatoes, 13, 15, 72, 317; blight of, 138; domestic markets for, 119n, 317; exported to the United States, 181, 317; varieties of, 138n; *see also* Colorado potato beetle

Poultry, 11, 75, 155, 274, 287; exported to British Isles, 287; exported to the United States, 181, 181-2, 287; improvement, 155, 274

Poultry Association of Ontario, 352

Poultry fairs, 287

Precambrian Shield, 1, 2, 63

Pre-emption. *See* Squatter's rights

Prescott: brewery, 241; garrison market, 36; horse-racing, 168n; railway interest, 180, 187

Prescott County: agricultural society, 164n; draining, 314-5; grain-growing, 117, 119; Granger movement, 345; livestock industry, 119; lumbering, 115; pork-packing, 119; settlement, 305; shanty market, 119, 302, 302n; tobacco-growing, 316; see also Ottawa District

Presqu'Ile (now Erie), Pa.: garrison market, 26

Prince Edward County: agricultural societies, 164, 165, 336, 352; clover-growing, 99n; dairy industry, 186, 253, 263-4; essay, 388; fruit-growing, 319; grain-growing, 90-1, 105, 186-7, 242; gypsum, 165; hop-growing, 220, 220-1, 315-6; implements, 99n; livestock industry, 153, 185, 186-7, 193-4, 267; politics, 352; trade with the United States, 185, 186-7; wool-growing, 77; see also Bay of Quinte

Prince Edward District. See Prince Edward County

Prince Edward Island: reciprocity with, 1850, 175; see also Maritime Provinces

Prosperity: 1796-1800, 26; 1812-1815, 36-7; 1815-1819, 37-8; 1825-1830, 44, 47-8; 1843-1846, 136-7; 1849-1850, 176-7; 1853-1857, 72n, 198-9, 202-3, 207-8; 1865-1866, 228-9

Pumpkins, 22

Quebec (Lower Canada): agricultural societies, 337n; fruit market, 210, 211, 322; grain-growing, 9, 47, 125, 217-8; livestock industry, 141, 268-9, 269n, 275; ploughing, 13-4; shanty market, 302n; source of livestock, 9, 11, 140, 145, 145n, 150; see also Eastern Townships, Montreal region

Quebec, P.Q.: agricultural beginnings at, 9; agricultural society, 162; flour and grain market, 216-7, 236-7

Quebec and Lake Huron Railway (projected), 293, 296

Queenston: cattle fairs, 159; potash market, 32

Quinte, Bay of. See Bay of Quinte

Rafts: in grain trade, 29, 107; in livestock trade, 45

Railway building, 187-9, 308-9; agricultural effects of, 198-9, 212, 233-4, 234-5, 308-9

Rakes, 97, 201-2, 311

Raleigh: exhibition, 165

Ranney, Hiram, dairyman, 251, 252, 254, 256

Reapers, 96-7, 199-201, 310, 312

Rebellion of 1837, agrarianism in, 124n, 130-1, 348

Reciprocity Treaty of 1854, 187-95, 225, 229-30, 254, 278-9, 358

Red Fife wheat, 102-5, 247

Red River settlement, 39; see also Manitoba

Red top, 73

Reform Party before 1837, agrarian qualities of, 348

Renfrew: agricultural society, 340n; cattle fair, 282

Renfrew County: agricultural society, 340n; climate, 3; dairy industry, 260, 302; grain-growing, 243, 302; Indian agriculture, 5; livestock industry, 76n, 278; shanty market, 301-2; see also

Bathurst District, Bonnechere Valley, Madawaska Valley, Opeongo Road

Renting of land, 67-8, 68

Rhode Island: source of Lower Canada horses, 145

Rice, wild, 98n

Rice Lake Plains, 5, 64

Richmond: agricultural society, 168

Richmond Hill: cattle fair, 160, 161; farmers' club, 169; tariff resolutions, 131n

Riddell, Walter, essayist, 387

Rideau Canal region: construction market, 46, 117n; mining, 307; trade with the United States, 181

"Rights" to land, 33, 64, 69, 295

Rochester, N.Y.: grain market, 124n, 177, 191; milling industry, 124n, 177-8, 191; source of implements, 202; source of seeds, 100

Rollers, 95, 311

Rome and Cape Vincent Railroad, 188

Romney Marsh (Kent) sheep, 272

Root crops in rotations, 323, 323n

Ross Township: livestock industry, 76n

Rouen ducks, 155

Royal George horses, 268

Russell County: draining, 314-5, 315; exhibition, 341; grain-growing, 117; lumbering, 115; settlement, 305; shanty market, 302, 302n; tobacco-growing, 316; see also Ottawa District

Rye, 22, 86, 86n, 88, 239, 243; domestic market, 88; exported to Europe, 243, 243n; exported to the United States, 181; production statistics, 86, 86n, 239

St. Catharines: winery, 321-2

St. Catharines region: livestock industry, 151; poultry industry, 155

Saint John, N.B.: fruit market, 321

St. Johns: milling industry, 28

St. Joseph Island: agriculture, 24n

St. Lawrence County, N.Y.: dairy industry, 251, 262

"St. Lawrence County (N.Y.) butter," 262

St. Lawrence Lowlands, 1, 2

St. Lawrence River counties: climate, 3; dairy industry, 251; grain-growing, 27, 29, 101, 117, 119, 137-8, 176-7, 207; livestock industry, 119, 285; mixed farming, 207; pork-packing, 119; settlement, 17, 18n, 51n, 356; shanty market, 118, 119; soil exhaustion, 196; trade with the United States, 181; see also Dundas County, Glengarry County, Grenville County, Leeds County, Stormont County

St. Mary's: egg trade, 286

St. Thomas region: livestock industry, 151, 284; see also Elgin County

San Francisco, Calif.: sheep market, 278

Sandwich: cattle fair, 161

Sarnia: grain trade, 233

Saugeen Township: settlement, 55

Sault Ste. Marie: agriculture at, 24; fruit market, 322; fur-trade provision market, 24

Schooners in grain trade, 107n, 233-4

Scotland. See British Isles

Scott, J. W., dairyman, 255

Seaforth region: egg industry, 286; livestock industry, 275; *see also* Huron County

Seeders, 95, 201, 311

Selkirk, Lord, and Merinos, 152, 152*n*

Sewing machines, 215, 306-7

Shanghai hens, 155

Shanty market: in Muskoka District, 300; in Ottawa Valley, 46, 88-9, 110-1, 116, 116-7, 118, 119, 206, 209, 281, 301-2, 302*n*, 358; in Ottawa-Huron region, 297-8, 300; in Trent Valley, 120

Sheep: *before 1812*, 14, 14*n*, 15, 23, 140; *1812-1850*, 52, 76-7, 126-7, 127-8, 152-3; *1850-1867*, 181, 184-5, 194-5, 208-9, 223, 225-7, 267, 267*n*, 271-2, 272*n*, 287*n*; *1867-1880*, 271-3, 275-8, 280, 287*n*; exported to British Isles, 280; exported to the United States, 181, 183, 184-5, 194-5, 223, 226, 226*n*, 228, 277-8, 278; imported from British Isles, 152*n*, 153, 267*n*; imported from the United States, 126-7, 127-8, 140, 152-3, 227; improvement, 152, 165, 227, 267, 267*n*, 271-3; kinds or breeds of (*see also* Cheviot sheep, etc.), 141, 152-5, 271-3; methods of raising, 76-7; *see also* Lambs, Wool

Sheep fairs, 283*n*

Shetland ponies, 147*n*

"Shiners," 111*n*, 160

Shire horses, 147-8, 148*n*, 269

Shorthorn cattle. *See* Durham cattle

Shropshire Down sheep, 272-3, 273*n*

Shropshire swine, 152

Siberian wheat, 101-2

Silos, lack of, 244*n*

Simcoe, Lt. Gov. J. G.: and agricultural society at Niagara, 157, 158; and free grants, 290; and land speculators, 33-4

S i m c o e   County: agricultural societies, 168, 340; essays, 388; grain-growing, 6-7, 90-1, 244*n*, 248, 324, 324*n*; implements, 199-200; Indian agriculture, 6-8; land speculation, 64-5; livestock industry, 6, 195; racial groups, 50; settlement, 50; shanty market, 300; trade with the United States, 195; vegetable-growing, 6

Smith, Andes, dairyman, 254, 254*n*, 257*n*

Smiths Falls: implement works, 311*n*, 312*n*; turkey fair, 287

Smuggling of agricultural produce into the United States, 179*n*, 185

Soil exhaustion, 7, 89, 196, 197, 206, 242, 246, 324, 324-5

Soils of Ontario, 1, 2; pioneer classification of, 20

Sorghum, 219-20, 315

Soule's (Genesee White Flint) wheat, 100

Southdown sheep, 153-4, 165, 272-3, 276-7, 278

Squashes, 5, 6

Squatters, 67, 112-4, 114-5

"Squatters' rights," 67, 295

Squirrels, 78*n*

Stamford Township: fruit-growing, 320; oak-plains, 5

Standardbred horses, 268

Steam engines, 312-3, 313*n*

Steamships: in butter trade, 260; in grain trade, 107, 231, 233, 234; in poultry trade, 287; in vegetable trade, 318

Stone, F. W., livestock breeder, 149, 278

Stormont County: dairy industry, 253; lumbering, 115; see also Cornwall region, Eastern District, St. Lawrence River counties

Stoves, 72n, 215

Stranding of settlers in lumbering areas, 113-4, 300, 302

Stratford: cheese board, 259; cheese-and-butter train, 259; livestock association, 352

Straw cutters, 310n

Strawberries, 322

Stumping, 74

Suffolk Punch horses, 269, 269n

Suffolk swine, 273, 273n

Sunflowers, 6

Superphosphates, 325

Superstitions, 61

Surface features of Ontario, 1-3, 296-7

Surveying, 12n, 16n

Swine: before 1812, 10, 11-2, 14, 14n, 15, 22; 1812-1850, 77, 128, 141, 151-2; 1850-1867, 183-4, 195, 209, 223-5, 273-4, 287n; 1867-1880, 243, 273-4, 285-6, 287n; exported to the United States, 129, 183-4, 195, 225; imported from British Isles, 151-2; imported from the United States, 45, 140, 224, 273, 286; improvement, 151-2, 273-4; kinds or breeds (see also Berkshire swine, etc.), 141, 151-2, 152n, 273, 273n; methods of raising, 22, 77, 88, 96, 258, 285-6; see also Pork, Pork-packing industry

Talbot settlement: livestock industry, 151

Tariffs: American (see United States, tariffs); imperial (see also Corn Laws), 45; provincial, 44, 125, 130, 131-2, 132, 133-4, 134, 176, 357

Taxes, 214n

Tecumseth Township: settlement, 50

Tedders, 311

Teeswater: creamery, 263

Tenant farming, 62n, 68, 68n

Teviotdale: cattle fair, 282n

Thames Valley: dairy industry, 30-1; French-Canadian agriculture, 51; grain-growing, 87, 107n; Indian agriculture, 52, 74; livestock industry, 31, 127-8; settlement, 63; soil exhaustion, 206; see also Elgin County, Essex County, Kent County, Middlesex County, Oxford County

Thistles, 92, 92n, 96, 182n

Thompson, E. W.: on Canada Corn Act, 137; on soil exhaustion, 196; president of the Agricultural Association of Upper Canada, 137, 196

Thorah Township: agricultural society, 168

Thoroughbred horses, 146, 146n, 267

Thorpe, Judge, and agricultural society at York, 158

Threshing: custom, 312; with flail, 97, 99n; with horses or oxen, 97-8, 99n; with machinery, 98-9, 312

Threshing machines, 98-9, 312, 336

Threshing-bee, 312n

Tilbury East Township: agricultural society, 336

Tile Drainage Act, 1878, 314

Timothy, 73; seed exported to the United States, 195, 195n

Tobacco, 8, 40-2, 221, 316, 358-9; exported to Quebec, 40-1, 221; in Ohio, 40n; methods of culture, 41

Tomatoes, 79

Tools, superiority of American to British, 72n

Topknot hens, 155

Toronto (formerly York): agricultural convention, 1846, 171; agricultural societies, 158, 162, 163, 164, 338; brewery, 241; cattle fair, 159; depression, 1835, 123, 123n; elevator, 234n; exchange, 235-6; exhibitions, "Industrial," 338, 339, local, 162, 165-6, 338, 339, provincial, 171-2, 269n, 272n, 273n, 337; fruit market, 210, 319, 321, 322; garrison market, 25; grain trade, 29, 177-8, 191, 219, 234-5, 235-6, 236-7, 237, 238; horse-racing, 168n; linseed-oil mills, 317; livestock market, 126, 134, 208, 210, 210n; milling industry, 216; population, 1850, 63; pork-packing industry, 223-4, 285-6; tobacco market, 221; town market, 30, 159; wool market, 226

Toronto, University of. See University of Toronto

Toronto and Sydenham Road, 290

Toronto Exchange, 235-6

Toronto Globe, agrarian tendency of, 350

Toronto region: dairy industry, 252-3; grain-growing, 81, 91, 103, 123, 244, 247; hemp-growing, 43; implements, 96; labour shortage, 1853, 199; livestock industry, 126, 146, 147, 148n, 193n, 274-5; superior farming, 81n; trade with the United States, 193n; see also York County

Toronto Township: cattle fair, 160

Transactions of the Board of Agriculture and of the Agricultural Association of Upper Canada, 330, 387-8

Transactions of the Board of Agriculture of Upper Canada, 330, 387-8

Travellers' accounts of Upper Canada criticized, 81n, 374-5

Trees, 4, 20, 306

Trent Valley: shanty market, 120

Turkey fairs, 287

Turkeys, 75n, 78n; exported to British Isles, 287; exported to the United States, 181-2

Turnips, 72-3, 284

United States: agricultural market in general, 354, 357, 358-9; dairy market, 178-9, 179n, 181, 181-2, 228, 253, 253n, 262; egg market, 178-9, 179n, 181, 181-2, 286-7; flax market, 222-3, 317; flour and grain market, 26, 123-4, 176, 177-8, 178, 179, 181, 191-2, 216-7, 217, 228, 233, 243, 244, 245, 358-9; fruit market, 211, 319, 320, 322; hay market, 182, 182n; livestock market, 31-2, 129, 129n, 149, 178-9, 179, 179n, 181, 182-3, 183, 183-4, 184-5, 192-3, 193-4, 194-5, 195, 210, 223, 223n, 225, 226, 226n, 228-9, 267, 274-5, 278, 278-80, 358-9; potato market, 181, 317; poultry market, 181, 181-2, 287; source of flour and grain, 17, 37, 38, 116, 124-5, 125, 131, 135, 135n, 136, 175-6, 192, 231-3, 244; source of fruit, 211; source of livestock, 10, 17, 37, 38, 39, 45, 126-7, 127-8, 133n, 140, 140n, 144, 146, 151, 152-3, 165, 224, 227, 267, 273, 286;

source of meat, 37, 39, 45, 116, 128, 133n, 210n, 224; source of vegetables, 38; source of wool, 154; tariffs (*see also* McKinley Tariff), 123, 178n; vegetable market, 181, 317, 318; wool market, 178-9, 182, 194, 194n, 226, 226n, 276-7

United States Agricultural Society, exhibition of, 342

University of Toronto: experimental farm at, 330-1; professor of agriculture at, 328, 330-1, 331; veterinary course at, 332

Upper Canada. *See* Ontario

Upper Canada, Board of Agriculture of. *See* Board of Agriculture of Upper Canada

Upper Canada Agricultural and Commercial Society, 158

Upper Canada Agricultural Society, 162

Utica, N.Y., speculators in Upper Canada, 129n

Vankoughnet, Hon. Philip, colonization policy of, 290, 292

Vegetables, 9, 22, 78-9; exported to Quebec, 318; exported to the United States, 181, 317, 318; imported from the United States, 38

Vermont: immigration from, 19, 30-1; livestock industry, 127, 145; source of grain, 17; source of provisions, 37

"Vermont Dairy butter," 262

Vespra Township: settlement, 50

Veterinary colleges, 332

Victoria County: grain-growing, 242, 248; shanty market, 300; *see also* Trent Valley

Vine Growers' Association, 321

Virginia: livestock industry, 31; source of horses, 267

Wade, John: livestock breeder, 149; on Red Fife wheat, 105; on Siberian wheat, 102

Wages of agricultural labourers, 55n, 213

Wars, effects of: American Civil, 192, 216-30, 232-3, 253, 281, 309; Crimean, 198, 204, 206; Franco-Prussian, 247; French Revolutionary, 25; Italian, *1859*, 205; Napoleonic, 27-8, 43; War of 1812, 36-7

Waterloo: cattle fair, 281, 282n

Waterloo (now Cataraqui). *See* Cataraqui

Waterloo County: agricultural society, 339; flax-growing, 222; grain-growing, 237; immigrants' market, 46; implements, 95; livestock industry, 147, 153, 193, 209, 269n, 284; oak-plains, 5; settlement, 51n; trade with the United States, 193; *see also* Grand River Valley, Waterloo Township, Wellington District

Waterloo Township: settlement, 53, 63-4

Watertown, N.Y., New York State Fair at, 342

Welland Canal: construction market, 46; grain trade, 46, 233, 234; milling industry, 135; rural opposition to, 130-1

Welland County: agricultural society, 343, 343n; essay, 388; exhibition, 343; horse-racing, 343, 343n; livestock industry, 272; oak-plains, 5; *see also* Grand River Valley, Niagara District, Niagara peninsula, Stamford Township

Wellington County: agricultural society, 340; essay, 388; flax-growing, 316-7; grain-growing, 237, 239, 242, 244n, 248; labour scarcity, 199; livestock industry, 193, 209, 269n, 284; settlement, 51n; trade with the United States, 193; see also Guelph region, Guelph Township, Wellington District

Wellington District: agricultural societies, 146, 164, 164n, 165-6, 167n; exhibitions, 146, 165-6, 167n

Wentworth County: agricultural societies, 158, 342; exhibition, 342; livestock industry, 152n, 284; oak-plains, 5; see also Dundas Street, Gore District, Grand River Valley, "Grimsby country," Hamilton region, Niagara peninsula

West Gwillimbury Township: settlement, 50

West Highland cattle, 270n

Western District: agricultural society, 161, 164, 167; exhibition, 167

Western Fair at London, 337-8

Wheat: before 1812, 15, 25-6, 28, 29; 1812-1850, 5, 47-8, 73, 81, 85, 85-6, 86n, 89, 89-90, 97, 97n, 100-5, 105, 106-7, 117, 123, 125, 134, 136-7, 175-8, 196, 354, 357-8; 1850-1867, 86, 186, 197, 197-8, 198, 204-5, 206, 226-7, 239; 1867-1880, 239, 245-9, 306; competition with dairying, 251, 253; competition with fruit-growing, 318-9; competition with wool-growing, 226-7; enemies (see Cutworms, Black stem rust, Grasshoppers, Hessian fly, Wheat midge, Wheat smut); exported to British Isles, 25-6, 27-8, 28, 38-9, 47-8, 122, 134-5, 136n, 197-8, 204, 232-3; exported to the United States, 123-4, 176, 177-8, 191-2, 216-7, 228, 233, 245; fall, 99-100, 100, 239, 245-9; imported from British Isles, 103; imported from Manitoba, 247; imported from the United States, 17, 39, 101-2, 124-5, 125, 131, 135, 135n, 136, 175-6, 191-2, 231-3; improvement, 100-2, 165, 246, 336n; production statistics, 86, 86n, 239, 248; spring, 12, 100-1, 204-5, 239, 247; superiority of Upper Canada, 28, 48, 99-100; varieties (see Black Sea wheat, etc.); see also Crops, Grain trade

Wheat midge, 104-5, 125, 137-8, 186, 196, 203-4, 205, 207, 245-6

Wheat smut, 245, 313n

Whitby: grain market, 199

Whitby Township: agricultural society, 168; settlement, 57

White Flint wheat, 100

White Leghorn hens, 274

White Topknot ducks, 155

Winchester: dairy industry, 262-3; Granger movement, 345

Windmills, 12, 14-5

Windsor region: market gardening, 318; see also Essex County

Wine-making, 9n, 321-2

Wineries, 321-2

Wire fences, 314

Wisconsin: grain-growing, 104; livestock industry, 194n, 225

"Wolf-in-the-tail," 76, 76n

Wolves, 78n

Wood, Hon. S. C., and Ontario Agricultural Commission, 326

Woodstock: dairy market, 260; trade with the United States, 129

Wool, 14n, 76-7, 141n, 152-5, 225-6, 227, 275-7; competition with dairying, 276, 276n; competition with wheat-growing, 226-7; dealers, 194n; exported to British Isles, 226n; exported to the United States, 178-9, 182, 194, 194n, 226, 226n, 276-7; imported from the United States, 154

Wool fair, 77

Wool Growers' Association, 227

Woollen mills, 277

Wright, Philemon, livestock breeder, 150n

Yonge Street: grain-growing, 90; livestock industry, 148, 154; settlement, 63, 290; superior farming, 63

York. *See* Toronto

York County: agricultural society, 205; dairy industry, 251, 253; depression, *1857*, 205; essay, 388; grain-growing, 89, 90-1, 242, 246; land speculation, 205; oak-plains, 5; settlement, 19; *see also* Home District, Lake Ontario counties, Markham Township, Toronto region, Yonge Street, York Township

York Township: farmers' club, 169-70

Yorkshire horses, 269

Yorkshire swine, 152, 273, 273n